Real World, Real Speakers

Bringing **Public Speaking** to Life

Presentations in Everyday Life is a hands-on, practical text that strives to motivate and empower students to become more effective, ethical communicators. Based on information gathered in a survey of presenters and professionals from a variety of vocational backgrounds, this book focuses on teaching students practical presentation skills for real-world speaking situations. Written in an encouraging, accessible format, this text provides the principles for learning how to develop and deliver powerful messages in any number of communication contexts.

Building on the well-received first edition, the second edition includes expanded content and new features inspired by suggestions from students and faculty who have used the book as well as the most current communication research. Strengthened by additions such as a video CD-ROM, online speech preparation toolkit, new tools for practicing presentation skills, and cutting-edge research, the second edition of *Presentations in Everyday Life* continues to deliver the best how-to strategies for becoming a highly effective speaker.

Public Speaking Gets Practical

Presentation Principles in Action

Assessing a Website

Directions: In addition to the general tests for assessing supporting material discussed in this chapter, special criteria should be applied when evaluating websites and Web sources. Use the following checklist to assess the validity and reliability of supporting material found on two websites of your choice. For the first website, select a site that is, in your opinion, a *good* site for researching valid supporting material. For the second website, select a site that is, in your opinion, a *questionable* or *poor* site that may not provide credible, recent, consistent, relevant, or valid information. Be prepared to present your evaluations of both websites.

Website Assessment

Web Site #1 URL: Host:	Web Site #2 URL: Host:	Assessment Criteria and Questions
		CRITERION #1: AUTHORITY
Acceptable Unacceptable Cannot Determine Comments:	_____ Acceptable _____ Unacceptable _____ Cannot Determine Comments:	1. Are the *sponsor's* identity and purpose clear? 2. Are the *author's* identity and qualifications evident? 3. If the material is protected by copyright, who is the copyright holder? 4. Can you verify the legitimacy of the webpage's sponsor (e.g., a phone number or postal address to contact for more information)? 5. Are you sure that the named source is actually operating the site? 6. Have you run the names of unfamiliar topics, sources, and authors through a search engine to learn more about them and what other people have said about them?
		CRITERION #2: ACCURACY
Acceptable Unacceptable Cannot Determine Comments:	_____ Acceptable _____ Unacceptable _____ Cannot Determine Comments:	1. Are the sources of factual information clearly listed so that you can verify them in another source? 2. Has the sponsor provided links that can be used to verify claims? 3. Is statistical data well labeled and easy to read? 4. Is the information free of grammatical, spelling, and typographical errors that would indicate a lack of quality control?

New! Presentation Principles in Action provide students with hands-on application of chapter concepts through questionnaires, class exercises, speaking assignments, and assessment instruments, including "Pronunciation Drills," "Separating Facts and Opinion," and "Assessing a Website."

Adapting Persuasion to Cultural Differences

In Chapter 5, "Audience Analysis and Adaptation," we include a Mini-Module titled "Adapting to International Audiences" that discusses guidelines for adapting your speaking style to listeners from other countries. In this Mini-Module, however, we look at some of the ways in which different cultures respond to persuasive appeals. As was the case with presentation speaking style, we lack significant research in this area of study. At the same time, you should make every effort to understand, respect, and adapt to the ways in which culturally diverse audience members may respond to persuasive messages.

As we have noted, even within the United States, there are members of microcultures (Native American Indians, African Americans, Hispanic/Latino Americans, Asian Americans, and certain religious groups) that coexist within mainstream society. The members of these groups may be as collectivist and high context as audience members from other countries. In a highly individualistic culture such as that of the United States, listeners value individual achievement and personal freedom. In collectivist cultures (those of Asian and Latin American countries), audience members are more likely to value group identity, selflessness, and collective action. Audiences in collectivist cultures place less importance on the opinions and preferences of the individual than do audiences in individualistic cultures.[1] In the United States, appeals that benefit individuals—personal wealth, personal success, personal health and fitness—may be highly persuasive while appeals that benefit society and families are often overlooked. Think about the commercials that you see on television. They often focus on how *you* can become more successful, more attractive, and healthier; they rarely address collective benefits. When addressing a collectivist audience, however, you should think about collective benefits. How does your position help your collectivist audience's families, businesses, and communities?

Now let's explore how different persuasive strategies may be applied to audiences from high-context cultures in contrast with strategies used with low-context audiences in the United States. In low-context cultures such as those of the United States, England, and Germany, audiences expect messages to be explicit, factual, and objective. Words are valued and believed. For example, in the United States, persuasive appeals are often direct—do this; buy that; drink this; avoid that; just do it! In advertising, this would be termed a *hard-sell* approach to persuasion.

In contrast, high-context cultures such as those of Japan, China, and Mexico expect messages that are implied and situation specific. Nonverbal behavior is valued and believed more than words. A soft-sell approach would be a better persuasive strategy. When addressing a high-context audience, encourage listeners to draw their own conclusions. Demonstrate benefits and advantages rather than advocating action.

Differences between cultures are very real. At the same time, be cautious about how you interpret and use this information. You cannot assume that all members of a culture conform to one or more cultural dimensions. Are all Japanese collectivist and high context? Many young Japanese business professionals are learning and embracing American ways that include a more direct and self-centered approach to communication. Are all Australians individualistic? Although Australians are very independent and value personal freedom, they also live in a culture in which power distance is minimal. Public displays of achievement or wealth are frowned upon.[2] One of your authors lived in Australia for a year and was introduced to the *tall poppy syndrome.* If, in a field of poppies, one red blossom grows higher than the others, you chop it off. When people show off or try to rise above others, you cut them down to size, too. "He thinks he's a tall poppy" is used to describe someone who—in American terms—is "too big for his britches."

Unfortunately, the lack of significant research on attitude and behavior change in other cultures makes it difficult to provide universal guidelines or strategies for persuasion. There is no question, however, that differences do exist. Effective speakers spend extra time and energy investigating the attitudes, beliefs, and values of a culture before speaking in order to ensure that they understand, respect, and do their best to adapt to their listeners.

1. Sharon Shavitt and Michelle R. Nelson, "The Role of Attitude Functions in Persuasion and Social Judgment," in *The Persuasion Handbook: Developments in Theory and Practice*, ed. James Price Dillard and Michael Pfau (Thousand Oaks, CA: Sage, 2002), p. 150.
2. Shavitt and Nelson, p. 150.

Mini-Modules provide step-by-step instruction on presentation techniques many other books gloss over, such as "The Top Seven Sentence Problems," "The Habits of Creative Thinkers," and "Adapting Persuasion to Cultural Differences."

Features Students Can Use

Real World, Real Speakers

offer stories and examples from survey respondents, the authors, and professionals that demonstrate presentation principles and strategies in action.

Take Charge of the Situation

Logistics play a critical role in many presentations, particularly when the place and occasion speak louder than words. Such was the case when President George W. Bush spoke at Ground Zero on September 14, 2001. Bush's short, ten-sentence speech was given amidst the smoking remains of the Twin Towers in New York City. Like many official visitors, he toured the site and talked with the exhausted, grimy firefighters, police, medical personnel, and volunteers. When he heard the crowd chanting, "USA!" he climbed to the top of a rubble pile, put his arm around a firefighter's shoulder, and spoke to the crowd through a bullhorn. The following analysis of the occasion and logistics helps to explain the success of Bush's short speech.[1]

Occasion

The speech was delivered only three days after the September 11, 2001, tragedy. Workers were still combing through the rubble twenty-four hours a day. Whereas Bush had already been criticized for being "missing in action" immediately following the tragedy, his impromptu Ground Zero speech was a fitting match for the occasion.

- *Why Bush?* Because he was president of the United States.
- *What does the audience expect?* The immediate audience wanted both comfort and toughness from the president. The larger viewing audience wanted to see a strong leader taking charge.
- *What's proper?* A respectful and emotionally charged speech.

Logistics

Bush's short speech also addressed the four logistical questions in a way that made his speech a powerful moment in the midst of a tragedy.

- *Who?* The immediate audience—firefighters, police, medical personnel, and volunteers—needed a short, rousing endorsement and tribute from the president. The large audience of television viewers saw an intense and powerful president taking charge of an embattled scene.
- *Where?* Not only was the president speaking at Ground Zero; he was also speaking from the top of a rubble pile with his arm around a firefighter. The picture was dynamic and compelling.
- *When?* The president spoke only three days after the September 11 disaster. Workers were still putting out fires and searching the site for survivors. The president's compassionate and encouraging words gave his immediate and larger audience comfort and hope.
- *How?* When the audience shouted that they couldn't hear him, the president grabbed a bullhorn and climbed to a higher position so that his audience could both see and hear him. No sophisticated sound equipment, no manuscript, no lectern, no special lighting—he spoke impromptu. Anything other than an impromptu speech would have seemed inappropriate and insincere, given the occasion. Bush was not the awkward public speaker audience members had begun to dread but instead was an energetic leader taking charge of a desperate situation.

1. A transcript of this speech appears in the Appendix.

What's Proper?

Events or gatherings often have specific rules of protocol. **Protocol** is a term that refers to the expected format of a ceremony or the etiquette observed at a particular type of event. In diplomatic circles, the rules of protocol are written down and taken very seriously—addressing everything from where to seat a dignitary at dinner to how to address a member of the monarchy. In other circumstances, the "rules" of protocol are less formal or are part of a tradition. Thus, we expect a certain tone at a graduation ceremony and a very different tone at a political rally. At a funeral, a eulogy may be touching or funny, but it's almost always very respectful and short.

Tips

provide insider information drawn from the authors' extensive experience, including "Don't Tell Them Everything You Know," "Model Charismatic Teachers," and "Avoid Ethnocentrism and Stereotyping."

FAQs (Frequently Asked Questions)

provide short answers to some of the most commonly asked questions by students, from "How many key points should I include?" and "How do I avoid saying *um* and *uh* so often?" to "What should I do with my hands?"

Don't Speak Without a Clear Purpose

Dr. Terry L. Paulson, psychologist and author of *They Shoot Managers, Don't They?*, warns speakers about the hazards of speaking without a purpose: "There are so many messages and memos being hurled at today's business professionals [that] they are in information overload. It's like sipping through a fire hydrant. Don't unnecessarily add to the stream by including unnecessary fill, facts, and fluff. Volume and graphs will not have a lasting impression; having a focus will. Ask yourself early in the process: What do I want them to remember or do three months from now? If you can't succinctly answer that question, cancel your presentation."[1]

1. Quoted in Lilly Walters, *Secrets of Successful Speakers* (New York: McGraw-Hill, 1993), pp. 3–4.

Is It Ethical to Have a Private Purpose?

As the preamble to the communication ethics credo in Chapter 1 indicates, "questions of right and wrong arise whenever people communicate," and that includes whenever speakers make presentations. Becoming a "good" speaker involves more than delivering a well-organized presentation. A good speaker is committed to preparing and presenting an ethical presentation that is honest, fair, and beneficial to both the speaker and the listeners.

One of the most important ethical questions to ask yourself is this: Who will benefit if I achieve my purpose—will I, my audience, or my audience *and* I benefit? If your public and private purposes conflict or undermine each other, you may be on shaky ground. If you would be hesitant or embarrassed to tell your audience your private purpose, this may be a sign that it's ethically questionable. There is nothing wrong with having a private purpose such as wanting to get a good grade on your presentation or wanting to impress the boss with your speechmaking success. However, there *is* something wrong if achieving your private purpose would hurt or deceive your audience. As the ethics credo in Chapter 1 notes, truthfulness and honesty, freedom of expression, tolerance, and respect are essential to the integrity of communication. Both of us share that belief and apply it to every presentation we make or hear.

Having a clear purpose does not guarantee that you will achieve it. But without a purpose, little can be accomplished. In the workplace, the average employee spends a lot of time listening to other people, attending meetings, and reading memos or reports. If all that time spent doesn't accomplish something, it's obvious the communicators didn't spend enough time asking "why" questions. They didn't know their purpose.

Public and Private Purposes

There can be more than one answer to the question "What is my purpose?" The student speaker in the scenario who wanted to "give students the inside scoop" in the "Department Survival Guide" had a clear purpose. However, that same student may also have wanted to please the faculty members who requested the presentation or to use the speaking opportunity as a way to meet new students. Wanting to share the unwritten rules in a department survival guide is a *public purpose.* Wanting to please faculty members or to meet new students is a *private purpose.* Skilled speakers understand the absolute necessity for a public purpose, the advantages of a private purpose, and most important, the difference between the two.

If you were asked to state the goal of your presentation for a newsletter announcement or to a communication class instructor, you would be stating your **public purpose.** You may not need or even want to share your **private purpose,** the personal goal of your presentation. For example, many companies sponsor volunteer speakers bureaus, programs in which company employees volunteer and are scheduled to speak to community groups. Let's say that the volunteer speakers bureau of a local utility company publicly announces that its chief engineer will give an informative talk on ways to conserve energy. The presentation's public purpose will attract an audience. The private purpose, however, can explain why the utility company wants an audience in the first place: It wants to create goodwill and convince the public that the utility is interested in helping them conserve energy.

Why would a company employee volunteer for a speakers bureau, though? It's extra work, there is rarely extra pay, and the assignment could subject the speaker to harassment from a hostile audience. When we have asked such volunteer speakers why they are willing to do all that extra work, we have heard a variety of personal reasons. Most express private purposes that focus on personal and career goals. Some employees volunteer because their service looks good on their résumés or will

Public Speaking Gets Innovative

New **VideoLab** CD-ROM

The VideoLab CD-ROM adds a dynamic element to public speaking classes by reinforcing key concepts in an interactive, self-paced environment. This study tool provides digital video of student speeches that can be viewed in conjunction with corresponding outlines, manuscripts, note cards, and instructor critiques. A series of drills to help students analyze content and delivery follows each speech. Guidelines for integrating the VideoLab study tool into coursework are provided in the instructor's materials.

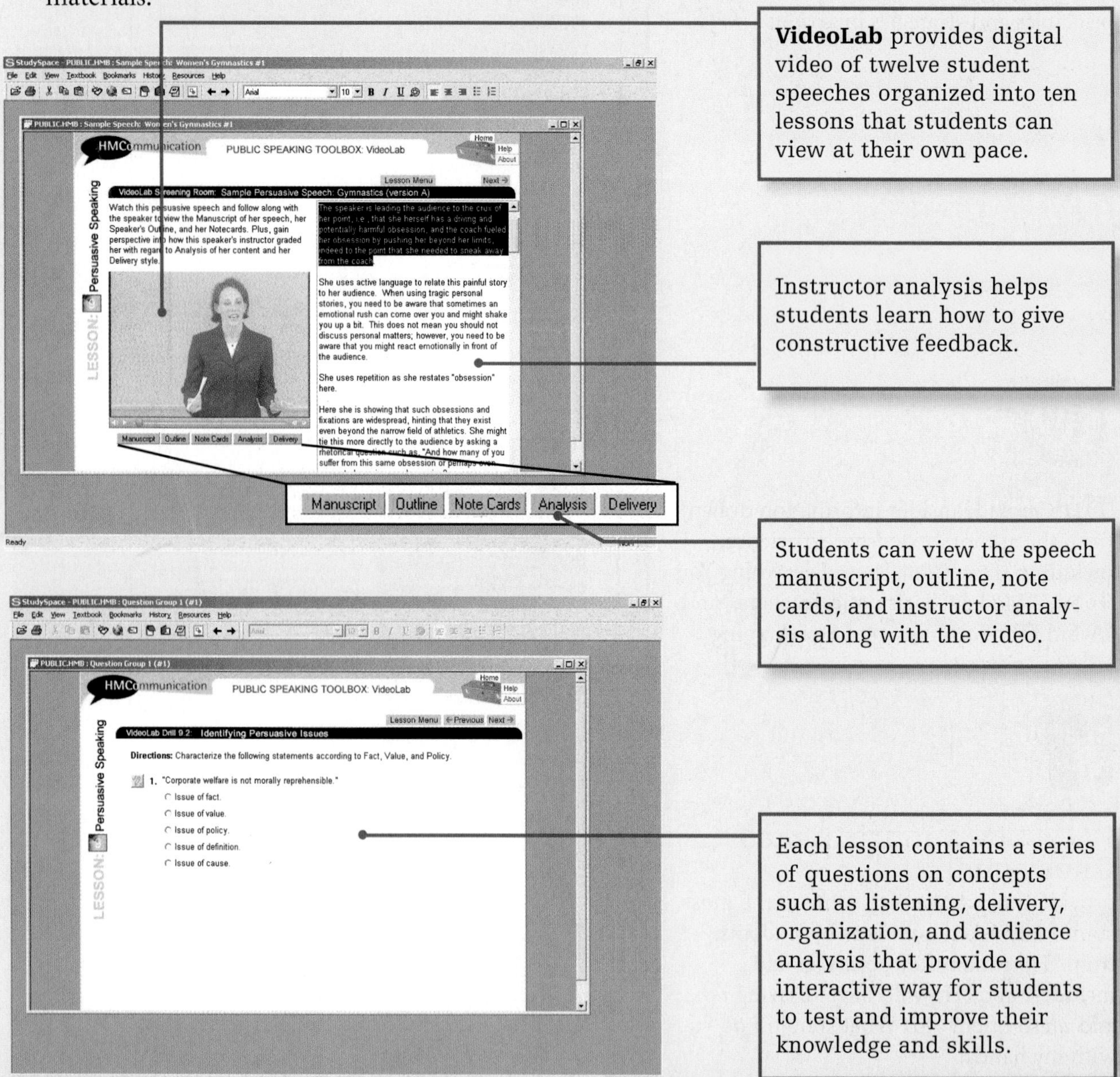

Technology Beyond the Classroom

Online SpeechStudio

The Online SpeechStudio, available in Eduspace®, is a speech preparation toolkit that helps students learn to model and compose organized, thoughtful speeches and build an online portfolio of their work. With resources tailored to all of the major types of speech design, the Online SpeechStudio gives students hands-on practice with every stage of the speech development process, including selecting a topic, conducting research, audience analysis, organizing a speech, and critiquing.

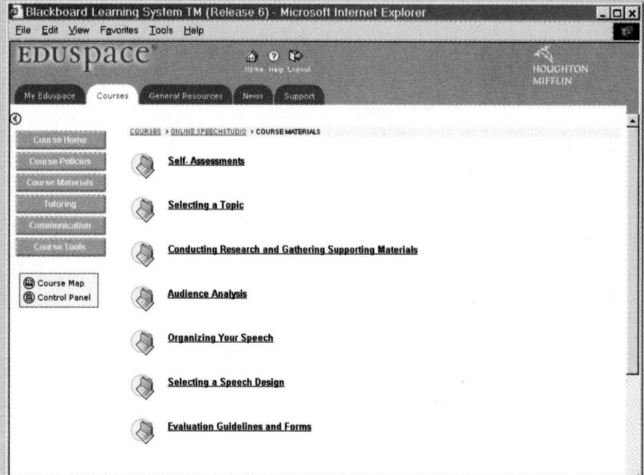

A **Complete Package** for Instructors and Students

The Instructor's Resource Manual, by Isa Engleberg, can be adapted to a variety of course formats and teaching styles. It includes:

- Sample **syllabi**
- Chapter-by-chapter **test bank** and **exercises**
- Ready-to-use **speaking assignments**, **writing assignments**, and **assessment instruments**
- Photo-ready **graphics** for use as transparencies or handouts
- **Guidelines** for using the manual
- Techniques for **videotaping** and **assessing** student presentations
- **Distance learning** guidelines and techniques

Additional instructor's ancillaries include a **computerized test bank**, a **PowerPoint presentation program**, a **companion website**, **real-world speeches videos**, the **Contemporary Great Speeches Video**, and other video opportunities.

Student resources include:

The **Speech Preparation Workbook**, containing activities and outline formats for the major presentations discussed in the textbook and assigned in the Instructor's Resource Manual.

The **Multicultural Activities Workbook for the Public Speaking Classroom**

A student-focused **companion website** with exercises and activities to further develop student skills. These include **A Cyber Evaluation (ACE)** online chapter quizzes, hot links to research sites, and links to all screen shots found in the text.

The **VideoLab CD-ROM**, which is available as a package option.

The **Online SpeechStudio** in Eduspace, a speech preparation toolkit containing resources to help students model and compose thoughtful, organized speeches.

About the Authors

Dr. Isa Engleberg

Isa Engleberg, Professor of Speech Communication at Prince George's Community College, has been named outstanding community college educator by the National Communication Association (NCA) and received the highest teaching honor from Prince George's Community College. She is an experienced author and recognized expert in group communications, having written four college textbooks on public speaking and group communication. Isa Engleberg is also serving as the 2003 NCA President.

Dr. John Daly

John Daly, past president of the National Communication Association (NCA) and prize-winning professor of both communication and management at the University of Texas, Austin, is one of the most renowned and sought-after teachers and scholars of communication. In addition to his commitment to undergraduate education, Daly has also acted as communication consultant to more than 300 public and private organizations. This is his first introductory public speaking text.

Presentations in Everyday Life

Strategies for Effective Speaking

SECOND EDITION

Presentations in Everyday Life

Strategies for Effective Speaking

SECOND EDITION

Isa N. Engleberg

Prince George's Community College

John A. Daly

University of Texas, Austin

Houghton Mifflin Company

BOSTON NEW YORK

Senior Sponsoring Editor: Mary Finch
Developmental Editor: Kristen Lefevre
Senior Project Editor: Audrey Bryant
Editorial Assistant: Sarah Cleary
Senior Production/Design Coordinator: Jennifer Meyer Dare
Senior Manufacturing Coordinator: Marie Barnes
Marketing Manager: Elinor Gregory

Cover image © Frank Herholdt/Getty Images

Printed in the U.S.A.

Library of Congress Catalog Card Number: 2002109437

ISBN: 618-26016-1

1 2 3 4 5 6 7 8 9-DOW-08 07 06 05 04

BRIEF CONTENTS

part six

Applications

CONTENTS

part one
The Basics

part four

Engaging Your Audience

16 Physical Delivery 353

17 Presentation Aids 372

part six

Applications

FAQS

TIPS

PREFACE

For all of our adult lives, each of us has studied, taught, consulted, coached, and written about human communication. We enjoy speaking in front of groups and look forward to listening to good presentations. We remain in awe of people whose presentations have the power to inspire and inform. Great speakers move people and nations–they can change the world with their words.

We both became interested in communication in high school, when we competed on our respective schools' debate and public speaking teams. In college, we both discovered that we could continue to compete and even take classes in speech communication! We knew that learning to speak comfortably in front of groups was more than a competitive skill; it was a survival tool.

Whether we were speaking to classmates, professors, colleagues, friends, or the public, our speaking ability helped determine whether we achieved personal and career success, whether we were respected by those around us, and whether we were included in the social and political life of our community. By the time we entered graduate schools, our career paths were clear. Both of us became communication professors. John Daly now teaches communication at the University of Texas at Austin. Isa Engleberg is a professor of communication studies at Prince George's Community College in Largo, Maryland. By the time this second edition is published, both of us will have served as president of the National Communication Association, the world's largest professional association of communication scholars and educators.

We also find ourselves seeking opportunities outside the classroom to help people become better speakers. Although most people don't make many public speeches, the presentations they do make are often critical to their personal and professional success. From our more than fifty combined years as communication instructors and speech coaches, we know that most people can become more effective presenters with study and practice.

Very simply, we wrote this book because we are passionate about the importance of good speaking. The challenge of helping speakers decide what to say and how to say it still excites and interests us. And it's something we want to share.

We are delighted by the enthusiastic response to the first edition of *Presentations in Everyday Life.* We are particularly proud when faculty members tell us that the textbook is academically strong *and* useful. And we're delighted when students tell us that they're keeping the book as a reference for making oral reports in other classes and as a guide to preparing effective presentations in out-of-class settings.

In the second edition, we have strengthened our commitment to offering our best advice on presentation speaking skills supported by the best communication theory and research in our field.

We Focus on Student and Speaker Needs

Presentations in Everyday Life: Strategies for Effective Speaking integrates the scholarship and theory of presentation speaking with the needs of today's diverse college students. Our research and writing have been guided by an overriding principle that asks, "What do speakers want and need to know?" Although we recognize that what speakers *want*

("I want to get rid of my nervousness") may not be what they *need* (to learn how to reduce and adjust to the natural consequences of presentation anxiety), we have honored their expressed concerns and provided practical, time-tested answers to their questions. At the same time, we have made a concerted effort to apply the best communication theory and research to practical strategies and skills.

Questions asked by students, colleagues, clients, and professional speakers led us to pose a critical question to ourselves: What do people want and need to know about presentation speaking? This question both inspired us to write this book and planted the seeds of the practical approach we take to the subject of presentation speaking. We actualize our real-world focus in two significant ways. We explain *how* to use communication strategies and skills when making a presentation, and we respond to the needs of a wide variety of speakers.

Emphasizing How to Speak

Unlike textbooks that primarily describe *what* to do when making a presentation or public speech, *Presentations in Everyday Life* teaches speakers *how* to do it. For example, rather than telling readers to make sure they speak loudly enough, we explain *how* to increase volume, *how* to speak with or without a microphone, and *how* to adjust to different surroundings (see Chapter 15, "Vocal Delivery"). Rather than just listing a variety of ways to organize an informative presentation, we explain *how* to select effective strategies for achieving a specific, informative purpose (see Chapter 18, "Developing Informative Presentations"). Teaching speakers *how* goes well beyond *what* because it gives them a repertoire of communication strategies and skills that can be adapted to any speaking situation.

Surveying Real-World Speakers

Although most students take a communication course for a semester, they will make presentations for the rest of their lives. Understanding this reality, we teamed up with Houghton Mifflin to design, conduct, and analyze some nontraditional market research: We sent surveys to individuals from all walks of life who had bought books on public speaking and presentations. We asked them what they wanted to learn and which communication strategies and skills they relied on the most in their professional lives. We also asked them to volunteer stories about their successes and frustrations as presenters.

The results of this research were both predictable and surprising. For example, although respondents acknowledged concerns about their delivery skills and speech anxiety, they were much more interested in learning how to prepare substantive, engaging presentations. Their insights and needs helped us link communication scholarship to the real world of presentation speaking. The stories they shared provide an added dimension to the textbook. Not only do they give us genuine and often amusing examples; they also reveal a sophisticated appreciation of the importance and consequences of effective communication.

We Believe in the Centrality of Communication Studies

We believe that the study of communication is, without a doubt, the most important of all the academic disciplines. As communication educators, we assume an awesome responsibility. We encounter students from all walks of life and cultures. We take students from cities, farms, suburbia, working careers, and other cultures and teach them the most important of all skills: how to communicate.

The principles found in this textbook empower learners. They provide a basis for understanding and learning how to effectively develop and deliver messages that affect their own lives and the larger world in significant and enduring ways. Although we focus on presentation speaking, the principles and skills in this textbook apply to all communication contexts—interpersonal, small group, and mediated communication. Learning the basic principles of presentation speaking provides a lifelong guide for becoming a more effective and ethical communicator.

We Combine Tradition and Innovation

We fully recognize that like us, the majority of instructors who adopt this textbook have strong opinions about course content as well as tried-and-true teaching methods. We know that a textbook is no substitute for the professional mastery that comes from years of teaching. At the same time, we know that some instructors will be new to the teaching profession and that their choice of textbooks may influence their development into seasoned professionals. In order to serve the needs of both types of instructors, we have retained the content and logical sequence of topics that can be found in other textbooks while adding several innovative features.

Tradition

Like most other textbooks in the field, ours begins with an introduction to the basic principles of presentation speaking and moves through considerations of topic selection, audience analysis, supporting material, organization, delivery, and the application of communication principles to informative, persuasive, and special occasion presentations. Our chapters, however, are self-contained by design, providing instructors with the flexibility to make assignments that mix different chapters in different ways, depending on their goals.

As a way of focusing on student needs, we have split several traditional chapters into smaller units. For example, whereas other textbooks may devote only one or two chapters to delivery, our Part V includes four chapters. One focuses on preparation and practice, the second addresses vocal delivery, the third highlights physical delivery and adapting to mediated presentations, and the fourth explores developing and using presentation aids. The appearance of twenty-two chapters should neither alarm instructors nor hinder instruction. Well-established course competencies and teaching techniques will work just as well with these smaller, more precise chapters. Our modular approach also enables us to cover the traditional topics and simultaneously provide a "home" and focus for materials that are missing from or randomly scattered throughout other textbooks.

Continued Innovation

We have retained the well-received innovations included in the first edition of *Presentations in Everyday Life.* For example,

- We emphasize *presentation* speaking rather than public speaking. As a broader term, *presentation speaking* includes public speaking (formal speeches delivered to *public* audiences in *public* settings) as well as the more common and less formal presentations given in everyday situations at college, work, and social gatherings.

- A unique Dynamic Presentation Model focuses on seven basic principles of presentation speaking (Purpose, Audience, Credibility, Logistics, Content, Organization, Performance), which are reinforced throughout the textbook and applied to all types of presentations.
- Chapter 2, "Listening and Critical Thinking," links these skill areas to each other and demonstrates their applicability to speakers and listeners alike.
- All of Chapter 3, "Building Presentation Confidence," focuses on communication apprehension for the purpose of helping students understand and deal with presentation anxiety.
- Chapter 6, "Speaker Credibility and Ethics," connects these two important concepts to one another and to the basic principles of presentation speaking.
- Chapter 10, "Organizational Tools," presents alternative methods (beyond outlining) of discovering and organizing the key points and supporting material in a presentation.
- Chapter 13, "Generating Interest," was created in response to the number one concern expressed by our survey respondents: "How can I make my presentations more interesting?" This unique, pivotal chapter focuses on the effective use of stories, humor, and audience participation.
- A sophisticated rhetorical strategy for information speaking forms the basis for Chapter 18, "Developing Informative Presentations," and focuses on matching topic characteristics and audience analysis with appropriate organizational patterns, supporting material, and explanatory strategies.
- Chapters 19 and 20, "Understanding Persuasion" and "Developing Persuasive Presentations," cover theoretical and practical approaches to persuasion, including clear explanations of critical theories and how they can be applied to everyday examples of persuasive communication.

Second Edition Features

The second edition of *Presentations in Everyday Life* includes new features inspired by two sources. Faculty members and students using the first edition have suggested organizational changes as well as the expansion of several innovative features and the inclusion of in-text exercises and assessment instruments. Cutting-edge communication research provided the second inspiration and basis for new and expanded content. For example,

- A new section at the end of every chapter, "Presentation Principles in Action," provides questionnaires, class exercises, speaking assignments, and/or assessment instruments related to chapter content.
- We place greater emphasis on cultural diversity and the skills needed for adapting to audiences with different perspectives and backgrounds throughout the textbook.
- Additional Mini-Modules address topics such as "The Public Speaking Tradition," "Adapting to International Audiences," "The Habits of Creative Thinkers," "The Top Seven Sentence Problems" and "Adapting Persuasion to Cultural Differences."
- An expanded critical thinking section in Chapter 2, "Listening and Critical Thinking," includes two new features: (1) "Critical Thinking Habits" such as "Rethinking Your Purpose," "Testing Your Thinking," and "Thinking About Words" and (2) a section on using Bloom's Taxonomy and theories of intellectual development as a basis for adapting to different ways of thinking.

- An expanded section on finding topics for classroom presentations strengthens Chapter 4, "Purpose and Topic."
- A new section on conducting and using effective audience surveys provides a powerful research tool in Chapter 5, "Audience Analysis and Adaptation."
- A brand-new Chapter 12, "Engaging Language," departs from traditional treatments of language by linking word choice to a presentation's purpose, audience, speaker credibility, logistics, content, organization, and performance. The chapter introduces the Four Cs of Speaking Style (*Clear, Committed, Colorful,* and *Captivating*) as a framework for providing practical advice about selecting effective and memorable language that is matched to a presentation's purpose and a speaker's style.
- A major expansion of Chapter 13, "Generating Interest," provides a new section devoted to finding and shaping effective stories and a summary of research on ways to convey clear and memorable messages.
- Updated chapters on delivery in Part V include new features on using notes effectively and adapting delivery to different cultures.
- A revised and updated Chapter 17, "Presentation Aids," incorporates better visual examples and cautions speakers about the pitfalls of using distracting presentation aids.
- New research and theories of persuasion in Chapters 19 and 20 include discussions of heuristics, persuasive campaigns, Psychological Reactance Theory, and applications of Toulmin's Model of Argument.
- New sections on eulogies and sales presentations strengthen Chapter 21, "Developing Special Presentations."
- A new section on presenting in virtual groups in Chapter 22, "Developing Group Presentations," describes strategies and skills for effective presentations using videoconferencing and collaborative presentation technology.
- The expanded Appendix includes new student presentations as well as new public speeches.

Our Pedagogy Focuses on the Real World

To help readers understand and master materials presented in this textbook, we have developed special pedagogical features that reflect our teaching styles and professional consulting expertise. The questions that open each chapter and those that appear in the Frequently Asked Questions (FAQs) features emerged from recurring questions we have been asked by students, survey respondents, clients, and instructors. The TIPs reflect "trade secrets" we share with our students and clients. All of these features help students master the content because they are based on many years of successful teaching, scholarly research, and personal experiences. We know these features work because we have used them to great advantage with thousands of speakers.

- **Opening Questions.** Every chapter opens with a set of questions commonly asked by students, instructors, and/or survey respondents. The chapter content answers these questions and the end-of-chapter summaries repeat them, this time with brief answers based on the chapter's content.
- **FAQs (Frequently Asked Questions).** We provide short answers to frequently asked questions such as "How many key points should I include?" (Chapter 10), "How do I avoid saying um and uh so often?" (Chapter 15), "What should I do with my hands?" (Chapter 16), and "How do I find common ground?" (Chapter 19).

- **TIPs.** Advisory paragraphs provide "insider information," cautionary notes, or reminders such as "Never tell an audience that you are nervous" (Chapter 3), "Appeal to varied learning styles" (Chapter 17), and "Evidence can change attitudes" (Chapter 20). TIPs provide sound advice in an encouraging tone.
- **Real World, Real Speakers.** Stories told by respondents to our survey, the authors, students, and professional speakers appear throughout the text to illustrate communication principles and strategies. The stories also reinforce the power of narratives as a rhetorical device.
- **Mini-Modules.** Most chapters include a Mini-Module, a brief, boxed discussion of an optional technique often ignored by other textbooks, such as "Adapting to International Audiences" (Chapter 5), "Interviewing for Information" (Chapter 8), "Using a Microphone" (Chapter 15), and "Handling Hostile Questions" (Chapter 21).
- **Slides.** Every chapter includes several summary and preview lists of core principles and strategies such as "Top-Ranked Speaking Skills" (Chapter 1), "A Purpose Statement Should Be . . ." (Chapter 4), "Tests of Supporting Material" (Chapter 8), and "Benefits of Eye Contact" (Chapter 16). These are also available as downloadable PowerPoint slides from the companion website.
- **Presentation Principles in Action.** The end of every chapter provides one or more questionnaires, class exercises, speaking assignments, and/or assessment instruments related to the chapter content. Examples include a "Listenability Test," "Personal Report of Public Speaking Anxiety," "Applying the NCA Ethics Credo," "Assessing a Website," "Separating Facts and Opinion," "Creativity Scale," "Writing Apprehension Test," "Assessing a Story," "Pronunciation Drills," "Visual Aid Assessment," and "Creative Brainstorming," along with a variety of speaking assignments and assessment forms.

We Support Varied Learning Styles

We took on the challenge of adapting our textbook to the varied learning styles of our readers. We know, for example, that some students learn better by reading about the principles and strategies of good speaking. Others need real-world examples to demonstrate the principles in action. Some learners always pose questions that must be answered before they can master a skill.

We have tried to practice what we preach about audience adaptation:

- For students who learn best by reading about communication principles, we offer detailed explanations of both theories and speaking strategies, supported by multiple examples.
- For those experiential learners who need to see principles in action, we have included many excerpts from student and real-world presentations throughout the textbook and complete presentations in the Appendix.
- For learners with a visual orientation, we have included summary and preview slides, charts, tables, photographs, diagrams, drawings, website screens, and highlighted FAQs and TIPs.

And to keep all of our readers interested and engaged, we have included scenarios, dialogues, outlines, real-world stories, Mini-Modules, and short questionnaires written in clear, vivid language and even with a sense of humor. These strategies, which we also recommend in Chapter 13 for generating interest, are more than good writing principles. They help us capture reader attention and ultimately enhance interest, understanding, and learning.

We Offer a Complete Package for Instructors and Students

By enlisting the resources of our publisher, we provide a full range of ancillary materials for both instructors and students.

The comprehensive **Instructor's Resource Manual,** by Isa N. Engleberg, can be adapted to a variety of course formats and teaching styles. The Instructor's Resource Manual includes the following elements:

- Sample **syllabi**
- A chapter-by-chapter **test bank** of objective and essay questions
- Ready-to-use **speaking assignments** for every chapter
- Ready-to-use **writing assignments** for every chapter
- Ready-to-use **assessment instruments,** including presentation evaluation forms, student feedback forms, and self-evaluation forms
- Chapter-by-chapter **exercises** with accompanying teaching tips
- Photo-ready **graphics** for use as transparencies or handouts
- An instructor's **resource library**
- **Guidelines** for using the manual and its pedagogical features

Other instructor's ancillaries include the following:

- A **Computerized Test Bank,** available in both PC and Mac formats, includes all the test items from the Instructor's Resource Manual.
- A ***PowerPoint* Presentation Program** includes all the "Slides" from the text in addition to other downloadable assets.
- A **Companion Website** includes links to all screen shots shown within the chapters as well as research sites, exercises, the "Slides," and other ancillary materials for instructors and students alike.
- A **Contemporary Great Speeches Video** and a compilation of **Student Speech Videos,** in addition to other video opportunities, are available to textbook adopters. Ask your Houghton Mifflin representative for details.

Student resources:

- The **Speech Preparation Workbook** contains activities and skeleton outline formats for the major presentations discussed in the textbook and assigned in the Instructor's Resource Manual.
- The **Multicultural Activities Workbook for the Public Speaking Classroom**
- A student-focused **Companion Websit**e includes exercises and activities to further develop student skills, such as **A Cyber Evaluation** (**ACE**) online chapter quizzing, hot links to research sites, and links to all screen shots found in the text.
- The **Student CD-ROM** is available for free with the text.

Acknowledgments

We extend our sincere appreciation to the following reviewers, whose excellent suggestions and comments helped shape the final form of *Presentations in Everyday Life:*

Bernard Armada, *University of St. Thomas;* Cameron Basquiat, *Community College of Southern Nevada;* Tim Borchers, *Moorhead State University;* Harold Borden, *El Camino*

Community College; Audrey Boxman, *Merrimack College;* R. D. Britton, *Suffolk Community College;* Brant Burleson, *Purdue University;* Jeff Butler, *University of Central Florida;* Lori A. Byers, *Spalding University;* David Douglass, *Willamette University;* Kerry Egdorf, *University of Wisconsin–Milwaukee;* John Ernst, *Heartland Community College;* James Ferris, *University of Wisconsin;* Barbara Franzen, *Central Community College;* John Gore, *Indiana University–South Bend;* Nichola Gutgold, *Pennsylvania State University–Lehigh Valley;* Robert E. Gwynne, *University of Tennessee–Knoxville;* Todd Holm, *Truman State University;* David S. Hopcroft, *Quinebaug Valley Community Technical College;* Kimberly Howard, *Walla Walla College;* Karen Huck, *Central Oregon Community College;* Richard Ice, *St. John's University;* Susan Jasko, *California University of Pennsylvania;* Corwin King, *Central Washington University;* Charles J. Korn, *Northern Virginia Community College–Manassas;* David LeVasseur, *West Chester University;* John MacKay, *Bowling Green State University;* Rick Maxson, *Drury University;* Janette Kenner Muir, *George Mason University;* Nicholas C. Neupauer, *Butler County Community College;* Andrea Pearman, *Tidewater Community College;* Lori Polacheck, *Itawamba Community College;* Mary-jo Popvici, *Monroe Community College;* Terri Reherman, *San Juan College;* Kellie W. Roberts, *University of Florida;* Glynnis Holm Strauss, *Coastal Bend College;* Mary Triece, *University of Akron;* Jennifer Van Kirk, *University of Illinois at Urbana-Champaign*; Beth M. Waggenspack, *Virginia Polytechnic Institute and State University;* Karin A. Wilking, *Rochester Community and Technical College.* Special thanks are extended to Dianna Wynn, *Courtroom Intelligence.*

Although the title page of this book puts our names front and center, this project would never have seen the light of day without the work of Kristen LeFevre, our talented Development Editor at Houghton Mifflin Company. Kristen took on the daunting task of piloting the second edition of this book through choppy seas. Her patience, good sense, and professionalism helped us transform reviewer suggestions and the new features we insisted on including into a highly coherent, cutting-edge edition of *Presentations in Everyday Life.*

Certainly, it takes a team of publishing professionals to create an outstanding textbook. We extend our heartfelt thanks to our former editors, George Hoffman and Adam Forrand, who paved the way for our wonderful new editor, Mary Finch. We also thank Brigitte Maser, Donna LaVerdiere, Elinor Gregory, Barbara LeBuhn, Nancy Blodget, Audrey Bryant, and Ann Schroeder, whose contributions in marketing, designing, photo researching, art development, and production personify the principle of group synergy. We finally thank Houghton Mifflin's College Division and its president, June Smith, for making a major commitment to us by supporting this project with exceptionally talented professionals.

Isa N. Engleberg
John A. Daly

part one

The Basics

chapter one

Presentation Speaking

- What do real-world speakers want to know about presentation speaking?
- What's the difference between a presentation and a public speech?
- What basic principles underlie all types of presentation speaking?
- How do speakers and listeners work together to communicate?
- How can I become a more effective speaker?

There are dozens of public and presentation speaking books on the shelves of most retail bookstores. Some of their titles are practical—*Speaking Your Way to the Top*, *Writing Great Speeches*, *High-Impact Presentations*. Other titles are somewhat bizarre—*I Can See You Naked*, *I'd Rather Die than Give a Speech*, and *What to Say When You're Dying on the Platform*. Both types of titles provide some insight into their topics. The practical titles presume a compelling need for presentation speaking skills in business and career settings. The "weird" titles tap into the underlying anxiety that often accompanies the prospect of having to speak in front of an audience. Both sets of titles have merit. Most people will have to make presentations, even though making them can create anxiety.

By calling our book *Presentations in Everyday Life: Strategies for Effective Speaking*, we place it squarely in the practical category. Our subtitle—*Strategies for Effective Speaking*—indicates that being an effective speaker requires strategic decision making about everything from organizing your message to developing a strong and clear speaking voice. To become an effective speaker, you must go well beyond the books that offer "secrets," "checklists," and "recipes for success." We believe that effective communication—be it between two people or in front of thousands—requires an understanding of communication theory and research. To that end, we dedicate ourselves to backing up our advice with that of the best communication scholars and researchers we know. *Presentations in Everyday Life* does more than offer advice about *what* to do when you have to speak—it explains *how* to speak and *why* the advice works.

The Real World of Presentation Speaking

How do you become a better speaker? This question prompted us to write this textbook. In cooperation with the Market Research Department of our publishers, Houghton Mifflin Company, we designed and conducted a national survey aimed at answering this question. Instead of surveying faculty or students, we sent a questionnaire to people at business addresses who had bought one or more commercially available books on public speaking within a one-year period. We wanted to learn which topics were most important to consumers beyond the college classroom.[1] After all, you may be a student speaker for only one brief semester—and a "real-world" speaker for the rest of your life!

Our questionnaire included a checklist and one open-ended question: "Can you tell us about a situation in which you had to prepare and deliver a speech or presentation and why you think it was successful or unsuccessful?" The respondents' answers are gems. We read stories about speaking triumphs and disappointments. People shared their "secrets" of good speaking as well as their anxieties. We discovered that even the most experienced and successful speakers are still looking for ways to improve. You will find some of these real-life stories throughout this book and, we hope, will identify with the challenges these speakers faced and learn from the ways in which they met those challenges.

What Matters to Presenters

Without going into significant detail, we would like to share a few notable results from our survey. But please do not draw any broad conclusions. Remember that this survey was sent to a specific type of audience—working professionals who had purchased a book on public speaking during a one-year period. And as with any other opinion survey, there are no "right" answers. Rather, our results give a rough sketch of what motivated book buyers wanted to learn about becoming better speakers.

What do you think mattered most to our book buyers? The top six concerns are listed below.

After analyzing the results of our survey and thinking about our own students' needs, we concluded that regardless of a presenter's level of speaking experience and ability, everyone has questions about how to become a better speaker. Sometimes the questions are enormous in scope: Where do I start? Sometimes they're very specific: What should I do with my hands when I speak? Because the answers to questions like these can make a big difference in a presentation's outcome, we have structured this entire book around asking the questions our students ask us most often and exploring their answers.

TOP-RANKED SPEAKING SKILLS

1. **Keeping your audience interested**
2. **Beginning and ending your presentation**
3. **Organizing your presentation**
4. **Selecting ideas and information for your presentation**
5. **Deciding what to say (choosing a topic or an approach)**
6. **Understanding and adapting to your audience**

Why Speaking Skills Matter to You

Several years ago, an article appeared in the *New York Times*[2] with the headline "Meek and Mumblers Learn Ways of Getting a Word In." The article describes how more and more people are devoting time, money, and energy to improving their speaking skills. Why? The article's examples demonstrate how important presentation speaking has become for achieving personal and career success.

- One 14-week public speaking course offered by Dale Carnegie & Associates, Inc., attracted 117,000 students and garnered $100 million in revenue.
- Toastmasters International, the best-known nonprofit organization whose mission is to improve public speaking, has enjoyed a 7 percent annual increase in membership for the last decade.
- An estimated 45 percent of all medium and large corporations provide some public speaking training for their employees.
- Corporate clients can pay up to $3,000 per day for one-on-one instruction and $15,000 for group lessons in public speaking.
- Special medical clinics offer 16-week treatments for presentation anxiety; these can cost from $800 to $2,000 per person.

Speech training has become a big business for good reasons. Despite and because of our increased interaction with technology and media, we have more opportunities to speak today than we had only a decade ago. In the introduction to her book *Simply Speaking,* Peggy Noonan, who was one of President Ronald Reagan's speechwriters, notes:

> *The changes that have swept modern businesses have contributed to a talking boom. As more and more businesses become involved in the new media technologies, as we become a nation of fewer widgets and more Web sites, a new premium has been put on the oldest form of communication: the ability to stand up and say what you think in front of others. At the business conference, in the teleconference and the seminar, businessmen and businesswomen are increasingly called on to speak about their industry, their plans, the realities within which they operate, what government is doing or not doing to make things better or worse. And they're not alone. Teachers and professors and reporters and doctors are out there too.*[3]

Effective presentations have enormous power. Famous speeches—President Abraham Lincoln's *Gettysburg Address,* Martin Luther King Jr.'s *I Have a Dream*—have literally shaped the world we live in. The best presentations can delight us, inspire us, and even make us cry. Responsible speakers employ this power to make the world a better place. Unethical speakers have used the same power to bring tyranny and death to millions.

Presentations have consequences. When you deliver a dazzling presentation, you enhance your personal credibility and influence the lives of others. Most famous

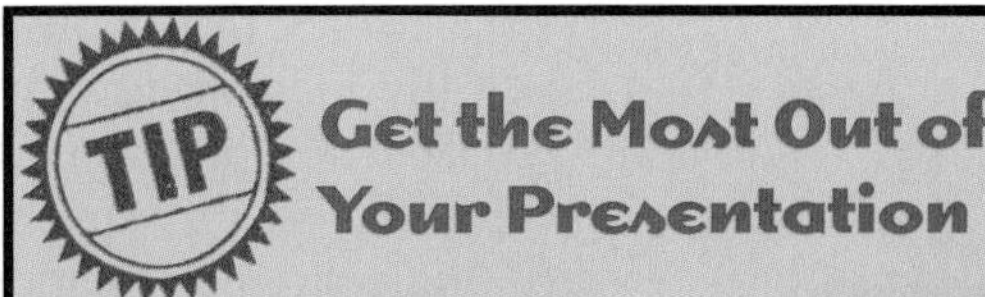

Get the Most Out of Your Presentation

"We live in a competitive world. An effective presentation allows you, as well as your knowledge, talent, and abilities, to stand out from the rest of the crowd,"[1] writes Robert Pike, a leading communication consultant and trainer. He also maintains, "How you [give presentations] will either raise or lower your credibility and make a difference in your ability to influence others."[2] There is more to a presentation than meets the eye (and ear) of your audience. Since you *will* have to speak, why not take advantage of the opportunity? In addition to sharing a message, use your presentation as a way to stand out and be noticed.

1. Robert W. Pike, *High-Impact Presentations* (West Des Moines, IA: American Media, 1995), p. 8
2. Pike, p. 9

Bobby Drozek, a student at Marlboro College in Vermont, argues for the installation of cable television at a monthly town meeting where students and faculty each have a vote.

leaders—be they in business, religion, or government—have the ability to present ideas clearly and persuasively. Even great people who are not famous—distinguished teachers, doctors, preachers, and community leaders—understand that presentation speaking skills are prerequisites for success.

Effective presentation skills can be evidenced by the difference between knowing something and being able to explain it. Effective speaking can mean the difference between having a good idea and knowing how to share it with others. The ability to prepare and deliver a successful presentation is illustrated by the difference between interesting audience members and inspiring them to action.

No matter what your current or future profession may be, it will most likely require you to make presentations. Thus, learning to become an effective presenter is a wise personal investment.[4] Since you *will* give presentations, be prepared to do them well.

What Is Presentation Speaking?

Perhaps you are sitting in a college course titled Public Speaking and wondering why we've been talking so much about *presentation* speaking. We chose this term deliberately because we believe that *presentation speaking* is a broader, more inclusive term than *public speaking.* The key word here is *public.*

The American Heritage Dictionary of the English Language defines *public* as "of, concerning, or affecting the community or the people; participated in or attended by the people or a community; connected with or acting on behalf of the people, community, or government." In brief, the word *public* refers to the "community or people as a whole."[5] When you hear the term *public* or *public audience,* what do you envision? A staff meeting? Probably not. You probably see a lone figure standing on a stage facing a large audience. Now, what do you think of when you hear the term *presentation* or *presentation speaking*? A political rally? Probably not. You probably see a professional person addressing a group of colleagues in a meeting or someone talking to an informal group of interested listeners.

As we see it, **public speaking** is a special type of presentation speaking that occurs when speakers address public audiences in community, government, and/or organizational settings. Public speeches are usually open and accessible to the public and press and have the potential, if not the purpose, of affecting people beyond the immediate audience. **Presentation speaking** is a much broader term and refers to *any* time speakers use verbal and nonverbal messages to generate meanings and establish relationships with audience members, who are usually present at the delivery of a presentation.[6] We prefer the term *presentation speaking* for three reasons:

PRESENTATIONS

- **Are more common than public speeches**
- **Are less formal than public speeches**
- **Are more important to employers**

Reviewing the Public Speaking Tradition

Presentation speaking has a lengthy and distinguished history. Thousands of years ago—long before most people used reading and writing to share knowledge and test ideas—speech was the primary means to achieve a variety of goals. Citizens and their rulers used speech in legislative assemblies and courts of law. Philosophers used speech to ask questions and discuss great ideas. Military leaders used speech to explain campaigns and motivate soldiers. It is not surprising that the most effective speakers were also the most influential citizens, rulers, philosophers, teachers, and military leaders. The roots of presentation and public speaking lie in ancient fields.

The most important group of early speech theorists and teachers in Western civilization lived in Greece and Rome. Ancient Athens was an oral society in which citizens (all male in those times) were expected to express their views clearly and persuasively in law courts, in political assemblies, and on special public occasions. One of the most famous and influential philosophers was Aristotle, one of Plato's students, who created his own school of philosophy. Aristotle's famous *Rhetoric,* written during the late fourth century B.C., established many of the public speaking strategies we use today. His definition of **rhetoric** as the ability to discover "in the particular case what are the available means of persuasion"[1] focuses on strategies for selecting the most appropriate persuasive arguments for a particular audience in a particular circumstance. His division of proof into logical arguments (*logos*), emotional arguments (*pathos*), and arguments based on speaker credibility (*ethos*) remains a hallmark for teaching persuasive speaking.

In ancient Rome, we encounter the revitalization of the five great canons of classical Greek rhetoric. Speakers were taught to devise the best ideas for an argument (*inventio,* invention) and to arrange those ideas effectively (*dispositio,* organization). The words selected to express ideas effectively (*eloquotio,* style) relied on the speaker's ability to think critically and recall (*memoria,* memory) as well as on the ability to deliver a speech effectively (*pronuntiatio,* delivery). The great statesman and orator Cicero and the lawyer-rhetorician Quintillian enlarged on these ideas in their own works on rhetoric.

In the broadest sense, the origins of Western thought and Western civilization began with the philosophers and rhetorical theorists of ancient Greece and Rome. In *The Rhetoric of Western Thought,* James Golden and his colleagues put it this way: In ancient Greece and Rome, effective public speaking was "an instrument for conveying truth to the masses, as a culturally important subject which merited scientific classification and analysis, and as practical training essential for every free citizen."[2]

As an inheritor of that tradition, you can begin your quest to become a more effective speaker by knowing that centuries of thought and theory form the basis for the strategies and skills you will study in this textbook.

1. Lane Cooper, *The Rhetoric of Aristotle* (New York: Appleton-Century-Crofts, 1932), p. 7.
2. James L. Golden, Goodwin F. Berquist, and William E. Coleman, *The Rhetoric of Western Thought,* 4th ed. (Dubuque, IA: Kendall/Hunt, 1989), p. 14.

Presentations Are More Common

Most of you will make many presentations but few public speeches. Your presentations will *not* be directed to the community or to "people as a whole." Of course, there are exceptions. If you decide to run for office or to become active in community issues, you will have to speak in front of public audiences. If you become famous—as either an expert or a celebrity—you will be invited to make public speeches. But in general, you are much more likely to be asked to make a presentation in smaller, private settings. For example, presenters teach classes, summarize sales strategies, coach middle school soccer teams, and brief the media at crime scenes.

As we've indicated, *presentation speaking* is a broad term. It encompasses everything from small, intimate talks in private settings to major speeches in front of large public audiences. By using the broader term, we can cover more kinds of speaking situations and still zero in on the kinds of presentations you will be asked to make.

Presentations Are Less Formal

Generally, a public speech is more formal than a private presentation. Usually, presentations are delivered from notes rather than written out and delivered word for word. Given the workplace setting of most presentations, you are also more likely to use visual aids during a presentation. And although some politicians and public figures are increasing their use of visual aids, most public speakers simply stand behind a lectern and speak.

Presentations usually allow and even encourage more interaction between the speaker and the audience. Both the speaker and the audience members may question each other. There may even be a brief pause for a discussion among listeners. On the other hand, in public speaking, the speaker speaks, the audience listens, and if questions come, they come only after the speech is finished.[7]

Presentations Are More Important to Employers

In 1997, the Business–Higher Education Forum, in affiliation with the American Council on Education, conducted a study in which employers were asked how best to prepare college students for the world of work. The subsequent report placed (oral) communication skills at the top of the list.[8] In 2000, the National Association of Colleges and Employers conducted a survey in which employers were asked to rank, in order of importance, a list of ten skills they seek in college graduates. The results: Oral communication skills were first on the list.[9]

Businesses need good presenters, not public orators. When employers are asked about the skills they are looking for in new employees, *public* speaking is not at the top of their lists. What does emerge, however, is a clear preference for communication skills, including the ability to present ideas and information to colleagues and clients. In fact, most business settings use the term *presentations* rather than *public speaking*. When we work as consultants, we are never asked to prepare a public speaking seminar. Instead, we are asked to provide training sessions that focus on presentation skills. The titles of many popular books on speaking also reflect this business orientation: The American Management Association publishes *How to Prepare, Stage & Deliver Winning Presentations.* Career Press publishes *Secrets of Power Presentations.* Robert W. Pike, a nationally recognized communication trainer, is the author of *High-Impact Presentations.*[10]

Chita Roa-Marquez, a nurse from New Jersey, understands the difference between presentation speaking and public speaking. In her response to our survey, she wrote: "As a nurse supervisor by profession, I make a lot of presentations (about new procedures, trends, and in-service training). As founding president of a nonprofit organization, I do a lot of public speaking (welcoming addresses, keynote speeches, or being the mistress of ceremonies at a public event)."

Presentation Speaking and Conversational Speaking

People who spend hours talking to their friends, family members, and coworkers often freeze up when they're asked to give a five-minute presentation. A manager who can drop in on a colleague to discuss a new project may panic when asked to give a talk

Real World Real Speakers

Trust Yourself and Your Speaking Style

One of your authors once worked for a man who seemed to have two personalities—one for conversations and one for presentations. His conversational speaking style was very friendly and relaxed, with a great sense of humor. Colleagues looked forward to talking with him because he made them feel so comfortable. They felt like his equal in all discussions. Everyone thought he was a great boss. His presentation speaking style, however, was totally different. He'd get up in front of a group, and his voice would go down in pitch. He'd use lots of technical terms. He'd become stiff and formal. He'd even research jokes to tell. Although he had strong interpersonal communication skills, he was an awful speaker. He didn't seem like himself. He put people off. Even his jokes were bad. Only those who worked with him knew this wasn't what he was really like. Unfortunately, he lost several top management jobs because he came across as cold and technical when speaking in front of groups. It's too bad he didn't trust using the conversational speaking style that everyone knew and liked.

explaining that project to a group of vice presidents. A neighbor who complains about the condition of the street may back off when asked to describe those conditions at the weekly city council meeting. Why is it that we treat presentation speaking and conversational speaking so differently? We devote Chapter 3, "Building Presentation Confidence," to one reason—presentation anxiety. Fear of speaking in front of groups can turn ordinarily confident people into nervous wrecks.

There is, however, another reason that people regard presentation speaking and conversational speaking as different forms of communication. A lot of people think that presentation speaking requires a very different kind of speech—different vocabulary, a different way of talking, different physical behavior. Experienced speakers know that using a conversational speaking style can create a friendly atmosphere in which audience members are comfortable and motivated to listen. We will see in Chapter 12, "Engaging Language," that choosing the style and language that best suit your audience is a critical part of presentation speaking. In general, effective speakers rely on words that are simple, short, and direct rather than on the more formal language used in a term paper or business report.

You don't have to become a different person when you speak in front of an audience. However, that doesn't mean you should use exactly the same style for both conversational and presentation speaking. There are some differences. For a presentation, you should make sure that you are speaking loudly enough to be heard. You should also spend more time preparing. At the same time, don't give up a speaking style that has worked for you for years in most other communication situations. Trust yourself and let your personality be an important part of your speaking style.

Basic Principles of Presentation Speaking

At the heart of this textbook is a decision-making system based on a few carefully chosen communication principles. These principles can help you make critical decisions about your presentation from the minute you find out you will have to speak to the minute you've said your last word. By applying these principles, you should be able to make effective decisions about what to say, be able to explain the reasons that your decisions make sense, and be able to evaluate your decisions by assessing the success of your presentation.

The Seven Principles

The basic principles of presentation speaking include seven decision-making points that encourage critical thinking. We have selected a single word to represent the key element in each principle. Are the principles represented by these seven words all you need to know about effective speaking? No. As you can see from the upcoming chapter headings, we cover many more than seven topics in this textbook. The seven principles, however, represent the most basic decisions you will have to make when preparing and delivering a successful presentation. Each principle answers key questions about presentation speaking.

PRINCIPLES OF PRESENTATION SPEAKING

Purpose: Determine your purpose.
Audience: Connect with your audience.
Credibility: Enhance your believability.
Logistics: Adapt to the location and occasion.
Content: Select appropriate content.
Organization: Organize your content.
Performance: Practice your delivery.

Purpose: Why are you speaking? When determining the purpose of your presentation, ask yourself these questions: What do I want my audience to know, think, believe, or do as a result of my presentation? Given my purpose, how do I focus and narrow my topic?

Audience: Who is in your audience? To understand your audience, ask yourself: How do the characteristics of my audience—such as demographics, interests, and attitudes—affect my purpose? How can I learn more about my audience? In what ways can I adapt to my audience in order to improve my presentation?

Credibility: Are you believable? Presentations can enhance your credibility. Ask yourself: How can I become associated with my message in a positive way? What can I do to demonstrate my expertise on this topic? What will assure the audience that I am worthy of their trust? Am I an ethical speaker?

Logistics: Where and when will you speak? When considering the location and occasion of a presentation, ask yourself: Why am I speaking to this group at this time in this place? How can I plan for and adapt to the logistics of the place where I will be speaking? Does the occasion require special adaptations?

Content: What ideas and information should you include? When searching for and selecting materials for your presentation, ask yourself: Where and how can I find good ideas and information for my presentation? How much and what kind of supporting material do I need? Have I found the best sources? Which ideas and information should I include?

Organization: How should you arrange your content? When organizing your presentation, ask yourself: Is there a natural order to the ideas and information I want to include in my presentation? What are the most effective ways to organize my presentation in order to adapt it to my purpose, audience, logistics, and content? How should I begin and end my presentation? How do I link its major sections?

Performance: How should you deliver your presentation? Asking yourself questions about delivery before you get up to speak can improve the quality of your performance. Ask yourself: What form of delivery is appropriate for my purpose, audience, and setting? What delivery techniques will make my presentation more effective? How much and what should I practice?

Applying the seven principles of presentation speaking requires more than checking off items on a "To Do" list. Each principle affects the others. For example, even the best-organized presentation won't achieve its purpose if it offends the audience or uses words they don't understand. Likewise, a flawlessly prepared but poorly delivered presentation may not capture its audience's attention. Any decision made about one principle will have an impact on the others.

Moreover, later decisions can affect earlier ones. If, while practicing your presentation, you discover that you've gone far over the time limit, you should go back and reduce the amount of information in your presentation or cut some of the key points. If you can't find the information you need, or if your research doesn't prove the point you want to make, you may need to modify or change your purpose.

FAQ ?

What are Encoding and Decoding?

Most of the terms that describe the communication process are self-explanatory, but we're often asked to explain two of them in more detail: *encoding* and *decoding*. In a very real sense, most of this book is devoted to strategies for effectively encoding and decoding messages in a presentation speaking context. When we communicate with each other, we convert our ideas into messages by using language as well as vocal and physical delivery. Thus, encoding is the decision-making process we use to create and send messages. Think of it this way: You go to a store looking for the perfect greeting card to send to a friend. None of the cards you look through captures what you want to say, so you buy a blank card. After several tries at writing the greeting, you're stumped. You can't find the right words to express your ideas and feelings. You have an encoding problem. In presentation speaking, you can avoid encoding problems by considering all seven principles—purpose, audience, credibility, logistics, content, organization, and performance—in advance and avoid being caught with little or nothing to say.

Decoding converts a "code" into an understandable form. Thus, it is the decision-making process we use to interpret, evaluate, and respond to messages. In presentation speaking, decoding involves more than hearing and seeing a speaker. Audience characteristics, motives, interests, knowledge, attitudes, and learning styles influence the decoding process and contribute to a listener's ability to receive a message as it was intended by a speaker. Communication problems occur when encoding (the speaker's intended message) and decoding (the listener's interpretation of that message) do not match.

How Communication Works

The seven principles of presentation speaking work for a reason: They have emerged from centuries of studying what communication is and how it functions. These definitions and functions can be expressed in **communication models,** which identify and name the steps or components involved in the communication process. Models also show how these components relate to and interact with each other. And they can help explain why a presentation did or did not achieve its intended purpose—or even predict whether or not it will.[11]

Figure 1.1 Basic Communication Model

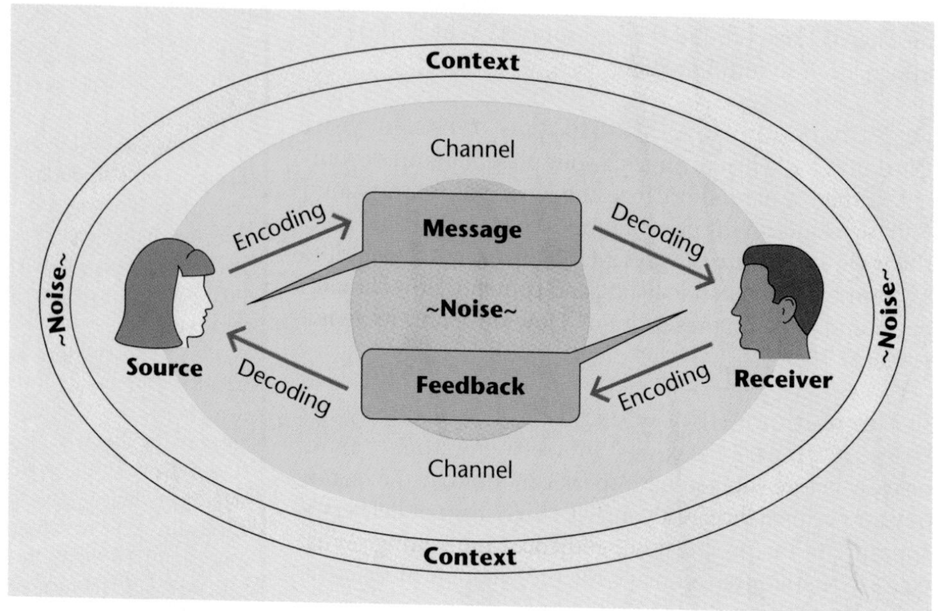

How do communication models, as in Figure 1.1, characterize the interaction between speakers and listeners? They always include a **message,** the content of the presentation itself. As the **source** of that message, the speaker **encodes** it with specific words and actions and then sends that message out into the world. The **channel** is the medium (sight and sound) through which the message travels. The message, though, doesn't really mean anything until it arrives at a **receiver,** a person who **decodes** the message and decides what it means.

The speaker (source) and the audience (receiver) rely on each other to give messages their meaning. Communication is not a one-way street. Rather, it is a transaction between a speaker and one or more listeners. In a business transaction, we exchange money for goods. In a **communication transaction,** we exchange messages in order to share meaning.

Finally, all communication takes place in a **context**—a surrounding environment that can affect every aspect of the communication process. Context can be *physical*—the size of a room, the lighting, the attractiveness or comfort of the setting. Context can also be *psychological*—the mood of the audience, the temperament of the speaker, the unsettling effects of a recent event. All presentations occur in a certain setting at a certain time under certain conditions. All of these factors contribute to a context that affects how we speak and listen to one another.

The Dynamic Presentation Model

In the same way that communication models represent the interaction between communicators, a model of presentation speaking that we have developed reflects the dynamic relationship between your presentation and your audience. We use the word *dynamic* to signify the fact that presentation speaking is a complex, compelling, and

Figure 1.2 The Dynamic Presentation Model

The source of the message—you—is represented by the wheel on the left.
The receiver—your audience—is represented by the wheel on the right.

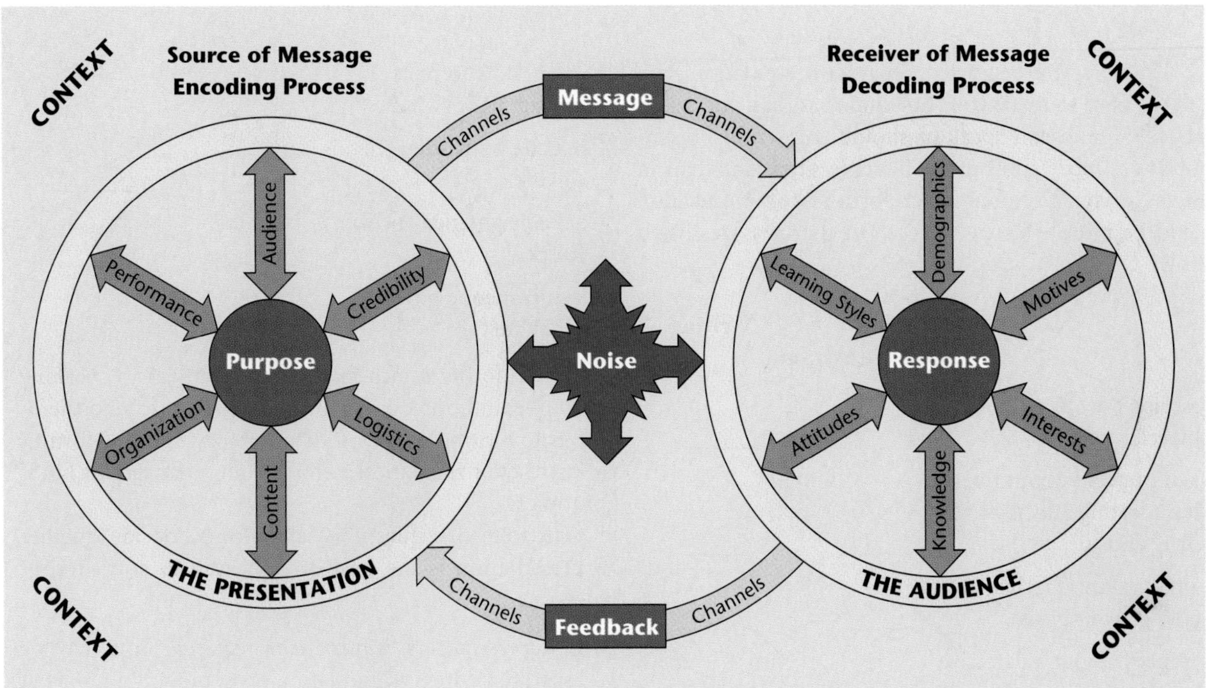

even chaotic process. During a presentation, many things happen at once. Figure 1.2 "freezes" a presentation to illustrate our model's interacting components.

The Presentation. Let's start with the left "wheel," representing a speaker's presentation. At the center or hub of the wheel is the first and most important decision-making point: determining the purpose of your presentation. All subsequent decisions you make will connect to and revolve around this point. The spokes on the wheel represent the remaining six principles.

Purpose should guide the ways in which you adapt to your audience and to the logistics of your presentation. Purpose likewise should influence your decisions about gathering, selecting, and organizing the ideas and information you will include in that presentation. All the "purposeful" choices you make in the planning stages in turn will affect your decisions about how to present yourself as a credible source and how best to deliver your message. All these spokes connect the hub (purpose) to the outer "surface" or "rim" of the wheel, the presentation itself. Thus, a well-prepared speaker delivers a message that reflects strategic decisions about every principle.

The presentation wheel is a dynamic representation of what happens when a speaker encodes a message. However, having a purpose is not enough; the hub of a wheel won't get you anywhere. Successful encoding also involves deciding how to construct and place each spoke of the wheel on the hub so that the wheel is strong and headed in the

Choosing the Best Form for Your Message

Before you begin to prepare a presentation, you need to make your first and most basic decision: Should you speak or should you write? Presentations are more appropriate in some situations than in others. In your opinion, which form of communication would be more effective for each of the messages listed below?

	Oral Presentation	Writing
Describe how to assemble a bicycle.	______	______
Warn preteens about the long-lasting effects of drug abuse.	______	______
Convince your teacher to change your grade.	______	______
Complain about a defective product to a company.	______	______
Share a recipe for lemon poppy-seed pound cake.	______	______
Explain how to repair a broken light switch.	______	______
Persuade nonvoting friends to vote.	______	______
Coax a frightened speaker to speak.	______	______
Teach someone how to meditate.	______	______

What do the topics that lend themselves to speaking have in common? What about the topics that lend themselves to writing? Can you definitely say that one form is always better than another for certain messages or kinds of topics?

The following questions can help you decide whether a presentation is the best or only way to convey your message:

- *Is a presentation requested or required?* You may be asked to address a graduating class, present a report at a staff meeting, offer a toast at a wedding, or introduce a guest speaker. In such cases, not only does the nature of the event require a presentation, but the audience

right direction. Keep in mind that a missing spoke or a weak one can cripple a wheel. Likewise, failing to consider one or more principles can prevent a speaker from reaching an audience and achieving the presentation's purpose.

The Audience. At the center or hub of the audience's wheel is its response. In an ideal communication transaction, the speaker's purpose and the audience's response would be the same. For example, if your purpose is to persuade audience members to donate five dollars to the local Red Cross chapter, you have a successful transaction when everyone in the audience donates five dollars. However, in the real world of presentation speaking, perfect transactions are extremely rare. More than likely, some audience members will donate nothing, some will give you their pocket change, others will produce the $5 bill, and a few inspired listeners may give you more than five dollars.

Chapter 5, "Audience Analysis and Adaptation," explores the factors represented by the spokes of the audience wheel. By considering and adapting to these factors, a speaker has a better chance of matching purpose and response—the message the audience "gets" is the message the speaker intended.

The audience wheel is a dynamic representation of what happens when audience members decode a message. Depending on the spokes of the audience wheel (demographics, motives, interests, knowledge, attitudes, and learning styles), listeners may interpret, evaluate, and respond to a message in a variety of ways that have little to do also expects certain qualities in the presentation—inspiration for a commencement speech, clarity and brevity in a report, good cheer at a wedding, and background information about a guest speaker.

- *Is immediate action needed?* If an unexpected problem arises, there may not be time to write a memo or publish a report. If an audience must be made aware of a problem in order to take immediate action, a presentation may be the best way to respond. If a crisis requires that everyone be told about a situation as quickly as possible, a presentation would be much more effective than a written report.
- *Is the topic controversial?* Confronting a controversy in person can often produce better results than trying to deal with the problem in writing. A face-to-face situation gives a speaker the opportunity to explain the problem and correct misunderstandings as they arise. Audience members can listen, ask questions, and challenge ideas. Although this kind of speaking can be difficult and even intimidating, audiences would prefer to hear about most controversies from a speaker. The exceptions are topics that can be too upsetting to discuss before a large audience, such as news about a personal tragedy or announcements about budget cuts. In these cases, written messages or one-to-one conversations can soften the blow.
- *Will the audience have questions?* Any subject, whether it's controversial or not, may prompt audience questions. A new or complex procedure may best be introduced in a presentation that encourages audience questions and comments. In a controversial or emergency situation, answering audience questions may be the most important part of a presentation. A presidential press conference, for example, may begin with a short statement about a new or ongoing crisis and be followed by the many and varied questions of the White House press corps.
- *Will YOU make a difference?* It is difficult to ignore someone talking to you face to face. It is much easier to ignore an e-mail, a memo, or a report. The emotion in a speaker's voice and the physical energy of a presentation are difficult to capture in a written message. Audiences know that you're taking a bigger risk when you put yourself and your message in front of them rather than communicate through the safety and distance of a written message. A presentation can be the most effective form of communication simply because *you are there.* Your willingness to "put yourself on the line" makes your message more personal and important. The more your message depends on you, the more you need a presentation.

with the speaker's intended message. On the other hand, when a speaker considers the audience "spokes," the speaker and the audience may share a common meaning.

Message, Channel, and Feedback. There are three other essential components in the Dynamic Presentation Model. The first is the message—the presentation itself. Your message is more than the content of a presentation; it includes the way in which you have transformed your purpose into words and action.

The **channel** is the medium through which you transmit the message to your audience. Anything that affects the senses of sight, hearing, touch, taste, or smell can be used as a communication channel. In most speaking situations, hearing and sight are the principle channels used to transmit a message. However, the more channels you use, the more likely your message will be understood and appreciated. For example, would you rather write a letter to your best friend, talk to your friend on the telephone, or communicate with your friend in person? Given the choice, most of us would spend time with our best friend. Whereas writing only uses the sight channel, and talking on the phone only uses the sound channel, face-to-face communication can engage all channels of communication. The more channels you use, the richer the communication experience

The third element, **feedback,** is critical to a presenter's success. Feedback is any verbal or nonverbal response from your audience that you can see or hear. Are your audience members smiling or frowning, leaning forward or falling asleep, taking notes or

Feedback works both ways. The success of this jazz musician's workshop depends on his ability to respond to student feedback when he speaks and performs—and on his giving appropriate feedback to students when they speak and perform.

raising their hands, applauding or grumbling, asking questions or challenging your conclusions? Audience feedback helps you to assess how well your message is being received and whether you are likely to achieve your purpose. Feedback is also a critical element in the meaning-creation process; it is your audience "speaking" to you—encoding and sending you their own messages. If you "listen" to audience feedback and decode its meaning, you can even adjust your message and delivery while you are speaking. We strongly believe that feedback-induced adaptation is critical to a presenter's success.

Noise

Presentation speaking is not, unfortunately, a perfectly predictable or reliable process. As the wheels in our model turn and interact, they may encounter "bumps" and obstacles in their path that can inhibit a message from reaching its receivers as it was intended to do. **Noise** is a communication term used to describe these inhibiting factors. Noise can be *external*—such as a police siren outside the window, a soft speaking voice, or a difficult-to-understand accent. Noise can also be *internal* and psychological. *Psychological* noise occurs when a listener is preoccupied with personal thoughts and therefore misses or misinterprets a message.[12] Psychological noise affects speakers, too. For example, the "noise" of worrying about how you look or focusing on an audience member who is frowning may inhibit your ability to speak effectively.

Effective speakers are as sensitive to potential and real noise as they are to audience feedback. If noise is physical, they can try to reduce or eliminate it—for example, by closing a window or speaking with more volume and clarity. If noise is psychological, they can try to overcome their internal or audience distractions. Noise is an unpredictable and ever-present phenomenon in every speaking situation.

Use Feedback to Gauge Audience Reactions

Our survey respondents frequently cited the ability to adapt to feedback as being critical to their success. Harold Stocker, president of Stocker and Associates, a marketing and design company in Bartlett, Illinois, emphasized that when speaking to a large or small group, "you *know* when they are with you." A company president and CEO who did not wish to be named wrote about what happened when he "fumbled through a presentation and rambled on: I noticed that I was losing audience interest, which unnerved me even more. I guess, in the truest sense, that was audience feedback." Lewis A. McLeod, who works as an air-quality program manager for the Confederate Salish and Kootenai Tribes in Montana, commented that "there was and always seems to be plenty of feedback and questions from students at the local tribal college. For that reason alone I feel the presentations were successful." Cheryl Draper-Shaw, a registered nurse in Red Springs, North Carolina, wrote: "I know they have listened when they ask questions or make comments." Experienced speakers are sensitive to audience reactions. They use feedback—whether positive or negative—to assess and adjust their presentations.

Noise can be highly disruptive, regardless of whether it is in the room, in the audience's mind, or in your head. Ineffective speakers seem oblivious to noise—they keep speaking even when a nearby siren drowns out their talk or a traumatic event distracts their audience.

Effective speakers are proactive. They think ahead and anticipate the potential sources of noise. Then they try to prevent that noise from happening or from interfering with their presentation. Don't wait for noise to derail your presentation; be

Leslie Walker, the great-great-great niece of Harriet Tubman, speaks to a third-grade class about her famous relative. Would her talk be different if she were speaking to a university class, a public audience, or a group of history professors?

prepared to dampen, eliminate, and/or adapt to any noise you may encounter. If unexpected noise does occur, don't ignore it. Determine its source and significance; then adapt. And remember that regardless of the kinds of noise you may encounter in most speaking situations, "the show must go on."

In an ideal speaking situation, the speaker has a clear central purpose and strong "spokes" to support a presentation. The message the presentation conveys moves through a channel without any interfering noise. Listeners receive a message that takes their feedback into account and has been adapted to the characteristics represented by the audience wheel's "spokes." And most critically, in an ideal speaking situation, the speaker's purpose and the audience's response overlap into a mutually beneficial transaction, as Figure 1.3 below shows. Effective speakers accept the fact that they may never create or deliver a perfect presentation. At the same time, they never stop trying to reach that ideal.

Becoming an Effective Speaker

A presentation can often be the most efficient and effective way to communicate. Presentation speaking can make immediate and personal contact with an audience in a way that cannot be duplicated by writing and can reach many people with an efficiency that cannot be matched in one-to-one conversations.

Reading this textbook will not make you a better speaker. Speaking will. Like many skills, presentation speaking requires knowledge *and* practice. It also requires as much preparation as a lawyer gives to an important case, as a tennis pro gives to a championship tournament, and as a great chef gives to a royal banquet. Some speakers are luckier than others. They seem to have an instinct that tells them when and how to achieve their goals through presentation speaking. Most of us are not that fortunate. We need to consciously learn the strategies and skills of preparing and delivering effec-

Figure 1.3

A Successful Communication Transaction

A speaker's purpose and the audience's response are brought together by a message and feedback-induced adaptation.

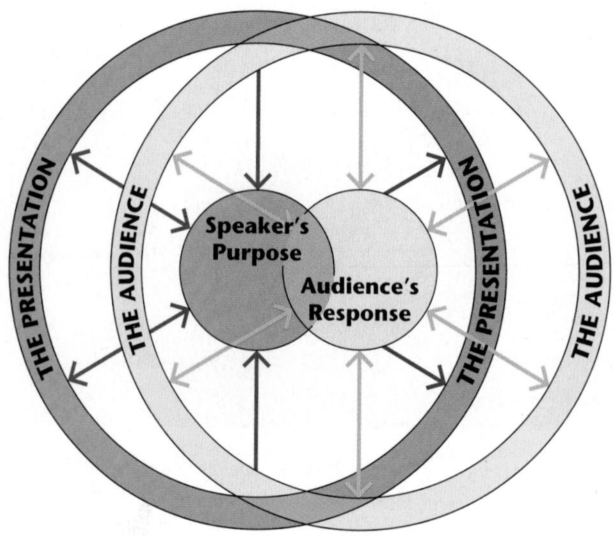

tive presentations. However, you *can* become a confident and successful speaker, and we're here to help. At the very least, you should understand the importance of cultural sensitivity, the responsibility to communicate ethically, and the value of making strategic decisions.

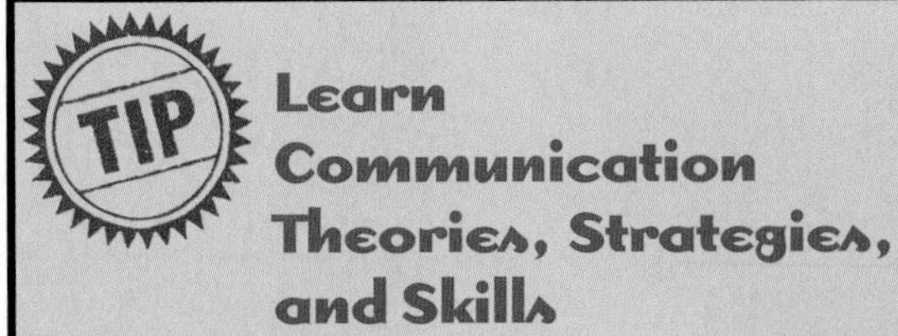

Learn Communication Theories, Strategies, and Skills

Effective speakers understand that communication theories, strategies, and skills form the foundation of effective presentations.[1]

Theories are statements or general principles that explain why and how the world works. Consider the impact of Einstein's theory of relativity and Darwin's evolutionary theories on the way you understand the world around you. Theories can also help you understand why some speakers succeed and others fail. They do not necessarily tell you what to do or say. Nevertheless, without theories, we would have difficulty understanding why or how to use a particular strategy or skill. Throughout this textbook, a wide range of theories are presented to help you understand and make effective decisions about the development of your presentations.

Strategies represent the specific plans of action you select to help you achieve your purpose. Well-chosen strategies can help you analyze and adapt to your audience and decide how to organize the key points of your presentation. The most effective strategies are based on strong theories and good research. If you don't understand theory, you won't know why strategies work in one situation and fail in another.

Skills are the tools you use to prepare and perform a presentation. They range from writing talent to performance ability. Skills also include the ability to do research, think critically, and create an outline. Like strategies, skills are most effective when they are grounded in theory. Without theories and strategies, you may not understand when and why to use a particular skill to its best advantage.

1. Based on an adaptation of Senge's theories, methods, and tools in building learning organizations in Peter M. Senge et al., *The Fifth Discipline Fieldbook: Strategies and Tools for Building a Learning Organization* (New York: Doubleday, 1994), p. 31.

Cultural Sensitivity

Effective speakers understand, respect, and adapt to the diverse world in which they live and speak. The global reach of modern technology and transportation as well as the unprecedented demographic changes of the recent past and projected future place speakers and audience members in a rich, multicultural environment.

Many years ago, a white American businessman could predict the gender, race, average age, and even religion of most audience members—they would look like him, speak like him, and share many of the same attitudes, beliefs, and values. Today, such audiences are rare. Many years ago, hospital nurses could predict the gender, predominant race, and average age of most colleagues and the doctors for whom they worked. Today, hospitals are multicultural communities in which a thirty-five-year-old woman from India might be an orderly, a nurse, a doctor, or a chief administrator.

We live and speak in a multicultural world. Not surprisingly, speakers and audience members from different cultures communicate differently. Culturally sensitive speakers develop effective strategies when communicating with diverse audiences within and outside the borders of their home community and country. In Chapter 5, "Audience Analysis and Adaptation," we consider the ways in which cultural dimensions and cultural values affect audience analysis and adaptation. Here we offer an introduction to several intercultural principles that can help you make strategic decisions as you develop and deliver presentations to a wide range of audience members.[13]

Understanding, respecting, and adapting to cultural diversity begin with comprehending *culture* as a concept. **Culture** can be defined as the common characteristics and collective perceptions that distinguish one group of people from another. Cultures extend well beyond race, ethnicity, and geography. Thus, a peanut farmer from Georgia and a New York advertising executive can have very different cultural perspectives, as would a Nigerian, an Indonesian Moslem, and a Navaho tribal member. When you think about cultural diversity, consider how factors such as age, gender, religion, education, socioeconomic status, sexual orientation, range of abilities, common history, language, and political perspectives affect values, beliefs, and behaviors.

Also, *within* most cultures there are groups of people—members of **microcultures**—that coexist within the mainstream society.[14] In the United States, Native American Indian tribes can be considered microcultures—as can African Americans,

David Tsui, Director of Hong Kong's Economic and Trade Office, speaks to the Chamber of Commerce in Syracuse, New York. In such a situation, both speaker and audience members should respect and adapt to cultural differences.

Hispanic/Latino Americans, Asian Americans, and members of large and small religious groups.

For the most part, intercultural communication research has been conducted in and applied to personal relationships, business management settings, and education and health care environments. We know much less about the ways in which intercultural differences operate in presentation speaking. Even though the mass media may broadcast programming, news, and advertisements to the most remote corners of the globe, we do not know which presentation speaking theories, strategies, and skills are most effective with diverse audiences. However, experience teaches us that understanding and respecting cultural differences are the first steps to becoming a culturally sensitive and adaptive speaker. Cultural sensitivity often separates effective speakers from those who are misinterpreted or rejected by audience members from diverse cultures.

Barriers to Cultural Sensitivity. Understanding the dimensions of cultural variability will not help you become a better speaker if you view them as hard and fast rules. Are all American audiences composed of individualistic, fact-focused listeners? Of course not. Within American mainstream culture, microcultures may vary significantly. Can you assume that all audiences from Denmark expect equality between speakers and listeners, and prefer to hear innovative ideas? You do so at your peril. Cultural dimensions are broadly drawn pictures of a group of people who, in general, share some common characteristics. A group of young Japanese executives may be just as individualistic as American executives. An audience of African Americans may be more group-centered and more willing to accept uncertainty than a group of European Americans. Understanding cultural differences does not give you a fail-safe system for adapting to an audience. Rather, it helps you to understand how cultural differences can be used to anticipate and adapt to a variety of audiences.

Intercultural Strategies and Skills. Understanding the dimensions of cultural variability and the barriers to cultural sensitivity goes a long way when you are preparing effective presentations. In addition, we offer several suggestions that can further enhance your credibility and help you achieve the purpose of your presentation.[15]

1. **Do your intercultural homework.** Learn as much as you can about the characteristics and customs of speakers and audience members from other cultures and microcultures.
2. **Evaluate *your* ethnocentric beliefs.** Do not let ethnocentrism distort your presentation. Understand how *your* culture and *your* culture-based perspectives may differ from those of other speakers and audience members.
3. **Develop *better* stereotypes.** Identify the legitimate characteristics and expectations of speakers and audience members from other cultures and microcultures.
4. **Empathize.** Imagine the communication challenges facing speakers and audience members from cultures that are different from your own. Try to acknowledge or accommodate their views when speaking and listening.
5. **Expect the unexpected.** Culturally sensitive speakers and audience members develop a high tolerance for cultural differences. They initially accept the things that they do not understand and work hard to comprehend and appreciate the differences that make cultures distinct.
6. **Watch your tongue.** Make sure that you never belittle or make fun of other cultures or microcultures. Be aware that using words with negative, culture-bound meanings can lead to unfortunate misunderstandings.

Avoid Ethnocentrism and Stereotyping

Learning about cultural diversity and the dimensions of cultural variability can lead to perilous consequences if you succumb to the twin obstacles of ethnocentrism and stereotyping.[1]

Ethnocentrism is a belief that your culture is superior to others. Ethnocentrism is not about pride in your country or culture; instead, it is a mistaken belief that your culture is a superior culture—and that with it come rights and privileges that are or should be denied to others. Ethnocentric speakers believe that

- [Their] culture should be the role model for other cultures.
- People would be happier if they lived like people in [the speakers'] culture.
- Most other cultures are backward when compared with [their] culture.[2]

Ethnocentric speakers run the risk of offending audiences when they imply that they represent a superior culture or believe in superior values. Ethnocentrism can apply to a speaker's race, ethnic background, religion, socioeconomic status, gender, and even neighborhood.

Stereotypes occur when you make generalizations about a group of people that oversimplify their characteristics. Unfortunately, stereotyping usually attributes negative traits to an entire group when, in reality, only a few people of the group possess those traits. For example, a famous study of college students found that even in the mid-1990s, African Americans were stereotyped as lazy and loud, whereas Jews were described as shrewd and intelligent.[3] Such stereotypes lead to **prejudices**—negative attitudes toward a cultural group as a whole, based on little or no direct experience with that group. Whereas stereotypes foster opinions about a group, prejudices reflect how you feel about that group.

Ethnocentrism and stereotyping—as well as the resulting prejudices—affect both speakers and audience members. When a speaker and audience member view each other in ethnocentric or stereotypical terms, the speaker's message is less likely to reach the listener as intended. In fact, it is more likely to reach the listener as an ignorant and offensive message.

1. James W. Neuliep, *Intercultural Communication: A Contextual Approach,* 2nd ed. (Boston: Houghton Mifflin, 2003), Chapter 3.
2. Items from Neuliep and McCroskey's Generalized Ethnocentrism (GENE) Scale, in James W. Neuliep, *Intercultural Communication: A Contextual Approach,* 2nd ed. (Boston: Houghton Mifflin, 2003), pp. 29–30.
3. Data from P. G. Devine and A. J. Elliot, "Are Racial Sterotypes Really Fading? The Princeton Trilogy Revisited," *Personality and Social Psychology Bulletin* 21 (1995): 1139–1150.

Communicating Ethically

Sadly, the strategies and skills in this textbook can be used and have been used for less-than-honorable purposes. Unscrupulous speakers have misled trusting citizens and consumers. Bigoted speakers have used hate speech to oppress those who are "different." Self-centered speakers have destroyed the reputations of their rivals with public pronouncements.

Chapter 6, "Speaker Credibility and Ethics," devotes a major section to the ethical obligations of good speakers and good listeners. Here we present the National Communication Association's (NCA) Credo for Ethical Communication.[16]

The National Communication Association Credo for Ethical Communication

Questions of right and wrong arise whenever people communicate. Ethical communication is fundamental to responsible thinking, decision making, and the development of relationships and communities within and across contexts, cultures, channels, and media. Moreover, ethical communication enhances human worth and dignity by fostering truthfulness, fairness, responsibility, personal integrity, and respect for self and others. We believe that unethical communication threatens the quality of all communication and consequently the well-being of individuals and the society in which we live. Therefore, we, the members of the National Communication Association, endorse and are committed to practicing the following principles of ethical communication:

- We advocate truthfulness, accuracy, honesty, and reason as essential to the integrity of communication.
- We endorse freedom of expression, diversity of perspective, and tolerance.
- We endorse freedom of expression, diversity of perspetive, and tolerance of dissent to achieve the informed and responsible decision making fundamental to a civil society.
- We strive to understand and respect other communicators before evaluating and responding to their messages.
- We promote access to communication resources and opportunities as necessary to fulfill human potential and contribute to the well-being of families, communities, and society.
- We promote communication climates of caring and mutual understanding that respect the unique needs and characteristics of individual communicators.
- We condemn communication that degrades individuals and humanity through distortion, intimidation, coercion, and violence, and through the expression of intolerance and hatred.
- We are committed to the courageous expression of personal convictions in pursuit of fairness and justice.
- We advocate sharing information, opinions, and feelings when facing significant choices while also respecting privacy and confidentiality.
- We accept responsibility for the short- and long-term consequences of our own communication and expect the same of others.

We strongly support the NCA Credo for Ethical Communication. We also believe in its underlying assumption that ethical communication is a vital ingredient in everyday interactions as well as in a civil and democratic society.

In Latin, the word *credo* means "I believe." Thus, an ethics credo is a belief statement about what it means to be an ethical communicator. We strongly believe that an effective and credible communicator must be an ethical communicator. The NCA credo sets clear standards for all communicators and has specific applications to presentation speaking.

Making Strategic Decisions

We wrote this book to help you make strategic decisions about preparing and delivering a successful presentation. We don't ask you to memorize tons of communication theory or research. Rather, we apply theory and research to all aspects of the presentation speaking process. Seeing theory in action will help you to make your own decisions as you develop and deliver your presentations. As most experienced speakers know, there's more to speaking than simply following a set of rules. Effective speaking depends on the ability to think critically and to make strategic decisions at key points in the presentation speaking process. In this textbook, we apply the best of communication theory and research to the real-life speaking situations you will face in your future.

Summary

What do real-world speakers want to know about presentation speaking?

They want to know how to keep an audience interested, how to begin and end a presentation, how to select and organize appropriate content, how to choose a good topic, and how to adapt to an audience.

What's the difference between a presentation and a public speech?

Presentation speaking occurs any time speakers use verbal and nonverbal messages to generate meanings and to establish relationships with audience members. Public speaking is a type of presentation speaking that occurs when speakers address public audiences in community, government, and/or organizational settings.

What basic principles underlie all types of presentation speaking?

The following questions represent seven basic principles to consider when preparing a presentation: (1) What is your purpose? (2) Who is in your audience? (3) How can you enhance your credibility? (4) What are the logistics? (5) What content should you include? (6) How should you organize your content? (7) How should you practice and deliver your presentation?

How do speakers and listeners work together to communicate?

Speakers and audiences rely on each other to give messages their meaning. In an ideal speaking situation, the speaker's purpose and the audience's response overlap in a mutually beneficial transaction.

How can I become a more effective speaker?

You can begin the process of becoming a more effective speaker by understanding the importance of cultural sensitivity, the responsibility to communicate ethically, and the value of making strategic decisions.

Presentation Principles in Action

Public Speaking Survey

On a 5-point scale, in which 5 is Extremely Important, and 1 is Not at All Important, how would you rate the following topics or areas in their importance to your becoming a better public speaker? **(Please circle one number for each item.)**

ITEM	Extremely Important	Very Important	Somewhat Important	Not Very Important	Not at All Important
1. Selecting ideas and information for your presentation	5	4	3	2	1
2. Overcoming/reducing nervousness/stage fright	5	4	3	2	1
3. Understanding and adapting to your audience	5	4	3	2	1
4. Adapting to the location/ occasion of your presentation	5	4	3	2	1
5. Determining the purpose of your presentation	5	4	3	2	1
6. Deciding what to say (Choosing a topic or approach to your presentation)	5	4	3	2	1
7. Organizing your presentation	5	4	3	2	1
8. Beginning and ending your presentation	5	4	3	2	1
9. Using your voice effectively	5	4	3	2	1
10. Using gestures, body language, and eye contact effectively	5	4	3	2	1
11. Speaking with or without notes	5	4	3	2	1
12. Answering audience questions	5	4	3	2	1
13. Using humor in your presentation	5	4	3	2	1
14. Enhancing your credibility/ believability	5	4	3	2	1
15. Using visual aids and technology effectively	5	4	3	2	1
16. Choosing appropriate and effective words	5	4	3	2	1
17. Convincing/influencing your audience	5	4	3	2	1

ITEM	Extremely Important	Very Important	Somewhat Important	Not Very Important	Not at All Important
18. Keeping your audience interested	5	4	3	2	1
19. Practicing/rehearsing your presentation	5	4	3	2	1
20. Telling stories effectively	5	4	3	2	1
21. Outlining your presentation	5	4	3	2	1
22. Making special types of presentations (toasts, introductions, eulogies, awards)	5	4	3	2	1
23. Presenting to/in small groups/teams	5	4	3	2	1
24. Speaking impromptu/off-the-cuff	5	4	3	2	1
25. Other:	5	4	3	2	1

How Ethnocentric Are You?

The GENE (Generalized Ethnocentrism) Scale is composed of twenty-two statements concerning your feelings about your culture and other cultures. In the space provided please write the number that reflects the degree to which each statement applies to you by indicating whether you (5) Strongly Agree, (4) Agree, (3) Are Undecided, (2) Disagree, or (1) Strongly Disagree with the statement. There are no right or wrong answers, and some of the statements are similar to others. Be honest! Work quickly and record your first response.

1._____ Most other cultures are backward when compared with my culture.

2._____ My culture should be the role model for other cultures.

3._____ People from other cultures act strangely when they come to my culture.

4._____ Lifestyles in other cultures are just as valid as those in my culture.

5._____ Other cultures should try to be more like my culture.

6._____ I'm not interested in the values and customs of other cultures.

7._____ People in my culture should learn a lot from people in other cultures.

8._____ Most people from other cultures just don't know what's good for them.

9._____ I respect the values and customs of other cultures.

10._____ Other cultures are smart to look up to our culture.

11._____ Most people would be happier if they lived like people in my culture.

12._____ I have many friends from different cultures.

13._____ People in my culture have just about the best lifestyles anywhere.

14._____ Lifestyles in other cultures are not as valid as those in my culture.

15._____ I am very interested in the values and customs of other cultures.

16._____ I apply my values when judging people who are different.

17._____ I see people who are similar to me as virtuous.

18._____ I do not cooperate with people who are different.

19._____ Most people in my culture just don't know what is good for them.

20._____ I do not trust people who are different.

21._____ I dislike interacting with people from different cultures.

22._____ I have little respect for the value and customs of other cultures.

To determine your ethnocentrism score, complete the following four steps.

Step 1: Add your responses to scale items 4, 7, and 9.

Step 2: Add your responses to scale items 1, 2, 5, 8, 10, 11, 13, 14, 18, 20, 21, and 22.

Step 3: Subtract the sum from step 1 from 18 (i.e., 18 minus the step 1 sum).

Step 4: Add the results from step 2 and step 3. This is your generalized ethnocentrism score. Higher scores indicate higher ethnocentrism. Scores above 55 are considered high ethnocentrism.

Source: The GENE Scale, developed by James W. Neuliep and James C. McCroskey, is designed to measure a person's level of ethnocentrism. See James W. Neuliep, *Intercultural Communication: A Contextual Approach,* 2nd ed. (Boston: Houghton Mifflin, 2003), pp. 29–30.

Key Terms

channel 15
communication model 11
communication transaction 12
context 12
culture 19
decoding 12
encoding 12
ethnocentrism 21
feedback 15
message 12
microculture 19
noise 16
prejudices 21
presentation speaking 8
public speaking 8
receiver 12
rhetoric 7
skills 19
source 12
strategy 19
stereotypes 21
theory 19

Notes

1 In collaboration with the authors of *Presentation Speaking in Everyday Life,* Houghton Mifflin's Market Research Department conducted a survey to examine the importance of traditional topics usually covered in public speaking textbooks. Approximately two thousand copies of a two-page questionnaire were mailed to individuals who had recently purchased a commercially available public speaking book and who had used a business address to secure the purchase. Two hundred eighty-one usable questionnaires were returned, resulting in a response rate of 11 percent. Respondents were geographically dispersed. Twenty-five percent worked in industry. Workers in government (10%), health (10%) and nonprofit organizations (10%) made up 30 percent of respondents. Nine percent came from the financial industry; another 9 percent worked in technology-related industries. Approximately 25 percent of the respondents, including business owners and independent contractors, worked in "other" occupations. The public speaking survey is reproduced in this chapter.

2 "Meek and Mumblers Learn Ways of Getting a Word In," *New York Times,* 29 May 1989, pp. 1 and 24.

3 Peggy Noonan, *Simply Speaking: How to Communicate Your Ideas with Style, Substance, and Clarity* (New York: HarperCollins, 1998), p. x. Copyright © 1998 by Peggy Noonan. Reprinted by permission of HarperCollins Publishers, Inc.

4 Thomas Leech, *How to Prepare, Stage & Deliver Winning Presentations* (New York: AMACOM, 1993), pp. 9 and 17.

5 *The American Heritage Dictionary of the English Language,* 4th ed. (Boston: Houghton Mifflin, 2000), p. 1416. Copyright © 2000 by Houghton Mifflin Company. Reproduced by permission from *The American Heritage Dictionary of the English Language, Fourth Edition.*

6. The Association for Communication Administration's 1995 *Conference on Defining the Field of Communication* produced the following definition: "The field of communication focuses on how people use verbal and nonverbal messages to generate meanings within and across various contexts, cultures, channels, and media. The field promotes the effective and ethical practice of human communication." See *www.natcom.org/publications/Pathways/5thEd.htm.*

7 Leech, p. 4.

8 Business–Higher Education Forum, *Spanning the Chasm: Corporate and Academic Cooperation to Improve Work-Force Preparation* (Washington, DC: Business–Higher Education Forum in affiliation with the American Council on Education, January 1997), p. 5.

9 National Association of Colleges and Employers, *Job Outlook, 2000.* See *www.jobweb.org/pubs/pr/pr11800.htm.*

10 Thomas Leech, *How to Prepare, Stage & Deliver Winning Presentations* (New York: AMACOM, 1993); Marjorie Brody, *Speaking Your Way to the Top: Making Powerful Business Presentations* (Boston: Allyn & Bacon, 1998); William Hendricks et al., *Secrets of Power Presentations* (Franklin Lakes, NJ: Career Press, 1996); Robert W. Pike, *High-Impact Presentations* (West Des Moines, IA: American Media, 1995). There are many other commercially available, business-oriented books on speaking that use the terms *presentations* and *presentation speaking* rather than *public speaking.*

11 Rob Anderson and Veronica Ross, *Questions of Communication: A Practical Introduction to Theory,* 2nd ed. (New York: St. Martin's, 1998), p. 68.

12 Dominic A. Infante, Andrew S. Rancer, and Deanna F. Womack, *Building Communication Theory,* 2nd ed. (Prospect Heights, IL: Waveland, 1993), p. 32.

13 For more information about the nature of cultures and microcultures, see James W. Neuliep, *Intercultural Communication: A Contextual Approach,* 2nd ed. (Boston: Houghton Mifflin, 2003), Chapters 2 and 3. Also see Myron W. Lustig and Jolene Koester, *Intercultural Competence: Interpersonal Communication Across Cultures,* 3rd ed. (New York: Longman, 1999); Guo-Ming Chen and William J. Starosta, *Foundations of Intercultural Communication* (Boston: Allyn & Bacon, 1998); Judith N. Martin and Thomas K. Nakayama, *Experiencing Intercultural Communication* (Mountain View, CA: Mayfield, 2001).

14 See James W. Neuliep, *Intercultural Communication: A Contextual Approach,* 2nd ed. (Boston: Houghton Mifflin, 2003), pp. 21 and 78–105. Other authors describe *microcultures* as *cocultures.* Using either of these terms is preferable to using the older, somewhat derogatory term *subcultures.*

15 Based on suggestions for improving rhetorical communication across cultures in James C. McCroskey, *An Introduction to Rhetorical Communication,* 8th ed. (Boston: Allyn & Bacon, 2001), p. 157.

16 The credo for ethical communication was developed at the 1999 Communication Ethics Credo Conference sponsored by the National Communication Association. The credo was adopted and endorsed by the Legislative Council of the National Communication Association in November 1999. The complete credo is available on the NCA website *www.natcom.org/policies/External/EthicalComm.htm.* Used by permission of the National Communication Association.

chapter two

Listening and Critical Thinking

- What role does listening play in presentation speaking?
- How can I become a better listener?
- How do I "listen" to an audience?
- What role does critical thinking play in presentation speaking?
- How do I become a more effective critical thinker?

Successful presentations require effective listening and critical thinking. If your audience can't or won't listen, why are you speaking? If you have not given serious thought to the development and delivery of your presentation, why *should* they listen?

When it comes to presentation speaking, listening and critical thinking cannot be separated. Unfortunately, and all too often, we entrust effective listening to the audience and critical thinking to the speaker. If such a separation were possible, you could present almost any well-organized, well-delivered message and be guaranteed that an audience of good listeners would accept everything you said without question. However, the real world of presentation speaking is quite different. Your ability to think critically and listen effectively is as important when you are speaking as when you are an audience member.

As a speaker, you need to think critically in order to analyze what you learn about your audience before and during a presentation. Only then can you make strategic decisions about how to achieve your purpose. As an audience member, you should think critically about what you see, hear, and feel about a speaker and his or her message. Only then can you decide what to do or what to believe. Both kinds of critical thinking, however, require effective listening.

What Is Listening?

We define effective **listening** as the ability to understand, analyze, respect, appreciate, and appropriately respond to the meaning of another person's spoken and nonverbal messages.[1] At first, listening may appear to be as easy and natural as breathing. After all, everyone listens. In fact, just the opposite may be closer to the truth. Although most of us can *hear*, we often fail to *listen* to what others have to say. Hearing and listening are not the same thing. Hearing requires only physical ability; listening requires thinking ability. People who are hearing impaired may be better listeners than those who can hear the faintest sound.

Listening is what audiences are supposed to do when speakers talk. In fact, listening is our number one communication activity. Although percentages vary from study to study, Figure 2.1 shows how most of us divide up our daily communication time.

One study of college students found that listening occupies more than half of their communicating time.[2] In the corporate world, executives may devote more than 60 percent of their workday listening to others.[3]

Yet despite all of the time we spend listening, most of us aren't very good at it. For example, immediately after listening to a short talk, most of us cannot accurately report 50 percent of what was said. Without training, we listen at only 25 percent efficiency.[4] And of that 25 percent, most of what we remember is distorted or inaccurate.[5]

As a speaker, you must learn to adjust to and compensate for the poor listening habits of your audience. As an audience member, you will find that your listening ability affects whether you understand and accurately interpret what you hear in a presentation. This dual responsibility on the part of the speaker and audience ensures that

Figure 2.1

Time Spent Communicating

Source: Isa Engleberg and Dianna Wynn, *Working in Groups*, 3rd ed., p. 124. Copyright ©2003 by Houghton Mifflin Company. Reprinted with permission.

Communication Activity	Percentages
Listening	40–70%
Speaking	20–35%
Reading	10–20%
Writing	5–15%

presentations achieve their purpose. As we indicated in Chapter 1, "Presentation Speaking," a successful communication transaction occurs when a speaker's purpose and an audience's response are brought together by a message. Without effective listening, the transaction will fail to produce shared meaning.

Types of Listening

Listening is a complex behavior. Researchers have identified several types of listening, each of which employs unique listening skills.

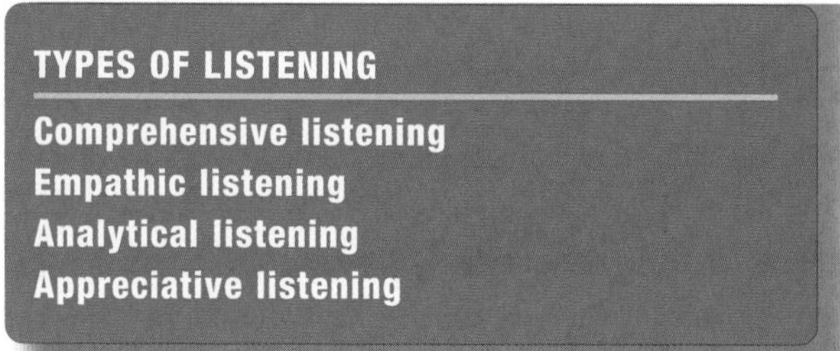

Comprehensive Listening. Comprehensive listening answers this question: What does the speaker mean? **Comprehensive listening** focuses on accurately understanding the meaning of a speaker's spoken and nonverbal messages. Later in this chapter, we discuss how to "listen" to nonverbal communication—the messages speakers send without using words.

Comprehensive listening involves two basic steps. First, make sure you accurately hear what is said while simultaneously paying attention to nonverbal cues such as facial expressions, gestures, posture, and vocal quality. Second, make sure that you accurately interpret the speaker's meaning. Can you identify the key points as well as the claims and evidence she uses to support an argument? After all, if you don't comprehend what a person says, you can't be expected to respond in a reasonable way.

Suppose a speaker is trying to persuade you to participate in a voter registration drive. As a comprehensive listener, you may wonder whether "Join the voter registration drive" means that you (1) should, in general, support voter registration, (2) should volunteer and help register voters, or (3) should register to vote. The way in which you interpret the meaning of a single comment can determine your response to the whole presentation.

Audience members aren't the only ones who need strong comprehensive listening skills. During a question-and-answer session, speakers need to understand audience questions. In addition, comprehensive listening can be just as important before you speak. It's the type of listening you should use when someone asks you to speak so that you can be sure that you understand the presentation's purpose, audience, logistics, and occasion.

Empathic Listening. Empathic listening answers this question: How does the speaker or audience feel? **Empathic listening** goes beyond understanding what a person means; it focuses on understanding and identifying with a person's situation, feelings, or motives. Can you see the situation through the speaker's eyes? To put the question another way, how would you feel in a similar situation?

By not listening for feelings, you may overlook the most important part of a message. Even if you understand every word a person says, you can still miss the anger, enthusiasm, or frustration in a speaker's voice. An empathic listener doesn't have to agree with or feel the same way that a speaker does, but he should try to understand the type and intensity of feelings that the speaker is experiencing. For example, suppose a speaker says that voting is a waste of time. An empathic listener may wonder whether the speaker means that (1) she is stressed and may have more important things to think about, (2) she is frustrated because there aren't any good candidates to vote for, or (3) the line is usually so long at the polling station that standing in it wastes her precious time.

Audience members can be empathic listeners in simple ways. For instance, smiling and nodding at someone who is speaking communicates attention and interest. What's more, if you act as though you're listening, you may actually end up listening more effectively and retaining more information!

Analytical Listening. Analytical listening answers this question: What's my opinion? Of the four types of listening, **analytical listening** focuses on evaluating whether a message is logical and reasonable. Analytical listening asks you to make a judgment based on your evaluation of the speaker's arguments. Is the speaker right or wrong, logical or illogical? Good analytical listeners apply critical thinking skills and understand why they accept or reject a speaker's ideas and suggestions.

A speaker makes the following proposal: "Suppose we post signs and offer free rides to the voting polls." An analytical listener might have questions such as these: (1) Will voters misinterpret the ride as pressure to vote for a particular candidate? (2) Wouldn't voters want to check to see that all drivers have adequate car insurance? (3) Is there enough time to design, print, and post the signs before the election?

A listener needs analytical listening skills in order to judge the validity of an argument and the factors that separate credible sources from biased ones. To listen analytically, you should evaluate presentations by testing the ways in which they apply the seven basic principles of presentation speaking (as Figure 2.2 shows), to assess the strength and merit of a speaker's ideas and opinions.

Appreciative Listening. Appreciative listening answers this question: Do I like, value, or enjoy what the speaker is saying? **Appreciative listening** applies to *how* speakers think and speak—the ways in which they choose and use words and their ability to use humor, tell stories, argue persuasively, or demonstrate understanding. Appreciative listening can reward a speaker who is able to capture and eloquently describe a complex concept or proposal. When a speaker's words, stories, or sense of humor delight us, we listen appreciatively. Appreciative listening skills can help us enjoy and acknowledge good presentations.

Suppose that a speaker suggests there is no greater duty in a democracy than that of expressing your opinion at the polling booth on Election Day. An appreciative listener

Figure 2.2 Questions for Analytical Listening

Purpose Questions:

____Is the speaker's purpose clearly stated? If not, what is the speaker trying to achieve?

____Could the speaker have a hidden or an ulterior motive?

____Did the speaker achieve his or her purpose?

____Was achieving the *speaker's* purpose worth the time *you* spent listening?

Audience Questions:

____Does the speaker seem to understand the nature and characteristics of the audience?

____Does the speaker appear to understand and respect the audience's attitudes and beliefs?

____Does it seem as though the speaker is trying to take advantage of the audience in any way?

____Could this presentation be delivered to *any* audience, or has the speaker made an effort to adapt it to this audience's interests and needs?

Credibility Questions:

____As far as you can determine, is the speaker well informed about the topic?

____Does the speaker seem to be sincere and trustworthy?

____Does the speaker appear to be genuinely interested in the topic and the audience?

____Do you trust and believe this speaker?

____Would you invite this speaker to address an audience of colleagues or friends?

Logistics Questions:

____Has the speaker stayed within the time limit? If not, what has been the effect of too little or too much speaking?

____Has the speaker adapted to the setting of the presentation (considering the size of the room and the audience, using amplification, using presentation aids)?

____If the presentation is taking place on a special occasion, has the speaker adapted to that occasion?

____Could this presentation be delivered to any audience in any setting, or has the speaker effectively adapted to this setting and occasion?

Content Questions:

____Does the speaker seem well informed?

____Is the information relevant to the topic or purpose of the presentation?

____Does the speaker identify her or his sources of information?

____Does the information seem reasonable and believable? If not, what is the problem?

____Does the speaker appear to be misleading the audience?

Organization Questions:

____Is the presentation clear and easy to follow?

____Are the key points identified and well supported?

____Does the speaker go off on tangents that have little to do with the purpose or the key points of the presentation?

Performance Questions:

____Was the speaker's delivery effective?

____Could you hear and understand what the speaker said?

____Did the speaker's gestures, posture, and dress enhance the presentation?

____Did the speaker use equipment and presentation aids well?

____Did the speaker look directly at the audience?

____To what extent did the speaker's delivery affect your opinion of his or her message?

might think that (1) the speaker phrased that idea eloquently; (2) when seen as a patriotic duty rather than as a time-consuming chore, voting seems worthwhile; or (3) the tone of the speaker's voice communicated genuine sincerity.

Learning to Listen

You *can* learn specific listening skills, and as we'll soon see, most of them apply two basic principles: (1) use your extra thought speed and (2) apply the "golden listening rule." Once you understand and apply these principles as overriding listening strategies, you can begin to work on specific listening skills.

Planning to Listen

What if we told you that next week you will have to make a presentation that really matters to a very important group of people. We bet that you would spend a lot of time planning that talk. Now, suppose we told you that next week you will be attending a meeting to listen to an important presentation. How much time would you spend preparing? Our guess is that you would spend much less time preparing to listen. We believe that planning to listen can be just as important as planning to speak. Here are five suggestions that can help you plan to listen:

- *Do some prior study.* The more you know about a topic, the more you will get out of hearing a presentation about it. In some classes, communication instructors ask students to announce their topics a week in advance so that listeners can start thinking about what they will be hearing.
- *Identify and narrow your listening goals.* Find a personal reason for listening. Ask yourself this question: What do I want from or what can I gain from listening to this presentation? Narrow your list of goals into three questions you want answered. When you hear the speaker address the related topics, listen carefully and ask yourself whether your questions have been answered satisfactorily.
- *Match your listening style to the presentation's purpose.* Thomas Leech, a communication consultant, suggests that "by knowing which listening hat to wear, listeners can get more out of the presentation and properly direct their own efforts."[1] For example, if you're attending a presentation designed to entertain, you probably won't need to listen analytically. However, you would want to listen analytically to a speaker who was trying to persuade audience members to change their opinions or behavior. At an informative presentation filled with detailed facts and figures, you would apply your comprehensive listening skills. And if you're listening to someone tell a good story or read a passage from literature, empathic and appreciative listening may be most appropriate. Good listeners can rely on any and all of the four listening styles when necessary.
- *Generate some questions in advance.* When you go to a presentation with questions in mind, you will listen better because you'll be paying attention to whether or not the speaker answers them. If you discover that the speaker has avoided or has not developed the topic you were curious about, ask your question during a question-and-answer session. The audience may appreciate your question and benefit from the answer.
- *Share the message.* Listen as though you've been asked to report on what you've heard. After the presentation ends, make a point of telling someone else what you heard. If you know in advance that you will be reporting on what you have heard, you will have to listen more carefully. Also, by reporting, you will have to repeat the message and will be more likely to remember what was said.

1. Thomas Leech, *How to Prepare, Stage, & Deliver Winning Presentations* (New York: AMACOM, 1993), p. 266.

Use Your Extra Thought Speed

Most people talk at about 125 to 150 words per minute. According to Ralph Nichols, a respected listening researcher and author, if thoughts were measured in words per minute, most of us could think at three or four times the rate at which we speak.[6] Thus, we have about 400 words' worth of spare thinking time for every minute during which a person talks to us.

Thought speed is the speed (words per minute) at which most people can think, compared to the speed at which they can speak. So what do we do with all that extra thinking time? Poor listeners use their extra thought speed to daydream, engage in side

Is Listening a Skill or a Habit?

You know what a habit is. It's something you do so frequently and have done for so long that you've stopped thinking about why, how, and whether you do it. We believe that effective listening is also a habit—something that is second nature to people.

Stephen R. Covey, the author of *The Seven Habits of Highly Effective People*, defines *habit* in a way that captures the essential components of good listening. In his opinion, habits require knowledge, skills, and desire. Knowledge plays a role similar to that of theory—it describes *what to do* and *why to do it.* Skill is *how to do it.* And desire is the motivation, the reason that you *want to do it.* Covey maintains that in order to make something a habit, you have to do all three.[1] This is especially true in listening, which relies as much on a listener's motivation (*want to do it*) as it does on knowledge and skill.

Given the many thousands of examples Covey could have used to explain his definition of habit, he turns to the art of listening to illustrate how the three components of an effective habit interact with one another:

> *I may be ineffective in my interaction with my work associates, my spouse, or my children because I constantly tell them what I think, but I never really listen to them. Unless I search out correct principles of human interaction [knowledge], I may not even* know *I need to listen.*
>
> *Even if I do know that in order to interact effectively with others I really need to listen to them, I may not have the skill. I may not know how to really listen deeply to another human being.*
>
> *But knowing I need to listen and knowing how to listen [are] not enough. Unless I* want *to listen, unless I have the desire, it won't be a habit in my life. Creating a habit requires work in all three dimensions.*[2]

1. Stephen R. Covey, *The Seven Habits of Highly Effective People* (New York: Simon & Schuster, 1989), p. 47.
2. Covey, p. 47.

conversations, take unnecessary notes, or plan how to confront a speaker. Good listeners use their extra thought speed productively when they

- Identify and summarize key points
- Pay more attention to nonverbal behavior
- Analyze arguments
- Assess the relevance of a speaker's comments

Conscientious audience members don't waste their extra thought speed—they use it to enhance comprehensive and analytical listening.

Apply the Golden Listening Rule

The **golden listening rule** is easy to remember: Listen to others as you would have them listen to you. Unfortunately, this rule can be difficult to follow. It asks you to suspend your own needs in order to attend to someone else's.

The golden listening rule applies to the speaker, too. As a speaker, you know your material, but your audience is hearing it for the first time. You may have spent hours crafting your message; your audience may not have given much thought to the issue. You may believe what you're saying; the listener may be skeptical.[7] Conscientious speakers understand and adapt to the ways in which audience members listen to a presentation.

Develop Good Listening Habits

Although using your extra thought speed and applying the golden listening rule are basic listening principles, ways to practice them may not be obvious. Developing the following six habits can improve your listening ability and help you apply the two basic principles of effective listening. When and how you use these skills depend on whether you are the speaker or an audience member, whether you are speaking to a large or small group, and whether you have the flexibility to interact with the speaker or audience members during or after a presentation.

THE SIX HABITS OF EFFECTIVE LISTENERS

1. **Overcome distractions.**
2. **Listen for big ideas.**
3. **"Listen" to nonverbal behavior.**
4. **Make it personal.**
5. **Paraphrase.**
6. **Listen before you leap.**

Comprehending and respecting speakers on both sides of a controversial question require the application of the golden listening rule: Listen to others as you would have them listen to you.

Overcome Distractions. Distractions can take many forms.[8] Loud and annoying noises, uncomfortable room temperature and seating, frequent interruptions, distracting decor, and outside activities are environmental distractions. A speaker's delivery can also be distracting. It's hard to listen to a speaker who talks too softly, too rapidly, or too slowly or who speaks in a monotone or with an unfamiliar accent. Even a speaker's mannerisms and appearance can be distracting. Remember the concept of noise in our communication model? Reducing the noise—physical or psychological—that interferes with the communication process can improve your entire audience's ability to listen to your message.

One important form of psychological noise is listener bias. A bias can be either of two things: your own prejudice or an unfair attitude which you hold that stems from prior experience. Bias can also be a preference that inhibits you from making an impartial judgment.[9] If, for example, you "know" you disagree with a viewpoint that is going to be discussed, either you won't listen or you'll spend your time criticizing the speaker. Pro-life audiences may not want to listen to a pro-choice speaker—and vice versa. A gun-control advocate may not have an easy time getting a group of gun owners to listen. Please understand that there's nothing wrong with criticizing a speaker *after* you've listened comprehensively and analytically to a presentation. The problem results when you let your bias prevent you from listening as a responsible audience member.

When a distraction is environmental, you are well within your rights as a listener or speaker to shut a door, open a window, or turn on more lights. In large groups you may need to ask permission to improve the group's surroundings. If, for example, the room's temperature is too cold or hot, don't hesitate to interrupt your presentation and ask someone to adjust the thermostat—or to do it yourself. Not only will *you* feel more comfortable, but the audience will also thank you for making it easier to listen. Be a hero. Help your audience by taking action to overcome environmental distractions whenever possible.

Depending on the circumstances and setting of a presentation, you may be able to take direct action to reduce behavioral distractions. If an audience member's behavior is distracting, you may be well within your rights to ask that person to stop talking or moving around. After all, if she is distracting you, the person is probably also distracting others. If a presenter speaks too softly or uses visual aids that are too small, a conscientious audience member may ask him to speak up or to explain what is on a visual.

Listen for Big Ideas. Good listeners can identify a speaker's purpose, central idea, and key points. Poor listeners tend to listen for and remember isolated facts.

Admittedly, sometimes the fault lies with the speaker. When faced with a disorganized speaker who keeps talking long after making a point, listeners may lose track and drift off. In a small group setting, a good listener who senses such problems could interrupt the speaker and ask, "Could you help me out here and summarize your point in a couple of sentences?" Such an interruption is not rude when it is the only way to get the speaker to clarify an important issue. There's also a big difference between asking for a summary and yelling out, "Hey, what's your point?" Although it is tempting for listeners to blame poor speakers when they can't figure out the message, good listeners try to cut through facts and irrelevant comments in order to identify the most important points and main ideas.

One way to listen for "big" ideas is to borrow a plan-to-listen tip. Plan to tell someone else what you've heard. We know that when people believe they have to report back on what they've heard, their comprehension increases significantly. Ask yourself the audience's side of the purpose question: What does the speaker want me to know, think, believe, or do after hearing this presentation? Then try to list the key points or ideas the speaker used to achieve that purpose.

"Listen" to Nonverbal Behavior. Speakers don't always put everything that's important into words. Very often, you can understand a speaker's meaning by noting and interpreting nonverbal communication. **Nonverbal communication** is a general term used to describe the messages that we send without using words. It applies to body language, physical appearance, facial expression, and eye contact as well as to the emotions and emphasis communicated by the tone of a person's voice. Good listeners know that nonverbal behavior can communicate as much as or more meaning than words alone. They pay attention to the "mismatch" between verbal and nonverbal messages, such as when a speaker says, "I'm delighted to see you here today" while cringing and turning toward the door.

A change in a speaker's vocal tone or volume may be another way of saying, "Listen up; this is very important." A presenter's sustained eye contact may be a way of saying, "I'm talking to you!" Facial expressions can reveal whether a thought is painful, joyous, exciting, serious, or boring. Even gestures can be used to express a level of excitement that words cannot convey.

If, as research indicates, more than half of our meaning is conveyed nonverbally,[10] we are missing a lot of important information if we fail to "listen" to nonverbal behavior! Even Sigmund Freud suggested that "he that has eyes to see and ears to hear may convince himself that no mortal can keep a secret. If his lips are silent, he chatters with his fingertips; betrayal oozes out of him at every pore."[11] No wonder it is difficult to conceal what we mean and feel during a live presentation.

Correctly interpreting a speaker's nonverbal responses can tell a listener as much as or more than the spoken words. At the same time, the nonverbal reactions of listeners (head nods, smiles, frowns, eye contact, and sitting posture) can affect the quality, quantity, and content of a speaker's message. Even the setting of a presentation (a nonverbal aspect) can communicate a wealth of meaning about the status, power, and respect given to speakers and listeners.

Make It Personal. All of us have had trouble listening and remembering presentations we were not interested in or concerned about. Why expend the energy to listen if you won't be affected? If a politician talks about improving a shopping district many miles from your neighborhood, why pay attention? If an instructor lectures on a subject that won't be on the exam, why take notes? If the boss describes his recent fishing trip in agonizing detail, who cares? We hope you've begun to understand how and why you should listen in such circumstances. First the how: Find a way in which the speaker's message could affect you. Will the proposal increase your taxes? Will the lecture help you learn or apply other material? Will remembering details of the boss's fishing trip earn you brownie points in the future? Find a personal reason to listen even when the information seems uninteresting or irrelevant.

Paraphrase. **Paraphrasing** is the ability to restate what people have said in a way that indicates that you understood them. Too often we jump to conclusions and incorrectly assume that we know what a speaker means and feels. Paraphrasing is a listening check that asks, "Am I right? Is this what you mean?"

Paraphrasing requires finding new words to describe what you have heard rather than repeating what a person has said. In addition to rephrasing the meaning of the speaker's message, a paraphrase usually includes a request for confirmation. Paraphrasing can be used for many purposes:

To clarify meaning: "When you said that you weren't going to the conference, did you mean that you want one of us to go instead?"

To ensure understanding: "I know that you said you approve, but I sense you're not happy with the outcome. Am I way off?"

To summarize: "What you seem to be saying is that it's not the best time to change this policy. Am I right?"

By rephrasing what we have heard and requesting confirmation, we can use paraphrases to help confirm our perceptions. Effective paraphrasing requires us to use our extra thought speed to produce a statement that follows the golden listening rule.

Listen Before You Leap. One of the most often-quoted pieces of listening advice to come from Ralph Nichols's writings is that "we must always withhold evaluation until our comprehension is complete."[12] Good listeners make sure that they understand a speaker before reacting either positively or negatively.

Sometimes when we become angry, friends may tell us to "count to ten" before reacting. Taking the same precaution is also good advice for listening. Counting to ten, however, implies more than withholding evaluation until you understand completely. You may comprehend a speaker's words perfectly but be infuriated or offended by

Real World Real Speakers

"Listen" to Nonverbal Feedback

A highly respected and successful courtroom attorney told a story about how audience feedback let him know that his client had no chance of avoiding jail time. He was defending one of four suspects in an armed bank robbery. Right after the robbery, the police followed a lead to a city row house and found four men matching the descriptions of the bank robbers asleep in one bedroom. Under one bed they found the exact amount of money stolen from the bank. The lawyer's client contended that he lived at the house and that three of his friends had asked to crash for the night. The lawyer made these final arguments to the jury: My client is the unfortunate victim of circumstance. Because he let his buddies crash at his house, he has been accused of a crime he didn't commit. Just because there were four bank robbers doesn't mean that my client is one of them.

As he spoke, the jury's chairwoman nonverbally "told" him that he would lose his case. A small, amused smile crept across her face as the lawyer spoke. Almost imperceptively, her head moved back and forth in a "no." When he said that his client had no idea that a bank had been robbed, another juror raised one eyebrow with a look that said, "Okay, you've done your best to defend your client, but you and I know he's guilty as sin." Sure enough, the jury found all four suspects guilty as charged.

what you hear. If an insensitive speaker refers to the women in the audience as "girls," it may take your counting to twenty to allow you enough time to collect your thoughts and maintain your ability to listen comprehensively. If a speaker tells an offensive joke, you may have a double reaction—anger toward the speaker and disappointment with those who laugh. Try to understand the effects of offensive comments and emotionally laden words without losing your composure or concentration.

Limit counterarguing. All of us have a tendency to criticize mentally or to refute speakers as we listen to them. Certainly, when you're highly involved with a topic, it's difficult to control this tendency. We recommend maintaining a balance between uncritical acceptance of a speaker's message and flat-out rejection. Effective listeners engage their analytical listening skills to track and assess the validity of a speaker's message; they don't use their listening time to develop harsh or personal attacks.

When you listen before you leap, you are not approving of or condoning what someone says. Instead, you are using your extra thought speed to decide how to react to controversial, prejudiced, or offensive comments. Listening before you leap gives you time to adjust your reactions in a way that will help clarify and correct a statement rather than offend, disrupt, or infuriate a speaker or other audience members.

Listening to Your Audience

One of the most important and difficult speaking skills to learn involves "listening" and adapting to your audience during a presentation. Here, we are not talking about listening to their comments or questions after your presentation. Instead, we are talking about watching and listening for their feedback *during* your presentation. As we indicated in Chapter 1, feedback is the verbal and nonverbal responses audience members communicate as they listen to a speaker. Feedback tells you a great deal about whether your audience is responding positively or negatively to your presentation.

Everyone in an audience reacts in some way. Sometimes that reaction is crystal clear. Audience members may smile or frown. They may nod "yes" or "no" as they listen. They may break into spontaneous applause or refuse to applaud. They may sit forward at full attention or sit back and look bored. At other times, they may stare at you with blank faces or appear distracted. Feedback can help you determine the kind of effect that you are having on your audience.

As you speak, look at and listen to the ways in which audience members react to you. Do they look interested or bored, pleased or displeased? If you can't see or hear reactions, ask for feedback. There is nothing wrong with stopping in the middle of a presentation to ask audience members if they understand you. Not only does such feedback help you adapt to your audience; it also tells listeners that you are interested in their reactions. Asking for feedback also helps your audience listen. By asking the audience questions or seeking confirmation, you are helping everyone understand and respond to the same message.

Adjusting to Audience Feedback

As important as it is to "listen" to your audience, it is just as important to listen to yourself. The ability to monitor and understand the effects of what you say will make you a more successful speaker. Two skills can enhance your ability to listen to yourself. First, translate feedback into useful information about the way you speak and listen so that you can answer questions such as these:

- Are audience members actively listening to me, or do I seem to be talking to a blank wall?
- Do audience members seem to understand what I am saying, or do they seem confused by my remarks?
- Do I feel my voice rising and my heart racing when I talk about an emotional issue or address an argumentative audience member?

Good speakers silently ask and answer these questions as they speak. Then they use a second important skill—they make mid-presentation corrections. If an audience seems confused, the speaker may slow down and re-explain a concept. If the audience looks bored, the speaker may add an interesting or amusing story to rekindle their interest. If the audience seems hostile, the speaker may try to defuse the tense atmosphere by acknowledging the legitimacy of the audience's concerns, announcing a question-and-answer session scheduled for *after* the talk, or beginning with an amusing story about how another speaker handled an inhospitable audience.

Learning to "listen" as a speaker is just as important as learning to listen as an audience member. Both skills require critical thinking, a willingness to withhold evaluation until comprehension is complete, and the courage to make mid-performance adjustments as you speak.

Adapting to Different Listeners

Just as audience members have different backgrounds and abilities, they also have different ways of listening. Some audience members may only listen for and remember a few facts. They may not be able to identify or analyze your central idea or key points

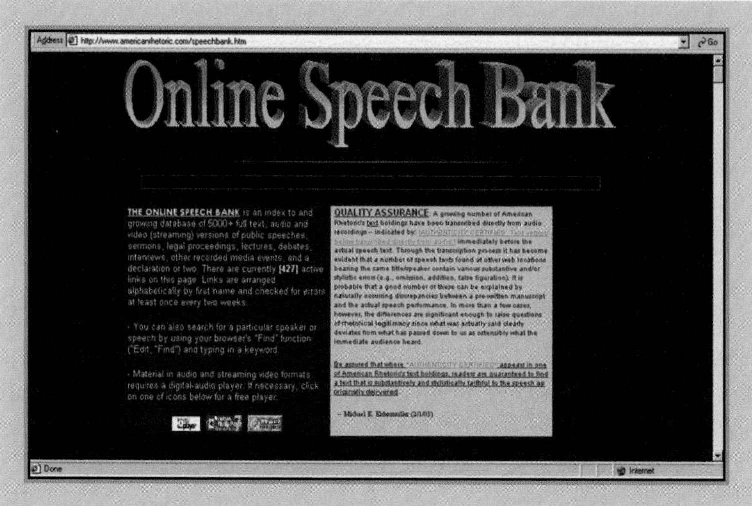

On Houghton Mifflin's Public Speaking website, www.hmco.com/college/communication, you'll find video clips of major presentations by speakers with different backgrounds and perspectives. How do such differences affect the way you listen to a speaker's message?

because they may have underdeveloped empathic, analytical, or appreciative listening skills. Other audience members may be skilled at almost all forms of listening.

Listening behavior may also differ between men and women. Researchers tell us that men may be more likely to listen to the content of what is said while women may focus more on the relationship between the speaker and the audience. Males tend to hear the facts while females are more aware of the mood of the communication. In other words, men tend to focus on comprehensive and analytical listening while women are more likely to be empathic and appreciative listeners.[13]

Cultural differences can also influence the ways in which audience members listen and respond to a presentation. One study concluded that international students perceive U.S. students to be less willing and less patient as listeners than those from African, Asian, South American, or European cultures.[14] Myron Lustig and Jolene Koester, communication professors and the authors of *Intercultural Competence,* offer an explanation of such perceived differences in listening behavior. English is a speaker-responsible language in which the speaker structures the message and relies primarily on words to provide meaning. Japanese, however, is a listener-responsible language in which speakers indirectly indicate what they want listeners to know. Listeners must rely on nonverbal communication and an understanding of the relationship between the speaker and the listener to interpret meaning.[15] Thus, an English-speaking listener may feel as though a Japanese speaker is leaving out important information whereas the Japanese listener may think that the English speaker is overexplaining or talking down to him or her. Such misunderstandings and perceived discourtesy are due to speaking and listening differences rather than to substantive disagreement.

The habits of effective listening and critical thinking go hand in hand. Adapting your presentation to the diverse listening and thinking styles of audience members can be a complicated and challenging task for even the best critical thinkers. Fortunately, critical thinking and listening are skills that can be taught, learned, practiced, and transformed into lifelong habits. The responsibility for effective thinking and listening rest with both the speaker and the audience, as Figure 2.3 indicates. Not only are these habits essential to developing effective presentations; they are also critical elements in *all* forms of communication.

Figure 2.3 Critical Thinking and Listening as Speakers and Audience Members

Speaker	Audience Member
Rethink your purpose.	Identify the speaker's purpose.
Understand how your audience thinks.	Understand how *you* think and feel.
Take time to think.	Take time to think.
Test your thinking on others.	Test your thinking on others.
Think about your words.	Think about the speaker's words.
Avoid wishful thinking.	Avoid wishful thinking.

What Is Critical Thinking?

Although critical thinking has strong links to listening, it is not the same thing. Nor is critical thinking the same as day-to-day, "automatic" thought. Rather, **critical thinking** is the particular kind of thinking we use to analyze what we read, see, or hear in order to arrive at a justified conclusion or decision. It is a conscious process that when effective, always has an outcome. It can result in a conclusion, decision, opinion, or behavior.[16] It can even result in a presentation.

Critical thinking puts your mind to work on complex problems—from considering a career change or resolving a family crisis to making an effective job-related presentation or critiquing a major public speech. When you think critically, you "talk to yourself" about what you are doing and why you are doing it when you make important decisions. In the case of speechmaking, those decisions impact all seven principles of presentation speaking.

After many years of teaching, coaching, and speaking, we have learned that the best and brightest speakers tend also to be excellent critical thinkers. Whereas actors perform lines written by a playwright, speakers write their own lines. Whereas athletes may model their behavior after superstars and Olympic medal winners, good speakers develop their own styles. Whereas an author can spend days, weeks, or years writing a significant article or book, speakers are often required to get up and make a significant presentation with little advance notice. To succeed, speakers must be able to think critically.

At every stage of the encoding process, you will need to make critical decisions: What is the purpose of my presentation? How should I adapt to my audience? What is the best way to arrange the room in which I will be speaking? How much research do I need to do? How should I organize my content? How can I make my

Does Critical Thinking Require Criticizing?

A common confusion about critical thinking is that it means criticizing. Definitions of the word *criticize* include "to find fault with" and "to judge the merits and faults of."[1] The word *critical* is a broader, less fault-finding term. *Critical* comes from the Greek word for critic (*kritkos*), which means to question, to make sense of, to be able to analyze.[2] Critical thinking is a way of analyzing what we read, see, and hear in order to make intelligent decisions about what to do or believe. It is *not* a way to tear down an argument or criticize a speaker. Critical thinking requires specific skills: You need to be able to identify what you're being asked to believe or accept and to evaluate the evidence and reasoning you're given in support of the belief. You need the ability to judge the credibility of sources. You should be able to develop and defend a position on an issue, to ask appropriate questions, to be open-minded, and to draw reasonable conclusions.[3]

1. *The American Heritage Dictionary of the English Language*, 4th ed. (Boston: Houghton Mifflin, 2000), p. 432. Copyright © 2000 by Houghton Mifflin Company. Reproduced by permission from *The American Heritage Dictionary of the English Language, Fourth Edition*.
2. John Chaffee, *Thinking Critically*, 7th ed. (Boston: Houghton Mifflin, 2003), p. 51.
3. Robert H. Ennis, "Critical Thinking Assessment," *Theory into Practice* 32 (1993): 180.

Effective speakers use critical thinking to make strategic decisions at every key point in the presentation speaking process—even when they're interacting with others.

presentation interesting? What form of delivery should I use? Critical thinking skills can help you answer these questions. Those answers in turn can help you develop a presentation that achieves your purpose, meets your audience's needs, and thus establishes and enhances your credibility.

Audience members must be critical thinkers, too. Otherwise, they may misunderstand messages or be deceived and exploited by speakers. Critical thinkers intelligently evaluate speakers and their messages. They recognize the differences between fact and fiction, between valid and invalid arguments, between credible experts and biased sources, and between skilled persuasion and intimidating coercion. When one audience member does not think critically, the consequences are unfortunate for that particular listener. When most audience members, television viewers, and citizens do not think critically, the consequences can undermine the foundation of a democratic society.

At this point you may be wondering how you can apply critical thinking to presentation speaking. Learning how to think critically requires a great deal more than reading this chapter or learning a set of presentation speaking rules. As we indicate in Chapter 1, "Presentation Speaking," effective speakers use critical thinking to make strategic decisions at key points in the presentation speaking process. Critical thinkers work their way through decisions about purpose, audience, credibility, logistics, content, organization, and performance. In fact, every chapter in this textbook offers critical thinking strategies and skills that can help you become a more effective speaker.

In this early chapter, however, we take an introductory look at three strategies that can help you become a more critical thinker and, as a result, a more effective speaker and a more discerning audience member.

ENHANCE YOUR CRITICAL THINKING

1. Identify different types of claims.
2. Separate facts from inferences.
3. Develop good critical thinking habits.

Identify Different Types of Claims

Brooke Noel Moore and Richard Parker, the authors of *Critical Thinking*, contend that critical thinking requires the "careful, deliberate determination of whether we should accept, reject, or suspend judgment about a claim—and of the degree of confidence with which we accept or reject it." What is a claim? Moore and Parker write that "claims are statements that we accept as true or false."[17] There are, however, several types of claims that go well beyond determinations of truth.

A **claim** is a statement that identifies your position on a particular issue or topic. Speakers make many kinds of claims in the course of a presentation. Claims answer the question "What am I trying to explain or prove?" In addition to claiming that something is true or false, you may claim that something is good or bad, probable or improbable, or a reasonable or unreasonable course of action. Understanding each type of claim can help you—as a speaker—develop a strong and well-justified presentation. As an audience member who understands the nature of claims, you will have better tools for analyzing the quality of someone else's presentation.

Claims of Fact.

Claims of fact state that something is true, that an event occurred, that a cause can be identified, or that a theory explains a phenomenon. For example, "Our final exam is scheduled for May 12 at noon" is a simple claim of fact. Whether this claim is true or not requires some research, but it should be fairly easy to verify as true or false. Claims of fact such as "The death penalty deters criminals" are controversial and may be difficult to prove one way or the other. But the statement is still a claim of fact. Critical thinkers can research the topic and apply logical reasoning when determining whether the claim is, in actuality, a fact.

Claims of Conjecture.

A **claim of conjecture** suggests that something will or will not happen in the future. For example, you could say, "Candidate X will be elected president." Although you cannot predict the future, you can make well-informed decisions based on good information. Claims of conjecture usually rely on subclaims of fact. For example, claims of fact related to a candidate's background, previous campaign successes, and survey results can help you make a well-informed claim of conjecture.

Claims of Value.

Claims of value assert that something is worthwhile—good or bad, right or wrong, or best, average, or worst. "My instructor is the best professor at the college" is a claim that places value on someone. Claims of value are difficult to prove because they involve personal opinions and beliefs. Yet, on a daily basis, we are bombarded with claims of value—everything from slick advertisements about a "best" brand to the personal opinions of friends.

Claims of Policy. **Claims of policy** recommend a particular course of action. "Our association should develop guidelines for dealing with inquiries from the press and electronic media" is an example of a claim of policy. When thinking about a claim of policy, you may need to analyze supporting claims of fact, conjecture, and value in order to justify why you are advocating a particular policy or course of action.

In Chapters 19, "Understanding Persuasion," and 20, "Developing Persuasive Presentations," we revisit these claims in terms of how they relate to developing persuasive presentations. For now, you, as both a speaker and a listener, should be aware of the different types of claims.

If a speaker claims that one product is better than another, are you being asked to accept a claim of fact or of value? If you campaign for a political candidate, are you supporting a claim of conjecture or of policy? Understanding the different types of claims can help you select appropriate strategies for achieving the purpose of your presentations. As an audience member, understanding the different kinds of claims gives you a means of separating facts from wishful thinking about the future, value statements, and suggested courses of action.

Separate Facts from Inferences

In a single day, you will encounter hundreds of claims. Some of those claims will be made by friends, colleagues, and family members; others by speakers, government agencies, and commercial businesses. In addition to understanding the different types of claims, critical thinkers know how to separate facts from inferences. Remember that a claim of fact is a statement that can be proven true or false. An **inference,** however, is the process of drawing a conclusion based on claims of fact.

Critical thinking can help you separate provable facts from unprovable inferences. Why is this important? When you accept an inference as a fact, you are "jumping to conclusions" that may not be justified. When you assume that an inference is "true," you may be led down a path that leads to a poor decision. For example, the claim "My car broke down three times last month" is a claim of fact. You can document the truth of this statement. However, the claim "My car will probably break down next month" is a claim of conjecture. If you know why your car has been breaking down, you may be able to conclude that future breakdowns are likely, but you cannot claim this inference as a fact.

Here's another fact/inference example that could impair a speaker's credibility and effectiveness.

Claim: Almost 90 percent of the students in my audience are African American.

Inference: Therefore, my audience is politically liberal and votes for Democrats.

Although your claim about the percentage of African Americans in your class can be determined by surveying your audience, you cannot and should not jump to the conclusion that they are liberal and vote for Democrats. Even if voting research indicates that the majority of African Americans support Democratic candidates, you cannot assume that the members of this particular audience share these characteristics.

Develop Good Critical Thinking Habits

Earlier in this chapter, we discussed the importance of developing good listening habits. The same is true of critical thinking. You must know *what* and *why* to think critically, know *how* to think critically, and *want* to think critically in order for it to become a habit.

We offer five habits of effective critical thinking that—with knowledge, skill, practice, and a desire to improve—can help you think critically about presentation speaking.

FIVE HABITS OF CRITICAL THINKERS

1. **Rethink your purpose.**
2. **Think like your audience.**
3. **Take time to think.**
4. **Test your thinking on others.**
5. **Avoid wishful thinking.**

Rethink Your Purpose. Your answer to the purpose question—"What do I want my audience to know, think, believe, or do as a result of my presentation?"—comes with an admonition. What *you* want to accomplish may have little connection to what the audience needs or wants. Don't let your own biases and passions blind you to the attitudes and interests of your audience. After all, don't many professors treat their courses as the most important in the college? Don't most major movie producers think they have backed a sure-fire box office hit? Do you often find yourself puzzled when others lack your enthusiasm for a favorite food, movie, book, sports team, or political candidate?

Remember: Most speakers care more, want more from, and know more about their presentations than the audience does. So rethink your purpose. Look for ways to make your interests and needs compatible with those of your audience. If you and your audience do not share similar needs, interests, attitudes, and values, consider modifying your purpose to one that is more realistic and achievable.

Think Like Your Audience. Try to understand how your audience thinks. Visualize yourself in the audience. Imagine how the audience members think, feel, and listen. Will they be interested in your message? How will they analyze and respond to what you say? Turn the golden listening rule—listen to others as you would have them listen to you—into a critical thinking rule. Analyze and adapt to *how* others listen in order to get them to listen to you.

If you cannot discern how a specific audience may think, here are some general tendencies found in most audiences:

- Audiences tend to remember vivid, dramatic information as well as negative or distressing information.

Take the Haney Test

One way to demonstrate the differences between facts and inferences is to test yourself by taking a short quiz developed by William V. Haney.[1] Read the following story and assume that all of the information presented in it is accurate and true. Read the story carefully because it has ambiguous parts designed to lead you astray. Next, read the statements about the story and indicate whether you consider the statements true, false, or ambiguous by labeling them *T*, *F*, or "*?*" *T* means that the statement is definitely true on the basis of information presented in the story. *F* means that it is definitely false. The question mark (*?*) means that it may be either true or false and that you cannot be certain on the basis of the information in the story.

Story:

You arrive home late one evening and see that the lights are on in your living room. There is only one car parked in front of your house, and the words Harold R. Jones, M.D., *are spelled out in small gold letters across one of the car's doors.*

Questions About the Story:

1. __T__ The car parked in front of your house has lettering on one of its doors. (This is a true statement because it is stated in the story.)
2. __?__ Someone in the family is sick. (This could be true, and then again it might not be. Perhaps Dr. Jones is paying a social call at your home, perhaps he has gone to the house next door or the one across the street, or maybe someone else is using his car.)
3. __F__ No car is parked in front of your house. (This is a false statement because the story contradicts it.)
4. __?__ The car parked in front of your house belongs to a woman named Johnson. (This answer may seem very likely to be false, but can you be sure? Perhaps the car has just been sold. Perhaps Dr. Jones's wife is using his car, and her last name is *Johnson*.)

1. William V. Haney, *Communication and Interpersonal Relationships: Text and Cases* (Homewood, IL: Irwin, 1992), pp. 231–232.

- Audiences tend to have great confidence in their own beliefs and opinions and to question the truth of information that runs counter to those beliefs.
- Audiences tend to see their own behavior as more justified than others' behavior.
- Audiences tend to assume that others have the same motives that they do.

In light of these predispositions, try out your critical thinking. What do these tendencies tell you about how to develop and deliver an effective presentation? What kinds of information and examples should you use to support your claims? How should you present claims that may differ from the audience's assumptions and opinions?

Take Time to Think. Critical thinking takes time. In day-to-day decision making, we often grab the first idea that pops into our heads. Critical thinking, however, requires time to test ideas and to let alternative ideas emerge.

You need time to produce a wide range of well-developed ideas before deciding which ones will meet your own and your audience's needs. Good ideas need time to percolate—time to seep into one another and produce even better ideas. In his book *Becoming a Critical Thinker,* Vincent Ruggiero puts it this way: "Be open to ideas at all times. You may find that insights occur to you when you don't expect them—while you shower, walk from class to class, or sleep through the night."[18] Putting more time into critical thinking can result in better decisions about every key principle in the speechmaking process.

Test Your Thinking on Others. All of us have experienced moments in which we have deluded ourselves about something we strongly believe. As speakers, we also make flawed decisions about presentations. We may believe that everyone in the audience will be glued to every word we say, exhibiting high levels of interest and agreement. However, critical thinkers avoid such self-deception by testing and retesting their messages.

A friend, family member, or colleague can provide valuable insights, good suggestions, and words of warning about potential problems. Even though you have been rethinking your purpose, trying to think like your audience, and devoting considerable time to strategic decision making, you still may have overlooked something.

Audience members who read or hear your presentation for the very first time may have very simple but important observations and questions. They may be confused by a complex or abstract idea, may be unwilling to accept a claim or argument that you think is foolproof, may feel manipulated by a proposal, or may be upset by an inappropriate example or word. If your test audience doesn't have an immediate reaction, ask questions. In their opinion, what was your central idea or purpose? At what points were they most interested, bored, supportive, or suspicious? Were there any words they didn't understand?

Ask your reviewer to read or listen comprehensively, empathically, analytically, and appreciatively. You don't have to adopt every suggestion from a critic, but you should consider her or his reactions seriously. At the same time, you may be delighted to discover that you've made excellent strategic decisions and that your work-in-progress is ready to go.

Avoid Wishful Thinking. Speakers and audience members have a tendency to say and hear things that they want to believe. However, just because you *want* something to be a certain way does not mean that it is or will be that way. Horoscopes are a great example of wishful thinking. Read any horoscope. In most cases, it seems to address you. How can that be? The answer: Horoscopes offer hope and the promise of dreams come true. They seduce us into wishful thinking with promising words about our future.

In terms of presentation speaking, just because you think that your ideas are compelling does not mean that your audience will share your opinion. Just because you believe that you have a right to go overtime because your information is so interesting and important, don't assume that your audience shares your interest and passion. A wishful thinker may believe, "My presentation will be successful because I've worked long and hard on it." Sadly, long, hard work expended without critical thinking about the basic principles of presentation speaking may lead to a disappointing outcome.

How do you know if you're engaging in wishful thinking? One way is to separate what you can *know* (based on critical thinking) from what you *believe* (often the result of wishful thinking). Make up a sentence that begins with the words *I believe that.* Replace the word *believe* with the word *know* and see if your statement is still reasonable. In many cases, wishful thinking only reinforces unreasonable claims, weak arguments, and unachievable goals. The following are two examples of sentences that substitute *believe* for *know.*

> *I* believe *that my presentation will be a success because I worked so hard. I* know *that my presentation will be a success because I worked so hard.*
>
> *I* believe *that students will learn more if we increase teachers' salaries. I* know *that students will learn more if we increase teachers' salaries.*

In both cases, the *believe* sentences demonstrate wishful thinking by someone who cannot *know* the outcome of his or her "wishes." Successful presentations require more than hard work—they require critical thinking, informed decision making, and plenty of practice. Improving the quality of education requires more than higher pay for teachers; a host of complex factors contribute to student learning.

Audience members who engage in wishful thinking may make excuses for a speaker who does not say what they want or expect to hear. For example, an audience member may think, "I'm sure he doesn't believe that, but he had to say it to get elected" as a way to preserve a positive opinion about a political candidate. Thinking, "She must be tired—that's why her presentation lacked energy and volume" may help an audience member accept a less-than-wonderful performance by a usually compelling speaker.

In March 2003, President George W. Bush demonstrated the political value of converting beliefs into knowledge at a White House press conference when he said, "I believe we'll prevail. I *know* we'll prevail."

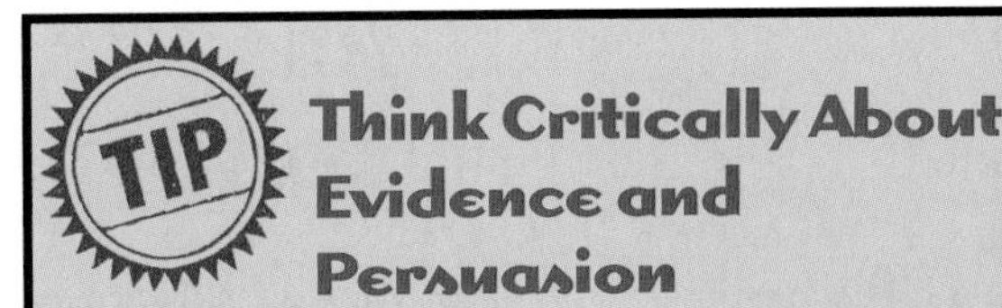

Think Critically About Evidence and Persuasion

In addition to learning the critical thinking strategies and skills described in this chapter, you should think critically about the quality of evidence used to support the claims in a presentation as well as about the validity of arguments used in persuasive speeches. Chapter 8, "Supporting Material," provides a set of recommendations and criteria for testing the validity of the supporting material you hear or use to support the claims in a presentation. These tests of evidence include the following:

- Is the source identified and credible?
- Is the information recent?
- Is the information consistent?
- Is the information relevant?
- Is the statistical method valid?

In Chapter 19, "Understanding Persuasion," and Chapter 20, "Developing Persuasive Presentations," critical thinking lies at the heart of every effective strategy. When developing a persuasive presentation, critical thinkers focus on

- Understanding, categorizing, and adapting to audience attitudes, beliefs, and values
- Selecting appropriate persuasive strategies based on an audience's critical thinking and listening habits
- Developing strong and appropriate persuasive arguments
- Organizing arguments to maximize persuasion
- Avoiding fallacies of argument

In addition to helping a speaker develop an effective presentation, critical thinking about supporting material and persuasive arguments helps audience members judge the quality of a presentation and the credibility of a speaker.

Adapting to Different Ways of Thinking

Life would be much easier (and very boring) if everyone thought alike. If everyone were an effective listener and a first-rate critical thinker, communicating would be easy—if you just said what you meant, you would be understood. Fortunately, our different ways of thinking make life more interesting and more challenging whenever we communicate. Different ways of thinking enhance human creativity, improve cooperative problem solving, and make the world a more interesting place. Regardless of whether you are speaking in your hometown or across the globe, understanding and adapting to different ways of thinking are just as important as understanding and adapting to cultural diversity.

In Chapter 1, we discuss the importance of becoming a culturally sensitive speaker. Here we look at how cultural differences affect the way we think—as speakers and as audience members. In addition to exhibiting cultural differences in thinking, speakers and listeners may differ in terms of the ways in which they learn and think about messages.

Bloom's Taxonomy

Benjamin Bloom and his colleagues contend that thinking skills can be categorized in a hierarchy beginning with the simplest level of behavior and moving to the most complex. Thus, whereas some thinkers can remember basic information, ideas, and principles, more advanced thinkers can apply and analyze knowledge. Bloom and his colleagues offer six major categories of thinking—the most basic ones must be mastered before higher-order thinking can develop.

The following questions can help you understand which types of thinking skills you use most often.[19] Check as many statements as apply to the way that you think.

I am comfortable and confident when asked…

1. _____ To recall information (dates, events, places, names, ideas) or to define, describe, label, quote, or list.

2. _____ To comprehend meaning, to interpret facts, to order and group, to summarize and describe, or to explain or paraphrase.

3. _____ To apply knowledge, to solve problems using skills or knowledge; to demonstrate, show, construct, or compute.

4. _____ To analyze knowledge and opinions, to identify or organize components, to compare and contrast, or to explain.

5. _____ To synthesize old ideas to create new ones; to draw conclusions; to rearrange, plan, create, design, or invent.

6. _____ To evaluate theories, strategies, arguments, and evidence; to critique ideas based on standards or criteria; to recommend, convince, judge, conclude, or justify.

The most effective critical thinkers are comfortable and confident when they are required to recall, comprehend, apply, analyze, synthesize, or evaluate what they hear, see, or read. Critical thinking is much more difficult if you or an audience member find it difficult to apply concepts, analyze ideas, synthesize information, or evaluate an

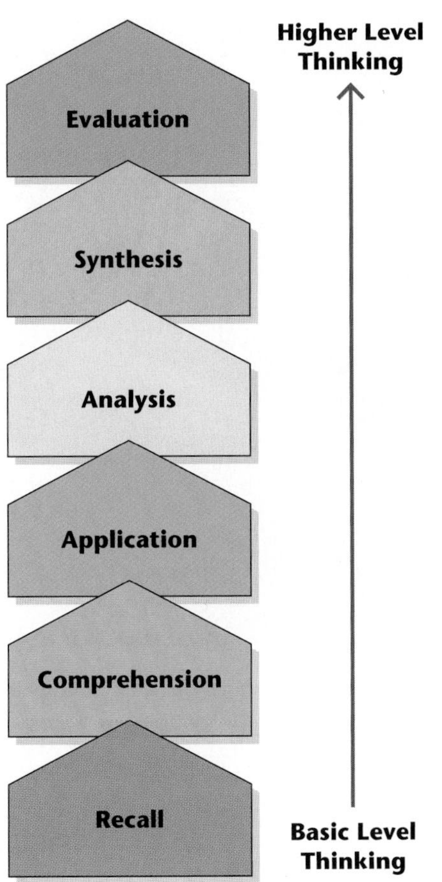

Figure 2.4

Bloom's Taxonomy of Thinking

argument. Do not assume that your audience thinks the way you do. Although you may be able to grasp the weaknesses of an argument or to synthesize a series of ideas into a unified concept, don't assume that your audience shares this ability.

Intellectual Development

Researchers have also investigated how and why people respond so differently to the challenge of critical thinking. It is not surprising that some people have not developed the habit of thinking critically. They are passive thinkers who prefer to receive knowledge from others without questioning their conclusions. Active, critical thinkers analyze knowledge and draw their own conclusions. The following types of knowledge represent different levels of thinking, beginning with the most passive, noncritical level of thinking and continuing to the most active critical thinking level.[20]

- *Knowledge as Facts.* At this basic level, thinkers expect speakers and writers to present knowledge, suggest opinions, and recommend behavior. They want to be told what to think and what to do rather than engaging in critical thinking.
- *Knowledge as Personal Opinions.* These thinkers may know the facts, but they believe that one opinion is as good as any other. They rely on their instincts or feelings, and they often substitute wishful thinking for critical thinking.

Skillful attorneys try to adapt to a jury's level of intellectual development. Whereas some jury members will rely on presented facts and opinions to make decisions, others will test those facts and opinions in order to draw informed conclusions.

- *Knowledge as Tested Conclusions.* At this level, thinkers apply logic and critical thinking rules to test facts and opinions. Their strict reliance on rules and procedures may prevent them from understanding how facts and opinions impact their lives and the world around them.
- *Knowledge as Personal Commitments.* Sophisticated critical thinkers go beyond objective testing of facts and opinions to draw personal conclusions. They understand that a presentation's context and audience have as much to do with the meaning of a message as the speaker's intentions. They advocate their own beliefs and values, but they listen to and respect those of others.

Speakers and listeners who view knowledge as facts or as a series of opinions do *not* think critically. Those who embrace the habits of effective critical thinking understand that knowledge should be tested but also must reflect a position that is reasonable and applicable to other situations.

FAQ Do Feelings Count in Critical Thinking?

If you study and read about critical thinking, you soon notice a bias against emotional thinking. Some writers go so far as to describe critical thinking as a process that excludes "emotionalism" or "relies on reason rather than emotions." We do not share this condemnation of emotions. Instead, we believe that divorcing decision making from emotions can lead to poor decisions.

Emotions are a component of everyday decisions. Why don't consumers buy the cheapest, safest, easiest-to-repair automobiles on the market? Why do people make donations to college football teams rather than to local charities? Why does an employer rely on intuition or a hunch when hiring a new employee, even though another applicant's résumé is stronger than that of the person who is offered the job? Are these irrational decisions? Perhaps. But they're not unreasonable given the amount of pleasure, pride, and productivity we can expect to receive from a car, a football team, and a new employee.

Sometimes our emotions trigger a response that defies logical analysis. In some cases, our instincts may be more reliable than a conclusion based on a detailed analysis of options. Critical thinkers understand that effective decision making is an art, not a science. The art of presentation speaking relies on communication science as well as the artful wisdom that comes with mature human experience.

When Benjamin Bloom and his colleagues developed their hierarchy of cognitive thinking skills, they also identified another important domain of thinking and learning based on various types of feelings and emotions.[1] Antonio Damasio, a neurologist, maintains that emotions play a crucial role in critical thinking. In his studies of patients with damage to the emotional centers of their brains, Damasio found that lack of feelings also impaired rational decision making.[2]

Emotions, gut feelings, instincts, hunches, and practical wisdom can help you make good decisions. They help you understand how decisions affect others. They give you a way of assigning value when considering competing options. They make your decision making human rather than robotic.

In his popular book *Emotional Intelligence*, Daniel Goleman embraces Damasio's view of emotions. Goleman urges us to harmonize head and heart. Although strong feelings can create havoc in a person's reasoning, lack of feeling can also be disastrous, especially when weighing important life decisions.[3]

Despite our acceptance of emotions as part of the critical thinking process, we acknowledge some of their hazards as well. Emotions must be *balanced* with critical thinking. Our intuitions are not always correct. Think about these popular sayings: "Opposites attract" and "Absence makes the heart grow fonder." Are these statements true? As much as your personal experiences may confirm both of these maxims, social science research suggests that both are wrong. Now consider the next two sayings that social scientists claim are true in most close relationships: "Birds of a feather flock together" and "Love the one you're with." Even though the latter two maxims are correct and the former two are wrong—most people believe they are all true!

1. Benjamin S. Bloom, Bertram B. Mesia, and David R. Krathwohl, *Taxonomy of Educational Objectives* Vol. 1, *The Affective Domain*, and Vol 2, *The Cognitive Domain*. (New York: David McKay, 1964).
2. See two works: Antonio R. Damasio, *Descartes' Error: Emotion, Reason, and the Human Brain* (New York: Penguin U.S.A., 1994); and Antonio R. Damasio, *The Feeling of What Happens: Body and Emotion in the Making of Consciousness* (San Diego: Harvest/Harcourt, 1999).
3. Daniel Goleman, *Emotional Intelligence* (New York, Bantam, 1995), pp. 27–29 and 52–53.

Summary

What role does listening play in presentation speaking?

The ability to listen enables an audience to understand, analyze, respect, and appreciate the meaning of a speaker's message. Speakers must learn to adjust to and compensate for the poor listening habits of many audience members.

How can I become a better listener?

In addition to using your extra thought speed to analyze what you hear and to applying the golden listening rule, you can employ the six habits of effective listening to enhance your ability to listen: Overcome distractions, listen for big ideas, "listen" to nonverbal behavior, make it personal, paraphrase, and listen before you leap.

How do I "listen" to an audience?

You "listen" to an audience by looking for and responding to feedback. Responding and adapting to audience feedback have an added advantage of helping your audience to listen to and understand your message.

What role does critical thinking play in presentation speaking?

Effective speakers use critical thinking to make strategic decisions at key points in the presentation speaking process by working their way through decisions about purpose, audience, credibility, logistics, content, organization, and performance.

How do I become a more effective critical thinker?

Critical thinkers—regardless of whether they are speakers or audience members—know how to identify different types of claims, can separate facts from inferences, and develop five critical thinking habits: rethinking or identifying the speaker's purpose, understanding how the audience thinks, taking time to think, testing their thinking on others, and avoiding wishful thinking.

Presentation Principles in Action

Assessing Listenability

Directions: Think about all of the times that you have listened to presentations and public speeches in a variety of situations (listening in classrooms, in political settings, at religious services, at work, or at special occasions such as weddings, retirement dinners, or graduations). Every listener responds differently to the communication behaviors and characteristics of a speaker. Some behaviors or characteristics will be more important to you than others in determining how easy or difficult it is for you to listen. The following chart lists several factors that make listening either difficult or easy, with a focus on the listener's perceptions of speaker behaviors and characteristics that contribute to the ease of listening.

Rate the following items on a seven-point scale in terms of how important they are to listenability in a presentation speaking situation.

7 = Extremely Important

6 = Very Important

5 = Somewhat Important

4 = No Effect

3 = Somewhat Unimportant

2 = Very Unimportant

1 = Extremely Unimportant

Presentation Speaking Listenability*

ITEMS	7	6	5	4	3	2	1
1. **Confidence.** Speaker appears confident, relaxed, natural.							
2. **Content and Structure.** Speaker uses good reasoning and logic, chooses interesting topics, organizes well, seems knowledgeable.							
3. **Verbal Delivery.** Speaker speaks clearly and uses appropriate volume, rate, and pitch.							
4. **Nonverbal Expressiveness.** Speaker uses appropriate facial expressions, gestures, movements, and eye contact.							
5. **Audience Involvement.** Speaker relates messages to listeners' interests, knowledge, feelings.							
6. **Verbal Clarity.** Speaker explains things clearly, using appropriate vocabulary; avoids rambling.							
7. **Personal Appropriateness.** Speaker is well groomed, polite, and credible; seems ethical.							

***Listenability**-Factors important in making listening easy for you.

On completing the previous instrument, ask yourself these questions:

- What do the results tell me about my obligations as a speaker when developing a presentation?
- What do the results tell me about my own listening habits and how I can improve them?
- What do the results tell me about the seven basic principles of presentation and how they relate to the listening process?
- How do my results compare with those of other students in my class?

Source: The Presentation Speaking Listenability Assessment was inspired by and based on a study that attempted to identify listenability factors in interpersonal and public speaking settings. See Ethel C. Glenn, Philip Emmert, and Victoria Emmert, "A Scale for Measuring Listenability: The Factors That Determine Listening Ease and Difficulty," *International Journal of Listening* (1995): 44–61.

The Haney Test

Directions: Read the following story. Assume that all the information presented in it is definitely accurate and true. Read it carefully because it has ambiguous parts designed to lead you astray. You can refer back to the story whenever you wish. Next, read the statements about the story and indicate whether you consider each statement true, false, or ambiguous.

T means that the statement is *definitely true* on the basis of the information presented in the story.

F means that the statement is *definitely false.*

? means that the statement may be either true or false and that you cannot be certain which it is on the basis of the information presented in the story. If any part of a statement is doubtful, insert a question mark (*?*).

Answer each statement in turn, do not go back to change any answer later, and don't reread any statements after you have answered them. Doing so would distort your score. Your instructor has the answer key.

The Story

A businessman had just turned off the lights in the store when a man appeared and demanded money. The owner opened a cash register. The contents of the cash register were scooped up, and the man sped away. A member of the police force was notified promptly.

Statements About the Story

1. T F ? A man appeared after the owner had turned off his store lights.
2. T F ? The robber was a *man*.
3. T F ? The man who appeared did not demand money.
4. T F ? The man who opened the cash register was the owner.

5. T F ? The store owner scooped up the contents of the cash register and ran away.
6. T F ? Someone opened the cash register.
7. T F ? After the man who demanded the money scooped up the contents of the cash register, he ran away.
8. T F ? Although the cash register contained money, the story does *not* state *how much.*
9. T F ? The robber demanded money of the owner.
10. T F ? A businessman had just turned off the lights when a man appeared in the store.
11. T F ? It was broad daylight when the man appeared.
12. T F ? The man who appeared opened the cash register.
13. T F ? No one demanded money.
14. T F ? The story concerns a series of events in which only three persons are referred to: the owner of the store, a man who demanded money, and a member of the police force.
15. T F ? The following events occurred: Someone demanded money, a cash register was opened, its contents were scooped up, and a man dashed out of the store.

Source: William V. Haney, *Communication and Interpersonal Relationships: Text and Cases* (Homewood, IL: Irwin, 1992), pp. 232–233, 241. The correct answers and their explanations can be found in the *Instructor's Resource Manual* to accompany *Presentations in Everyday Life,* Second Edition, which is available from the College Division of the Houghton Mifflin Company, Boston, MA.

Key Terms

analytical listening 31
appreciative listening 31
claim 43
claims of conjecture 43
claims of fact 43
claims of policy 44
claims of value 43
comprehensive listening 30
critical thinking 41
empathic listening 31
golden listening rule 34
inference 44
listening 29
nonverbal communication 36
paraphrasing 37
thought speed 33

Notes

1 Sections of this chapter are based on Chapter 6 of Isa N. Engleberg and Dianna R. Wynn, *Working in Groups: Communication Principles and Strategies,* 3rd ed. (Boston: Houghton Mifflin, 2003).

2 Larry L. Barker et al., "An Investigation of Proportional Time Spent in Various Communication Activities by College Students," *Journal of Applied Communication Research* 8 (1980): 101–109.

3 Andrew D. Wolvin and Carolyn G. Coakley, *Listening,* 5th ed. (Madison, WI: Brown & Benchmark, 1996), p. 15.

4 Ralph G. Nichols, "Listening Is a 10-Part Skill," *Nation's Business* 75 (Sept. 1987): 40.

5 S. S. Benoit and J. W. Lee, "Listening: It Can Be Taught," *Journal of Education for Business* 63 (1986): 229–232.

6 Nichols, p. 40.

7 Alan M. Perlman, *Writing Great Speeches* (Boston: Allyn & Bacon, 1998), p. 91.

8 Madelyn Burley-Allen, *Listening: The Forgotten Skill,* 2nd ed. (New York: Wiley, 1995), pp. 68–70.

9 *The American Heritage Dictionary of the English Language,* 4th ed. (Boston: Houghton Mifflin, 2000), p. 176.

10 Mark L. Knapp and Judith A. Hall, *Nonverbal Communication in Human Interaction,* 4th ed. (Fort Worth, TX: Harcourt Brace, 1997), p. 466.

11 As cited in Knapp and Hall, p. 391.

12 Ralph G. Nichols, "Do We Know How to Listen? Practical Help in a Modern Age," *Speech Teacher* 10 (1961): 121.

13 See Deborah Tannen, *You Just Don't Understand: Women and Men in Conversation* (New York: William Morrow, 1990), pp. 149–151; Diana K. Ivy and Phil Backlund, *Exploring Gender Speak* (New York: McGraw-Hill, 1994), pp. 206–208 and 224–225.

14 Wolvin and Coakley, p. 125.

15 Myron W. Lustig and Jolene Koester, *Intercultural Communication Across Cultures,* 3rd ed. (New York: Longman, 1999), p. 249.

16 For other definitions and discussions of critical thinking, see Brooke Noel Moore and Richard Parker, *Critical Thinking,* 5th ed. (Mountain View, CA: Mayfield, 1998); John Chaffee, *Thinking Critically,* 6th ed. (Boston: Houghton Mifflin, 2000); Richard W. Paul, *Critical Thinking: How to Prepare Students for a Rapidly Changing World* (Santa Rosa, CA: Foundation for Critical Thinking, 1995).

17 Moore and Parker, p. 5.

18 Vincent R. Ruggiero, *Becoming a Critical Thinker,* 4th ed. (Boston: Houghton Mifflin, 2002), p. 51.

19 Adapted from Benjamin S. Bloom and David R. Krathwohl, "Taxonomy of Educational Objectives: The Classification of Education Goals," in *Handbook I: Cognitive Domain,* ed. Benjamin S. Bloom (New York: Longman, Green, 1956). Also see L. Anderson and David R. Krathwohl, *Taxonomy for Learning, Teaching and Assessing: A Revision of Bloom's Taxonomy of Educational Objectives* (New York: Longman, 2001). Several websites also provide effective summaries of Bloom's Taxonomy. Use *Bloom's Taxonomy* as a search phrase.

20 The four stages of thinking are based on the work of two researchers who examined thinking as a component of intellectual development. William Perry's early research was further developed by Mary Belenky and her colleagues. See Kelvin L. Seifert, Robert J. Hoffnung, and Michelle Hoffnung, *Lifespan Development,* 2nd ed. (Boston: Houghton Mifflin, 2000), p. 447; Joanne Gainen Kurfiss, *Critical Thinking: Theory, Research, Practice, and Possibilities,* ASHE–ERIC Higher Education Report No. 2 (Washington, D.C.: Association for the study of Higher Education, 1988), pp. 51–58; William G. Perry Jr., "Cognitive and Ethical Growth: The Making of Meaning," in *The Modern American College,* ed. Arthur W. Chickering and Associates (San Francisco: Jossey-Bass, 1981), p. 79.

chapter three

Building Presentation **Confidence**

- Where does presentation anxiety come from?
- What makes some speakers look so confident?
- How can preparation reduce presentation anxiety?
- Do relaxation techniques really work?
- How can breaking the rules help me to become a more confident speaker?
- How do practice and focus build confidence?

Whether you call it presentation anxiety, communication apprehension, stage fright, or talking terror, you wouldn't be human if the thought of giving a speech or presentation didn't make you a bit nervous. On the first day of a public speaking class at our respective institutions, we often ask students what their goals are for the course. An overwhelming number of students only give answers related to fear of speaking. No other answer comes close. Students write that they want to "gain confidence," "overcome anxiety," "stop being nervous," "get rid of the jitters," and "calm down."

In fact, about 75 to 85 percent of the U.S. population experiences some form of anxiety when faced with the prospect of making a presentation.[1] In most studies, Americans report that they fear public speaking more than heights, death, financial difficulties, and snakes.[2] Even people such as Barbra Streisand, Billy Graham, Jane Fonda, and Lily Tomlin who are known for their public performances and presentations have reported that they suffer from extreme stage fright.[3] It's hard to believe that people would rather fall off cliffs, die, lose their jobs, or be thrown into a snake pit than make a presentation. Most people probably would choose to give a speech rather than suffer any of the previously mentioned horrors. Nevertheless, for many Americans the *thought* of making a presentation is incredibly frightening. In this chapter, we focus on the causes of presentation anxiety and what you can do to reduce it and become a more confident speaker. This last sentence is an important one. As we've indicated, most people experience some anxiety when they make an important presentation. It would be unnatural not to. In fact, that "keyed up" feeling is a positive and normal reaction to speaking and demonstrates that you care about what you have to say. The issue, then, is not whether you experience presentation anxiety but rather how you label it and transform it. And that is the focus of this chapter.

What Is Presentation Anxiety?

Presentation anxiety is a natural reaction to a unique kind of social situation—the task of getting up to speak in front of a group of people. Speakers cite many reasons for getting nervous—such as "I could forget what I want to say," "My audience will hate me," or "I'll make a huge, embarrassing mistake." However, the probability of any of these things happening is very small. It's *imagining* their happening that creates anxiety.

Presentation anxiety is also a physiological response to stress. Physical symptoms such as sweaty palms and a perspiring forehead, a fast pulse, shallow breathing, cold extremities, flushed skin, nausea, trembling hands, quivering legs, and "butterflies" in the stomach are the body's reaction to the release of stress hormones such as adrenaline.[4] Yet these symptoms also resemble those that accompany many *positive* experiences. Suppose you're waiting for the exciting conclusion of a football game, the ending of an adventure movie that has had you at the edge of your seat, or the arrival of a loved one whom you haven't seen for many years. How would you feel? You'd be physically aroused, just as you are when making a presentation—pounding heart, shortness of breath, flushed skin. Many of the physical sensations of excitement are the same as those of anxiety. It's the way in which you interpret them that is important. You can think of making a presentation as an exciting adventure or as a frightening, even horrifying event. It all depends on how you choose to label it. Let's look at what the "anxiety" label means.

How Confident Are You?

To assess your level of communication confidence, complete this brief questionnaire:

Presentation Confidence Survey*

For each statement please indicate whether you (1) strongly agree, (2) agree, (3) neither agree nor disagree, (4) disagree, or (5) strongly disagree.

1. I have no fear of making a speech. 1 2 3 4 5
2. I feel relaxed when giving a speech. 1 2 3 4 5
3. Giving a speech really scares me. 1 2 3 4 5
4. My thoughts become confused and jumbled when I'm giving a speech. 1 2 3 4 5
5. I face the prospect of giving a speech with confidence. 1 2 3 4 5

Now score yourself using this formula: Your score = 12 minus (items 3 + 4) plus the sum of (items 1 + 2 + 5). If your score is quite high (the possible range is from 5 to 25), you're probably very nervous about making presentations in most situations. If your score is quite low, you have a low level of anxiety when planning or making a presentation. Most scores fall in the middle range—indicating a moderate level of speaking anxiety. Regardless of your level of anxiety, however, you will still have to make presentations. Thus, it's important to learn how to deal with your apprehensions in various settings.

*There are longer, more sophisticated instruments for assessing your level of communication apprehension and stage fright. See Richmond and McCroskey in the Notes section of this chapter.

Presentation anxiety is a speaker's individual level of fear or anxiety that is associated with either real or anticipated communication to a group of people or an audience.[5] What does this mean? First, look at the phrase *a speaker's individual level of fear or anxiety.* All this says is that some speakers are more frightened than others. Some people look forward to presentation speaking; others would do almost anything to avoid it.

Second, note the phrase *real or anticipated communication.* This says that anticipating all the things that could go wrong makes some people more nervous than making an actual presentation, while others are most nervous *during* a presentation. In fact, for many speakers, less than a minute after beginning a presentation, their anxiety subsides as their heart rates begin a gradual and fairly steady decline.[6]

Third, see how the definition mentions a *group of people or an audience.* This means that some people are just as nervous when speaking to a small group of three people as others are in front of an audience of thousands. Again, those anxious feelings are perfectly natural in either setting—and may be as much a sign of excitement as of nervousness.

Sources of Presentation Anxiety

One of the keys to building presentation confidence is to understand the sources of the nervousness and discomfort that you may feel when speaking to a group or an audience. Although everyone has his or her own personal reasons for being nervous, researchers have identified some of the key fears that underlie presentation anxiety.[7] See if you can recognize yourself in any of the sections that follow.

At a job fair, interested students must appear confident and competent when speaking to recruiters. The first few seconds in such encounters make long-lasting impressions.

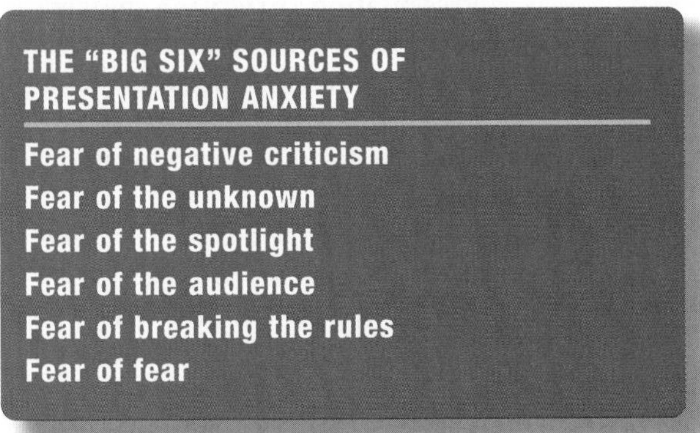

Fear of Negative Criticism. Presentations happen in front of an audience that watches and evaluates you. Some researchers maintain that the fear of a negative evaluation is the number one cause of speaking anxiety.[8] In part, presentation anxiety anticipates the possible anguish and embarrassment of being evaluated as a poor speaker—or failing.

Before a presentation, you may worry about what audience members will think of you and your talk. During a presentation, you may experience heightened anxiety if you begin to think that your audience is not interested or approving. And afterwards you may be haunted by worries about audience members' final judgments. "Did they like it?" and "How'd I do?" are not idle or innocent questions; they are ways of determining whether you have succeeded or failed.

Speakers who have learned and believe that their talking is grounds for criticism are rarely confident speakers. Virginia Richmond and Jim McCroskey, experts in the study of communication apprehension, found that a person's level of presentation anxiety is determined in part by the extent to which she or he was rewarded for or deterred from communicating as a child.[9]

So how do you turn the fear of negative criticism on its head? Scan your audience for positive reactions—a nod, a smile, or an alert look. When you find them, focus on them: Seeing positive feedback generally reduces presentation anxiety. When you sense that your listeners like you and your message, that reaction means your presentation is succeeding.

Fear of the Unknown. Most people fear the unfamiliar, and making a presentation falls into that category for many inexperienced speakers. Even if you have had some experience making presentations, you may still become anxious if you don't know much about your audience or topic. In unfamiliar settings, the size and shape of a room, unexpected background noises, the ways in which lights and microphones operate, and whether and where audience members will sit all have the potential to unnerve a speaker. Even a familiar room and audience can look quite different from the podium.

The switch to an uncommon or unexpected role can transform a usually confident person into a tangle of nerves. Imagine that you are asked to stand up and explain a new procedure or introduce a guest in the audience. If you were attending an event or a meeting and expecting to be a listener, being called on to switch roles and to be a presenter instead could be unsettling, to say the least.

So how do you reduce your fear of the unknown? For starters, remind yourself that since you're taking this course, presentation speaking *won't* be an unknown anymore! If you're asked to give a presentation, whether months or moments in advance, you'll know what to do.

Fear of the Spotlight. One of the primary reasons many people give for having presentation anxiety is knowing that they will be the main focus of their audience's attention. Whereas a little attention may be flattering and pleasurable, standing alone in the spotlight makes many people nervous. In such a situation your audience is watching everything that you do; they are there to hear what you have to say. It's hard to imagine anything more conspicuous. Moreover, feeling conspicuous can lead to excessive self-consciousness, which in turn may cause you to focus on yourself rather than on your message. The more self-focused you are, the more likely you will experience nervousness.

Since excessive self-focus can limit your effectiveness as a speaker, try this trick to break the habit: Focus your attention on a few friendly faces in the audience rather than on your notes or on yourself. Not only will this technique make you less self-conscious, but it will also engage your audience in your presentation and focus their attention more on your message—and less on you!

Fear of the Audience. Sometimes the characteristics of the audience can heighten a speaker's anxiety. Talking to two people is quite different from speaking to two thousand, so it's no surprise that large audiences arouse more anxiety than small ones.

Large audiences also tend to be composed of people with varying backgrounds, interests, and purposes—and this diversity can make some speakers nervous. They may worry that adapting to one part of a diverse audience means running the risk of

Real World Real Speakers

Giving a Presentation Makes Me Feel . . .

In our classes we often ask students to describe how they feel when asked to make a presentation. We've received responses that range from a sense of empowerment to total terror, as the following illustrate:

- Giving a presentation makes me feel powerful. Although nervousness enters the picture, so does a feeling of power. The thought of having everybody's full attention and being able to convey my point of view makes me feel as though I'm in charge.
- Giving a presentation makes me feel scared. I feel as though people aren't listening to me but instead are looking at my shoes or clothes, so I worry that I have both earrings in or that my blouse is buttoned correctly. You're on the spot with twenty pairs of eyes staring at you.
- I'm very quiet and shy in front of most people, especially people I don't know. Because I'm a quiet person, I'm not comfortable with just coming out and speaking to someone—which is just like giving a speech because you are speaking to people you've never met.
- Giving a presentation makes me feel extremely nervous. My heart starts racing so fast that it makes me breathless. My knees, and the rest of my body, start to tremble, and I feel like I'm going to lose control. I've tried taking deep breaths to calm myself when I feel this way. I've also tried medication, but it doesn't work. The last time I enrolled in a speech class, I dropped out because I was so nervous about giving a speech and embarrassing myself.

We are pleased to report that all four of these students did quite well in the course.

excluding another part. More likely, though, fear of the audience relates to the fear of the unknown we discussed earlier. If you don't know much about your audience—and what you do know is that you don't have much in common with them—you're likely to feel somewhat apprehensive.

One way in which you may differ from your audience is in your status. A junior-level financial officer suddenly asked to present a major report to a group of senior vice presidents would probably be more anxious about speaking than if she were assigned to talk to a group of beginning finance students. Why? Because of the relative imbalance between her status level and her audience's.

As we discuss in Chapter 5, "Audience Analysis and Adaptation," you can learn a lot about your audience and use the information that you gather to develop a presentation uniquely suited to their needs. You may find areas of common interest, reducing the perceived gaps between you and your audience. And you may find that you have been invited to present because you know more about a given topic than your "higher status" audience does. Increasing your knowledge about your audience can decrease your anxiety.

Fear of Breaking the Rules. Many speakers experience presentation anxiety because they are burdened with too many **rigid rules** and misconceptions about what makes a presentation good or bad. The rules of speaking are not like the rules of baseball or the laws of physics. "Three strikes and you're out" works in baseball; this rule doesn't apply to presentations. "What goes up must come down" is fine in applied physics but not in presentations. Unfortunately, some speakers believe that the "rules" they find in textbooks or learn about in a communication class are hard and fast. At best, the rules are generalizations that can be applied to many situations. At worst, some rules are wrong. We wish we had a dollar for every student who has been told to look at a spot on the back wall above the heads of the audience rather than to establish direct eye contact. For fear of saying "uh" or "um" in a presentation, speakers have overrehearsed to the point of sounding like robots.

Novice speakers sometimes take all the rules about a good presentation too seriously. They become anxious because as they are speaking, they find themselves not adhering to every rule. Experienced speakers know, however, that no two presentations are alike and understand that rules are only rough guides. They know that sometimes these rules should be bent or broken.

Fear of Fear. One of the biggest problems with presentation anxiety is that it grows on itself. If, for example, you start feeling a slight tremor of fear, you may become more conscious of that feeling, which in turn can generate even more anxiety. Don Green, who applies the techniques of sports psychology to helping musicians overcome performance anxiety, suggests a quick and simple method for breaking the fear cycle: Give a name to your fear; then tell "Pete" or "Ruth" to scram![10] We explore other methods for ending this cycle in the rest of this chapter.

Sources of Confidence

Successful speakers know two very important facts about presentation anxiety: They know that it's very common, and they know that it's usually invisible. Remember that 75 to 85 percent of the U.S. population experiences presentation anxiety. This means that most audience members will understand your feelings, wouldn't want to trade

Exhibitors at trade shows repeatedly make the same presentation on topics they know well, growing more confident and competent each time.

places with you, and might even admire your courage for being up there. If you do appear a bit nervous, most listeners will know how you're feeling and won't let it interfere with their impression of you or your presentation. Despite most people's worst fears, audiences tend to be kind to speakers. They are willing to forgive and forget an honest mistake. Since no one in your audience expects you to be perfect, why should you? Indeed, audiences are usually on your side.

Also, remember that in most cases your anxiety is invisible. Audiences cannot see or hear your fear. They cannot see a pounding heart, an upset stomach, cold hands, or worried thoughts. They do not notice small changes in a voice or remember occasional mistakes. In fact, most speakers who describe themselves as being nervous appear confident and calm to their audiences. Many speakers think that they display far more anxiety than audience members actually report seeing. Even experienced speech teachers, when asked about how anxious a speaker is, seldom accurately estimate the speaker's anxiety.[11]

If you find yourself feeling a little anxious before your next presentation, remind yourself of these two vital facts. They can help you transform your anxiety into presentation confidence.

REMEMBER: PRESENTATION ANXIETY IS ...

shared by your audience
and
usually invisible

Becoming a Confident Speaker

A good side effect of presentation anxiety's being so common is that psychologists and communication researchers have developed many effective methods for helping anxious speakers cope. We hope you find some that can work for you in the pages that follow![12]

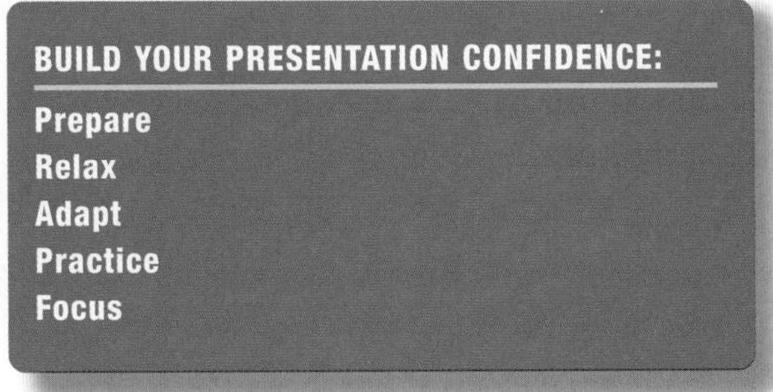

Prepare

"Be prepared" is more than the Boy Scouts' motto; it is one of the guiding maxims of successful speakers. Not only does conscientious and thorough preparation make your presentation better; it also makes you a better presenter. Why? Remember that fear of the unknown contributes to presentation anxiety. Preparation is one way of changing something unfamiliar into something familiar. Novice speakers often report that a symptom of their nervousness is their feeling of being lost and confused as they speak. Preparation can replace this sense of confusion with confidence.

Good preparation requires that you know as much as possible about where and to whom you are speaking, what you are going to be talking about, and how you are going to deliver your message. We urge you to master the preparation process, check out the place where you will be speaking beforehand, choose a familiar topic, and avoid taking on more than you can handle.

Master the Preparation Process. Does speaking anxiety affect the ways in which people prepare presentations? John Daly and his colleagues answer this question with a definite *yes.*[13]

Scholars and teachers have observed that, in general, anxious speakers are less effective and successful than confident speakers. Not surprisingly, their fear of speaking may distract and distress them while they speak. But there may be another good reason why anxious speakers don't speak as well as confident speakers do—they don't know *how* to prepare and deliver a good presentation.

Daly and his colleagues report that anxious speakers are less likely to prepare in ways that are essential for a successful presentation. In short, they don't focus on the seven principles of presentation speaking. Rather than working their way through orderly decisions about purpose, audience, credibility, logistics, content, organization, and performance, they become "lost" in the process. They experience difficulty coming up with relevant content, they hunt for "perfect" words, they backtrack over already completed material, and they spend time reassuring themselves that they have adequately covered their topic.[14] They end up focusing on themselves and their fears rather than on making orderly and strategic decisions about the speechmaking process.

Be prepared to speak by learning how to prepare a presentation. If necessary, use a checklist to mark whether you've applied all seven principles of presentation speaking. After all, how can you expect your presentation to be successful if you don't know how to prepare it? Reading this textbook and mastering its principles, working diligently on speaking assignments, adequately rehearsing your presentations, and having others analyze your presentations can help you understand and master the preparation process.

Check It Out. Pilots check out their airplanes before taking off, champion golfers check out the course before playing a round, and good speakers check out the places where they will be speaking before they speak. Check out the seating, the microphone, the lighting, and the equipment *before* you speak. That way you make the unfamiliar familiar—*and* you don't have to worry about technical difficulties during your presentation. Make sure that you can see your notes and have a place to put them. Make sure the lectern isn't too high or too low. If you can, you may want to rearrange the audience's seating. Practice a few sentences of your presentation before anyone gets there so that you'll have a feel for the sound of the room. Checking out the setting beforehand can help you feel more confident about approaching the podium and your audience when it's time to do the real thing.

If you can't get to the place where you will be speaking in advance, ask the person who invited you about the facilities, equipment, and other logistical details. As Chapter 7, "Logistics and Occasion," discusses in more detail, knowing about where, when, and why you're speaking reduces the novelty of the speaking situation and can help to reduce your anxiety.

Real World Real Speakers

Spend Hours to "Be Prepared"

Lilly Walters, the author of *Secrets of Successful Speakers,* advocates hours of preparation as a way of reducing stage fright. To make her point, she tells stories about several famous speakers and their preparation of formal and impromptu speeches (which are spur-of-the-moment comments). Mark Twain, one of the highest-paid speakers of his era, said, "It takes me at least three weeks to prepare an impromptu speech." A friend of Winston Churchill, England's great prime minister, wrote, "Winston has spent the best years of his life writing impromptu speeches." Churchill estimated that it took him six to eight hours to prepare a forty-five-minute speech. For an important presentation, you may need to spend as much as one hour preparing for each minute of the presentation.[1]

1. Lilly Walters, *Secrets of Successful Speakers* (New York: McGraw-Hill, 1993), pp. 32–33. Her information about Winston Churchill is taken from William Manchester, *The Last Lion: Winston Spencer Churchill* (New York: Dell, 1983), p. 32.

Speak About a Familiar Topic. Speakers who know what they're talking about feel more comfortable and less anxious. If you have ever made a presentation about something you knew little about, you know what it feels like to be unprepared. You may fear questions you can't answer, fear that you don't have enough to say, and even fear that you are wrong about something you do say. You can nip nervousness in the bud by picking a topic that you already know and care about. If you do this, you'll find it's much easier to prepare your presentation, and you'll feel more confident delivering it. You won't have to worry that audience members will think you're uninformed or that questions following your talk will be ones that you can't answer. Your interest in your topic will show and will engage your audience.

Begin in Your Comfort Zone. If you aren't a confident swimmer, you probably won't jump into the deep end of a pool. If you aren't an experienced midwife or physician, you should be reluctant to deliver a baby. And if you aren't a confident speaker, you shouldn't talk in dangerous territory. Try to begin by speaking in your comfort zone. If your level of anxiety is high, don't deliver your presentation for the first time to an audience of two thousand people. Instead, try it out on a group of friends or coworkers first. If your topic is complicated, make sure that the beginning of your presentation is clear and well rehearsed. Tell a story you know very well, or make sure the beginning of your presentation is the one part that you know best. By starting in "shallow water," you can gradually make your way into deeper water without fear of drowning.

Relax

One well-accepted way of reducing presentation anxiety is to learn how to relax and minimize its symptoms. Relaxation techniques reduce nervous feelings by substituting feelings of calmness. You can begin this process by learning simple relaxation exercises that lessen many of the physical symptoms of presentation anxiety—rapid heartbeat, stomachache, shaky hands and legs, and trembling voice. Many of the books and courses that teach meditation and relaxation techniques can help you prepare for any situation that makes you nervous or anxious. However, some meditation techniques require time and privacy. Since you cannot excuse yourself from an auditorium stage to meditate right before your presentation, try to develop a set of short tension-reducing techniques that you can use in the few minutes or seconds before speaking. (See the TIP on page 68.)

Memorize the First Minute

Because we know that a speaker's nervousness is often most intense at the very beginning of a presentation, we suggest that you try memorizing the first minute of your presentation. If you're worried that you can't memorize the beginning, keep practicing it until you feel very comfortable with your opening. Then, make sure that you have your notes handy for quick reference. Having the opening down pat gives great comfort and confidence to many speakers. Memorizing or feeling comfortable with your introduction can reduce anxiety and get you rolling.

Systematic Desensitization. A technique of behavioral therapy called **systematic desensitization**[15] can be especially effective as a relaxation technique for reducing performance anxiety. Sometimes we associate fear with certain situations, things, or experiences such as flying, insects, elevators, snakes, or presentation speaking. One way of breaking the fearful response bond is to learn a new, relaxed response to the same situation.[16] Systematic desensitization begins by training speakers to achieve deep muscle relaxation. In this relaxed state, they are then asked to imagine themselves in a variety of communication situations—ranging from one that is very comfortable to those that produce more anxiety. Karen Dwyer, author of *Conquering Your Speechfright*, has noted, "When you can visually imagine yourself in all the steps in the speechmaking process and maintain deep relaxation at the same time, you will have broken your fearful response to public speaking."[17] Systematic desensitization is a therapy developed by psychologist Joseph Wolpe to help clients with phobias and serious anxieties. Clients are taught to visualize a series of anxiety-provoking situations while maintaining a state of relaxation and, as a result, weakening the bond between the anxiety and the feared object. To accomplish this goal, clients are asked to imagine an item from a sequence of increasingly fear-provoking situations called a *desensitization hierarchy*.[18]

How would this technique apply to presentation speaking? Figure 3.1 shows a hierarchy of presentation speaking situations.

Figure 3.1 **A Desensitization Hierarchy for Presentation Anxiety**

Even anxious speakers would feel comfortable thinking about the first few items of this hierarchy. As the process progresses, however, the situations become more anxiety-producing. By trying to relax even when visualizing these situations, the anxious speaker can slowly learn to associate presentation speaking with relaxation rather than with nervousness.

1. You are reading a newspaper article about a politician's speech.
2. You are watching a television newscast in which speakers are shown speaking at a meeting.
3. You are listening to someone give a presentation at work.
4. You learn that you will have to give a presentation at work next month.
5. You are starting to gather ideas and information for your presentation.
6. You are learning a lot about the size and composition of your audience.
7. You are preparing your notes for the presentation.
8. You are practicing your presentation in private.
9. You are practicing your presentation in front of a good friend or family member.
10. You see yourself arriving at the place where you will present your talk.
11. You see yourself walking to the podium and preparing to speak.
12. You see yourself beginning your presentation.

Break the word *relax* into two syllables: *re* and *lax*. Breathe in slowly through your nose while saying the sound *re* (ree) silently to yourself, holding the long *e* sound all the while you are inhaling. This should take just about three seconds. Then breathe out slowly, also for about three seconds, thinking the sound *lax* (laks) silently to yourself, and hold the *a* sound while exhaling. Inhale and exhale, thinking, "REEE-LAAAX" four or five times. By the time you finish this thirty-second relaxation exercise, your pulse should be slower and, hopefully, you will also feel calmer. A word of caution, though: If you inhale and exhale too deeply and for too long, you could end up feeling lightheaded or faint rather than relaxed and calm. Try to find the pace that helps you relax before beginning your presentation.

If using the word *relax* doesn't work, try *calm down* or *no fear*. As long as there are vowels to hold for three seconds, any two-syllable phrase that suggests tension reduction can work. If repeating a word or phrase doesn't work for you, try something simpler. A small yawn or quiet sigh right before you speak can relax your neck and throat muscles. Tensing and relaxing your stomach muscles before you speak can squeeze a lot of tension out of your body. Find the relaxation exercise that works for you, and you'll be rewarded with a calmer body and mind.

Systematic desensitization works amazingly well. The underlying notion is that presentation anxiety arises when you mentally associate fear with speaking. After your successful treatment, a sense of relaxation will arise when you think about making a presentation. Any number of studies confirm that the technique works.[19] It is also a method used by almost every professional sports team to aid players in coping with "clutch" moments. Watch a basketball game. A "clutch" moment occurs when, for instance, a game is tied, and one team has one free throw left that will allow it to win if a basket is made. The player making the shot may "choke"—shoot the ball and entirely miss the hoop. If she does, there's no win. Watch carefully how this player acts as she prepares to take the shot. Note how relaxed she is. Every muscle appears to be almost limp. What you are seeing is systematic desensitization at work. The player has learned that the more nerve-wracking the situation, the more relaxed she has to be.

Understanding how systematic desensitization works can help you overcome presentation anxiety. The big idea here is that if you can teach yourself to relax, you'll be less nervous. Certainly this is easier said than done. But try deep breathing, peaceful meditation, stretches, or other tension-releasing techniques before your next presentation. They should help.

Cognitive Restructuring. Whereas systematic desensitization assumes that a relaxed body will relax your mind, cognitive restructuring goes a step further. **Cognitive restructuring** assumes that presentation anxiety is caused by worrisome, irrational, and nonproductive thoughts (cognitions) about speaking. Thus, reducing anxiety, fear, and nervousness requires changing or restructuring those cognitions.[20]

Consider the transcript on page 69 of a cognitive restructuring session between a teacher and a student.

As you can see, the process tries to change the speaker's unrealistic beliefs about making a presentation. Most of the time, you won't make big mistakes. Most of the time people won't laugh at you, and even if they do laugh, it isn't the end of the world.

Jerry Lynch, a sports psychologist, works with athletes who become anxious or fearful when it's time to perform.[21] He recommends that they adopt affirmations to restructure the way that they think. "Watch what you say," he cautions. "When you say, 'I can't,' you lose power. Your body immediately backs down." Lynch urges his athletes to write and repeat strong positive statements about their performances. The same technique can work for speakers. The next time that you feel anxious, try telling yourself these positive statements: "My message is important." "I am a well-prepared, skilled speaker." "Apprehension gives me extra energy."

The thing to remember about cognitive restructuring is that it helps you to become more realistic about what will happen when you make a presentation. The experience won't be all that bad. You'll survive. And remember this, writes speechwriter Peggy

Teacher:	Well, why are you so scared about making a presentation?
Student:	I don't know...maybe because I know people will laugh at me if I make a mistake.
Teacher:	Now, let's think about that. Why do you think you'll make a mistake...a mistake that will make people laugh at you?
Student:	I just know I could.
Teacher:	Sure you could, but the walls in this office could collapse, too. So let's assume you make a mistake, as rare as that might be. What's the harm?
Student:	I'd be embarrassed.
Teacher:	You're right. Embarrassing things happen to all of us—even when we're not making presentations. We survive, don't we?
Student:	Yeah, but I would feel bad.
Teacher:	Sure you would, but only for a little while...

Noonan: "Every great speaker in history has flopped somewhere along the way, most of them more than once. So relax. It's only a speech."[22] Challenge and then banish the irrational, negative beliefs that get in the way of speaking success.

Visualization. Closely related to cognitive restructuring is **visualization,** a procedure that encourages people to think positively about presentation speaking by taking them through the entire speechmaking process.[23] Many professional and Olympic athletes use visualization to improve their performance. Dr. Marcia Middel, a psychologist and former All-American swimmer, helps athletes and musicians to overcome performance anxiety through visualization.[24] They are told to find a quiet place where they can relax and visualize a picture of themselves in competition. For example:

> *Create a mental picture of yourself diving into the pool. Now, enter that picture; hear the sounds you usually hear; smell the air; feel the sweat on your body; tune into what the diving board feels like under your feet or the water around your body. If you are hoping to improve a particular technique, then remember a time [when] you did it very well. Recreate that moment[;] then carefully perform the technique until you have executed it flawlessly in your head. Rehearse this image for a few minutes each day.*[25]

Speakers can use visualization to overcome presentation anxiety. Before you make your presentation, sit back and picture the entire event. Imagine walking into the room with confidence and energy. Think about how many smiles you'll receive as you talk, think about the heads nodding in agreement, think about the looks of interest you'll see in the eyes of your audience, think about how smoothly you will deliver your message, and think about your successful conclusion. And then congratulate yourself. Many speakers find visualization a powerful method of building confidence.

Professional athletes such as Swedish golfer Annika Sorenstam use visualization to enhance their performance and confidence.

Sharing Your Fears with Friends. Discussing and sharing your anxieties with others can have several positive results. Because a majority of people fear presentation speaking, you will discover that you are not alone. It's also easy to believe that your fears are worse than anyone else's until you begin talking about them. You'll probably find that even the most confident-looking speakers can have upset stomachs and moments of panic. Remember that presentation anxiety is natural. You may not like the feeling of it, but it's one you share with most other people.

Discussing your speaking fears with others can also help you to correct misperceptions you may hold about your presentations. If you tell a friend or your instructor that you stumble over your words, you may find out that they've never noticed it. What seems like a major stumble to you may be nothing more than a pause to your audience. If you think that your voice shakes while you are speaking, you may find out that your listeners don't hear any shakiness. Remember that audiences can't see most symptoms of presentation anxiety. Likewise, confirming that your symptoms are invisible to your audience can be very reassuring.

Last, sharing your anxieties can help you to substitute positive thoughts for negative ones. If you tell your friends you were afraid that your audience noticed your shaky hands, they may tell you that everyone was too far away to notice and that, in fact, you looked poised. Rather than thinking, "I was a nervous wreck," substitute the thought "My friends tell me I looked calm."

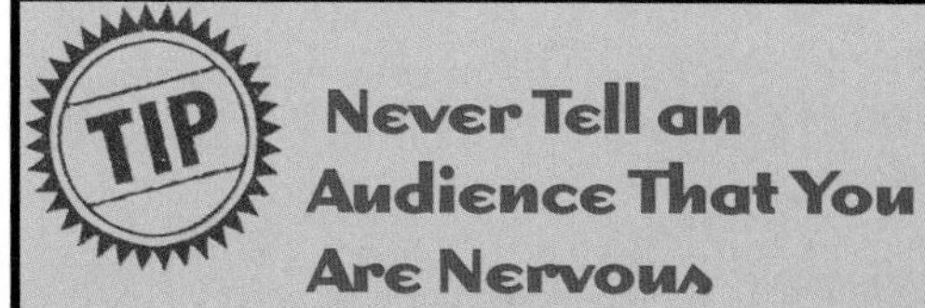

Never Tell an Audience That You Are Nervous

Some novice speakers take sharing a little too far—they figure that if friends will be supportive of their fears, most audiences will be, too. Unfortunately, sharing your anxieties with the audience tends to backfire. It only makes audience members more aware of your nervousness and makes you feel more self-conscious. Don't describe or discuss your speaking anxiety with your audience. Don't apologize before, during, or after your presentation. Don't tell your audience that you haven't prepared well enough. Don't burden them with all the problems you've had getting ready. If you are well prepared and have practiced your presentation, there won't be any need to apologize. Talk privately with your friends or instructor about presentation anxiety. Speak confidently to your audience.

Adapt

A presentation is not a permanent, written document. Unexpected events, questions from audience members, and late-breaking news may mean that you have to modify your well-prepared presentation on the spot. Doing this can be difficult for anxious speakers, who may be too busy concentrating on their own feelings to veer away from their planned presentations. However, anticipating potential problems and bending or breaking rigid rules can help even the most nervous speaker become more flexible and confident.

Anticipate and Address Potential Problems. Related to checking out your physical surroundings (see page 65) is assessing, in advance, what might create problems for you during a presentation. Once you've identified what makes you conscious of your nervousness or what could lead an audience to conclude that you're nervous, you can devise strategies to mask or modify these difficulties.

For instance, suppose that you notice that your hands shake when you hold your notes during a presentation. The sense that everyone might see them trembling might raise your anxiety level. The solution is simple: Eliminate the display of shaking. How? Since flimsy paper will shake in speakers' hands, no matter how comfortable they are about speaking, use stiffer note paper or lay your notes on a lectern or clipboard to eliminate much of the noticeable shaking. Or what should you do if a visible rash creeps up your neck whenever you speak? Again, the answer is simple: Mask it. Wear a buttoned-up shirt, a turtleneck, or a scarf. Thinking ahead about potential problems gives you the time to resolve them. Don't wait until you're speaking to deal with things that hinder your performance.

Bend or Break the Rules. Many years ago, a psychologist at UCLA, Mike Rose, researched why people experienced writer's block.[26] After watching many writers, he found that those with writer's block had rigid rules about writing. They believed, for example, that you had to have a perfect first sentence before you could go on to write the next sentence. These writers slaved over that first sentence for hours, often feeling that they would "never get it right." Writers who didn't suffer from writer's block knew that an opening sentence was important but decided not to worry about it if nothing immediately came to mind. The difference between "blocked" and comfortable writers was that the former group let the rules run them while the latter group ran the rules. Don't be too tied to beliefs that you might have about what a "good" speaker looks and sounds like.

There are no “must” rules of speaking. This book is, of course, filled with advice. But every piece of advice should be adapted to *your* purpose, *your* audience, and *your* situation. Is it sometimes all right to put your hands in your pockets while speaking? Yes. Is it acceptable, in some situations, to sit down rather than to stand when speaking? Sure! Rules are best understood as guidelines for speaking, not as commandments. Sometimes breaking a commonly accepted rule can make your presentation more interesting and memorable. Smart speakers use rules when they aid their presentations and dismiss them when they get in the way.

Apprehensive speakers can be reluctant to abandon the “safety” of their rules, yet they may also feel more confident in communication contexts with fewer rules. For instance, most people are far more comfortable answering questions than they are making presentations. You’d think it would be the opposite since a speaker has to think “on her feet” when answering questions, whereas she can do most of her thinking about a presentation beforehand. Because people have far fewer rigid rules about what good question-and-answer sessions ought to be like, they find them less nerve-wracking. On the other hand, almost everyone has strong notions of what presentations should be like. Drop the rules if they don’t produce the results you want.

Practice

If you’re good at something, you will usually be more confident when doing it, and the best way to become good at something is to practice. Knowing how to make effective presentations is the best way to ensure that you will succeed with them. In fact, the best piece of insider information we can give to anyone learning a skill is this: practice, practice, practice. If you’ve spent time practicing your presentation, you have less reason to be nervous. You know that you can make it through the presentation, no matter how anxious you are. Don’t memorize your entire speech (what if you forget it?); just practice it often. Even though both of us have made thousands of presentations to hundreds of different groups, we still practice before going “on stage.” Our secret of success is that there is no secret. Although it takes valuable time to practice, the payoff is a confident and seemingly effortless presentation.

Michelle Crawford practiced her lines and prayed with her mother before speaking to the Wisconsin Legislature about how the state’s new welfare program had transformed her life. Then Governor Tommy G. Thompson beams at Ms. Crawford’s success.

Real World Real Speakers

Forget About Yourself . . . and Your Fear

Peggy Noonan, who was one of President Reagan's speechwriters, describes herself as being near-phobic about speaking in front of groups. After having a horrible experience in seventh grade—she had been asked to read aloud from "The Song of Hiawatha" and was in such a panic that she lost her voice and nerve—she didn't give another speech until she was forty years old. An interesting thing happened to her about halfway through that presentation:

> *But what I remember most, the key thing, is that about halfway through the speech I improved, became more focused and more sure, because my mind fastened on what I was saying,* and I wanted to be understood. *. . . I realized: When you forget yourself and your fear, when you go beyond self-consciousness because your mind is thinking about what you are trying to communicate, you become a better communicator. . . . This is the beginning of the end of self-consciousness, which is the beginning of the end of fear.*[1]

1. Peggy Noonan, *Simply Speaking: How to Communicate Your Ideas with Style, Substance, and Clarity* (New York: HarperCollins, 1998), p. 8.

Focus

Experienced speakers know that one of the best ways to build presentation confidence is to concentrate on the message and audience rather than on themselves. Speakers who worry about how they look and sound often feel more anxious than speakers who concentrate on what they have to say. Just as professional athletes and musicians channel their nervous energy into the sport or the music, excellent speakers convert nervousness into energy that focuses on their message.[27] Focusing on getting your message across to your audience means that you won't have enough time to think about your fears. Conveying that you care about your message gives your presentation an added measure of courage, conviction, and confidence. Janice Bryant, a nurse and social worker with Home Hospice in Sherman, Texas, discovered this effect when making a presentation to a local United Way board about hospice care. "It was very successful," she wrote, "because for the first time I was able to put aside my nervousness and convey the true emotions of my topic."

If you want to torture someone involved in a sport, ask the athlete to think of every movement he or she makes while playing. Ask a tennis player to note where his arms and legs are as he serves. Ask him to think about how high the ball goes before he hits it. Very quickly, any serve he would make would be ruined if he applied this focused self-attention during a match. The same is true during a presentation. If you concentrate all of your attention on how you look and sound rather than on what you have to say, you can be guaranteed a less-than-wonderful presentation and a higher level of anxiety. On the other hand, speakers who focus on achieving their purpose report low tension levels.

This observation explains why research studies have found that people with high levels of presentation anxiety find it hard to remember very much about their audience, the room they were in, or even what they said. They can recall, however, the negative feelings and worries they had during the presentation.[28] Giving less thought to yourself and more thought to reaching the audience with your message can reduce your level of anxiety and improve the quality of your performance and presentation.

The Triangle of Terror

Presentation anxiety, fear of snakes, and fear of heights usually top the lists of people's fears. If, however, you fear snakes, you can try to avoid them as well as learn which ones are dangerous and which ones are harmless. You may even be able to trace your emotional response to stories about Adam and Eve's unfortunate encounter with a snake in the Garden of Eden. Fear of presentation speaking is a different matter. To begin with, you cannot avoid speaking. Nor can you easily separate presentations into dangerous and harmless encounters. Presentation anxiety is a complicated phenomenon that reflects a triangle of terror as illustrated in Figure 3.2.

The **triangle of terror** represents three interacting components of presentation anxiety and how they affect your head, heart, and habits. Understanding your level of presentation anxiety and becoming more confident require an appreciation of all three components:

Head: What kinds of fearful thoughts do you have about presentation speaking?

Heart: What kinds of emotional and physical distress do you experience before, during, and even after a presentation?

Habits: To what extent have you mastered the seven principles of presentation speaking?

Your analysis of and answers to these questions can help you to decide on a strategy that will transform the triangle of terror into speaking confidence. Experiment with the various methods for coping with presentation anxiety, as illustrated in Figure 3.3.

Figure 3.2 The Triangle of Terror

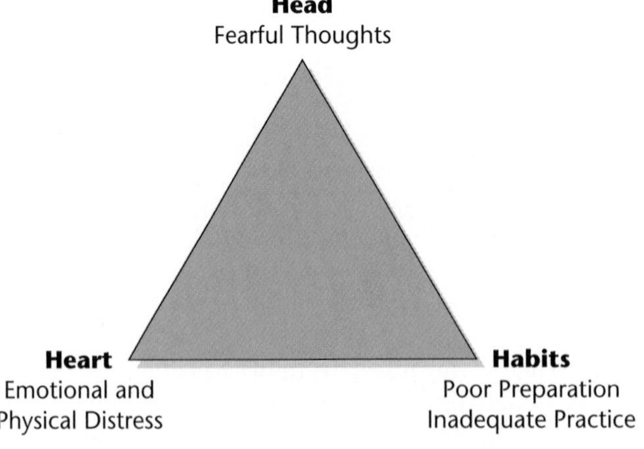

Figure 3.3 Strategies for Transforming the Triangle of Terror into Presentation Speaking Confidence

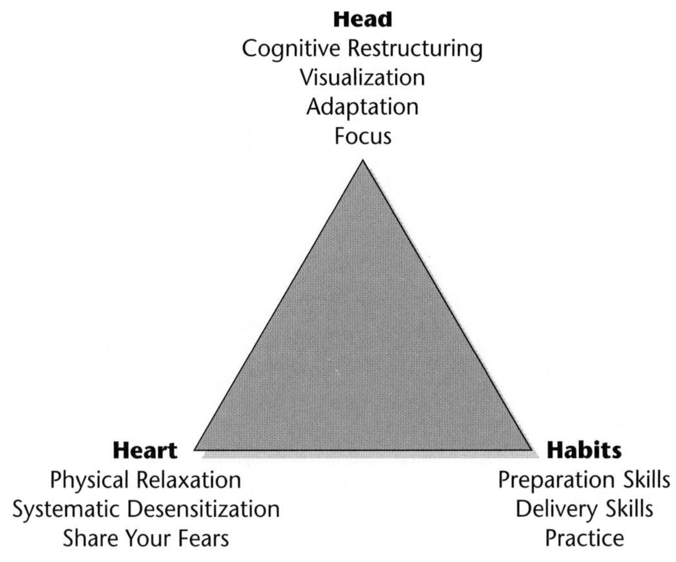

Head: Develop a realistic assessment of your attitudes and beliefs about presentation speaking.

Heart: Analyze where, when, and why you experience emotional and physical distress.

Habits: Keep working to improve your preparation and delivery skills.

Just Do It

Experience is a great teacher. One of the best ways to change presentation anxiety into presentation confidence is to speak. It's like learning to swim. You can read about how to tread water and listen to all the advice that your swimming instructor and friends may give you, but in the end you have to get in the water and try it. So take your first plunge with a positive mental attitude. Learn to say, "I can do it, and I will do it" rather than "I'm scared." And remember this: Always give your talk. No matter how frightened you are, you *can* do it. Making the decision to give a speech is the first step in building skills and confidence.

We're not saying it's easy. Building confidence will take conscientious work on your part. Moreover, it won't happen overnight. You'll have to practice the various skills we've described, a number of times, with a variety of presentations in different situations. Eventually, they'll become second nature. Practice will give you the tools to project confidence in yourself and in your message.

Summary

▶ Where does presentation anxiety come from?

Sources of presentation anxiety include fear of negative criticism, fear of the unknown, fear of the spotlight, fear of the audience, fear of breaking the rules, and fear of fear.

▶ What makes some speakers look so confident?

Successful speakers may be just as nervous as unsuccessful speakers, but they also know that presentation anxiety is natural and usually invisible. They also know how to cope with anxiety by using a variety of methods that help them prepare, relax, adapt, practice, and focus.

▶ How can preparation reduce presentation anxiety?

Preparation helps to reduce fear of the unknown. Preparation strategies that help to reduce presentation anxiety include mastering the preparation process, checking out the place where you will be speaking in advance, speaking about a familiar topic, and beginning in a comfortable setting.

▶ Do relaxation techniques really work?

Relaxation techniques help to reduce nervous feelings by substituting feelings of calmness. Effective relaxation techniques include systematic desensitization, cognitive restructuring, and visualization.

▶ How can breaking the rules help me to become a more confident speaker?

Some speakers become too tied to rigid rules that prevent them from adapting to their purpose, audience, and logistics.

▶ How do practice and focus build confidence?

Practice can improve both skills and confidence. Focus teaches you to concentrate on your message rather than on yourself. Conveying that you have practiced your presentation and care about your message gives your presentation an added measure of courage, conviction, and confidence.

Presentation Principles in Action

Personal Report of Public Speaking Anxiety (PRPSA)

Directions: This instrument is composed of thirty-four statements concerning feelings about communicating with other people. Indicate the degree to which the statements apply to you by marking whether you (1) Strongly Agree, (2) Agree, (3) Are Undecided, (4) Disagree, or (5) Strongly Disagree. Work quickly; just record your first reaction.

1. _____ While preparing for giving a speech, I feel tense and nervous.
2. _____ I feel tense when I see the words *speech* and *public speaking* on a course outline when studying.
3. _____ My thoughts become confused and jumbled when I am giving a speech.
4. _____ Right after giving a speech, I feel that I have had a pleasant experience.
5. _____ I feel anxious when I think about a speech coming up.
6. _____ I have no fear of giving a speech.
7. _____ Although I am nervous just before starting a speech, I soon settle down after starting and feel calm and comfortable.
8. _____ I look forward to giving a speech.
9. _____ When the instructor announces a speaking assignment in class, I can feel myself getting tense.
10. _____ My hands tremble when I am giving a speech.
11. _____ I feel relaxed while giving a speech.
12. _____ I enjoy preparing for a speech.
13. _____ I am in constant fear of forgetting what I prepared to say.
14. _____ I get anxious if someone asks me something about my topic that I do not know.
15. _____ I face the prospect of giving a speech with confidence.
16. _____ I am in complete possession of myself while giving a speech.
17. _____ My mind is clear when I am giving a speech.
18. _____ I do not dread giving a speech.
19. _____ I perspire just before starting a speech.
20. _____ My heart beats very fast just as I start a speech.
21. _____ I experience considerable anxiety while sitting in the room just before my speech starts.
22. _____ Certain parts of my body feel very tense and rigid when I am giving a speech.

23. ______ Realizing that only a little time remains in a speech makes me very tense and nervous.

24. ______ While giving a speech, I know I can control my feelings of tension and stress.

25. ______ I breathe faster just before starting a speech.

26. ______ I feel comfortable and relaxed in the hour or so just before giving a speech.

27. ______ I do poorly giving speeches because I am anxious.

28. ______ I feel anxious when the teacher announces the date of a speaking assignment.

29. ______ When I make a mistake while giving a speech, I find it hard to concentrate on the parts that follow.

30. ______ During an important speech, I experience a feeling of helplessness building up inside of me.

31. ______ I have trouble falling asleep the night before a speech.

32. ______ My heart beats very fast while I present a speech.

33. ______ I feel anxious while waiting to give my speech.

34. ______ While giving a speech, I get so nervous I forget facts I really know.

Scoring the PRPSA

Step 1: Add the scores together for items 1, 2, 3, 5, 9, 10, 13, 14, 19, 20, 21, 22, 23, 25, 27, 28, 29, 30, 31, 32, 33, and 34.

Step 2: Subtract the total for step 1 from 132.

Step 3: Add the scores together for items 4, 6, 7, 8, 11, 12, 15, 16, 17, 18, 24, and 26.

Step 4: Add the total for step 3 to your total for step 2.

Scores should range between 34 and 170. If your score is below 34 or above 170, you have made a mistake in calculating the score.

Score	Level of Speaking Anxiety	Percentage of Speakers
34–84	Low level of anxiety	5%
85–92	Moderately low anxiety	5%
93–110	Moderate anxiety	20%
111–119	Moderately high anxiety	30%
120–170	Very high level of anxiety	40%

Source: Virginia P. Richmond and James C. McCroskey, *Communication, Apprehension, Avoidance, and Effectiveness*, 4th ed. (Scottsdale, AZ: Gorsuch Scarisbrick, 1995), pp. 131–132.

Key Terms

cognitive restructuring 68
presentation anxiety 59
rigid rules 62
systematic desensitization 67
triangle of terror 74
visualization 69

Notes

1 Michael T. Motley, *Overcoming Your Fear of Public Speaking: A Proven Method* (Boston: Houghton Mifflin, 1997), p. 3; Virginia P. Richmond and James C. McCroskey, *Communication: Apprehension, Avoidance, and Effectiveness*, 4th ed. (Scottsdale, AZ: Gorsuch Scarisbrick, 1995).

2 In *Conquer Your Speechfright* by Karen Kangas Dwyer (Fort Worth, TX: Harcourt Brace, 1998), Dwyer cites *The Book of Lists* by Wallenchinksy, Wallace, and Wallace (New York: Bantam Books, 1977), in which fear of public speaking ranks as the number one "common fear" in America. Similar data can be found in The Bruskin Report, *What Are Americans Afraid Of*? (Research Report No. 53, 1973).

3 Motley, p. 3.

4 Sharon S. Brehm, Saul M. Kassin, and Steven Fein, *Social Psychology*, 4th ed. (Boston: Houghton Mifflin, 1999), p. 510.

5 This definition is based on James McCroskey's definition of *communication apprehension:* "an individual's level of fear or anxiety associated with either real or anticipated communication with another person or persons." See Richmond and McCroskey, p. 41.

6 Motley, p. 27.

7 We have tried to summarize some of the considerable research related to communication apprehension. Four available sources that report the results of this research are John A. Daly and James C. McCroskey, eds., *Avoiding Communication: Shyness, Reticence, and Communication Apprehension* (Thousand Oaks, CA: Sage, 1984); Richmond and McCroskey, *Communication;* Dwyer, *Conquer Your Speechfright;* and Motley, *Overcoming Your Fear of Public Speaking.*

8 See Dwyer, p. 23.

9 Richmond and McCroskey, p. 64.

10 Ralph Blumenthal, "First Divers, Now Divas: Exorcising the Jitters," *New York Times*, 18 August 1999, pp. B1 and B4.

11 Lori J. Carrell and S. Clay Willmington, "The Relationship between Self-Report Measures of Communication Apprehension and Trained Observers' Ratings of Communication Competence," *Communication Reports* 11 (1998): 87–95.

12 Also see John Daly and Isa Engleberg, "Coping with Stagefright: How to Turn Terror into Dynamic Speaking," *Harvard Management Communication Letter* 2 (June 1999): 1–4.

13 John A. Daly, Anita L. Vangelisti, and David J. Weber, "Speech Anxiety Affects How People Prepare Speeches: A Protocol Analysis of the Preparation Process of Speaking," *Communication Monographs* 62 (1995): 283–398.

14 Daly et al., p. 396.

15 For more on systematic desensitization, see Richmond and McCroskey, pp. 97–102, and Dwyer, pp. 73–86. A narrated audiotape on deep muscular relaxation is also available: Larry L. Barker, *Listening to Relax: A Deep Relaxation Guide from Head to Foot* (Fort Worth, TX: Harcourt Brace, 1996).

16 Dwyer, p. 40.

17 Dwyer, p. 40.

18 Douglas A. Bernstein et al., *Psychology*, 5th ed. (Boston: Houghton Mifflin, 2000), pp. 571–572.

19 See Mike Allen, John E. Hunter, and William A. Donohue, "Meta-Analysis of Self-Report Data on the Effectiveness of Public Speaking Anxiety Treatment Techniques," *Communication Education* 38 (1989): 54–76; Gustav Friedrich et al., "Systematic Desensitization," in John A. Daly et al., *Avoiding Communication: Shyness, Reticence, and Communication Apprehension* (Creskill, NJ: Hampton, 1997), pp. 305–329.

20 Dwyer, p. 40 and pp. 53–72; Richmond and McCroskey, pp. 102–105.

21 Delaine Fragnoli, "Fear of Flying," *Bicycling* 38 (1997): 46–47.

22 Peggy Noonan, *Simply Speaking: How to Communicate Your Ideas with Style, Substance, and Clarity* (New York: HarperCollins, 1998), p. 205. Copyright © 1998 by Peggy Noonan. Reprinted by permission of HarperCollins Publishers, Inc.

23 Joe Ayres and Tim S. Hopf, "Visualization: Is It More than Extra-Attention?" *Communication Education* 37 (1989): 1–5; Joe Ayres and Tim S. Hopf, "Visualization: Reducing Speaking Anxiety and Enhancing Performance," *Communication Reports* 5 (1992): 1–10; Joe Ayres and Tim S. Hopf, *Coping with Speech Anxiety* (Norwood, NJ: Ablex, 1993); Joe Ayres, Brian Heuett, and Debbie Ayres Sonandre, "Testing a Refinement in an Intervention for Communication Apprehension," *Communication Reports* 11 (1998): 73–84.

24 Wendy DuBow, "Do Try This at Home," *Women's Sports and Fitness* 19 (1997): 78.

25 DuBow, p. 78.

26 Mike Rose, "Rigid Rules, Inflexible Plans, and the Stifling of Language: A Cognitivist Analysis of Writer's Block," *College Composition* 13 (1980): 389–401.

27 Blumenthal, p. B1.

28 John Daly, Anita Vangelisti, and Samuel Lawrence, "Public Speaking Anxiety and Self-Focused Attention," *Personality and Individual Differences* 10 (1989): 903–913.

part two

Preparation

chapter four

Purpose and Topic

- What do I want my audience to know, think, feel, or do?
- How do I refine my purpose?
- Can the type of presentation help me find a good topic?
- How do I find an appropriate topic?
- How do I narrow my topic?

Students in public speaking classes and presentation training seminars often ask their instructors, "What should I talk about?" The question is important but may be unique to a communication class. "What should I talk about?" is rarely asked by presenters outside of the classroom. Although almost all college-level public speaking textbooks devote an entire chapter to choosing a topic, most commercial books on making presentations ignore this subject. Why? They do so because of the special nature of teaching and training sessions. Whether you are taking a three-credit college course or are enrolled in a one-day seminar on presentation speaking skills, the goal is learning *how* to develop and deliver effective presentations. Outside of the classroom, though, the goal is achieving a specific purpose *through* an effective presentation.

Presentations outside of the classroom are a means to an end. In the classroom, they are the subject of study and the graded end product. Because most presentations take place outside of the classroom, this chapter explores how to determine your purpose and topic from both perspectives.

Topic Versus Purpose

In the world outside of the communication classroom or training seminar, presenters usually choose or are invited to speak because they are experts on a subject, because events call for a presentation on a particular topic, or because they are recognized celebrities. What they should talk about is rarely a concern. A noted scientist invited to give a commencement address at a college graduation knows that a highly technical presentation would be inappropriate. The same speaker, if asked to make a presentation at a chemical engineering convention, knows that the audience would expect a discussion of complex scientific data.

Within the walls of a college classroom or a training seminar, your speaking situation is unique. You aren't being asked to speak because you're an expert or because the audience is eager to hear your presentation. In fact, you probably have been given a speaking assignment by an instructor who wants to teach you how to apply communication principles.

Like many other students, you may find choosing a topic for an in-class presentation difficult. Unless your instructor specifies a topic area, you have a world of topics from which to choose. The wide range of choices can be overwhelming and bewildering. As a result, many students ask a common and understandable question: What should I talk about?

Presenters outside of the classroom are less concerned with this question. Instead, they focus their attention on *how* to achieve a specific purpose in front of a specific audience. You can do the same: Shift your focus to the purpose of your presentation, and let that goal guide your topic choice.

Real World Real Speakers

Let Your Purpose Be Your Guide

At an annual ProMax media convention in Toronto, Canada, actor Christopher Reeve, who had been paralyzed in a horseback-riding accident, was invited as a keynote speaker. Almost every one of the several thousand professionals working in the field of radio, television, and film promotion attended the session. Sitting in his wheelchair at center stage and speaking in the slow, halting voice his breathing apparatus required, Mr. Reeve talked about how his accident had changed the way he viewed his past, his present, and his future life. A hush fell over the audience during the entire presentation. Many listeners were moved to tears by the speaker's courage and determination. When invited to speak, Christopher Reeve can talk about anything he wants to. To his credit and with enormous credibility, he uses such opportunities to garner support for spinal injury research and to champion the rights of the disabled.

Determining Your Purpose

Asking, "What do I want to achieve as a result of my presentation?" is *not* the same as asking, "What should I talk about?" **Purpose** asks, "What do I want my audience to know, think, feel, or do as a result of my presentation?" Purpose focuses on *why*: Why

Client and Consultant Scenario

Speaker: I have to make a presentation to the production department.

Consultant: Why?

Speaker: You mean *what,* don't you? On what topic?

Consultant: No. I mean *why.* Why are you making this presentation?

Speaker: Because I've been told to.

Consultant: Why?

Speaker: Because management wants our employees to keep better track of customer questions and complaints.

Consultant: Why?

Speaker: Because better records tell us how well the product works and what problems customers are having with it.

Consultant: So why are you speaking?

Speaker: To convince the production department to keep better records of customer input so we can improve services and make a better product.

Consultant: Congratulations. That's your *purpose.*

Student and Instructor Scenario

Student: I've been asked to give a talk to new students in our department.

Instructor: Why?

Student: Why have *I* been asked, or why do the new students need to hear a talk by a fellow student?

Instructor: Both.

Student: Well, I guess they chose me because I've been very involved in the department—between classes and cocurricular activities, I practically live in the department.

Instructor: Not to mention that you're a pretty good speaker. But why do new students need to hear *you* talk? Why not a faculty member?

Student: I know the kinds of questions students have. After all, I'm one of them. New students might feel more comfortable asking me a question than they would asking a professor.

Instructor: Does this suggest a purpose and a topic area?

Student: I sure don't want to talk about the official stuff! They can bore themselves by reading that in the catalog and the department handbook.

Instructor: So what's your purpose?

Student: To give new students the inside scoop—the unwritten rules, the unofficial tips.

Instructor: Does this purpose suggest a topic?

Student: How about "Department Survival Guide"?

Instructor: Good. That's a presentation they'll appreciate.

am I speaking, and what outcome do I want? We believe that identifying your purpose is the critical first step in developing an effective presentation. In Chapter 1, "Presentation Speaking," the Dynamic Presentation Model indicates that decisions about your purpose are at the center or "hub" of the encoding process. You must know *why* you are speaking before you can select or develop a topic. Even if your only reason for speaking is that your instructor has assigned the task, your decisions about a topic should be influenced by the nature and potential outcomes of that assignment. In order to illustrate the difference between purpose and topic, we offer two brief scenarios—one between a client and a communication consultant, the other between a student and a communication instructor.

What question did the consultant and the instructor keep asking? "Why?" And why did they keep asking it? Because presentation speaking is a means to an end. By first asking yourself *why* you are speaking, you determine your strategic goal. You focus on what you want to accomplish, and this establishes a *purpose* for speaking. Use your purpose to pinpoint the outcome you want to achieve, not the information you want to include.[1]

Don't Speak Without a Clear Purpose

Dr. Terry L. Paulson, psychologist and author of *They Shoot Managers, Don't They?*, warns speakers about the hazards of speaking without a purpose: "There are so many messages and memos being hurled at today's business professionals [that] they are in information overload. It's like sipping through a fire hydrant. Don't unnecessarily add to the stream by including unnecessary fill, facts, and fluff. Volume and graphs will not have a lasting impression; having a focus will. Ask yourself early in the process: What do I want them to remember or do three months from now? If you can't succinctly answer that question, cancel your presentation."[1]

1. Quoted in Lilly Walters, *Secrets of Successful Speakers* (New York: McGraw–Hill, 1993), pp. 3–4.

Is It Ethical to Have a Private Purpose?

As the preamble to the communication ethics credo in Chapter 1 indicates, "questions of right and wrong arise whenever people communicate," and that includes whenever speakers make presentations. Becoming a "good" speaker involves more than delivering a well-organized presentation. A good speaker is committed to preparing and presenting an ethical presentation that is honest, fair, and beneficial to both the speaker and the listeners.

One of the most important ethical questions to ask yourself is this: Who will benefit if I achieve my purpose—will I, my audience, or my audience *and* I benefit? If your public and private purposes conflict or undermine each other, you may be on shaky ground. If you would be hesitant or embarrassed to tell your audience your private purpose, this may be a sign that it's ethically questionable. There is nothing wrong with having a private purpose such as wanting to get a good grade on your presentation or wanting to impress the boss with your speechmaking success. However, there *is* something wrong if achieving your private purpose would hurt or deceive your audience. As the ethics credo in Chapter 1 notes, truthfulness and honesty, freedom of expression, tolerance, and respect are essential to the integrity of communication. Both of us share that belief and apply it to every presentation we make or hear.

Having a clear purpose does not guarantee that you will achieve it. But without a purpose, little can be accomplished. In the workplace, the average employee spends a lot of time listening to other people, attending meetings, and reading memos or reports. If all that time spent doesn't accomplish something, it's obvious the communicators didn't spend enough time asking "why" questions. They didn't know their purpose.

Public and Private Purposes

There can be more than one answer to the question "What is my purpose?" The student speaker in the scenario who wanted to "give students the inside scoop" in the "Department Survival Guide" had a clear purpose. However, that same student may also have wanted to please the faculty members who requested the presentation or to use the speaking opportunity as a way to meet new students. Wanting to share the unwritten rules in a department survival guide is a *public purpose.* Wanting to please faculty members or to meet new students is a *private purpose.* Skilled speakers understand the absolute necessity for a public purpose, the advantages of a private purpose, and most important, the difference between the two.

If you were asked to state the goal of your presentation for a newsletter announcement or to a communication class instructor, you would be stating your **public purpose.** You may not need or even want to share your **private purpose,** the personal goal of your presentation. For example, many companies sponsor volunteer speakers bureaus, programs in which company employees volunteer and are scheduled to speak to community groups. Let's say that the volunteer speakers bureau of a local utility company publicly announces that its chief engineer will give an informative talk on ways to conserve energy. The presentation's public purpose will attract an audience. The private purpose, however, can explain why the utility company wants an audience in the first place: It wants to create goodwill and convince the public that the utility is interested in helping them conserve energy.

Why would a company employee volunteer for a speakers bureau, though? It's extra work, there is rarely extra pay, and the assignment could subject the speaker to harassment from a hostile audience. When we have asked such volunteer speakers why they are willing to do all that extra work, we have heard a variety of personal reasons. Most express private purposes that focus on personal and career goals. Some employees volunteer because their service looks good on their résumés or will

Figure 4.1 Public Purpose, Private Purposes

Public Purpose	Private Purposes
I want to persuade my audience to visit the National Gardens in June to see the largest display of late flowering azaleas in America.	(1) I want to attract more visitors to the gardens in order to increase our entry fee receipts. (2) I want to impress my boss by showing her how in my new role as assistant director of public services, I can attract more visitors to the gardens.
I want to persuade my audience that all children should be immunized before starting kindergarten.	(1) I want my research on the need for immunization to help me prepare a booklet for the clinic where I work. (2) Given the instructor's comments about her young children, I hope this topic will interest her and will help me earn a good grade.

help them when it's time for a promotion. Others do it to improve their presentation speaking skills and to take advantage of the training provided by the company.

In a communication class, the private purpose often relates to the speaker's academic goals. Use your speaking opportunity for achieving your private purposes—an A, the personal admiration of your class, a future recommendation from your instructor, and even improved speaking skills.

Don't miss the opportunity to get the most out of your presentation. As long as the different purposes don't conflict or undermine each other, there is nothing wrong with a presentation that tries to achieve both a public and a private purpose.

We want to emphasize that a presentation should have only one public purpose but may have several private purposes. Figure 4.1 illustrates some of each.

Private purposes are not in and of themselves unethical, but deceptive purposes are. Keep asking yourself, "Who will benefit if I achieve my private purpose—will I, my audience, or my audience *and* I?" Be honest with yourself about your purpose, and even more important, be honest with your audience.

The Purpose Statement

When you know *why* you want to speak, you're ready to state your purpose and, in the process, figure out if it's a good basis for a presentation. Writing a **purpose statement** that clearly specifies the goal of your presentation will help give your purpose a reality check. "My purpose is to tell my audience all about my job as a phone solicitor" is too general and is probably an impossible goal to achieve in a time-limited presentation. "My purpose is to make my audience aware of two common strategies used by effective phone solicitors to overcome listener objections" is better. Effective purpose statements

A PURPOSE STATEMENT SHOULD BE . . .

Specific and Clear
Achievable
Relevant

Real World Real Speakers

Serving a Higher Purpose

Several ministers answered our survey and reminded us of the importance of purpose in developing a presentation. The Reverend Bill D. Nickell, who has been a pastor of the First Assembly of God Church in Canyon, Texas, for twenty years, told us that he has to prepare four sermons a week. The Reverend Glenn Ridall Jr., pastor of the Stewartstown Baptist Church in Stewartstown, Pennsylvania, wrote that he delivers two to three sermons a week and other presentations for special occasions and holidays.

In both cases, the pastors have found the Bible a rich source of topics on which to base a sermon. The key, however, is finding the passage or story that illustrates a message of importance to a congregation. The purpose of the sermon—strengthening the family, accepting the word of God with absolute faith, opening one's heart to others—is supported by and based on scripture. The Bible is not necessarily the topic but is the foundation and means of helping the ministers achieve their purposes.

share three characteristics: They are specific and clear, achievable, and relevant to audience needs and interests.

Specificity and Clarity. A general, vague, or confusing purpose statement won't help you prepare your presentation. A specific statement, though, can give you both scope and direction. Think of your purpose statement as the description of a destination. Telling a friend, "Let's meet in New York City" is too general and vague. "Let's meet at the Gramercy Park Tavern at 5:30 P.M. on Tuesday" is a clear and specific statement that will make sure that both of you end up in the same place at the same time. A specific purpose statement ensures that both you and your audience know where you're going.

Achievability. A purpose statement should establish an achievable goal. Inexperienced speakers often make the common mistake of trying to cover too much ground or asking too much of their audiences. A presentation is a time-limited event. An audience of less-than-perfect listeners can absorb only a limited amount of information. Changing audience attitudes about a firmly held belief can take months rather than minutes. Both of us have advised well-meaning students and clients to scale down the goals of their presentations. What is the likelihood that a student speaker can convert a class to his religion during a ten-minute presentation? What is the likelihood that a speaker can convince every person at a rally to donate $100 to the campaign of a relatively unknown political candidate? A purpose statement can be specific, but it may not be achievable.

Rather than seeking to convert the whole class to your religion, you may be more successful if you try to dispel some misconceptions about it. Rather than asking for $100 for a candidate's campaign, you may ask audience members to take home campaign flyers or to consider signing up as campaign volunteers. Achieving one small step may be much more realistic than attempting a gigantic leap into unknown or hostile territory.

Relevance. Even if your purpose statement is specific and achievable, you may still have difficulty reaching your goal if your topic is irrelevant to your audience's needs or interests. Describing the characteristics of semiconductors or the different varieties of tree toads may fascinate you, but if you can't find a reason that the topic would be relevant or interesting to your listeners, you may find yourself talking to a bored or annoyed audience. Political candidates usually focus their attention on the issues that matter to a particular audience. Advocating tax breaks for new businesses may not be of much interest to (and may even antagonize) a group of parents who want more funding for public schools.

Drafting a specific, achievable, and relevant purpose statement is not an academic exercise; it is a means of producing a valuable tool that can help you determine how to prepare and organize your presentation. All elements of your presentation should be specifically related to your purpose statement.[2] As we indicate in our Dynamic Presentation Model in Chapter 1, all encoding decisions related to the audience, credibility, logistics, content, organization, and performance should be driven by your purpose. You will save yourself time and effort by staying focused on a clear and achievable goal.

From Purpose to Topic

Purpose asks, "What do I want my audience to know, think, feel, or do as a result of my presentation?" Topic completes the previous question by adding "about what?" Your **topic** is the subject matter of your presentation.

Presentation topics can range from recycling to rap music to repairing refrigerators. A topic is often a simple word or phrase: *recycling*. Yet two presentations that discuss the same topic can be different because they have opposing purposes. "I want my audience to support recycling as an environmental policy" is quite different from "Recycling is costly and ineffective as an environmental policy."

Always make sure your purpose and topic are specific, achievable, and relevant to your audience—no matter what their age may be.

Topics for Classroom Presentations

The somewhat artificial nature of the classroom setting can make it difficult to decide on a purpose and topic for a class presentation. For example, your assignment tells you only that you have to give an informative presentation on a topic of your own choosing, organized or delivered in a certain way, in a specific number of minutes. You're not making a presentation because the situation demands it (a condition that would help you identify the purpose) but because your instructor does! When choosing a topic to meet these unique demands, begin by asking several questions.

QUESTIONS FOR CHOOSING A TOPIC

1. **What type of presentation is assigned?**
2. **What topics interest me?**
3. **What do I value?**
4. **What do I know about these topics?**
5. **What will appeal to my audience?**

Inside and outside a classroom, these questions can be the key to finding a good topic when the choice is yours. By considering each question, you should be able to find a topic that suits you, your audience, and your purpose.

What Type of Presentation Is Assigned?

Another way to determine your purpose and to select an appropriate topic is to understand the type of presentation you are being asked to make. Traditionally, presentations have been divided into three types.

The information provided by a crewman's brief presentation can reassure passengers and prepare them for an emergency.

Informative Speaking. An **informative presentation** is designed to instruct, explain, describe, enlighten, demonstrate, clarify, correct, or remind. Teachers spend most of their lecture time trying to inform students. Sometimes an informative presentation explains a complex concept or demonstrates a new procedure. Sometimes it updates old information or clears up misunderstandings. Informative presentations can take the form of a report to a committee or a formal lecture to a large audience. Informative presentations tend to be uncontroversial; they concentrate on sharing information. We cover informative presentations in more detail in Chapter 18, "Developing Informative Presentations."

Persuasive Speaking. A **persuasive presentation** is designed to change audience opinions and/or behavior. These changes may be directed toward an idea, a person, an object, or an action.

Idea: Kindness should be the golden rule.
The Big Bang Theory best explains the creation of the universe.

People: Abraham Lincoln was our greatest president.
Homosexuals should be granted equal protection under the law.

Object: Broccoli is the perfect food.
SUVs are dangerous vehicles.

Actions: Wear seat belts.
Restrict your salt and fat intake.

Advertisers try to persuade customers to buy their products. Political candidates do their best to persuade audiences to elect them. Persuasive presentations occur in courtroom arguments, in religious services, in blood donation drives, around the dinner table, and in daily conversations.

Different types of persuasive presentations have different goals. Some try to strengthen or weaken an existing attitude; others are designed to change audience attitudes. Some persuasive presentations try to create positive or negative feelings; others attempt to whip an audience into an emotional frenzy. A persuasive presentation can convince an audience to take action, or it can encourage an audience to consider unpopular viewpoints. Chapters 19, "Understanding Persuasion," and 20, "Developing Persuasive Presentations," provide more detail on persuasive presentations. For now, just remember that different types of persuasive presentations require different strategies and seek different outcomes.

Entertainment Speaking. A presentation that entertains often takes place in informal settings. As the name implies, **entertainment speaking** tries to amuse, interest, divert, or "warm up" an audience. Stand-up comedy is a form of entertainment speaking. After-dinner speakers amuse audiences too full to move or to absorb serious ideas and complex information. Speakers at a retirement party often "roast" a coworker to the delight of colleagues, friends, and family.

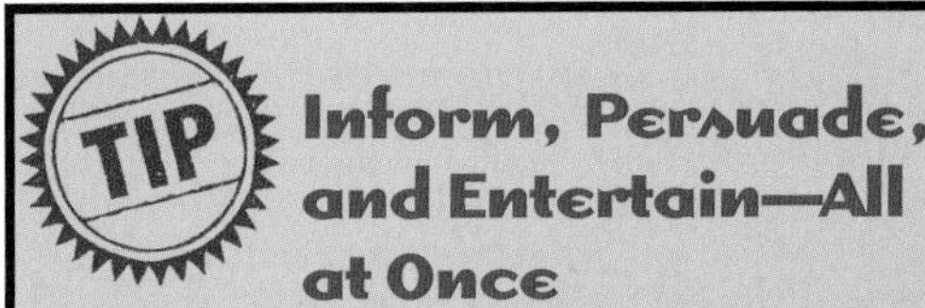

Though determining your purpose will help you decide whether you should be trying to inform, to persuade, or to entertain, it's not always an either/or decision. Some skilled speakers, regardless of their purpose, will try to do all three. For example, the purpose of a college professor's lecture usually is to inform. In order to inform, however, a good teacher also may try to persuade students that the information is important, relevant, and interesting. Such persuasion can motivate students to listen and learn. The professor may also try to entertain students so that they will pay better attention to an informative lecture. Regardless of which type of presentation you have been assigned or have chosen to make, there may be benefits to including components that inform, persuade, and entertain. Presentations that only inform or persuade or entertain are rare. Make your presentation more interesting and compelling by considering how you can include all three types of speaking.

Make sure that you understand the type of presentation you have been asked to prepare and deliver. If your audience or instructor wants an informative presentation, relying on a series of jokes or emotional pleas won't impress your listeners or meet audience expectations. If your audience wants to be entertained, a complex statistical analysis or a series of persuasive arguments will not amuse them. First and foremost, make sure that you know what kind of presentation is expected and then meet those expectations.

What Topics Interest You?

Sometimes when we ask students what topics interest them, we are greeted with blank stares. What do you like to do, we ask—on the job, in your spare time, with your family or friends? It hasn't occurred to them that a topic they find interesting could also interest an audience. When asked, "What do you like to do in your spare time?" students often tell us that they're too busy to have spare time. They eat, sleep, go to classes, study, work, and may even have families to raise. Yet as busy as all of us are, there is always something that we enjoy doing above and beyond the daily grind—a sport, a hobby, an activity. What do we look forward to when the schoolwork is done, when the kids are out or in bed, when we've left work?

The enormous range of interests in one class can be astounding—from mountain climbing to nineteenth-century German philosophers. In one semester, for instance, we heard student presentations on the topics listed in Figure 4.2.

There are several ways to get in touch with the ideas, things, and people you find interesting. Answering "leading questions" can help (see pp. 98–99), or you can do some brainstorming. Create a chart in which you list potential topics under broad headings—sports, food, hobbies, places and destinations, famous people, art and music, important events, personal goals, public and community issues, objects and things, theories and processes, natural and supernatural phenomena, campus concerns. By the time you finish filling in your interests on such a chart, you may have dozens of good topics for a presentation. You might even try mind mapping, an organizational technique described in Chapter 10, "Organizational Tools," as a way to get your creative juices flowing.

What Do You Value?

Your **values** guide how you think about what is right or wrong, good or bad, just or unjust, correct or incorrect. Values trigger your emotions and guide your actions.[3] Take an inventory of your values when looking for a topic.

The Institute for Global Ethics has identified eight universal human values: love, truthfulness, fairness, freedom, unity, tolerance, responsibility, and respect for life.[4] How do your values influence your feelings and behavior about the value-laden issues on the next page?

Figure 4.2

Topics Based on Student Interests

Interpretation of Dreams
The Elvis Cult
Investment Strategies
The Perfect Chocolate Chip Cookie
Drink More Water
Collecting Baseball Cards
Genealogy and Your Family Tree
Wine Tasting
Exercise and Long Life
Haunted Houses
Being a Big Brother/Big Sister
Afro-Cuban Jazz
Financial Planning
School Vouchers
Sign Language and Fingerspelling
Restoring Cars

Avoid Toxic Topics

We would be remiss if we didn't include a word of warning about what we call *toxic topics.* Toxic topics are subjects that have the potential to turn an audience against you. Only the most skilled speakers know how to approach and talk about such topics without turning off their audience. We classify toxic topics into three categories: those selected by speakers who are *overzealous,* those that *"overpromise,"* and those that *offend* an audience.

Overzealous speakers often choose controversial topics with the best of intentions. For example, a student with strong religious beliefs may try to convert the class to a particular religion by conjuring up fiery visions of the fate that befalls nonbelievers. Some pro-life and pro-choice speakers may go too far when presenting evidence to support their respective positions—displaying pictures of aborted fetuses or telling gruesome stories about botched abortions in the days when abortions were illegal. We've learned one important lesson from listening to such speeches: Overzealous speakers rarely persuade anyone. Instead, they turn off most listeners and damage their credibility.

Some topics "overpromise"—that is, they offer promises that cannot be kept. Can you believe a speaker who claims that you will lose twenty pounds in two weeks without dieting, that you can double your money in a no-risk investment scheme, or that you can grow hair on a bald head with a secret herbal treatment? Unfortunately, some gullible audience members (often poor listeners who lack critical thinking skills) *do* believe such speakers. If you pick a topic that promises something that audience members may regard as too good to be true, be careful how you introduce and develop your content. An audience of critical thinkers and effective listeners will be highly skeptical if you cannot deliver what you promise.

The topics we find most toxic are those that offend or insult a person or a particular group of people. For example, soon after the September 11 tragedy, we read and heard pronouncements such as "A sinful America deserved September 11," "Jews committed the September 11 attack on the World Trade Center in New York," or "Muslims go to heaven if they kill Americans." Could you listen to such presentations without becoming distressed or alarmed?

Be sensitive to your audience's background, attitudes, beliefs, and feelings when you choose a topic. If you are unsure about the effect of your choice of topic, ask potential audience members whether your presentation could be interpreted as overzealous, overpromised, or offensive. If there is even a hint of a *yes* when they answer, consider finding another topic.

Love: Marital infidelity

Truthfulness: Plagiarism

Fairness: Affirmative action

Freedom: Gun control

Unity: Labor unions

Tolerance: Hate speech

Responsibility: Parental accountability

Respect for Life: Human cloning

Be cautious when searching your personal values for a topic. They may be very different from those of your audience members. Also, remember that cultures differ in what they value. For example, most Americans strongly value individuality—personal freedom, independence, and individual achievement. Other cultures may value group goals more than individual goals. Note how basic American and Chinese values differ in Figure 4.3.[5]

Figure 4.3

American and Chinese Values

American Values	Chinese Values
Independence	Obedience to and respect for parents
Belief in God	Honoring ancestors
Progress	Industry (working hard)
Equality of all humans	Tolerance of others
Privacy	Harmony with others
Patriotism	Humbleness
Suspicion of authority	Loyalty to superiors

What Do You Know About These Topics?

Everyone is good at something. Everyone knows more about a few things than most other people do. Almost everyone can claim to be an expert in some area. A fruitful source of topics is your work experience. The following scenario is based on a conversation one of us had with a student who was searching for a suitable topic:

Student: But my job isn't interesting—to me or to an audience.

Professor: What do you do?

Student: Phone solicitation. You know, when someone calls you at dinnertime and asks you to subscribe to a newspaper or magazine you don't want.

Professor: I hate those calls, especially during dinner.

Student: I know. Most people do. So there's no way I can use this as a topic for my presentation.

Professor: Are you good at your job?

Student: I've been doing it part-time for three years. I always go beyond my quotas.

Professor: How come?

Student: Well, there's a knack to it. I know what works—how to get people to listen—how to get over their objections.

Professor: You mean you've become an expert at getting people to listen to your pitch and to buy your product over the phone?

Student: Expert? I don't know about that. But I sure know the tricks of the trade.

Professor: Are the tricks a company secret?

Student: No. We're trained, but we also develop our own styles.

Professor: I know I can't speak for the rest of the class, but I'd like to know more about the strategies you use when you call.

Student: Really?

Professor: Absolutely. You have the makings of a terrific presentation.

Figure 4.4

Topics Based on Personal Experience

- Shoeing a Horse
- Volunteering for Suicide Hotlines
- Teaching a Parakeet to Speak
- Doing Missionary Work in China
- Playing the Cello
- Editing a Video
- Closing a Sale
- Therapeutic Massage
- Drawing Blood
- Duties of a Night Watchman
- Spiking a Volleyball
- Brewing Beer
- Instructing in Aerobics
- Growing Tomatoes
- Butchering a Side of Beef
- Weight Lifting

Many of the best presentations are based on personal experiences. Don't underestimate your experiences and skills. Rely on your expertise and enlighten your audience. That's what some of our former students did. Their topics are listed in Figure 4.4.

What Will Appeal to Your Audience?

Questions about your audience are more difficult to answer than questions about your own interests and expertise. The interests of your listeners can differ in as many ways as there are people in the audience. Chapter 5, "Audience Analysis and Adaptation," will discuss audiences and audience analysis in detail. As you consider potential topics, try to think of how to make each one appeal to your audience. If you are interested in the interpretation of dreams, relate the theories to the kinds of dreams most people have experienced. If your topic is haunted houses, you can make it more immediate by describing ghostly sightings in *local* haunted houses. And if you plan to compare recipes you've collected in your search for the perfect chocolate chip cookie, you should share the most delicious samples with your audience. Find the links between your interests and those of your audience.

Stanley Singer, a former Navy submarine veteran, talks to students about patrolling the seas underwater. His personal experiences and expertise held the class spellbound.

Don't Tell Them Everything You Know

Know your purpose. Drop what is unimportant. Stick to the essentials. So then how do you decide what to include in your presentation? Begin by categorizing what you know into three categories:

1. Content that would be *nice* for my audience to know.
2. Content that my audience *should* know.
3. Content that my audience *must* know if I want to achieve my purpose.

You can represent these three categories in concentric circles:

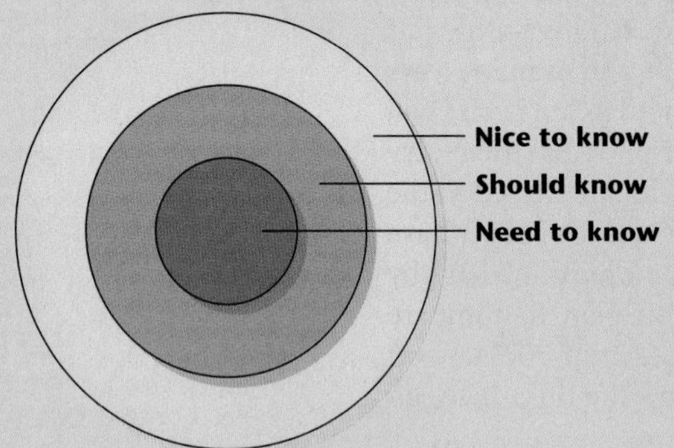

Once you have categorized your ideas and information, drop everything in the *nice to know* category from your presentation. Focus your attention on what your audience *must* know. Only consider the material in the *should know* category if you've run out of material to support your topic. More than likely, however, you will have more than enough ideas and information in the *must know* category. In fact, you may discover that some of the *must know* information really belongs in the *should know* category. Focus on material that will help you achieve your purpose. Drop or save the rest for another presentation.

Narrow the Topic

So you've found a presentation topic that clearly has an informative, persuasive, or entertaining purpose that interests you, appeals to your audience, and draws on your expertise. But have you found a topic that you can manage? If, as we have recommended, you have written a specific, appropriate, and relevant purpose statement, your topic should be well focused and ready for further development. However, you may still need to narrow or modify your topic in order to achieve your purpose or to adapt to your listeners' needs. There's an old saying: "Don't bite off more than you can chew." For presentations, the saying should read instead: "Don't bite off more than your audience can digest."

Although you may be an expert on your topic, your audience may be hearing about it for the first time. Don't bury them under mounds of information. Ask yourself: If I only have time to tell them one thing about my topic, what should it be? Chances are that conveying a single important idea will be enough to achieve your purpose.

Let's say your purpose is to demonstrate the difficulty and danger of serving as a volunteer firefighter, but you don't have enough speaking time to explain all the risks of firefighting. You could narrow your topic by focusing on how hard it is to break down a fire-engulfed door or on the skills needed to safely carry a victim from a burning building. Although you would like to share more information, you can still achieve your purpose by choosing a narrow, specific topic.

Look at how these students narrowed some broad, general topic ideas into better topics for classroom presentations:

Broad:	The History of Rock Music
Better:	Chubby Checker and the Twist
Broad:	A Review of Greek Mythology
Better:	The Origins of Aphrodite
Broad:	Preparing a Five-Course Dinner for Eight
Better:	Setting the Table for a Formal, Five-Course Dinner
Broad:	Converting the Class to My Religion
Better:	Explaining the Purpose of Baptism
Broad:	Advances in Semiconductor Technology
Better:	What Is a Semiconductor Device?

As we indicated in Chapter 2, "Listening and Critical Thinking," most listeners will not remember most of what you say. In fact, audience members are more likely to remember their impression of you rather than the details of your presentation. Consider who's listening as you narrow your topic to achieve your purpose.

Search the Web

If you like surfing the World Wide Web and need a good topic for a presentation, you have a wonderful resource to call on. Not only can you research a topic on the Web; you can also search for a topic there. All of the major search engines such as Google and Yahoo! have directories that suggest topic areas. Other websites offer reference materials—some free, some for a small fee—that begin with extensive indexes that cover a wide range of topics. The following categories represent a composite list of topic areas included in such website directories.

- Agriculture
- Animals and Pets
- Arts and Entertainment
- Automotive
- Business and Economy
- Cities and Towns
- Computers and Technology
- Education
- Geography
- Health and Fitness
- History
- Hobbies and Games
- Home and Garden
- Jobs and Careers
- Money
- Music
- News and Media
- Parenting and Family
- People and Relationships
- Philosophy
- Recreation and Sports
- References
- Religion and Spirituality
- Science
- Shopping
- Society and Culture
- Teens
- Travel
- Women's Issues
- World

Within each of these areas, you will find dozens of subtopics. For example, the *Health and Fitness* directory on one site includes a long list of topics beginning with *Alternative Medicine;* moving through *Disabilities, Diseases/Conditions, Fitness/Wellness, Medicine/Allied Health, Mental Health,* and *Recovery/Addiction;* and concluding with *Women's Health.* The *Disease* directory begins with *AIDS* and ends with *Thyroid Disease.* Looking up just one of the diseases—*Chronic Fatigue Syndrome/Fibromyalgia*—resulted in more than a dozen subjects ranging from the history of fibromyalgia to personal stories of sufferers.[6] If you can't come up with a good topic on your own, a Web search will help you find hundreds of potential topics.

Summary

▶ What do I want my audience to know, think, feel, or do?

Determine the purpose of your presentation. You must know *why* you are speaking before you can select or develop an appropriate topic. All presentations should have a public purpose, a stated goal that can be shared with an audience. Some presentations also have a private purpose that achieves a personal goal.

▶ How do I refine my purpose?

Ask yourself, "What do I want my audience to know, think, feel, or do as a result of my presentation?" Make sure your purpose statement is specific and clear, achievable, and relevant.

▶ Can the type of presentation help me find a good topic?

Presentations to inform, persuade, or entertain have different goals that require different types of preparation.

▶ How do I find an appropriate topic?

In choosing a topic for an assignment, try to answer the following questions: (1) What type of presentation is assigned? (2) What topics interest me? (3) What do I value? (4) What do I know about these topics? (5) What will appeal to my audience?

▶ How do I narrow my topic?

Narrow your topic by asking: If I only have time to tell my audience one or two things about my topic, what should they be?

Presentation Principles in Action

Leading Questions Lead to Good Topics

You don't have to be the world's greatest expert to give a presentation; you just have to be interested enough to begin collecting ideas and information. Completing the following statements may help you find topics worth researching and developing into a presentation.

1. I've always wanted to know more about

   a. ______________________________

   b. ______________________________

2. If I could make one new law, I would
   a. ______________________________
   b. ______________________________
3. If I had an unexpected week off, I would
   a. ______________________________
   b. ______________________________
4. I've always wanted to be able to
   a. ______________________________
   b. ______________________________
5. If I could give away a million dollars, I would
   a. ______________________________
   b. ______________________________
6. The world would be a better place if
   a. ______________________________
   b. ______________________________

Key Terms

Notes

1 Gerald M. Phillips and Jerome J. Zolten, *Structuring Speech* (Indianapolis: Bobbs-Merrill, 1976), p. 70.
2 Thomas Leech, *How to Prepare, Stage, & Deliver Winning Presentations* (New York: AMACOM, 1993), p. 46.
3 Milton Rokeach, *The Nature of Human Values* (New York: Free Press, 1973), p. 3.
4 Rushworth M. Kidder, *Shared Values for a Troubled World* (San Francisco: Jossey-Bass, 1994).
5 Based on research cited in James W. Neuliep, *Intercultural Communication: A Contextual Approach*, 2nd ed. (Boston: Houghton Mifflin, 2003), pp. 52–65.
6 In addition to the large search engines such as Yahoo! and Google, specialized websites offer a wealth of potential topics. For example, *www.about.com* is composed of individual sites run by professional "Guides" who are carefully screened and trained. Each Guide builds a comprehensive site that includes reviewed content, relevant links, "how-tos", forums, and answers to questions. For example, the about.com site on *chronic fatigue syndrome/fibromyalgia* is guided/edited by a former medical technologist who lives with chronic fatigue syndrome and who currently works as a lecturer in communication studies at a large southern university.

chapter five

Audience Analysis and Adaptation

- How do I focus my presentation on a particular audience?
- What do I need to know about my audience?
- How can I gather useful information about my audience?
- How do I effectively analyze and adapt to the results of my audience research?
- What techniques can help me adapt to my audience during a presentation?

The presence of a living, breathing audience makes presentation speaking different from most other forms of communication. Whereas writers have little control over when, where, or why they are read, speakers often can decide when, where, or why they speak. Writers, filmmakers, and TV producers do not usually see their audience's immediate reactions (although they may hear or read about them later). However, speakers not only see their audience's immediate reactions; they can also adapt to the responses. The writer writes alone, and the reader reads alone; the speaker and the audience work together and form a unique relationship. Audiences make presentations unpredictable, anxiety-producing events. They also make speechmaking one of the most personal, exciting, and empowering forms of communication.

Audience-Focused Communication

You've spent hours of time and thought determining your purpose and narrowing the topic of your presentation. You know what you want to accomplish. Now it's time to develop the presentation itself. Right? Not necessarily. Instead, now you need to focus your attention on your audience. It's time to put their interests and needs above yours. Because a presentation is *not* a presentation unless it has an audience, being a truly effective speaker requires understanding, respecting, and adapting to the people who will be listening to you. Always remember that presentations are made to and for audiences.

Audience-focused communication is all around you. In advertising and marketing, it's called *targeting.* Each ad for a product takes aim at a target market: sweetened breakfast cereals for kids, athletic shoes for teenagers, convenience foods and detergents for homemakers, beer for sports fans. In marketing, the primary purpose is to sell the product, but the means and methods of selling can be as different as the customers in the audience. In a presentation, this process is called audience analysis and adaptation.

As we indicated in Chapter 1, "Presentation Speaking," the process of developing a presentation begins with identifying your purpose. The second principle to consider in that process is analyzing the people in your audience. **Audience analysis,** the ability to understand and adapt to listeners, separates good speakers from great ones and is critical to improving your presentation. A thoughtful, deliberate analysis of the audience and their likely responses to your presentation can help you plan what to say and how to say it.[1] How you go about achieving your purpose should depend on your audience. The examples you include in your presentation, the words you use, and even your delivery style should be adapted to your audience's interests and needs.

The goals of audience analysis are to find out something about your audience, to interpret those findings, and as a result, to select appropriate strategies that will help you achieve the purpose of your presentation. Fortunately, there are some fundamental audience analysis steps that can help you attain this goal. As obvious as these steps may seem, they can require hours of research and thinking to complete. But if you don't address them, your presentation may miss the mark.

AUDIENCE ANALYSIS STEPS

1. **Ask relevant questions about your audience.**
2. **Gather information that answers audience research questions.**
3. **Analyze the researched information about your audience.**
4. **Adapt your presentation on the basis of your audience analysis.**

WIIFT?

WIIFT ("wif-it") is a popular acronym used in sales training that stands for the question "What's In It For Them?" It's a way of reminding sales professionals to focus on customer characteristics, needs, interests, attitudes, and values rather than on WIIFM ("What's In It For Me?"). The same advice applies to speakers: Concentrate on your audience rather than on yourself. Why should they listen to you? What do they want? What do you have to offer them? If your audience sees no reason to listen, they won't. Help them understand what's in it for them, or they won't invest their attention or devote critical thinking to your message. Presentations are made to and for audiences. As long as you keep that in mind, you will understand why you should focus your attention on WIIFT.

Understanding and adapting to your audience has several practical advantages beyond those linked to achieving your purpose.[2] A thorough understanding of your audience can help you focus your presentation and decide how to narrow your topic. If, for example, you discover that your audience is very familiar with the concept of *emotional intelligence,* you don't have to explain its basic tenets. An audience-focused approach can also simplify and shorten your preparation time by using the audience as a criterion for deciding what to include or exclude. You would give different examples of how understanding emotional intelligence can improve decision making to an audience of college administrators than you would to an audience of fashion designers. Putting the audience at the center of your thinking can help you customize your presentation. Also, by focusing your presentation on the audience, you are likely to feel more comfortable and confident when you finally address them face to face.

Researching Your Audience

You get to know your audience by asking relevant research questions about its members. Seven basic questions apply to all audiences. In some cases, the answers may be obvious, particularly when you know the people in the audience or have addressed them before. In other cases, you will have to spend a lot of time and effort answering the following questions.

AUDIENCE RESEARCH QUESTIONS

Who are they?
Why are they here?
What do they know?
What are their interests?
What are their attitudes?
What are their values?
What are their learning styles?

Audience Characteristics

Answering these audience research questions can help you paint a portrait of your audience's characteristics—a combination of their demographics, motivations, knowledge, interests, attitudes, values, and learning styles. As our Dynamic Presentation Model in Chapter 1 shows, these characteristics are found in every audience and are well worth knowing.

Who Are They? Answers to this question reveal many audience characteristics. Are the people in your audience predominantly male or female, old or young, rich or poor? You should be trying to gather as much **demographic information** as you can about the people who will be watching and listening to you.

You can collect both general and specific demographic information about your audience. Considering general demographic characteristics such as the ones listed in Figure 5.1 can help you think about your presentation in broad terms.

If you know that the audience is composed of a particular group or will be meeting for a special reason, you can gather more specific demographic information such as the characteristics listed in Figure 5.2. An audience of college undergraduates will differ from an audience of airline pilots. A group of homeowners will differ from a group of students living in a dormitory.

Whether they are general or specific, knowing something about the demographic characteristics of your audience helps you to target your presentation. For example, you can assume that everyone in an audience of college students has earned the equivalent of a high school diploma. You probably can conclude that a Baptist youth group will be more familiar with the New Testament than the members of a Jewish or Muslim youth group would be. If the people in your audience are members of a single group or organization, think about the characteristics that brought them together. What do they have in common? Are they all taking the same class? Do all of them have children in the daycare center you're working with? Do they own or manage local businesses?

When adapting to audience demographics such as age, gender, nationality, race, education level, and socioeconomic background, you must strive to understand and

Figure 5.1 **General Demographic Characteristics**

Age	Gender	Marital Status
Race	Religion	Ethnic Background
Occupation	Income Level	Place of Residence

Figure 5.2 Specific Demographic Characteristics

Health and Physical Characteristics	Career Goals
Hobbies	Common Interests
Working Hours and Conditions	Recreational Activities
Dress and Appearance	Political Affiliations
Club/Association Memberships	Choice of Vacations
Newspaper/Magazine Subscriptions	Choice of Automobiles
Employment Positions	Military Experience

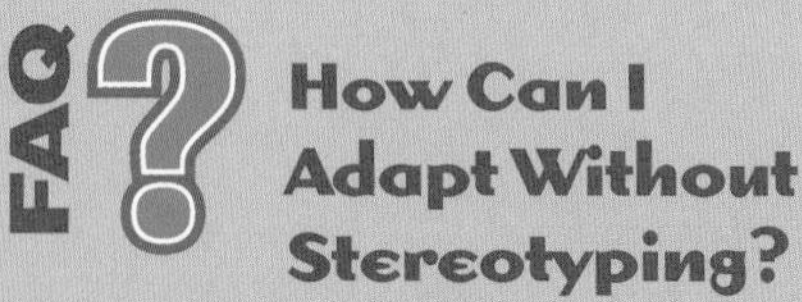

Too often we form "one-size-fits-all" opinions about people based on visible or obvious demographic characteristics such as their age, race, gender, occupation, nationality, or religion. As we indicate in Chapter 1, these oversimplified conceptions, opinions, or images of a person or a group of people are called **stereotypes.*** Stereotyping can inhibit effective audience analysis and adaptation. So how do you avoid it? First, there are the obvious suggestions—never use racial slang terms; don't tell sexist or racist jokes; don't use stereotyped references. Second, don't try to mimic or look like the members of a cultural group to which you don't belong. You'll only look and sound foolish and probably will be resented by your audience. Third, don't make universal assumptions about your audience: They will live in mostly white neighborhoods if they're white and in mostly black neighborhoods if they're black; they will like chow mein if they're Chinese and fried green tomatoes if they're Southern.

Avoiding stereotyping requires a deeper understanding and respect for others. If a person dislikes the music, political candidates, clothes, and hobbies that you like, you should make every effort to respect these differences of opinion rather than ridicule the person for having such opinions. Learn as much as you can about your audience and acknowledge the differences you discover. Then concentrate on communicating a message designed to share meaning with your audience.

* For insights into the effects of stereotyping, see Alberto Gonzalez, Marsha Houston, and Victoria Chen, eds., *Our Voices: Essays in Culture, Ethnicity, and Communication*, 3rd ed. (Los Angeles: Roxbury, 2000).

respect the differences you discover. Be careful not to stereotype audiences according to their demographic characteristics. Stereotyping audience members (Asians are good students; all women want children; New Yorkers are aggressive) can do more harm than good.

Considering demographic characteristics goes well beyond race and ethnic background. For example, consider age. We know that, in general, younger audiences are more susceptible to persuasion than older audiences, whose members are often more set in their ways. Yet knowing the audience's ages may not be enough to tell you how to approach the group. Try persuading a teenage audience that opera is a higher art form than the music they listen to and love. But show an older audience a way to save money on taxes, and we'll show you audience members willing to change their ways!

We are not suggesting that you ignore an audience characteristic such as age but rather that you also consider other factors such as education, income, political affiliations, interests, and occupations. Asking how differences in audience characteristics are relevant to your purpose and topic matters most. Moreover, remember that *your* own age, nationality, race, education level, and socioeconomic background may be just as critical in determining how well an audience listens to you.

Researchers in the fields of psychology, anthropology, sociology, and communication have identified several dimensions of cultural variability that can be used to differentiate cultures. Figure 5.3 presents a brief description of four important dimensions and how they may affect speakers and audience members.[3]

Why Are They Here? Asking why an audience is assembled is not the same as asking about their demographic characteristics. As much as you may want your audience to be there because they are interested in you and your presentation, this is not always or even usually the case. Answers to the question "Why are they here?" can tell you a great deal about your audience that will help you meet them where *they* are rather than where

Figure 5.3 Cultural Dimensions

Cultural Dimension	Definition and Cultural Examples	Speaker Behaviors	Audience Reactions
Power Distance	Degree of equality among individuals in a group, audience, or culture. **High power distance:** Inequality between high- and low-status members. Malaysia, Guatemala, Panama, Philippines, Mexico, Venezuela **Low power distance:** More equality and interdependence among members. New Zealand, Denmark, Israel, Austria	**High power distance** speakers may be direct, give explicit directions, and expect compliance from audience members. **Low power distance** speakers may be less direct and more focused on trying to accommodate audience opinions and needs.	**High power distance** audience members may accept opinions and follow orders from high-status speakers. **Low power distance** audience members may distrust or resent direct orders from speakers and expect more respect and adaptation.
Uncertainty Avoidance	Degree of comfort in uncertain, unpredictable, and unknown situations. **High uncertainty:** Prefer rules, plans, and routines. Greece, Portugal, Guatemala, Belgium, Japan **Low uncertainty:** Comfortable with ambiguity and unpredictability. Hong Kong, Sweden, Denmark, Jamaica, Singapore	**High uncertainty** speakers may be nervous and tense when speaking to strangers and prefer to make well-prepared, well-organized presentations. **Low uncertainty** speakers may be less structured and willing to offer innovative ideas and to take risks with an audience.	**High uncertainty** audience members may seek predictable, clear instructions that conform with existing beliefs and values. **Low uncertainty** audience members may take suggestions but also may feel independent of and be willing to challenge the speaker.
Individualism–Collectivism	Preference for independence or interdependence. **Individualism:** Value individual achievement and personal freedom. United States, Australia, Great Britain, Canada **Collectivism:** Value group identity and collective action. Asian and Latin American countries	**Individualistic** speakers may focus on personal achievements and seek credit for their work. **Collectivist** speakers may emphasize how they share audience values and how their messages will benefit listeners and the greater good.	**Individualistic** audience members may look for ways in which a speaker's message can satisfy their personal needs. **Collectivist** audience members look for ways in which a speaker's messages may benefit their group or community.
High or Low Context	Degree to which meanings are based on verbal or nonverbal cues and personal or impersonal relationships. **High context:** Messages are implied, situation sensitive, and relationship dependent. Japan, China, Greece, Mexico **Low context:** Messages are explicit, factual, and objective. England, United States, Germany	**High context** speakers may consider background and history of the speaker-audience relationship, focus on nonverbal cues, and adapt to audience feedback. **Low context** speakers may present facts in a clear, direct, and explicit speaking style.	**High context** audience members may need time to review information and react, and are conscious of the speaker's relationship to the audience. **Low context** audience members may have difficulty understanding subtle nonverbal cues and the importance of going beyond "just facts" and the roles of speaker-audience relationships.

Figure 5.4 Why Are They Here?

Reason for Attending	Examples
Audience members are required to attend.	A college class, a mandatory training session, a talk by a supervisor
Audience members always attend.	A monthly service club meeting, a weekly staff meeting, a popular social event
Audience members are interested in the topic.	A topic related to their personal and/or professional interests
Audience members are interested in the speaker.	A political candidate, a celebrity, a newly hired executive or manager
Audience members will be rewarded.	Earn "points" with the speaker, boss, or instructor; paid to attend; receive credit for professional development
Audience members are not sure why they are attending.	Accompanying a friend, taking notes for a colleague or boss, substituting as a group representative, having nothing else to do

Sometimes an audience may be so varied that it's impossible to find a best way to reach everyone. In such cases, it helps to identify and concentrate on key audience members—the people who have the authority or ability to make things happen. They may be opinion leaders or other respected audience members. Other audience members may take their cues from the ways in which these people react to a presentation or speaker. If key people seem interested and responsive, others will mimic their behavior. If they seem bored or annoyed, others will be, too. If you cannot reach everyone in an audience, try to reach those who have influence. How do you find out who these key audience members are? Check the nonverbal communication of audience members: Who gets the most handshakes? Who is given a prominent seat or is accompanied by an entourage? Who commands attention? If you can't tell who is most important by observing an audience, ask. Ask the person who invited you about audience members who have influence or hold senior-level positions. You may even discover that the most important and influential person in the audience is the person who invited you.

you are. Audiences attend meetings and presentations for many different reasons, as Figure 5.4 illustrates.

Needless to say, the audience members who are interested in the topic or who stand to benefit from attending a presentation will be quite different from those who don't know why they are there or who are required to attend. Each type presents its own special challenges for a speaker. A highly interested and well-informed audience demands a compelling, knowledgeable, well-prepared speaker. An audience required or reluctant to attend a presentation may be pleasantly surprised and influenced by a dynamic speaker who has the ability to give audience members a reason to listen. Moreover, entire audiences rarely fit into one type of group. You may find yourself speaking to an audience that includes several people representing each reason for attending.

What Do They Know? Because audience members possess various levels of education and knowledge, figuring out what they know about your topic is an important step in determining what to include in your presentation. Audience knowledge is based on several factors: educational level, demographic characteristics, and interest or expertise in a topic. Assessing your audience's knowledge level can be challenging, particularly when you are addressing a diverse audience.[4] You can meet this challenge by asking yourself several questions:

- How much do they know about the topic?
- How much background material do I need to cover?
- Will they understand my vocabulary and specific, topic-related terminology or jargon?
- Have they heard any of this before?

Answering these tough questions is essential to matching your presentation to an audience's level of understanding and knowledge. As Michael Hattersley, a columnist for the *Harvard Management Update,* maintains, "Nothing is more boring to audiences than a rehash of overly familiar information, and nothing more frustrating than trying to decipher a presentation pitched way over their heads."[5]

The level of education completed can tell you something about your audience's general knowledge and vocabulary. Demographics can tell you something about their experiences and expertise in areas as diverse as childcare, religious training, and firsthand experience with cultural and historical events. An audience being introduced to a new management theory or scientific concept—regardless of their education levels, demographic characteristics, or interests—may need a carefully worded and basic-level introduction to a complex topic.

Don't Underestimate Your Audience

Even though you may know more than your audience, don't treat them like children or as if they are uneducated. Dr. Arthur Furst, professor emeritus at the University of San Francisco, stated it well in his survey response: "I always assume my audience is intelligent but not acquainted with my topic of discussion." The burden of providing a clear explanation or valid argument is on you, not on your audience. If you insult the basic intelligence of the people sitting in your audience, you will never achieve the purpose of your presentation.

What Are Their Interests? Answering these questions—Who are they? Why are they here? What do they know?—can help you gauge your audience's interests, which are often what bring people to hear a presentation. Ignoring this important factor can result in a less-than-effective presentation. As we see it, there are two types of audience interests: self-centered interests and topic-centered interests.

Self-centered interests are aroused when a presentation can result in personal gain or loss. A political candidate's position on tax increases can result in more or fewer taxes for audience members. A proposal to restructure a company or an organization can result in more or less power for employees. A talk by a personnel director can provide information about how to get a more desirable job. In all of these cases, the listener stands to lose or to gain something as a result of the presentation or its outcome.

Audience members also have topic-centered interests—subjects they enjoy hearing and learning about. Topic-centered interests can include hobbies, favorite sports or pastimes, or subjects loaded with intrigue and mystery. However, topic-centered interests often tend to be personal. A detailed description of a Civil War battle may captivate the Civil War buffs in the audience but bore the other members. The presentation of a new approach to management may intrigue those who enjoy management theory but alienate the hands-on administrators who find such theories restrictive and impractical in real-world settings. Whether self-centered or topic-centered, listener interests have a significant effect on how well an audience pays attention to you and your message.

What Are Their Attitudes? When you ask about **audience attitudes,** you are asking whether the people in your audience agree or disagree with your purpose statement, how strongly they agree or disagree, and what you can do to influence their opinions and/or behavior. There can be as many opinions in your audience as there are people. Some audience members will already agree with you before you begin your presentation. Others will disagree no matter what you say. Some audience members will be neutral or have no opinion; they will neither agree nor disagree. Figure 5.5 shows a wide range of opinions that can be found in an audience listening to the same presentation. In Chapters 19, "Understanding Persuasion," and 20, "Developing Persuasive Presentations," we focus on ways of adapting a persuasive

When Knight Ridder, Inc., bought the Kansas City Star, *CEO Anthony Ridder had to consider audience attitudes and reactions when he announced the big purchase to a group of anxious employees.*

presentation to listeners who agree with you, to those who disagree, and to those who are neutral. Once you understand why an audience agrees or disagrees with you, you can begin the decision-making process of matching persuasive strategies to audience attitudes.

Figure 5.5 Spectrum of Audience Opinions

The speaker's stated purpose is "to convince the audience that imposing longer jail sentences will deter and reduce crime." Audience members may hold a variety of opinions on the issue.

Strongly Agree	Agree	Neutral	Disagree	Strongly Disagree
If criminals know they won't be back on the streets within a short period of time, longer jail sentences will deter them and reduce crime.	Because criminals are sometimes released before they have served their sentences, longer jail sentences may help deter and reduce crime.	There are good, strong arguments on both sides of the issue. *or* I don't know very much about this issue.	Because longer jail sentences cost more and are unfairly given to poor and minority defendants, longer jail sentences may not be a wise course of action.	Longer jail sentences do not deter or reduce crime; they only create more hardened, dangerous criminals.

To make matters even more complicated, there can be many different reasons why people have the same opinion. For example, audience members who oppose longer jail sentences for convicted criminals may do so for various reasons:

- The jails are too crowded now, and there's no money or public support to build new ones.
- Longer sentences do not prevent or stop crime.
- Rehabilitation should be stressed instead of jail time.
- Rich people will get off; the poor will be the ones who spend more time in jail.
- Long sentences are cruel and unusual punishment for some crimes.
- Longer jail sentences won't work if criminals can get out on early parole.

Not only can a wide range of opinions be found in one audience; an equally wide range of *behaviors* may also be present, as Figure 5.6 shows.

As with opinions, there can be many different reasons why people behave in certain ways. For example, audience members who volunteer to work on Robin Brown's campaign may do so for several reasons. One audience member may like Brown's position on education; another may want to see her shake up the old guard; a third may hope that she will appoint active campaign workers to government and community board positions.

Adapting to audience knowledge, interests, and attitudes can produce a winning combination for most speakers. Ignoring these factors can lead to failure. Here are two examples in which presenters ignored these factors:

- A student speaker tried to convince her class to join her church and to become born-again Christians. She warned the audience that failure to embrace her religion would condemn their souls to hell. The result: Although the speaker was sincere in her beliefs, listeners of different religions and other Christian denominations resented her talk and were offended by her warning.
- A new, eager manager decided to use his time during a staff meeting to describe the principles and value of understanding emotional intelligence (EI) in team decision making. He gave a highly informative presentation that included recent research on EI, studies demonstrating its value in decision making, and recommendations for ways to incorporate EI into the business's

Figure 5.6 Spectrum of Audience Behavior

The speaker's purpose is "to convince the audience that Robin Brown is the best candidate for mayor because she supports zero tolerance of crime." Audience members may behave quite differently, depending on their attitudes about an issue.

Strongly Agree	Agree	Neutral	Disagree	Strongly Disagree
Because I don't feel safe in my own neighborhood, I will volunteer my time to work on Brown's campaign.	Because crime in our city is on the rise, I will vote for Brown on Election Day.	I don't know whether crime is a voting issue. *or* I still don't know whether I'll vote for Brown or D'Angelo.	Because I think there are more pressing issues facing our city than crime, I will vote for D'Angelo on Election Day.	Because I think "zero tolerance for crime" is just a code phrase for licensing police brutality, I will volunteer my time to work on D'Angelo's campaign.

planning process. What he failed to realize was that the audience had been through extensive training in emotional intelligence and probably knew more about the topic than he did. The result: The other managers, who had looked forward to welcoming a new member to their team, were disappointed with his presentation and disturbed by his arrogance in assuming that he knew more than they did.

What Are Their Values? In Chapter 4, "Purpose and Topic," we advise you to take an inventory of your values when looking for suitable topics for a presentation. The same kind of thinking applies to assessing your audience's values. Remember the American values we list in Chapter 4—independence, belief in God, progress, the equality of all humans, privacy, patriotism, and suspicion of authority. They also apply to audience members. Do *all* Americans share the values on this list? No. And certainly, they don't view them as equally important. Thus, if the male members of an audience value self-interest more than equality between the sexes, they might not support a program designed to hire more women in management positions. If audience members value religion and church attendance, they may be reluctant to accept the ideas of a nonbeliever or a person who is not a churchgoer.

When a speaker and an audience come from different cultures, value differences may be significant. Let's use American and Chinese values as an example. If, for instance, Chinese audience members value obedience to and respect for their parents, they may resist an American speaker's praise of personal independence. If a Chinese speaker describes the value of honoring one's ancestors above all else, an American Christian audience may view this belief as contrary to their faith in God.

Effective speakers identify their audience's values as a starting point for determining whether or not they share opinions about what is right or wrong, moral or immoral, good or bad. If your values differ from your audience's values in significant ways, you may have a difficult time achieving the purpose of your presentation.

What Are Their Learning Styles? You can go beyond audience characteristics and opinions to ask one additional question that relates to how audiences react to a presentation: *How do they think, listen, and learn?* In Chapter 2, "Listening and Critical Thinking," we covered the critical roles of effective listening and critical thinking in the speechmaking process.

In addition to differing in the ways that they listen and think, audience members differ in terms of how they learn. Certainly no two people think exactly alike. Not surprisingly, no two people learn in the same way. Each of you has your own unique learning style. Richard M. Felder has defined **learning style** as the characteristic strengths and preferences that exemplify the way that you take in and process information. Although you may learn best by focusing on facts, other learners may be more comfortable investigating theory. Whereas you may want to see a concept in action, others may want to read a detailed explanation of it. Although you may learn best by studying alone, others may prefer working in study groups in which they interact and learn with others.[6]

One of the learning style models we have used in our own presentations categorizes learning into three basic styles: *visual, auditory,* and *kinesthetic/tactile.* Visual learners prefer reading and seeing. They learn by reading about a concept, seeing information displayed on a word chart, and using flash cards or note summaries to trigger their memory. If they can't see it, there's a good chance that they won't learn it.

Auditory learners learn by listening. In classes, they may ask if they can audiotape the instructor's lectures. We often observe auditory learners talking about class material with other students as a way of re-hearing what they've just heard.

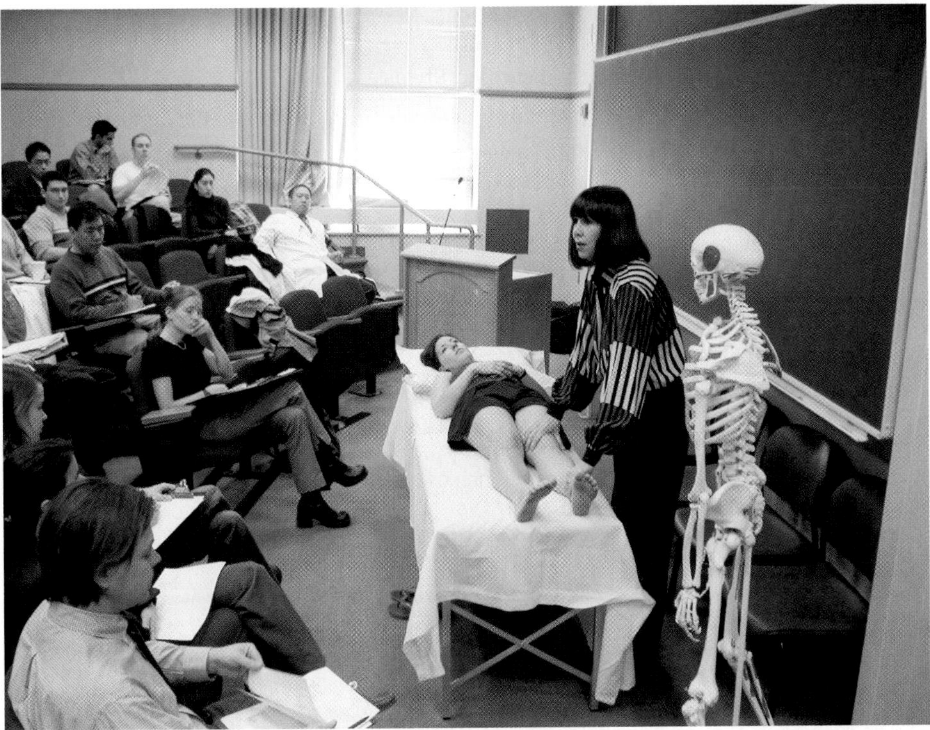

Students in a Harvard Medical School class use different learning styles to master course content and medical practices. How can the instructor adapt to visual, auditory, and kinesthetic/tactile learners?

The third type of learning style is called kinesthetic/tactile. *Kinesthetics* refers to the study of movement and activity. The term *tactile*—meaning touch—is also used to describe these learners. Kinesthetic/tactile learners want a hands-on approach. For example, in addition to reading a textbook or listening to lectures about presentation speaking or computer programming or a nursing procedure, they want to try doing it. Kinesthetic/tactile learners are the students who squirm in their seats when we've talked too long or when we assign lengthy readings. They like building models, practicing techniques, and figuring something out on their own rather than reading about it or following directions. Figure 5.7 illustrates some of the differences among these three learning styles.

All speakers need to take their audience's learning styles into account. Unless you are absolutely sure that there are only one or two learning styles in your audience (an unlikely occurrence), you should appeal to all three styles. Thus, in our own teaching we use a variety of techniques. When we lecture, we supplement our talks with visual aids by writing on the board, using presentation slides, or providing handouts. We often use personal examples that illustrate a concept or pause and ask students to paraphrase what we've just said. When possible, we use diagrams, graphics, and physical demonstrations to help the visual learners in addition to providing oral and written explanations for the auditory and visual learners. We also try to break up the class period or seminar with group discussions or activities for those who learn by doing. This variety of approaches makes our classroom presentations more dynamic and also accommodates the range of learning styles in our student audiences.

Figure 5.7 Learning Styles

Learning Styles		
Visual Learners	**Auditory Learners**	**Kinesthetic/Tactile Learners**
• Learn best by reading and seeing • Become distracted by noise and movement • Read and follow written and visual directions • Like teachers to write on the board or supplement the lecture with visual aids • Prefer reading newspaper and magazine articles to hearing a radio report • Remember faces but not names	• Learn best by hearing • Like to discuss concepts with others • Prefer classroom discussions and study groups • Repeat information out loud in order to remember it • Prefer TV and radio reports instead of newspapers and magazines • Remember names but not faces	• Learn best by doing • Like to touch, experiment, and rehearse • May copy notes over and over again to make them neat and organized • Move while learning • Like making models, posters, and diagrams • Can do two things at once • Remember what they did with others but not the people's faces or names

Gathering Audience Information

We've been talking about the basic research questions you should ask about your audience. But how do you gather that information? There are several ways, ranging from simple observation to using sophisticated survey methods. The method that will work best for you depends on how much time and energy you can devote to the audience analysis process. In general, though, two very basic techniques can tell you a great deal about your audience: Learn to look and listen and develop useful audience surveys.

Stop, Look, and Listen

As children, some of us were taught to *stop, look, and listen* when crossing the street. The same lesson applies to gathering information about an audience. Make sure that you stop and take the time to look at and listen to your audience.

Look. The simplest method is to observe your audience or to imagine what they will look like and try to answer as many questions as you can on the basis of their appearances. What percentage of your audience will be male or female? Will there be a wide age range? Is the audience likely to be racially diverse or fairly uniform? Do you picture audience members as formally or casually dressed?

Looking at your audience will tell you more about their characteristics than about their opinions. Nevertheless, you can draw a few conclusions about your audience's opinions and behavior from their appearances or their group membership. A young audience may be more likely to support a tax on social security income than an audience of senior citizens. A group of well-dressed corporate executives may be more conservative than an audience of community activists.

You also may want to observe their behavior. Are they restless, or do they appear eager to listen? Are they smiling or frowning? Do they look wide awake or tired? From your conclusions about their behavior, you may want to inject more or less energy into

On a tour of a fire station, a fireman looks and listens to his guests in order to make his presentation interesting and informative.

your presentation. You may want to shorten it or add more examples. Because audience feedback can send powerful messages to a speaker, your success may depend on how well you pay attention and adapt to such messages.

Listen. Simply put, ask questions about the people in your audience and listen to the answers! You won't always have the opportunity to look at your audience before your presentation. When that's the case, use the Listen technique.

You can get valuable information about your audience from the person who invited you to speak or from someone who has previously spoken to this group. If you can, arrange to talk to several audience members before you are scheduled to speak. Talk to as many people as you can, listen for common characteristics as well as for information about their opinions and behaviors, and take some notes about your conclusions. But be careful when asking about opinions. One person's opinion may be atypical.

The Look and Listen techniques are streamlined enough that you can even apply them during the few minutes you have before speaking. As you're waiting to speak, quickly scan the room. What audience characteristics and behaviors leap out? You will be able to see how many men and women are in your audience. You can quickly judge whether all ages seem to be represented or whether the audience consists of one age group. You can see how they're dressed.

Christina Stuart, a popular and widely published communication consultant, describes the benefits of prepresentation small talk as an audience analysis technique:

> *It always surprises me to see how speakers fail to chat with their audience at coffee breaks and mealtimes. I find these times an invaluable source of material and will often refer to a conversation which I have had with a member of the audience prior to my talk. For example, saying, "Someone was telling me during the coffee break that ..." can lead to my next point. It has the*

advantage of showing the audience that you are approachable and that you can relate to their problems and experiences. And you benefit from speaking face to face with the individuals who are your audience. It is also more relaxing than trying to fit in a final mental rehearsal.[7]

Survey Your Audience

In most speaking situations, you will only have time to look at your audience and listen to the answers to questions about them. There is, however, another way to gather valuable information about your audience: Use an audience survey. A **survey** is a series of written questions designed to gather information about audience characteristics and opinions.

Political candidates and elected officials rely on voter surveys to design political campaigns and public addresses. Corporations rely on consumer surveys to develop new products, improve existing products, and successfully market their products to a public audience. Television networks use viewer surveys to determine which shows will live or die.

If politicians, corporations, and networks rely on audience surveys, why shouldn't you? One reason is that you may not have the time, opportunity, or permission to develop, administer, and analyze the results of an audience survey. Another reason is that you may not know how to do it.

Audience surveys should be carefully constructed. It is easy to write poor questions and just as easy to draw the wrong conclusions from answers. Without training in questionnaire design and analysis, you should be very careful and cautious. At the same time, a good questionnaire can give you valuable information about the characteristics and opinions of your audience. (See the audience survey in Figure 5.8.)

There are hundreds of books, articles, and even courses on how to develop and conduct surveys. Obviously, we cannot tell you everything you need to know about survey research here. But there are some basic guidelines that can help you write a useful audience survey.

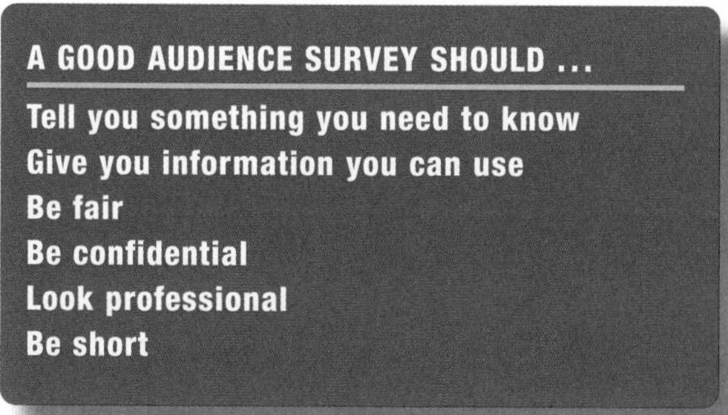

A good survey should tell you something you need to know, something you don't already know about your audience. Don't use a survey to ask obvious questions: Should the U.S. oppose terrorism? Do you want to earn more money? Any answer other than *yes* to these questions would be so unusual that you would wonder about the person's motives or sanity.

A good survey should give you information that you can use. Don't use a survey to ask questions unrelated to the purpose of your presentation. A question such as "Do you exercise regularly?" does not tell you whether *regularly* means twice a day, week, or

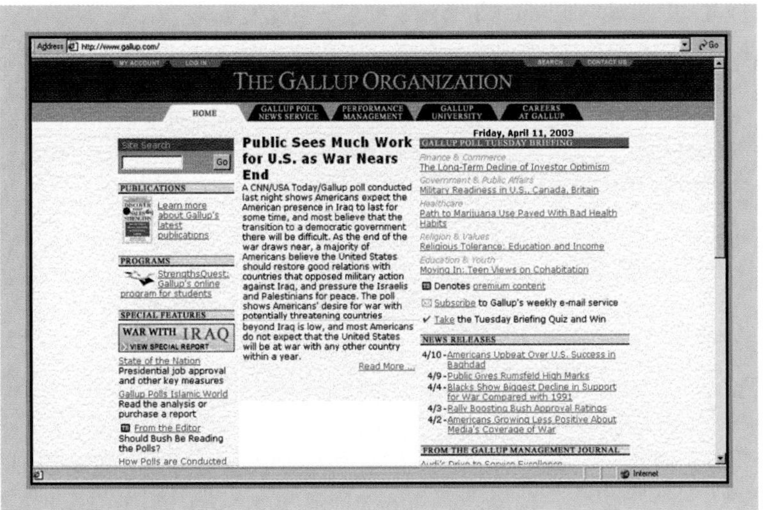

The Gallup polling organization's website www.gallop.com, provides detailed information about many audience characteristics—from product preferences and social interests to audience knowledge of and opinions about political issues and candidates.

month. An open-ended question such as "Why do you support Robin Brown for mayor?" could give you a useless answer—"Because she is the best candidate." The following examples show you how the previous questions can be made more useful.

Poor Question: Do you exercise regularly?

Good Question: How often do you engage in aerobic exercise?

_____ rarely
_____ once or twice a month
_____ once or more a week
_____ daily
_____ ____________________ (fill in your own answer)

Poor Question: Why do you support Robin Brown for mayor?

Good Question: List three reasons why you think Robin Brown is the best candidate for mayor.

A good survey should be fair. If you don't word your questions carefully, you won't get an accurate picture of your audience. *Yes* or *no* questions often exclude audience members who don't know the answer or who are undecided. Questions such as "Are you against gun control?" or "Do you favor stricter prison sentences?" don't leave room for answers such as "It depends on the circumstances" or "I haven't made up my mind yet."

A good survey should be confidential. Survey takers are more likely to give you honest information about themselves, their opinions, and their behavior if you don't ask for their names and identifying information. Respect your audience's privacy. If you know that the audience is predominantly female or African American or under thirty years old, don't ask questions that would make it easy to identify the few minority members.

A good survey should look professional. It should be clear, easy to use, and duplicated so that each audience member has an individual questionnaire to complete. Audience members are more likely to give serious thought to a professional-looking survey than to one that has been scribbled and slapped together at the last minute.

Figure 5.8 Sample Audience Survey

AUDIENCE SURVEY

The Role of Government and the Importance of Political Involvement

Demographic Information:

Please provide the following demographic information:

1. **What is your age?**
   ❑ 18–25 ❑ 26–35 ❑ 36–50 ❑ Over 50
2. **What is your gender?**
   ❑ Female ❑ Male
3. **Do you have children?**
   ❑ Yes ❑ No
4. **Do you live with your parents?**
   ❑ Yes ❑ No
5. **Do you have health insurance?**
   ❑ Yes ❑ No
6. **Are you registered to vote?**
   ❑ Yes ❑ No

   6a. If yes, what political party?
   ❑ Republican ❑ Democrat ❑ Independent ❑ Other: ______________
7. **Do you vote in most elections?**
   ❑ Yes ❑ No
8. **What is your annual income level?**
   ❑ Less than $10,000
   ❑ $10,000 to $24,999
   ❑ $25,000 to $49,999
   ❑ $50,000 to $74,999
   ❑ More than $75,000
   ❑ I do not work at this time

Survey Questions:

Listed below are various areas of government spending. Indicate whether you would like to see more or less government spending in each area. Remember that if you indicate you favor much more, it might require a tax increase to pay for it.

1 Spend much more
2 Spend more
3 Neither increase nor decrease spending
4 Spend less
5 Spend much less
6 Undecided

A good survey should be short. Find out only what you need to know. Most people don't like taking the time to answer a long questionnaire. A long survey also gives away too much information about your presentation and can ruin the effect you are trying to achieve.

Please circle the appropriate number:

The environment	**6**	**5**	**4**	**3**	**2**	**1**
Health	**6**	**5**	**4**	**3**	**2**	**1**
Law enforcement	**6**	**5**	**4**	**3**	**2**	**1**
Education	**6**	**5**	**4**	**3**	**2**	**1**
Military defense	**6**	**5**	**4**	**3**	**2**	**1**
Retirement benefits	**6**	**5**	**4**	**3**	**2**	**1**
Unemployment benefits	**6**	**5**	**4**	**3**	**2**	**1**
Culture and arts	**6**	**5**	**4**	**3**	**2**	**1**

Below are listed several potential roles for the government. Indicate whether you would like to see the government assume these responsibilities by using the following scale:

1 Definitely should be
2 Probably should be
3 Probably should not be
4 Definitely should not be
5 Undecided

Please circle the appropriate number:

Provide a job for everyone who wants one.	**5**	**4**	**3**	**2**	**1**
Keep prices under control.	**5**	**4**	**3**	**2**	**1**
Provide healthcare for the sick.	**5**	**4**	**3**	**2**	**1**
Provide a decent standard of living for the elderly.	**5**	**4**	**3**	**2**	**1**
Provide industry with the help it needs to grow.	**5**	**4**	**3**	**2**	**1**
Provide a decent standard of living for the unemployed.	**5**	**4**	**3**	**2**	**1**
Give financial assistance to college students from low-income families.	**5**	**4**	**3**	**2**	**1**

How interested would you say you personally are in politics?

- ❑ Very interested
- ❑ Fairly interested
- ❑ Somewhat interested
- ❑ Not very interested
- ❑ Not at all interested
- ❑ Can't choose

Source: University of Chicago National Opinion Research Center General Social Survey. The questionnaire deals with people's attitudes toward the government. Survey excerpts can be found in Earl Babbie, *The Practice of Social Research,* 8th ed. (Belmont, CA: Wadsworth, 1998), pp. 160–162.

Types of Survey Questions. When you create a survey, try to figure out which kinds of questions will give you accurate, useful, and fair information about your audience: Survey questions can be divided into two broad types: open-ended and close-ended questions.

Open-ended questions allow respondents to provide specific or detailed answers. These types of questions often begin with wording such as "What do you like most about . . . ?" or "Please explain why." Here are a few examples:

- If you have never donated blood, please explain the reason or reasons why you haven't.
- What qualities do you look for in a new employee?
- What religious beliefs are shared by Christians, Muslims, and Jews?

Close-ended questions force audience members to choose an answer from a limited list. As a student and consumer, you are probably familiar with the following four types of close-ended questions.

Agree/Disagree. For each statement, indicate whether you (1) strongly agree, (2) disagree, (3) neither agree nor disagree, (4) disagree, or (5) strongly disagree.

1. I feel relaxed when giving a speech. 1 2 3 4 5
2. My thoughts become confused when I give a speech. 1 2 3 4 5

Multiple Choice. In your opinion, what percentage of your daily communicating time do you spend listening?

_____ More than 70%

_____ 40–70%

_____ 20–35%

_____ 10–20%

_____ 5–15%

Ratings. How would you rate the following items in terms of their importance to you in becoming a more effective speaker?

	Extremely Important	Very Important	Somewhat Important	Not Very Important	Not at All Important
1. Organizing your presentation	5	4	3	2	1
2. Adapting to your audience	5	4	3	2	1

Checklist. Which values are most important to you? You may check one or more answers.[8]

_____ Individuality and self-interest take precedence over group interests.

_____ Personal privacy is an unalienable right.

_____ All forms of authority, including government, should be viewed with suspicion.

_____ Personal success depends on acceptance among your peers.

_____ You should believe in God and belong to an organized religious institution.

_____ Men and women are equal.

_____ All human beings are equal.

_____ Progress is good; America is a symbol of progress.

Survey Administration. Once you have developed and duplicated a good survey instrument, you must determine the best way to distribute and collect your questionnaires. If you are speaking to a classroom audience, you can hand out your survey before class and collect it at the end of class. Alternatively, your instructor may set aside part of one class period for this process.

It is much more difficult to distribute and collect a survey outside of a classroom setting. You must have the permission and cooperation of the group or organization that you will be addressing, and you must have plans in place to collect the responses. You may want to provide stamped, preaddressed envelopes so that respondents can send their questionnaires directly to you. Unfortunately, response rates for mailed surveys tend to be quite low, so you may want to see if the group that invited you to speak would be willing to distribute and collect the survey for you. With appropriate software or the services of an outside vendor, you can e-mail surveys to a population and have the software collect and graph the results for you. Regardless of what method you choose, the effort is well worth your time and attention because a good survey can provide the keys to understanding and adapting to the people in your audience.

Analyzing and Adapting to Your Audience

Everything you learn about your audience tells you something about how to prepare your presentation, but you have to analyze what you have learned in order to apply it effectively. This step is not always easy, particularly if you're saturated with tons of information about your audience. How do you separate the useful from the useless? How do you develop or change a presentation to address a particular kind of audience?

Audience analysis and adaptation requires you to go back to your purpose statement and apply your answers to the basic audience research questions. Identify which audience factors can help you to achieve the purpose of your presentation as well as which will require you to adjust your purpose to fit your audience profile. Then examine the content of your presentation and customize it for your audience.

Let's look at how two speakers applied their audience research to two very different types of presentations—an informative presentation on growing tomatoes and a persuasive presentation on the harmful effects of television violence. Note how the answers to our seven audience questions affected the ways in which each speaker modified her preliminary purpose into one that better suited her audience.

Preliminary Purpose. To provide information on growing tomatoes.

Who are they? They are twenty women and eight men who belong to the local garden club. All but three are over forty. They have known one another for many years.

Why are they here? They are attending a monthly club meeting at which they discuss group-selected topics. Many attend for social reasons, too.

What do they know? They already know a lot about growing tomatoes but want to improve the health and output of their plants.

What are their interests? They are very interested in plants of all kinds, but a few may be more interested in growing flowers than in growing tomatoes. Fortunately, the group picked the topic, a factor indicating their high level of interest.

What are their attitudes? They are avid gardeners, but they may be a bit wary about *my* ability to tell them something new and interesting about tomatoes.

What are their values? They probably value independence and hard work given the personal dedication it takes to be a successful gardener and an active member of the garden club. Given the diversity of club members, they probably embrace equality.

What are their learning styles? Like most audiences, they will represent a variety of learning styles. My guess is that they will be hands-on learners who like listening to details and who also enjoy sharing their own experiences and opinions.

Revised Purpose. To share my knowledge of the latest and best research on improving the health and output of a tomato plant in this growing region.

Preliminary Purpose. To warn the class about the effects of television violence.

Who are they? They are twenty-five college students, the majority of whom range in age from eighteen to twenty-nine. Three are over thirty; two are over forty. They are taking a required communication course. About 50 percent have younger siblings; 20 percent are the parents of young children. Most of those without children say they plan to have children in the future.

Why are they here? They are in class because attendance is required. They may be preoccupied with thoughts about their own presentations or about personal matters.

What do they know? They have probably read or heard about the effects of television violence but may not be familiar with specific studies. They are aware of the television rating system.

What are their interests? Most of them are mildly interested; those with children are more interested.

What are their values? Given that most class members plan to raise families and that 20% are parents, this topic appeals to a wide range of traditional family values—protect and nurture children; preserve and strengthen the family; promote a safe and caring world.

What are their attitudes? Most of them believe that television violence is something of a problem, but their positions are not very strong. A few have strong opinions—believing either that television violence is very harmful or that controlling television content could ban many of the programs they enjoy.

What are their learning styles? I know most of my classmates and have seen all three learning styles at work. In addition to a well-organized presentation for auditory learners, I will use video clips of TV violence to illustrate my point for visual learners. I will also provide a handout that describes the rating code used by broadcasters to designate the amount of violence, profanity, and sexually explicit material in a program. Then I will show several more video clips and ask the kinesthetic/tactile learners to try rating the examples.

Revised Purpose. To urge listeners to support measures that protect children from the harmful effects of frightening TV shows and movies using examples and research from Dr. Joanne Cantor's television violence study.[9]

As a way of illustrating the value of customizing your presentation, we provide two examples of student presentations that used audience survey results to make major modifications. The following adjustments are described in the students' own words.

Donate Your Organs. As a result of my survey, I learned that most of the people in class were not organ donors, so I did have an audience that needed persuading. The majority of those who were not donors have heard of the program, but since 36 percent had not, I decided to provide this information. Since the nondonors didn't know how to become donors, I included information on the various methods available to them. Almost 75 percent had never considered becoming a donor, and all but one of the nondonors had some objections (fear of giving organs, guarantee the donor is dead, want to be buried with all of their parts, don't want to donate unhealthy organs). I decided to address some of the objections and to show them that these concerns should not prevent them from donating their organs to those in need.

How Safe is Nuclear Energy? Most of the students in my audience believe that nuclear power is unsafe and has no future in the United States. Surprisingly, many think that fossil fuels are very safe. I took this to mean that they were looking at nuclear energy only in terms of immediate dangers (a terrorist attack, a meltdown, a leak, or an accident). They were not thinking of our long-term energy needs or about alternative energy sources. Thus, I decided to focus on our long-term energy needs and the advantages of using a variety of energy sources to ensure and safeguard our future.

Although these answers are used merely as illustrations, they demonstrate that different topics and different audiences produce very different responses to audience questions. Good analysis selects and uses those responses that provide insight into preparing a presentation that adapts to audience interests and needs.

Your willingness to research, understand, and respect your audience can mean the difference between failure and success. Georganne Millard, a motivational speaker and radio talk-show host in Purchase, New York, describes how she successfully speaks to audiences of older adults: "Most of my speeches are given to an elderly audience, and as I am in midlife, it's obvious there is a generation gap. Therefore, I preface all my presentations with stories about my 'grandma' and her trials and tribulations. That way everyone understands and can then relate to my topic."

Mid-Presentation Adaptation

Thus far, we have explored ways of gathering and analyzing audience information and ways to adapt to audiences *before* you speak. Just as crucial is having the confidence to engage in these important activities *during* a presentation. Sometimes, no matter how well you've prepared for an audience, you run into the unexpected. What if an audience of engineers or top executives bring their spouses or families to your presentation? Do you ignore the unexpected guests or acknowledge and adapt to them? What if the chief executive officer or company president shows up at a training workshop for clerical workers? Do you continue the presentation that you planned, or do you try to adjust it in a way that would make participants feel more comfortable in the presence of their boss? What if your carefully researched and well-organized presentation doesn't seem to be working? If your audience members seem restless, bored, or hostile, how can you adjust to that negative feedback? And finally, what do you do

Adapting to International Audiences

Have you ever listened to someone speak in a foreign language that you had studied in school? Were you able to understand every word? Did you find the experience difficult or frustrating? Imagine what it must be like for a non-native speaker of English to understand your presentation. Even in other English-speaking countries, you may find it difficult to "translate" some terms into Standard American English. For example, in Australia, to *shout* is to pay for a round of drinks in a pub. A *rubber* is the same thing as the eraser you use to rub out a pencil mark. In British English, the *underground* is the same as an American *subway,* and a *subway* is a pedestrian tunnel beneath a crowded English street.

Unfortunately, we lack significant research on the differences in presentation speaking styles in other countries. We do know, however, that there *are* differences in the ways in which speakers and audiences develop and react to presentations. For example, an article in the *New York Times* entitled "To Some in Europe, the Major Problem Is Bush the Cowboy" notes that "to European ears, the president's language is far too blunt" and that he puts things in "black-and-white certainties." The same article quotes a German government official who criticizes Bush's confrontational speaking style and his "jabbing of his finger at you. It's Texas, a culture that is unfamiliar [to] Germans. And it's the religious tenor of his arguments."[1]

European reactions to President Bush's pronouncements underscore the importance of understanding, respecting, and adapting to cultural differences. The guidelines we offer are derived from general intercultural research and from observations we have made when speaking to international audiences, both at home and abroad. Through trial and error, we have learned that adapting to international audiences requires special strategies and skills.

Speak Slowly and Clearly.

Unless audience members are fluent in English, they must translate your words into their own language as you speak. In corporate and government settings, you may be lucky enough to have the services of a translator who translates your words over a headphone system—much like what you see in newscasts from the United Nations or in international conferences. Even so, the best of translators can have difficulty keeping up with rapid speech. Help your listeners by slowing down and speaking as clearly as you can. However, we do *not* mean speaking at a snail's pace or increasing your volume to the point of shouting at your audience. They are not hearing impaired. But they do need more time to absorb what you are saying. In addition to speaking at a slower rate, pause once in a while so that they can catch up with you and enjoy a brief mental break.

Use Visual Aids.

Instead of the visual aids that work best for American audiences, international audiences prefer visuals that use complete statements and full sentences rather than key words. Most non-English speakers are better readers than listeners. If you display slides or give them handouts, use more words. Then give them time to read those words and take notes. If they can't catch every word you say or display, give them a handout to read that will help them understand and remember your message.

Be More Formal.

In general, use a more formal style when speaking to international audiences. United States speakers and

if you are informed, at the last minute, that your twenty-minute presentation must be shortened to ten minutes in order to accommodate another speaker?

Expect the Unexpected

The confidence to make midcourse changes depends on good advance preparation. If you have prepared well and have practiced your presentation, you should be able to deviate from your plan with little trouble. Remember that one of the ways in which a audiences often interact informally—using first names and a friendly, informal speaking style. However, in German-speaking countries, John Daly might be referred to as *Herr Doctor Professor Daly*. In Australia, Isa Engleberg may be called *Isa* in discussions and question-and-answer sessions, but be introduced as *Dr. Engleberg* for a public presentation. In addition, this formality goes well beyond names and titles. When speaking to international audiences, dress professionally, consider developing a manuscript for your presentation, and adopt a more formal speaking style. If you discover that an international audience is comfortable with an informal style, you can loosen up and become more casual. If, however, you begin in a casual style and discover that your audience disapproves, it's very difficult to become more formal as you speak.

Adapt to Cultural Perspectives.

Consider the dimensions of cultural variability that typify your audience. If you are speaking to an audience that expects a certain distance to be maintained between supervisors and subordinates, don't urge them to hang out with the boss at a local bar. Both you *and* your boss may lose their respect. If you are a typical, individualistic American who likes to boast about your accomplishments, you may find a collectivist audience disturbed by your apparent arrogance and lack of concern for others. If you are addressing an audience from a high-context culture, be less direct. Let them draw conclusions for themselves rather than "telling" them what to think or do. Give them time to get to know and trust you.

Avoid Humor.

Humor rarely translates. Even in this country, a joke that makes a Californian laugh may be lost on a New Englander. Multiply that problem many times over when speaking to an international audience. Jokes that rely on puns or funny sayings don't translate into other languages. If you poke fun at yourself, and your audience expects a formal presentation, they may think you are foolish. Humor can backfire. Don't expect an international audience to translate your hilarious story accurately. They may misinterpret your point and may even take offense at your story.

Avoid U.S. Clichés.

Every language and culture has unique clichés. A *cliché* is an overused expression familiar to everyone in a particular culture. Clichés can be simple expressions, such as "without further ado," or be linked to a familiar activity or sport, as in "he struck out with the boss." Translating culture-bound expressions can produce strange results. For example, a colleague from Yugoslavia has her own unique interpretations of common U.S. sayings. Once she combined "He's a chip off the old block" with "He's got a chip on his shoulder" and said, "He's a chip off the old shoulder." Rather than worrying about a "tempest in a teapot," she talks about coping with a "storm in a cup of water."

Respect Their Politics.

Whenever possible, we try to read the local newspapers or listen to the news before addressing an international audience. Usually, there are English news translations. If not, ask someone to tell you about the events and news on everyone's mind. This information can help you understand why an audience may disagree with the politics of the U.S. government or the actions of a U.S. corporation. It can also help you respond to hostile questions by acknowledging your audience's point of view. When challenged with political questions, we answer them honestly while pointing out that America is a richly diverse country with multiple viewpoints that don't always support U.S. government policies.

1. "To Some in Europe, the Major problem Is Bush the Cowboy," *New York Times*, 24 January 2003, p. A1.

presentation differs from written communication is in the presenter's ability to adapt to a living, breathing audience right on the spot. Speakers who stubbornly stick to their outlines or manuscripts and refuse to accommodate or adapt to their audiences will never be highly successful. Those who see their presentation as a game plan that can be modified before and during the game are much more likely to achieve their purpose.

To effectively adapt to your audience during a presentation, you need to do three things at once: deliver your well-prepared presentation, correctly interpret the feedback you receive from the audience, and successfully adapt your presentation on the basis of

Real World Real Speakers

Connect, Correct, Continue

Tim Norbeck, the chief executive officer of the Connecticut Medical Society, provided us with his real-world advice about paying attention to audience reactions during a presentation: "I speak to groups frequently, usually on specific subjects related to health care. Although people tell me that my talks are well received, I know that this is the case by watching their reactions during a speech. If the audience stays riveted, you know that you have connected. I strongly believe that to keep the audience's interest, you must use interesting and relevant stories and humor—to connect them to the points you are trying to make. If a speaker is observant, he or she will always know whether a speech is successful or not."

your interpretation. Interpreting feedback requires that you look at your audience members, read their body language, and sense their moods. As one writer puts it: "Want to know how you're doing? Look at your audience."[10] Are they looking directly at you with interest? Do they look bored or distracted? Watch how they interact with each other. Are they nodding and smiling or having side conversations? Audience members who sit forward as they listen tend to be more interested than those who sit back.

Let the Audience Help You

If audience feedback suggests that you're not getting through, don't be afraid to interrupt your presentation by asking **comprehension questions.** A question such as "Would you like more detail on this point before I go on to the next one?" does more than get your audience's attention. It also involves your audience, assesses their understanding, and keeps you in control of the situation.[11]

Think about adjusting your presentation in the same way in which you would adjust your conversation with a friend. If your friend looks confused as you speak, you might ask what's wrong. If your friend interrupts with a question, you probably will answer it or ask if you can finish your thought before answering. If your friend tells you that he has a pressing appointment, you are likely to shorten what you want to say. The same is true with an audience. If the faces and body language of audience members indicate that they're confused, re-explain what you're saying. Unless you're in a very formal setting, you can ask them why they seem puzzled. You can even encourage them to ask questions during your presentation if time allows. However, if you choose this tactic, make sure that their questions don't detract from the message you want to share.

Finally, if your talk is running too long, or the audience is becoming restless, don't ignore the problem; adapt to it. Cut your presentation, highlight the key points, or choose to cover one important point rather than two. And be gracious. Don't abuse the time limit and run the risk of annoying your audience or host.

The whole point of audience analysis is putting your listeners first. They are why you are there. Ron Hoff, the author of several trade books on presentation speaking, has said it as well as anyone: "Here's the point: the minute you start to worry about yourself—how much *you've* got to cover, how late *you* already are, whatever—thereby ignoring the condition of your audience, you're headed for deep trouble. Audiences inevitably put *their* needs ahead of *your* needs. It's not even close."[12] Effective audience analysis and adaptation ensure that the audience's needs are first, and always first, in the heart and mind of a presenter.

Summary

▶ How do I focus my presentation on a particular audience?

Audience-focused presentations depend on effective audience analysis, which includes researching your audience, analyzing the results of your research, and adapting your presentation to that analysis.

▶ What do I need to know about my audience?

You need to know useful information about audience demographics, the reasons that they are attending, and their levels of knowledge as well as their interests, attitudes, and learning styles.

▶ How can I gather useful information about my audience?

Methods for gathering information about your audience range from very simple observational techniques to sophisticated survey methods. The technique that will work best for you is often determined by the amount of time and energy you can devote to the audience analysis process.

▶ How do I effectively analyze and adapt to the results of my audience research?

When analyzing the results of audience research, go back to your purpose statement and integrate the answers to your audience questions into your goal. Then adjust your presentation in a way that adapts to the audience's characteristics, interests, and needs.

▶ What techniques can help me adapt to my audience during a presentation?

Learn to read, interpret, and adapt to the feedback that you receive from an audience during your presentation.

Presentation Speaking in Action

Who Are We?

You can begin learning how to develop and use an audience survey by constructing one for your class. Begin with the following questions and then add eight more questions. Don't ask obvious questions such as asking students to identify their gender—you can look at your class and make that determination.

Once you have constructed your own questions, compare them with the questions asked by other students. As a class, you may be able to develop a single questionnaire that can help all the members learn more about their shared audience.

1. Age ❑ under 21 ❑ 21–25 ❑ 26–35 ❑ 36–50 ❑ over 50
2. Major: ______________________ ❑ Undecided
3. Culture:
   - ❑ African American
   - ❑ Asian American
   - ❑ European American
   - ❑ Latino/Hispanic American
   - ❑ Native American
   - ❑ Mixed Specify: ______________
   - ❑ International Specify: ______________
   - ❑ Other: ______________
4. In your opinion, which learning style do you prefer? Rank the styles in order of preference with 1 being your first preference and 3 being your least preferred learning style.

   _____ Visual Learner

   _____ Auditory Learner

   _____ Kinesthetic/Tactile Learner

5. ______________________________
6. ______________________________
7. ______________________________
8. ______________________________
9. ______________________________
10. ______________________________
11. ______________________________
12. ______________________________

Key Terms

audience analysis 101
audience attitudes 107
close-ended question 118
comprehension questions 124
demographic information 103
learning styles 110
open-ended question 118
stereotypes 104
survey 114

Notes

1 Michael Hattersley, "The Key to Making Better Presentations: Audience Analysis," *Harvard Management Update* 2 (Oct. 1996): 5.

2 See Dennis Backer and Paula Borkum Backer, *Powerful Presentation Skills* (Chicago: Irwin, 1994), p. 1. The authors include the results of an unattributed national survey: "Knowledge of the listeners was cited as one of the most important pieces of information necessary to prepare and present a speech."

3 Although there are dozens of excellent intercultural communication textbooks that summarize the many dimensions of cultural variability, we have based our descriptions on the work of James W. Neuliep, *Intercultural Communication: A Contextual Approach*, 2nd ed. (Boston: Houghton Mifflin, 2003), Chapter 2. In addition to describing several cultural dimensions, Neuliep also provides a series of self-assessment instruments and indexes designed to measure a reader's cultural attitudes, beliefs, and values. Significant primary sources include Geert Hofstede, *Culture's Consequences* (Beverly Hills: Sage, 1984); Geert Hofstede, *Culture and Organizations: Intercultural Cooperation and Its Implications for Survival:* (London: McGraw-Hill, 1991); Edward T. Hall, *The Silent Language* (Greenwich, CT: Fawcett, 1959); Edward T. Hall, *Beyond Culture* (Garden City, NY: Anchor, 1997).

4 Thomas Leech, *How to Prepare, Stage, & Deliver Winning Presentations* (New York: AMACOM, 1993), p. 51. Leech provides a series of excellent quotations from experienced speakers highlighting the importance of taking audience knowledge into account. Examples: "Perhaps the single most important thing in making a presentation is understanding.... the degree of knowledge and interest by principal audience members. My own observation is that very few people who make presentations understand that.... People don't do much homework regarding the sophistication of audiences.... If audience members can't understand your language, don't relate to your references, or can't follow your line of discussion, it is highly unlikely that they will grasp your message."

5 Hattersley, p. 6.

6 Volumes have been written about learning styles. Education textbooks and journals usually address this topic in sections that discuss instructional methods and pedagogy. For example, Donald C. Orlich and his colleagues explore a variety of learning style variables in Chapter 5, "Sequencing and Organizing Instruction." See Donald C. Orlich et al. *Teaching Strategies: A Guide to Better Instruction*, 6th ed. (Boston: Houghton Mifflin, 2001). A Web search of *learning styles* will produce numerous helpful sites provided by experts who specialize in learning style research and applications. For example, Dr. Richard M. Felder's site at North Carolina State University examines four learning style models that have been used effectively in engineering education.

7 Christina Stuart, *How to Be an Effective Speaker* (Chicago: National Textbook, 1988), p. 119.

8 The items on this checklist are based on Francis Hsu's "Postulate of Basic American Values" found in H. N. Seelye, *Teaching Culture: Strategies for Intercultural Communication*, 3rd ed. (Lincolnwood, IL: National, 1993), pp. 128–129.

9 See Joanne Cantor, *Mommy, I'm Scared: How TV and Movies Frighten Children and What We Can Do to Protect Them* (San Diego: Harcourt Brace, 1998).

10 Ron Hoff, *I Can See You Naked* (Kansas City, MO: Andrews and McMeel, 1992), p. 169.

11 Stuart, p. 115. The author recommends using comprehension questions for smaller audiences as a way of remaining in control by confining your comments to the material you have already presented.

12 Hoff, p. 210.

chapter six

Speaker Credibility and Ethics

- What factors determine whether the audience will perceive me as a good speaker?
- How can I enhance my credibility as a speaker?
- How does my character influence the success of a presentation?
- How can I ensure that I am treating my audience fairly and ethically?
- What can audience members do to ensure that they are treating a speaker fairly and ethically?

A well-prepared presentation and an effective speaker are not the same thing. If they were, you could hire a speechwriter and work with a speech coach to be guaranteed success. As we've indicated before, presentations differ from other forms of communication simply because *you are there.* Being willing to "put yourself on the line" can make your message more personal, more vital, and more effective. In this chapter, we emphasize how important you and your credibility are in determining whether an audience listens to, learns from, and responds to your presentation.

The concept of *speaker credibility* is over two thousand years old. Even in ancient times, speech coaches (yes, there were speech coaches way back then) recognized that the characteristics and qualities of a speaker were just as important as the speech. In his *Rhetoric,* Aristotle wrote about *ethos,* a Greek word meaning "character": "The character [ethos] of the speaker is a cause of persuasion when the speech is so uttered as to make him worthy of belief.... His character [ethos] is the most potent of all the means to persuasion."[1] Aristotle's concept of *ethos* has evolved into what we now call speaker credibility. In Chapter 19, "Understanding Persuasion," ethos will appear again as one of the most powerful ways to persuade an audience.

Studies of speaker credibility have demonstrated its significance. For example, in one study two different audiences listened to an audiotape of the same presentation. One audience was told that the speaker was a national expert on the topic. The other audience was told that the speaker was a college student. After listening to the presentation, each audience was asked for their reactions. Can you guess the results? The "national expert's" speech persuaded more audience members to change their minds than the speech by the "student" did.[2] Aristotle's contention about ethos is as true today as it was in ancient Greece. Audience perceptions about the speaker influence a presentation's success. Learning how to enhance your credibility is well worth the effort and is the topic of this chapter.

Components of Speaker Credibility

Speaker credibility represents the extent to which an audience believes you and the things you say. *The American Heritage Dictionary* defines *credibility* as the "quality, capability, or power to elicit belief."[3] In other words, the more credible you are in the eyes of your audience, the more likely you are to achieve the purpose of your presentation. If your audience rates you as highly credible, they may excuse poor delivery. They are so ready to believe you that the presentation doesn't have to be perfect.[4]

In order to become a more credible speaker, it's important to understand which qualities contribute to your credibility. Of the many factors researchers have identified as major components of speaker credibility, three have an especially strong impact on the believability of a speaker: character, competence, and charisma.[5]

COMPONENTS OF SPEAKER CREDIBILITY

- **Character**
- **Competence**
- **Charisma**

Figure 6.1

Character

Adjectives listed on the left side of the following word pairs describe a speaker of good character.

Honest	Dishonest
Kind	Cruel
Friendly	Unfriendly
Open	Closed
Fair	Biased
Respectful	Rude
Dedicated	Disloyal
Caring	Unconcerned

Character

Character relates to a speaker's honesty and goodwill. Are you a person of good character—trustworthy, sincere, and fair? Do you put the good of the audience above your own? When you speak, do you come across as friendly, sincere, and honest? When you're presenting an argument, is your evidence fair, are any reservations acknowledged, and is the conclusion warranted? Figure 6.1 shows these and other aspects of character. Of the three components of speaker credibility, character may be the most important. If your listeners don't trust you, it won't matter if you are an international expert or the most exciting speaker that ever electrified an audience.

As shown later in this chapter, a speaker of good character is seen as a good person. In this case, "good" means being ethical—doing what is right and moral when you speak in front of an audience. Unfortunately, a presentation can be used for unethical as well as ethical purposes. A speaker can help an audience or can take advantage of it, can present accurate information or can mislead an audience with false information, and can support a worthy cause or support a selfish one. In other words, the audience's opinion of your character determines whether they will believe you. If an audience *thinks* you are dishonest, you will have little chance of achieving your purpose. If you *are* dishonest, you don't deserve to achieve your purpose. But if you are honest, and the audience sees you as honest, their perception of you will help you to achieve your purpose.

Competence

Competence relates to a speaker's expertise and abilities, as the qualities in Figure 6.2 illustrate. In the best of all speaking situations, an audience will believe you are competent if you are a recognized expert. Proving that you are competent can be as simple as listing your credentials and experience. An audience is unlikely to question a recognized brain surgeon, a professional baseball player, or an international dress designer, as long as each sticks to discussing brain surgery, baseball, or dress design. Sometimes experts can use the prestige they have in one field and transfer it to another. A brain surgeon may speak about the need for national health care, a baseball player may warn

Figure 6.2

Competence

Adjectives listed on the left side of the following word pairs describe a competent speaker.

Experienced	Inexperienced
Well prepared	Unprepared
Qualified	Unqualified
Up-to-date	Out-of-date
Trained	Untrained
Informed	Uninformed
Intelligent	Unintelligent

In 1992, Rigoberta Menchú, a leader of the Committee of the Peasant Union in Guatemala, won the Nobel Peace Prize for her work as a leading advocate of Indian rights and ethnocultural reconciliation throughout the Western Hemisphere. Here, she brings enormous credibility and public visibility to a human rights symposium in Texas.

youngsters about the dangers of drug abuse, and a dress designer may suggest inexpensive ways of looking stylish.

If you were the captain of an eighty-foot sailboat that set a speed record sailing from Portugal to Boston, an audience will believe and probably will enjoy your tales of high-sea adventure. If a professor of oceanography describes Atlantic Ocean currents, an audience is likely to accept the information without question. Fortunately, you don't have to be a celebrated sea captain or have a Ph.D. to be an expert. A student, an auto mechanic, a waiter or waitress, a mother or father of six children, a minister, a chef, a nurse, and a government employee can all be experts. Such speakers can rely on their own life experiences and opinions to demonstrate competence.

But what happens when you aren't an expert? How can you demonstrate that you know what you're talking about? The answer lies in one word: research. As Chapter 8, "Supporting Material," discusses, you must thoroughly research the ideas and information you will need for your presentation. Whereas skimming *The Joy of Cooking* will not make you an expert chef, thorough research can give you enough up-to-date content to become a well-informed speaker. Although you may only use a small percentage of the supporting materials you collect, you can rely on your hours of research to give you confidence. Letting an audience know how much time and effort you have put into researching your topic, or sharing your surprise at discovering new ideas and

TIP Model Charismatic Teachers

Most of you can recall a wonderful, charismatic teacher who stood above the rest. These outstanding and dynamic teachers exhibited energy, enthusiasm, vigor, and commitment. Everyone wanted to get into their classes. What did they do to inspire and arouse their students? What was the source of their charisma? Research on teaching and learning has noted a teacher characteristic that may provide an answer to these questions and a model for those of you seeking to enhance your personal charisma.

The concept is called **immediacy.** Defined as perceptions of physical and psychological closeness, immediacy includes both verbal and nonverbal behaviors that, taken together, enhance student learning and motivation.

Some of the *nonverbal* characteristics of high immediacy include consistent and direct eye contact, smiling at students, appropriate and natural body movement and gestures, vocal variety, and maintaining closer physical distance. *Verbal* immediacy is associated with a sense of humor, a willingness to engage in conversations with students, self-disclosure, using inclusive language ("us" and "we"), offering feedback, seeking student input, and openness to meeting with students. Immediate teachers influence positive perceptions of interpersonal closeness, sensory stimulation, warmth, and friendliness.[1]

Think about charismatic speakers or teachers you've seen and heard. Were their bodies glued to a desk or lectern? Or did they come from behind that barrier, gesture openly, and move closer to (or even into) the audience? Did they smile and look at the group, use an expressive voice, and actively engage listeners in the discussion—even if they did nothing more than get people to nod their heads or raise their hands? Did they share personal feelings, relate life experiences, and use inclusive language? Immediate teachers and charismatic speakers have a lot in common. Recall how they behaved, or watch a charismatic speaker in action. Chapters 14 through 17 focus on performance skills that can help you to build the skills you need to unlock the mysteries of charismatic speaking.

1. Timothy G. Plax and Patricia Kearney, "Classroom Management: Contending with College Student Discipline," in *Teaching Communication*, ed. Anita L. Vangelisti, John A. Daly, and Gustav W. Friedrich, 2nd ed. (Mahwah, NJ: Lawrence Erlbaum, 1999), p. 276. Also see John A. Daly and Anita L. Vangelisti, "Skillfully Instructing Learners: How Communicators Effectively Convey Messages," in *Handbook of Communication and Social Interaction*, ed. John O. Greene and Brant R. Burleson (Mahwah, NJ: Lawrence Erlbaum, 2003), pp. 892–895.

information, demonstrates that you have worked hard to become a qualified and competent speaker. If you don't have firsthand experience or cannot claim to be an expert, let your audience know what efforts you have made to be well prepared. The following are some examples: "We conducted a study of over 2,000 individuals and found. . . ." "After reviewing every textbook on this subject written after 1995, I was surprised that the authors didn't address. . . ." "I have spoken, in person, to all five of our county commissioners. They all agree that. . . ."

Charisma

Charisma is a quality reflected in your level of energy, enthusiasm, vigor, and commitment. A speaker with charisma is seen as dynamic, forceful, powerful, assertive, and intense. President John F. Kennedy and Martin Luther King Jr. were charismatic speakers who could motivate and energize audiences. So was Adolf Hitler. People can disagree about a speaker's message yet still find that speaker charismatic. Figure 6.3 on the right illustrates the elements of charisma.

Are you a dynamic speaker? Can you inspire and arouse the emotions of an audience with your words? Are you eager to share your opinions with other people? Is your delivery animated, energetic, and enthusiastic? If your answer is "yes" to any of these questions, *charisma* may be a component of your speaking style. If your answers to the previous questions are "no," do not despair. Charisma is a valuable characteristic for a speaker, but it is not essential for success. A gentle speaker who is competent and trusted can be more successful than a charismatic speaker of questionable motives. In fact, some speakers have too much energy and intensity; they can frighten and exhaust an audience. Nevertheless, there is no question that an emotionally charged sermon or convention address can motivate thousands of people.

Despite Mother Teresa's soft-spoken intensity (see the Real World, Real Speakers box), a key factor in determining whether a speaker has charisma is his or her delivery. Charisma often has more to do with how a speaker delivers a presentation than with what the person is saying. Speakers who have strong and expressive voices will be seen as having more charisma than speakers with hesitant or unex-

Real World Real Speakers

Mother Teresa's Soft-Spoken Charisma

Charisma does not have to rely on fireworks. Soft-spoken speakers can be very charismatic. Mother Teresa, the Catholic nun whose tireless work with the sick and poor in India earned her the Nobel Peace Prize, was one of these. Mother Teresa's words reached around the world. Her credibility was unimpeachable, her confidence unshakable. Yet she was "soft-spoken as a breeze. Her incredible intensity, her commitment, made her dynamic. She had that magical quality called charisma—drawing others to her and making them want to follow her lead."[1]

Peggy Noonan, one of Ronald Reagan's speechwriters, describes a National Prayer Breakfast in 1994 at which Mother Teresa spoke:

> *She was small and moved slowly, hunched forward slightly.... [She] looked weathered, frail, and tough as wire.... No thank you, no smile. She just stood there holding the speech and looking down at it.... For twenty-five minutes she just read ... her text.... She finished her speech to a standing ovation and left as she had entered, silently, through a parted curtain, in a flash of blue and white. Her speech was a great success in that it was clear and strong, seriously meant, seriously stated, seriously argued and seriously received.... She softened nothing, did not deflect division but defined it. She came with a sword. She could do this, of course, because she had ... a natural and known authority. She had the standing of a saint.*"[2]

1. Gay Lumsden and Donald Lumsden, *Communicating with Credibility and Confidence* (Belmont, CA: Wadsworth, 1996), p. 37.
2. Peggy Noonan, *Simply Speaking: How to Communicate Your Ideas with Style, Substance, and Clarity* (New York: HarperCollins, 1998), pp. 197–204. Copyright © by Peggy Noonan. Reprinted by permission of HarperCollins Publishers, Inc.

pressive voices. Speakers who gesture naturally and move gracefully will be perceived as having more charisma than those who look uncomfortable and awkward in front of an audience. Speakers who can look their audiences in the eye will be regarded as having more charisma than those who avoid any sort of contact with members of the audience. Practicing and developing your performance skills can enhance your charisma in the same way that preparation can help you become a more competent speaker.

Another way to enhance your charisma is to show an audience how committed you are to your purpose. Demonstrate that your actions speak louder than your words. Are you merely concerned about the homeless, or do you volunteer your time and energy at a local homeless shelter? Do you oppose nuclear energy, or do you demonstrate in front of nuclear power plants and donate one paycheck a year to antinuclear organizations? Do you complain about higher tuition and cutbacks in student services, or do you write to your college's board of trustees expressing your concerns? By showing that you are active and committed to your purpose, you can better stimulate an audience to join you.

Active	Passive
Enthusiastic	Dull
Bold	Timid
Energetic	Tired
Confident	Hesitant
Stimulating	Boring
Dynamic	Lethargic

Figure 6.3

Charisma

Adjectives listed on the left side of the following word pairs describe a charismatic speaker.

Developing Credibility

You can develop or heighten your credibility, but please understand one very important fact: *Speaker credibility comes from your audience.* Only the audience decides whether or not you are believable. Several of our colleagues contend that credibility does not exist in any absolute or real sense; it is based solely on audience perceptions.[6] Thus, even if you are the world's greatest expert on your topic and deliver your carefully written and well-prepared presentation with skill, the ultimate decision about your credibility lies with your audience. Think of it this way: Credibility is "like the process of getting a grade in school. Only the teacher (or audience) can assign the grade to the student (or speaker), but the student can do all sorts of things—turn in homework, prepare for class, follow the rules—to influence what grade is assigned."[7] Teachers give grades, judges award prizes, reviewers critique books, and audiences determine your level of credibility. At the same time, there are things you *can* do—find out what you have to offer your audience, prepare an interesting presentation, and show your audience why you're uniquely qualified to deliver it—to influence your audience's opinion of you and your presentation.

DEVELOPING SPEAKER CREDIBILITY

Take a personal inventory
Be well prepared
Toot your own horn

Take a Personal Inventory

In order to enhance your credibility, you have to believe that you have something to offer an audience. We have worked with speakers who believed that they didn't have special skills or unique experiences, but such beliefs are usually unfounded. Every person can do or has done something that sets her or him apart from everyone else. It's just a matter of discovering what that something is. The Personal Inventory Mini-Module on p. 136 can help you identify the unique gifts and talents that contribute to your credibility.

Be Well Prepared

An effective presentation has a clear purpose, is adapted to the audience and occasion, is well prepared and organized, and is skillfully delivered. Your success as a speaker also depends on the relationship between you and your audience, and a well-prepared presentation gets that relationship off on the right foot. Likewise, lack of preparation communicates many negative messages to an audience. It says that you don't care enough about the audience to be well prepared. You didn't do enough research or didn't take enough time to organize your content. You didn't rehearse what you had prepared. If you don't have time to prepare for your audience, why should they have time for you? Conversely, a thoroughly researched, well-organized, and confidently delivered presentation conveys your respect for your audience. A respected audience will respond in kind.

Toot Your Own Horn

A presentation lets you show an audience that your ideas and opinions are based on more than good preparation. They are based on your experience, your accomplishments, and your special skills and traits. There's nothing wrong with using words such as *I, my,* and *me* if they are appropriate. But remember this: You can use too many *I, my,* and *me* words. You could step over the line and be accused of boasting. For example, one of us once sat through an honors student awards ceremony in which faculty members presented a variety of awards to outstanding students. Two of the almost three dozen presentations annoyed the audience. They were delivered by faculty members who used the word *I* instead of focusing on the student who was being honored: "As chairman of the department and an expert in this field of study, *I* decided. . . ." "As outgoing president of the association, *I* was the first person to. . . . " By using the awards presentation to spotlight themselves, the speakers undermined their own credibility.

As the Tip on page 138 notes, having someone else introduce you is one way to bolster your credibility. However, you can use your own

Can I Fake Charisma?

Students and clients sometimes ask us whether they should try to fake charisma. We answer this question with an absolute *no*. You either have charisma, or you don't. If being highly energetic and enthusiastic while you speak does not come naturally, don't fake it. You won't fool your audience and may even alienate them. "Faking" charisma is unethical. Pretending to be energetic and enthusiastic about a message you don't believe in deceives and misleads your audience.

However, any speaker can have charismatic moments. Think about your life experiences. Think of something you've done that will inspire people. Have you ever helped or saved someone in trouble? Have you ever faced down a threat? Have you ever succeeded when you thought you would fail? Have you heard an inspiring story about someone else? Use these examples and stories in your presentation. Tell them simply and sincerely, speaking from the heart. Let your enthusiasm for the story translate into energy. When you're telling a good story that's meaningful to you, a charismatic moment can materialize.

So should you fake charisma? No. You can, however, become charismatic when you carefully select and care about what you say.

NAACP President Kweisi Mfume walks toward the podium at Baltimore City Community College. His competence, character, and charisma led Baltimore citizens and leaders to appeal to him to run for mayor. With regrets, he declined the honor.

Personal Inventory: Learn More About Yourself

If you doubt that you have the right stuff to become a highly credible speaker, we urge you to take a personal inventory. Find the answers to these three questions: (1) What are my experiences? (2) What are my achievements? (3) What are my skills and traits?

What are my experiences? An experience that seems routine to you may be a new experience for your listeners. Answer the following questions to help yourself identify those special experiences that make you unique.

- Where have I lived or worked (in another town, city, state, country)?
- What kinds of jobs or duties have I had (unusual, technical, dangerous, satisfying, interesting, unique)?
- What special events have I attended (legendary concerts, historic sporting events, special holiday celebrations, famous political marches, renowned speeches)?
- What experiences have had a great impact on my life (meeting a famous person, childbirth, the illness or death of a friend or family member, involvement in a dangerous situation, physical disability, drug or alcohol abuse, a religious conversion, a visit to a foreign country, combat experience, learning from a great teacher)?

Something as simple as living or working in a different state can add a dimension to your personality. Many audiences enjoy hearing stories about places they've never been and the kinds of people they rarely meet. You can use personal experiences in examples, stories, definitions, and analogies. Personal information can add character and interest to you and to your presentation.

What are my achievements? You don't have to land on the moon to achieve something important. What seems like an everyday accomplishment to you may be an impressive achievement to your listeners. The following questions may help you to identify those achievements that make you unique.

- What can I do that most people cannot (play the cello, manage a swimming pool, reconstruct a computer, write a song or a short story, raise money for charities, decorate cakes, train a horse, design clothing, speak Turkish)?
- What awards or contests have I won (a scholarship, a prize in an art show, an award for public service, a sporting championship, a cooking contest, a TV or radio quiz, the lottery)?
- What are my special hobbies or interests (mountain climbing, collecting autographs, playing the stock market, doing crossword puzzles, studying Buddhism, following a musical group or singer)?

What are my skills and traits? Once you have answered questions about your experiences and achievements, you can begin to uncover dozens of your skills and traits. You may not recognize some of your special skills and personality traits because you have been using them for so long. Go back to the list of your experiences and achievements and think about the skills that you have used as well as the personality traits that have surfaced. For example:

- If you have won a sporting event, what qualities helped you to succeed (hard work, discipline, leadership, good sportsmanship, ability to learn the rules, accepting a coach's harsh criticism, analyzing the opponent, working well with team members, being competitive)?
- If you have organized a trip to a concert with a group of friends, what did you have to do to make it happen (coordinate schedules; research concert dates, times, and ticket prices; order or wait in line to buy tickets; collect money for tickets while remaining cheerful, helpful, enthusiastic, polite, and patient)?

You have unique qualities that can help enhance your credibility as a speaker. Take the opportunity of giving a presentation to use and display your experiences, accomplishments, skills, and traits.

introduction—and your entire presentation—to enhance your credibility by presenting your credentials during the presentation and by demonstrating a thorough understanding of your topic.[8] If you're an expert, find a way to tell the audience: "In my thirty years of college teaching..." "When I was honored by the Chamber of Commerce..." In none of these cases would you be exaggerating or boasting. Rather, you would be explaining how and why you know what you're talking about.

Every person has unique skills, experiences, outlooks, and drives. A presentation that emerges from those unique qualities reflects well on the person who gives it and enhances that speaker's credibility.

Ethos and Ethics

A discussion about speaker credibility would not be complete without giving attention to the relationship between ethos and ethics. The words *ethos* and *ethics* are very similar. Both come from the Greek word meaning "character." And as we indicated in our discussion of character as a component of credibility, the apparent "goodness" of a speaker is very important in determining whether that speaker will be believed by an audience. **Ethos,** Aristotle's term for speaker credibility, and *ethics,* however, are not the same thing. What makes them different is their sources.

Remember that the audience determines a speaker's credibility (*ethos*). A speaker's *ethics,* on the other hand, are personal. They are the speaker's beliefs about what is right or wrong, moral or immoral, good or bad. **Ethics** are a set of personal principles of right conduct, a personal system of moral values.[9] Only you can determine how ethical you are.

The National Communication Association's *Credo for Ethical Communication* in Chapter 1 provides a summary of personal belief statements about what it means to be

Two former ecstasy users—residents of a rehabilitation center—testify on drug abuse before the Senate Government Affairs Committee in Washington, D.C. How credible is the testimony of these speakers?

Figure 6.4

Let Someone Else Introduce You

One of the best ways to strengthen your credibility is to have someone introduce you to the audience. The introducer usually tells the audience something about the speaker's background, experiences, achievements, and skills—qualities and factors that demonstrate character, competence, and charisma. A good, well-delivered introduction can motivate an audience to listen to you. Like the first few moments of your own presentation, such an introduction can focus audience attention and interest, preview your topic area, establish an appropriate mood, and put *you* squarely into the presentation. In short, it can help you to achieve your purpose.

If the person who will be introducing you asks for information, don't be shy. Provide a list of your accomplishments. You can even write out what you would like the person to say, selecting those items most relevant to your purpose and audience. If you have the opportunity to craft one, a custom-made introduction can be an invaluable tool in creating an atmosphere that lets your character, competence, and charisma shine.

an ethical communicator. Each of the principles in this credo should be applied to how you communicate—whether you're talking to one person or to an audience of one thousand listeners. For example, the ethics credo states, "We advocate truthfulness, accuracy, honesty, and reason as essential to the integrity of communication." If you want to be a credible speaker, it is your responsibility to be truthful, accurate, honest, and reasonable when you prepare and deliver a presentation.

A very ethical speaker, however, may have low ethos because the audience perceives the speaker as uninformed, aloof, or boring or because the audience has no advance knowledge of the speaker's good reputation. Likewise, a speaker may be highly credible with one audience and yet be judged unethical by other observers on other occasions. Richard Johannesen, who studies communication ethics, uses Adolf Hitler to illustrate this point. Today, we assess Hitler as an unethical person and an unethical communicator, yet many of his contemporary Germans seemed to grant him a very high ethos level.[10] Because audiences will hold you accountable for what you say, ethical communication is *your* obligation.

Roger Ailes, a television producer and political media adviser, wrote a book titled *You Are the Message: Secrets of the Master Communicators.* His title sums up a lot of the research on speaker credibility. As Ailes says:

Real World Real Speakers

Create a Credible Impression

Gary Reynolds, a manager for Amoco, told us about a successful presentation he made at a retirement dinner. Note how he enhanced his own credibility in front of an audience that knew him and his level of expertise very well. As he tells it, "I memorized a substantial [number] of facts and figures in an area that was widely known by the attendees and honoree but about which I had no knowledge. The area was of great interest to the honoree, and everyone else in the audience knew how ignorant I was about it. But because I spouted a myriad of facts and delivered my presentation without notes the honoree hugely appreciated the presentation, and my peers were humorously amazed."

Mr. Reynolds understood that his audience would be judging him *and* his message. He went to great lengths to ensure that he was respected for the effort that he had made (character), that he knew what he was talking about (competence), and that his delivery would help him to appear energetic and confident (charisma). Mr. Reynolds spent a great deal of time and effort creating an impressive and believable presentation.

> *When you communicate ..., it's not just the words you choose to send the other person that make up the message. You're also sending signals of what kind of person* you *are—by your eyes, your facial expression, your body movement, your vocal pitch, tone, volume, and intensity, your commitment to your message, your sense of humor, and many other factors. The [audience] is bombarded with symbols and signals from you. Everything you do in relation to other people causes them to make judgments about what you stand for and what your message is.... Unless you identify yourself as a walking, talking message, you miss that critical point.*[11]

In other words, the total *you* affects every aspect of your presentation and how your audience feels about you and your message. Your success as a speaker is directly affected by your ethos and ethics. Your presence *does* make a difference.

Good Speeches by Good Speakers

We like to think of an ethical speaker as a good person who speaks well. Becoming a good speaker involves more than making decisions about your purpose, the audience, or your organizational pattern. A good speaker is also someone who is committed to being an ethical speaker and makes presentations that are true, fair, and beneficial to all.

A presentation can have significant and long-lasting effects on an audience. Like any tool, it can be applied with skill to achieve a useful purpose, or it can be used to damage and destroy. Although a hammer can be used to build a home, it also can be used to punch holes in a wall. One unethical presentation can affect the way an audience sees you in all future encounters. Thus, we believe that a good speaker must ask and answer important ethical questions at every point in the speechmaking process. Ethical decision-making is more than a means of improving speaker credibility; it is a moral obligation of every good speaker.

ETHICAL DECISION-MAKING FOCUSES ON

Purpose
Audience
Logistics
Content
Organization
Performance

Ethical Decisions About Purpose

Who will benefit if you achieve your purpose—you, your audience, or you *and* your audience? If your public and private purposes conflict or undermine each other, you may be headed for an unethical decision. Unfortunately, audiences can be and are deceived by speakers who appear to be honest but whose private purposes are selfish and even harmful to their audiences. When Reverend Jim Bakker asked millions of TV viewers for contributions to support his religious work, he used their good-faith money to build a large personal financial empire. There was a conflict between his public and private purposes.

If your stated public purpose is to tell people to "join the Handy-Dandy Health Spa because it has the best equipment and trainers," but your private purpose is to get a fifty-dollar bonus for every member you recruit, you are standing on shaky ethical ground. If the spa does not have the best equipment and trainers, your need for fifty dollars should be weighed against your audience's right to know the truth. If you would be ashamed or embarrassed to reveal your private purpose to an audience, you should question the honesty and fairness of your public purpose. There's nothing wrong with having a private purpose such as wanting to get an A on your presentation or impressing the boss with your speechmaking success. On the other hand, there *is* something wrong when achieving your private purpose means deceiving your audience.

FAQ: Should I Imitate a Speaker Whom I Admire?

There's nothing wrong with using a good speaker as a model. But don't get carried away. Don't try to mimic your idol. Only James Earl Jones can or should sound like James Earl Jones. Don't be too attached to beliefs you may have about what a "good" speaker looks and sounds like. It's much easier and more comfortable to let the real *you* come through. Say what you have to say, and trust your instincts.

Peggy Noonan, who was President Reagan's speechwriter, goes even further when she offers this advice: "Don't imitate the high oratory of past presidents and generals. Say it the way you'd say it if you were speaking, with concentration and respect, to a friend. Your own style will emerge with time as you write and speak. . . . And while it is good to be inspired by these speeches [by famous leaders], . . . it is not good to be daunted by them, to think, 'This isn't as good as Kennedy's inaugural [so] I might as well throw in the towel.'"[1]

What matters is that you sound like yourself, not like some famous actor, past president, or orator. Being an ethical speaker means being true to who you are and how you normally communicate.

1. Peggy Noonan, *Simply Speaking: How to Communicate Your Ideas with Style, Substance, and Clarity* (New York: HarperCollins, 1998), pp. 205 and 47. Copyright © 1998 by Peggy Noonan. Reprinted by permission of HarperCollins Publishers, Inc.

Ethical Decisions About the Audience

Are you being fair to your audience? Are you using the information that you have gathered about audience members to help or to harm them? The more you know about your listeners, the easier it is to tell them what they

Real World Real Speakers

Speechcraft or Stagecraft?

By delivering his "I Have a Dream" speech in front of the Lincoln Memorial, Martin Luther King Jr. linked himself and his message to the president who signed the Emancipation Proclamation. By campaigning at a company that manufactures American flags in 1988, presidential candidate George Bush Sr. linked himself and his candidacy to the symbols connected with the flag—patriotism and American values. When President Clinton criticized powerful drug companies for pursuing "profits at the expense of our children," he did so during a visit to a local health clinic where children got free immunization shots. George W. Bush's "Top Gun" landing on the aircraft carrier Abraham Lincoln preceded his declaration that major combat had ended in Iraq. How did these speakers use the place and the occasion at which they were speaking to help them achieve their purposes? To what extent did these speakers succeed in enhancing their credibility and effectiveness by choosing where they were speaking? What did their decisions reveal about their character?

want to hear. However, telling an audience what they want to hear may not be the same as telling them what they *need* to hear. It may be difficult to convince audience members who want "no new taxes" that more money is needed for education and job training. Simultaneously promising "no new taxes" and a reduction of government waste to pay for education and public services can earn a politician votes but may not serve the public good.

Market researchers and political pollsters can tell their clients what an audience wants. A good speaker has the ethical responsibility to weigh what an audience wants to hear against what is truthful, fair, and beneficial. A good speaker also has the responsibility not to pander to audience wishes. You would rightly question the character of a politician who tells an audience of teachers and parents that education is her first priority and then tells a group of builders and bankers that tax breaks for developers come first. Changing your message as you move from group to group may demonstrate good audience analysis and adaptation, but it is unethical if the messages conflict with one another.

Ethical Decisions About Logistics

At first, where and when you speak may seem to have nothing to do with ethical decision-making. But just as decisions about your purpose and your audience can be used to manipulate or even to trick listeners, decisions about logistics can also be used unethically.

Time limits can be used as an excuse to withhold important information: "If time allowed, I could explain this in more detail, but trust me. . . ." An ethical speaker might say, "Because I have limited time, I've prepared a handout of well-respected sources that support my position. . . ." Uncomfortable physical conditions can also be used as an excuse for quick and uncritical decisions: "We've tried to get the air conditioner working, but since we can't, let's cut off debate and vote so we can get out of here." An ethical speaker might say, "I know it's hot, but considering how important this issue is, let's keep talking to ensure that we make a responsible decision." Good speakers should consider how their decisions about logistics and occasion may affect their messages and the audience's beliefs about their credibility.

Ethical Decisions About Content

You face many ethical choices as you research, select, and use supporting material in your presentation. As described in Chapter 8, the ethical speaker is responsible for ensuring the validity of all ideas and information used in a presentation. You must identify and qualify your sources. You should know whether the information is recent, complete, consistent, and relevant. You should be sure that statistics are valid. And you must not plagiarize. Ethical speakers never, ever represent someone else's words or ideas as their own.

Ethical speakers learn as much as they can about their topics. They recognize that most controversial issues have good people and good arguments on both sides. Ethical speakers also demonstrate respect for those who disagree with them. By making ethical decisions about content, you ensure that your presentation will be forthright and fair.

Ethical Decisions About Organization

As Chapter 9, "Organization," and Chapter 10, "Organizational Tools," explain, good organization requires answering two basic questions: What should I include? and How should I organize my content? These may not seem like ethical issues, but deciding to leave out information can be as unethical and unfair as including false information. Should you add valid information that does not support your purpose? Should you include opponents' arguments that could damage your case? Should you present only one side of an argument when the other side is reasonable and well supported? Should you use emotional examples to cover up your lack of valid statistics? Unfortunately, there are no simple answers to these questions. As you will see in Chapter 19, "Understanding Persuasion," and in Chapter 20, "Developing Persuasive Presentations," acknowledging the other side of an argument can enhance your credibility by demonstrating your awareness of other points of view. Emotional examples can be powerful forms of supporting material as long as they complement other types of valid supporting material.

Deciding what to include and what to leave out of your presentation directly affects your credibility. While determining how to organize a presentation, an ethical speaker tries to be truthful and fair when deciding what to include and how to organize that material.

Ethical Decisions About Performance

Although the chapters on performance and delivery are yet to come, it's not too early to say a few words about ethical performance. The good speaker uses his or her performance to communicate, not to distract the audience from the truth. A highly emotional performance can be more convincing than sharing the most up-to-date and valid statistical information. If the emotions are real, they are appropriate. However, when an emotional response is inappropriate, it's unethical to fake emotions or to incite them in your audience.

Even a speaker's appearance can deceive an audience. A speaker could dress in poor-quality, threadbare clothing as part of a plea for money. A speaker can fake weakness or illness to gain sympathy. A phony accent can make a speaker appear to be a very different person. A good speaker uses an honest communication style and avoids acting out a false role.

The Good Audience

Throughout this chapter, we have emphasized the importance of being an ethical speaker. We've also seen how your success as an ethical speaker depends on the relationship between you and your audience. After all, it's the audience that either does or does not regard you as competent, charismatic, and of good character.

The ethical speaker has the responsibility of being honest, fair, and concerned about the audience, but audiences have important ethical responsibilities, too. Good audiences are good listeners. They listen for ideas and information with open minds. They withhold evaluation until they are sure that they understand what a speaker is saying. Good audiences are active listeners—they listen to understand, to empathize, to analyze, and to appreciate. They think critically about a speaker's message. However, not all audience members are "good" at these skills. Many don't or won't listen because they have decided, even before the presentation begins, that they don't like the message or the speaker. In Chapter 19, a major section is devoted to adapting to an audience that is unwilling to listen or hostile to your ideas.

Your audience is more likely to appreciate and listen to you if they think you have character, competence, and charisma. Although competence and charisma are important characteristics of a good (effective) speaker, character determines whether you are seen as a good (ethical) speaker. The audience has the final say, though, and also has an ethical responsibility to do unto the speaker as they would have the speaker do unto them. An open-minded, unprejudiced audience is essential in order for a genuine transaction to occur between speakers and listeners.

Summary

▶ What factors determine whether the audience will perceive me as a good speaker?

The most important factors affecting the believability of a speaker are character, competence, and charisma.

▶ How can I enhance my credibility as a speaker?

Three ways in which you can enhance your credibility are to take a personal inventory of your experiences, achievements, skills, and traits; to be well prepared; and to "toot your own horn."

▶ How does my character influence the success of a presentation?

Speaker credibility (ethos) can be the most important factor in determining whether you achieve the purpose of your presentation.

▶ How can I ensure that I am treating my audience fairly and ethically?

Good speakers make ethical decisions about all aspects of a presentation, including its purpose, audience, logistics, content, organization, and performance.

▶ What can audience members do to ensure that they are treating a speaker fairly and ethically?

Audience members should use effective listening and critical thinking skills when evaluating a speaker and his or her message.

Presentation Principles in Action

The NCA Ethics Credo Applied

Directions: Review the preamble and principles of the National Communication Association's "Credo for Ethical Communication" in Chapter 1. The following table lists each of the Credo's nine principles of ethical communication with an example that demonstrates its application to the college classroom. Consider each principle and its corresponding example. Then supply a second example that demonstrates your understanding of each principle as it applies to presentation speaking. The example can be personal, hypothetical, or taken from current events or history.

NCA Credo for Ethical Communication

Ethical Principles	Examples
1. Truthfulness, accuracy, honesty, and reason are essential for ethical communication.	• Students should accurately quote and cite the sources of information in their papers and presentations. •
2. Freedom of expression, diversity of perspective, and tolerance of dissent are fundamental to a civil society.	• Instructors should encourage the free expression of ideas in the classroom, particularly when they differ from those of the instructor and majority of class members. •
3. Ethical communicators understand and respect others before evaluating and responding to their messages.	• Students should strive to understand unfamiliar or controversial beliefs and values before making judgments about them. •
4. Access to communication resources and opportunities are necessary to fulfill human potential and contribute to the well-being of families, communities, and society.	• All students should have access to and training in the use of up-to-date computers and electronic communication. •
5. Ethical communicators promote climates of caring and mutual understanding that respect the unique needs and characteristics of individual communicators.	• Instructors should relate to students on an individual basis in order to consider their individual needs and characteristics. •
6. Ethical communicators condemn communication that degrades individuals and humanity through distortion, intimidation, coercion, and violence and through the expression of intolerance and hatred.	• Statements that disparage or stereotype others should not be tolerated in the classroom. •

Ethical Principles	Examples
7. Ethical communicators express their personal convictions in pursuit of fairness and justice.	• Instructors should encourage students to express well-informed political and personal beliefs in public settings. •
8. Ethical communicators share information, opinions, and feelings when facing significant choices while also respecting privacy and confidentiality.	• Instructors should keep students informed about their progress privately and confidentially. •
9. Ethical communicators accept responsibility for the short- and long-term consequences of their own communication and expect the same of others.	• Students who are penalized for plagiarism, cheating, or classroom disruption should accept the consequences of their actions. •

Key Terms

character 130
charisma 132
competence 130
ethics 137
ethos 137
immediacy 132
speaker credibility 129

Notes

1 Lane Cooper, *The Rhetoric of Aristotle* (New York: Appleton-Century-Crofts, 1932), pp. 8–9.

2 Dan O'Hair, Gustav W. Friedrich, and Linda Dixon Shaver, *Strategic Communication in Business and the Professions,* 3rd ed. (Boston: Houghton Mifflin, 1998), p. 498.

3 *The American Heritage Dictionary of the English Language,* 4th ed. (Boston: Houghton Mifflin, 2000), p. 427. Copyright © 2000 by Houghton Mifflin Company. Reproduced by permission from *The American Heritage Dictionary of the English Language, Fourth Edition.*

4 Malcolm Kushner, *Successful Presentations for Dummies* (Foster City, CA: IDG Books Worldwide, 1997), p. 21.

5 The earliest and most respected source describing the components of a speaker's credibility is Aristotle's *Rhetoric.* As translated by Lane Cooper (New York: Appleton-Century-Crofts, 1932, p. 92), Aristotle identified "intelligence, character, and good will" as "three things that gain our belief." Aristotle's observations have been verified and expanded. In addition to those qualities identified by Aristotle, researchers have added variables such as objectivity, trustworthiness, coorientation, dynamism, composure, likability, and extroversion. Research has consolidated these qualities into three well-accepted attributes: competence, character, and dynamism. We have used the term *charisma* in place of *dynamism.*

6 O'Hair et al., p. 498.

7 Kushner, p. 21.

8 Jo Sprague and Douglas Stuart, *The Speaker's Handbook,* 5th ed. (Fort Worth; Harcourt Brace, 2003), p. 257.

9 *The American Heritage Dictionary,* p. 611. Copyright © 2000 by Houghton Mifflin Company. Reproduced by permission from *The American Heritage Dictionary of the English Language, Fourth Edition.*

10 Richard L. Johannesen, *Ethics in Human Communication,* 2nd ed. (Prospect Heights, IL: Waveland, 1983), p. 109. Also see Richard L. Johannesen, *Ethics in Human Communication,* 4th ed. (Prospect Heights, IL: Waveland, 1996), pp. 10–11.

11 Roger Ailes with Jon Kraushnar, *You Are the Message: Secrets of the Master Communicators* (Homewood, IL: Dow Jones-Irwin, 1988), p. 20.

chapter seven

Logistics and Occasion

- What do I need to know about the place where I'll be speaking?
- What materials and equipment should I use?
- How long should I speak?
- Should I change my presentation for different occasions?
- What should I wear?

People make presentations for many different reasons at a variety of times and locations, in front of different sizes of audiences, using a wide range of media. Just as every audience is different every time you speak, so too are the occasion and the place where you speak. And just as you need to understand and adapt to your audience, you need to understand and adapt to the logistics and occasion of your presentation.

Why Place and Occasion Matter

As important as determining the purpose of your presentation, adapting to your audience, and enhancing your credibility are, it can be easy to overlook a critical step—analyzing and adapting to the occasion and the place where you will be speaking. You need to investigate and analyze important questions about where, when, how, why, and to whom you are speaking. Asking and answering these questions lets you tailor your presentation to the occasion and can minimize the risk that something unexpected or unwanted will get in the way of its effectiveness.

Why do filmmakers scout for the perfect location? Why do advance staff check and recheck every detail before a politician gives a speech? Why do couples spend so much time searching for the ideal wedding site? The answer is this: They want to make sure that the location not only matches the purpose and tone of the occasion but also adds value and impact to the event. They do their best to ensure that nothing goes wrong. Your presentation can benefit from the same kind of "advance" work.

Logistics

Whether you are speaking at a family barbecue or a formal banquet, a prayer meeting or a party, take a critical look at the place where you will be speaking *before* deciding what you want to say. Adapting to the place where you will be speaking requires critical thinking about logistics. The term **logistics** comes from the military and describes the strategic planning, arranging, and use of people, facilities, time, and materials relevant to your presentation.

Proper attention to the logistics of your presentation can help ensure its success. As management communication consultant Thomas Leech put it, "When presentations go smoothly, audience members scarcely notice anything about the mechanics; when something goes wrong, that may become the most dominant and lasting impression: *'I don't recall anything he said, but I'll never forget what he did.'*"[1] Although there is a great deal to consider about the logistics of every presentation, answering four general questions can make your presentation more effective.

LOGISTICS QUESTIONS

People: *Who* and how many people are in the audience?
Facilities: *Where* will I be speaking?
Time: *When* will I speak?
Materials: *How* will I display materials?

Who?

Answering the first question—Who is in my audience, and how many people will be there?—helps you determine how the size of your audience could or should affect the preparation and presentation of your message. If there are only fifteen people in your audience, you probably don't have to worry about whether they can hear you. If there are five thousand people in your audience, though, you should plan to use a microphone and will need to make sure it's supported by a good sound system. In Chapter 15, "Vocal Delivery," we include a Mini-Module on how to use a microphone most effectively.

Knowing the size of your audience also helps you figure out what kinds of presentation aids might work best. If there are five hundred people in the audience, projecting images onto a large screen would be more effective than using a small chart or demonstrating a detailed procedure. If you want to distribute handouts, passing them out is fine for a small audience. For a large audience, it would be better to leave a stack by the doorway for audience members to take as they enter or leave the room.

The size of an audience also affects the amount of eye contact you can establish, the extent to which you can ask an audience to interact with you, and the amount of time it takes an audience to get settled.

Where?

Make sure you know as much as you can about the facility in which you will be speaking. Will you speak in an auditorium, at a barbecue, in a classroom, or on television? Figure 7.1 lists some of the questions to consider when thinking about where you will be speaking.

A speaker talks to an emergency crew about a hazardous chemical cleanup. How would the logistics of this situation affect his presentation?

Figure 7.1 **Find Out About the Facilities**

- Will the presentation take place inside or outside?
- What are the size and shape of the room?
- Will the room be formal or informal (a ballroom, an auditorium, a locker room, a community center, an art gallery)?
- Does the room have good ventilation (heating, air conditioning, air circulation)?
- Will the audience sit or stand?
- If the audience is seated, what are the seating arrangements (rows, tables)?
- Will the audience fill the space or be scattered?
- What kind of lighting will there be?
- Will there be a speaker's platform (podium, lectern, table for materials or equipment)?
- Will there be a public-address system?
- Will there be any distracting sights or sounds?

With answers to the questions listed in Figure 7.1, you're ready to take the next step: figuring out how to adapt to the place where you will be speaking. You can make the logistics work *for* you rather than against you. If you have the opportunity to control the physical arrangements of the place where you will be speaking, take full advantage of it. Adjust the seating arrangements, lighting, and sound system to match your needs as a speaker.

Seating Arrangements. Ask in advance about the seating arrangements for your audience. Will they be seated in a theater-style auditorium, around a long conference table, or at round tables scattered throughout a seminar room? If, for example, an audience of one hundred people is expected in an auditorium that can seat eight hundred, you may want to request that the balcony or side sections be closed off so that the audience will be seated in front of you.

If you will be asking audience members to read handouts or to write, try to set up a seminar-style arrangement in which every listener has a desk arm or table to write on. If you intend to involve the audience in small-group discussions during or after the presentation, make sure the chairs are movable. However, if you have a lot of information to share in a short period of time and need your audience's undivided attention, straight rows of chairs or auditorium seating can reduce the interaction among audience members.

Seating arrangements can also affect where you stand and where you put any equipment or presentation aids. Something as basic as placing a screen in front of an audience can divert or focus the "spotlight" on the speaker.

In addition to learning as much as you can about the facility in which you will be speaking, check out the neighborhood in advance. Find out what's going on near the room or building where you will be speaking.

Several years ago, one of us was scheduled to conduct a communication seminar in a large hotel's conference center. The room was attractive and set up perfectly. What wasn't perfect were the events scheduled for the neighboring meeting rooms. Next door on the right, the Dallas Cheerleaders were holding auditions. In the room on the left, a beer distributor was sponsoring its annual sales celebration. Imagine the noise from a cheerleading audition combined with the non-stop traffic and uproar caused by beer distributors sneaking a peek at the hyped-up cheerleaders. Disaster awaited the seminar scheduled between these two boisterous events.

If possible, make sure that you know what's going on in adjacent rooms or nearby buildings so that you have time to find another room or place for your presentation if necessary. A college football game or community parade occurring a few blocks away may make it impossible for your audience to get to or park near the place where you will be speaking.

Lighting. In many speaking situations, you can't do much about lighting. Most lights can only be turned on or off, with no options in between. In more sophisticated

Positioning a Screen

If you intend to use a screen, don't place it in the center of the room. Don't angle it toward the audience on the left side of the room (from the audience's point of view), either. Instead, angle the screen toward the audience on the right side. Why? For one thing, you, not your presentation aids, should be the center of the audience's attention. If your screen is in the center of the room, you will be stuck on either the right or the left side of the room, unable to move across the room without walking in front of the screen. You will be "cornered." So why put it on the right side but not the left? There are two reasons, both having to do with the fact that people read English from left to right. When readers scan an image, they generally start at the left side and move toward the right. Consequently, your audience's attention will be drawn to a screen on the left rather than to you in the middle. What is more important, however, is that when you point at a screen on the left side, you will be forced to point to the ends of sentences, phrases, or words rather than to the beginnings. When the screen is placed on the right side (from the audience's perspective), you will be able to point to the beginnings of items—the points where your audience's eyes will naturally be focused. Figure 7.2 shows a floor plan for correct screen placement.

Figure 7.2 Placing the Screen

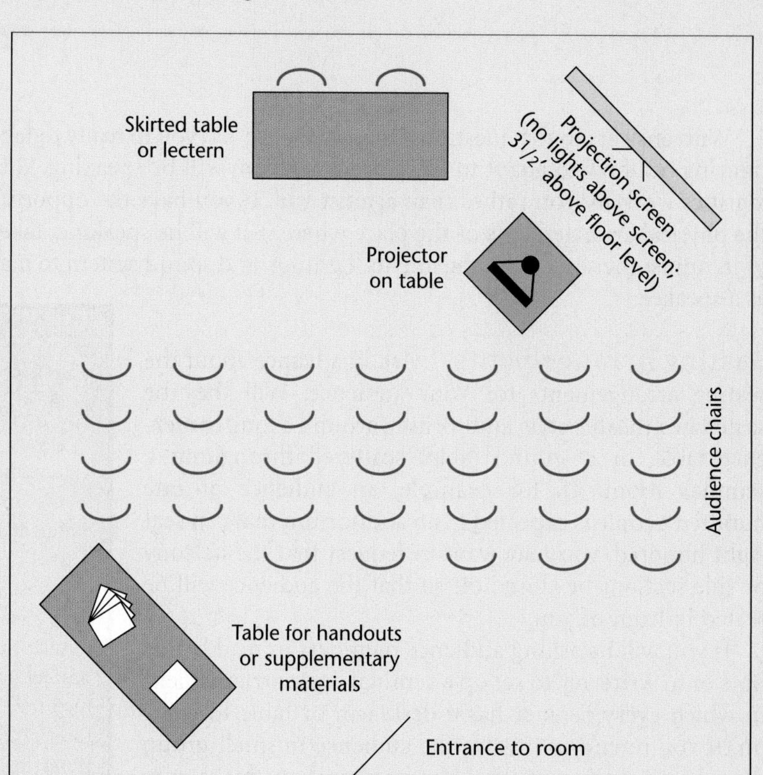

settings, you may be able to dim lights as required for a slide presentation or to use theater lights to spotlight your location.

Remember that electricity isn't the only source of light. Windows let in natural light during the day, so if there aren't any curtains, you may have trouble displaying projected images. If the room is too dark, you may have just as much difficulty keeping your audience's attention focused.

Sound. Different rooms have different acoustics. The term **acoustics** refers to the science of sound. Good acoustics help your voice carry and sound strong and natural. Poor acoustics may make your voice echo, may distort it as it bounces off multiple surfaces, and can create "dead zones" where you can barely be heard at all. Although you can rarely change a room's acoustics, you can adapt to them. If your voice will not carry to the far reaches of the audience, arrange for the use of a microphone or ask your audience to move closer to you.

If the room has a strange echo or distorts your voice, consider moving away from the podium and closer to your audience. Since you can't move the walls of the room, move yourself to a position that improves the carrying power and quality of your voice. If you're lucky, there may be a technician available to test your voice and to adjust the room's sound system *before* the audience arrives as well as *during* your presentation. Paying attention to the acoustics of a room can help you decide how to deliver your presentation and whether to arrange for a sound system support.

Don't Leave Them In the Dark

Although adjustable lighting has considerable advantages over simple on/off switches, use it carefully. If you are going to display videotapes, overhead transparencies, or computer-generated slides, turn the lights down, but don't leave your audience in the dark. You never want the lights any dimmer than they need to be. If the room is too dark, your audience may drift off to slumberland in the glow of your beautiful slides. If you intend to turn off your overhead projector when you're not displaying a slide, remember that the room will become even darker without that light source. Another problem can arise if you dim the lights sufficiently to let everyone see your slides or overheads. The room may become too dark for you to read your notes.

Obviously, you need to find a middle ground—partially dimming the lights might be one solution, but getting a lectern with a light would be better. The more you know about the lighting system in a room, the better you can plan how to speak and how to use your presentation aids.

When?

When will you be speaking—in the morning, during a busy workday, before a ceremony, or after a meal? Are you scheduled to speak for five minutes or for an hour? Asking questions about the time and duration is essential to planning a successful presentation. After all, if you've prepared an hour's worth of material and then discover that you have only ten minutes to speak, what do you cut? Figure 7.3 lists some questions concerning when you will be speaking.

Your answers to the questions in Figure 7.3 may require that you make major adjustments to your presentation. Say you're scheduled to speak at 8 A.M. Because your audience may not be fully awake, adjust your presentation so that it's crisp and clear as well as kind and gentle to help them ease into the day. However, if you're scheduled for a 4:30 P.M. presentation, your audience may be very tired after a long day's work. If that's the case, plan on using a more energetic speaking style to perk up your audience. And if you have to speak to an audience after a five-course banquet, you may find that a short or humorous approach is the only way to compete with their desire for an after-dinner nap. Speaking before or after a dinner or social event can put you in a difficult spot. You must gain your audience's attention and interest right from the start to counter the distraction of what came before your presentation or what's going to happen after it.

Of all the questions to consider about when you will speak, perhaps the most important and, unfortunately, the most ignored one is how long you are *scheduled* to speak. Make sure that you know how much time you've been given and adjust your

- At what hour will I be speaking?
- For how long am I scheduled to speak?
- How long do I want to speak?
- Where am I in the order of speakers?
- What comes before or after my presentation (other speakers, lunch, entertainment, cocktails, questions and answers)?
- Is there anything significant about the date or time of my presentation (birthday, holiday, anniversary)?

Figure 7.3

Ask About Time and Duration

FAQ: What If I Need More Time to Say Something Important?

Although we often give advice about staying within a time limit, many speakers dismiss our warning. "But I have something really important to say, and I *have* to talk longer!" they exclaim. What these speakers fail to understand is that just because *they* believe that their message is important or interesting, this doesn't mean that it's important or interesting to the audience. Part of your responsibility as a speaker is to spark that interest and focus the listeners' attention.

If you often exceed your time limit, try this exercise. Imagine that you've just been told that you have to give your presentation in half the time you were promised. Which sections or subsections of your presentation would you cut? Ask yourself whether anyone would miss what you've cut. Ask yourself whether you can still achieve your purpose without the material you've cut. Now, take another look at your presentation. You may discover that the shortened version is crisper and more focused. Don't add back what you've cut unless the material is absolutely essential. Do your best to stay within the time limit you've been given. Doing so demonstrates respect for your audience, and they will appreciate your self-discipline and kind consideration.

Here's a logistics strategy we recommend for speakers who are worried about time limits. Prepare *two* presentations. One is the well-prepared presentation you want to give that also meets the announced time limit. The second presentation is equally well prepared but is 25 percent shorter. By having two presentations, you know exactly what you will say if you have to cut the length of your comments. You may even find that using the shorter version may be the best choice regardless of the amount of time you're allowed to speak because you will have worked so hard to capture and share the essence of your message.

presentation accordingly. Unless you're a famous celebrity or an extraordinary speaker, most audiences will become impatient if you exceed the time limit. Whether you're scheduled for five minutes or for an hour, never add more than 10 percent to your allotted time. Better yet, aim for 10 percent less!

Plan your presentation so that it fits well within your time limit. Time yourself, keeping in mind that real presentations often take longer than the one you have practiced. Put a watch right next to you when you speak. Ask someone to give you a signal when it's time to begin your conclusion. And when that signal comes, don't ignore it, even if it means skipping major sections of your presentation. Your audience gave you their time; don't take more than you've been given.

Common sense and an alert eye on the audience can help you adapt to timing issues as they arise. If you're the third speaker on a panel, and the first two have spoken for so long that they've used up most of your time, don't be stubborn and also speak too long. Be honest and fair with your audience. If they're scheduled to be somewhere else in fifteen minutes, tell them you will shorten your presentation to accommodate them and do just that. If, on the other hand, an audience doesn't want to let you go and keeps asking for more, give it to them. Use your common sense. Watch and analyze your audience's feedback. If they're squirming in their seats, checking their watches, or beginning to slip out of the room, cut to your conclusion. If you use your time wisely, you will be using it well.

How?

Once you've considered the audience size as well as the setting and the time of your presentation, you're ready to make decisions about the materials and equipment you will need and how best to integrate them into your presentation. Materials and equipment include lecterns, projection screens, and microphones. You'll also have to make decisions about the clothes you will wear (which we discuss a little later in this chapter) or arranging for technical assistance.

Figure 7.4 lists some questions to consider when deciding what materials and equipment you'll need for a presentation.

Knowing where you will be speaking also enables you to make decisions about the materials and equipment you may need and how to adapt accordingly. Although you may have a great set of slides to show, there may not be a screen or a convenient place to put or to plug in a slide projector or computer. Although you may like using a lectern, some places cannot provide one. It's best to know in advance what is—and just as important, what isn't—available at your presentation's location so that you can consider those factors during the planning stages.

When planning how to use equipment and presentation aids, make the necessary physical arrangements and then prepare yourself to make do with less in the unlikely event that your arrangements fall through. It is possible to be heard by an audience of one thousand people without a microphone. It is possible to describe a procedure if your demonstration video malfunctions. If a media technician doesn't show up, you should know how to run the equipment on your own. But why make it difficult for yourself when careful logistical planning and preparation can provide what you need?

Assuming that everything you need is in the room in which you will be speaking, make sure that each piece of equipment is working. Turn on every machine. Boot up your computer and click through a few slides (and don't forget to backtrack to the beginning of your presentation). Make sure that you know how to operate any unfamiliar equipment. Don't forget the small things, and don't assume they will be where you expect them to be on the day of your presentation. Are there pens, pointers, cords, and even extra batteries and bulbs available? A good friend of ours recently made an important training presentation. He carefully prepared his overheads, arrived long before his scheduled speaking time, made sure that the overhead projector was plugged in, and then, after he was introduced, discovered that there was no screen on which to project his slides!

Once you've checked out the equipment and the room from your vantage point, walk to the back of the room and see what the most distant members of your audience will be seeing. Do you need to angle the flip charts or the screen in a particular direction? Is the projector in focus? Are the chairs arranged in a way that will allow everybody to see you and the screen clearly? Are there any barriers that will block the view of some audience members?

All of these preparatory steps take time. In the same way that bands do a sound check before a concert begins, experienced speakers always check the room and equipment *before* their presentations and never assume that everything is in working order.

FAQ Should I Use a Lectern?

Before answering this question, we want to clarify two terms that are frequently but mistakenly used interchangeably: *lectern* and *podium*. A **lectern** is "a stand that serves as a support for the notes or books of a speaker," whereas a **podium** is "an elevated platform, as for an orchestra conductor or a public speaker."[1] You approach and stand on a podium. You put your notes on (and may be tempted to clutch the edges of) a lectern. If the lectern is small, and you know you will need a glass of water or a place to put a display object, find a table to put next to the lectern.

Generally, you will need a lectern if your presentation is formal or to be made before a large audience. For more informal talks and presentations to small groups, you may have nothing more than an assigned place to stand or sit. Chapter 16, "Physical Delivery," provides advice on how to take advantage of a lectern and how to avoid using it as a crutch or a barrier between yourself and your audience.

1. *The American Heritage Dictionary of the English Language*, 4th ed. (Boston: Houghton Mifflin, 2000), pp. 998 and 1354. ©2000 by Houghton-Mifflin Co. Used by permission from *The American Heritage Dictionary of the English Language*, 4th ed.

- What equipment, if any, do I need to be seen and/or heard?
- What equipment, if any, do I need for my presentation aids to be seen?
- What equipment *don't* I need?
- Is there a lectern (adjustable, with a built-in light or microphone, big enough to hold my notes)?
- Are there any special arrangements that I need to make (requests for water, a timer, special lighting, or a media technician?

Figure 7.4

Do an Equipment Check

Occasion

When either of us is asked to make a presentation, our first questions do not focus on whether the audience expects a PowerPoint presentation or whether we'll have a lectern for our notes. Instead, we usually ask, "What's the occasion?" Once we know *why* an audience will be assembled, we can ask better questions and make better decisions about logistics.

OCCASION QUESTIONS

Motive: Why is the audience assembled?

Speaker: Why are *you* speaking on this occasion?

Expectations: What is expected for this occasion?

Protocol: What is appropriate for this occasion?

When you're a student preparing a speaking assignment for a class, you don't have to worry much about the occasion or the setting of a presentation. You know where you will be speaking (the classroom), when you will be speaking (the date and time of the class), and how long you can speak. You also know what type of presentation your speaking assignment requires. Given that you're probably in the same room every time your class meets, you even know what materials and equipment you can use to enhance your presentation. You know the audience, the instructor's expectations, and the criteria that will be used to determine your success.

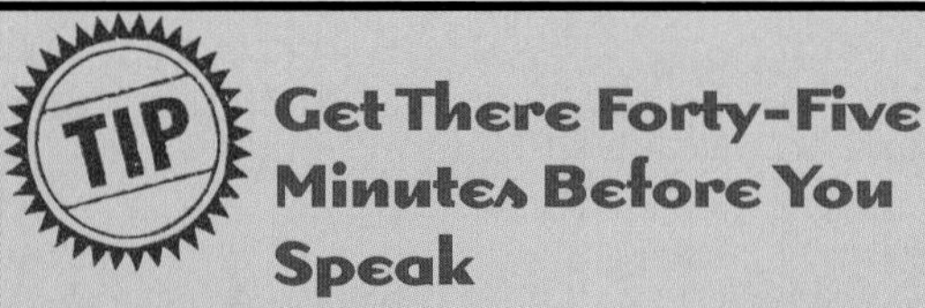

Even before it's time to speak, there is a lot you can do to make sure that your presentation is ready to go. Make sure that everything you need is in the room, that the equipment works, and that you know how to dim or brighten the lights as needed. Even if the staff responsible for preparing the room and providing equipment have "guaranteed" that everything will be there, you may be in for an unpleasant surprise. The overhead projector that you requested may not be there; a critical cord for the computer may be missing; the flip chart may only have three pieces of paper on it. Whenever you can, show up at least forty-five minutes before you have to speak, and check out the room. That gives you enough time to find equipment if something is missing or to make last-minute changes so that you can speak without your presentation aids.

Real-world speakers do not have the luxury afforded student speakers or seminar participants. Not only do speakers outside of the classroom have to spend time planning for the logistics of a presentation; they also must give serious consideration to the occasion of a presentation. When we use the term **occasion,** we mean the reason that an audience has assembled at a particular place and time. The occasion for a presentation can be as public and formal as witnessing the inauguration of a U.S. president or as routine as giving a brief status report at a staff meeting. Certainly, the logistics of these occasions differ, but so do the speaker's motivation, tone, and role. Whereas logistics ask about *who, where, when,* and *how,* occasion asks *what* and *why.*

Would you give the same presentation at a memorial service as at a pep rally? Of course not. Because each occasion dictates a very different type of presentation, considering the nature of the occasion is important. You must

President Bush declares the end of major combat in Iraq aboard the aircraft carrier USS Abraham Lincoln. Why was Bush both praised and criticized for speaking from this unique location?

take into account the nature and significance of the event as well as the circumstances that motivated the audience to attend the presentation.

What's the Occasion?

Every occasion exists for a reason. College classes or training seminars provide occasions during which student speakers can improve their ability to make effective presentations. The workplace presents numerous speaking occasions. One day, you may be given a few minutes with a group of senior managers to explain why you want to hire a new employee. On another day, you may be required to present a quarterly report to your department. The agendas for these staff meetings dictate the kinds of presentations you may be required or may need to make. On a larger scale, you may choose to attend a public forum in which you are given three minutes to explain your position on a particular issue. Or you may ask or be invited to speak at the memorial service of a family member, a good friend, or a colleague. In all of these cases, the occasion has as much to do with how you prepare and present your remarks as it does with your purpose and audience.

If you were to tell someone about having to make a presentation, and she then asked, "What's the occasion?" what would you say? Whether you answer, "Oh, it's just an assignment I have to do for my speech class" or "I've been asked to testify on behalf of legislation protecting disabled adults," make sure that you understand the reason for the event and what kind of presentation best suits the occasion.

Why Me?

Is your audience assembled because they want to hear *you* or because they are interested in your topic? Are you speaking because you were assigned the task or because you were invited to speak? In some cases, a group may want you to speak because they have heard that you're an expert on a topic they're interested in. Sometimes, you may be chosen to speak because you've won an award, because you're well known, or just because you're available and won't say *no* when asked. For example, if you're the chair of an awards committee, or you know the award recipient, you may be asked to present an award at a banquet. If you're a marketing expert, you may be asked to address the sales force to broaden their understanding of your company's marketing goals and product development efforts.

Speakers are not picked randomly. They are chosen because they are the most knowledgeable, most able, or most appropriate persons to make presentations. So when you're chosen to make a presentation, always ask yourself, "Why have *I* been invited to speak to *this* audience in *this* place and on *this* occasion?"

What Does the Audience Expect?

The occasion of a presentation also reveals something about your audience's expectations. Are they assembled for a mandatory training session, to be entertained, to kill time, or to learn a new skill or principle? Successful speaking involves adapting to the audience's expectations. (Chapter 5, "Audience Analysis and Adaptation," discusses this in detail.) If you've been asked to give a toast at a wedding, don't bemoan the high divorce rate. If asked to talk about methods of lowering taxes, don't spend your time campaigning for a political candidate.

The occasion also raises audience expectations about the way a presentation will be delivered. Business audiences often expect speakers to pepper their presentations with sophisticated, computer-generated graphics and visual aids. Audiences at political events have become accustomed to the sound bite on television and expect to hear short, crisp phrases in live public speeches, too. Think about what style of presentation *you* would expect to hear at a particular occasion. Then try to match your speaking style to those expectations.

Utah Jazz forward Karl Malone proudly points to the logo for his new charity, the Karl Malone Foundation for Kids, during a press conference. As founder of the charity, he was the most appropriate speaker for this occasion, and the audience expected to hear his comments.

Real World Real Speakers

Take Charge of the Situation

Logistics play a critical role in many presentations, particularly when the place and occasion speak louder than words. Such was the case when President George W. Bush spoke at Ground Zero on September 14, 2001. Bush's short, ten-sentence speech was given amidst the smoking remains of the Twin Towers in New York City. Like many official visitors, he toured the site and talked with the exhausted, grimy firefighters, police, medical personnel, and volunteers. When he heard the crowd chanting, "USA!" he climbed to the top of a rubble pile, put his arm around a firefighter's shoulder, and spoke to the crowd through a bullhorn. The following analysis of the occasion and logistics helps to explain the success of Bush's short speech.[1]

Occasion

The speech was delivered only three days after the September 11, 2001, tragedy. Workers were still combing through the rubble twenty-four hours a day. Whereas Bush had already been criticized for being "missing in action" immediately following the tragedy, his impromptu Ground Zero speech was a fitting match for the occasion.

- *Why Bush?* Because he was president of the United States.
- *What does the audience expect?* The immediate audience wanted both comfort and toughness from the president. The larger viewing audience wanted to see a strong leader taking charge.
- *What's proper?* A respectful and emotionally charged speech.

Logistics

Bush's short speech also addressed the four logistical questions in a way that made his speech a powerful moment in the midst of a tragedy.

- *Who?* The immediate audience—firefighters, police, medical personnel, and volunteers—needed a short, rousing endorsement and tribute from the president. The large audience of television viewers saw an intense and powerful president taking charge of an embattled scene.
- *Where?* Not only was the president speaking at Ground Zero; he was also speaking from the top of a rubble pile with his arm around a firefighter. The picture was dynamic and compelling.
- *When?* The president spoke only three days after the September 11 disaster. Workers were still putting out fires and searching the site for survivors. The president's compassionate and encouraging words gave his immediate and larger audience comfort and hope.
- *How?* When the audience shouted that they couldn't hear him, the president grabbed a bullhorn and climbed to a higher position so that his audience could both see and hear him. No sophisticated sound equipment, no manuscript, no lectern, no special lighting—he spoke impromptu. Anything other than an impromptu speech would have seemed inappropriate and insincere, given the occasion. Bush was not the awkward public speaker audience members had begun to dread but instead was an energetic leader taking charge of a desperate situation.

1. A transcript of this speech appears in the Appendix.

What's Proper?

Events or gatherings often have specific rules of protocol. **Protocol** is a term that refers to the expected format of a ceremony or the etiquette observed at a particular type of event. In diplomatic circles, the rules of protocol are written down and taken very seriously—addressing everything from where to seat a dignitary at dinner to how to address a member of the monarchy. In other circumstances, the "rules" of protocol are less formal or are part of a tradition. Thus, we expect a certain tone at a graduation ceremony and a very different tone at a political rally. At a funeral, a eulogy may be touching or funny, but it's almost always very respectful and short.

When inquiring about the protocol of an occasion, you are asking what customs or rules may require special adaptation on your part. Understanding customs or rules of delivery style, timing, language, or dress can help you plan what you want to say, organize your message, choose the most appropriate delivery style, and even select what to wear for your presentation.

How do you determine the protocol of an occasion? Unless you've been to a similar event, you should ask those who have invited you to speak or those who have attended before. We naturally ask such questions when we are invited to a wedding, an awards banquet, or a fundraising event. Is the wedding formal? Is the awards banquet a black-tie event? Is the fundraiser a casual daytime event or a Saturday-evening extravaganza? For example, if you have never been to a christening, a bar mitzvah, or the breaking of a fast during the month of Ramadan, you would probably ask several questions about how to behave—such as when to arrive, what to wear, and whether you should bring a gift. Before you begin researching, writing, or rehearsing a presentation, make sure that you know about any customs or "rules" that may apply.

Dress and Appearance

Deciding how to dress for a presentation requires an understanding of the occasion: why an audience is assembled, why you are the speaker, what the audience expects for the occasion, and what the "rules" of protocol are. In short, your clothes should fit the occasion.

In a college classroom or training seminar, a few speakers may carefully select what they will wear on the days when they are scheduled to speak, particularly if the speaker's outfit is part of the presentation. For example, demonstrating your martial arts skills is much easier if you're wearing your karate outfit and your hard-earned black belt. Wearing your uniform may add emphasis to your presentation about joining the National Guard. Yet for the most part, students and trainees do not give a lot of thought to what they will wear when they speak in class. Outside of the classroom, however, speakers devote significant attention to what they wear and to the impression their appearance will create for their audience.

We are often asked, "What should I wear when I make a presentation?" Our answer is always this: Dress to create a positive impression. Long before an audience hears what you say, they will see you, so wear something that will match the purpose and tone of your presentation. What you wear can affect your audience's initial and lasting impressions of you and your message.

Dress for Success

John T. Molloy, the well-known author of *New Dress for Success*, emphasizes how important it is for your clothes to fit the occasion. Given that the first and often most important statement a speaker makes to an audience is a nonverbal one, Molloy urges presenters to dress to fit audience expectations. He contends that if you dress inappropriately for an audience, you will lose them for the first few minutes. Rather than focusing on you and your message, they will be criticizing or be distracted by what you are wearing.[2]

Your appearance is part of your presentation, and like everything else, it benefits from planning. If your clothes don't match your purpose or the occasion, you can send a mixed message. For instance, how would you react to a student giving a graphic and emotional speech about child abuse while wearing a T-shirt with a large yellow "happy" face on the front? Would you believe a speaker talking about "get-rich-quick" investment opportunities who showed up in a wrinkled, poorly tailored suit? In both cases, the message and the outfit conflict. Your clothing should help you achieve your purpose, not distract you or your audience from it.

Wardrobe Guidelines

The clothes you wear for a presentation are more important in some settings than in others. A well-tailored suit may be perfect for an important corporate presentation but inappropriate for a company picnic, a talk on bass fishing, or a cooking class. What you normally wear to work will usually be perfectly appropriate for a presentation in a staff meeting. However, the clothes you usually wear to class may be too casual or inappropriate for an important, graded presentation. Your clothes don't have to be expensive, and they don't have to make a fashion statement. What matters most is that they reflect your purpose, fit your audience and the occasion, and are appropriate and comfortable for you.[3]

Be Comfortable. Rarely will either of us wear brand-new clothes or shoes when we are scheduled to make a presentation. We know that if your shoes hurt, you won't move about naturally, and you'll be preoccupied with pain. If you discover when you stand up to speak that your new clothes have become creased and crumpled, you may find yourself worrying about them rather than concentrating on your presentation. An outfit that looks and feels good while you're standing in front of a store's three-way mirror may be constricting and unattractive when you are sitting on a stage or are at a podium. If you perspire a great deal, wear cool fabrics and colors that mask wet stains. Presentations are stressful enough as it is, so don't wear something that adds another source of discomfort.[4]

In addition to avoiding new, untested outfits, choose clothing that fits loosely. If your clothes are tight, you will have trouble walking, gesturing, and sitting. Loose clothes allow you to point up, bend down, and reach without embarrassment or worry. However, don't confuse loose clothes with sloppy clothes. Your clothes should be comfortable *and* flattering.

An experienced speaker who asked to remain anonymous told us the following story: "Once, at the last minute, I was asked to sit on a large stage with several other speakers who were scheduled to speak to an audience of about five hundred people. When I walked on stage, I knew I had worn the wrong dress. It was a buttons-all-the-way-down-the-front dress, and it was short. Sitting on the stage created an immediate problem. In a seated position, the dress rode up several inches above my knees, and the button at the hem of the dress opened a slit another two inches. I had to keep one hand on the base of the dress so it wouldn't be more revealing. Before I knew it, my name was being called to speak. I found myself feeling unusually flustered and agitated as I walked to the lectern. It should have been an easy-to-give presentation. Instead, my concern about a dress prevented me from being fully prepared and fully composed."

Be Appropriate. You can use what you've learned about your audience to select an outfit that fits the style and customs of the occasion. For example, one of us once addressed a group of academic administrators in Singapore, an Asian city-state only a few miles from the equator. The year-round temperature and humidity were near 90. Some buildings lacked air conditioning. Wearing a tailored suit would have been

How does this guide's clothing affect his presentation about a festival at Mission San Juan Capistrano in California?

stifling. Cotton-blend pants and skirts with loose-fitting shirts and blouses were perfectly acceptable and appropriate.

Generally, it's a good idea to wear standard business clothing for a presentation. For men, that means a dark business suit or a conservative sports coat with an appropriately matched pair of pants. In more casual settings, a light-colored sports jacket is fine. You can always remove your jacket and tie if that's necessary.

Women have a tougher time when it comes to choosing a presentation wardrobe. In formal settings, a two-piece suit is always appropriate. Solid colors, high necklines, and comfortable high heels are safe bets. Tailored suits and dresses are more authoritative and professional than frills and cute prints. There's nothing wrong with wearing a pantsuit or slacks and a blouse if you've determined beforehand that such outfits are going to be predominant in your audience.

Real World Real Speakers

Look Like What You Do

Dan Alexander is Neiman Marcus's top salesman. He works at the Tyson's II Galleria store in northern Virginia. A native Washingtonian, he has been in the garment business for forty years. In 1998, he was more than the company's top African American salesman; he was the number one associate, ringing up two million dollars in sales. In addition to working with customers, he has conducted seminars on the art of sales. How does he dress for such occasions? On the day he was interviewed for the business section of the *Washington Post*,[1] he wore a three-button navy suit with working buttonholes on the sleeves. His white shirt had French cuffs and a point collar. He wore a deep blue silk tie with a subdued diamond pattern, and a pale blue handkerchief tucked discreetly into the breast pocket of his jacket. His trousers were cuffed and broke gently over a pair of black Oxfords, which were brilliantly shined but not to a flashy military sheen. "You want to look like what you do," he said.

1. Robin Givhan, "Secrets of a Supersalesman," *Washington Post*, 6 December 1998, pp. H1 and H12.

One of our colleagues recently moved from a faculty position at a large East Coast college to a communication department at a small college in a ranching and oil-rich section of Texas. During her first year at the new college, one of her students showed up for his first major speech wearing a nice cowboy hat, pressed jeans, a dress shirt, and polished Western boots. She started to dock him points for his attire but quickly realized that what he wore was perfectly appropriate and professional for many business settings in that part of the country. The overall impression mattered, not specific "dress-for-success" rules.

If there is a rule of thumb about selecting appropriate clothing, it is this: Be as conservatively dressed as the key members of your audience. If you know in advance that everyone will be wearing cowboy boots, exercise outfits, or fishing clothes, use your best judgment and consider joining them. Your wardrobe should enhance your presentation, not hurt it.

Be Yourself. Despite all of the advice on how to dress for a successful presentation, the objective is to look appropriate and professional—but not to look like a clone. If you look better in light colors and like to wear them, don't buy a dull, dark suit. But please understand that for many men, the classic dark suit is a "power garment" that helps establish authority, credibility, and likableness.[5]

At the same time, don't abandon a signature piece of clothing or accessory. Some of our most distinguished colleagues wouldn't look right without these unique items. Sam would not be Sam without his bow tie. Judith would look unusual in anything but bright colors and high heels. Ellen needs her dark eye glass frames. A special suit style, a set of complementary colors, a type of eyeglass frame, or a "signature" tie is not inappropriate if it is part of someone's unique personality. Being yourself means finding clothes and colors that fit *your* style, *your* body shape, and *your* coloring. Looking professional does not mean that you must copy the latest look in a fashion magazine. Find the outfit that enhances your presentation and your credibility.

When preparing for your presentation, give your clothes the kind of attention that supersalesman Dan Alexander does (see Real Word, Real Speakers). In fact, a salesperson and a speaker have a lot in common. Both have a purpose; both have an audience;

both adapt to the interests and needs of their listeners. Like the supersalesman at Neiman Marcus, a good speaker should look appropriate for the purpose, audience, and occasion of a presentation.

Grooming and Accessories

As important as clothing is to your appearance, so also is something even closer to you—your body. Hair that falls in your face and requires rearranging throughout a presentation will annoy you and your audience. If you have long hair, put it up or pull it away from your face for a tighter, tailored look. An unshaven face, unwashed hair, and smeared makeup have no place in most speaking settings. If you're wearing a suit or sports jacket, button one of the coat buttons when you stand to speak. Take things out of your pockets, whether they're pens in your shirt pocket or the change and keys in your pants pocket. Women should leave their purses with a friend or colleague.

If you wear makeup, it should look natural. As tempting as it may be to wear bright lipstick, heavy eye shadow, blush, and thick dark eyeliner around your eyes, resist the temptation. At the very least your makeup should be understated and carefully applied.

As is the case with your presentation wardrobe, there is a rule of thumb about grooming and accessories. Nothing on your body should draw attention to itself. If you wear bracelets, they shouldn't clang together. If your earrings dangle and reflect light, they could be distracting. If your tie displays a big pattern of cartoon characters, it may not be appropriate. Your presentation should be the center of an audience's attention. If something about your appearance could distract your listeners, fix it or leave it far from the lectern.

Although the way in which you dress can have a significant impact on your presentation, your message matters more. An expensive suit and perfect hair cannot camouflage a poorly prepared presentation.

Link Purpose, Audience, and Place

At this point in the preparation process, you should have identified your purpose (Chapter 4, "Purpose and Topic"), analyzed your audience (Chapter 5, "Audience Analysis and Adaptation"), and decided how you will adapt to the occasion and place where you will be speaking. All of these decisions should be made before you begin preparing the content of your presentation. At the same time, we urge you to be flexible. As you do your research, you may discover that your purpose will change due to audience expectations or the time limit you've been given. As you organize your content and plan your speaking strategies, you may find that you will need more presentation aids (or none) to make your point. If, as you practice, you discover that you are more comfortable using extensive notes, you may need to make sure that a lectern will be available at the front of the room.

Purpose, audience, logistics, and occasion are linked. Devoting attention and critical thinking to all four will, in the long run, save you time and help you develop and deliver a more effective presentation.

Summary

What do I need to know about the place where I'll be speaking?

You should know enough about the place's logistics to be able to plan for and adapt to the people, facilities, time allotted for, and materials relevant to your presentation.

What materials and equipment should I use?

Make sure that you know what materials and equipment will be available before you decide whether to use them in your presentation. Rather than being caught unaware, arrive far in advance to make sure that everything you need is present and in good working order.

How long should I speak?

Speak for as long as you are scheduled to speak. Be prepared to shorten your presentation if circumstances require doing so.

Should I change my presentation for different occasions?

Adapt your presentation to the nature of the occasion, the reason that you are the speaker, the expectations of the audience, and the protocol of the occasion.

What should I wear?

Your clothes should be comfortable, appropriate for the setting and occasion, and in a style that suits your personality and purpose.

Presentation Principles in Action

Dress For the Occasion

Directions: You can find a wealth of advice on how to dress for success in professional settings by searching both commercial bookstores and the World Wide Web. The following chart represents a distillation of such advice for both men and women. Think about the different professional settings and occasions at which *you* may be asked to speak either now or in the future. Then consider the kinds of clothing and accessories you would wear based on the principles discussed in this chapter: Be comfortable, be appropriate, and be yourself.

Depending on your gender, rate the items on the chart for men or women in terms of how well they represent how *you* would dress when addressing an audience in a professional setting: (5) I would *always* dress this way; (4) I would *often* dress this way; (3) I would *sometimes* dress this way; (2) I would *occasionally* dress this way; (1) I would *never* dress this way.

After completing your ratings, ask yourself whether you believe these recommendations are appropriate or too rigid. On what occasions or under what logistical circumstances would you break these rules?

Women: Dressing For a Presentation

WOMEN	Always	Often	Sometimes	Occasionally	Never
1. Conservative long-sleeved blouse (white is best, pastel is next best)	5	4	3	2	1
2. Minimal makeup	5	4	3	2	1
3. Neat, professional hairstyle	5	4	3	2	1
4. Conservative two-piece business suit (solid dark blue or gray, or muted pattern)	5	4	3	2	1
5. Polished shoes, low or moderate heels, conservative color	5	4	3	2	1
6. No visible body piercing beyond conservative pierced earrings	5	4	3	2	1
7. Conservative hosiery at or near skin color	5	4	3	2	1
8. Minimal perfume	5	4	3	2	1
9. Minimal jewelry	5	4	3	2	1
10. Only one set of earrings	5	4	3	2	1
11. Portfolio or briefcase rather than purse	5	4	3	2	1
12. Manicured nails in clear or conservative-colored polish	5	4	3	2	1

Men: Dressing For a Presentation

MEN	Always	Often	Sometimes	Occasionally	Never
1. Conservative long-sleeved shirt (white is best)	5	4	3	2	1
2. Silk tie with a conservative pattern	5	4	3	2	1
3. Professional watch, only a wedding ring and/or school ring	5	4	3	2	1
4. Conservative two-piece business suit (solid dark blue or gray, or muted pattern)	5	4	3	2	1
5. Matching belt and shoes	5	4	3	2	1
6. Dark, laced, polished shoes and black socks	5	4	3	2	1
7. No earrings or visible body piercing	5	4	3	2	1
8. Neat, professional hairstyle	5	4	3	2	1
9. Neatly trimmed mustaches and/or beards	5	4	3	2	1
10. Minimal cologne	5	4	3	2	1
11. Trimmed and clean finger nails.	5	4	3	2	1
12. Professional briefcase or portfolio	5	4	3	2	1

Source: A variety of sources was used to create these charts. See John T. Molloy, *New Dress for Success* (New York: Warner, 1988) as well as websites such as *www.jobsearch.about.com/library/howto/htdress.htm* and *www.worktree.com/tb/IN_dress.cfm.*

Key Terms

acoustics 150
lectern 153
logistics 147
occasion 154
podium 153
protocol 157

Notes

1 Thomas Leech, *How to Prepare, Stage, & Deliver Winning Presentations* (New York: AMACOM, 1993), p. 170.
2 John T. Molloy, *New Dress for Success* (New York: Warner, 1988), pp. 358–359.
3 Leech, pp. 220–222.
4 Leech, p. 220.
5 Molloy, p. 62

part three

Content and Organization

chapter eight

Supporting Material

- What forms of supporting material should I use?
- How can I tell if my supporting materials are valid?
- Can I use personal knowledge as support?
- How do I find good supporting material in a library?
- How do I conduct research online?
- How much credit should I give to the sources of my supporting material?

Imagine that you're at a party chatting about aerobic exercise with a person you've just met. This person says, "You really ought to give up step classes and take Tai Bo instead." You ask why, and all she can say is "Because it's great!" You think to yourself, "Why should I listen to her if she can't give a better reason than that?" Often, audiences find themselves in a similar situation: A presenter offers some new information or asks them to do something, and unless the speaker can back up the information or request, chances are the audience won't pay much attention.

A good presentation not only makes a point but also backs up that point with relevant, interesting, and accurate supporting material. As soon as you know the purpose of your presentation, you should begin collecting ideas and information that support it. This entire process can be as simple as spending a few hours thinking about your purpose or as all-encompassing as spending months doing research. In this chapter we look at different forms of supporting material and where and how to find them.

Support Your Ideas

Expert speakers are information specialists. They know their subjects well and can recite names, dates, statistics, stories, and sayings about their topics. Just as devoted baseball fans know their team's statistics, expert speakers know their subjects and can tailor their presentations to suit a variety of audiences, occasions, and purposes.

Most speakers aren't experts, though, and need to search for supporting material. **Supporting material** consists of ideas, opinions, and information that help to explain and/or advance a presentation's main ideas and purpose. Facts, opinions, statistics, and stories are just a few of the forms of supporting material speakers use in their presentations.

Types of Supporting Material

Information comes in many different forms. You will find definitions in dictionaries, background and historical information in encyclopedias, facts and figures online and in almanacs, true-life stories in magazines and on homepages, and editorial opinions in newspapers and online newsletters. The best presentations use a mix of supporting material; they don't rely on just one type. Why? Most audiences would find an unending list of statistics boring. They might find a speaker who tells story after story frustrating, particularly if there's no clear reason for his telling the stories. Variety is the spice of life, and different forms of information can give a presentation added life and vitality. Let's explore the options available to you and look at situations in which different types of supporting material work particularly well.

TYPES OF SUPPORTING MATERIAL

- Facts
- Statistics
- Testimony
- Definitions
- Analogies
- Descriptions
- Examples
- Stories

Facts. A **fact** is a verifiable observation, experience, or event known to be true. "*Chicago* won the 2002 Oscar for Best Picture" is a fact, but "*The Hours* should have won" is an opinion. Facts can be personal ("I went to the 2003 Kentucky Derby") or the official record of an event (the 2003 Kentucky Derby winner failed to capture the Triple Crown). They are usually short statements that can be proven true or false. Most presentations—regardless of their purposes—are supported to some extent by facts. Facts provide support by using something certain or knowable to demonstrate or prove something less well-known. Facts are most effective when the audience has no trouble accepting them as true. When an old-time TV detective asked for "just the facts, ma'am," he was looking for factual material to support his case. In the following example, a speaker links factual information about a fairly well-known disease to the recent appearance of a new form of it.

> *Hepatitis types A and B have been around and well known by doctors for many decades. But hepatitis C was not identified until quite recently—1989 to be exact.[1] And unlike the case with the A and B versions, very few hepatitis C victims survive.*

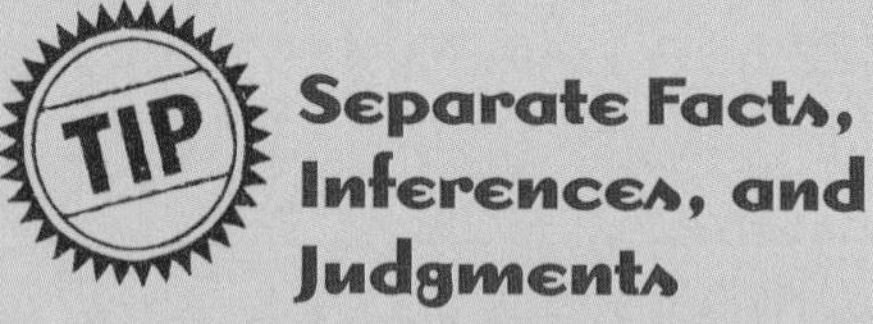

Separate Facts, Inferences, and Judgments

If you use facts as supporting material, make sure that they are really facts—not inferences or judgments. In Chapter 2, "Listening and Critical Thinking," we point out that whereas a fact is a statement that can be proven true or false through observation, an inference goes beyond the facts to reach a conclusion that may not be verifiable. Thus, a statement such as "Mia always turns her work in on time" can be a fact based on an instructor's records and observations. However, a claim such as "I'm sure Mia will continue to turn her work in on time" is an inference.

In addition to distinguishing between facts and inferences, be just as careful that you do not present personal judgments as facts or inferences. A **judgment** is a statement that expresses your opinion or makes an evaluation, as in "Mia is a responsible and reliable person."[1] Most presentations contain facts, inferences, and judgments. Facts provide the basis for reasonable inferences and sound judgments. If your inferences are based on proven facts, you can have a lot more confidence in the judgments you put forward in your presentation.

1. John Chaffee, with Christine McMahon and Barbara Stout, *Critical Thinking, Thoughtful Writing: A Rhetoric with Readings*, 2nd ed. (Boston: Houghton Mifflin, 2002), pp. 393–409.

Statistics. **Statistics** organize, summarize, and analyze numerical information that has been collected and measured. Statistics are also used to predict events ranging from economic trends to the winners of football games. Although many people equate statistics with facts, statistics are factual only if they have been collected and analyzed fairly. Even if all of your friends prefer chocolate to vanilla ice cream (a fact), you cannot conclude that 100 percent of the population prefers chocolate (a statistic). To draw conclusions about the ice cream flavors most people prefer, you would have to survey a larger and more representative group of people. In a presentation, statistics are effective support when you want to describe what a population is like as well as what a population likes. Note how the student speaker in the following excerpt uses statistics to bolster her point about geographic illiteracy.

> *The* Los Angeles Times *reported on a survey conducted by a California State University professor in which students were told to name and locate the leading trading partner with the United States. The students named Japan, but then none could find it. The leading trade partner to the United State is Canada, and only 29 percent of those students located Canada on a map.*

Testimony. **Testimony** refers to statements or opinions that someone has said or written. In advertising, testimony from celebrities associates a product with a famous person (if I buy X, I'll be like that person), while testimony from "real" people associates a product with someone "just like me." Testimony in a presentation works the same way and can add believability to your presentation. In Chapter 19, "Understanding Persuasion," we describe how celebrity endorsements work to persuade audiences.

You can support your presentation with testimony from books, speeches, plays, magazine articles, radio or television, courtroom testimony, interviews, or homepages. You can quote real people—politicians, scientists, celebrities, experts—living or from years gone by. Sometimes a quotation, whether it comes from the president of the United States or from Big Bird on *Sesame Street,* can make your point better than you can. In the following example, a student uses an expert's testimony to support her point.

> *My own childhood experiences may not be enough to convince you that something should be done to control media violence viewed by children. Instead, listen to the words of Dr. Joanne Cantor, a communication professor and author of the recent book* Mommy, I'm Scared: *"From my 15 years of research on mass media and children's fears, I am convinced that TV programs and movies are the number-one preventable cause of nightmares and anxieties in children."*[2]

Definitions. **Definitions** explain or clarify the meaning of a word, phrase, or concept. A definition can be as simple as explaining what *you* mean by a word or as detailed as an encyclopedia or unabridged dictionary definition. Use definitions when your presentation includes words or ideas that your audience may not know or may misunderstand. In the following excerpt, a speaker uses two very different definitions of the same term to talk about the musical form known as "the blues."

> *Not sure what the blues are? The* New Encyclopaedia Britannica *states that "as a musical style, the blues are characterized by expressive pitch inflections (blue notes), a three-line textual stanza of the form AAB, and a 12-measure form." Well, that's okay for some, but have you ever heard Muddy Waters sing "You Can't Lose What You Never Had"? The encyclopedia definition just doesn't cut it. That's why I like to use an old bluesman's definition: "The blues ain't nothin' but the facts of life."*

Presentation aids can enhance the impact of supporting materials by conveying ideas and information in memorable ways. For example, rather than trying to define or describe the blues, playing a Howlin' Wolf or Muddy Waters recording can accomplish the same objective. A piece of sheet music for a blues song would show exactly what a three-line stanza and a twelve-measure form look like. Not only can presentation aids help audiences remember the information in your presentation; they can also be an effective source of information on their own. We focus on presentation aids in Chapter 17, "Presentation Aids."

Analogies. **Analogies** identify similarities. In a sense, they compare definitions of one concept to another. Analogies can identify similarities in things that are alike—"If the traffic plan worked in San Diego, it will work in Seattle." Analogies also can identify similarities in things that are not really alike—"If a copilot must be qualified to fly a plane, a U.S. vice president should be qualified to govern the country." Analogies are a useful way of describing a complex process or relating a new concept to something the audience understands very well. Here's how Jesse Jackson, a masterful speaker, used an analogy to define the Rainbow Coalition, a political group committed to fostering diversity:

> *America is not like a blanket—one piece of unbroken cloth, the same color, the same texture, the same size. America is more like a quilt—many patches, many pieces, many colors, many sizes, all woven and held together by a common thread.*[3]

Descriptions. **Descriptions** help to create a mental image of a scene, a concept, an event, an object, or a person. They provide more details than definitions by offering causes, effects, historical background information, and characteristics. In the description that follows, a speaker expands the definition of the blues by describing the musical style's origins and essence.

> *The impact of the blues goes well beyond the Mississippi Delta and the urban blues of Chicago. The* New Grove Dictionary of Music and Musicians *describes the influence and importance of the blues as follows: "From obscure and largely undocumented rural, (African) American origins, it became the most extensively recorded of all folk music types.... Since the early 1960s blues has been the most important single influence on the development of Western popular music." Not bad credentials for a musical form that's too often called the devil's music.*

Examples. An **example** provides a reference to a specific case or instance in order to make an abstract idea more concrete. We've used examples throughout this book to clarify, emphasize, and reinforce our points. Examples can be brief descriptions or detailed stories. By choosing examples carefully, you can customize your presentation for a particular audience. The first example that follows supports a claim about the popularity of Muzak; the second contrasts the contributions of male and female blues singers.

> *No wonder Muzak has so many fans—fans like AT&T, IBM, and Xerox.*

> *Today most of us associate the blues with male performers—Muddy Waters, Howlin' Wolf, B. B. King, and Buddy Guy. In the 1920s, the blues stars were women—Ma Rainey, Bessie Smith, Victoria Spivey, and Alberta Hunter.*[4]

Stories. **Stories** are accounts or reports about something that has happened. Audiences often remember a good story, even when they can't remember much about a presentation. Stories should be interesting, but what's more important is that they reinforce your point. Almost nothing else has the impact of real stories about real people in the real world. Here, Vivian Hobbs, a former attorney who recently lost her fight to survive a crippling disability, used a personal story in the beginning of a commencement address about the triumph of human will:

> *I was in an automobile accident just after high school, which left me in a wheelchair. I was trying to deal with that, a new marriage, and other personal and financial problems, not the least of which was an uncertainty about what I could do—about the extent of my own potential.*[5]

In Chapter 13, "Generating Interest," we devote a major section to the value and the techniques of telling good stories during a presentation.

Vary Your Supporting Materials

Try to use at least three different forms of supporting materials in a presentation. To see why, consider the following selection from an article titled "The Shadow Epidemic," about hepatitis C, a form of liver disease. The article appeared in *The New Yorker* magazine and was written by Dr. Jerome Groopman, a cancer and immunology specialist.

> *Approximately four million Americans, nine million Europeans, and a hundred and seventy million people worldwide are infected with hepatitis C. In contrast, about a million Americans are thought to be HIV positive. Some 4 percent of people between the ages of thirty and fifty are believed to carry the virus; among black American men, it's 10 percent. Each year, there are an estimated thirty thousand new infections and ten thousand deaths. There is no broadly effective treatment, and if none is developed over the next decade, the death rate from hepatitis C could rise to thirty thousand a year—a mortality rate roughly equal to that of AIDS in 1996.*[6]

If you were to hear someone read the previous paragraph in a presentation, would you understand and remember most of the statistics? Would you be able to separate the statistics on hepatitis C from those on HIV infections? Certainly, the epidemic appears to be serious, but the long list of medical statistics makes the nature of the epidemic and its frightening outcome difficult to grasp. Don't misunderstand us—this is excellent and compelling information. But if you want to include Dr. Groopman's data about hepatitis C in a presentation, you should try to combine it with other types of supporting material such as examples, testimony from patients and other doctors, descriptions of the disease, and even the use of presentation aids to display and compare statistics.

Test Your Supporting Materials

Speakers use supporting materials to enhance their presentations and to demonstrate their depth of knowledge about their topics. However, information that's not accurate and up-to-date undermines this function. Test every piece of supporting material before adding it to your presentation. Is it the *best* information? Is it valid? **Valid** means that the ideas, opinions, and information are well founded, justified, and

TESTS OF SUPPORTING MATERIAL

1. **Is the source identified and credible?**
2. **Is the information recent?**
3. **Is the information consistent?**
4. **Is the information relevant?**
5. **Is the statistical information valid?**

true. Do 75 percent of American families recycle cans, bottles, or paper? Are the history and evolution of the blues really separate from those of jazz? Five questions can help you test your information to determine its validity.

Is the Source Identified and Credible? This is the first and most important question to ask when you're trying to determine your information's validity. Although you may not know what percentage of Americans recycle, there are sources that do know. References such as *The Information Please Almanac, The World Almanac,* or the *New York Times Almanac* have been in business for many years. Their continued success depends on their ability to collect and publish information that is true and up-to-date. Also, check newspapers. Their reputations depend on their ability to publish accurate information. There are, however, big differences among newspapers. The sensational and often bizarre *National Enquirer* may be fun to read, but the *Wall Street Journal* is more likely to contain reliable information.

Also, make sure that you use objective sources of information. A source can be **biased,** meaning that it states an opinion so slanted in one direction that it may not be objective or fair. As a researcher, you must be alert to potential bias. If the source has a strong opinion or will gain from your agreement, be cautious. For years, tobacco companies publicly denied that cigarette smoking was harmful, even though their own research told them otherwise. Now, we recognize that the tobacco companies' pronouncements were biased and untrue. What biases do you think special interest groups such as the National Rifle Association, Pro-Choice or Pro-Life groups, NORML

Columbine High School teacher Patty Nielson, seated next to Senate Minority Leader Tom Daschle, tells her story of surviving the fatal shooting incident at her school. Why is her story an effective way of supporting a plea to control guns and gun violence?

(National Organization to Reform Marijuana Laws), the AARP (the American Association of Retired Persons), and the Teamsters Union may have? The information that they publish could be misleading; the opinions may be unfounded. However, just because sources are biased doesn't necessarily mean they aren't telling the truth.

No matter where you get your information, you must be able to identify its source and determine whether that source is qualified and credible. If you're using an article, what magazine does it come from, and who wrote it? Always note your source as completely as possible, including the date of publication and page number. Is the author a recognized authority on the subject? Is the person a recognized expert, a first-hand observer, a scientist, or a respected journalist?

Is the Information Recent? Ask yourself this question if the information you're considering will be subject to change or if you will be using it to make claims about events or to predict outcomes. In these cases, you would probably be better off using magazine or newspaper articles and reliable Web sources rather than books. Health books written before 1985 won't have much to say about AIDS. Books written in the early 1990s on how to use a library will not contain much advice about the use of computerized index systems, the Internet, or CD-ROMs. But if your topic is philosophical, historical, or timeless, there is nothing better than using an old book to discover new information. When you are collecting and recording information, note the source's publication date. In this rapidly changing information age, your data can become old news in a matter of hours.

Is the Information Consistent? Check to ensure that the information you want to include reports facts and findings similar to other information on the same subject. Another way to look at this question is to ask whether the information makes sense. If every doctor and medical expert tells you that penicillin will *not* cure a cold, why believe a friend who recommends it as a treatment? If the evidence clearly shows that cigarette smoking is dangerous, the fact that your grandmother smoked two packs a day and lived to be eighty-five doesn't mean you should ignore the warnings.

At the same time, information that is different can be interesting and worth noting. If most reports indicate that cutting down on salt and animal fats will reduce cholesterol and high blood pressure, you may be suspicious of a study that says salt and fat intake are okay. Yet some studies that compared U.S. salt intake with that in other countries concluded that salt may not be as dangerous as once was thought. When a French study reported that drinking red wine dampens the dangerous effects of fat intake, liquor stores began providing free copies of the study to their wine-drinking customers. Despite such studies, however, it may be wiser to wait for more information before making a presentation that recommends abandoning a low salt/low fat diet and taking up a red wine diet.

Is the Information Relevant? Make sure that the information is related to your purpose and topic. Say you were speaking about the divorce rate of American marriages. Just because Elizabeth Taylor married eight times does not demonstrate that stable marriages are on the way out. As the U.S. Census Bureau knows, fifty million Americans marry and stay married to one person. If you're trying to persuade an audience that *Seinfeld*'s high TV ratings as a network program in the 1990s justify its selection as the best commentary on life in the last decade of the twentieth century, your evidence may be irrelevant to the millions of people who can't relate to the New York City lifestyle depicted on *Seinfeld.*

Is the Statistical Information Valid? Interpreting statistics is an art and a science. Most of you probably don't know how to use the sophisticated research methods required to produce valid statistical results. Instead, you have to rely on the numbers reported by others. The problem with choosing and using the best statistical information is that you may have no idea whether the research that produced the statistics is valid. For example, if 100 percent of the physics professors at one college are African American and 100 percent of the physics professors at a neighboring college are European American, you may wonder whether a charge of discrimination could be justified—until you learn that there is only one physics professor at each college.

Incorrect statistics can come from poorly designed research or from people who misinterpret the numbers. Statistics can be informative, dramatic, and convincing. They also can mislead, distort, and confuse. Use them carefully.

Research Strategies

You may have a general idea of which forms of supporting materials you want to use, but finding the specific pieces requires research. **Research** is a systematic search or investigation designed to find useful and appropriate supporting material. Even if you already know something about your topic area, good research can make you look and sound a lot better. For example, you may know that Americans watch a lot of television; research lets you know that the average American watches TV more than four hours a day.[7] Although everyone may know that communication skills are important for business success, research lets you know that many managers rank communication skills first in importance of all the skills needed to succeed in business.[8]

A good researcher with a good research strategy becomes an effective investigator who has a systematic plan for searching the available sources of information in the same way in which a detective searches for clues. The information you need is out there; you just have to find it. Investigative research involves knowing how to uncover valuable resources. That said, the research process starts with *you.*

You Are a Source

Yes, you! When speakers ask us whether they can use their personal experiences and knowledge as a form of support, we encourage them to do so. In fact, if you are an expert on a topic, have a unique background or life experience, or work in an unusual job or field, you may be the best source of ideas and information about it. A stamp collector, a carpenter, a musician, and a refugee from Kosovo or East Timor will all be able to share stories and information that can be new and interesting to an audience.

You can be a good source of ideas, even if you're not an expert. The reason that you are speaking, the experiences you have had, your ethnic or religious background, your job or hobby, or your strong beliefs and opinions are valuable sources of ideas as well as information. If you're going to make a presentation about drunk driving, you might want to describe an accident you witnessed or were involved in that was caused by a drunk driver. Note how this student used his own experiences as supporting material for his presentation:

Even though I'm a guy, I wanted to make a presentation about how to avoid rape. I admit that rape isn't something I thought about much—that is, I didn't think about it at all until last month, when my older sister called me in tears to tell me that she'd just narrowly escaped a sexual assault. Visions of a stranger trying to attack my sister in the dark of night flashed through my mind. But was I ever wrong—the attack took place at lunchtime, and the attacker was a man she'd been dating for a few weeks. Turns out that what little I thought I knew about rape was wrong!

We give, however, a word of caution about relying on yourself as a resource. If you use your own ideas and opinions, make sure that they are based on fact. You may believe that capital punishment deters criminals, yet your additional research may reveal that criminologists who have studied this question disagree. You may believe that colds are caused by working up a sweat in damp, cold weather; research may tell you that exposure to a virus is the cause of a cold, regardless of the weather. Although you may be an excellent source of ideas and information, you should also check some other sources to reinforce your views. That's where libraries and online research come in.

Libraries

Before leaping to the World Wide Web, we want to reinforce the value and techniques of doing library research. For those of you who may think that libraries are becoming obsolete, think again. From your local branch library to the Library of Congress, libraries contain valuable information you can't find anywhere else. Learn to use libraries to their fullest potential.

USING THE LIBRARY

- **Find the right library**
- **Get facts and figures from the reference collection**
- **Get recent material from periodicals and newspapers**
- **Get background and general information from books**

Find the Right Library. Not all libraries are alike, so before you start your library research, make sure you're in the right one! Your local public library may have everything you need if your topic and audience are general. You'll be able to find popular magazines, local and national newspapers, encyclopedias, and general interest books in most public libraries. In some large cities, the central branch of a public library can be as comprehensive as a college or university library.

A second type of library—college and university libraries—tends to be larger than most public libraries and holds vast collections of academic resources. Whereas a public library might have a few dozen books on music, a university with a strong music department will have in its library shelves books and recordings that deal with almost every form of music. Academic libraries subscribe to specialized journals covering topics from accounting to zoology in such great detail that these publications may be too technical for your needs.

A third kind of library, the special collections library, can be found at museums, professional schools, performing arts centers, corporations, government agencies, or nonprofit organizations. As the name implies, these libraries hold highly specialized collections of books, magazines, and special documents related to specific fields. If you need highly specialized information and cannot find it at a college library, contact a special library for permission to visit and conduct your research. Most public and college libraries have a directory that you can consult to find special collections libraries in your area.

A fourth type of library is much closer to home. In fact, it *is* your home. The books, magazine, and newspapers you have in your home may contain valuable supporting material. As soon as you have determined your purpose and topic, start looking for ideas and information right at home. You may find a vital piece of information in a newspaper or magazine article that you overlooked before selecting your topic. If your home has an encyclopedia, you can do some general reading to prepare yourself for your trip to a public, college, or special collections library. Some people have in their homes their own "special collections" built around interests, beliefs, and hobbies. Our friend Karla loves 1950s fashion magazines and probably has a better "collection" than most libraries. Our friend Sid loves to fish and has just about every magazine and guidebook on bass fishing that exists. And, as you might have guessed, one of us has an extensive collection of blues music and literature. For some information, there's no place like home.

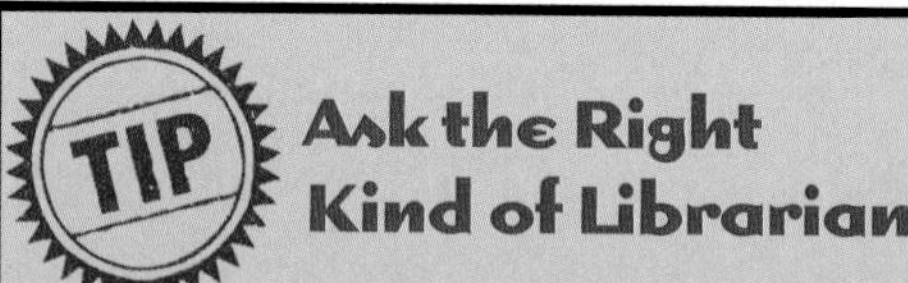

This Tip could begin and end with the following piece of advice: Ask a librarian for help. If you do, you will spend your research time more efficiently because you will be guided by a person qualified to help you find the information you need and to direct you to the best source for it. But make sure you ask the right kind of librarian. Not everyone who works in a library is a trained professional with a degree in library science. The person who checks out books may only be a clerk or a student intern.

Look for or ask to talk to a reference librarian—someone who helps library patrons find what they need. Be prepared to tell the librarian the purpose and topic of your presentation as well as to give a brief description of the audience and the place where you will be speaking. By providing the librarian with specific information, you will gain a partner who can help and direct you. Not only can librarians assist you with your research; they also can show you the best way to use their library. Rather than wander aimlessly through rows of shelving, you can ask a librarian to point you in the right direction and guide you through your search.

Get Facts and Figures from the Reference Collection. All libraries have a reference collection. Reference books are just what their name suggests—you refer to them, consult them, skim through them. They are not meant to be read in their entirety. Unfortunately, you cannot check them out of the library. Even so, they are one of the first places to look for supporting material.

Reference materials can give you a broad overview of a topic or very specific information. The information is there; it is your job to find it. Reference books and CD-ROMs are available on almost every subject. Figure 8.1 lists and describes some of the different types of references, many of which are also on CD-ROM, that you can find in most libraries.

Figure 8.1 gives you only a brief description of some of the many resources in a library's reference collection. Encyclopedias and almanacs are most useful for finding general background information and specific facts. A popular reference book like *Bartlett's Familiar Quotations* can give you access to thousands of famous passages, phrases, and proverbs to use as testimony in your presentation. But remember that the information you gather from a library's reference collection is only the raw material for your talk. A presentation is much more than a list of famous quotations and interesting facts.

Get Recent Material from Periodicals and Newspapers. Whereas reference collections contain factual and background information, periodicals and

Figure 8.1 Reference Collection Resources

Encyclopedias	Contain information on almost all subjects; they are a good place to start your research. (*Encyclopedia Americana, International Encyclopedia of Social Studies*)
Yearbooks	Summarize the events of one year; they can cover many subjects or specialize in one field of study. (*Britannica Book of the Year, Yearbook of Science and the Future*)
Dictionaries	Provide information about words—their spelling, meaning, pronunciation, origin, and use. (*The American Heritage Dictionary of the English Language, Anchor Bible Dictionary, Roget's Thesaurus*)
Almanacs and Abstracts	Collect up-to-date facts and statistical information. (*Statistical Abstract of the United States, The Information Please Almanac*)
Handbooks and Manuals	Provide broad, factual information on one subject. (*Occupational Outlook Handbook, Chilton's Auto Repair Manual*)
Atlases	Contain a collection of maps, some with statistical charts and special maps showing population, climate, and so forth. (*The Time Atlas of the World, Atlas of the Oceans*)
Biographical References	Provide brief articles or background information about noteworthy and famous people. (*Who's Who in America, Contemporary Authors*)

newspapers provide recent, up-to-date information. Periodicals include scholarly journals as well as the most current and popular magazines. Newspapers can give you the local, national, and international news of the day along with feature articles, commentary, and editorial opinions.

In order to find articles on specific subjects in periodicals, you should use the library's periodical index. Today, almost all such indexes can be found on CD-ROM. Depending on your choice of library, you may find different systems in use. Computerized indexes can contain references to hundreds of magazines as well as listings for national newspapers.

One of the richest sources of current information is the newspaper. Here, too, there are special indexes. There is a *New York Times Index*, a *Washington Post Index*, a *National Newspaper Index*, and the *NewsBank*. Again, depending on the library, you may find that all of these indexes are on CD-ROM. Many large libraries also subscribe to newspaper and news organization websites on which you can find daily updates of news stories and feature articles. Look up *www.nytimes.com* or *www.cnn.com* to see for yourself.

Get Background and General Information from Books. It may surprise you to find books listed at the end of a list of library resources. But there is no point in searching for books if you're in the wrong library or haven't checked the available references and periodicals. Choose books carefully and avoid checking out a pile of them that may not contain what you need.

Books are marvelous resources, particularly when you need background information on a general topic or a thorough understanding of a writer's theory or research. There are, however, drawbacks to using books as your *only* source of information. Books can become dated very quickly. Between the time an author writes a book and the time you check it out of the library, several years can pass.

A second drawback to using books as a sole resource is the amount of time it can take to find the piece of information you need. You don't have to read an entire book while researching a presentation. Just read those parts that relate to your topic. Review the table of contents at the front of the book and the index at the back to focus your search on a few relevant sections or pages. Does this mean that books should not be read cover-to-cover? Of course not. Good books are always a delight to read. But if you have a presentation to research and can't take the time to read an entire book, don't feel guilty about skipping large sections in order to find the supporting materials you need.

Computerized, online library catalogs have made the process of selecting books much easier. Now you can use key words in a computer search to find library books related to your topic. In most libraries you can print a list of book titles and their authors, publishers, dates, call numbers, and library locations. The printout can also include whether the books are available, on loan, or in the reference collection. Libraries, like computers, have become user friendly.

At this point you may be feeling overwhelmed. It may seem as though there are so many places to look for information that you could spend your whole life researching and run out of time to prepare your presentation. But that is exactly why it's important to use the library systematically. Match the type of information you're seeking with the appropriate kind of source material. Efficient and productive research will turn up materials uniquely suited to your presentation's purpose, topic, audience, and occasion.

With the advent of the Internet and the extraordinary reach of the World Wide Web, some speakers have abandoned libraries. Don't join the exodus. Libraries are still gold mines of information in which, if you are a skilled researcher, you can find most of the supporting materials you need for a presentation. At the same time, the World Wide Web is a rich source for finding information on almost any conceivable topic. Use both—you'll double your chances of finding the best supporting material for your presentation.

TIP Differentiate between Your Primary and Secondary Sources

When conducting research and deciding which supporting materials to use, consider whether you need or are using primary or secondary sources of information. A **primary source** is the document, testimony, or publication in which information first appeared. For example, a journal article that contains the results of an author's original research would be a primary source. A magazine or newspaper that reports on the original research or writing done by someone else is a secondary source. **Secondary sources** report, repeat, or summarize information from one or more other sources. Look carefully at secondary sources of information to determine, if possible, the primary source. Publications like *Newsweek*, *USA Today*, and *Parade Magazine* rarely conduct their own research. As secondary sources, they publish information they have obtained from primary sources.

Electronic and Online Research

Most of the resources available in libraries are also available online. The Internet puts the world at your fingertips. We do not have the space in this book to teach you how to use the Internet—and besides, it changes so quickly that we would surely be guilty of providing out-of-date information. So rather than describe how to get information from the Web, we will instead concentrate on some advantages and disadvantages of online research.

Advantages. The advantages of searching the World Wide Web for supporting materials are apparent to anyone who has tried. For example, when we were looking for up-to-date information on the issue of plagiarism from online sources, we went online and found what we needed in minutes.

You will find thousands of databases, personal webpages, publications, research, and visuals online.[9] Fortunately, there are a number of online search services that provide indexes and access to all this specialized information. General directories such as the *Internet Public Library* (*www.ipl.org*) at the University of Michigan or *The Library of Congress* (*www.lcweb.loc.gov*) and popular search engine directories often provide directories of selected sites related to specific topics.

Most of you are familiar with one or more **search engines** such as Google, Yahoo! and MSN Search. These Web "catalogs" help you find what you need by matching key words to websites that include those terms. Most popular search engines can be used in two ways: Type in a term or click on one of many indexed topics that have proved popular. Of course, unless you carefully select your key terms, you can end up with thousands of sites that have little to do with your topic.

In addition to basic search engines, **meta search engines** (sometimes called metacrawlers) don't search the Web themselves to build listings. Instead, they tap several basic search engines all at once. The results are then blended together into one page.[10] Like the search engines they explore, meta search engines come and go. As we write this chapter, some of the most popular meta search engines are Metacrawler, WebCrawler, and Excite as well as strangely named sites such as Dogpile, Ithaki, and Ixquick. By the time this textbook has been published, there may be many more sophisticated search engines and meta search engines that are even easier to use and more efficient at targeting the information you need. For a list of the best current meta search engines, go to our publisher's website at *www.college.hmco.com/.*

Why Did I Get A Recipe for Bean Dip When I Was Looking for the L. L. Bean Catalog?

There are millions and millions of websites out there. Finding the ones that meet your research needs can be a mind-boggling challenge. At first you may be tempted to engage a search engine in pursuit of a single word. Single-word searches will give you thousands of sites, most of which will be totally useless. A better idea is to do a what is called **Boolean search** to target the research material you need.*

- Use *AND* (or, in some cases, a + sign) if you want *both* words to appear in a document: blues AND Chicago.
- Use *OR* if only one of the words must appear in a document: blues OR zydeco.
- Use *NOT* (or in some cases a – sign) in front of words that must *not* appear in a document: blues NOT zydeco.
- Use quotation marks to specify a multiword phrase: "rhythm and blues," "devil's music," "jump blues."
- Use an asterisk as a substitute for letters that might vary: "juke*joint," "jook*joint."
- Use parentheses to group a series of possible terms and combine it with another term: (blues OR zydeco) AND "recording companies."

*There are many sources of information describing how to use Boolean operators with search engines or in computerized library indexes. Named after the ninteenth-century mathematician George Boole, Boolean operators provide a way of narrowing your search and reducing the number of "hits" you get. Try entering "Boolean operators" or "Boolean + operators" on any major search engine, and you'll find several thousand webpages giving you everything from simple to highly complex explanations of Boolean operators.

Disadvantages. Despite the enormous benefits of electronic research, there are significant disadvantages. The first problem is that the sources on the Internet do not cover all possible kinds of information (at least they don't today, but who knows what the future will bring?). If you want the latest news or very current information, using the Internet may be your best bet. But if you're looking for commentary on a classic novel, specialized research reports on an academic topic, or a reliable explanation of a political issue or historical movement, Internet sources may not be comprehensive or objective enough to meet your research needs.

A second disadvantage to using the Internet for research is that it can be difficult to test the validity of the information you find. Some trustworthy websites include those of major newspapers and magazines, professional associations, government agencies, libraries, legitimate media outlets, and well-known experts. Unfortunately, there are also highly biased sources. Because no one can possibly screen everything on the Internet for accuracy, it can be difficult to separate reliable from unreliable sources. Both of us have listened to student presentations in which all of the information was taken from highly questionable sources found on the Internet. Using less-than-credible Web sources can jeopardize the believability of an entire presentation. William Miller, president of the Association of College and Research Libraries, notes, "Much of

Interviewing for Information

Print and online sources are excellent for some kinds of information, but sometimes asking an expert can give you material you won't get any other way. Once you know the purpose and topic of your presentation, start looking for someone who can tell you more about it—a professor, a police officer, a lawyer, a store manager, a chef—and see if you can schedule an interview with the person. Call or write to set up an appointment with someone you want to interview several days or weeks before you would like to meet with him or her. Indicate what you would like to discuss and how long you expect the interview to last. Setting up an appointment in advance demonstrates your respect for the interviewee and gives you time to prepare.

As with any presentation (and yes, an interview *is* a kind of presentation), careful planning is the key to success. Ask yourself these questions:

- *Why am I conducting this interview?* Narrow the focus of your information-gathering interview by pinpointing what you want or need to know that you cannot find some other way.
- *Whom am I interviewing?* The more you know about the person whom you are going to interview, the more prepared you will be. Make sure that you know your interviewee's area of expertise and job functions. Think about your interviewee as a one-person audience and apply the techniques discussed in Chapter 5, "Audience Analysis and Adaptation," to gather background information.
- *What do I want or need to know?* You will need to do some background research before your interview. Find out about the organization for which that person works. The more you know about your topic before the interview, the easier it will be to understand and appreciate the interviewee's comments.
- *What questions should I ask and in what order?* No matter whom you are interviewing, come prepared with a series of questions. Begin with a general question such as "What interests or abilities led you to this job?" Then, move on to specific questions that will give you detailed information. What you learn in the first few minutes can tell you which of your specific questions to use. You can ask for lists of achievements, most difficult problems, or suggestions for change. However, don't interview to get information you've already found through research. Use the interview to learn something new.
- *How can I get the interview off to a good start?* Treat your interview as an important event. Show up at the appointed time appropriately dressed. Have your questions typed on clean paper. At the beginning of the interview, remind your interviewee why you need his or her information and advice. This can take the form of a thank-you—"Thanks so much for taking twenty minutes out of your day to talk with me about your company's commitment to community service. I know you're the driving force behind it, and I'm looking forward to hearing about what got you started." Demonstrating what you know about the topic and why you want to interview this person shows that you are well prepared and professional.
- *How do I keep the interview running smoothly?* Your behavior during the interview should be as professional as your dress and your level of preparation and planning. When you speak, make sure that your voice is clear and easy to hear. Establish eye contact with the person whom you are interviewing throughout the course of the interview. Keep track of the time, dropping a few of your questions if you're running overtime. And remember that it's okay to smile, gesture, lean forward, take notes, and even frown if it's appropriate. Your engaged, animated responses will keep the interview moving.
- *Do I need to follow up?* When your interview is over, there's one more step to remember. Send a thank-you e-mail or note. Call with a follow-up question that gives you a chance to personally thank your interviewee. Not only will you be doing the right thing and making a good impression, but you will also be ensuring your ability to return to your interviewee for more information.

Interviewing is as much an art as a skill. One of the keys to conducting a successful interview is good listening. Good listening will tell you if your questions have been answered before you ask them. Good listening can also give you new insights that can lead to new questions. Listen carefully and modify your questions according to the answers you hear. If all goes well, all your questions will be answered as you have a fascinating discussion with an interesting and cooperative expert.

Why not bookmark several meta search engines? For example Altavista, www.altavista.com, provides a very large directory and a great search engine.

what purports to be serious information [on the Web] is simply junk—neither current, objective, nor trustworthy."[11]

In addition to the questions asked about any type of information (see pages 173–176), there are special questions to consider when evaluating Internet information and its sources. Anyone can put anything on the Internet. Make sure that your sources are trustworthy and that your information is valid. Always test information that you have found on the Internet by asking these four additional questions: (1) Who posted the information? (2) Why did they post it? (3) When was the information written versus when was it posted? (4) Do other published sources verify this information? (See pages 188–189 for criteria that can help you assess the validity and reliability of supporting material found on websites.)

Documentation

All forms of supporting material used in a presentation (including information from Internet sources and interviews) should be documented. **Documentation** is the practice of citing the sources of your supporting material in a presentation. In-speech documentation enhances your credibility as a researcher and communicator and informs listeners about the sources and validity of your information and ideas.

Even if an author or a website grants you permission to reproduce material for personal use, you still must give the source of that information credit in your presentation.[12] Getting permission can become a complicated process requiring that you pay a publisher or an author for the right to use his or her material. In most college settings, permission doesn't obligate you to pay an author, but it does require you to include an acknowledgment of the rightful author and the source in your presentation or references.

Documenting Your Sources in Writing

In a written report, documentation follows one of several accepted formats such as Modern Language Association (MLA) style, American Psychological Association (APA)

FAQ So What Should I Say to Document Supporting Material?

Your spoken citation should include just enough information to allow an interested listener to find the original source you're citing. Generally, it's a good idea to provide the name of the person (or people) whose work you are using, say a word or two about that person's credentials, and mention the source of the information: "Dr. Joanne Cantor, a University of Wisconsin professor, drew this conclusion in her book *Mommy, I'm Scared:* 'Media violence...'" When the information is time-sensitive, you should include the date of publication or posting. Sometimes, when a person or reference is well known, you don't have to do much more than say, "In his last State of the Union Address, President Bush said...." or "As the great psalm begins, "The Lord is my shepherd; I shall not want...." To document electronic sources orally, you could say, "An article on plagiarism in the *Purdue News*, found at *www.purdue.edu*, reports that...." You could also display the complete website addresses on a slide (as long as you give listeners enough time to copy them). If you want your audience to have complete citations, prepare a bibliography as a handout.

style, the prescriptions of *The Chicago Manual of Style* (published by the University of Chicago Press), or many others. The documentation section in any of these organizations' manuals will provide models of how to format a reference, endnote, or footnote. Depending on which style manual you use, there are very specific rules for documenting electronic sources.

Documenting electronic sources is much like documenting print sources. One difference is that there are two types of electronic sources. There are those that change, such as websites or online resources. Then there are those that don't change, such as a computer program or a database stored on a CD-ROM. This is an important distinction. If you are using an electronic source that changes, make sure that you provide the date on which you used the source. Why? Because the information could be different on the following day. When working with a permanent CD-ROM, treat it like a book or journal and make sure that you provide the date of publication, not the date on which you used the source. Here are two examples of citations from online sources:

Julie J. C. H. Ryan, Student Plagiarism in an Online World, Prism, *http://www.asee.org/prism/december/html/ student_plagiarism_in_an_onlin.htm, December 1998.*

Purdue University Online Writing Lab, Avoiding Plagiarism, http://owl.english. purdue.edu/handouts/research/r_ plagiar.html, © 1995–2003.

Always be prepared to provide a list of the references you used to prepare your presentation—just as you would for a written report. In most speaking situations, you will not be required to provide such a list. We recommend, however, that you keep a list of your references for your own use. If nothing else, it will remind you of which sources you used in the event that you are challenged about information or asked to repeat or to update your presentation. There are situations, however, in which you may be asked to provide your references—either for your instructor or for informing audience members and colleagues.

Documenting Your Sources in Presentations

In a presentation you should document the sources of supporting material "out loud." We are not suggesting that you read complete citations to your audience. Imagine how strange it would be to read aloud the previous examples of online citations on plagiarism. Think how awkward it would sound to provide the detail required by any of the publication manuals in the middle of your presentation. The last thing you want to do is to clutter your talk with complete citations or long Internet addresses. What you should provide is enough oral information to credit the sources of your information. If you believe that your audience should have access to the information you have used, you may provide a handout listing your references.

Not Documenting Your Sources is Plagiarism

Why does documentation matter? Because without it you could fall into the trap of plagiarizing your source materials, intentionally or not. To **plagiarize** is "to use and pass off (the ideas or writings of another) as one's own; to appropriate for use as one's own passages or ideas from (another)."[13] The word *plagiarism* comes from a Latin word, *plagium,* which means "kidnapping." Thus, when you plagiarize, you are stealing or kidnapping something that belongs to someone else. Simply put, when you plagiarize, you fail to document and give credit to the sources of your information. Unfortunately, some speakers believe that prohibitions against plagiarism don't apply to them. Others know that they apply but think they can get away with it. Still others plagiarize without even realizing that they are doing it.

Plagiarism Hurts Everyone. Although most speakers don't intend to commit "literary theft," plagiarism occurs more often than it should, often with serious consequences. In colleges, students have failed classes, been expelled from programs and schools, or been denied a degree when caught plagiarizing. In the publishing business, authors have been sued by writers who claimed that their ideas and words had been plagiarized. Well-respected scientists, politicians, university officials, and civic leaders have been tarnished with charges of plagiarism.

Avoiding Plagiarism. Most speakers don't set out to plagiarize. Ignorance, however, is no excuse. Almost every teacher has had students who turned in entire articles from magazines or encyclopedias as their original work. "But," say the accused students, "we were told to find and share research." This is true, but presenting someone else's work as your own is not research—it's plagiarism. Give credit where credit is due. The person who published or posted those original ideas spent a lot of effort creating them and should be recognized for that effort.

The key to avoiding plagiarism is to identify the sources of your information in your presentation. A second key is understanding that changing a few words of someone else's work is not enough to avoid plagiarism. If they're not your original ideas, and most of the words are not yours, you are ethically obligated to tell your audience who wrote or said them and where they came from.

This requirement applies equally to material you find on the Web. The World Wide Web has added a new dimension to the problem of plagiarism. In an article in *Prism,* a publication of the American Society for Engineering Education, author Julie Ryan explains that "the proliferation of Web pages and electronic publications makes plagiarism easier to accomplish and harder to recognize."[14] She describes the problem as follows:

> *A few words typed into a Web search engine can lead a student to hundreds, sometimes thousands, of relevant documents, making it easy to "cut and paste" a few paragraphs*

Is It Ever Okay to "Borrow" a Phrase or an Idea?

It's one thing to slip in a quotation and pretend it's your idea and wording. It's another thing to use a familiar phrase in a new context to support an idea. For instance, politicians often use phrases borrowed from other sources. So do writers. Throughout this textbook, we have alluded to phrases taken from literature and popular sources. For example, on page 178 we wrote that for some information, "there's no place like home." Anyone who's seen *The Wizard of Oz* knows that Dorothy used that magic phrase in order to get back home to Kansas. Using a familiar phrase like this in other contexts can make an idea more interesting and memorable. Besides, think how awkward the following acknowledgment would be: "For some information, 'there's no place like home,' as Dorothy said to her family and friends in the 1939 movie *The Wizard of Oz.*" Making an allusion to a famous quotation is not plagiarism as long as the phrase is well known and is used to interest or inspire audience members who will recognize the phrase.

Senator Barbara Boxer points to a California gold mine that was formerly a Native American sacred land site during testimony before the Senate Indian Affairs Committee. How does her use of a photograph as supporting material enhance her presentation?

from here and a few more from there until the student has an entire paper-length collection. Or a student can find a research paper published in one of the hundreds of new journals that have gone online over the past few years, copy the entire text, turn it into a new document, and then offer it up as original work without having to type anything but a cover page. Even recycling efforts and ghost writers have gone global with Web sites offering professionally or student-written research papers for sale, some even with a money-back guarantee against detection."[15]

Fortunately, the Web also provides instructors with the same access to information. Given time and a good search engine, many would-be plagiarizers have been caught and appropriately punished.

The bottom line is this: Plagiarism is not just unethical and illegal; it represents the theft of a person's hard work and good ideas. Diana Hacker, author of *The Bedford Handbook,* expresses this idea quite eloquently when she explains that any writing you do (whether for a research paper or for a presentation) is a collaboration between you and your sources: "To be fair and ethical, you must acknowledge your debt to the writers of these sources."[16]

A presentation is more than a collection of statistics, examples, quotations, stories, and famous phrases from other sources. Supporting material helps you explain, clarify, convince, and interest your audience. Use it to spice up your presentation, demonstrate a principle, or prove a point. Don't use information in place of ideas. Use information to support ideas. And when you use it, give the person who wrote it or the publication that printed it the credit it deserves for supplying you with the raw materials you needed for your presentation.

Summary

▶ What forms of supporting material should I use?

Select the best quality of material and use more than one type of the following forms of supporting material for your presentation: facts, statistics, testimony, definitions, analogies, descriptions, examples, and stories.

▶ How can I tell if my supporting materials are valid?

Test your supporting material by asking whether the information you want to use is credible, recent, consistent, relevant, and statistically accurate.

▶ Can I use personal knowledge as support?

You may be an excellent source of information, as long as you make sure that your facts are accurate and your opinions well founded.

▶ How do I find good supporting material in a library?

After making sure you have found the right library and sought the services of a professional librarian, look for materials in the reference collection, in periodicals and newspapers, and in appropriate books.

▶ How do I conduct research online?

Use an appropriate search engine to help yourself find the material you need. Narrow your search to a very specific term or phrase in order to maximize the efficiency and effectiveness of your research.

▶ How much credit should I give to the sources of my supporting material?

Provide enough information about your sources so that a listener could locate that information. To be fair and ethical, you must acknowledge your debt to those who wrote the ideas and information you have used in a presentation.

Presentation Principles in Action

Assessing a Website

Directions: In addition to the general tests for assessing supporting material discussed in this chapter, special criteria should be applied when evaluating websites and Web sources. Use the following checklist to assess the validity and reliability of supporting material found on two websites of your choice. For the first website, select a site that is, in your opinion, a *good* site for researching valid supporting material. For the second website, select a site that is, in your opinion, a *questionable* or *poor* site that may not provide credible, recent, consistent, relevant, or valid information. Be prepared to present your evaluations of both websites.

Website Assessment

Web Site #1 URL: Host:	Web Site #2 URL: Host:	Assessment Criteria and Questions
_____ Acceptable _____ Unacceptable _____ Cannot Determine Comments:	_____ Acceptable _____ Unacceptable _____ Cannot Determine Comments:	**CRITERION #1: AUTHORITY** 1. Are the *sponsor's* identity and purpose clear? 2. Are the *author's* identity and qualifications evident? 3. If the material is protected by copyright, who is the copyright holder? 4. Can you verify the legitimacy of the webpage's sponsor (e.g., a phone number or postal address to contact for more information)? 5. Are you sure that the named source is actually operating the site? 6. Have you run the names of unfamiliar topics, sources, and authors through a search engine to learn more about them and what other people have said about them?
_____ Acceptable _____ Unacceptable _____ Cannot Determine Comments:	_____ Acceptable _____ Unacceptable _____ Cannot Determine Comments:	**CRITERION #2: ACCURACY** 1. Are the sources of factual information clearly listed so that you can verify them in another source? 2. Has the sponsor provided links that can be used to verify claims? 3. Is statistical data well labeled and easy to read? 4. Is the information free of grammatical, spelling, and typographical errors that would indicate a lack of quality control?

Web Site #1 URL: Host:	Web Site #2 URL: Host:	Assessment Criteria and Questions
______ Acceptable ______ Unacceptable ______ Cannot Determine Comments:	______ Acceptable ______ Unacceptable ______ Cannot Determine Comments:	**CRITERION #3: OBJECTIVITY** 1. Is the reason that the sponsor is providing each piece of information evident? 2. Is the information content separate from advertising or opinion? 3. Is the sponsor's point of view presented clearly with well-supported arguments? 4. If the site is not objective, does it acknowledge opposing points of view?
______ Acceptable ______ Unacceptable ______ Cannot Determine Comments:	______ Acceptable ______ Unacceptable ______ Cannot Determine Comments:	**CRITERION #4: CURRENCY** 1. Is the material recent enough to be accurate and relevant? 2. Are there any indications that the material is kept up to date? 3. Do you see statements indicating where data from charts and graphs were gathered? 4. Is there an indication that the site is complete and not still being developed?

Source: Based on John Chaffee, with Christine McMahon and Barbara Stout, *Critical Thinking, Thoughtful Writing*, 2nd ed. (Boston: Houghton Mifflin, 2002), pp. 534–536, 614.

Just the Facts or Just My Opinion?

Directions: The following excerpts come from two articles in well-respected publications. Look at the sample statements, any of which could serve as supporting material in a presentation. Indicate whether the samples represent facts (historical or observable facts/valid statistics) or opinions (inferences or judgments).

Are They Facts or Opinions?

Fact or Opinion?		Supporting Material
SOURCE		Business–Higher Education Forum. *Spanning the Chasm: A Blueprint for Action* (Washington, D.C.: American Council on Education and the National Alliance of Business, September 1999).
Fact	Opinion	1. The Business–Higher Education Forum's 1997 report, *Spanning the Chasm,* revealed that . . . students must now graduate with highly developed cross-functional, flexible skills in leadership, teamwork, problem solving, time management, self-management, adaptability, analytical thinking, global consciousness, and basic communications, including listening, speaking, reading, and writing.

Fact or Opinion?		Supporting Material
Fact	Opinion	2. Today... the whole of human knowledge doubles every five years.
Fact	Opinion	3. American college graduates are entering the workplace ill-equipped to effectively contribute in a fast-paced world economy.
Fact	Opinion	4. Foreign language courses help students understand world cultures and develop a global consciousness and should be required.
Fact	Opinion	5. Erie Community College received a $122,240 grant to develop a model credit-bearing apprenticeship program.
SOURCE		Scott Turow,* "To Kill or Not to Kill," *The New Yorker,* January 6, 2003, pp. 40–47.
Fact	Opinion	1. Illinois, which has a death penalty, has a higher murder rate than the neighboring state of Michigan, which has no capital punishment but roughly the same racial makeup, income levels, and population distribution between cities and rural areas.
Fact	Opinion	2. I respect the right of a majority of my fellow citizens to decide that [capital punishment] ought to be imposed on the most horrific crimes.
Fact	Opinion	3. The justice that survivors [family members of murder victims] seek is the one embedded in the concept of restitution: The criminal ought not to end up better off than his victim.
Fact	Opinion	4. Capital punishment for slaying a woman is imposed at three and a half times the rate for murdering a man.
Fact	Opinion	5. Sometimes a crime is so horrible that killing its perpetrator is the only just response.

*In 2000, Turow served on an Illinois commission to recommend reforms of the state's capital punishment system.

Key Terms

analogy 172
biased 174
Boolean search 181
definition 171
description 172
documentation 183
example 172
fact 170
judgment 170
meta search engine 181
plagiarism 185
primary source 180
research 176
search engine 181
secondary source 180
statistics 170
stories 172
supporting material 169
testimony 171
valid 173

Notes

1 Jerome Groopman, "The Shadow Epidemic," *The New Yorker*, 11 May 1998, pp. 48–49.

2 Joanne Cantor, *Mommy, I'm Scared: How TV and Movies Frighten Children and What We Can Do to Protect Them* (San Diego: Harcourt Brace, 1998), p. 5.

3 Jesse Jackson, Rainbow Coalition speech given at the 1984 Democratic Convention, 17 July 1984. For an analysis and complete text of the speech, see James R. Andrews and David Zarefsky, *Contemporary American Voices* (New York: Longman, 1992), pp. 355–362.

4 Daphne Duval Harrison, *Black Pearls: Blues Queens of the 1920s* (New Brunswick, NJ: Rutgers University Press, 1988).

5 Vivian Hobbs, Commencement Address at Prince George's Community College, Largo, Maryland, 1991. See Appendix for complete address.

6 Groopman.

7 *New York Times 1999 Almanac* (New York: Penguin, 1998), p. 395.

8 Jerry L. Winsor, Dan B. Curtis, and Ronald D. Stephens, "National Preferences in Business and Communication Update," *Journal of the Association for Communication Administration* 31 (1997): 170–179.

9 A useful compilation of subject-specific library resources and websites can be found in Diana Hacker, *Research and Documentation in the Electronic Age*, 2nd ed. (Boston: Bedford Books, 1999). In addition to general advice on Internet research, the booklet lists sources in the humanities, history, social sciences, and sciences and features a large section on how to document sources according to different style manuals.

10 A specialized website, Search Engine Watch, provides tips on using search engines more effectively. See *www.searchenginewatch.com.*

11 Quoted from *Chronicle of Higher Education*, 1 August 1997, p. A44, in Ann Raimes, *Keys for Writers*, 2nd ed. (Boston: Houghton Mifflin, 1999), p. 73.

12 Diana Roberts Wienbroer, *The McGraw-Hill Guide to Electronic Research and Documentation* (Boston: McGraw-Hill, 1997), p. 26.

13 *The American Heritage Dictionary of the English Language*, 4th ed. (Boston: Houghton Mifflin, 2000), p. 1340. Copyright © 2000 by Houghton Mifflin Company. Reproduced by permission from *The American Heritage Dictionary of the English Language, Fourth Edition.*

14 Julie J. C. H. Ryan, "Student Plagiarism in an Online World," *Prism*, December 1998, p. 1, as retrieved online at *www.asee.org/prism/.*

15 Ryan, p. 2.

16 Diana Hacker, *The Bedford Handbook* (Boston: Bedford Books, 1998), p. 570.

chapter nine

Organization

- Why is organization so important?
- How do I select the key points for a presentation?
- How do I link my purpose, central idea, and key points?
- Are there established organizational formats that I can follow?

Many popular books on presentation speaking include a three-step guide to organization that we call the "Tell 'em Technique." It goes like this: "Tell 'em what you're gonna tell 'em—tell 'em—then, tell 'em what you told 'em." As simple as the Tell 'em Technique seems, it does capture three important tips about how to organize a presentation. Audiences benefit if they know what the main ideas of a presentation will be. They also benefit if they hear the main ideas more than once. And finally, a summary of the main ideas helps them remember what they have heard. There is, however, more to good organization than the Tell 'em Technique, which tells you *what* to do but not *how* to do it. How do you select the best ideas and information for your presentation? How do you arrange those ideas? There's no one right way, but there *are* many ways in which you can use organizing principles to help yourself get the most out of your speaking opportunities. We explore these principles in this chapter.

Why Organization Matters

Years of teaching, coaching, and communication consulting have led us to conclude that most speakers underestimate how important organization is to the success of their presentations.

As an audience member, you already know how much it matters. You no doubt find a well-organized presentation easier to listen to and remember than a poorly organized one. You probably find it difficult to understand and remember the words of a speaker who rambles and doesn't connect ideas. In fact, you may never want to hear that speaker again. Researchers confirm that audiences react positively to well-organized presentations and speakers and negatively to poorly organized ones.[1]

This idea is not new. Cicero, the great Roman senator and orator, identified two initial tasks required of every effective speaker. The first was to determine the key points; the second was to put those key points into an orderly sequence. Cicero used the Latin word *inventio* to describe the speaker's attempt "to find out what he should say."[2] He identified the second step, *dispositio,* as the task of arranging ideas and information for a presentation in an orderly sequence. The selection and arrangement of ideas and information can help audience members make decisions about important issues and select a course of action. For example, if a speaker is trying to help audience members assess the benefits of competing insurance plans, a disorganized presentation will neither describe each plan

ORGANIZATION HELPS THE AUDIENCE

Understand the message
Remember the message
Decide how to react

Real World Real Speakers

Don't "Shoot from the Hip"

The president/CEO of a large company who responded to our survey—but who wishes to remain nameless—shared this story: "I had to make some brief remarks after taking over the presidency of a state association. I knew I had to make this speech but did not spend time organizing my thoughts or writing an outline. I did not have notes and did not rehearse. Just shot from the hip. The more I talked, the more I felt I fumbled and rambled on, and I soon noticed I was losing the interest of the audience, which unnerved me even more. My brief speech was not a success."

clearly nor help the listeners decide which plan is best or which to choose. They may feel even more confused after hearing the presentation than before they heard it.

Organization also helps you as a speaker. If you are well organized, you are much more likely to achieve the purpose of your presentation. Organization helps you to decide how many and what kinds of research and supporting materials you will need for your presentation. If, for example, your purpose is to report on the need for repairs at the community swimming pool, you do not have to spend time researching the hourly pay rate of lifeguards.

Organization also helps you to determine a clear and effective arrangement of the content that you want to include. Not only does it tell you which ideas should come first or last; organization also keeps you focused on the development of each idea. Equally important and not surprisingly, well-organized speakers are seen as more competent and confident than disorganized speakers.

ORGANIZATION HELPS THE SPEAKER

Gather ideas and information
Arrange those ideas strategically
Enhance his or her credibility

How to Get Organized

Building a strong presentation is like building a house, and organization is the blueprint. Collecting ideas and information for your presentation is similar to choosing and collecting the materials you would need to build a house. Although just about every house includes wood, nails, windows, doors, siding, wiring, and plumbing, piling all those building materials on a home site would not give you a house. You would still need a detailed blueprint or plan to tell you what you're building, what you need to build it, and how to put the pieces together. Similarly, most presentations have a purpose and supporting materials that advance and support them—but just "piling up" your ideas won't result in an effective presentation. The **organization** of a presentation helps you to stay focused on your purpose while you're deciding what to include in your talk and how to put it all together in an effective way. Your purpose and the needs and interests of your audience help you decide what to include on your "blueprint." Communication scholars even use the term **framing** to describe the organizational process. Much like a presentation, a picture frame and a house frame capture and arrange critical content.

Before you can put all the pieces of a presentation into a pattern, structure, or order, though, you must decide which pieces to use. Considering your purpose, your audience, your credibility, the occasion, and the logistics of the situation can help you make these decisions.

- *Consider Your Purpose.* When deciding what to include in your presentation, always begin with your purpose (see Chapter 4, "Purpose and Topic"). Include ideas and supporting material that will help you to achieve your purpose. Leave out anything that's not relevant. If your purpose is to teach new employees how to fill out a performance evaluation form, you won't need to talk about the history of the evaluation system. If, however, your purpose is to explain why the performance evaluation form is so complicated, information about its history and development might be just what you need.
- *Consider Your Audience.* Having analyzed your audience (see Chapter 5, "Audience Analysis and Adaptation"), you're in a good position to select ideas and supporting material that will interest and influence its members. Say your purpose is to gain support for a tax increase. To an audience of government employees, you might explain how a tax increase could prevent staff layoffs. To members of a neighborhood organization, you might explain that a failure to increase revenues through taxes would result in fewer police patrols.
- *Consider Your Credibility.* Will your good character and expertise be evident to your audience (see Chapter 6, "Speaker Credibility and Ethics")? If not, consider including a separate section—or at least some supporting material—designed to enhance your credibility. After all, if audience members don't trust or believe you, your organization won't matter. Share personal stories and examples that demonstrate your commitment, trustworthiness, or expertise. Look for ways to connect your experiences and values to those of your audience. And always remember that audiences will dismiss you and your well-organized presentation if they perceive you as unethical.
- *Consider the Logistics and Occasion.* Use what you know about where, when, and why you will be speaking (see Chapter 7, "Logistics and Occasion") to guide your selection of ideas and supporting material. Let's say that you know you will have only ten minutes to speak, and you have five advertising campaigns that you want to describe as examples of a marketing company's effectiveness. You likewise would know that you would have time to focus on only one or two of them or to provide a brief highlight of each campaign.

Considering these factors will help you to determine what ideas to include, in a general sense. Now it's time to get specific and think about how to shape those ideas into a well-organized, effective presentation.

Select Your Key Points

At this point in the preparation process, you may have heaps of excellent ideas and supporting material but no plan for organizing them. The first step in organization requires answering a single question: What are the key points that I want to cover in

This speaker uses a flip chart to clearly list key points of her presentation to a Spanish-speaking audience on preventing depression.

my presentation? The **key points** of a presentation represent the most important issues or the main ideas that you want your audience to understand and to remember during and after your talk. Finding and selecting your key points (Cicero's *inventio*) are the first step in developing a clear organizational format for your presentation. So how do you do this? Look for a pattern or a natural grouping for your ideas and information.

Depending on your purpose and topic area, this can be an easy task or a huge puzzle. Inexperienced speakers often feel overwhelmed by what seems to be mountains of unrelated facts and figures. Don't give up! Finding a pattern is similar to assembling a patchwork quilt or planting a flower garden. You have all the pieces or plants; now it is time to look for similarities in shape and color as well as to figure out how all the pieces can be combined to create a complete picture.

One way to begin your search for a pattern is to apply the "4Rs of Organization" to the ideas that you're considering for inclusion. The 4Rs represent a series of critical thinking steps that can help you find an effective organizational pattern for your presentation.

THE 4Rs OF ORGANIZATION

Review
Reduce
Regroup
Refine

Review. Find an uninterrupted block of time and a quiet place and bring all of your ideas and supporting material to the table. Reread and critique what you've written or collected. Does the information you've collected support your purpose, or is it marginal or irrelevant? Have you determined the key points that you want to make in your presentation? Evaluate the amount of supporting material you've gathered. Is there enough? Or is there too much to include in your presentation? What common ideas have appeared in most of your research? Which ones seem most interesting, relevant, and important? Will you need some vital statistics or dramatic testimony to back them up?

By thinking critically and unemotionally about your material, you may find that certain ideas and information jump out as must-include "keepers," whereas others can be put aside for another day. Both of us have found that a way of organizing the ideas and information that we have collected for a presentation often emerges during the process of carefully reviewing our materials.

Reduce. Once you have reviewed your ideas and information, try to boil the "keepers" down to their essential points. In a presentation, less can be more. Rather than risk overwhelming your audience with too much information, choose a few key items that they will notice and remember. Great chefs know that reduction is the secret of a great sauce. In cooking, reduction is more than just boiling off water—it's a way of intensifying flavors and changing the chemical composition of the other ingredients. The same is true in a presentation. Reduction looks for and organizes the essence of a presentation; it boils away the extras. Finding the essence of your presentation will help you create an organizational pattern that will give you and your message more impact.

Regroup. Try regrouping the ideas and relevant supporting material that you want to include in your presentation into different categories. If you plan to talk about a problem, you may want to put illustrative stories about the problem into one group and statistics and research that analyze the problem into another. Or you might consider categorizing the problem along a timeline—how did it start, when did it become serious, what's the current status, and what will happen if the problem is not solved? If your presentation will focus on a set of accomplishments by your organization, you could try several different groupings—achievements that have won awards, the impact of selected accomplishments on groups of people or organizations, a history of the organization's achievements, or the practical value of encouraging outstanding efforts by employees. Regrouping your ideas and information may help you to identify an organizational pattern that will best suit the purpose of your presentation.

Refine. Once you have reviewed, reduced, and regrouped your material, it is time to refine—time for the finishing work. Sometimes this can be the most important step because it puts your key points into a form that will make your presentation more memorable. If, for example, you were listing the accomplishments of an organization, you might group them in terms of how *ready, willing,* and *able* the organization is to serve its public.

Very often, refining means rewording an idea in a creative way. Refining can also help you to find a useful or familiar "hook" on which to hang your key points. For example, the 4Rs of Organization use a common first letter to help you to remember how to use this technique. Labeling each section of a presentation about the organization's accomplishments with *ready, willing,* or *able* uses a popular saying as the basis for refining your ideas.

Link Your Key Points and Central Idea

Now that you've discovered and selected your key points, you must directly link them to your central idea. A house that does not connect the framing to the foundation will not stand. Similarly, a presentation that does not connect its key points to the central idea will not achieve its purpose.

Your purpose and your central idea may not be the same. Your purpose states what *you* want your audience to know, think, believe, or do as a result of your presentation. Your **central idea** is a sentence or thesis statement that summarizes the key points that you want your *audience* to understand and remember. The central idea also can provide a brief preview of the organizational pattern you will follow to achieve your purpose. As the overall structure of your presentation emerges during the *regrouping* stage, you should connect your key points to your central idea. If you find that it takes more than one sentence to state your central idea, go back to the drawing board. You may be trying to do too much, or you may not have a clear purpose or organizational pattern. The following three examples illustrate how topic area, purpose, and central idea are different but closely linked to one another.

Topic Area:	Growing tomatoes
Purpose:	To teach the audience how to grow healthy tomatoes
Central Idea:	Growing healthy tomatoes requires good soil, bright sun, plenty of water, and a watchful eye.
Topic Area:	Refugee families
Purpose:	To increase donations to the church's refugee assistance program
Central Idea:	Because the church's refugee families program has been a blessing for all of us—the families, our church, and you—please continue to make financial contributions to our ministry.
Topic Area:	Muzak
Purpose:	To make the audience more aware of the purpose and power of Muzak
Central Idea:	The next time that you hear Muzak playing your song, you will remember how pervasive it is, how it originated, and how it tries to lift your spirits and productivity.

Notice how the statement of the central idea in the previous examples identifies the topic area and the purpose of a presentation while previewing the organizational pattern. As you review, reduce, regroup, and refine your material, your central idea may go through many revisions. But by the time you are ready to speak, the central idea should be clear and should state what you are going to say and in what order you will say it to achieve your purpose.

Keep It Simple

Even the best listeners in your audience will not be able to remember everything that you say. Keeping your overall structure simple and clear will improve the chances that your audience will retain your central idea, a few of your key points, and the best pieces of supporting material that you include. Television news reports and newsmagazines structure their material so that a sixth-grader can follow a story. Approach your presentation in the same way. Don't be tempted to include ten reasons for change, two hundred years of history, or twenty-five charts just because that material is available. Instead, pick out the most important reasons, the key events, or the most dramatic charts.

Several years ago both of us attended an address by a well-respected colleague. The presentation got off to a good start, but after twenty minutes the audience began to get restless. Just then, the speaker announced that he would conclude by sharing ten major recommendations with us. You could almost hear the audience groan. It was just too much! As the presentation dragged on, the recommendations merged into one another. We left the assembly without a clear understanding of what had been said. We had to read the address in printed form before we could begin to appreciate the speaker's message and key points. The presentation was neither simple nor clear, and as a result, it did not achieve its purpose.

At this point in the organizational process, you may be wondering how to consolidate your key points into a clear and coherent presentation. If a clear organizational pattern doesn't emerge as you review, reduce, regroup, and refine your material, you may be able to apply one or more commonly used patterns to meet your organizational needs.

Organizational Patterns

Even the most polished presentation speakers sometimes find it difficult to see how their ideas and information fall into an organizational pattern. If you're in a similar position, do not despair. Several commonly used organizational patterns can help you clarify your central idea and find a format for your presentation.

ORGANIZATIONAL PATTERNS

- **Topical**
- **Time**
- **Space**
- **Problem-Solution**
- **Causes and Effects**
- **Scientific Method**
- **Stories and Examples**
- **Comparison-Contrast**
- **Memory Aids**

Arrange by Subtopics

Topical arrangement involves dividing a large topic into smaller subtopics. Subtopics can describe reasons, characteristics, techniques, and procedures. For example, you could divide the topic of alcoholism into its symptoms and treatments, or you could devote your entire presentation to describing available treatments.

Ask Common Questions

Topical arrangement is not restricted to a series of subtopic statements. If you can transform your subtopics into commonly asked questions, your audience will become more involved and more willing to listen to your answers. For example, you could arrange the key points in a presentation on justifications for the death penalty as follows:

1. The *deterrence* factor
2. The *cost* factor
3. The *revenge* factor

A series of common and frequently asked questions about the death penalty give you a more interesting and compelling approach to this topic. Think about how an audience might react to the following questions:

1. Does the death penalty *deter* others from committing murder?
2. What *costs* more—life in prison or the process leading to execution?
3. Do victims' families have a right to *revenge* and emotional closure?

Using common questions as key points provides a way of addressing your audience directly with a series of thought-provoking questions.

For a presentation on growing tomatoes, you could divide the topic into different types of tomatoes or growing techniques. You could support a political candidate by describing her or his stand on different issues or by listing the candidate's qualifications and contributions to the community. If your ideas and information can be divided into discrete categories, topical arrangement can provide a clear pattern of organization. For example:

Topic Area: Facial expressions in different cultures
Purpose: To appreciate that some facial expressions don't always translate between cultures
Central Idea: Americans and native Japanese often misinterpret facial expressions depicting fear, sadness, and disgust.[3]
Key Points: A. Fear
B. Sadness
C. Disgust

Sequence in Time

Some topics lend themselves to a **time arrangement,** which orders information according to time or calendar dates. Most step-by-step procedures begin with the first step and continue sequentially through the last step. Giving recipes, listing assembly instructions, and describing technical procedures often require a time arrangement, as do presentations on historical events. You also can use time arrangement for a past-present-future pattern or for a before-after pattern. For example:

Topic Area: Running meetings
Purpose: To explain how to use meeting time effectively and efficiently
Central Idea: Well-run meetings have a definite beginning, middle, and end.
Key Points: A. Convening the meeting
B. Giving the opening remarks
C. Following the prepared agenda
D. Ending the meeting

Position in Space

Observing where people and places are located as well as where events take place may help you alert your audience to your key points. **Space arrangement** is not used as often as time arrangement, but it's just as obvious a pattern for certain topics. If your information can be placed in different locations, you may want to use space arrangement as an organizational pattern. Travel books often divide a map into sections in order to describe different regions of a country. A proposed highway system is hard to

Speakers often use time arrangement when demonstrating the steps of a recipe or cooking technique. The chicken must be prepared and properly trussed before it can be roasted.

describe unless you can show where it will go and what it will displace. You can use space arrangement to discuss a topic involving different locations, such as city, state, and federal taxes or national holidays in Canada, Mexico, and Brazil. Here is an example of spatial organization:

Topic Area: Brain structure

Purpose: To explain how different sections of the brain are responsible for different functions

Central Idea: A guided tour of the brain begins in the hindbrain, moves through the midbrain, and ends in the forebrain, with side trips through the right and left hemispheres.

Key Points:
A. The hindbrain
B. The midbrain
C. The forebrain
D. The right and left hemispheres

Present Problems and Solutions

A **problem-solution arrangement** can be used to describe a situation that is harmful (the problem) and then offer a plan to solve the problem (the solution). Problems can be as simple as a squeaking door, a burned cookie, or a misunderstood procedure or as serious and as widespread as drunk driving, poor quarterly earnings, African famine, low employee morale, or acid rain. Solutions likewise can be just as different, ranging from oiling a door hinge to airlifting tons of food and medicine to another continent. As Chapter 20, "Developing Persuasive Presentations," discusses in more detail, problem-solution patterns work especially well for persuasive presentations.

Opt for Options

Very often there is more than one answer to a question or more than one solution to a problem. *What's the best diet plan? What's the best way to treat cancer? What's the best way to finance a college education?* When a problem brings to mind many possible solutions or remedies, you may want to share those options with your audience. As in a problem-solution arrangement, begin your presentation by describing the nature and significance of the problem. However, instead of offering a single plan for solving the problem, discuss the available options. Then tell the advantages and disadvantages of each option or provide a good reason that explains why one option is better than the others.

For example, suppose your central idea is that community colleges are an excellent option for cash-strapped students and families. Your presentation would begin with a section describing the high costs and consequences of financing a college education. Then you would describe and evaluate several funding options such as college savings plans, college loans, scholarships, and enrollment at a local community college before transferring to a four-year college. If your goal is to familiarize audience members with the options, you can invite your listeners to make their own decisions. If, however, you want to advocate community college enrollment as the most practical option for cash-strapped students and their families, you can give them reasons illustrating why they should opt for the community college alternative. In either case, your organizational pattern begins with a statement of the problem followed by an informed discussion of the options.

They can also be used in informative presentations, as this outline shows:

Topic Area: Poor participation in meetings
Purpose: To provide suggestions for solving common "people problems" in meetings
Central Idea: Learning how to deal with a few common behavioral problems in groups will improve a group's performance.
Key Points: A. Nonparticipants
B. Loudmouths
C. Interrupters
D. Whisperers
E. Latecomers and early leavers

Show Causes and Effects

A **causes and effects arrangement** either presents a cause and its resulting effect, or details the effects that lead to a cause. In cause-to-effect, you describe or identify a situation, object, or behavior that results in another situation, object, or behavior. We have heard speakers claim that eating red meat causes disease and depression, that lower taxes result in more business investment and personal savings, and that large classrooms, inadequate discipline, and low teacher salaries explain the decline in educational achievement. In effect-to-cause, you can describe situations, behavior, or objects and then identify their causes—the reasons that they occur. We have heard speakers claim that sleepiness or lack of energy can be caused by an iron deficiency, that the decrease in lake fish is caused by acid rain, and that low voter turnout may be due to the belief that voting doesn't make a difference anymore. As these examples show, causes and effects arrangements work particularly well when you want to establish a relationship among occurrences or to justify a course of action or conclusion.

Be careful with causes and effects, though. The fact that one occurrence follows another does not mean that the first causes the second. Perhaps a third factor is to blame. Sleepiness or lack of energy can also be caused by too many late-night parties. The decrease in lake fish can also be caused by too much fishing. Remember that there was a time when people believed that bad luck was caused by walking under ladders, breaking mirrors, or having a black cat cross their path. In the following outlines, a speaker identifies the causes (biological and environmental) of an effect (overeating).

Topic Area: Overeating
Purpose: To understand the multiple factors that influence eating habits
Central Idea: Identifying the causes of overeating can help you begin to minimize its effects.
Key Points: A. Biological causes
B. Environmental causes

Real World Real Speakers

The Path to a Guilty Verdict

On April 19, 1995, the Alfred P. Murrah Federal Building in Oklahoma City was blown up. Federal intelligence linked Timothy McVeigh and Terry Nichols to the crime. Imagine what it must have been like for prosecutors in the 1997 Terry Nichols trial to win their case. They had to prove that Nichols, a man with an ironclad alibi for the day of the Oklahoma City bombing, was a coconspirator with convicted bomber Timothy McVeigh. Although there was, in the words of prosecutor Beth Wilkinson, "an avalanche of evidence" against Nichols, most of it was circumstantial. Nothing put him at the scene of the crime; no one testified that he had planned or had taken credit for the bombing.

At the beginning of her three-hour summation to the jury, Ms. Wilkinson presented a large poster on which, in the upper left-hand corner, the Alfred P. Murrah Federal Building was pictured *before* the bombing. In the lower right-hand corner, there was a photo of the building *after* the bombing. Prosecutor Wilkinson organized her summation by taking the jury on a journey along a winding road that connected the two buildings. At critical "stops" along the road, she focused on key pieces of evidence—Nichols's purchase of fertilizer, his theft of bomb-making materials, his phone calls to McVeigh. She walked her jury from one piece of evidence to another—all leading to the bombing that claimed 168 lives. Not only did she use a spatial arrangement pattern to help her lead the jury clearly and logically to the picture of the bombed building, but she also led them to find Nichols guilty.

In the next example, a speaker contends that television has harmful effects on children.

Topic Area: Children and television

Purpose: To describe the harmful effects that television has on children

Central Idea: Television has a negative influence on children and their families because it displaces time that could be spent on more important activities.[4]

Key Points:
A. Television has a negative effect on children's physical fitness.
B. Televison has a negative effect on children's school achievement.
C. Televison is a hidden competitor for more important activities.
D. Television watching may become a serious addiction.

Arrange Scientifically

Scientists address a wide variety of physical, biological, and psychological questions ranging from "Is the universe expanding?" and "Do commonly prescribed diuretics significantly reduce high blood pressure?" to "What is the relationship between speaker preparedness and presentation anxiety?" In order to ensure the validity of such research, a scientific method is applied to the ways in which such research is conducted and shared. **Scientific method arrangement** follows a well-established organizational pattern that is the mainstay of scientific reporting. When sharing the results of a scientific study or explaining the development of a theory—either your own or the work of an eminent scientist—consider using an organizational pattern that follows the steps prescribed by journals that publish scientific research.

Usually, there are five basic sections in a scientific research report: (1) an explanation of the research question and why it is important; (2) a review of previous research on the topic in question; (3) a description of the scientific methods used to study the research question; (4) a presentation of research results, often including statistical tests that link the results to the research question; and (5) a discussion section that interprets the results and their implications.[5]

The following example outlines a presentation explaining the results of a study on the relationship between presentation anxiety and the preparation process.

Topic Area: Presentation anxiety and the preparation process

Purpose: To explain why anxious speakers should study and master the process of preparing an effective presentation

Central Idea: Learning effective preparation skills can improve the quality of your presentation *and* reduce your level of speech anxiety.

Key Points:
A. Research question: What is the relationship between speaker anxiety and preparation skills?
B. Review of previous research
C. Study method
D. Study results
E. Discussion and Implications: Learning effective preparation skills may reduce speech anxiety.

Tell Stories and Give Examples

Sometimes a series of dramatic stories can be so compelling and interesting that they can easily become the backbone of a presentation. Such stories can be used as an organizational pattern or, as we indicated in Chapter 8, "Supporting Material," they can be used as supporting material for presentations organized in other ways.

Sometimes selecting a series of appropriate stories or examples is all you need to do to organize your presentation. Television commercials use this technique. You see a series of people who have been made happy, rich, beautiful, healthy, sexy, or clean by a product. In a presentation, you tell stories or provide a series of examples to support your point. Dramatic stories about successful artists or professionals who escaped from youthful poverty and prejudice can be the key points of your presentation, as this outline illustrates:

Topic Area: Leaders and adversity

Purpose: To convince listeners that disabilities are not a barrier to success

Central Idea: Many noteworthy leaders have lived with disabilities.

Key Points:
A. Franklin D. Roosevelt, president of the United States
B. Jan Scruggs, disabled soldier and Vietnam Memorial founder
C. Helen Keller, deaf and blind advocate

Compare and Contrast

A **comparison-contrast arrangement** shows your audience how two things are similar or different. This pattern works well when an unfamiliar concept is easier to explain by comparing it to a familiar concept or when you are trying to demonstrate the advantages of one alternative over another. For example, you can compare and contrast the features of one car with those of another in its price class. You can compare and contrast the rate of growth and yield of tomato plants grown with or without fertilizer. You can compare and contrast the story of a refugee family helped by a church assistance program with that of a family who relied on government services. For example:

Topic Area: Family sedans
Purpose: To recommend a way of evaluating medium-sized cars
Central Idea: Comparing performance, comfort, fuel economy, and reliability can help you to select and purchase a new mid-sized car for your family.
Key Points: A. Performance
B. Comfort
C. Overall fuel economy
D. Predicted reliability

A special form of the compare-contrast arrangement is called a **figurative analogy.** As discussed in Chapter 8, an analogy is a description that shows the ways in which two things are similar and suggests that what is true about one thing will also be true about the other. A figurative analogy notes similarities in two things that are not obviously comparable. The following example compares student success to horse racing.

Topic Area: Student success in college
Purpose: To identify the multiple factors that affect student success in college
Central Idea: Predicting student success is like picking the winning horse at the racetrack and must include considerations of a student's high school record, parents' education, teachers, and advisers as well as the college's type of campus.
Key Points: A. High school grades and test scores = Track record
B. Parents' education = Horse's breeding record
C. Teacher = Trainer
D. Adviser = Jockey
E. Type of campus = Track conditions

Use Memory Aids

Journalists use the Who, What, Where, When, and Why questions to remind themselves of the key parts of a news story. First aid instructors teach the ABCs of First Aid—Open the Airways, check for Breathing, and check for Circulation. Music teachers have their 3Bs (Bach, Beethoven, and Brahms), and the 4-H Club has used its name to remind members of its fourfold aim of improving head, heart, hands, and health. Throughout this textbook you have already seen and will continue to see **memory aids arrangements** such as these used as organizational patterns and as ways of helping you remember what you've read. You can use them alone to organize your presentation or in combination with any of the other organizational patterns we've been discussing. Here's an example:

Topic Area: Organizing a presentation
Purpose: To provide an effective method for selecting the key points of a presentation
Central Idea: The 4Rs represent a series of critical thinking steps that can help you develop an effective organizational pattern for your presentation.

Ordering the Key Points

Once you have identified the key points that will directly support your central idea and have chosen the organizational pattern that you want to use, you may find yourself faced with a very common question: Which key points should go first, second, or last?

In many cases, the organizational pattern you've chosen will dictate the order of your key points. If, for example, you are using time arrangement, the first step in a procedure should come first. If you are looking at a historical event, you can begin at the beginning and work your way forward to the finish.

But what if your format does not dictate or suggest an order? In these cases, identify and place your strongest ideas in strategic positions. Do you "put your best foot forward" and lead with your strongest idea? Or do you "save the best for last"? Unfortunately, there is no single answer. Your answer depends on many factors, such as the audience's attitude toward you and your message, the occasion of the presentation, and the strategies you intend to use to achieve your purpose. That said, we offer some tips related to these factors:

- *Strength and Familiarity.* If one of your ideas is not as strong as others, place it in the middle position. For example, in illustrating the Stories and Examples organizational format, we used the example of a presentation on leadership and physical disabilities that featured examples—stories about President Roosevelt, Jan Scruggs, and Helen Keller. Whereas most audiences would have some familiarity with the first and third individuals, they probably wouldn't recognize Jan Scruggs (who, by the way, is a disabled Vietnam veteran who founded the Washington Vietnam Veterans Memorial and authored *To Heal a Nation*[1]). Thus, we put the least familiar story in the middle of the presentation in order to start and end with better-known examples.
- *Audience.* Whether you lead from strength or "end with a bang" depends on your best judgment about how to achieve your purpose, given what you've learned about your audience. If your audience wants information about current projections, make sure that you satisfy that need early. Other points related to future sales projections can come later. If an audience is not very interested in your topic, don't begin with your most technical, detailed point. You may be better off beginning with a point that explains why understanding the topic is important. If you are facing a hostile audience or speaking about a controversial topic, you may want to begin with a key point that focuses on the background of an issue or on the reasons that there is a need for change.
- *Logistics.* In addition to audience factors, the logistics of a situation can affect the order of key points. If you're one of a series of presenters, you may end up with less time to speak than was originally scheduled. Plan your presentation so that your most important key points come first. That way, if you *do* have to shorten your presentation, your audience will still have heard the main thing you came to say.

There aren't any hard and fast rules about ordering your points. Just make sure that they follow a logical progression and are ordered in a way that helps your audience to understand and remember what you tell them.

1. Jan C. Scruggs and Joel L. Swerdlow, *To Heal a Nation: The Vietnam Veterans Memorial* (New York: HarperCollins, 1992).

Key Points: A. Review
B. Reduce
C. Regroup
D. Refine

Please note that these commonly used patterns of organization are neither strategies nor solutions to organization problems.[6] They are only arrangements to consider when looking for an effective organizational pattern. And even though many presentations will fit one or more of these common formats, there is nothing wrong with coming up with your own original pattern.

Match the Format to the Content

A little earlier in this chapter, we introduced you to the 4Rs of Organization. Let's look at how this technique can be applied to matching an organizational pattern to the content of a presentation. Suppose you wanted to give a talk on the uniquely American musical form known as the *blues.* As you *review* the material you've gathered, you may discover that a lot of it focuses on famous blues musicians—that emphasis would imply a topical arrangement that lists individual artists and describes their contributions. You can now *reduce* the number of influential artists you will talk about and *regroup* them by years, areas of the country, or special contributions. You could further *refine* your topical arrangement by using a famous song title as the heading for each key point.

On the other hand, your *review* of your research might instead suggest a causes and effects arrangement that would demonstrate how the blues influenced other forms of music such as the rock revival of the 1960s and rap music in the 1990s. Again, think about how to *reduce* these influences to the major forms of music, *regroup* them by era or type, and *refine* your presentation by labeling each form.

In a third *review* of your research, you might note that the blues migrated from the Mississippi Delta region to cities such as Memphis and Chicago. You then might try space arrangement that follows the railway lines moving north and northeast. *Reduction* would limit your consideration to major migration routes. *Regrouping* could organize your material by early and late migrations or East Coast versus Midwest migrations. *Refining* might suggest the names of famous northbound trains as headings for each section of your presentation.

Choose the approach—the contributions of individual musicians, the influence of the blues on contemporary music, or the migration of the blues—that best adapts to your purpose, the people in your audience, and the logistics and occasion of your presentation.

There are many ways to organize the content of your presentation. You may find that one format is perfect or that a combination of patterns is best. It's important to note that there are many other organizational patterns such as advantages-disadvantages, using famous quotations as key points, dos and don'ts, and checklists. In Chapter 20, "Developing Persuasive Presentations," and Chapter 21, "Developing Special Presentations," we suggest additional patterns of organization for different types of presentations.

One of the reasons that both of us spend so much of our preparation time thinking about and experimenting with ways to organize our remarks is that the time is so well spent. Remember that deciding how to organize is part of the overall strategy for making a presentation. Organization provides you with a framework that can tell you what to include in your presentation, in what order to include it, and for what effect.

Isn't Organizing the Same as Outlining?

Leonard Rampulla, a New York architect who also serves as president of a professional organization, told us: "[Although] there is a comfort level using my voice and gestures and answering questions, my delivery was more successful when I was well organized and used an outline." Mr. Rampulla understands the value of organization and the utility of an outline. He also understands that they are not the same thing.

Organizing a presentation requires careful attention to selecting key points and appropriate supporting material and then to putting all the pieces of a talk in their proper place and order. Organization provides a strategic framework that links your purpose to the audience's willingness and ability to listen, understand, and respond to your message. Organization is a strategy. Outlining, on the other hand, is a technique, as you will see in Chapter 10, "Organizational Tools."

Summary

▶ Why is organization so important?

Organization helps a speaker gather ideas and information, develop a rhetorical strategy, and enhance credibility. Organization also helps an audience understand, remember, and react to what you say.

▶ How do I select the key points for a presentation?

Consider your purpose, the audience, the occasion, and the logistics of the situation. Then apply the 4Rs of Organization—review, reduce, regroup, and refine.

▶ How do I link my purpose, central idea, and key points?

Make sure that your central idea summarizes the key points of your presentation and, if appropriate, provides a brief preview of the organization you will follow to achieve your purpose.

▶ Are there established organizational formats that I can follow?

Common organizational patterns include topical arrangement, time arrangement, space arrangement, problem-solution, causes and effects, scientific method, stories and examples, comparison-contrast, and memory aids.

Presentation Principles in Action

Match the Organizational Patterns

Directions: Each of the following examples illustrates how to use one (or more) of the organizational patterns listed below. Try to match each outline with an appropriate pattern or patterns.

A. Topical Arrangement
B. Time Arrangement
C. Space Arrangement
D. Problem-Solution
E. Causes and Effects
F. Scientific Method Arrangement
G. Stories and Examples
H. Comparison-Contrast
I. Memory Aids
J. Mixture of Patterns

1. _____ The Three Stages of Pregnancy
   First trimester
   Second trimester
   Third trimester

2. _____ The Qualities of Good Running Shoes
   Cushioning
   Stability
   Motion control

3. _____ Four Basic Techniques for Playing Volleyball
   Setting
   Bumping
   Spiking
   Serving

4. _____ The Richest Source of Diamonds
   South Africa
   Tanzania
   Murfreesboro, Tennessee

5. _____ The Legacies of Presidents Reagan, Bush, and Clinton
   Domestic issues
   International issues
   Political issues

6. _____ The Lives of Homeless Families
   The Khoo family
   The Taylor family
   The Arias family

7. _____ Aspirin Can Reduce Heart Attacks
   Can aspirin reduce heart attacks?
   What does the research say?
   What are the implications of this research?

8. _____ The "Throw, Row, Then Go" Rules of Lifesaving
   Throw a life preserver to the victim.
   Row a boat or surfboard to the victim.
   Go (swim) to the victim as the last resort.

9. _____ Slowing the AIDS Epidemic
   AIDS is a devastating disease.
   A cure has not been found.
   Current treatments can slow the spread of AIDS.

Key Terms

causes and effects arrangement 202
central idea 198
comparison-contrast arrangement 204
figurative analogy 205
framing 195
key points 196
memory aids arrangement 205
organization 194
problem-solution arrangement 201
scientific method arrangement 203
space arrangement 200
time arrangement 200
topical arrangement 199

Notes

1 Some of the best research on the value of organizing a presentation was done in the 1960s and 1970s. See Ernest C. Thompson, "An Experimental Investigation of the Relative Effectiveness of Organizational Structure in Oral Communication," *The Southern Speech Journal* 26 (1960): 59–69; Ernest C. Thompson, "Some Effects of Message Structure on Listeners' Comprehension," *Speech Monographs* 34 (1967): 51–57; James McCroskey and R. Samuel Mehrley, "The Effects of Disorganization and Nonfluency on Attitude Change and Source Credibility," *Communication Monographs* 36 (1969): 13–21; Arlee Johnson, "A Preliminary Investigation of the Relationship Between Organization and Listener Comprehension," *Central States Speech Journal* 21 (1970): 104–107; Christopher Spicer and Ronald E. Bassett, "The Effect of Organization on Learning from an Informative Message," *Southern Speech Communication Journal* 41 (1976): 290–299.

2 One of the best overviews of Cicero's contributions to rhetoric appears in Lester Thonssen and A. Craig Baird, *Speech Criticism: The Development of Standards for Rhetorical Appraisal* (New York: The Ronald Press, 1948), pp. 78–91. Also see James L. Golden, Goodwin F. Berquist, and William E. Coleman, *The Rhetoric of Western Thought,* 4th ed. (Dubuque, IA: Kendall/Hunt, 1989).

3 Steve Emmons, "Emotions at Face Value," *Los Angeles Times,* 9 January 1998, pp. E1 and E8.

4 See Marie Winn, "The Trouble with Television," in *Taking Sides: Clashing Views on Controversial Issues in Mass Media and Society,* ed. Alison Alexander and Jarice Hanson, 5th ed. (Guilford, CT: Duskin/McGraw-Hill, 1999), pp. 22–28.

5 See the chapters on reading and writing quantitative and qualitative research reports in Joann Keyton, *Communication Research: Asking Questions, Finding Answers* (Boston: McGraw-Hill, 2001), pp. 314–345.

6 Katherine E. Rowan, "A New Pedagogy for Explanatory Public Speaking: Why Arrangement Should Not Substitute for Invention," *Communication Education* 44 (1995): 236–250.

chapter ten

Organizational **Tools**

- How do I go about shaping my ideas into a presentation?
- How can outlining help me organize my presentation?
- How do I connect one idea to another?
- Can I be both creative and well organized?

Determining and ordering the key points of a presentation are two different but related functions. Chapter 9, "Organization," describes strategies for surveying the ideas and information you have collected to determine the key points that will best suit your purpose. Ordering involves arranging the specific parts of a presentation in an effective sequence. Do you recall the two basic tasks Cicero required of every effective speaker? Creating a well-organized presentation requires both of them: determining the key points (*inventio*) and putting those points into an orderly sequence (*dispositio*). We explored *inventio* in Chapter 9. Now, we will look at *dispositio* in more detail.

Fortunately, there are several techniques or tools for arranging your ideas and information in a well-organized presentation with a clear beginning, middle, and end. These tools can shape your content and strengthen your message. Although they are not unique to speechmaking, these techniques can prove invaluable when you're deciding how to sort and where to strategically place the key points of a presentation.

Getting Ready to Outline

Almost every presentation and public speaking book ever written advocates outlining as a means of organization. So do we, yet we also recognize that outlining has its limits and appreciate that not everyone finds outlining equally useful. Outlining is a planning tool, not an end in itself. Outlining helps you organize and order your ideas. Thomas Leech, a communication consultant and executive speech coach, observed that "presenters sometimes say that they don't outline because it will constrain their thought process and take away their natural flow. Yet a presentation must be constrained. It must be tightly packaged, with all the extraneous ideas and materials excluded. An audience deserves and will insist upon a concisely organized message that achieves its goals in the least possible time."[1]

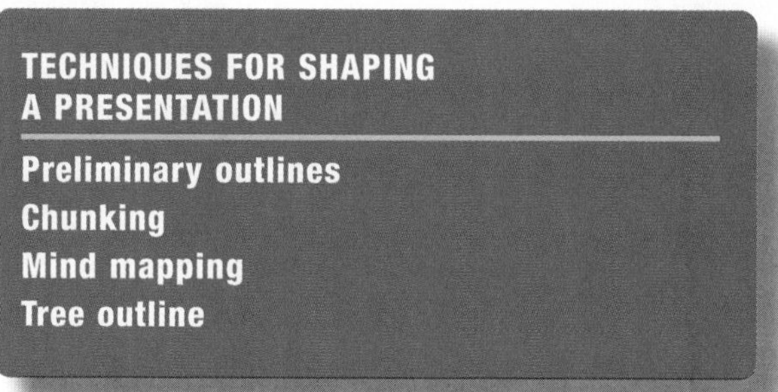

Preliminary Outlines

Outlines give you a clear and logical framework on which to hang your ideas and supporting material. They are not born fully grown during the speechwriting process with every detail and subpoint in place. Outlines grow. They begin in a preliminary form

TOPIC AREA:

I. Introduction
  A. Purpose/Topic
  B. Central Idea
  C. Brief Preview of Key Points
    1. Key point #1
    2. Key point #2
    3. Key point #3 (or more)

II. Body of the Presentation
  A. Key Point #1
    1. Supporting Material
    2. Supporting Material
  B. Key Point #2
    1. Supporting Material
    2. Supporting Material
  C. Key Point #3
    1. Supporting Material
    2. Supporting Material

III. Conclusion

Figure 10.1

Model Preliminary Outline

with a few basic building blocks. An informal **preliminary outline** puts the major pieces of your message in a clear and logical order. In its simplest form, a preliminary outline looks like this:

I. Introduction
II. Body of Presentation
III. Conclusion

Figure 10.1 shows an expanded preliminary outline for a presentation that you can use as a model.

You can use this model to organize almost any presentation. Naturally, you would modify the outline, depending on the number of key points and the types and amount of information you would be using as supporting material. There should be at least one piece of supporting material under each key point. If you think that you know what your key points will be, try developing the details of your presentation according to this model.

Chunking

Why do phone numbers have dashes or dots in them? Put another way, what's easier to remember—a series of ten random numbers or a three-digit area code, a three-digit local exchange number, and a four-digit number to complete a phone number?

Figure 10.2 Organize by Chunking

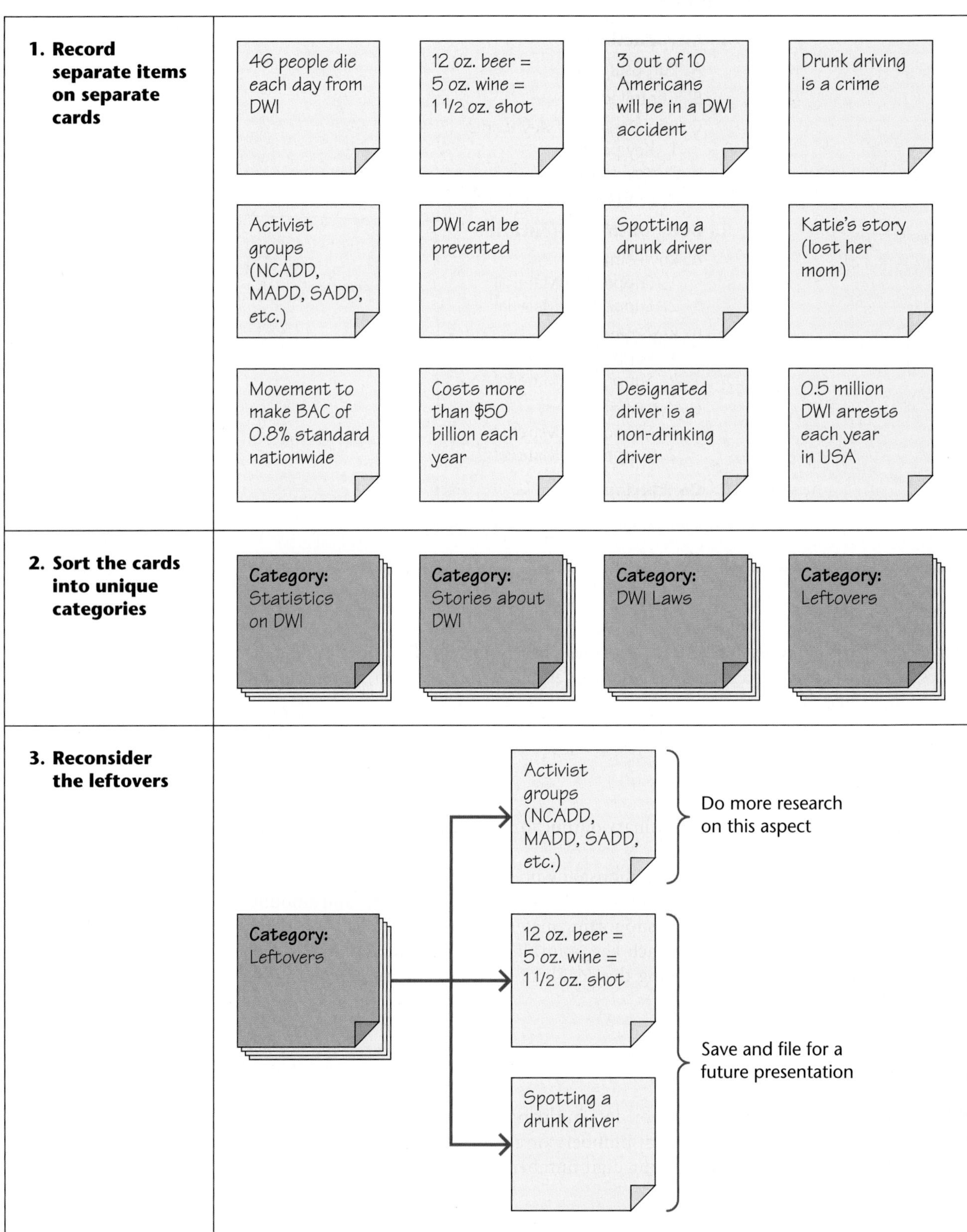

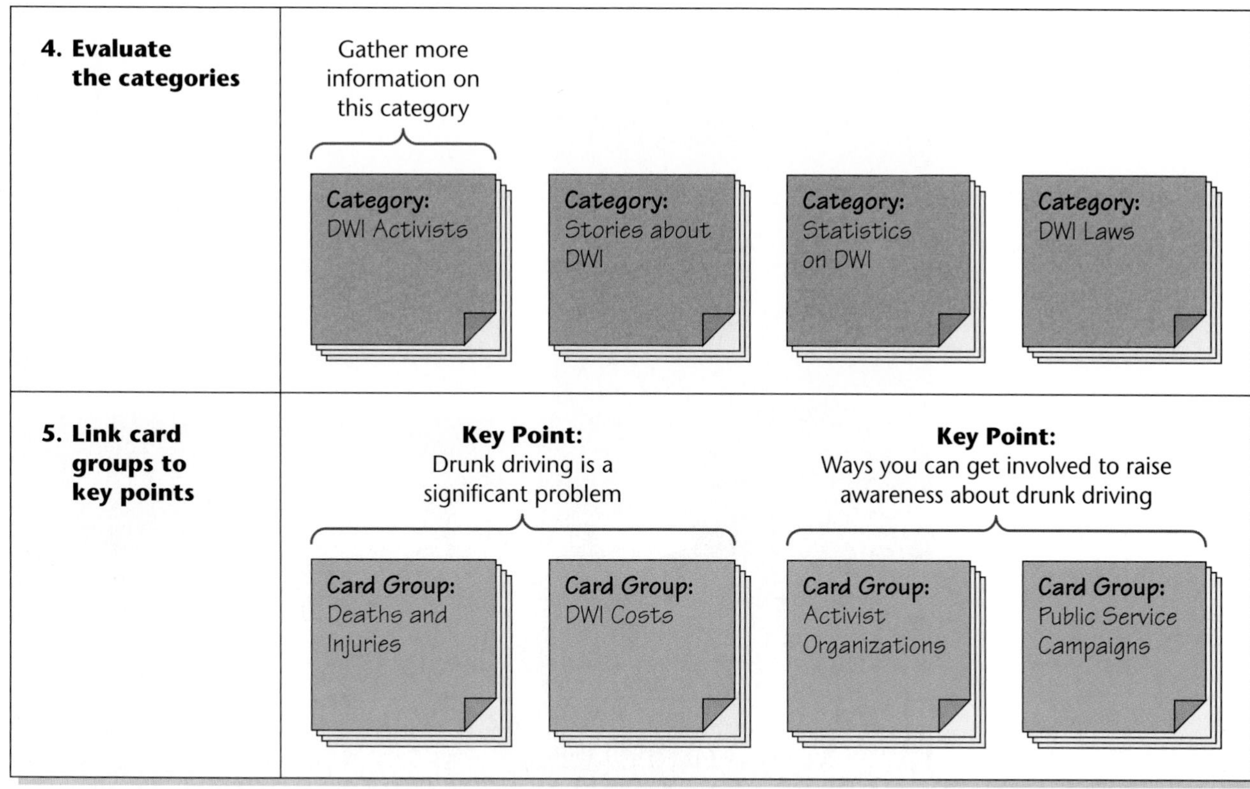

You know the answer because you can recall many phone numbers with relative ease. The dashes or dots in phone numbers illustrate the concept of chunking, a principle that also applies to presentation speaking. **Chunking,** as its name implies, is the process of sorting the ideas and supporting material you have gathered for a presentation into unique categories or "chunks."

Although the chunking process requires time for recording, sorting, and critical thinking, we know several excellent speakers who swear by chunking as the best way to find an effective organizational pattern for their presentations. The chunking process is illustrated in Figure 10.2 and works like this:

1. *Record separate items on separate cards.* Every time you come up with a good idea or piece of supporting material for your presentation, record it on a 3 × 5-inch card. Post-Its work well, too. Put only *one* idea, phrase, example, quotation, story, and so forth on each card or Post-It. Keep it simple to make sorting easier.

2. *Sort the cards into unique categories.* When you have finished gathering and recording your ideas and supporting material on cards, sort them into non-overlapping categories. For example, in a presentation on drinking and driving, stories about alcohol-related car accidents could be put in one pile, demographic statistics on the kinds of people most likely to drive while intoxicated could go in another pile, suggested changes in drunk driving laws could go in a third pile, and so on.

Texas Governor Tick Perry studies a draft of his State of the State speech. Paying attention to a presentation's organizational structure can be just as important as rehearsing the words in it.

3. *Reconsider the leftovers.* After you have sorted your cards into unique categories, do you have any remaining cards that cannot be placed in a pile? Maybe they don't apply to your topic or to the purpose of this presentation. Maybe you need to gather more information about this aspect of the topic. Maybe your entry isn't specific enough to file. If you decide not to use the ideas or information on a card, consider saving those cards. They may come in handy for a future presentation.

4. *Evaluate the categories.* Do some piles contain only two or three cards while others have dozens of cards? Does this mean that you need more information on an important subtopic? Are you missing important information? For example, are you missing a pile on the number of DWI deaths and injuries in the United States or in your home state? Have you forgotten to research current laws?

5. *Link card groups to key points.* Give each pile of cards a name. For example, a pile of cards that includes statistics on DWI deaths and injuries could be labeled "Deaths and Injuries." Another pile that documents the financial impact of drunk driving could be labeled "DWI Costs." Both piles could be used to support a key point that drunk driving is a significant problem.

By the time you have finished the chunking process, you will have the basic building blocks of your presentation. Your remaining task will be to arrange those key points and their supporting material in a suitable order for your presentation.

Mind Mapping Is	Mind Mapping Is Not
A creative way to generate key points	Structured thinking
A starting point for reviewing, reducing, and regrouping key ideas	An analytical tool
A free flow of ideas that can help you make connections among ideas and supporting material	A technique for evaluating key points

Figure 10.3

Mind Mapping

Mind Mapping

Not everyone is skilled at outlining or chunking. Moreover, a preliminary outline may not be the best way to *begin* organizing a presentation, particularly when a linear, logical progression of ideas may be difficult to develop or may not be the ideal way to achieve your purpose.

We recommend that you use a technique called **mind mapping** because it encourages the free flow of ideas and lets you define relationships among the ideas. Rather than forcing your content into a predetermined organizational pattern, you can discover connections that suggest one or more organizational patterns for your presentation (see Figure 10.3).

In the late 1960s, Tony Buzon (editor of the *International Mensa Journal,* a publication for people with genius IQs) came up with the concept of mind mapping as a way to harness the potential of the whole brain. Mind mapping can help you generate ideas while your brain is in a highly creative mode of thought.[2]

How do you mind map? Start with a clean sheet of paper. Write your subject or central idea in the middle of a blank page. Then, write down the ideas you hope to cover in your presentation. Don't be afraid to fill the page. Neatness doesn't count. Initially, there are no bad ideas. What is important is that you have a one-page conglomeration of the many ideas that you could include in your presentation. If possible, put related ideas near each other on the page and draw a circle around that group of ideas. If groups of ideas are related, let your circles overlap or draw lines between those circles.

Figure 10.4 shows a mind map for a presentation on Muzak created by Julie Borchard, a student who was preparing to compete in an informative speaking contest. It's a hodgepodge of words, phrases, lists, circles, and arrows. After completing such a mind map, you can label circled ideas as key points and put them in a logical order. The entire text of Julie's presentation is included in the Appendix.

Because there was so much interrelated material to be included, Julie found the mind map a useful way to begin the organizational process. Note how almost every idea on the mind map in Figure 10.4 is included in the presentation.

Mind mapping is a very useful tool when you have lots of ideas and information about a topic but are having trouble deciding how to arrange the ideas for a presentation. Mind maps let you see all of your ideas without superimposing an organizational pattern on them. They also let you postpone the need to arrange your ideas in a pattern until you have collected enough information to think about how you want to organize the content of your presentation.

Tree Outline

If you can't outline with ease, don't think chunking or mind mapping would work for you, or need more help sorting your ideas and information, you might want to

Figure 10.4 Muzak Mind Map

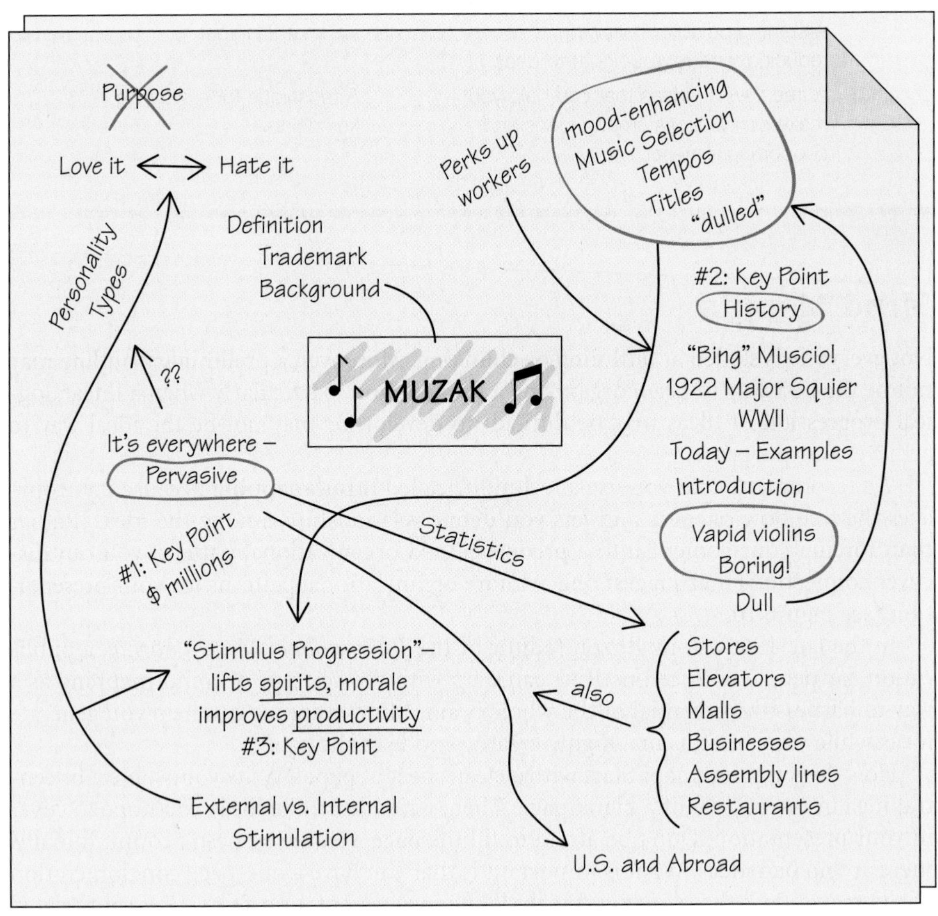

try another organizational technique. It's known by a variety of similar names: tree outlines, idea trees, organization trees.

Let's start with the most lifelike example—the **tree outline.** Although an outline and a tree are not alike, there are some characteristics that have similar functions and relationships. You can think of your central idea as the tree's trunk, your key points as its limbs, and your supporting materials as branches extending from each limb. Your words are the leaves. Figure 10.5 shows a tree outline.

In a tree outline, all of the limbs (key points) are directly attached to the trunk (central idea). All branches (supporting material) are attached to respective limbs, and all leaves (words) are attached to branches. A limb cannot be attached to a branch or a leaf. Note that the tree outline follows the model preliminary outline (see Figure 10.1).

I. Introduction

   A. Central Idea = Trunk
   B. Preview of Key Points = Limbs #1, #2 and #3

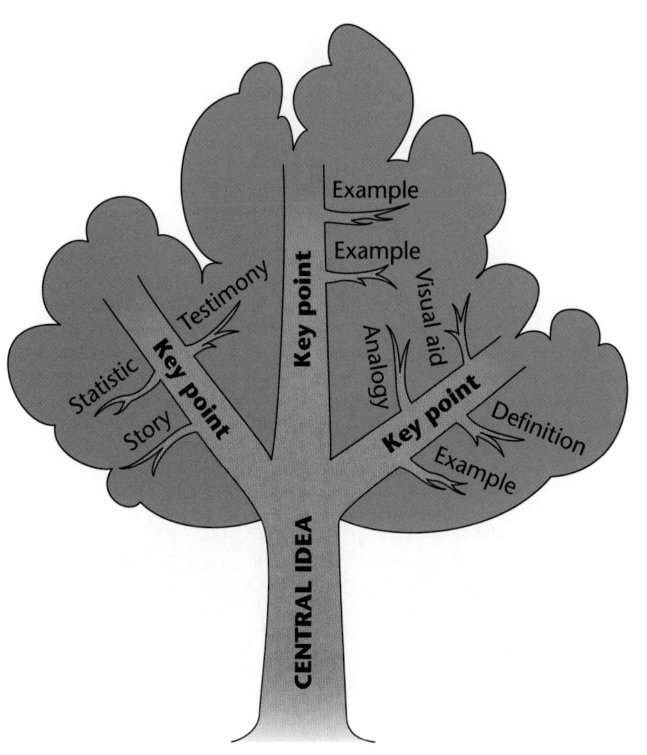

Figure 10.5

Tree Outline

II. Body of Presentation

  A. Limb #1
    1. Branch and Leaves
    2. Branch and Leaves

  B. Limb #2
    1. Branch and Leaves
    2. Branch and Leaves

  C. Limb #3
    1. Branch and Leaves
    2. Branch and Leaves

III. Conclusion

Your tree may look quite different, depending on the organizational pattern that you use. For example, suppose that you have decided to give a presentation on the need to support local refugee families. After reviewing your material, you decide that telling a series of dramatic stories about real-life refugee families would be the most effective way to present your message. In such a presentation, there would be only one central idea: People should help support the refugee families in your community. Thus, instead of having several limbs with branches attached, you would go straight from the trunk to the branches for your supporting material. As Figure 10.6 shows, this tree outline would resemble a pine tree.

Organizational Patterns Do Grow on Trees. Using the tree outline is a great way to experiment with different organizational patterns. For example, if you were using a problem-solution format, your tree might have just two limbs—one

Figure 10.6

Pine Tree Outline

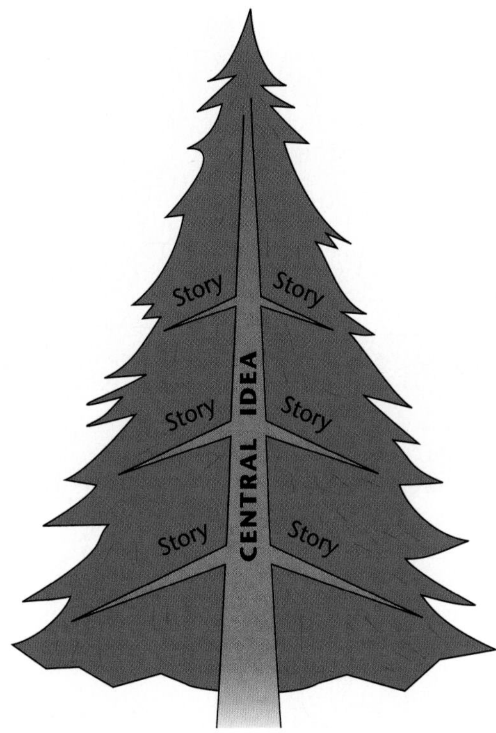

labeled "problem" and one labeled "solution." After reviewing your material, however, you might discover the need for a third limb, labeled "causes." Causes are neither the problem nor the solution; rather, they explain why there is a problem or why there isn't a solution. So what began as a tree with two mighty limbs has become one with three limbs (problem, causes, solution).

By experimenting with a tree outline, you may find that you have limbs with no branches and/or branches with no limbs. You may have planned to compare the safety of fossil fuel energy to the dangers of nuclear energy but find you have no branches (supporting material) for the "fossil fuels are safe" limb. Or you might have lots of branches on rubber production, but they don't belong on a tree trunk (central idea) labeled "How to Change a Tire."

The Organization Tree. An **organization tree** is a more structured version of the tree outline. Although it doesn't look like a tree, it still maintains the relationships depicted in the tree outline. Figure 10.7 is a worksheet for preparing an organization tree and was developed by Marya Holcombe and Judith Stein, the authors of *Presentations for Decision Makers.*[3]

How do you use this worksheet?

1. On the far left of the organization tree worksheet, fill in your central idea—the one concept that you want the audience to understand and remember.
2. In the center section, fill in your key points—those ideas that would be the major branches on a tree outline. Each key point should be separate and should not be a subtopic of another key point.
3. To the right of each key point, add detailed supporting material. Make sure that each piece of supporting material is directly linked to the key point to which it is attached.

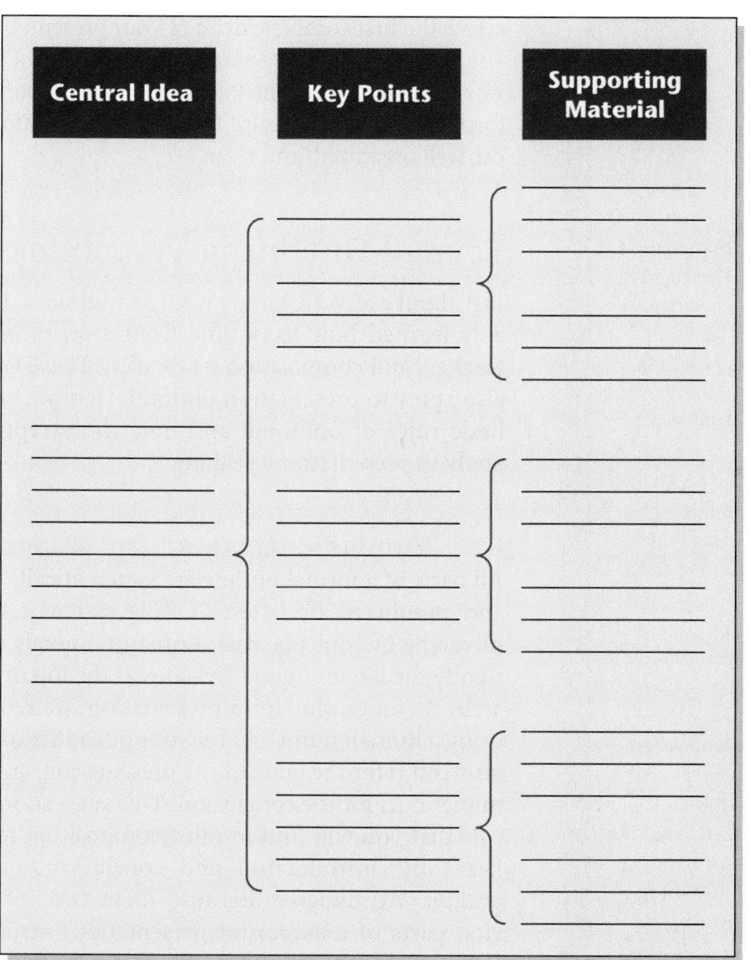

Figure 10.7

Organization Tree Worksheet

Not only does the organization tree add more structure than a mind map does; it also puts the ideas and information in a hierarchical order. The central idea is more fundamental than each of the key points. The key points are more prominent than the supporting material. An organization tree provides a pattern for your presentation. It shows you whether or not your key points directly relate to your central idea and whether or not you have adequate supporting material for each key point.[4]

The Formal Outline

Preliminary outlines, mind maps, and tree outlines help you to develop and arrange your ideas into a sketch of a presentation. Refining these sketches into your actual presentation often requires the creation of a formal outline. A **formal outline** is a comprehensive written framework for a presentation that follows established conventions concerning content and format. Whereas informal outlines help you plan your presentation—particularly while your key ideas are still evolving—a formal outline helps you

How Many Key Points Should I Include?

Including too many ideas or key points is one of the most common mistakes speakers make when outlining their presentations. Not surprisingly, then, one of the questions we hear most often is this: How many key points should I include? We wish there were a definitive answer. Generally, we suggest that there should be at least two key points and no more than five. Three are ideal. In fact, scholars have discovered that audience members expect and anticipate that speakers will make three points in their speeches.[1] Of course, there are exceptions. Remember the pine tree outline? That presentation advocating community help for refugees focused on dramatic stories that supported a single central idea which was also the key point.

If you have too many key points, try to boil them down. Audiences usually seem able to understand and remember three key points better than four or five. Ask yourself these questions: Which ideas are the most essential? Which ones will help me achieve my purpose? Which ones are most likely to interest and affect my audience? Apply the 4Rs technique discussed in Chapter 9. Carefully review, reduce, and, if possible, regroup your key points. It's better to cut one of your key points than to sacrifice your whole presentation to a bored or restless audience.

1. John Heritage and David Greatbach, "Generating Applause: A Study of Rhetoric and Response at Party Political Conferences," *American Journal of Sociology* 92 (1986): 110–157.

create the first complete draft of your presentation. Once you identify your key points and feel confident about the way in which you want to arrange and support them, a formal outline can ensure that your presentation is logical, well organized, and clear.

Formal Outlining Principles

Just about everyone knows what an outline is. You probably learned how to outline from a series of English teachers and composition textbooks.[5] These techniques also apply to presentation outlines. Here we offer three basic rules of outlining and note the exceptions that apply to presentation speaking.

Use Numbers, Letters, and Indentation. All parts of a formal outline are systematically indented and numbered or lettered.[6] This system reflects the hierarchy of your material. Roman numerals (I, II, III) signify the largest major divisions at the top of the hierarchy. In an outline for a presentation, we recommend using a Roman numeral *I* for your introduction, Roman numeral *II* for the body of the presentation, and Roman numeral *III* for the conclusion. This suggestion breaks a rule that you will find in most composition textbooks: Leave the introduction and conclusion out of the outline. We disagree. Because these two sections are vital parts of a successful presentation's structure, we recommend including them in a formal outline.

After using Roman numerals to establish the major sections of a presentation, follow standard outlining rules about letters, numbers, and indentation: Indented capital letters (*A, B, C,* and so forth) are used for subtopics that fit under a major division. In a presentation, capital letters can be used to designate the key points. Further indented Arabic numbers (*1, 2, 3,* and so forth) are even more specific. In a presentation, Arabic numbers can be used to list supporting material, evidence and reasoning, or any other subdivision of a key point. If you need a fourth level, you would indent and use lowercase letters (*a, b, c,* and so forth). As you move from Roman numerals to capital letters to Arabic numbers to lowercase letters, your information should become more and more specific. Remember the tree outline. You start with a single trunk, move to limbs (*A, B, C*), then to branches (*1, 2, 3*), and finally to small twigs and leaves (*a, b, c*).

Divide Your Subpoints Logically. Each major subpoint should include at least two points indented under it or none at all. If there is an *A*, there must be a *B*; for every *1*, there must be a *2*. In other words, all headings or subpoints must have at least two parts because you cannot logically divide something into just one part. Why? Think of it this way: Can you cut a piece out of a cake with only one slice from the middle to the edge? No. Instead, you need two cuts to remove a slice (or none at all if you want a really big piece—the whole cake!).

Wrong:
I.
  A.
II.

Right:
I.
  A.
  B.
II.

Keep the Outline Consistent. Use either a topic, a phrase, or a full sentence for each key point in your outline rather than mixing styles. When you get to the Arabic number level, you may need more than a word or a phrase to record supporting material, but you should try to use a consistent style to label each level throughout the outline. Also, use a consistent grammatical form: If you begin each subpoint with a verb, don't switch to beginning with nouns halfway through the outline. Don't change styles or grammatical forms in the same outline. Not only will consistency make your outline easier to read and use; it will also force you to work on finding the best and most precise words, phrases, and/or sentences for each section.

Wrong:
I. Consistent Style
II. Use a consistent grammatical form.

Right:
I. Keep the outline consistent in style.
II. Use a consistent grammatical form.

Right:
I. Consistent style
II. Consistent grammatical form

Why, you may ask, are there such strict rules? The reason has little to do with the obsessions of English teachers. These rules can help you to create a clear and useful outline. Consistent headings, consistent style, and consistent grammatical structure keep your outline clear and provide a dependable structure for organizing your presentation.

The Benefits of Outlining

A formal outline is a planning tool, a blueprint for your presentation. It tells you where every piece of your presentation goes—from the introduction through the conclusion. However, its benefits don't stop there. Besides helping you organize your presentation, a formal outline also serves other important functions.

OUTLINING HELPS YOU

Select and order your supporting material
Enhance your word choice
Change and adapt your presentation
Check your structure
Reveal flaws in logic

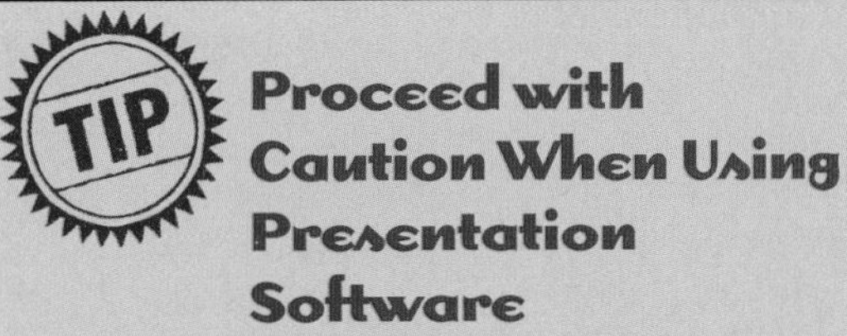

Just a dozen or so years ago, few speakers used sophisticated software to prepare and give their presentations. Today colleges and corporations are demanding that everyone learn to use one or more **presentation software** packages such as PowerPoint, Corel Presentations, or Freelance. Most of these packages encourage beginners to use the software's fill-in-the-blank outline. Perhaps you've already tried this and are wondering why we're spending so much time talking about outlining a presentation when there are already programs that will do it for you. The answer is that these packages *don't* organize! Rather, they convert material that you input into outlines or convert your outline into a storyboard of visual aids.

You can't rely on software packages to organize your presentations for you. Unless you have reviewed, reduced, regrouped, and refined your materials (see Chapter 9), you'll most likely end up with a flashy but fragmented presentation. Presentation software may help you put on a good-looking show, but it's no substitute for good organization.

Selecting and Ordering Supporting Material. A formal outline helps you pull together the results of your gathering and ordering ideas and information. With your key points in place, you can then insert your related supporting materials, identifying each by its form under each key point. A quick scan of your formal outline will reveal at a glance whether you have too many statistics and not enough testimony or stories. If this is the case, you can modify the presentation by substituting different forms of supporting material in your outline.

Enhancing Word Choice. A formal outline also requires that you use very specific word choices when writing the beginning of your presentation, stating your central idea, labeling your key points, and even making a smooth transition from one section to another. Ideally, you should include the exact wording of your central idea and key points on your formal outline. Also include references to or the exact wording of the supporting material that you intend to use. By paying careful attention to wording, you can make sure that it's consistent, clear, and memorable. Unless you are reading your presentation from a manuscript (something we discuss in Chapter 14, "Performance and Practice"), a formal outline may be the only written record of your presentation.

Making Changes and Adaptations Easier. In the same way that builders modify blueprints as they work, you can adjust your formal outline. A formal outline allows you to make changes in any part of your presentation quite simply. For instance, once you have your key points outlined, you can easily test different organizational patterns for them by arranging the sections and their related subsections in different sequences. If you find a great piece of supporting material at the last minute, you can just add an Arabic number for it under the appropriate capital letter. A formal outline allows you to update material at the last minute without disturbing the outline format. With a few quickly drawn arrows to guide your way around a section that should be cut, an outline can help you modify your presentation at the last minute.

Checking Structure. A formal outline lets you check each subpoint against its key point and each key point against your central idea. As you construct a formal outline, keep asking yourself questions such as these: Do subpoints 1 and 2 support the major A point? Do the A and B points support the central idea? If they don't, you may not be well organized, or you may not have selected appropriate supporting material for your presentation. If, for example, your list of key points (A, B, C, D, E, F, G, and so forth) begins to look like alphabet soup, find a way to consolidate those ideas into a few major categories with more subcategories. If, on the other hand, you are straining to find a B point to follow an A point, your first key point may be too broad. Remember: A well-developed outline provides and checks the structure of your message.

Revealing Flaws. Outlines can also help you look for errors, flaws, and digressions. The outline of a presentation can reveal whether a section is lacking supporting material. It can also reveal whether two sections are saying the same thing and whether every section is relevant to your central idea.[7] An added advantage of having a formal outline is that you can share it with someone else before you speak. In reviewing your outline, a helpful reader may find phrases that are unclear, terms that are ambiguous, or supporting material that doesn't support a main idea.

A good formal outline is more than an organizational tool. It is a safety net that helps you arrange and rearrange ideas and supporting materials, and catch and correct errors. It also forms the basis for flexible speaking notes that you can use to rehearse and deliver your presentation. Using a formal outline can shape your content, strengthen your message, and enhance audience understanding.

Presentation Outlines

Formal outlines provide a great way to organize your material and to double-check the content of your message. Formal outlines are not, however, the same as speaking notes. The notes that you use during a presentation should not be as long or detailed as a formal outline. Generally, we like using a short outline—one that includes little more than a list of key points and reminders of supporting material. Other speakers whom we know use full sentence outlines in which each key point is written out word for word. Rarely, however, do speakers use a complete formal outline as speaking notes. Figure 10.8 shows a simplified complete sentence outline for a presentation on the importance of customer service. Note that the introduction, central idea, key points, and conclusion are written out, whereas reminders about the type and substance of supporting material are put in parentheses.

Presentation outlines rarely conform to all the rules of formal outlining. Rather, speakers use these rules as guidelines to help them create a clear and compelling

---

Figure 10.8 Complete Sentence Outline

I. Introduction

A. Question: What will be the most important factor for competitive business success in the year 2000 and beyond? (Gallup Poll of CEOs, owners, and company presidents)

B. Answer:
18% said operating efficiency
25% said product/service quality
27% said *customer service*

C. Central Idea: Become a service-centered business if you want to succeed.

II. Body

A. Your job security and business success depend on how valuable you are to your customers. (Stories, statistics, and descriptions of successful employees and businesses)

B. Customers will replace you with better service providers. (When the product and price are the same, service is the only area in which you can be different from the competition. Ask audience for examples.)

C. Develop a reputation for responsiveness. (Nordstrom, Saturn, Ritz Carlton Hotels, the local hospital)

III. Conclusion

Customers are the lifeblood of your business. They are not dependent on you; you are dependent on them. So remember the secret of keeping good customers: Exceed their expectations! And you'll succeed in business!

The Douglass Archives of American Public Address website at Northwestern University, www.douglass.speech.nwu.edu, provides numerous examples of historic American speeches on a variety of issues.

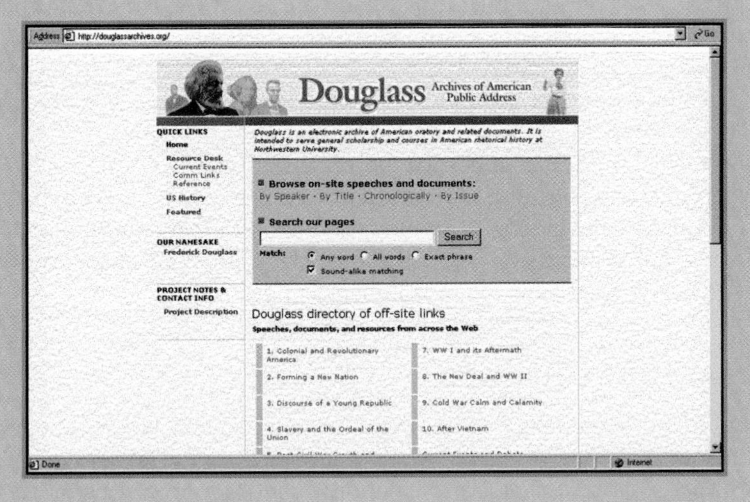

presentation. Figure 10.9 shows the detailed outline for Julie Borchard's presentation on Muzak (see Figure 10.4 for her mind map). The outline provides a lot of detail because it was used to prepare a manuscript version of the presentation. You can read the complete text of this award-winning presentation in the Appendix.

Notice that this outline does not conform to all of the outlining rules we cited. Although it does use numbers, letters, and indentation, it is not consistent in style or in grammatical form. Because the speaker used parts of the outline as her speaking notes for a well-rehearsed presentation, she needed only a word or phrase to remind her where she was. Nevertheless, she wrote her central idea and preview of key points as entire sentences to make sure that she got the wording exactly right. In addition, she identified the different types of supporting material in her outline to make sure that a variety of types were included in the presentation.

Connecting Your Key Points

Even though an outline shows how you've structured and developed your key points, it's missing the "glue" that attaches the key points to each other. **Connectives** are this glue and include the internal previews, internal summaries, transitions, and signposts that connect the pieces of your presentation to form a coherent whole. Without them, even a well-organized presentation can sound choppy and awkward.

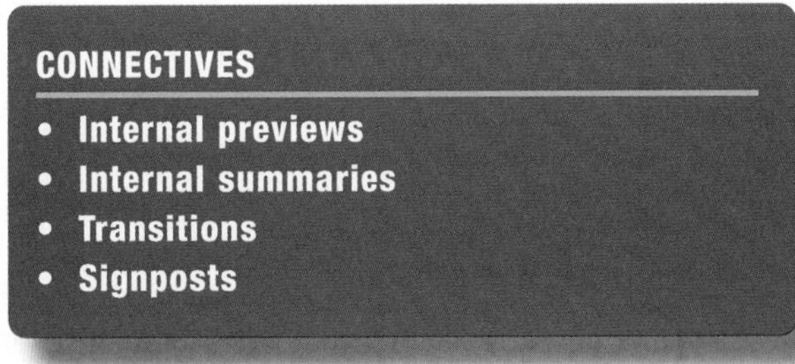

Figure 10.9 Complete Presentation Outline

MUZAK

I. Introduction

A. Play a sample of Muzak on a tape recorder to gain audience's attention.

B. Provide descriptions

1. By creators: sonorous design, sound energy
2. By the public: spineless melodies, vapid violins

C. Muzak

1. Trademarked brand name for background music (definition)
2. Muzak dominates the field (quotation from the president of Muzak).

D. Central Idea and Key Points

1. You can become more enlightened about Muzak
   a. By understanding how pervasive Muzak is
   b. By understanding how it originated
   c. By understanding how it lifts spirits and increases productivity

II. Body

A. Key Point #1: Pervasive (*USA Today* article)

1. Statistics: Size of business, number of listeners
2. Poll results: People like Muzak.
3. Statistics: American companies using Muzak

B. Key Point #2: Origins and Development

1. 1922: Major George O. Squier
2. 1937: "Fatigue and Boredom in Repetitive Work" (Wyatt and Langdon Study)
3. 1945: 75% of World War II industries (Nye Study)
4. 1972: Studies of Muzak and worker productivity (Manhattan Blue Cross/Blue Shield Study)

C. Key Point #3: Lifts Spirits and Improves Productivity

1. Work patterns and "stimulus progression" (*USA Today* article)
   a. Tempos
   b. Titles
2. Music Forms: "Dulled" recordings (quotation by Muzak executive)
3. Uses
   a. Major corporations and the federal government (examples)
   b. Restaurants, supermarkets
   c. Hospitals (St. Joseph's Hospital)
4. Personality Types and Muzak
   a. Need for external stimulation (study by Mose)
   b. Need for quiet (quotation from Perpetual Savings and Loan executive)

III. Conclusion

A. Size and Success of Muzak

B. Quotation: "Bing" Muscio, former President of Muzak

C. The sound of Muzak is here to stay.

Just as the chapter titles and headings in this textbook help you understand and follow what is being discussed, connectives help your audience follow, understand, and remember your message. In fact, connectives matter far more in spoken than in written communication.[8] A reader can go back to see how a writer connects ideas. Listeners don't have that luxury. They need wording such as "My next point is," "on the other hand," or

"It's time to talk about solutions" to alert and prepare them for important ideas in a presentation. Connectives help link one part of a presentation to another, clarify how one idea relates to another, and identify how supporting material bolsters a key point.

Internal Previews

One of the first connectives likely to appear in a presentation is the internal preview. In the introduction of a presentation, an **internal preview** reveals or suggests your key points to the audience. It tells them what you are going to cover and in what order. In the body of a presentation, an internal preview describes how you are going to approach a key point. Depending on your topic and your audience, you may need an internal preview only in your introduction. If your key points are complex with many subpoints, however, you may also want to include internal previews within the body of your presentation.

Here's how one student internally previewed his presentation on weight loss:

> *How do researchers and doctors explain obesity? Some offer genetic explanations; others psychological ones. Either or both factors can be responsible for your never-ending battle with the bathroom scale.*

Internal Summaries

Internal summaries are closely related to internal previews. The obvious difference is that a summary ends a section, whereas a preview begins one. **Internal summaries** are a useful way to reinforce important ideas. They also give you an opportunity to pause in a presentation and repeat critical ideas or pieces of information. Here's how the same student concluded a section on the genetic factors that influence overeating:

> *So remember, before spending hundreds of dollars on diet books and exercise toys, make sure that your weight problem is not influenced by the number and size of your fat cells, your hormone level, your metabolism, or the amount of glucose in your bloodstream.*

Transitions

The most common type of connective is the **transition**—a word, number, brief phrase, or sentence that helps you move from one key point or section to another. Transitions act like lubricating oil to keep a presentation moving smoothly. Transitions can be quite simple and can consist of little more than a word or phrase. They can also be one or two complete sentences that help you move from one major section of a presentation to another. We underline some common transitions in the following examples:

> *Yet it's important to remember . . .*
>
> *In addition to metabolism, there is . . .*
>
> *Next, we'll see . . .*
>
> *On the other hand, some people believe . . .*
>
> *Of equal importance is . . .*
>
> *Another reason why he should be elected is . . .*
>
> *Finally, a responsible parent should . . .*

As simple as these transitions may seem, they can serve an important purpose by helping you and your audience move smoothly through a presentation.

Transitions can also function as mini-previews and mini-summaries that link the conclusion of one section to the beginning of another. For example:

Once you've eliminated these four genetic explanations for weight gain, it's time to consider several psychological factors.

Signposts

A final type of connective is the signpost. Quite simply, **signposts** are short phrases that, like signs on the highway, tell or remind your listeners where you are in a presentation. For example, the previously mentioned student said he would discuss four genetic explanations for weight gain, so he began each explanation with numbers—first, second, third, and fourth: "Fourth and finally, make sure your glucose level has been tested and is within normal levels. . . ." Not only did his audience know that he had reached the fourth explanation; they also knew that he was concluding the "genetics" section and was moving on to the "psychological" explanations for overeating.

Along with alerting you of a destination, road signs also can make you aware of road hazards and even scenic outlooks. Signposts within a presentation can do the same thing. They can focus attention on an important statistic or idea. They can also highlight an eloquent phrase or special insight. For example: "Even if you can't remember his every accomplishment, please remember one thing: Alex Curry is the only candidate who has been endorsed by every newspaper and civic association in this county." Here's another example: "As I read this section of Toni Morrison's novel, listen carefully to how she uses simple metaphors to describe the cemetery scene."

Generally, audiences like to hear internal previews, internal summaries, transitions, and signposts during a presentation. Just as most travelers like to know where they are, where they've been, how they got there, and where they're going, audiences likewise appreciate a speaker who uses connectives well. Using connectives effectively requires you to pay careful attention to the places in your presentation that need links to other sections. In a short, uncomplicated talk, simple transitions may be all that is needed. However, in an important and complex presentation, you may need to use all four kinds of connectives. Either way, connectives will make your presentation much easier to understand and much easier to deliver with confidence.

Creative Organization

Chapters 9 and 10 have emphasized how important it is to have a clear plan for organizing the ideas and supporting material you wish to include in your presentation. We have suggested a variety of reliable organizational formats and have recommended several tools to help you explore and then organize your content. At this point, good organization may seem to be like a jigsaw puzzle in which your ideas and supporting material are dropped into the "right" pattern or outline. But we don't see it that way. Rather, we see these formats and tools as avenues to creativity. Creativity plays an important role in discovering and arranging the ideas that you want to include in a presentation.

What Is Creativity?

If you want your presentation to be both unique and memorable, try thinking creatively about its organization. Lee Towe, president of Innovators International, Inc.,

The Habits of Creative Thinkers

Scott Isaksen describes *creative thinking* as the process in which you make and communicate meaningful new connections by devising unusual new possibilities.[1] Although it's impossible to describe the creative process in precise terms (it wouldn't be all that creative if we could), we can describe four common stages in the creative process and recommend four methods for enhancing your own creativity. Generally, there are four stages in the creative process:[2]

- *Investigation.* You gather ideas and information and use that material to better understand the topic or problem.
- *Imagination.* You remove mental roadblocks (for example: I've never done this. No one will like it. It's expensive.) and try to generate as many new ideas and approaches as you can possibly imagine.
- *Incubation.* You allow a period of time to pass during which imaginative ideas are allowed to percolate and recombine in new ways. You may want to take a break or focus your attention on another issue or on day-to-day living during the incubation stage.
- *Insight.* The "Aha" moment when a new approach or solution emerges. When you recognize this breakthrough moment, you may build upon or improve the idea.

Given the benefits of creative thinking, we recommend four methods for enhancing your own creativity during the process of developing a presentation:[3]

1. *Suspend judgment.* Almost nothing inhibits creativity as much as negative responses to new ideas: "That won't work." "That's too bizarre." Keep your mind open to new ideas. Withhold evaluation until you have generated a lot of ideas. Let one idea build upon another. Fight your natural tendency to analyze and criticize. The kernel of a creative idea can be found in a seemingly stupid or utterly impossible suggestion.
2. *Ask, "What if?"* One of the reasons that you may be reluctant to think creatively is that you have preconceived notions about what can and can't be done. Instead, ask, "What if?" What if you had unlimited funds and could do whatever you wanted without worrying about costs? What if you could call upon a celebrity to endorse your idea? What if you could hire a special effects expert to produce your presentation slides? What if your audience were paying to hear you speak? A million-dollar idea can often be implemented for a lot less. An award-winning design can be created if the basic idea is creative. Rousing words can be crafted by a talented speaker who doesn't have celebrity credentials.
3. *Make associations.* Once you are able to put your judgments on hold and ask good questions, you are ready to begin making new connections. Here are three examples: Bill Bowerman increased sales of Nike shoes in the early years of the company by transferring the design of a waffle he was eating to the bottom of a new line of shoes. A device for lifting bed frames in a factory inspired master mechanic Elisha Graves Otis to build the first elevator (and make skyscrapers possible). Pyrex cookware was born when Dr. Jesse Littleton sawed off the bottom of a glass battery jar and used it to bake a chocolate cake for coworkers at Corning Glass Works. The lesson: Apply concepts isolated in one part of your brain to problems that may seem totally irrelevant.[4]
4. *Use metaphors.* Sometimes you can discover a highly creative approach by exploring common metaphors. Jury consultants tell us that finding the right metaphor can mean the difference between a winning argument and a lost case. In organizations, metaphors are often used to explain a complex process or procedure. For example, the metaphor of an emergency room has been used to redesign the registration process at some colleges. Students who don't need any help can register online or over the telephone. Those who need help are met by a kind of "triage nurse," a college advisor who can answer simple questions, direct them to a clerk for processing, or send them to a private room where they can receive "intensive care" from a "specialist" counselor. The beauty of a metaphor is that it forces you and your audience to look at a topic in new and creative ways.

1. Scott G. Isaksen, "Human Factors for Innovative Problem Solving," in *Handbook for Creative and Innovative Managers*, ed. R. L. Kuhn (New York: McGraw-Hill, 1988), pp. 139–146. Also, the Center for Creative Learning, Inc., provides an extensive bibliography of the history, research, and impact of creative problem solving. See *www.creativelearning.com/bibliography.htm.* © 2002.
2. Based on creative problem-solving strategies in Isa N. Engleberg and Dianna R. Wynn, *Working in Groups: Communication Principles and Strategies*, 3rd ed. (Boston: Houghton Mifflin, 2003), pp. 225–229.
3. In addition to Engleberg and Wynn, see Lee Towe, *Why Didn't I Think of That? Creativity in the Workplace* (West Des Moines, IA: American Media, 1996), pp. 18–36.
4. Towe, p. 33.

defines **creativity** as consisting of two parts: creative thinking and creative output.[9] *Creative thinking* is the process of searching for, reviewing, reducing, and regrouping ideas *without* making judgments. Mind mapping is a good example of creative thinking in action. When you mind map, you begin with a blank page rather than with a formal organizational pattern. Once you have put your ideas on paper, you also have a flexible tool to review, reduce, and regroup them. Finally, a mind map allows you to reserve judgment about how to refine and organize your ideas until your mind map is finished.

Creative output is the second component of creativity and consists of connecting and combining previously unrelated elements. For example, the circles and arrows you draw on a mind map allow you to combine ideas from various points on your page. Mind mapping, however, isn't the only way to think creatively about organization. Creativity requires a mental flexibility that allows you to mix thoughts and ideas from many different sources.

Creative Applications

A presentation on growing tomatoes can be ordered topically and creatively. How can you improve upon the following organization pattern? "You can grow healthy tomatoes by (1) planting them in a sunny place, (2) giving them plenty of fertilizer and water, and (3) keeping pests and weeds under control." What about comparing tomatoes to caring for a newborn baby? "You can be the proud parent of healthy tomato plants by (1) making their garden 'nursery' safe and comfortable, (2) giving them special food and formula that will help them grow up strong and healthy, and (3) seeing that they don't come down with the usual diseases." The tomatoes/newborns analogy makes the organizational pattern more interesting and more memorable. However,

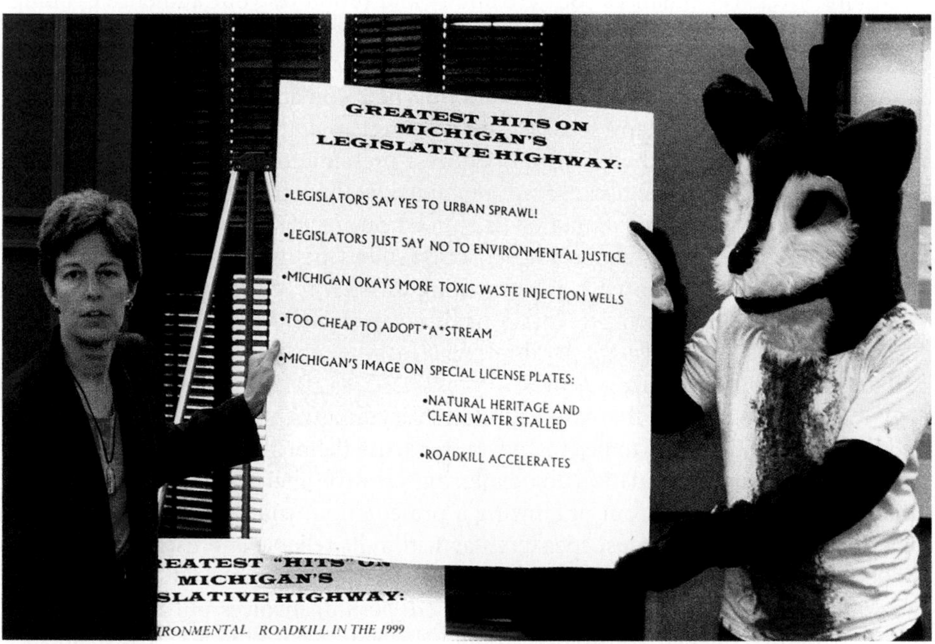

Alison Horton, director of the Michigan chapter of the Sierra Club (accompanied by Roger the Roadkill Deer) covers five key points about Michigan's environmental record. She refers to the state's environmental legislation as "roadkill," saying lawmakers have lost touch with citizens' values.

Real World Real Speakers

From Songs to the Sacred

Patricia Phillips, a customer services expert who lives in Alexandria, Virginia, uses excerpts from popular songs to begin each major section of her training seminar. Notice how each of the following song titles lends itself to customer service: "I Can't Get No Satisfaction" by the Rolling Stones, "Help" by the Beatles, "Respect" by Aretha Franklin, "Don't Be Cruel" by Elvis, and "Don't You Come Back No More" by Ray Charles. These well-known songs give Pat an upbeat and creative way to move into each new section of her seminar.

Another speaker, who works in a human relations department, uses the Bible's Ten Commandments to describe a company's work rules: "Thou shalt have no other jobs other than this one." In other words, if you're caught working at a second full-time job, you may be fired. He worded another rule as "Honor thy supervisor that thy days may be long with this company."

remember that using analogies is not the only way to produce creative organizational patterns.

On the other hand, creativity runs some risks. For example, suppose that the audience members were unfamiliar with the songs that Patricia Phillips (see "Real World, Real Speakers" box) referred to? They might find her presentation more confusing than memorable. What if using the Ten Commandments as a creative organizational pattern offended Christian and Jewish members of the second speaker's audience? If you wanted to use such a pattern, what could you say or do to avoid misunderstandings and people's taking offense?

Although there are potential dangers and costs to using creativity, almost nothing else more effectively enhances your credibility and promotes your audience's willingness to listen and learn. Using other creative organizational patterns such as a series of famous quotations, colors, or visual aids as signposts to the key points of your presentation can help an audience remember and thus help you achieve your purpose.

Despite its benefits, many speakers are reluctant to embrace using creativity as a means of discovering the best way to organize a presentation. Lee Towe suggests that many of us are not creative because we are guided by three noncreative habits: inertia, instruction, and imitation.[10] Some of us suffer from *inertia* (we've always organized presentations this way, so why change?), *instruction* (this is how we were taught to organize a presentation, so why do something different?), or *imitation* (we've heard good speakers organize their presentations this way, so we'll stick with these models). Instead, try a dose of *innovation* (by thinking creatively, we'll find interesting, effective, and unique ways to organize our presentations).

We are not suggesting that you abandon everything we've included in Chapter 9 and this chapter in a quest to be creative. Instead, use the principles of organization to give yourself a firm foundation for exploring creative alternatives. Before you can "think outside the box" about organizing a presentation, you ought to know exactly what that box is and why most speakers stay within its reliable and useful confines.

Remember Cicero's initial tasks for every effective speaker. The first (*inventio*) requires a search for main ideas; the second (*dispositio*) involves putting those ideas into an orderly sequence. If using creativity helps you to find the best ideas and supporting material for your presentation and helps you to put your content into an effective and orderly sequence, don't hesitate to release your creative talents.

Summary

How do I go about shaping my ideas into a presentation?

Techniques that can help you shape your ideas and information into an effective presentation include preliminary outlines, mind mapping, tree outlines, and organization trees.

How can outlining help me organize my presentation?

Outlining is only one of many ways to begin the organizational process. A formal outline, however, effectively concludes the organizational process by packaging your message in a concise manner that excludes extraneous ideas and materials.

How do I connect one idea to another?

Using connectives such as internal previews, internal summaries, transitions, and signposts will join the pieces of your presentation to form a coherent whole.

Can I be both creative and well organized?

Creativity can enhance your ability to review, reduce, regroup, and refine good ideas for a presentation that is organized and interesting.

Presentation Principles in Action

Organizational Jigsaw Puzzle

Directions: Develop a presentation outline for one or more of the three presentation topics listed using the subtopics provided. You may delete or add subtopics in order to create an effective organizational pattern and outline. Consider using mind mapping, chunking, or the tree outline as a way to develop your outline.

TOPIC: Collecting Fossils

Identifying fossils
How fossils are formed
Geologic time
How and where to collect fossils
Paleozoic era
Cenozoic era
Jurassic period
How fossils are useful
What are fossils?
Types of fossils
Myths about fossils
Mesozoic era
Cambrian era
Pleistocene period

TOPIC: The Care and Treatment of Common Shoulder Problems

The importance of early treatment
Causes of shoulder injuries
The anatomy of the shoulder
Diagnosing shoulder injuries
The role of physical therapy
Shoulder sprains and separations
General and arthroscopic surgery
How the shoulder moves
Shoulder injury symptoms
Heat treatment
Cortisone injections
Oral medication
Shoulder exercises
Torn rotator cuff

TOPIC: A Visit to the Greater Miami Area of Florida

Coconut Grove Arts Festival
The Grand Cafe, Coconut Grove
The Breakers Hotel, Palm Beach
Hy-Vong Vietnamese cuisine
The best beaches
Hurricanes
Golf and tennis
Airports and rental cars
Cruises
The Art Deco District
South Beach
The Fountainebleau Hotel
Citrus fruit
Everglades National Park
Collecting seashells
Little Havana
Average temperatures
Films and television shows

How Creative Are You?

Directions: If you were asked to take one minute to list all of the uses you can for a balloon, you might come up with a list that looks like this:

- A toy for a child
- Birthday decorations
- A flat balloon as a bookmark
- A large balloon as a way to travel
- Prom decorations
- Popping a balloon to get attention
- A balloon cut into strips to use as rubber bands

You can evaluate creative output like this by using four criteria developed by E. Paul Torrance:

1. *Quantity:* Did you come up with eight ideas per minute?
2. *Variety:* Did you have multiple categories of answers? For example, birthday decorations and prom decorations fall under the category of "Decorations."
3. *Elaborateness:* Did you visualize ways in which your ideas would interact with bigger ideas or with the surroundings? For example, "filling a balloon and releasing it into the sky" is a simple idea, whereas "asking people to put a note saying, 'Raising tuition will lower intelligence' into helium balloons released from the state capital" is an elaborate idea.

4. *Uniqueness:* Did you have unusual ideas on your list? For example, most people respond that balloons could be used as party decorations, but only one or two people might suggest using balloons to fill empty spaces in packing crates.

Use the balloon exercise as a model for the following activity. In three minutes, list all the uses you can imagine for *one* of the following items: a brick, pencil, pie pan, nail, or penny.

Item: ____________________

Creativity Scale

Give yourself one point for each use you put on the previous list. Speakers with high scores find it easier to come up with creative organizational patterns for their presentations. You may also wish to track your answers in terms of their variety, elaborateness, and uniqueness.

Number of uses noted in three minutes	Rating
0–6	**A Good Start**
7–12	**Average.** Solid foundation for progress
13–18	**Commendable.** You've started real creativity.
19–24	**Proficient.** You're able to introduce many categories.
25–30	**Expert.** You've broken the eight-item-per-minute barrier.
30+	**Master**

Source: Lee Towe, *Why Didn't I Think of That? Creativity in the Workplace* (West Des Moines, IA: American Media, 1996), pp. 9–12. Also see work of E. Paul Torrance, Torrance Center for Creative Studies, University of Georgia, at *www.coe.uga.edu/torrance.*

Key Terms

chunking 215
connectives 226
creativity 231
formal outline 221
internal preview 228
internal summary 228
mind map 217
organization tree 220
preliminary outline 213
presentation software 224
signposts 229
transitions 228
tree outline 218

Notes

1 Thomas Leech, *How to Prepare, Stage, & Deliver Winning Presentations* (New York: AMACOM, 1993), p. 97.

2 Tony Buzon, *Use Both Sides of Your Brain*, 3rd ed. (New York: Plume, 1989). Two websites of note include the 3M Meeting Network's advice on mind mapping, *www.3m.com./meetingnetwork/readingroom/ff_concepts_mindmapping.html* and *www.mindmapper.com.*

3 Marya W. Holcombe and Judith K. Stein, *Presentations for Decision Makers: Strategies for Structuring and Delivering Your Ideas* (Belmont, CA: Lifelong Learning Publications, 1983), p. 35.

4 Holcombe and Stein, pp. 36–37.

5 The rules of outlining contained in this chapter represent a composite of guidelines and conventions found in various handbooks for writers. See Ann Raimes, *Keys for Writers: A Brief Handbook*, 3rd ed. (Boston: Houghton Mifflin, 2002); H. Ramsey Fowler and Jane E. Aaron, *The Little, Brown Handbook*, 7th ed. (New York: Longman, 1998); Diana Hacker, *The Bedford Handbook*, 5th ed. (Boston: Bedford Books, 1998); Melinda G. Kramer, Glenn Leggett, and C. David Mead, *Prentice-Hall Handbook for Writers*, 12th ed. (Englewood Cliffs, NJ: Prentice-Hall, 1995); Lynn Quitman Troyka, *Simon and Schuster Handbook for Writers* (Englewood Cliffs, NJ: Prentice-Hall, 1987).

6 Troyka, p. 40.

7 Troyka, p. 37.

8 Jo Sprague and Douglas Stuart, *The Speaker's Handbook*, 6th ed. (Belmont, CA: Thomson/Wadsworth, 2003), p. 142.

9 Lee Towe, *Why Didn't I Think of That? Creativity in the Workplace* (West Des Moines, IA: American Media, 1996), p. 7.

10 Towe, p. 14.

chapter eleven

Introductions and Conclusions

- Why do introductions matter so much?
- How do I link my introduction to my topic?
- How can I acknowledge the speaking situation in my introduction?
- What do good conclusions do?
- What's the best way to end my presentation?

Real estate agents know that first impressions can sell a house. They call this "curb value" and tell sellers to mow their lawns, paint the front door, and bake fresh-from-the-oven chocolate chip cookies before hosting an open house. Movie promoters hire teams of creative artists to design posters and previews to entice potential audiences to see their productions. Large corporations invest millions of dollars in designing annual reports to make a strong first impression that communicates success to investors. First impressions definitely count.

Most of us try to make a good first impression. We make sure that every detail of our clothing is perfect for an important meeting or job interview. We clean up our homes for visits from bank appraisers, our bosses, or our parents. We work on our appearances from head to toe in order to make a splash at a party or club. Some people even practice their handshakes to make sure that they communicate just the right combination of confidence and sincerity. First impressions count in our professional and in our personal lives. They also count in presentations. What you say, how you say it, and how you look contribute to an audience's initial reaction to you. Making a good first impression is one of the most important components of an effective presentation.

By the same token, last impressions also last. Why do political candidates often jockey to be the last speaker at a rally? Why do films run the best songs and soundtrack tunes in the final credits? Why do elegant restaurants hire pastry chefs and teams of bakers to make sure that their desserts are as beautiful as they are delicious? The answer is that politicians, filmmakers, and restauranteurs know that we tend to pay attention to and remember the last thing that we see or hear. Because first and last impressions are critical, we discuss them separately from the rest of a presentation.

Introductions as Mini-Presentations

The introduction to your presentation is so important that it deserves almost as much attention as an entire presentation does. If you find the first chapter of a book confusing, you may not read any further. If the first few minutes of a TV movie bore you, you may zap to a new channel. If a salesperson offends or ignores you, you may leave the store. And if the beginning of your presentation isn't interesting, you may lose your audience. Although they may not walk out on you, they might tune you out, misunderstand you, forget you, or even worse, remember you as a poor speaker. On the other hand, a good beginning can create a positive, lasting impression and pave the way for a presentation that achieves your purpose.

Psychologists describe the power of first impressions as the **primacy effect.** They note that we recall items that are presented first. The primacy effect is most powerful at the beginning of a presentation, the point at which audience attention to some new stimulus is at its peak.[1] The best introductions capitalize on the primacy effect.

To create an effective introduction for your presentation, you must first understand what it can and should accomplish. Not only does the beginning of your presentation introduce you and your topic to the audience; it also introduces your audience to you. Your introduction gives the audience time to adjust, to settle in, to block out distractions, and to focus its attention on you and your message. At the same time, it gives you a chance to get a feel for the audience, to calm down, and to make any last-minute adjustments to what you want to say and how you want to say it. A good introduction establishes a relationship among three elements: you, your message, and your audience. It can also set the emotional tone for the rest of your presentation.

EFFECTIVE INTRODUCTIONS

1. **Focus audience attention**
2. **Connect to your audience**
3. **Put *you* in your presentation**
4. **Set the emotional tone**
5. **Preview your message**

Focus Audience Attention

Focusing audience attention may be *the* most important goal for the beginning of a presentation. In order to learn from or act on your presentation, your audience has to listen to it! So how do you get and keep your audience's attention? As we'll see shortly, you might begin with a direct or personal question, report an unusual example or statistic, or tell a fascinating story. No matter which technique you use, your goal is to use the first few seconds of your presentation to focus the audience on you and your message.

You can gain an audience's attention by exploding a firecracker, but once the smoke clears, your audience may be more frightened than interested. Inexperienced speakers often use inappropriate strategies to gain audience attention. Shock tactics can backfire. Jokes may evoke a laugh, but they lose their impact if the joke's topic is unrelated to the presentation or if the rest of the presentation is dull as dust. If, however, you choose an appropriate attention-getting introduction, the results can last an entire presentation.

Connect to Your Audience

One of the best ways to capture your audience's attention is to relate your purpose and topic to the audience's characteristics, motives, interests, needs, and attitudes. Give your listeners a selfish reason to listen to you by explaining how your presentation will help them. Tell a story about how people have benefited from listening to what you have to say. Your goal is to get your audience focused on and interested in what you are about to say.

An introduction that works wonders on one audience may fall flat on a second audience. Every audience is unique. Every introduction also should be unique and specially designed to connect you and your purpose to that particular audience.

The animal trainer talking about the Swainson's Hawk at the Rocky Mountain Raptor Reserve in Colorado has to compete with her winged friend for audience attention.

Put You in Your Presentation

You can craft an attention-getting and interesting introduction that doesn't put *you* in your presentation. But why not make a good beginning better? If you can link yourself to your topic or purpose, your audience is much more likely to pay attention and stay interested. You can give an informative presentation about baseball, but your audience will listen more intently if they know that you are or have been a baseball player, a lifelong fan, an umpire, or a baseball-card collector. If you are trying to convince an audience to stay sober while driving, your message will be much more persuasive if your audience learns that you are a drug abuse counselor or a recovering alcoholic or were the victim of a drunk driver. However, you don't need direct experience with your topic to put yourself in your presentation. Putting *you* in your introduction involves personalizing your message. If your audience sees that the topic affects you, they are more likely to let it affect them.

We devote most of Chapter 6, "Speaker Credibility and Ethics," to ways of putting *you* into your *entire* presentation. What your audience members think about your competence and character can be just as important as what they think about the content of your message. Right at the beginning of your presentation, an audience starts to decide whether you know what you're talking about and if you can be trusted.

Set the Emotional Tone

There is another goal that speakers often overlook when crafting an introduction. Look at your introduction and think about the mood you want to create when you begin. Do you want your audience to be amused? relieved? worried? concerned? curious? Patrick Collins, author of *Say It with Power and Confidence,* urges speakers to make sure that their introductions set an appropriate emotional tone that suits their purposes.[2]

You set the emotional tone of your introduction with the language that you use and the way in which you deliver your presentation. Is a joke an appropriate introduction to a presentation on child abuse? If your audience has assembled to hear about a controversial issue, will they patiently listen to a long opening story? If you're launching a new product or program, your words and mood should be positive and upbeat right from the start. If you're sharing tragic or disappointing news, your opening words should be clear and your mood respectful and somber. Select a style for your introduction to your presentation that matches the emotional tone of what's to come.

Preview Your Message

Use the beginning of your presentation to give your audience a sneak preview about the subject of your talk. Better yet, give them a clear idea of how you are going to develop your central idea. As Chapter 9, "Organization," discusses, you can state your central idea and briefly list the key points or steps that you will take to achieve your purpose. You also can introduce your topic by making sure that any stories, examples, or statistics that you share in the introduction relate directly to your topic. In most presentations, your audience should know right from the start what you will be talking about.

Even though introductions can be extremely effective for focusing audience attention, establishing speaker credibility, setting the emotional tone, and previewing the message, many inexperienced speakers don't prepare them with enough care. Why not? Speaking anxiety may be part of the reason. Chapter 3, "Building Presentation Confidence," notes that many speakers are most nervous during the first few seconds of their presentations. A well-planned, well-delivered introduction may be the last thing on their list of worries. It should be one of the first. Planning and practicing an effective introduction can do more than make a good first impression; it can also reduce anxiety. The first few seconds of a presentation need and deserve a lot of attention and thought. After all, you can't make a first impression a second time.

Ways to Begin

There are almost as many ways to begin a presentation as there are speakers, topics, and audiences. We have divided several of the most common methods into two types. **Topic-specific introductory methods** rely on topic-related supporting material to capture attention, gain interest, enhance the speaker's credibility, focus on the topic, and set the appropriate mood. **Situation-specific introductory methods** rely on the speaker's adapting to the interests and concerns of a specific audience in a particular setting or situation.

Topic-Specific Introductory Methods

There are many topic-specific methods for beginning a presentation, but among the most successful are those that immediately start with a piece of supporting material that captures the audience's attention. These methods can be used separately or in combination with one another.

TOPIC-SPECIFIC INTRODUCTIONS

- **Use an interesting example or statistic**
- **Quote someone**
- **Tell a story**
- **Ask a question**
- **Use a presentation aid**

Use an Interesting Example or Statistic.

Sometimes your research will turn up an example or a statistic that is unusual or dramatic. When presented all by itself, a good piece of research can gain an audience's attention and interest. Here's how one student began his speech on America's "growing" population:

> *America is overweight. Approximately fifty million Americans are carrying around millions of extra pounds of fat. And it's getting worse. Several years ago, Yankee Stadium lost 9,000 seats during renovation because the new seats had to be three inches wider just to fit the "growing" population of America.*

Beginning with an interesting example or statistic can prompt your audience to start thinking about your topic. The image of fat Americans squeezing into stadium seats is likely to stay with an audience.

Quote Someone.

There are many great speakers and writers. Careful research can uncover a dramatic statement or eloquent phrase that is ideal for the beginning of your presentation. Rather than trying to write the perfect beginning, you may find that someone else has already done it for you. But remember to give the writer or speaker full credit.

Sometimes a good quotation can help an audience overcome their doubts, especially when the writer or speaker is a highly respected and expert source of information. In the following example, a student uses two quotations to begin his presentation about the use of marijuana.

> *"Marijuana, in its natural form, is one of the safest therapeutically active substances known to man." And "marijuana is about the safest drug you can give for treating the side effects cancer patients have to endure from chemotherapy." Who made these statements? The first was made by Francis Young, the chief administrative law judge of the Drug Enforcement*

Agency. The second was made by Dr. Lester Grinspoon, a professor of medicine at Harvard University.

Tell a Story. Speakers can have great success by beginning a presentation with stories about their personal hardships or triumphs. They also can share stories they read about or hear from others. Sometimes stories are private and personal; at other times they are fictional and designed to illustrate a concept or an idea. An eighteen-year-old student shares a very personal story in the following introduction:

> *When I was 15, I was operated on to remove the deadliest form of skin cancer, a melanoma carcinoma. Even though a plastic surgeon performed the surgery, I had horrible scars. My doctor injected 10 shots of steroids into each scar every three weeks to stop the scars from spreading. One year and two operations later, I was told it would be impossible to do anything to correct the scars until I am at least 25 years old. I now know that it wasn't worth a couple of summers of being tan to go through all that pain and suffering. Take steps now to protect yourself from the harmful effects of the sun.*

Ask a Question. Asking a question can attract your audience's attention and interest. Why? Because it encourages them to think about the answer.

> *Why is it hotter in the summer than in the winter? When twenty-three Harvard students were asked this question at their graduation, only two were able to give a correct answer.*

Asking a question is an effective way to begin a presentation, particularly if the question has a direct effect on the audience. A variation of *ask a question* is *let them guess.* Rather than leaving audience members thinking, "Yes, I've often asked that question" or "Yes, those are important questions," this method should elicit a response such as "I have no idea!"

> *Which of the following eight products are owned by American companies and made in America: Bic pens, Arrow shirts, Godiva chocolates, Vaseline petroleum jelly, Firestone tires, Holiday Inns, and Tropicana orange juice? All? Half? The answer is* one. *Godiva chocolate is made and sold by the Campbell Soup Company.*[3]

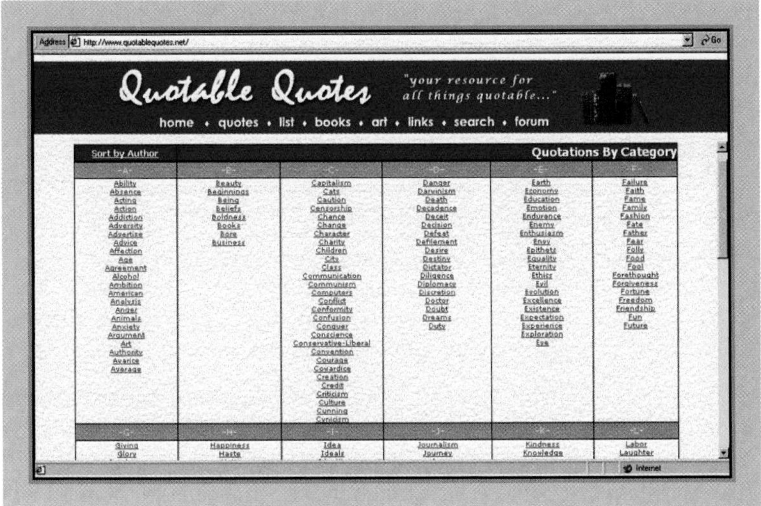

The Quotable Quotes website, www.quotablequotes.net, is just what it claims: "Your resource for all things quotable." The topic-based categories can help you find an appropriate quotation to use in the introduction of your presentation.

Use a Presentation Aid. A presentation aid such as a productivity chart, a cartoon, a product display, or a piece of taped music can help an audience focus its attention at the beginning of a presentation. In the following example, the student whose presentation on Muzak was outlined in Chapter 10, "Organizational Tools," began by playing a tape-recorded selection of some very smooth but dull music. After ten long seconds of recorded music, she began to speak.

> *It's been referred to by its creators as "sonorous design" and "sound energy, attractively arranged." On the other hand, to much of the American public, this product more often conjures up images of "spineless melodies" with "vacant volumes of vapid violins." In short, it's Muzak. And what you're hearing is an actual demonstration tape of Muzak. But Muzak isn't just any old song. According to its creators, it can reduce your stress, boredom, and fatigue and can increase your productivity.*

Situation-Specific Introductory Methods

As successful as the topic-specific methods for beginning a presentation may be, situation-specific methods can give you an added advantage. They let your audience know that you understand their specific interests and needs. Adapting your introduction to the characteristics of the audience, the nature of the occasion, or the circumstances of a situation demonstrates that your presentation is custom-made.

SITUATION-SPECIFIC INTRODUCTIONS

- **Refer to the place or occasion**
- **Refer to a recent or well-known event**
- **Directly address audience interests and needs**
- **Establish a personal link**

Refer to the Place or Occasion. An obvious, situation-specific way to begin a presentation is to refer to the place in which you are speaking or the occasion for the gathering. Consider this excerpt by General Douglas MacArthur, who led U.S. troops in the Pacific during World War II and the early years of the Korean War. Due to disagreements with fellow officers and President Harry S. Truman, he was relieved of his duties as general. On April 19, 1951, he addressed a joint session of Congress. He began his speech by referring to the place in which he was speaking rather than to himself:

> *Mr. President, Mr. Speaker, and distinguished Members of the Congress, I stand on this rostrum with a sense of deep humility and great pride—humility in the wake of those great American architects of our history who have stood here before me, pride in the reflection that this forum of legislative debate represents human liberty in the purest form yet devised. Here are centered the hopes, and aspirations, and faith of the entire human race.*[4]

A dozen years after General MacArthur's address, another famous American spoke in Washington, D.C. On August 28, 1963, Dr. Martin Luther King Jr. made his famous "I Have a Dream" speech on the steps of the Lincoln Memorial. By referring to the "shadow" of Abraham Lincoln, he was able to link his message to the man who signed the Emancipation Proclamation. Even his first few words echoed Lincoln's famous

Gettysburg Address that began "Four score and seven years ago." Dr. King began his speech as follows: "Five score years ago, a great American, in whose symbolic shadow we stand, signed the Emancipation Proclamation."[5]

Refer to a Recent or Well-Known Event. Events that have occurred shortly before your presentation or in the recent past can provide a means of gaining audience attention and interest. This method also applies to events that might occur even seconds before you speak. In formal speaking situations, you often will hear speakers begin by referring to what was said by the person who introduced them, particularly if the introducer has told a friendly or humorous story about the speaker or has praised her. This technique can make the speaker seem more human after a lengthy introduction.

Taking the microphone off its stand and addressing the audience with great personal conviction at an affirmative action rally at UCLA helps this speaker gain and maintain audience attention and interest.

You cannot, however, rely on being introduced or on thinking up a good line on the spot to follow an introduction. It's better to plan a strong beginning that refers to an event known to your audience. For instance, in the following introduction, a student refers to a recent local news story.

> *Last Friday, a front-page article in the* Journal *told a terrifying story: "Firefighters searching the burned-out shell of a popular all-night coffee shop made a grisly discovery early yesterday in the aftermath of a raging fire: the bodies of two male employees shot to death near a rear exit and, nearby, a third employee, critically wounded." Like you, I was horrified and shocked by this tragedy so close to home. But why, I wonder, does it take such a terrifying event to make us sit up and take notice of the crime problem in our own backyard?*

The "recent event" technique is a big part of political speechmaking. If you listen carefully to the news or watch the president's State of the Union address, you are bound to hear references to well-known recent events. President Franklin D. Roosevelt's words provide a famous example: "Yesterday, December 7, 1941—a date which will live in infamy—the United States was suddenly and deliberately attacked by naval and air forces of the empire of Japan."[6]

President George W. Bush's tribute at the Pentagon Memorial on October 11, 2001 echoed a similar theme: "On September 11th, great sorrow came to our country. And from that sorrow has come great resolve. Today, we are a nation awakened to the evil of terrorism, and determined to destroy it. That work began the moment we were attacked; and it will continue until justice is delivered."[7]

FAQ

Should I Say, "Ladies and Gentlemen"?

Perhaps you've noticed that speakers often begin formal presentations with phrases such as "Ladies and gentlemen" or "Mr. President, distinguished faculty members, students, alumni, and friends." Is this kind of acknowledgment necessary? It depends on the audience, the place, and the occasion. Very formal public settings pretty much require mentioning the officials or groups of people in attendance. Most ceremonial occasions—a major convention, a graduation, an acceptance speech, a televised address—likewise call for formal behavior. Using these introductory formalities is a way of thanking those who have invited you to speak and honoring the important people and groups who have come to listen to you. Even in somewhat less formal circumstances, such as speaking on a stage after having been introduced by someone else, you may want to formally acknowledge that person and others on the stage.

But sometimes formality can be out of place. Addressing a group of coworkers or peers in an informal setting as "Ladies and Gentlemen, distinguished colleagues ..." could seem stiff and unfriendly.

Directly Address Audience Interests and Needs. When there is a crisis, you need to address the problem at the outset. If budget cuts will require salary reductions, audience members will want to hear the details. They won't want to hear a humorous story, a clever question, or an unusual statistic. When a person's job or future is threatened, no time should be spent on clever beginnings. In fact, such introductions may even make the audience hostile. Get right to the point. Here's an example:

> *As you know, the state has reduced our operating budget by 2.7 million dollars. It is also just as important that you know this: All of you will have a job here next year—and the year after. There will be no layoffs. Instead there will be cutbacks in nonpersonnel budget lines, downsizing of programs, and, possibly, short furloughs.*

This speaker went directly to the central idea and the preview section of her presentation. Having first reassured employees that no one would be fired, she could then explain how the budget cutbacks, downsizing, and shorter furloughs would be implemented.

Establish a Personal Link. Use your introduction to link your background and experiences to those of your audience. Even though you may not know or may be quite different from the members of your audience, your experiences may be similar. For instance, a Jewish

Beginning with a Joke

Many public speaking books recommend beginning a presentation with a joke. As much as we enjoy a good laugh, we don't necessarily agree. Just because you've heard a good joke doesn't mean it would work as the introduction to your presentation. The audience may remember the joke but forget your message. Introductory jokes are great when they are perfectly matched to the topic and the audience. But if they aren't, save them for your friends.

Avoiding jokes doesn't mean avoiding humor in an introduction—an amusing example, a strange statistic, a funny story, or a great line from a comedian can work wonderfully. Some of the best speakers use humor in their introductions because they know that it's a sure way to gain audience attention and that it can give an audience a hint about the mood and direction of a talk. Some of the worst speakers use humor in their introductions because they can't think of any other way to begin. Because such speakers don't give their introductions a great deal of thought, their humor can be unrelated to the topic and, even worse, in poor taste.

Using humor effectively is more difficult than it seems, but these three guidelines always apply:

- First, the humor should be related to the topic or the speaker. When it is, humor can even be used to make a serious point. Note how this student began her presentation by comparing silly state laws to those controlling hand guns and assault weapons.

  There ought to be laws against some laws. In Weaverville, North Carolina, it's illegal to walk an unleashed miniature pig in public. On South Padre Island, Texas, it's illegal to wear socks or ties. In Topeka, Kansas, you can run afoul of the law if you put alcohol in a teacup. And in Ridgewood, New Jersey, you can't play with Silly String—in the summer.[1] *Yet in all of these states, it's perfectly legal to own and use certain types of guns—weapons that have no other function than shooting people.*

- Second, the humor in your introduction should be appropriate for the people in the audience. In 1983, Senator Jesse Helms was invited to be the commencement speaker at Grove City College. Like most other commencement speakers, the senator knew that his audience had probably heard many boring commencement addresses. Thus, he began:

  Mr. President, distinguished faculty members, alumni, friends of Grove City College—and, most especially, members of the graduating class, while it is an honor to have been invited to share this memorable occasion with you, I suppose that there have been few commencement speakers who have not contemplated the remark made by an irreverent classmate who speculated that if all the commencement speakers in America were laid end-to-end—that would be fine.[2]

- Third, it must be well delivered! We devote an entire section of Chapter 13, "Generating Interest," to using humor in a presentation.

In the previous examples, the speakers made light of their audience's expectations about them or their topic. They didn't tell jokes, yet their introductions gained the audience's attention and set a mood for what followed. If you're considering a humorous introduction, make sure that it relates to your topic. You might even test your introduction on a few friends—just give the introduction and then ask them what they think your presentation's topic is. If their guesses are too far afield, your introduction probably is, too.

Make sure that your introduction is appropriate. Give special consideration to the diversity of your audience and how different audience members might react to humor. Last, be sure to deliver your humor flawlessly. How? As the native New Yorker replied to the tourist who asked, "How do I get to Carnegie Hall?"—Practice, practice, practice.

1. "Banned in the U.S.A.," *Time*, 6 July 1998, p. 32.
2. For the complete text of Helms's commencement address plus commentary, see James R. Andrews and David Zarefsky, *Contemporary American Voices: Significant Speeches in American History, 1945–Present* (New York: Longman, 1992), pp. 317–321.

student told the following story at the beginning of a presentation on race relations to a predominantly African American audience.

> *When I was eight years old, I stayed home for a Jewish holiday in September. After I went to synagogue, my parents let me go outside to ride my bike. As I rode through the neighborhood, I encountered a group of kids coming home from school. Because I wasn't dressed for school and was riding my bike, they rightfully assumed I was Jewish. At first they began taunting me with the most terrible derogatory names imaginable. Then one of the kids picked up a two-by-four and tried to knock me off my bike. Even though he landed several direct blows, I kept pedaling until I outraced him. By the time I arrived home, I could barely walk. My back was badly bruised and my spine was damaged. To this day, I attribute my recurring back pains to that terrible day. And to this day, I am reminded of the pain that stays with you when people and prejudice breed hatred.*

Mix Your Methods

Many speakers combine introductory methods to begin their presentations. For instance, this student began her introduction to a persuasive presentation on geographical illiteracy with a familiar rhyme, a statistic, a question, and the worrisome results of a survey.

> *"In fourteen-hundred and ninety-two Columbus sailed the ocean blue and found this land, land of the free, beloved by you, beloved by me." Or so the historical rhyme reminds us. But, according to the National Geographic Society, over 48 percent of Americans don't know where Columbus landed. Do you? In fact, five to fifteen percent of Americans believe that Columbus set sail to find Europe.*

Regardless of how you begin your presentation, always ask yourself whether the method you're using will gain audience attention and interest, will put *you* in your presentation, will introduce your purpose or topic area, and will set the appropriate emotional tone. No matter how funny your joke, how inspiring your quotation, or how startling your statistic, your opening remarks won't accomplish anything unless they are linked to these introductory goals.

Starting Strong

In their eagerness to get going, some speakers don't give their introduction enough attention. Rather than applying the time-tested introductory techniques we've been exploring, they may fall into one or more common traps. If you know what these traps are, you can avoid them—and start strong!

Plan the Beginning at the End

Simply put, don't plan the introduction to your presentation before you've developed the body of it. There are many decisions to make when preparing a presentation; how to begin should not be the first. Because a strong introduction can help you achieve your purpose, it should be adapted to your audience and should relate to the content of your presentation. You have to know what the content is before you can preview your key points.

Generally, we recommend that your introduction should take no longer than 10 percent of your presentation time. If it takes more than that amount of time, audience members may begin to think, "Get on with it" or "Okay, okay, I catch your drift—now show me!" There are, of course, exceptions to the 10 percent guideline. If you are facing a distrustful or hostile audience, you may need more time to establish your credibility or to establish common ground with your audience. **Common ground** is a term we use to describe a belief, attitude, or experience shared by the speaker and the audience—a place where both you and your audience can "stand" without disagreement. In some situations, a speaker may need a longer introduction to create a more hospitable mood or to reduce audience concerns about the topic. In most cases, however, 10 percent of a presentation is ample time for achieving the goals of an introduction.

There's No Need to Apologize

Wouldn't it be strange if an actor came out onto the stage before a play to tell the audience that he hadn't memorized his lines very well and that he'd had a lot of trouble singing the first song in the second act? Why, then, do speakers apologize for their presentations before they give them? Too often, speakers begin with apologies or excuses. "I don't speak very often, so please excuse my nervousness." "I wish I'd had a few more days to prepare for this presentation, but I just found out that I had to make it on Tuesday." Comments like these do not accomplish very much. If your presentation is wonderful, the audience may be confused by your excuses. If it's awful (or you just think it is), let the audience draw their own conclusions. A presentation should start with a strong beginning and should not make excuses or apologize for the level of preparation or quality of delivery.

Avoid Using "My Speech Is About . . ."

Beginning statements such as "I'm going to talk about..." or "My topic is..." may be true, but they don't help you gain the audience's attention or interest. And even though they may introduce your topic, such statements will not necessarily make that important connection between your purpose and your audience.

Nevertheless, like all other rules, this one has exceptions. "I'm going to talk about how I was surrounded by killer sharks and survived" would probably make the most jaded audience listen! "My talk will be about the budget crisis and how it will affect your jobs" will likewise hold audience attention and interest. But you should usually try to avoid such beginnings. They communicate a lack of confidence and originality. Unless you have a good reason for choosing "My speech is about..." as a beginning, try not to use this method.

You Need More than a Great Beginning

A great beginning can accomplish a great deal. It can excite your audience and make them eager to hear more about you and your topic. But if the rest of your presentation doesn't live up to it, you can be headed for trouble. Remember the real estate agent's "curb value"? A newly mowed lawn won't make up for a leaky roof. Remember the movie poster that promises adventure and romance? No matter how eye-catching the poster, the movie had better live up to its image. A successful presentation can survive a less-than-great beginning, but a great introduction cannot save a poor presentation.

Last Impressions Last

What is true of introductions is also true of conclusions. Whether you like it or not, the final thing you say to an audience can determine how they think and feel about you and your presentation. It's no wonder that songs at the end of a concert are often the ones the audience has been waiting for. It's no wonder that the finale of a Broadway musical is often the most exciting number in the show. Even on a personal level we often worry about the last impression we make. For example, we send thank-you notes to show our gratitude or save a great dessert for the end of a meal. We know that last impressions can count just as much as first impressions and that last impressions last.

Remember the primacy effect and its implications for introductions? Psychologists have a similar term for explaining why we more accurately recall items presented last. It's called the **recency effect** and indicates that recall is even higher for items at the end of a list than for those at the beginning.[8] Final words can have a powerful and lasting impact on your audience. A good ending can ensure that the audience will remember the most important part of your message.

Conclusions as Mini-Presentations

What you say and do during the last few seconds of your presentation can determine whether and how well you achieve your purpose. Have you ever been disappointed by the ending of a book or a movie? Have you ever had a bad dessert ruin a decent meal? And have you ever squirmed in your seat when a speaker went on and on with a long, rambling conclusion?

The first step in deciding how to end your presentation is to understand its goals. Like the introduction, a conclusion should establish a relationship among three elements: you, your topic, and your audience. Like the beginning of a presentation, the ending should try to accomplish specific goals.

EFFECTIVE CONCLUSIONS SHOULD

1. **Be memorable**
2. **Be clear**
3. **Be brief**

Be Memorable

The most important goal of your conclusion is to make you and your message memorable. Before drafting your conclusion, ask yourself this question: "What is the one thing that I want my audience to remember at the end of my presentation?" Is it your central idea? Is it an image, a story, or a statistic? Audiences rarely remember all the details of a presentation. Instead, they remember a few ideas and a few images. The conclusion of your presentation gives you the opportunity to shape that idea or image into a lasting memory.

One way to make your conclusion memorable is to link your purpose to your audience's interests and needs. Give them a reason to remember you and your presentation. Show them how your message has affected you personally or how it can affect them as well.

Also, try to end on an emotional note that matches your message. If your presentation focuses on how to do something, try to get the audience excited about giving it a try. If your presentation gives your listeners a lot of new information, show them how to remember it and why they should. If you're trying to change your audience's attitude, show them how that change will help others, will solve a serious problem, or will make them feel good. But no matter what method you decide to use, you will want your audience to remember good things about you and your message.

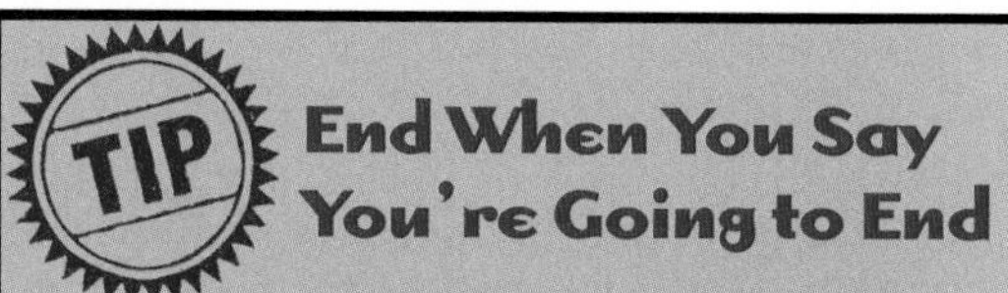

How do you react when you hear a speaker say, "And in conclusion..." and then he or she takes twenty minutes to actually conclude? The announced ending of a presentation should never go beyond a minute, no matter how long you have spoken. When you say you are going to end, end.

However, when we recommend that you should "end when you say you are going to end," we are not suggesting that the entire conclusion must be short. Sometimes a conclusion requires several minutes because you are building to an emotional climax, a complex conclusion, or a bold pronouncement. Rather, we strongly recommend that the words "In conclusion" or "Let me close by ..." should only be used to signal that the ending is very near. Don't frustrate or annoy your audience with several more minutes of talk when they are psychologically prepared for your presentation to end.

Be Clear

Being clear is just as important as being memorable. The last thing that you want your audience to do is to leave your presentation wondering what it was all about. What's the point of using a beautiful quotation or telling a funny story if it's not clear how it relates to your message? Again, ask yourself, "What is the one thing that I want my audience to remember at the end of my presentation?" Make sure that your conclusion repeats that one thing as clearly as possible. You may have to make that point more than once or word it several different ways in order to be sure that it's clear. Don't use the conclusion to add new ideas or to insert something that you left out of the body of the presentation. Use it to reinforce your central idea and to make your message sharp and clear.

Be Brief

When trying to make the ending of your presentation memorable and clear, you may be tempted to make it long. Resist this temptation! Whereas introductions may require some time to gain audience attention and enhance speaker credibility, conclusions should be short and sweet. As one old saying goes, "Be clear; be brief; be seated."

Ways to End

There are almost as many ways to end a presentation as there are ways to begin one. Some methods can help you make that final connection between your purpose and your audience. Other methods can strengthen the audience's final impression of you and your message. Each method can be used separately or combined with others.

WAYS TO END

- Summarize
- Quote someone
- Tell a story
- Share your personal feelings
- Use poetic language
- Call for action
- Bookend
- Mix your methods

Summarize

Reinforcing your key points in a succinct summary is the most direct way to conclude a presentation. It's clear and brief. And if you pay enough attention to the words you select for your ending, it can be memorable. In the following example, the speaker has reviewed and repeated the main points of her presentation in the form of questions to emphasize her central idea that America needs more women in Congress.

> *Now, if you ever hear someone question whether women are good enough, smart enough, and skilled enough to serve in the U.S. Congress, ask and then answer the three questions I posed today: Are women candidates caught in the "mommy trap"? Can women's issues attract big donors? And, are women too good to be "tough" in politics? Now that you know how to answer these questions, don't let doubters stand in the way of making a woman's place in the House.*

Quote Someone

What is true about quoting someone in the beginning of your presentation is just as true about using an ending quotation. Because quotations can be memorable, clear, and brief, people often use them as a finale to their presentations. Careful research can provide a quotation that will give your presentation a dramatic and effective ending.

Consider this example from the end of Barbara Jordan's keynote speech to the Democratic National Convention on July 12, 1976. Ms. Jordan, a congressional representative from Texas, was the first African American to deliver a keynote address at a major party's national political convention.

> *I am going to close my speech by quoting a Republican President and I ask you that as you listen to these words of Abraham Lincoln, relate them to the concept of national community in which every last one of us participates: "As I would not be a slave, so I would not be a master." This expresses my idea of Democracy. "Whatever differs from this, to the extent of difference, is no Democracy."*[9]

Tell a Story

Ending with a good story can be as effective as beginning with one. It can help an audience to visualize the outcome of your purpose. A well-told story can also help an audience to remember the main idea of your presentation. Dr. D. Stanley Eitzen, professor of sociology, delivered a speech at Bethell College in North Newton, Kansas, on September 25, 1989, about the dark side of competition. He left the audience with a story that summed up his central idea and message.

> *Let me conclude with a special example from the Special Olympics. A friend of mine observed a 200-meter race among three evenly matched 12-year-olds at a Special Olympics event in Colorado Springs. About 25 yards from the finish line, one of the contestants fell. The other two runners stopped and helped their competitor to his feet, brushed him off, and jogged together, hand in hand to the finish line, ending the race in a three-way tie. The actions of these three, especially the two who did not fall, are un-American. Perhaps... they did not understand the importance of winning in our society. To them, the welfare of their opponent was primary.... My message is that the successful life involves the pursuit of excellence, a fundamental respect for others—even one's competitors, and enjoyment in the process. Competition as structured in our society with its emphasis on outcome undermines these goals. I enjoin you to be thoughtful about the role of competition in your life and how it might be restructured to maximize humane goals.*[10]

Share Your Personal Feelings

One way of putting yourself into the ending of a presentation is to conclude by disclosing how you feel. Such an ending can touch the emotions of your audience and leave them with a strong memory of you, the speaker. People still remember how Martin Luther King Jr. closed the speech that he delivered on April 3, 1968. The next day King was assassinated.

> *I just want to do God's will, and He's allowed me to go up to the mountain, and I've looked over and I've seen the Promised Land. I may not get there with you, but I want you to know tonight that we as a people will get to the Promised Land. So I'm happy tonight, I'm not worried about anything, I'm not fearing any man. Mine eyes have seen the glory of the coming of the Lord.*[11]

Use Poetic Language

Being poetic is one of the best ways to ensure that your conclusion is memorable. Being poetic doesn't mean ending with a poem. Rather, it means using language in a way that inspires and creates memorable images. Use of language strategies such as repetition and metaphor can affect an audience as much as a singer can delight one with a song. If Martin Luther King Jr. had said, "Things will improve," his speech would not have had the impact that his use of the lyrics of the "Battle Hymn of the Republic" does: "Mine eyes have seen the glory." Making your words "sing" can make your presentation more memorable and effective.

Before people used the written word, everything was communicated orally. Long epic poems and stories were passed down from generation to generation by the revered members of the community—the storytellers. How did these people remember thousands of lines of poetry? One way was by using rhyme and rhythm. It is much easier to remember lines that rhyme. Interestingly, as the written word has become the dominant form of transferring knowledge, rhyme has faded. Look at the poetry of a few hundred years ago—it is much more rhythmic than its modern counterparts.

Rhyme and rhythm can make people remember what you said. Even during the O. J. Simpson trial, we heard, "If the glove don't fit, you must acquit."

One of the most dynamic American speakers is Jesse Jackson. On July 17, 1984, he concluded his speech at the Democratic National Convention poetically. Notice how he repeated the phrase "Our time has come" and the word *ground*. Reverend Jackson even adapted the beginning of the famous poem by Emma Lazarus carved into the base of the Statue of Liberty: "Give me your tired, your poor, Your huddled masses yearning to breathe free."

> *Our time has come. Our faith, hope and dreams will prevail. Our time has come. Weeping has endured for the night. And now joy cometh in the morning.*
>
> *Our time has come. No graves can hold our body down. Our time has come. No lie can live forever.*
>
> *Our time has come. We must leave racial battleground and come to economic common ground and moral higher ground. America, our time has come.*
>
> *We've come from disgrace to Amazing Grace, our time has come.*
>
> *Give me your tired, give me your poor, your huddled masses who yearn to breathe free, and come November, there will be a change because our time has come.*
>
> *Thank you and God bless you.*[12]

You don't have to be the leader of the Rainbow Coalition to be poetic at the end of your presentation. A young student ended a speech about respecting older people with the following short but poetic phrases:

> *For old wood best to burn, old wine to drink, old authors to read, old friends to trust, and old people to love.*

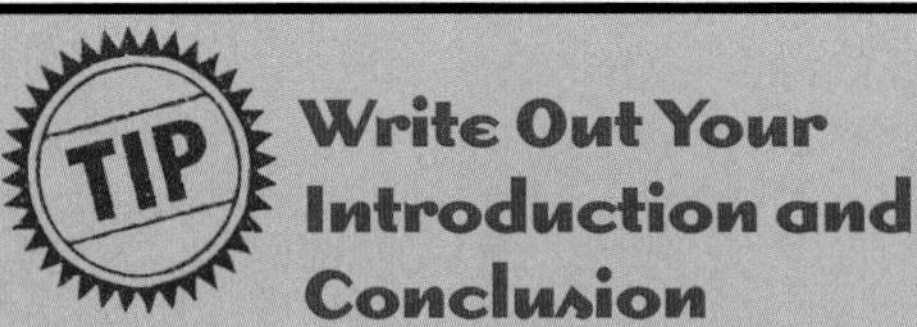

Unless you are very familiar with your audience or your topic, we recommend that you write out your introduction and conclusion word for word. In Chapter 14, "Performance and Practice," we recommend speaking from a brief outline or a list of key phrases for the entire presentation. However, the introduction and conclusion can be exceptions. Because the beginning and ending of a presentation matter so much, every word counts. But instead of reading from your manuscript, practice your introduction and conclusion so often that you won't need any notes (unless you're including a long quotation or complicated set of statistics). Because you will probably be most nervous at the beginning of your presentation, knowing your introduction by heart will also help you mask and minimize any nervous symptoms you may be feeling. Because you're not looking at notes, you can concentrate your full attention on your listeners rather than on your nervousness. As you close, you can again put aside your notes and deliver a well-crafted conclusion that allows you to focus on your audience and "clinch" your message.

Call for Action

One of the more challenging but effective ways to end a presentation is to call for action. Malcolm Kushner, a communication instructor and author, goes so far as to recommend that "every speech should end with a call to action. It doesn't have to be a call to action in the traditional sense (buy, give, vote), but it should ask every member of the audience to take some type of action. Because that's what really involves them."[13]

In a conclusion that calls for action, you are telling your audience to do more than merely listen to your presentation; you are asking them to *do* something. Even if you're just telling an audience to remember something, to think about a story you've told, or to ask themselves a question, you've asked them to become involved.

In the following example, Helen Keller ends a speech by calling for action. Born in 1880, Keller was left deaf, blind, and mute by disease at the age of nineteen months. With the help of Anne Sullivan, her dedicated teacher, she learned to read, write, and speak. In 1916,

Helen Keller delivered an antiwar speech at Carnegie Hall in New York City. She ended her speech with this call for action:

> *Strike against all ordinances and laws and institutions that continue the slaughter of peace and the butcheries of war. Strike against war, for without you no battles can be fought. Strike against manufacturing shrapnel and gas bombs and all other tools of murder. Strike against preparedness that means death and misery to millions of human beings. Be not dumb, obedient slaves in an army of destruction. Be heroes in an army of construction.*[14]

Bookend

If you can't decide which of the previously mentioned methods to use, consider ending your presentation with the same technique you used to begin it. We call this the *bookends method.* If you began your presentation with a quotation, end with the same or a similar quotation. If you began with a story, refer back to that story. If you began by referring to an event or incident, ask your audience to recall it.

A student speaker compared the human body to a machine in the introduction and conclusion of her speech. She began as follows:

> *Our bodies are miraculous machines. We fuel them, tune them up, and "exercise" them so they don't rust. If we notice a problem, we put them in the shop for repair, just like our cars. There, you may think, the similarity ends here because most of us trust our medical system more than our mechanics. After all, mechanics make mistakes. "The clamp came off," your mechanic tells you. "Our mistake—we'll fix it for you free of charge."*

After talking about the adverse effects of medical treatments in hospitals, she concluded her presentation this way:

> *Take care of your machine by demanding the same from your health care professionals as you would from your mechanic. When it comes to your body and your health, not everything can be fixed free of charge.*

Mix Your Methods

As was the case with beginnings, many speakers rely on more than one way to conclude a presentation. Think about your audience's learning styles. Restate your main points or tell a story they can visualize depending on whether they are auditory, visual, or physical learners. For instance, note how this student speaker used statistics and a personal story to end a presentation on alcoholism.

> *According to figures quoted in* Time *magazine, 18 million Americans are alcoholics, and that translates into better than one adult out of every ten. Very few, if any, of these people planned on becoming alcoholics. And many, like me, were well informed about the disease before falling victim. I've told you my story and alerted you to the role of denial in the hope that someday, if that doubt ever creeps into your mind and you find yourself asking whether you might have an alcohol problem, you'll remember my speech and take a harder, more objective look at that question. It could just save your life. It has saved mine.*

The conclusion of your presentation puts the final touch on all that has come before. Regardless of which way you conclude, you should always ask yourself whether the method you have decided to use will be memorable, clear, and brief. No matter how poetic you try to be or how many statistics you can read in two minutes, you won't accomplish much unless you link your method to the goals of ending.

Ending Effectively

Many beginning speakers—and even some veterans—don't pay much attention to carefully crafting their conclusions. Why? What's left of a person's speaking anxiety at the end of a presentation offers a partial explanation. Once you've presented your message, you may want to flee the podium and escape. Taking time to present a well-planned, well-performed ending may be the last thing you want to worry about. But because last impressions linger, the last thing you say can be just as important as the first.

Knowing that you have a well-prepared and strong ending for your presentation can help calm your nerves. The most effective endings match the rest of a presentation and make realistic assumptions about the audience.

Make Sure It Matches

Sometimes we tell students, "Don't go for fireworks without a reason to celebrate." In other words, don't tack on an irrelevant or inappropriate ending. If you have given a serious presentation about the need for better childcare, don't end with a tasteless joke about naughty children. If you have explained how to operate a new and complicated machine, you probably shouldn't conclude your presentation with flowery poetry. Match the mood and method of your ending to the mood and style of your presentation.

Have Realistic Expectations

What if you issue a call for action, and no one in your audience acts? What if you end with your favorite joke, and no one laughs? Certainly, you don't want to embarrass yourself or your audience at the end of a presentation. Don't expect miracles. Only an inexperienced speaker would expect everyone in an audience to sign an organ donation card following a presentation on eye banks. Most audiences will not act when called upon unless the request is carefully worded, reasonable, and possible. Don't end by demanding something from your audience unless you are reasonably sure that you can get it.

There is no best way to begin or end a presentation. Deciding which methods to use depends on your purpose, the audience, and the occasion. Regardless of your chosen method, a good introduction should link you, your topic, and your audience. By gaining audience attention and interest, putting *you* in your presentation, introducing your purpose or topic, and setting the appropriate emotional tone, your introduction can get you off to a strong start. A good ending also should link you, your topic, and your audience by being memorable, clear, and brief. Introductions and conclusions are not ornaments or frills; they are essential to making good first and last impressions.

Summary

Why do introductions matter so much?

The introduction of a presentation matters because that's when your audience creates and remembers its first impressions of you and your message. An effective introduction should attempt to focus audience attention and interest, connect to your audience, put *you* in your presentation, establish an appropriate emotional tone, and preview the topic.

How do I link my introduction to my topic?

Topic-specific methods include the use of interesting examples or statistics, quotations, stories, questions, and presentation aids.

How can I acknowledge the speaking situation in my introduction?

Situation-specific methods include making references to the place or occasion, to a recent or well-known event, and to audience interests and needs as well as establishing a link between you and your audience.

What do good conclusions do?

A good conclusion should be memorable, clear, and brief.

What's the best way to end my presentation?

Methods include the use of summaries, quotations, stories, personal feelings, poetic language, calls for action, and references to the introduction.

Presentation Principles in Action

Match the Methods

Directions: Read the introductions and conclusions provided below. Then identify the method or methods the speaker used in each example. In some cases, only one method is used; in other cases, there is a combination of methods. After matching the examples, choose the ones that are, in your opinion, the most effective in achieving the functions of a good introduction or conclusion.

Match the Beginnings

1. Uses an interesting example or statistic
2. Quotes someone
3. Begins with a joke
4. Tells a story
5. Describes the problem or topic
6. Asks a question
7. Establishes a personal link
8. Refers to the place or occasion
9. Refers to a recent or historical event
10. Uses presentation aids

Method: _____ How many of you hold a driver's license? Please raise your hand. Did you know that you also hold the keys to life and death whenever you drive? I am not talking about speeding. I am not talking about reckless driving or road rage. I am not even talking about drunk driving? I *am* talking about being an organ donor. (Based on a presentation by Dejai Burks, a student at Prince George's Community College, Maryland, a state in which drivers can designate organ donor status on their driver's license)

Method: _____ What is an HBCU? 30 percent of African Americans who hold doctorates earned their degrees from HBCUs, as did 35 percent of African American lawyers, 50 percent of black engineers, and 65 percent of black physicians. What is an HBCU? They are Historically Black Colleges and Universities. Yet despite their proud past, their future is in danger.

Method: _____ Many years ago, when I was a child, my grandmother used to say to me, "If anyone asks if you are Indian,... you tell them *no*. You tell them you are Choctaw." (Based on a speech by Owanah Anderson, a Choctaw Indian)

Method: _____ "To be, or not to be: That is the question." With these famous words, Hamlet pondered whether it was "nobler in the mind" to face the world with all "the slings and arrows of outrageous fortune" or to end his life "to die, to sleep." Today, doctor-assisted suicide has made decisions about suicide a controversial public issue.

Method: _____ [Hold up a soda can.] How many of these have you had today? [Hold up a bottle of water.] How many of these have you had today? Probably not enough. I learned this lesson the hard way. I began my "drinking" habit when I was in high school. I came down with mononucleosis. In addition to having the usual symptoms—sore throat, headache, and extreme fatigue—I became severely dehydrated and spent four days in the hospital. It was then that my body and I learned that I need more of this [hold up water bottle] and much less of this [hold up soda can—then throw it in the waste paper basket]. (Based on a class presentation by Nancy Trelstad, a student at Prince George's Community College)

Match the Endings

1. Summarizes
2. Quotes someone
3. Tells a story
4. Calls for action
5. Shares personal feelings
6. Is poetic
7. Uses a presentation aid
8. Refers to the beginning

Method: ______ Imagine Vic Damone instead of valium. Paul Simon instead of penicillin. Puccini instead of Prozac. Impossible? Well, given what you've just heard about Muzak's pervasiveness, development, and techniques, nothing should surprise you. Yes, the sound of Muzak is here to stay. (See Julie Borchard's "Sound of Muzak" speech in the Appendix.)

Method: ______ In a time when you have affirmative action being debated on one end, and HBCUs closing on the other, it's time to say, "I'm going to stand for something." (M. Christopher Brown, professor and researcher, Center for the Study of Higher Education at Pennsylvania State University)

Method: ______ The course of this conflict is now known, the outcome is certain. Freedom and fear, justice and cruelty, have always been at war, and we know that God is not neutral between them. Fellow citizens, we'll meet violence with patient justice—assured of the rightness of our cause, and confident of the victories to come. In all that lies before us, may God grant us wisdom, and may He watch over the United States of America. Thank you. (President George W. Bush, address to a Joint Session of Congress and the American people, September 20, 2001)

Method: ______ Why are Americans so fat? You now know the answer. It's simple—we eat more calories than we need. What can we do about it? You also know the answer. But this time, it's not as simple. I hope you take the advice I've offered in this presentation. Urge your school system to provide *daily* physical education for *every* grade. Urge them to provide more healthful food options in the school cafeteria and restrict access to junk food in vending machines. Urge your communities to create safe playgrounds, sidewalks, and walking trails. Show them that losing bad eating habits and learning to exercise are the best ways to lose weight and live right!

Method: ______ The past gave us reasons to neglect the severely mentally ill. The present shows the effect of our neglect. But the future gives us new hope for change. As Senator Edward Kennedy once said, "Few, if any, citizens in America have been more neglected or abused over the years. No population has been as worthy of our support, or received so little of it." Neglect and prejudice will get us nowhere. Only enlightened understanding and better care will bestow dignity on the beautiful minds buried in severe mental illness. (Based on a speech by Angela Thorpe, a student at Morgan State University)

Key Terms

common ground 249

primacy effect 238

recency effect 250

situation-specific introductory methods 242

topic-specific introductory methods 241

Notes

1 See Douglas A. Bernstein et al., *Psychology*, 5th ed. (Boston: Houghton Mifflin, 2000), p. 227; and Lester A. Lefton, *Psychology*, 5th ed. (Boston: Allyn & Bacon, 1994), p. 218.

2 Patrick J. Collins, *Say It with Power and Confidence* (Paramus, NJ: Prentice-Hall, 1998), pp. 60–61.

3 *Baltimore Sun*, 2 February 1992, p. D1.

4 For the complete text of MacArthur's farewell address plus commentary, see James R. Andrews and David Zarefsky, *Contemporary American Voices: Significant Speeches in American History, 1945–Present* (New York: Longman, 1992), pp. 27–33.

5 For the complete text of King's "I Have a Dream" speech plus commentary, see Andrews and Zarefsky, 1992, pp. 78–81.

6 For the complete text of Roosevelt's war message plus commentary, see James Andrews and David Zarefsky, *American Voices: Significant Speeches in American History, 1640–1945* (New York: Longman, 1989), pp. 474–476.

7 Office of the Press Secretary. Remarks by the President at the Department of Defense Service of Remembrance, The Pentagon, Arlington, Virginia, October 11, 2001. For the complete text of Bush's speech, see *www.september11news.com/PresidentBushPentagon.html.*

8 Bernstein, p. 227, and Lefton, p. 218.

9 For the complete text of Jordan's keynote address plus commentary, see Andrews and Zarefsky, 1992, pp. 279–282.

10 For the complete text of Eitzen's speech plus commentary, see Owen Peterson, *Representative American Speeches, 1989–1990* (New York: H. W. Wilson, 1991), pp. 119–128.

11 For the complete text of King's "I've Been to the Mountaintop" speech plus commentary, see Andrews and Zarefsky, 1992, pp. 114–120.

12 For the complete text of Jackson's Rainbow Coalition address plus commentary, see Andrews and Zarefsky, 1992, pp. 355–362.

13 Malcolm Kushner, *Successful Presentations for Dummies* (Foster City, CA: IDG Books, 1997), p. 137.

14 For the complete text of Helen Keller's, "Strike Against War" speech, visit the website *www.afb.org/afb/archives/papers/speeches/11speeches/11speech3.html.*

part four

Engaging Your Audience

chapter twelve

Engaging **Language**

- How do I choose appropriate and effective words for a presentation?
- What is the difference between oral and written style?
- How do I apply the principles of presentation speaking to language?
- What are the characteristics of an effective speaking style?

In Chapter 1, "Presentation Speaking," we describe the results of a national survey that asked people to identify the skills most important to becoming an effective speaker. "Choosing appropriate and effective words" ranked eighth, following "determining your purpose" and just ahead of "enhancing your credibility." When our students complete the same survey, "choosing appropriate and effective words" often ranks in the top three topics as an extremely important and desired skill. When we ask students to help us understand their reasons for choosing this item, they reply with comments such as these:

- "I'm afraid that right in the middle of speaking, I'll have trouble finding the words I need."
- "Sometimes when someone asks me a question at work, I fumble with the answer—not because I don't know the answer but because I can't find the right words to explain what I know."
- "I've listened to really good speakers, and I know that I can't speak as clearly or as eloquently."
- "When someone disagrees with me, I can't seem to explain my position—I can't find the right words."

This chapter focuses on helping you find appropriate and effective words for your presentations. We offer theories, strategies and skills for harnessing the power of language to promote the purpose of your presentation and to enhance your credibility as a speaker. We believe that every speaker can learn to *engage* (as in "to use" or "to employ") language and become an *engaging* (as in "compelling, interesting, and convincing") speaker.

The Power and Perils of Language

Well-chosen words lie at the heart of electrifying, memorable presentations. The right words teach, persuade, inspire, and delight audiences. How you use words can determine your ultimate success as a speaker. As Mark Twain, the great American humorist, observed, "The difference between the almost right word and the right word is really a large matter—'tis the difference between the lightning bug and the lightning." Well-chosen words can make the difference between a presentation that gets polite applause and one that gets people to stand up and cheer. The best words can give a presentation a unique flavor, emotional excitement, and brilliant clarity.

Martin Luther King Jr., who was well known for his nonviolent stand against racial segregation and discrimination, is revered for the stirring words of his "I Have a Dream" speech. Abraham Lincoln is remembered as the president who signed the Emancipation Proclamation and led the country during the Civil War between the states, but he is also venerated for the words he spoke in the Gettysburg Address. John F. Kennedy is celebrated as the brash young president who faced down the Soviets in Cuba and died from an assassin's bullet, but he is also remembered for his Inaugural Address, in which he challenged the audience to "Ask not what your country can do for you; ask what you can do for your country."

Reducing Writing Apprehension

Chapter 3, "Building Presentation Confidence," examines the sources and symptoms of presentation anxiety and offers a variety of methods for becoming a more confident speaker. Speakers who say they have difficulty choosing appropriate and effective words may be experiencing a similar phenomenon known as **writing apprehension,** the fear or anxiety associated with writing situations and topic-specific writing assignments. A high level of writing apprehension can affect your choice of college major or career as well as the quantity and quality of your writing.[1] As is the case with presentation anxiety, understanding the sources and symptoms of writing apprehension, along with developing good writing skills, can help anxious writers choose appropriate and effective words for their presentations.

Does the thought or the act of writing make you anxious? Take the Writing Apprehension Test at the end of this chapter to see how you compare with others who have taken the same test.[2] Similar to the Personal Report of Communication Apprehension in Chapter 3, the Writing Apprehension Test assesses your concerns about writing. If your score is low, you probably enjoy writing and seek opportunities to write. If, however, your score is high, you probably experience high levels of anxiety about "many kinds of writing and are likely to avoid it in most situations."[3]

Even if you don't experience writing apprehension, you may have negative attitudes about the writing process. One study of adults in various occupations found that 55 percent reported having negative feelings about writing.[4] Unfortunately, many of us have mistaken notions about writing that get in our way when we're looking for appropriate and effective words. We may spend too much time looking for *perfect* words rather than thinking of our first words as a first draft. We also may become stalled by grammatical rules. Fortunately, grammatical errors can be corrected in later drafts.

The methods we recommend for building presentation speaking confidence in Chapter 3 can also be applied to reducing writing apprehension:

- *Prepare.* Apply the seven basic principles of presentation speaking to the writing process: Determine your purpose, analyze and adapt to your audience, enhance your credibility, adapt your words to the writing assignment requirements or occasion, select appropriate content, organize your content, and edit and reedit what you've written.
- *Relax.* Relaxation can minimize the symptoms of writing anxiety. Try a variety of methods, including systematic desensitization, cognitive restructuring, and even visualization. Picture yourself writing with confidence and writing well.
- *Adapt.* Analyze and adapt to your audience and the occasion. Think about the kinds of words your listeners will understand and appreciate. When the words are appropriate and effective, don't worry about bending or breaking writing rules.
- *Write and rewrite.* It takes time to write and rewrite—just as it takes time to develop and practice a presentation. The payoff, however, is a much better presentation and a much more confident speaker.
- *Focus.* Focus on your message and your audience, not on your words. When students tell us that they have trouble finding the right words, we ask them a simple question: "What are you trying to say?" Very often, their answer supplies the exact words they need for their presentation.

1. John A. Daly, "Writing Apprehension and Writing Competency," *Journal of Education Research* 72 (1978): 10–14.
2. See Virginia P. Richmond and James C. McCroskey, *Communication: Apprehension, Avoidance, and Effectiveness*, 4th ed. (Scottsdale, AZ: Gorsuch Scarisbrick, 1995), pp. 125–126. Also see John A. Daly and Michael D. Miller, "The Empirical Development of an Instrument to Measure Writing Apprehension," *Research in the Teaching of English* 9 (1975): 242–249.
3. Richmond and McCroskey, p. 42.
4. Pearl Aldrich, "Adult Writers: Some Factors That Interfere with Effective Writing," *Research in the Teaching of English* 16 (1982): 298–300.

Note: For additional advice on overcoming writing anxieties, see Linda K. Fuller and Lilless McPherson Shilling, *Communicating Comfortably* (Amherst, MA: Human Resource Development, 1990).

Can your words achieve the same eloquence? We believe that every speaker has the potential to engage an audience with clear and powerful language. The power of language, however, poses potential hazards. Once the words are out of your mouth, you cannot take them back.

Words can be perilous. Senator Trent Lott lost his position as leader of the U.S. Senate in 2003 when his words of praise for retired Senator Strom Thurmond were interpreted as an endorsement of racial segregation. When President George Bush Sr. in 1988 told audiences, "Read my lips," declaring that there would be "no new taxes," he later had to eat his words—and jeopardize his chances of reelection—when his administration passed a large tax bill. When President Bill Clinton categorically denied that he had had "sexual relations with that woman, Miss Lewinski," his words came back to haunt him during the 1998 impeachment hearings. Words have great power, but they also create perils when speakers do not consider their full meaning and potential impact.

The Nature of Language

When you don't know the meaning of a word, what do you do? Most likely, you look it up in a dictionary. Depending on the word, however, you may find multiple definitions. Even if you pick the "right" definition, you still may be left wondering what a word means. For example, the first definition of *language* in *The American Heritage Dictionary of the English Language* reads as follows: Communication of thoughts and feelings through a system of arbitrary signals, such as voice sounds, gestures, and written symbols.[1]

Does this definition make everything clear? Is this how *you* would define *language?* Probably not. Yet most of you know exactly what you mean when you use the word *language.*

Language and Meaning

We have modified the dictionary definition of *language* to help clarify the relationship between language and meaning. **Language** is a system of arbitrary signs and symbols used to communicate thoughts and feelings. Every language on earth is a system—an interrelated collection of words and rules used to construct and convey messages.

In addition to having words with various meanings, languages have rules about how words are arranged, modified, and punctuated. "The went store he to" makes no sense until you rearrange the words into "He went to the store." And although "Him go to store" may be understandable, it violates several grammatical rules. In addition, the punctuation in our language helps us interpret the meaning of a phrase or sentence.

Languages are composed of arbitrary signs and symbols. A **sign** stands for or represents something specific. In many cases, a sign looks like or depicts a symptom of the thing it represents (see Figure 12.1). For example, the graphic depictions of jagged lightning and dark clouds on a weather map are signs of a storm. A hoarse voice can be the sign of a cold or throat infection. International traffic signs help drivers navigate the roads in foreign countries.[2]

Unlike signs, **symbols** do not have a direct relationship to the things they represent. Instead, they are an *arbitrary* collection of sounds and letters that stand for a concept. Nothing in the compilation of letters that make up the word *lightning* looks or sounds like lightning. The word *cloud* is neither white and puffy nor dark and gloomy. *The word is* **not** *the thing!* You cannot be struck by the word *lightning* nor get wet from the word *rain.*

Figure 12.1

Signs resemble the thing they represent.

SIGN **IDEA**

Watch for horse-drawn carriages! Driving in Amish communities is different from driving on other rural or urban highways. In Amish communities you will see horse-drawn buggies or equipment on the roadway as they travel to town or the fields.

Pay attention and be prepared to stop! There is a traffic light ahead.

This sign indicates that cyclists and pedestrians must share the walkway. Cyclists must yield to pedestrians.

Zia Native American sign for "the sun."

Showers

Rain

AM Showers

Cloudy

Mostly Cloudy

Partly Cloudy

Meteorological symbols for various weather conditions.

When you see or hear a word, you apply your knowledge, experience, and feelings to determine the meaning of the word. If, for example, someone talks about a steak dinner, you may have very different reactions to the word *steak,* depending on whether you are a rancher, a gourmet chef, a vegetarian, or an animal rights activist. And always keep in mind that you cannot eat the word *steak,* no matter how much your mouth waters at the thought.

C. K. Ogden and I. A. Richards provide a classic explanation of this phenomenon (see Figure 12.2). They use a triangle to explain the three elements in every language—the thinking person, the symbol (or sign) used to represent something, and the actual thing, idea, or feeling being referenced.[3]

Note that the Ogden and Richard's triangle does not have a solid base because the symbol and the referent are *not* directly related. The symbol must be mentally processed before it can have meaning.

Denotative and Connotative Language

The multiple meanings of words can be further understood by examining two major types of meaning: denotative and connotative.

Denotation refers to the objective, dictionary-based meaning of a word. Let's return to the word *steak.* A steak is a slice of meat, typically beef, usually cut thick and

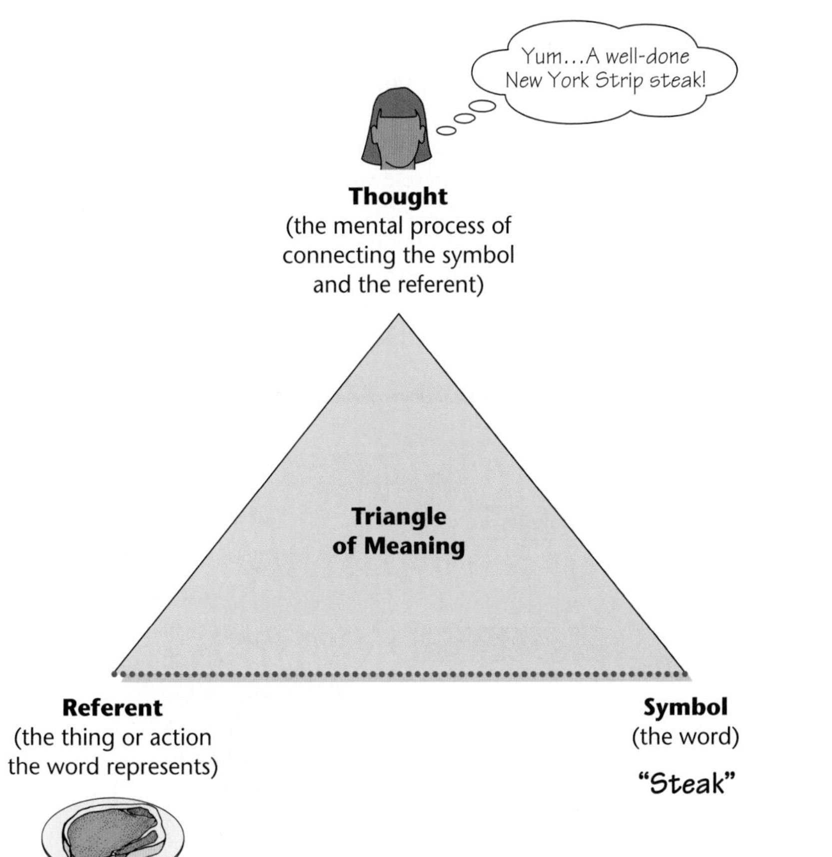

Figure 12.2

Ogden and Richard's Triangle of Meaning

across the muscle grain and served broiled, grilled, or fried. Remember that words usually have more than one definition. A steak can also be a thick slice of a large fish, such as a swordfish or salmon steak.

Connotation refers to the emotional response or personal thoughts connected to the meaning of a word. S. I. Hayakawa refers to connotation as "the aura of feeling, pleasant or unpleasant, that surrounds practically all words."[4] We evaluate the extent to which we like or dislike the thing or idea that the word represents.

Connotation, rather than denotation, is more likely to influence your response to words. As we noted with the word *steak,* it can mean a delicious, mouth-watering meal to a diner or chef as well as a disgusting slab of dead flesh to a vegetarian or animal rights activist.

Words that have similar dictionary definitions can have very different connotations for your listeners. How would you describe an *overweight* person: *fat, heavy-built, plump,* or *obese?* Is a *sexy* person *attractive, seductive, irresistible,* or *alluring?* If you choose a word with inappropriate connotations, your listeners may be confused, shocked, or offended. Effective speakers consider the possible connotations of every word they use.

General and Specific Meaning

You can minimize the misinterpretation of words by understanding that there are different levels of meaning in our language. Some words are highly abstract. An **abstract word** refers to an idea or concept that cannot be observed or touched. Words such as *love, freedom,* and *transportation* may not have the same meaning for everyone. The more abstract your language is, the more likely that your listeners may interpret your meaning in a way other than the way that you intended. **Concrete words** refer to specific things that can be perceived by our senses. Words like *engagement ring, American flag,* and *bicycle* narrow the number of possible meanings and decrease the likelihood of misinterpretation.[5]

Vivian Cook explains that there are three levels of meaning in language, ranging from the most abstract words to concrete words.[6] **Superordinate terms** are words in which objects and ideas are grouped together very generally, such as *vehicle, animal,* or *location.* **Basic terms** represent words that immediately come to mind when you see an object that represents a superordinate term, such as *car, van, truck; cat, chicken, mouse;*

Figure 12.3

Three Levels of Meaning

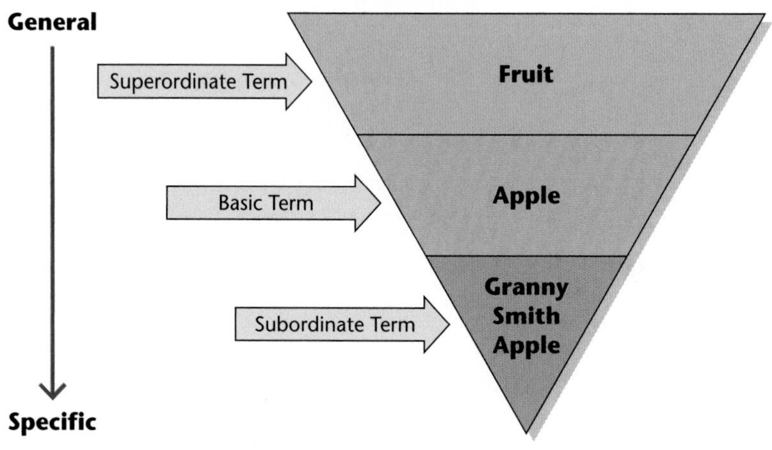

or *Bay Area, Quad Cities, Tri-State Area.* **Subordinate terms** are more concrete and specialized. The vehicle parked outside is not just a *car.* It is a *1988 red Mercedes sports car.* The animal purring on your lap is not just a cat; it is a blue-eyed Siamese cat named *Gatsby.* If you want to see the Golden Gate Bridge and Alcatraz, don't search the entire Bay Area; go directly to San Francisco.

Avoid using overly abstract words throughout a presentation. In order to be understood, abstract words need references to observable objects, people, or behaviors. For example, the Appendix includes a speech by Marge Anderson about the value of American Indian culture. At first, she offers general, abstract statements about the "differences" between Indians and non-Indians and the "issues" related to Indian casinos. Later, she describes the concrete benefits that have come with casino revenue—new schools, new health facilities, renovated elderly centers, twenty-eight thousand jobs for Indians and non-Indians, and $50 million dollars in federal taxes.

Clarifying what you mean by using concrete words prevents inaccurate inferences and misunderstandings. As you become more specific, your audience will have a clearer and more detailed picture of what you are trying to say.

Style

Style refers to the manner in which a presenter uses language to express a message. The notion of *style* is not just confined to speakers. Style is critical to the success of many endeavors. Champion athletes have unique styles of play (golf fans can recognize Tiger Woods's swing from a distance); internationally renowned opera singers have recognizable styles of singing (opera buffs can identify Luciano Pavarotti's voice in seconds); classic writers have distinctive ways of expressing themselves (theatergoers would never confuse Shakespeare's words with Arthur Miller's).

The same is true of speakers. Lani Arredondo describes language as "the fabric from which the verbal style of a presentation is fashioned.... Verbal style is composed of vocabulary, sentence structure and length, grammar and syntax, and techniques used for expressing the message."[7]

Effective speakers find their own unique style and understand the critical differences between oral and written language. Think of the contrast between Bill Clinton's speaking style and that of George Bush Sr. during the 1992 election campaign. Clinton had an "innate ability to explain things in terms that the average person could understand," speaking in complete sentences and paragraphs—in contrast with the "fractured prose of George Bush, whom it was virtually impossible to quote in a coherent sentence without the aid of ellipses and parentheses to patch his thoughts together."[8]

Does Grammar Matter?

Does grammar count in a presentation? You bet! But it may not be as crucial as you might think. In his book *If You Can Talk, You Can Write,* Joel Saltzman notes that when you are talking, you rarely worry about grammar or let it stand in the way of getting your point across. Do you ever say to yourself, "Because I don't know if I should use *who* or *whom,* I won't even ask the question?" Of course not. (However, you *should* know the difference between the two words.)

According to Saltzman, when you're talking, 98 percent of the time your grammar is fine and not an issue. As for the 2 percent of the time when your grammar *is* a problem, half of your listeners won't even notice your mistakes.[1]

We are not saying that grammar isn't important. However, worrying about it all the time may make it impossible for you to write or speak. If you have questions about grammar, consult a good writing handbook.[2] Also review the Mini-Module on sentence problems in this chapter on page 273.

1. Joel Saltzman, *If You Can Talk, You Can Write* (New York: Time Warner, 1993), pp. 48–49.
2. See Ann Raimes, *Keys for Writers: A Brief Handbook,* 3rd ed. (Boston: Houghton Mifflin, 2002). Also see Isa Engleberg and Ann Raimes, *Pocket Keys for Speakers* (Boston: Houghton Mifflin, 2004).

Use an Oral Style

There is a big difference between the words we use for written documents and the words we choose for spoken presentations. Our advice: *Say what you mean by speaking the way that you talk, not the way that you write.*

Oral and written styles differ in many ways. Primarily, oral style is characterized by the following features:

- **Shorter, familiar words**

This	Not This
Yes	Affirmative
Home	Residence
Large	Substantial
Clarify	Elucidate
Speaker	Orator

- **Shorter, simpler sentences**

This	Not This
He came back.	He returned from his point of departure.
Today the stock market crashed.	Today the stock market dropped so low that the drop was deemed to be a crash.

- **Personal pronouns (I, me, you, your, we, us, our)**

This	Not This
We want to hear from you.	This company wants to hear from its customers.
I have a dream.	Consider this dream.

- **Contractions**

This	Not This
But we won't let them.	But we will not let them.
I'm not going and that's that.	I am not going and that is that.

- **Informal, colloquial expressions**

This	Not This
Grab the phone and call.	Contact them by phone.
Give it a try.	You should attempt it first.
That was terrific.	You did an excellent job.

- **Incomplete sentences**

This	Not This
Great job!	You did an excellent job.
Old wood, best to burn. Old wine, best to drink.	Old wood burns the best. Old wine is best to drink.
Eight o'clock Wednesday night.	It's eight o'clock on Wednesday night.

Say what you mean, and say it simply. Forget about what you *think* is expected—formal language, perfect grammar, impressive vocabulary—and remember what you want to achieve—understanding, agreement, inspiration, memorability. Peggy Noonan reminds us why simple language works best: "Remember that speeches are

Figure 12.4

Use Clear and Simple Words and Sentences

This	Not This
I need help.	I require assistance.
I tried to find her.	I attempted to locate her.
This is a bad idea.	This idea represents an infeasible course of action.
People eat too much.	People do not control the size of their portions at meals.

words in the air. Your audience doesn't have a printed copy to which to refer to clear up any questions. All they have is you, speaking, up there, into a mike."[9]

The Appendix includes an informative presentation on using *CliffsNotes* by a former student, John Sullivan. Note how John uses an oral style in the introduction to his presentation.

> *Eight o'clock Wednesday night. I have an English exam bright and early tomorrow morning. It's on Homer's* Iliad. *And I haven't read page one. I forego tonight's beer drinking and try to read. Eight forty-five. I'm only on page 12. Only 482 more to go. Nine thirty, it hits me. Like a rock. I'm not going to make it.*

Although quite brief and grammatically incorrect, John's short words and sentences, personal pronouns, contractions, colloquial expressions, and informal style give a vivid picture of an unprepared and somewhat desperate student who is facing a major exam.

In addition to understanding the differences between oral and written style, make sure that you use the kinds of words and sentences that you would use in your everyday speech. When practicing your presentation, reconsider any complex words, phrases, or sentences. Ask yourself, "Is this really what I want to say? Is this really what I mean?" Short and simple words and sentences keep your style plain and direct. Clarity always beats formality, as the phrases in Figure 12.4 show.

You can look at the differences in written and oral styles by examining a student essay and presentation on the same topic that uses much of the same information. Notice the striking contrast between oral and written style in Figure 12.5.[10]

Find Your Own Style

Effective presenters understand themselves and find the style that suits them best. Some speakers do best with a formal speaking style in which every sentence is carefully crafted and rehearsed. Other speakers prefer an informal style in which key points are carefully worded, but stories and personal observations are shared informally.

Depending on your purpose, the audience and their expectations, the kind of personal image you want to project, and the logistics and occasion of the presentation, you may need to adapt your personal style. Throughout the rest of this chapter, we offer language strategies and skills that can help you find a style that best suits you and your message.

Figure 12.5

Differences in Written and Oral Style.

Excerpts from Essay on Neuromusicology	Excerpts from Presentation on Neuromusicology
"I haven't understood a bar of music in my life, but I have felt it" (qtd. in Peter 350). These words were spoken by Igor Stravinsky, who composed some of the most complex and sophisticated music of this century. If the great Stravinsky can accept the elusive nature of music and still love it, why can't we? Why are we analyzing it to try to make it useful? Ours is an age of information—an age that wishes to conquer all the mysteries of the human brain. Today there is a growing trend to study music's effects on our emotions, behavior, health, and intelligence. Journalist Alex Ross reports how the relatively new field of neuromusicology (the science of the nervous system and its response to music) has been developed to experiment with music as a tool and to shape it to the needs of society. Observations like these let us know that we are on the threshold of seeing music in a whole new way and using music to achieve measurable changes in behavior. However, this new approach carries dangers, and once we go in this direction, there can be no turning back. How far do we want to go in our study of musical science? What effects will it have on our listening pleasures? A short history lesson reveals that there has long been an awareness that music affects us, even if the reasons are not clear. Around 900 B.C., David (later King David) played the harp "to cure Saul's derangement" (Gonzalez-Crussi 69).	[Note: For the introduction to the presentation, the speaker plays a cut from "God Bless America" followed by a cut from *Sesame Street*'s theme music.] What did you think or feel when you heard "God Bless America"? What about the *Sesame Street* theme? I'm sure you're not surprised to learn that "God Bless America" reminds a lot of us of the September 11 tragedy, the 2003 War in Iraq, or patriotism. And the theme from good ol' *Sesame Street* probably put a smile on your face as you revisited the world of Kermit the Frog, Oscar the Grouch, and Big Bird. Why were your responses so predictable and so emotional? The answer lies in a new brain science—a science that threatens to control you by controlling the music you hear. Is resistance futile? In the next few minutes, we'll take a close look at and listen to the field of neuromusicology. Say what? *Neuro* meaning related to your brain and nervous system. And *musicology*—the historic and scientific study of music. Journalist Alex Ross put it this way: By understanding the nervous system and its response to music, neuro-musicologists study music as a tool and shape it to the needs of society. As New Age as all this may sound, there's plenty of history to back up the claims of neuromusicologists. For example, those of you who know your Bible know that King David played the harp to "cure Saul's derangement."

Ann Raimes, *Keys for Writers: A Brief Handbook,* 3rd ed. (Boston: Houghton Mifflin, 2003), pp. 152–158.

Top Seven Sentence Problems

Although audience members may miss or forgive a few grammatical errors, consistent grammatical problems can distract listeners and seriously harm your credibility. Rather than overwhelming you with dozens of rules, we describe seven sentence problems that we often hear when listening to student speakers.[1]

1. **Run-on sentences.** Run-on sentences are very common in presentations. When nervous speakers feel uncomfortable with the natural pause that comes at the end of a sentence, they often just keep going. They connect sentences with words such as *and* or *but*, even when such connections are inappropriate. Separate independent clauses into two sentences.

   Run-on sentence: My goal is not to turn you into a vegetarian, and I realize that, especially with Thanksgiving just a few days away, meat may be impossible for you to give up.

   Separate Sentences: My goal is not to turn you into a vegetarian. [Pause] I realize that with Thanksgiving just a few days away, you may find it impossible to give up meat. [Pause]

2. **Wrong verb forms.** Make sure that you use proper verb forms. Avoid nonstandard forms of verbs:

Wrong	Right
He brung	He brought
She should of went	She should have gone

We often hear students confuse the words lie and lay. Lie means to recline, as in "I was lying down when you called." Lay means to put or place, as in "Lay the map on the table."

3. **Tense shifts.** Avoid switching back and forth between past and present tense. When you maintain consistent tenses throughout your presentation, you help your audience understand what is happening and when.

   Tense shift: Getting the job was very difficult. The committee members ask many tough questions. (The first verb—was—is in the past tense; the second verb—ask—is in the present tense.)

   Revised: Getting the job was very difficult. The committee members asked many tough questions. (Both verbs are in the past tense.)

4. **Lack of subject-verb agreement.** Your subject and verb must always agree in person (*I, we, you, he, she, it, they*) and number (singular or plural). For example; singular third-person subjects (*he, she, it,* or singular nouns) need a singular verb.

Incorrect	Correct
He like	He likes
The teacher have	The teacher has
It pose a problem	It poses a problem

5. **Faulty pronoun case and reference.** Check to see that the subject and object pronoun are correct in relation to each other.

Incorrect	Correct
Me and my boss went to Florida.	My boss and I went to Florida.
Give the papers to Kathy and I.	Give the papers to Kathy and me.

One way to check your pronouns is to remove the pronoun or word that does not refer to you. You wouldn't say, "Me went to Florida" or "Give the papers to I." When you include yourself with another person, make sure that you use the correct personal pronoun.

6. **Adjective/adverb confusion.** Use the correct forms of adjectives and adverbs. Most speakers know the difference between an adjective like *soft* (He left the soft pillow on the bed) and the adverb *softly* (He tiptoed very softly). Many speakers have trouble with the adjective *good* (She is a good speaker) and the adverb *well* (She speaks well).

7. **Double negatives.** Double negatives should be avoided. A sentence such as "Those kids don't know nothing" should be "Those kids don't know anything." Double negatives may be customary in some dialects but should be avoided in formal speaking situations.

1. The Top Seven Sentence Problems are based on a similar section in Ann Raimes, *Keys for Writers: A Brief Handbook*, 3rd ed. (Boston: Houghton Mifflin, 2003), pp. 282–284. Also see Isa Engleberg and Ann Raimes, *Pocket Keys for Speakers* (Boston: Houghton Mifflin, 2004), Part 12, pp. 227–264.

Presentation Principles and Language

At every stage in the planning process, you should make strategic decisions about the words you choose for your presentation. From the point when you begin developing your purpose to the very last rehearsal before you get up to speak, think about your words and how you can make them work for you.

Language and Purpose

A powerful speech style can help you achieve your purpose. **Powerful speech** consists of words that express your confidence, whereas powerless speech conveys uncertainty. Powerful speech makes your purpose stand out.

James Dillard and Linda Marshall recommend ways of capitalizing on powerful speech.[11] They advise speakers to use simple and direct words and to avoid overusing the kinds of words that characterize powerless speech such as:

- *Qualifiers and hedges:* "sort of," "kind of," "I guess"
- *Hesitations and fillers:* "Uh," "Well," "You know"
- *Tag questions:* "..., right?" "..., don't you think?"
- *Disclaimers:* "I'm not an expert, but..." "I'm in the minority, but ..."
- *Intensifiers:* "Very surely," "Really," "Really, really"
- *Politeness:* "Please," "If you don't mind"

Don't dilute your presentation with powerless speech. If you seem unsure of or uncommitted to your purpose, your audience will be, too.

Language and Audience

Match your words to your listeners. If your audience can't understand your words, you won't achieve your purpose. The more you know about your audience members' characteristics and learning styles (see Chapter 5, "Audience Analysis and Adaptation"), the better you can choose the most appropriate language. If you start praising the virtues of "boarding" to an audience of senior citizens, they may think you're talking about living arrangements, not a snow sport. Take your audience into account as you select key words for your presentation.

In 1989, Dr. Henry Louis Gates Jr., an African-American scholar, delivered a speech at the *New York Times* President's Forum on Literacy.[12] What assumptions did Dr. Gates make about his audience by including the following quotation?

> *In the resonant words of W. E. B. DuBois: "I sit with Shakespeare, and he winces not. Across the color line, I move arm in arm with Balzac and Dumas, where smiling men and welcoming women glide in gilded halls.... I summon Aristotle and Aurelius and what soul I will, and they come all graciously with no scorn or condescension."*

Dr. Gates assumed that his audience was college educated and had read or would recognize the quotation from W. E. B. DuBois's 1903 book, *The Souls of Black Folk.* He also assumed that they understood DuBois's references to Shakespeare, Balzac, Dumas, Aristotle, and Aurelius. These assumptions were fine for his audience, but had he later been addressing a group of sixth-graders or recent Asian immigrants, many audience members would not have understood him.

At the beginning of the same presentation, Dr. Gates used a simpler style that made other assumptions about his audience:

Carly Fiorina, chief executive officer of Hewlett-Packard Company, delivers a keynote address at a meeting in Las Vegas. Ms. Fiorina can use her company's writing talent and resources to make her presentation compelling and memorable.

> *I grew up in a little town on the eastern panhandle of West Virginia, called Piedmont, population two thousand, supposedly (we could never find the other one thousand people). I started school in 1957, two years after the* Brown v. Board *decision, and in that year, 1957, my father bought a full set of the* World Book *encyclopedia.*

Even though his words are less complex and the story more folksy, Dr. Gates assumed his audience knew the importance of the Supreme Court's *Brown v. Board of Education* decision. Dr. Gates's mixing of styles—simpler at the start of his speech, more elaborate in the middle—demonstrates another fact about audiences: Variety keeps them interested.

In addition to adapting your words to the general characteristics of your listeners, make sure that you consider both the gender and cultures of audience members and avoid using exclusionary language.

Avoid Gender Bias in Your Language. For many years, the pronoun *he* was used to refer to an unspecified individual. Older textbooks used sentences such as "Every speaker should pay attention to his words." Interestingly, *he* was also used to refer to a student, teacher, or a professional while *she* was used to refer to a nurse or secretary. Today good speakers and writers use several techniques to avoid gender bias in pronoun use.

- *Use plural forms.* Instead of writing, "Every speaker should pay attention to his words," substitute "All speakers should pay attention to their words."
- *Avoid using a pronoun at all.* In some cases, you can rewrite a sentence and remove the pronoun altogether, as in "Good speakers pay careful attention to language."

Also, make sure that you use gender-neutral terms to describe jobs and professions. Even among performers, the word *actor* is replacing *actress* for women in theatre and film.

Gender-biased terms	Gender-neutral terms
Stewardess	Flight attendant
Mailman	Mail carrier
Actress	Actor
Fireman	Firefighter
Female soldier	Soldier
Chairman	Chairperson
Male nurse	Nurse
To "man" the booth	To staff the booth
Mankind	People, humanity, human beings

Avoid Cultural Bias in Your Language. Audience members who do not speak English as their first language may have difficulty understanding you—as you would have difficulty if you were listening to someone speak in a language that is not your native tongue. If your audience includes nonnative speakers of English, be careful how you choose your words. In Chapter 5, we offer special strategies and skills for speaking to international audiences. Many of those suggestions also apply to language choice:

- Keep your language clear and simple.
- Put complete statements and full sentences on visual aids, or provide a handout.
- Use a more formal style of speaking and address individuals by their formal titles.
- Avoid humor.
- Avoid U.S. clichés and colloquial expressions.

Use the names people prefer for their racial or ethnic affiliations. For example, *black* and *African American* are preferred terms; *Asian* is preferred to *Oriental.* Remember that the term *America* includes both North and South America. Avoid using stereotypical terms and descriptions for people that are based on the places where they come from.

Avoid Exclusionary Language. **Exclusionary language** uses biased terms that reinforce stereotypes or belittle other people. Do not emphasize differences by separating society into *we* to refer to people like *you* and *they* or *these people* to refer to people different from you. Use *we* to be truly inclusive of yourself and all your listeners.

Be aware of terms that are likely to offend. You don't have to be excessive in your zeal to be "politically correct," using *underachieve* for *fail* or *vertically challenged* for *short,* but do your best to avoid alienating your audience.

Pay special attention when choosing words to describe the following characteristics of people:[13]

- *Age.* Avoid derogatory, condescending, or disrespectful terms associated with age. Refer to a person's age or condition neutrally, if at all: not the *well-preserved little old lady* but the *woman in her eighties* or just the *woman.*
- *Politics.* Words referring to politics are full of connotations. The word *liberal,* for instance, has both positive and negative connotations. Take care with words like *radical, left-wing,* and *right-wing.*

- *Religion.* Devout Christians, Jews, and Muslims should not be labeled as *extremist* or *fanatic.* Never use the term *these people* when referring to a group with a different religion because it emphasizes differences. Even the word *we* should be avoided when it implies that all your listeners share (or should share) your religious beliefs.
- *Health and abilities.* Avoid descriptions like *confined to a wheelchair* and *victim* (of a disease). Instead, substitute *someone who uses a wheelchair* and *person with* (a disease). Never use the word *retarded.*
- *Sexual orientation.* Refer to a person's sexual orientation only if the information is necessary to your content. Do not assume that the sexual orientation of audience members is the same as your own.
- *The word* normal. One word to be especially careful about using is *normal*—when referring to your own health, abilities, physical characteristics, race, or sexual orientation. Some listeners could justifiably find that offensive.[14]

Language and Credibility

If you do not match your language to your audience, you may do more than lose their interest or agreement; you also may damage your credibility. If you make numerous grammatical mistakes and mispronounce many words, your audience may conclude that you are neither well prepared nor intelligent.

Most audiences admire a speaker who seems to know exactly how to choose appropriate and effective words. In fact, the richness of your vocabulary can enhance the audience's opinion of your credibility. Even when audience members don't understand every word or concept in your presentation, they may be impressed with your ability to engage language and speak eloquently.

We highly recommend using personal pronouns in your presentation as a means of enhancing your credibility. Personal pronouns put *you* in your presentation and help you establish a connection with your audience. Using the pronouns *you* and *your* frequently—and focusing your attention on people in different parts of the room as you do so—make each audience member feel singled out. A personal message is always more interesting than one for the masses.

"Ask not what your country can do for you. Ask what you can do for your country." If John F. Kennedy had instead said, "People should not ask what their country can do for them. People should ask what they can do for their country," do you think we would still remember his words? The second version does not have the impact of the first. *You* and *your* speak directly to an audience. Because the word *you* can be singular or plural, it allows you to speak to an entire audience as well as to each individual. It's personal. It asks you for your attention.

Make sure to put *you* in your presentation by using self-referential pronouns such as *I, me,* and *my.* By taking responsibility for your message, you establish your credibility (see Chapter 6, "Speaker Credibility and Ethics"). Telling a story about the time you saved a choking victim's life will interest audiences more than describing how other people have used the Heimlich maneuver to dislodge objects from choking people's windpipes. First-person accounts engage audiences. Using pronouns such as *we, us,* and *ours* intensifies the connection by highlighting the links between you and your audience. "We shall overcome" has significantly more power than "You shall overcome" or "I shall overcome." Personal pronouns bring your topic closer to you and to your audience.

Get Rid of Gobbledygook

Gobbledygook (the sound of which is supposed to imitate the nonsense gobbling of a turkey) is a noun that describes unclear and wordy jargon. **Jargon** is the specialized or technical language of a profession or homogenous group. Avoid jargon whenever possible.

William Lutz points out that all of us use jargon as "verbal shorthand that allows members to communicate with each other clearly, efficiently, and quickly"[1]. For example, when we were writing this textbook, we had to learn publishing jargon. We learned the difference between an *em dash* and an *en dash*. We learned to *stet* the *copy* we didn't want to change. We specified whether a subject should be a *#2 head* or *#3 head*. We were told when the *galleys* and then *page proofs* were due. We were even warned to keep our *AAs* (author's alterations in text) to a minimum in the final production stages. The list continues: *tearsheets, front matter, blues, F & G*. As long as we were using these words with our various editors, all was well. Using them outside the world of authors and publishers, however, would risk losing a listener's attention, understanding, and patience.

In some settings and on some occasions, the ability to use jargon properly is a sign of group membership and status. In other settings, jargon can make ideas difficult to understand and may even be used to conceal the truth. Some speakers use jargon to impress others with their specialized knowledge. Such tactics usually fail to inform others and often result in misunderstandings and resentment.

Acronyms and abbreviations unique to an occupation or organization are another form of jargon. One of your authors listened to the president of a professional association describe the benefits of membership to a group of undergraduate students. The speaker discussed the programs supported by the XYZ (not the actual letters of the association) association, the size of its membership, its scholarship opportunities, and the value of networking with other professionals. When the presentation was over and the speaker asked the students for questions, a hand shot up. "What does *XYZ* stand for?" the student asked. If you plan to use abbreviations, make sure that your audience understands what they mean.

In our opinion, the worst kind of gobbledygook occurs when speakers use big, multisyllable words in an attempt to impress an audience. Rudolf Flesch publishes a sixty-word blacklist in his book *Say What You Mean*. He contends that long words are a curse, a special language that comes between a speaker and audience. According to Flesch, people use such words to cloak themselves in a mantle of false dignity or to make themselves appear more powerful.[2] Why say *affirmative* when you mean *yes?* Why say *anticipate* instead of *expect?* Why use *obtain, procure,* or *secure* when *get* works just as well. Flesch writes, "*Get* is always better. It's the way we all talk. Get it?"[3]

1. William Lutz, *Doublespeak* (New York: Harper Perennial, 1990), p. 3.
2. Rudolf Flesch, *Say What You Mean* (New York: Harper & Row, 1972), p. 70.
3. Flesch, p. 88.

Language and Logistics

All communication takes place in a context—both physical and psychological. Understanding the context of your presentation will help you choose the most appropriate and effective words to use.

Have you ever heard someone say, "That's not what I meant. You took it out of context"? The characteristics of the physical place where you are speaking and the occasion of the presentation create a context. Whereas colloquial expressions and even risqué words may be appropriate in a toast at a bachelor party, they are likely to be inappropriate at a formal wedding reception. The words in a eulogy would be quite different from a casual greeting at a family reunion. Presenting a scholarly paper at an academic convention would probably involve using longer and more technical words than a presentation on personal safety at an elementary school would.

Chapter 21, "Developing Special Presentations," provides language choice suggestions for a variety of occasion-specific presentations, including introducing a presenter, welcoming an audience, making a toast, delivering a eulogy, making a sales presentation, answering audience questions, and speaking impromptu.

Language and Content

The challenge of choosing appropriate and effective words is not limited to speakers. Writers face a similar challenge. Readers sometimes suffer from the MEGO reaction to a piece of writing—"My Eyes Glaze Over." Even when ideas are well organized, readers become bored by wordiness, flatness, inappropriate word choice, clichés, and sentences constructed without interesting variation.

A similar affliction affects listeners. Audience members may suffer from the MMW reaction to a presentation—"My Mind Wanders"—even when the speaker is well prepared and well organized. As is the case with the MEGO reaction, speakers can prevent the MMW reaction by following the "4 Cs of Speaking Style."[15]

THE 4 Cs OF SPEAKING STYLE

- **Clear**
- **Committed**
- **Colorful**
- **Captivating**

Clear. Clarity always comes first. If you are not clear, your audience won't understand what you say and won't be impressed with how you say it. Use simple and direct words. Don't let long, fancy words get in the way of your message.

Marketing expert Jerry Della Femina writes: "Nobody has the time to try and figure out what you're trying to say, so you need to be direct. Most great advertising is direct. That's how people talk. That's the style they read. That's what sells products or services or ideas."[16] Clear, direct language informs and persuades.

To improve the clarity of your presentation, use declarative sentences. Think of the clarity in Martin Luther King Jr.'s affirmation: "I have a dream." Recall the simple eloquence of the Declaration of Independence: "We hold these truths to be self-evident: that all men are created equal; that they are endowed by their creator with certain unalienable rights; that among these are life, liberty, and the pursuit of happiness."

Committed. Committed speakers are both confident and dedicated to achieving their purpose. Have you ever heard a person say something like "It's a good idea, I think. Don't you agree?" or "Um,... I don't mean to be negative, but I wonder if possibly we might be making the wrong move here?" Making such cautious, powerless, qualified statements undercuts your meaning. Consider these alternative statements: "It's a good idea!" and "We're making the wrong move." These statements convey confidence and show that the speaker is committed and means what she or he says.

Committed speakers use active language. They use sentences with vivid, expressive verbs rather than bland forms of the verb *to be (be, am, is, are, was, being, been)* or verbs in the passive voice. *Voice* is a term that refers to whether the subject of a sentence performs or receives the action of the verb. If the subject performs the action, you are using an **active voice.** If the subject receives the action, you are using a **passive voice.**

A strong, active voice keeps your presentation moving. A passive voice takes the focus away from the subject of your sentence. "The *Iliad* was read by the student" is passive. "The student read the *Iliad*" is active. Because an active voice requires fewer words, it also keeps your sentences short and direct. With passive voice, the subject is the recipient of the action. With the active voice, the subject *performs* the action.

Less committed and confident speakers often have trouble using the active voice because they worry about sounding too direct. Look at the differences in these sentences:

Active voice: Sign this petition.

Passive voice: The petition should by signed by all of you.

The more passive the sentence, the less powerful the message. Tell your audience who is doing what, not what was done by whom.

Colorful. Colorful language elicits strong images in the minds of listeners. Communication researchers refer to this reaction as the **vividness effect.** They note that typically

Avoid Clichés

A **cliché** (pronounced klee-shay') is a trite or overused expression. Clichés are tired expressions that have lost their originality or force through overuse.[1] Here are some examples:

Crystal clear

Better late than never

Better said than done

Hit the nail on the head

White as a sheet

Clichés lack force because they are predictable rather than original. So how do you know if you're using a cliché? Try this simple test: Say the beginning of the phrase and see if you or others can guess the last word. If most people can guess the ending, you may be using a well-worn cliché.

Beginning of Phrase	End of Phrase
He's blind as a	bat.
The plan is dead as a	doornail.
It's selling like	hotcakes.
I'm as cool as a	cucumber.
Let's not beat around	the bush.

And remember, listeners from other cultures may not have a clue about your meaning when you use a cliché.

A critical look at these and other clichés reveals another weakness. They often make little sense. Are cucumbers cool? Do hotcakes sell well? Do you know anyone who has actually beaten around a bush? Is a doornail more dead than a wall or a floor nail? And although bats may not see well with their eyes, their radar system is far more powerful than our sense of sight.

Sometimes clever speakers will use a familiar cliché to make a point. You could use the phrase "blind as a bat" to launch a presentation about the misunderstandings we have about bats or a presentation about the marvels of modern radar. The cliché "white as a sheet" could be used in a presentation focusing on racial presumptions in the United States or in a presentation on the dangers of anemia. Even better, convert the cliché into something more interesting and original. Here's an example of how a student took the cliché "butterflies in my stomach" and transformed it into something fresh and memorable:

> *If the feeling in my stomach is caused by butterflies, there must be a horde of them, with horseshoes on.*[2]

1. See Ann Raimes, *Keys for Writers: A Brief Handbook*, 3rd ed. (Boston: Houghton Mifflin, 2003), p. 271.
2. Based on Diana Hacker, *The Bedford Handbook*, 5th ed. (Boston: Bedford, 1998), p. 279.

concrete words, use of descriptive details, and/or emotional language lend "color" to a presentation.[17] How do you achieve vividness and color? Use carefully chosen adjectives and adverbs to provide descriptive details. Unless you are going to use a presentation aid, language is the only means you have to create memorable images and emotional reactions.

Several years ago, one of our students began an award-winning persuasive speech with a story. Her clear and specific language created a powerful and unforgettable image. Try reading the following introduction out loud. You don't have to be dramatic—just let the words do it for you.

> *Picture two-year-old Joey. A hole in his throat so he can breathe. A tube jutting out of his stomach where a surgeon implanted a new esophagus. It all began when Joey found an open can of drain cleaner and swallowed some of its contents. However, this is not going to be a speech about poisoning and how to prevent it because Joey's tragedy was not caused by the drain cleaner. It occurred because Joey's mother followed an old set of first-aid instructions. She gave him vinegar. But instead of neutralizing the poison, the vinegar set off a chemical reaction that generated heat and turned Joey's tiny digestive tract into an inferno of excruciating pain.*

The student graduated many years ago, yet faculty members still refer to the "poor Joey" introduction as a model of colorful and effective language use.

A second way to add color to your presentation is to vary the intensity of your language. **Language intensity** refers to the degree to which your language deviates from bland, neutral terms.[18] You might say that your vacation was "okay," or that it was "good," or that it was "great!" Effective speakers use intense language to get attention and signal importance. Instead of using a word like *nice,* try *delightful* or *enchanting. Disaster* is a much more powerful word than *mistake.* A *vile* meal sounds much worse than a *bad* one. But don't go overboard—being too intense can boomerang. Listeners may feel that you've lost control. Effective speakers *vary* language intensity. On an important issue or point, they're more intense. Then they take a breather by using more neutral language so that the audience will be ready for the next important idea.

Research suggests that language intensity increases audience perceptions of all three components of credibility—competence, character, and charisma. However, speakers who are too intense—who don't vary their levels of intensity—may lose credibility in the eyes of the audience.[19]

Captivating. Poets, playwrights, and politicians have long understood the power of language to captivate an audience. **Captivating language** attracts and holds an audience by virtue of its beauty or brilliance. Captivating language can also elicit delight and a variety of emotions. Your choice of words can captivate an audience through the use of repetition (sounds and words), resemblances (similes and metaphors), or other rhetorical devices (antithesis, personification, rhyme) to "capture" and hold your audience's attention while making your ideas appealing and memorable.

CAPTIVATING LANGUAGE USES

- **Repetition**
- **Resemblances**
- **Rhetorical devices**

Repetition. The nature of presentation speaking makes repetition a necessary and powerful tool for all speakers. Because your listeners cannot go back and immediately rehear what you've said, repetition provides a way of captivating audiences by highlighting selected words, ideas, and phrases. Two types of repetition are commonly used by effective speakers: repetitions of sounds and repetitions of words.

Repetition can be as simple as beginning a series of words (or words placed closely together) with the same sound. This type of repetition is referred to as **alliteration.** At the opening of Julie Borchard's presentation on Muzak (see the Appendix), she refers to Muzak as the sound of "vacant volumes of vapid violins." Although alliteration may seem to be a subtle device, it is often found in phrases that audiences remember. One of the most quoted phrases from President Bush's 2003 State of the Union Address is this: "The dictator of Iraq is not disarming. To the contrary, he is deceiving." Newspaper headlines and editorials ran this line in next-day articles and editorials. Alliterations "capture" audience attention and are fairly easy to remember.

Repetition can also be extended to a word, a phrase, a clause, or entire sentences. Dr. Martin Luther King Jr. used the wording, "I have a dream" nine times in his famous 1963 speech in Washington, D.C. He used "let freedom ring" ten times. You can also repeat a short phrase within a single sentence. In President Abraham Lincoln's Gettysburg Address, the words *the people* are used three times in the famous concluding line: "and that government of the people, by the people, for the people, shall not perish from the earth."[20]

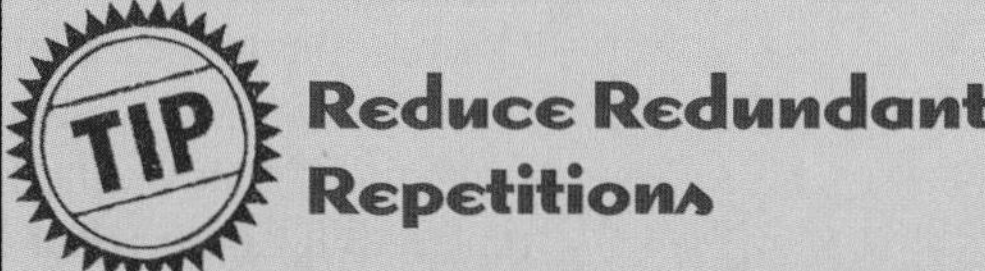

Be cautious with repetition and alliteration. These techniques lose their power if they're used excessively or haphazardly. Dr. Ronald Carpenter, a professor of English and communication studies, has cautioned: "Do not squander repetition on unworthy words!"[1] Here's an example of such overindulgence in these two sentences from President George Bush, Jr.'s acceptance speech at the Republican National Convention in 1992: "[Congress] is a body caught in a hopelessly tangled web of PACs, perks, privileges, partisanship, and paralysis. Every day, Congress puts politics ahead of principles and above programs." Rather than adding impact and motivation, the sentences sound a bit silly and are difficult to pronounce with dignity and style.

1. Ronald H. Carpenter, *Choosing Powerful Words* (Boston: Allyn & Bacon, 1999), p. 117.

Dr. Martin Luther King, Jr. repeated the phrases "I have a dream" and "Let freedom ring" multiple times during his eloquent, powerful March on Washington Speech, August 28, 1963.

Speechwriters have learned to use repetition as a way of involving and arousing audience members. In 1996, Vice President Al Gore addressed the Democratic National Convention on the eve of Bill Clinton's renomination. Gore ended seven paragraphs with the sentence "But we won't let them." For example, he said that the Republicans "want someone in that Oval Office who will rubber-stamp their plan. That's why they want to replace Bill Clinton. But we won't let them."[21] By the time Gore reached his third example, the audience was energized and eager to roar back, "But we won't let them!"

Repetition can drive home important ideas to the audience and help evoke action. Audience members anticipate repeated phrases during a presentation and remember them long afterwards. Also note that repetition within a single sentence often sounds better when used in groupings of three, as in Lincoln's conclusion that repeats *the people.*

Resemblances. Similes, metaphors, and analogies are powerful figures of speech that highlight resemblances. They compare two things that are usually quite different in most ways but have at least one quality in common.

A **simile** makes a direct comparison between two things or ideas, usually by using the words *like* or *as.*

A word fitly spoken is like apples of gold in pitchers of silver.

—Proverbs, 225–11

Float like a butterfly, sting like a bee.

—Muhammad Ali

Metaphors make a comparison between two things or ideas without using connective words such as *like* and *as.*

Art is a rebellious child, a wild animal that will not be tamed.

—Chilean novelist Isabel Allende

An iron curtain has descended across the continent of Europe.

—Winston Churchill

Similes and metaphors are based on analogies. As we discuss in Chapter 8, "Supporting Material," analogies compare similar things or contrast dissimilar things. For example, the analogy "Just as celebrated orchestra conductors must grasp the entire musical score while inspiring great performances from individual players, effective leaders must understand the big picture while motivating team members to perform at their full potential" can be expressed as a simile: "Effective leaders are like great orchestra conductors—they know the score and inspire great performances." It could also work as a metaphor: "Great leaders conduct an orchestra of talented team members."

Metaphors hold awesome power when they are well chosen and skillfully expressed—so much so that we often spend hours searching for good-match metaphors to use in our presentations. Metaphors are much more than a language technique; they move audiences from one realm of thought to another. Think of the many metaphors that we all use to describe the experience of love. *Love is a baseball game:* I made it to first base; I struck out; our separation is just a seventh-inning stretch. *Love is a journey:* We're at a crossroads; our relationship has hit a dead end; we can't turn around now.

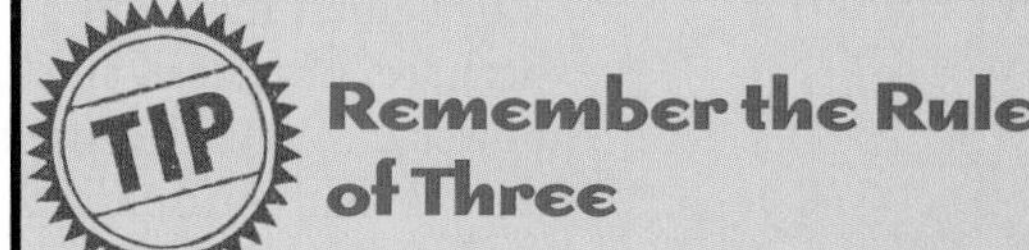

Remember the Rule of Three

In Chapter 10, "Organizational Tools," we note that three key points seem to be ideal for most presentations. Audience members often expect and anticipate that speakers will have three points—even to the extent that audiences prepare to applaud as they hear the third item in a series. The same is true of words and phrases listed in threes.

President George W. Bush's speechwriters often use the rule-of-three strategy. One early paragraph in Bush's 2003 State of the Union Address provides multiple examples. We note the repetition of three with numbers in parentheses:

In a whirlwind of (1) change and (2) hope and (3) peril, (1) our faith is sure, (2) our resolve is firm, and (3) our union is strong. (1) We will not deny, (2) we will not ignore, (3) we will not pass along our problems (1) to other Congresses, (2) to other presidents, and (3) [to] other generations. We will confront them with (1) focus and (2) clarity and (3) courage.[1]

1. *Washington Post,* 29 January 2003, p. A10.

Metaphors are potent tools. Ronald Carpenter offers the following list of common sources for metaphors that may help you find a suitable image for your presentation.[22]

- *Up and down. Up* is usually linked to happiness, health, life, and virtue, whereas *down* characterizes sadness, sickness, death, and low status. Martin Luther King Jr. referred to the "sunlit path of racial justice" as compared to the "dark and desolate valley of segregation."
- *Change of seasons.* In his 1992 inaugural address, President Bill Clinton asserted that by their votes for a Democratic candidate, "Americans have forced the spring," and "now we must do the work the season demands."
- *The sea.* Metaphors about the sea work across many cultures and stimulate deep emotional responses.[23] We turn again to Martin Luther King Jr.'s "I Have a Dream" speech for an example: "The Negro lives on a lonely island of poverty in the midst of a vast ocean of material prosperity."
- *Diseases.* The word *cancer* has powerful connotations. To call anything a "cancer" invokes suffering, fear, and death. The acronym *AIDS* has a similar impact.
- *Snakes.* The only fear that rivals fear of public speaking is fear of snakes. During World War II, Franklin Roosevelt described German submarines as "rattlesnakes." You can't get much lower than calling someone a "snake in the grass."
- *Natural phenomena.* Metaphors often use natural phenomena and weather images to describe serious consequences. We talk about being overwhelmed by "a flood" of requests or being "swamped" by work. We describe armed forces as moving and attacking with "lightning speed."

The best metaphors usually appeal to sensory experiences—what audience members see, hear, feel, smell, or taste. Sight and feeling (tactile sensation) are the most powerful. Why? Because sight and physical feelings last longer than hearing, smell, or taste. What you *see* lasts the longest—for hours, weeks, and even a lifetime. If your metaphor can invoke a strong visual image, you will create an indelible impression in the minds and memories of your audience.[24]

Rhetorical Devices. **Rhetorical devices** include a variety of language-based strategies that help speakers achieve their purpose. Here we look at three effective rhetorical devices: antithesis, personification, and rhyme.

RHETORICAL DEVICES

Antithesis: The balanced pairing of opposites

Personification: Explaining an abstract concept or complex idea in human terms

Rhyme: A catchy phrase with similar ending sounds of key words

When Neil Armstrong stepped on the moon in 1969, he spoke a line written for him by the poet James Dickey. Armstrong said: "That's one small step for man—one giant leap for mankind." When speakers use **antithesis,** they juxtapose two contrasting ideas to create a kind of balance between parallel words or phrases. Here's another example. In John F. Kennedy's inaugural speech, he said, "Let us never negotiate out of fear. But let us never fear to negotiate."

Antithesis is a powerful rhetorical device that can be difficult to write. Ronald Carpenter provides a method of developing a sentence that uses antithesis.[25] First, draw a seesaw like this:

Then pick two words with opposite meanings and put one on each side of the seesaw:

best worst

Next, write the remainder of a sentence that has approximately the same number of words on one side of the fulcrum as on the other. The key word is *balance.* Here's the result, taken from Charles Dickens's novel *A Tale of Two Cities:*

It was the best of times; it was the worst of times.

When Eleanor Roosevelt died, Adlai Stevenson used the following antithesis to describe her enduring spirit:

She would rather light candles than curse the darkness.

Carpenter identified two general rules for mastering antithesis. When you construct an antithesis, remember to check for (1) the level of balance and (2) brevity for easier recall.[26]

Personification can be colorful and captivating because it provides a human example of an abstract concept or complex idea. Presidents Ronald Reagan and Bill Clinton used this rhetorical device brilliantly. They put a human face on their ideas by telling personal stories—usually about an average U.S. citizen affected by the legislation or policy they were advocating.

Look back at the story about "poor Joey," the two-year-old boy who ingested drain cleaner. The speaker could have begun with statistics on dangerous antidotes for poison. Instead, she used personification to make the problem real and highly emotional. At a much simpler level, personification endows an inanimate object or abstraction with human qualities, as in "Flowers danced in the wind" or "Hunger lurked around every corner."

Rhyme occurs when words correspond with one another in terminal sounds. Rhyme can make a phrase easier to remember, even though it also gives the phrase a kind of singsong quality. A study of rhyme as a rhetorical device by psycholinguist Matthew McGlone concludes that rhyme makes ordinary statements more believable. A statement such as "Woes unite foes" was deemed more credible than one like "Woes unite enemies." Remember the O. J. Simpson trial in which attorney Johnnie Cochran rhymed "If it [the glove] doesn't fit, you must acquit"? This simple rhyme may have kept his client from being convicted of murder.[27]

What About Rhetorical Questions?

What are **rhetorical questions**? They are questions to which no answer is expected. Speakers use rhetorical questions to ask questions they either don't want the audience to answer out loud—questions they want the audience to think about—or to reach a predetermined conclusion. For example, in the Presentation Principles in Action section of this chapter, we include an excerpt from a speech by Jennifer Granholm, the governor of Michigan, who asks a series of rhetorical questions in which she contrasts continued funding of higher education with other state needs. She asks:

Is it college, or is it K–12? Is it college, or is it letting people out of jail? Is it college, or is it providing health care for senior citizens who have no other way to go?

Her hope is that the audience will accept her decision to cut state funding to colleges.

Many speakers use rhetorical questions. Many textbooks recommend the use of rhetorical questions as an effective and persuasive language strategy. However, research suggests that rhetorical questions may not generate persuasive thoughts in the minds of listeners. At the same time, these findings also indicate that there are no clear disadvantages associated with the use of rhetorical questions as stylistic devices. In some situations, rhetorical questions may help audience members recall an argument or emphasize a fact.[1]

Look at Governor Granholm's rhetorical questions again. If you are a college student, work at a college, or depend on colleges to train employees and local service workers, you may react to her rhetorical questions with critical questions of your own. Why does the cut have to come from college funding? Why not cut the state bureaucracy, get welfare cheats off the rolls, tax the rich corporations more, or raise the cigarette tax?

Rhetorical questions that involve audience members and get them to think critically have the potential to enhance your speaking style and credibility. At the same time, make sure that your questions don't challenge an audience's deeply held attitudes, beliefs, and values.

1. Barbara Mae Gayle, Raymond W. Preiss, and Mike Allen, "Another Look at the Use of Rhetorical Questions," in *Persuasion: Advances Through Meta-Analysis*, eds. Mike Allen and Raymond W. Preiss (Cresskill, NJ: Hampton Press, 1998), pp. 189–201.

Language and Organization

In Chapter 10, "Organizational Tools," we emphasize that a good, formal outline requires careful word choices when you are writing your introduction, stating your central idea, labeling your key points, and even making a smooth transition from one section to another.

Make sure that your central idea uses language that states exactly how you will go about achieving your purpose. If your key points are too long or awkwardly worded, you will have trouble saying them and, even more important, your audience will have difficulty remembering them. When organizing your presentation,

Style and Tone Go Hand in Hand

If you deliver your presentation in a monotone voice or emphasize the wrong words in a sentence, no one will appreciate your language. Even if your words are colorful and captivating, no one will be impressed if your voice doesn't highlight them.

Lani Arredondo contends that verbal style should generate an appropriate tone. **Tone** is the feeling or impression that an audience derives from a presentation.[1] Three factors affect the tone of a presentation:

1. *Language.* The kinds of words you choose communicate a tone. Your words can be businesslike, demanding, friendly, worrisome, sincere, or passionate. The following examples suggest how different verbal styles generate differences in tone:

   Bureaucratic and Pompous: Comprehensive analyses and assessments of departmental and interdepartmental operational strategies and procedures have determined the existence of conflicting organizational paradigms.

   Demanding and Confrontational: We have a problem here. You people need to shape up!

   Cooperative and Courteous: How many of you would like to improve your group's overall communication and teamwork?

2. *Performance.* Variation in your vocal delivery (volume, rate, pitch, fluency) and physical delivery (eye contact, facial expression, posture, gestures, appearance) can determine whether the audience notices important words and phrases, whether questions sound like questions, and whether exclamations receive appropriate emphasis. If your voice is unduly harsh, breathy, loud, or soft, you may not communicate the appropriate tone. Your voice and body are the instruments that convert your well-chosen words into the sounds and sights that reach your audience. Make sure that the tone of your performance matches the meaning of your words.

3. *Attitude.* After only a few seconds of listening, an audience will make decisions about your character. Are you friendly, sincere, and enthusiastic or brusque, impersonal, and condescending? Not surprisingly, audiences perceive a friendly, sincere, and enthusiastic speaker more positively than they perceive the opposite sort of speaker. Audience members use the language that they hear, the speaker's delivery, and the presenter's attitude to determine the tone of a message and to decide whether the message deserves their full attention and interest.

1. Lani Arredondo, *The McGraw-Hill 36-Hour Course: Business Presentations* (New York: McGraw-Hill, 1994), p. 147.

consider several tips for using words more effectively:

- Make sure that the wording of your key points is clear, committed, colorful, and captivating.
- Word your key points in a way that makes them easy to repeat and summarize at other places in your presentation.
- Use connectives (internal previews, internal summaries, transitions, and signposts) to help your audience follow, understand, and remember your message. Wording as simple as "My next point is" can alert and prepare listeners for important ideas.
- Look for creative ways to label your key points. Audience members are more likely to remember a presentation that compares growing tomatoes to caring for a newborn baby or an informative speech that covers the 4 Cs of Speaking Style.

Language and Performance

Let's begin with the biggest performance-related "problem" that faces speakers who want to choose and use appropriate and effective words: How can you plan words if you're speaking impromptu or extemporaneously? Students tell us, "Unless I write out my presentation and read it, I can't choose my words in advance." We agree. You can, however, make sure that you phrase your key points carefully and that you choose supporting materials, such as testimony and examples, that both inform and inspire. You can also write out and even memorize your introduction and conclusion to make sure that you get the most out of every word. You can practice telling stories you intend to share until the words become second nature to you. You can even identify and practice key phrases that you will repeat throughout your presentation.

As we note in Chapter 14, "Performance and Practice," even though most presentations are delivered informally and from notes, a few very important ones are delivered by using a manuscript. If your presentation will be quoted or made part of a public record, you may need to write out every word. If you are speaking in an emotional situation, you may want to have a manuscript to help you get through a difficult experience.

A manuscript gives you several other advantages. You can revise a manuscript many times to improve your choice of words. You can check a manuscript to test whether you have used an oral style. You can practice with a manuscript to make sure that your well-chosen words are easy to say. Even if you intend to convert your manuscript into a brief presentation outline or set of cards that highlight key points and supporting material, you may first want to work with a manuscript in order to choose appropriate and effective words.

Summary

▶ How do I choose appropriate and effective words for a presentation?

Choosing appropriate and effective words requires an understanding of the nature of language as a system of arbitrary signs and symbols used to communicate thoughts and feelings. Whereas the denotative meaning of words can be found in dictionaries, the connotative meaning is derived from the listener's emotional response or personal thoughts. Connotative meanings are more likely to influence you and your audience's responses to words. Clarify your meaning by using concrete words to prevent inaccurate inferences and misunderstandings.

▶ What is the difference between oral and written style?

Oral style uses shorter words and sentences, more personal pronouns, contractions, and colloquial expressions. Although grammar is important in the style, speakers often use incomplete sentences and repeated phrases to emphasize important ideas and information.

▶ How do I apply the principles of presentation speaking to language?

Consider the words that you intend to use as you make decisions about the seven principles of presentation speaking. Match your words to your purpose and audience. Use language that will enhance your credibility and adapt to the occasion and place where you will be speaking. Apply the 4 Cs of Speaking Style to the content of your presentation, paying special attention to the wording of key points and connectives. Use your vocal and physical delivery to link your overall style and the tone of your performance.

▶ What are the characteristics of an effective speaking style?

Enlist the 4 Cs of Speaking Style. Make sure that you choose clear and concise words that demonstrate your commitment to your purpose and audience. Enhance the power of your presentation by using colorful and captivating words and by utilizing a variety of language strategies, including repetition, resemblances, and rhetorical devices.

Presentation Principles in Action

Writing Apprehension Test (WAT)?

Directions: The following are a series of statements about writing. There are no right or wrong answers to these statements. Please indicate the degree to which each statement applies to you by marking whether you (1) strongly agree, (2) agree, (3) are uncertain about, (4) disagree, or (5) strongly disagree with the statement. Although some of these statements may seem repetitious, take your time and try to be as honest as possible.

1. _____ I avoid writing.
2. _____ I have no fear of my writing being evaluated.
3. _____ I look forward to writing down my ideas.
4. _____ My mind seems to go blank when I start to work on a composition.
5. _____ Expressing ideas through writing seems to be a waste of time.
6. _____ I would enjoy submitting my writing to magazines for evaluation and publication.
7. _____ I like to write my ideas down.
8. _____ I feel confident in my ability to express my ideas clearly in writing.
9. _____ I like to have my friends read what I have written.
10. _____ I'm nervous about writing.
11. _____ People seem to enjoy what I write.
12. _____ I enjoy writing.
13. _____ I never seem to be able to write down my ideas clearly.
14. _____ Writing is a lot of fun.
15. _____ I like seeing my thoughts on paper.
16. _____ Discussing my writing with others is an enjoyable experience.
17. _____ It's easy for me to write good compositions.
18. _____ I don't think I write as well as other people do.
19. _____ I don't like to have my compositions evaluated.
20. _____ I'm not good at writing.

Scoring: To determine your score on the WAT, complete the following steps:

Step 1. Add the scores for items 1, 4, 5, 10, 13, 18, 19, and 20.

Step 2. Add the scores for items 2, 3, 6, 7, 8, 9, 11, 12, 14, 15, 16, and 17.

Step 3. Complete the following formula:

WAT = 48 – Total from Step 1 + Total from Step 2

Your score should be between 20 and 100. If your score is below 20 or above 100, you have made a mistake in computing the score. The higher your score, the more apprehension you feel about writing.

Score	Level of Apprehension	Description
20–45	Low	Enjoys writing, seeks writing opportunities.
46–75	Average	Some writing creates apprehension; other writing does not.
76–100	High	Troubled by many kinds of writing, avoids writing in most situations

Source: Virginia P. Richmond and James C. McCroskey, *Communication: Apprehension, Avoidance, and Effectiveness,* 4th ed. (Scottsdale, AZ: Gorsuch Scarisbrick, 1995), pp. 42, 125–126. Also see John Daly and Michael Miller, "The Empirical Development of an Instrument to Measure Writing Apprehension," *Research in the Teaching of English* 12 (1975): 242–249.

Assess the Style

Directions: Read the following excerpts from three different presentations:

1. President George W. Bush's State of the Union Address, January 28, 2003
2. Washington State Governor Gary Lock's Democratic Response to the State of the Union Address, January 28, 2003
3. Michigan Governor Jennifer Granholm's comments on budget cuts to higher education, February 19, 2003

Review the speakers' styles and their language strategies. Pay special attention to the 4 Cs of Style. Which strategies do these speakers use? How well do they use them? What are the similarities and differences in these speakers' styles? Discuss your conclusions with the rest of your class.

The dictator who is assembling the world's most dangerous weapons has already used them on whole villages, leaving thousands of his own citizens dead, blind or disfigured.

Iraqi refugees tell us how forced confessions are obtained: by torturing children while their parents are made to watch. International human rights groups have catalogued other methods used in the torture chambers of Iraq: electric shock, burning with hot irons, dripping acid on the skin, mutilation with electric drills, cutting out tongues, and rape.

If this is not evil, then evil has no meaning.

And tonight I have a message for the brave and oppressed people in Iraq. Your enemy is not surrounding your country; your enemy is ruling your country.

—President George W. Bush, January 28, 2003
(*Washington Post,* 29 January 2003, p. A11)

This is not an easy time. But I often think about my grandfather, arriving by steamship 100 years ago. He had no family here; he spoke no English. I can only imagine how he must have felt as he looked out at his new country. There are millions of families like mine, people whose ancestors dreamed the American dream and worked hard to make it come true. They transformed adversity into opportunity.

Yes, these are challenging times, but the American family—the American dream—has prevailed before. That's the character of our people and the hallmark of our country. The lesson of our legacy is, if we work together, and make the right choices, we will become a stronger, more united and more prosperous nation.

—Washington State Governor Gary Lock, January 28, 2003
(*Washington Post*, 29 January 2003, p. A11)

It's not that I don't value higher ed, because I really do. The question: Is it college, or is it K–12? Is it college, or is it letting people out of jail? Is it college, or making sure you've got enough protective services workers for children who may be abused or neglected in their homes? Is it college, or is it providing health care for senior citizens who have no other way to go? Those are hard decisions, but if you have to rank them, college benefits fewer people than health care might.

—Michigan Governor Jennifer Granholm, February 19, 2003
(*Detroit Free Press*, 20 February 2003, p. A1)

Key Terms

Notes

1 *The American Heritage Dictionary of the English Language,* 4th ed. (Boston: Houghton Mifflin, 2000), p. 985.

2 Dominic A. Infante, Andrew S. Rancer, and Deanna F. Womack, *Building Communication Theory,* 2nd ed. (Prospect Heights, IL: Waveland, 1993), pp. 220, 221, and 232.

3 C. K. Ogden and I. A. Richards, *The Meaning of Meaning* (New York: Harcourt, Brace, 1936), p. 11.

4 S. I. Hayakawa and Alan R. Hayakawa, *Language and Thought in Action,* 5th ed. (San Diego, CA: Harcourt Brace Jovanovich, 1990), p. 43.

5 Isa N. Engleberg and Dianna R. Wynn, *Working in Groups: Communication Principles and Strategies,*

3rd ed. (Boston: Houghton Mifflin, 2003), p. 99.

6 Vivian J. Cook, *Inside Language* (London: Arnold, 1997), p. 91.

7 Lani Arredondo, *The McGraw-Hill 36-Hour Course: Business Presentations* (New York: McGraw-Hill, 1994), p. 147.

8 Thomas L. Friedman, "Now Clinton Decides Which Promises Came First," *New York Times*, 15 November 1992, Sect. 4, p. E1.

9 Peggy Noonan, *Simply Speaking: How to Communicate Your Ideas with Style, Substance, and Clarity* (New York: HarperCollins, 1998), p. 36.

10 Based on Isa Engleberg and Ann Raimes, *Pocket Keys for Speakers* (Boston: Houghton Mifflin, 2004), pp. 189–191.

11 James Price Dillard and Linda J. Marshall, "Persuasion as a Social Skill," in *Handbook of Communication and Social Interaction Skills*, ed. John O. Greene and Brant R. Burleson (Mahwah, NJ: Lawrence Erlbaum Associates, 2003), pp. 505–506.

12 For the complete text of Gates's speech plus commentary, see Owen Peterson, *Representative American Speeches, 1989–1990* (New York: H. W. Wilson, 1991), pp. 163–168.

13 Engleberg and Raimes, p. 224.

14 Engleberg and Raimes, p. 226.

15 MEGO and the 4 Cs of Speaking Style are based on two sources: Raimes, *Keys for Writers: A Brief Handbook*, 3rd ed. (Boston: Houghton Mifflin, 2004), p. 249; and Joseph Williams, *Style: Ten Lessons in Clarity and Grace*, 5th ed. (Reading, MA: Addison-Wesley, 1997).

16 A. Jerome Jewler, *Creative Strategy in Advertising*, 2nd ed. (Belmont, CA: Wadsworth, 1985), p. 41.

17 Lawrence A. Hosman, "Language and Persuasion," in *The Persuasion Handbook: Developments in Theory and Practice*, ed. James Price Dillard and Michael Pfau (Thousand Oaks, CA: Sage, 2002), pp. 375–376.

18 John W. Bowers, "Some Correlates of Language Intensity," *Quarterly Journal of Speech* 50 (1964): 415–420.

19 Hosman, pp. 376–377.

20 Garry Wills, *Lincoln at Gettysburg* (New York: Simon and Schuster, 1992), p. 263.

21 A complete text of Gore's address was obtained from the White House in 1999.

22 Ronald H. Carpenter, *Choosing Powerful Words* (Boston: Allyn and Bacon, 1999), pp. 109–111.

23 Michael Osborn, "The Evolution of the Archetypal Sea in Rhetoric and Poetic," *Quarterly Journal of Speech* 63 (1977): 347–363.

24 Carpenter, p. 111.

25 Carpenter, pp. 26–53.

26 Carpenter, p. 39.

27 *Forbes*, 5 October 1998, p. 45.

chapter thirteen

Generating Interest

- How do I interest audience members in my presentation?
- Why are stories so interesting?
- How should I use humor in my presentation?
- How can I directly involve my audience?

"How can I be more interesting when I speak?" It's understandable that many speakers ask this question. For one thing, novice speakers often *assume* they're not interesting; they can't imagine why an audience would want to listen to them talk about their topic. For another, they may have heard lots of boring presentations and may fear that theirs are doomed to be similar. Rarely is either assumption true. There is no reason that a well-prepared, audience-focused speaker should be dull or boring. In fact, all of us have listened to speakers who were so compelling that we were sorry to hear them end.

Although everything in this textbook is designed to help you make your presentations interesting and memorable, we also know that giving special attention to this issue can improve your chances of preparing and delivering a more successful presentation. In this chapter, we highlight several principles you can use to gain audience attention and interest. Whether you are presenting an informative briefing, advocating a persuasive position, or toasting a newlywed couple, there are many ways to make your presentation more interesting, more impressive, and more memorable. Spending time thinking about additional ways to interest and motivate your audience can transform an interesting presentation into a captivating one, changing a presentation that enhances your credibility into one that also puts you in a superstar category.

Overcoming Audience Disinterest

Effective speakers understand that audience analysis and adaptation are the keys to generating attention and interest in a presentation. Even while speaking, they monitor the audience's interest level. Immediate feedback provides a unique opportunity that only speakers get. A writer cannot tell if a reader is bored, whereas an observant speaker can sense a listener's lack of interest. A speaker can immediately adapt to feedback, while an author cannot.

Sometimes an audience's "I'm bored" feedback has little to do with you and your message. At other times, it's justified. To deliver an engaging presentation or to know when to modify a less-than-engaging one requires that you understand why audiences lose interest.

At the risk of simplifying a complex phenomenon, let's begin by acknowledging that audiences are often victims of two bad habits: short attention spans and poor listening skills. Two other bad habits can be attributed to the presenters: speaking too long and

DISINTEREST FACTORS

- **Limited attention span**
- **Poor listening habits**
- **Length of presentation**
- **Poor delivery**

delivering poorly. Learning to compensate for these habits is the first step in ensuring an interesting presentation.

Limited Attention Span

Even the most interesting speaker and topic cannot command 100 percent of an audience's attention 100 percent of the time. Life isn't like that. Audience members drift in and out of presentations, paying more attention to some sections than to others. They may be diverted for as little as half a second to as long as several minutes while thinking about personal problems, their upcoming day, lunch, or something else. **Attention span,** the amount of time an audience member can be attentive to sensory stimulation, differs for each of us according to age, intelligence, health, past experience, and motivation.[1] How long do you think the average adult can sustain undivided attention? Fifteen minutes? No. Try fifteen seconds![2]

You can stretch your audience's attention span by including a variety of attention-getting techniques:

- Use unusual and dramatic evidence.
- Use suspense to engage their curiosity.
- Use concrete words rather than abstract terms.
- Use colorful and captivating language.
- Demonstrate the *usefulness* of your information or advice.
- Involve their emotions.

FAQ Is It Television's Fault?

Some writers and researchers blame television for our short attention spans. Fifteen- and thirty-second commercials tell entire stories. Rarely does a television show go for more than fifteen minutes without a break. TV has taught our brains to disengage and think about something else. Consider the nightly TV news. How much time do most network news shows devote to a major story—a natural disaster, an economic crisis, a presidential scandal? Ten minutes? Five minutes? Guess again. News stories seldom get more than three minutes of air time. The entire day, around the world, is covered in about twenty minutes.[1]

Not only does television accommodate our short attention spans; programming is also designed to capture our attention with exciting videos and sound tracks. No speaker can compete with the technical whiz-bang of television. After all, what's the most boring thing on television? Talking heads. But no TV can do what live speakers do: engage and respond *personally* to their audiences.

1. Ron Hoff, *I Can See You Naked* (Kansas City, MO: Andrews and McMeel, 1992), pp. 75–76.

Poor Listening Habits

As we note in Chapter 2, "Listening and Critical Thinking," most audience members (and speakers) are not very good listeners. Therefore, it should not surprise you that an audience's listening ability is linked to its interest level. If an audience does not comprehend what you are saying, they may lose interest. If an audience does not appreciate what you are saying, they may tune out. If an audience is not analytical or empathic when they listen, your best arguments and stories will have little or no impact.

You can counteract the effects of poor listening. Look for more than one way to make and support your key points. For example, in addition to citing a statistic, give an example or tell a relevant story. Engage more of the audience's senses. Use a presentation aid or provide a handout to visually reinforce your spoken message.

Use organizational strategies to drive your ideas home. A good introduction can provide both a statement of your central idea and a preview of the key points in your presentation. As you move from key point to key point, use connectives to reinforce your message. Use internal previews and summaries to give the audience an additional opportunity to listen to each key point.

You can also help listeners by using a repetitive phrase to emphasize a point. For example, you may have heard politicians, members of the clergy, and motivational

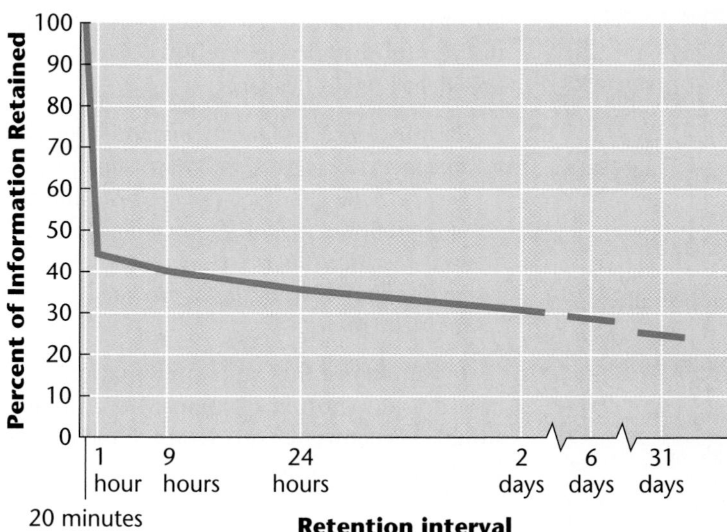

Figure 13.1

The Forgetting Curve

speakers repeat a word or phrase for this purpose. One of us heard a county executive do this to dispel an audience's negative perception of the police:

> *Our crime rate? It's down. Car thefts? Down. Break-ins? Down. Assaults? Down. Rape and homicide? Down. And the number of complaints about police brutality? Down!*

Limited attention span and poor listening habits combine to inhibit an audience's overall understanding and recall. About a hundred years ago, psychologists made two lasting discoveries about our memories.[3] One is the **forgetting curve** depicted in Figure 13.1.

Most audience members will forget a large portion of what they have seen or heard in a presentation. And most of that forgetting takes place in the nine hours that follow a learning experience such as listening to a presentation. Furthermore, the first hour of that nine-hour period will see the most information loss!

The second psychological finding, however, offers some hope. Some information—from algebraic formulas to bike riding—is retained in our long-term memory for decades. Although you may forget something you have learned if you do not use the information, it may be easy to *re*learn the material if the need arises.

All speakers should heed the implications of the forgetting curve and the fact that we save information in our long-term memories. Gaining and keeping audience attention—with a strong introduction, good evidence, well-organized content, engaging language, interest-generating features, and a memorable conclusion—can improve the audience's retention of your presentation.

Most speakers can learn to adjust to an audience's attention span and listening habits. Some also need to break their own speaker-based habits that can cause boredom: making overly long presentations and using lackluster delivery.

Length of Presentation

One reason why audience members dread presentations is that many of them just go on for too long. Peggy Noonan tackled the time issue as a presidential speechwriter. In the very beginning of her book, *Simply Speaking,* she puts this statement *first* on her

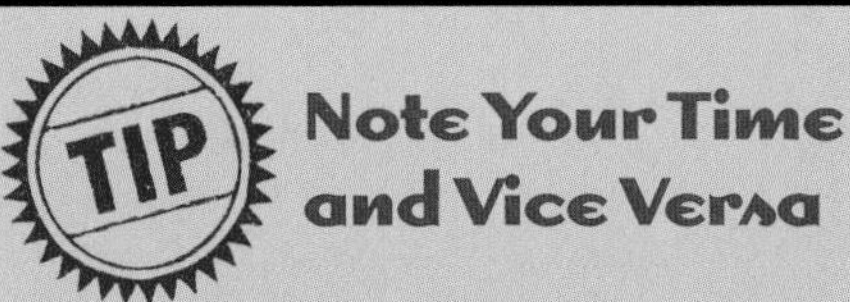

Note Your Time and Vice Versa

Recently one of us helped a colleague adjust some testimony he was preparing for a legislative hearing. He was told he had five to seven minutes to testify. What he wrote filled four single-spaced pages. Using an unrelenting red pen, we cut more than half of the copy. But he still ran overtime.

How do you calculate, during the preparation process, how long a presentation will be? Depending on the complexity of the material, the mood of the message, and your natural speaking rate, five double-spaced pages of manuscript can equal anywhere from seven to ten minutes of speaking time. Keep in mind that it's more difficult to gauge speaking time when using notes. The key is to repeatedly practice out loud what you want to say, while your presentation is still in the early stages of development. Time yourself and indicate the results right on your notes. Use a stopwatch to gauge the length of each section; you may discover that some sections go on for too long while others are brief and clear. Soon you'll be quite comfortable estimating how long it will take to deliver a presentation using notes.

list of preliminaries: "No speech should last more than twenty minutes."[4] She tells of learning that from President Ronald Reagan:

> *[Reagan] knew that twenty minutes is more than enough time to say the biggest, most important thing in the world. The Gettysburg Address went three minutes or so, the Sermon on the Mount hardly more.... So keep in mind what [Senator] Hubert Humphrey's wife is said to have advised him: "Darling, for a speech to be immortal it need not be interminable."*[5]

If you realize that your presentation will run long, how do you shorten it? Alan M. Perlman,[6] a professional speechwriter at Kraft Foods, recommends answering three questions to which we have added a fourth:

- Will the audience be able to reach this conclusion without my help? If the answer is *yes,* don't overburden an audience with unnecessary explanations, stories, or visuals.
- Is the audience already inclined to believe this? Don't spend a lot of time on a point if the audience already shares your opinion or belief.
- Does the audience really need to know this? If the answer is *no,* delete or shorten any statement, idea, or piece of supporting material that isn't directly relevant to your purpose.
- Is it relevant to your purpose? Show your audience how the information and advice you offer is directly related to every point you make. If it's not relevant, cut it.

Although it can be hard to distance yourself from your material, you should realize that it's not all equally important. Learning to assess your material honestly in light of the four previous questions makes controlling your presentation's length relatively easy.[7]

Poor Delivery

As emphasized in Part V, "Performance," poor delivery can undermine even the best-prepared presentation. One performance component has a particularly strong impact on audience interest levels: expressiveness. We define **expressiveness** as the vitality, variety, and sincerity that a speaker puts into his or her delivery. It is more than enthusiasm or energy. It is an extension of the speaker's personality and attitude.[8] If you feel good about yourself, are excited about your message, and are truly interested in sharing your ideas with an audience, you are well on your way to being expressive. Speakers who care about their topics and their audiences are usually much more expressive than presenters who are struggling through presentations they don't want to give. Also, the more expressive you are, the more likely you will be seen as a highly credible, charismatic speaker.

The Disney Corporation refers to its employees as "cast members." Everyone working on a Disney property is part of the show! When you speak to an audience, you are *performing* in every sense of the word. Presidents Ronald Reagan and Bill Clinton understood their roles as performers—as do good newscasters, salespeople, and religious leaders. The same is true of good speakers.

The Power of Stories

All humans have responded to stories, whether depicted in prehistoric cave paintings, written in novels, or told to children.[9] Throughout history, storytellers have acted as keepers of tradition. The ollahms and shanachies of Ireland, the African griots, the Navajo shamans, and the troubadours of medieval France were storytellers who held honored places in their societies.[10]

Stories have the power to captivate and educate. Audiences remember stories because they create lasting images. Joanna Slan, author of *Using Stories and Humor,*[11] claims that the ability to tell stories separates great presenters from mediocre ones. Time after time, she contends, speakers who are invited to reappear before the same audience will be asked, "Are you going to tell us the story about...?" In some cases, presenters are hired because a client wants the audience to hear a certain story that the speaker loves to tell.

Even corporations are learning the value of storytelling. The *New York Times* reported a rise in "executive storytelling" seminars, some of which can cost $3,000 to $4,000 for a personal two-and-a-half-hour session with a business executive. CEOs and corporate officers are mastering personal storytelling "as a way of enlivening speeches, sales pitches, training sessions, and other presentations on otherwise dry or technical topics."[12]

Stories also benefit speakers. If you're anxious, they can help to reduce your nervousness. Most of us find it relatively easy to tell stories, a situation which makes them

A traditional Aleut storyteller and environmental activist uses drumming to enliven the tales he tells young people on the Bering Sea coast in Alaska.

Telling Stories

Most of us are good storytellers in conversations. We can easily recount something that has happened to us or something that we have witnessed. Telling a story for a presentation, however, is not the same as describing the day's events. Unlike the everyday stories we tell and hear, a story for a presentation must be carefully selected and well told. It should conform to the following storytelling guidelines.[1]

- *Simple Story Line.* First and foremost, use a simple story line. Long stories with complex themes and multiple events are difficult to follow and just as difficult to tell. Can you summarize your story in fewer than twenty-five words? If not, don't use it—it's too complex.[2]
- *Limited Number of Characters.* Unless you are an accomplished actor or storyteller, limit the number of characters in your story. Good storytellers distinguish their characters by giving them unique voices—varying volume, rate, pitch, and tone. Doing this can be tough for the novice speaker. If your story has more than three or four characters, look for another story or drop the extra people. It can be difficult for both you and your audience to keep track of a lot of characters. Your story's characters must be consistent in the ways in which they behave and speak.[3] If they aren't, your listeners will lose trust in them and also lose trust in the story.
- *Exaggeration.* Exaggerate both content and delivery. Whether you are describing the whale of a fish that got away or the disaster that befell you on a vacation, the story will be more effective if you stretch reality. Exaggeration both makes a story vivid and helps you to highlight its message. The tone of your voice, the sweep of your gestures, and your facial expression add another layer of meaning and emphasis to your story. Think about the way in which you exaggerate your delivery when reading a story to a child. Use a similar kind of bigger-than-life performance for most stories. However, stay away from exaggeration when the story is very simple or very sad. Such stories should be told with simple dignity.
- *Audience Links.* Good stories provide a link to the audience. Stories don't work if the audience can't connect with the setting, characters, or topic. Even the most basic children's story about a barnyard full of animals can give us characters who share human feelings and experiences. If the audience can imagine themselves in a situation similar to that of a character in a story, they are much more likely to listen. Also, make sure that your story is appropriate for your audience. Be sensitive to what you have learned from your audience analysis. Don't tell stories that show insensitivity to audience members' ages, gender, race, religion, ethnic background, or income level. An insensitive, inappropriate story will sever your connection to the audience in an instant and will undermine your credibility.
- *Performance.* Rives Collins and Pamela Cooper suggest moving among four "circles of awareness" as you perform a story. Circle 1 is private. It evokes *your* feelings, memories, and imagined images as you tell a story. Even though you are not making eye contact with your listeners, they sense that you are experiencing the emotions and action of the story. Circle 2 focuses on the story's details and its characters. Rather than looking at your audience, you focus your eyes on a character or object in the story. If you truly see your story, the audience will see it, too. Circle 3 involves maintaining direct eye contact with one or two members of the audience as though a single listener represents the entire audience. You can wink, evoke a giggle, or share confusion or wonder with an individual listener. Circle 4 includes the entire audience as if it were a single listener. Good storytellers move among the four circles as they re-experience the story and share it with an audience.[4]
- *Practice.* Don't wait until you are standing at a lectern to see if your story works. Most stories get better after

less challenging to deliver. Most of us also find stories easy to remember, particularly when they relate events that we have experienced personally.

Stories are accounts of real or imagined events. They can be success stories, personal stories, stories about famous people, humorous stories, or even startling stories.

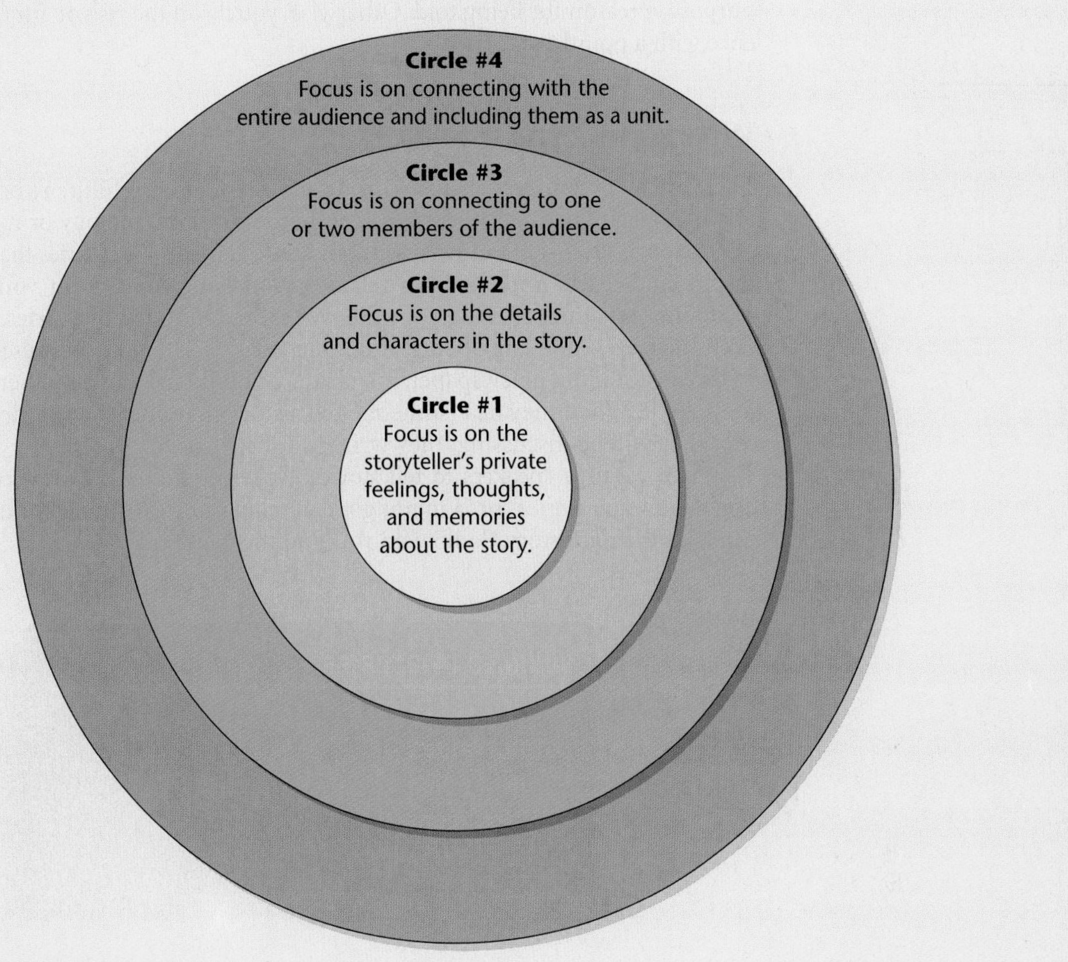

you've told them a few times. Practice telling your story to someone else—a friend, neighbor, colleague, or family member. Practice until you can tell the story without notes. Both of us have a repertoire of stories that we tell in our classes year after year. We know how to time each part of the story and how to exaggerate a point or a character's voice. We even know exactly how long to pause before or after the punch line of a story. Our storytelling skills come from lots of practice.

Finally, know when not to tell a story. If the story won't help you achieve the purpose of a presentation, leave it out.

1. William Hendricks et al., *Secrets of Power Presentations* (Franklin Lakes, NJ: Career Press, 1996).
2. Hendricks et al., p. 80.
3. Hendricks et al., p. 81.
4. Rives Collins and Pamela J. Cooper, *The Power of Story: Teaching Through Storytelling*, 2nd ed. (Boston: Allyn and Bacon, 1997), pp. 68–70.

The clergy use parables, stories with a lesson or moral, to apply religious beliefs to everyday life. We read fables, fairy tales, and folktales to children to demonstrate that "slow and steady wins the race" or that "there's no place like home." Ancient peoples have passed down stories—which we call *myths*—that commemorate famous events and people, explain natural and supernatural phenomena, and chronicle great adventures. Regardless of the type, however, stories must have a point that relates to your purpose, a reason for being told. Otherwise, you'll run the risk of annoying your audience with a pointless story.[13]

Where to Find Stories

There are many sources for stories. You can find stories in children's books and in holy books. You can highlight the exploits of heroes from mythology or movies to make a point. Sports celebrities and historical figures often have life stories that you can use to inspire and teach. You can also relate personal incidents from your childhood or recount events that changed your life. We are surrounded by stories. Good speakers keep their eyes and ears open for the ones that can be used in presentations. When they read a story in a newspaper, magazine, or book that can help them make a point, they clip it. When they hear someone tell a story that illustrates or dramatizes a concept they will be discussing, they write it down.

When we urge speakers to tell stories, we're often greeted with statements like "I don't know any stories" or "I'm not good at telling stories." But all of us can tell stories when it's the right story. So how do you find the "right" story?

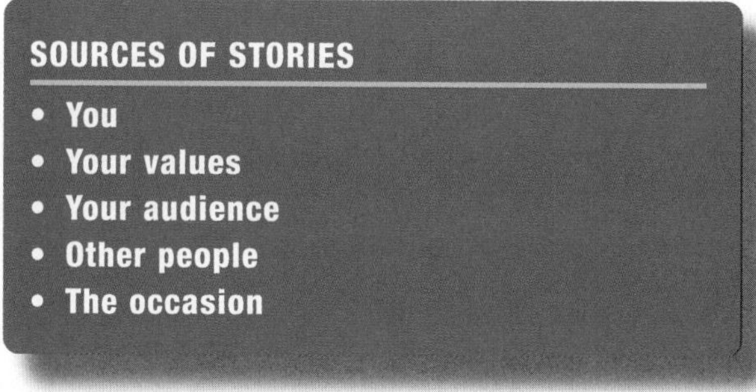

You. You are a living, breathing collection of stories. Rives Collins and Pamela Cooper suggest that one of the best ways to find stories is to rediscover your family's stories. They offer four suggestions for "priming" your personal story pump:[14]

1. *The story of your name.* Were you named for someone? Do you know how and why your name was chosen? Does your name have a meaning in another language? Does it reflect your ethnic background? Have you changed your name?

2. *When I was young in [location]_____.* Fill in the blank: When I was young *in Santa Rosa, at summer camp, in kindergarten, at the hospital, at my uncle's store, at my cousin's wedding, at the soccer finals*... What happened? Why do you remember it so clearly? What did you learn?

3. *Your family's "roots."* Where does your family come from? How far back can you trace your family? Are there any unique customs in your family? What's your family's ethnic background? Do you have a famous, notorious, or eccentric family member?

4. *Your special place.* Most of us can find stories if we think about places that have been very special to us. Special places can be your childhood bedroom, the vacant lot you played in with childhood friends, the dance studio where you learned to stand tall,

the farm where your family holds its annual reunion, the place where you were married, the first office you worked in, or the view from a nearby mountain top.

Your Values. What do you value? We're not talking about fur coats or fast cars, but rather about personal principles and standards. Eating a great meal may delight and "fill" you, but volunteering at a soup kitchen can ultimately be much more satisfying and fulfilling. What are your deep-seated values? Do they involve qualities such as justice, generosity, or honesty? Strong commitments to your family, the environment, or your profession? If you can identify something that you strongly value, there's probably a story there. For example, if you value hard work, you can tell a story about someone who gave all as well as someone who goofed off.

Your Audience. If you have spent time analyzing your audience, you may learn enough to find stories related to their interests, beliefs, and values. If your audience is deeply religious, you may share a story about a neighbor who gave up her worldly goods to work on a religious mission. If your audience loves sports, you may share a story about your own triumphs or trials as an athlete. If your audience is culturally diverse, you may share a story about how you, a friend, or colleagues succeeded in bridging cultural differences.

Other People. All of us know and have interacted with interesting people. Many of us have read about people with fascinating backgrounds and experiences. You can even interview people you know to uncover wonderful stories about their lives and knowledge. If, however, you are going to tell a story about someone you know, make sure that you have the person's permission. Don't embarrass a good friend or colleague by divulging a private story.

The Occasion. When and where are you speaking? What's happening in the news or in the neighborhood? Is Mother's Day coming up? Did it snow last week? You may want to find out if someone famous was born on the day that you're speaking. A story about a famous person's life may be relevant to your purpose and presentation.

Shaping the Story

Most good stories follow an organizational pattern—as do effective presentations. All good stories, no matter how short or how simple, share the same elements. Use the Story-building Chart in Figure 13. 2 to make sure that you have all the right pieces in the right order for your story.[15]

There are two additional features to note on the Story-building Chart. The first is that the chart provides a space for your story's title. Titling a story can focus your story on your presentation's purpose. A title such as "The Big Bad Man in the Back of the Building" suggests a very different story than one titled "The Happy Haven Behind Our House." At the bottom of the chart is a space for you to record the central point of your story. Make sure that the point of your story supports your purpose. If it's just an interesting story, cut it from your presentation, and save it for a friendly conversation.

Figure 13.3 shows how the Story-building Chart can be used to develop a good story as well as brief speaking notes. This story is based on a true incident experienced by one of your authors.

Figure 13.2

Story-building Chart

TITLE OF THE STORY:

BACKGROUND INFORMATION:

- Where and when does the story take place?
- What is going on?
- Did anything important happen before the story began?
- Provide an initial buildup to the story.
- Use concrete details.
- Create a vivid image of the time, place, and occasion of the story.

CHARACTER DEVELOPMENT:

- Who is in the story?
- What are their backgrounds?
- What do they look and sound like?
- How do you want the audience to feel about them?
- Bring them to life with colorful and captivating words.

ACTION OR CONFLICT:

- What is happening?
- What did you or a character see, hear, feel, smell, or taste?
- How are the characters reacting to what's happening?
- Let the action build as you tell the story.

HIGH POINT OR CLIMAX:

- What's the culminating event or moment of greatest intensity in the story?
- What's the turning point in the action?
- All action should lead to a discovery, decision, or outcome.
- Show the audience how the character has grown or has responded to a situation or problem.

PUNCH LINE:

- What's the **punch line**?
- Is there a sentence or phrase that communicates the climax of the story?
- The punch line pulls the other four elements together.
- If you leave out the punch line, the story won't make any sense.

CONCLUSION OR RESOLUTION:

- How is the situation resolved?
- How do the characters respond to the climax?
- Make sure that you don't leave the audience wondering about the fate of a character.
- In some cases, a story doesn't need a conclusion—the punch line may conclude it for you.

THE CENTRAL POINT OF THE STORY:

TITLE OF THE STORY: "You Never Know!"

BACKGROUND INFORMATION:
- Cocktail party in Melbourne, Australia
- Good talks with friendly, interested people (Quick examples: Prue, Margo, Neville)

CHARACTER DEVELOPMENT:
- Introduction to a distinguished gentleman
- Description of gentleman
- He asked many questions about my teaching area: communication and media studies.

ACTION OR CONFLICT:
- Became engrossed in discussion about U.S. broadcasting regulations
- Had lively discussion about the role of government in telecommunications regulation
- Ended our frank discussion to chat with other guests

HIGH POINT OR CLIMAX:
- Found and asked hostess, "Who is that delightful man? What does he do for a living?"

PUNCH LINE:
"Oh," she said, "he's our Federal Cabinet member in charge of telecommunications policies and regulations for the whole country."

CONCLUSION OR RESOLUTION:
- Felt stupid. Who am *I* to tell *him* about telecommunications policy?
- As he left, he came over to thank me for the most enjoyable talk he'd had all evening, adding, "I learned a lot about you Americans."

THE CENTRAL POINT OF THE STORY: You never know who you will be talking to—so make sure you know what you're talking about.

Figure 13.3

Story-building Notes

Why Stories Work

Storytelling is the oldest art form in the world.[16] Walter R. Fisher, a well-respected communications scholar, has devoted significant energy and intellect to studying the nature and purpose of **narratives,** a term that encompasses the process, art, and techniques of storytelling. Fisher sees storytelling as an essential aspect of being human. We experience life "as an ongoing narrative, as conflict, characters, beginnings, middles, and ends."[17] Good stories possess two essential qualities: probability and fidelity.[18]

Understanding these two qualities can help all storytellers improve their ability to select or write effective stories for a presentation.

Story probability refers to whether a story "hangs together" and makes sense. Stories that make sense have structural coherence (internal consistency—that is, one event leads to another) and character coherence (characters behave consistently). If you can't follow the events in a story, it probably lacks structural coherence. Likewise, if you can't tell why the characters do the things that they do, chances are the story doesn't have character coherence. Improbable stories are hard to follow and even harder to enjoy.

Story fidelity refers to the apparent truthfulness of a story. Speakers who fill their presentations with unbelievable stories will not earn their audience's respect. To test the fidelity of a story, ask the following questions:

- Do the facts and incidents in the story ring true and seem believable?
- Does the story address or support the speaker's point?
- Does the story omit, distort, or take out of context key facts and events?
- Does the story use logical arguments and patterns of reasoning?
- Does the story create the impact that the speaker intended?

Speakers whose stories pass this test are master storytellers. Former President Ronald Reagan was one such storyteller. Why is it, asks Walter Fisher, that President Reagan enjoyed a nearly unanimous evaluation as a "Great Communicator" despite the fact that he was also known for making factual errors, uttering inconsistent statements, reasoning in only a limited fashion, and frequently diverting attention from relevant issues?[19] One answer to this question is that Reagan's speaking talent was a triumph of acting, storytelling, presence, and performance.

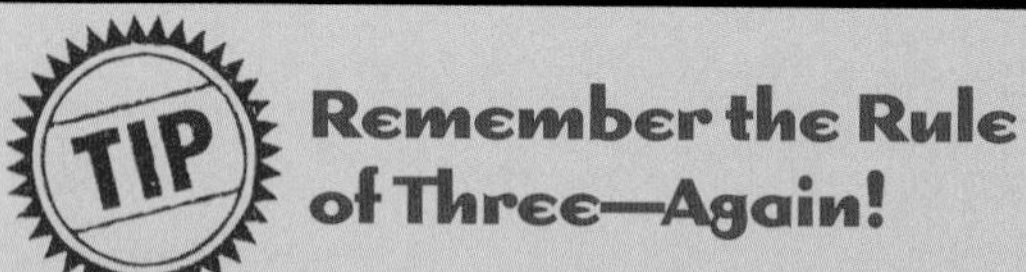

The rule of three also appears in two other chapters. In Chapter 10, "Organizational Tools," we note that audiences often expect and anticipate that speakers will have three points in their presentations. In Chapter 12, "Engaging Language," we apply the rule of three to words and phrases, as in Abraham Lincoln's words *of the people, by the people, for the people.*

In stories, the rule of three can be found everywhere:

Abraham, Isaac, and Jacob

The Father, Son, and Holy Ghost

Papa Bear, Mama Bear, and Baby Bear

The Three Little Pigs

Scarecrow, Tin Man, and Cowardly Lion

The Three Musketeers

Harry Potter, Ron Weasley, and Hermione Granger

The Three Stooges

Think of how many times a folktale character is given three wishes, three guesses, or three tries to overcome adversity. Indeed, storytellers have found magic in the rule of three.

The Value of Humor

Injecting humor into a presentation can capture and hold an audience's attention and help listeners remember you and your presentation. Humor can defuse anger, ease tension, and stimulate action. Audience members tend to remember humorous speakers positively, even when they are not enthusiastic about the speaker's message or topic. Humor also encourages listeners to have a good time while learning (and thus enhances learning). Since it has so many advantages, why not sprinkle some humor into your presentation?

Gene Perret, author of *Using Humor for Effective Business Speaking,* claims that humor can generate audience respect for the speaker, attract and hold listeners' attention, clarify obscure or complicated issues, and help an audience remember your main points.[20] Most of Perret's claims are easy to accept—with one exception. How, you may be wondering, can humor clarify obscure or complicated issues? Good humor is clear and understandable (or it won't get a laugh). Thus, understanding the principles behind the joke can help a listener understand your point of view. For instance, Perret once listened to a manager give a pep talk to a

A Laughing Club in Bombay, India offers members the benefits of therapeutic laughing.

production group that feared their entire line would be dropped and layoffs would begin. At the end of his talk, the manager "made his bottom line point empathetically. He said, 'I'm not saying all these things because your jobs are on the line. I'm saying them because mine is.' "[21]

Types of Humor

There are as many types of humor as there are funny speakers. The best humorous speakers know which type of humor to use in a particular situation in front of a particular audience. Some audiences respond well to one-liners, puns, funny stories, and goofy props. Others love funny quotations, cartoons, wacky definitions, lists, humorous letters, silly headlines, misspelled signs, absurd laws, funny song lyrics, and even light-bulb jokes. As is so often the case, the more you know about your audience, the better you can use humor to establish a connection with its members.

Using humor in a presentation does not necessarily mean telling jokes. It means poking fun and having fun. For example, in preparing the presentation about CliffsNotes that appears in the Appendix, John Sullivan worried because there was so little written about the topic. He had searched many sources and had even tried to interview Cliff Hillegass, the founder of CliffsNotes. In the following excerpt from his presentation, he poked fun at himself, at his sources of information, and at his discovery about the founder.

> *Yet for all the trust I put into CliffsNotes, I couldn't have told you one thing about them. Even though, according to no less a prestigious source than* People *magazine, over 50 million of these yellow and black pamphlets have been sold, you probably don't know too much about them, either. After exhausting* People *magazine and the* Nebraska Sunday World Herald Magazine, *I had to turn to Cliff himself. Yes, there is a Cliff behind CliffsNotes, and no, his last name is not Notes.*

FAQ: Is Humor Really the Best Medicine?

There's an old saying that "Laughter is the best medicine." Humor and laughter have been linked to good health and well-being, with claims that they can prevent Alzheimer's disease, boost immune systems, motivate bored students, and build morale in dreary offices.

In India, laughing clubs have become popular with people from all walks of life. What does a laughing club do? Its members get together on a regular basis—and laugh uproariously. Yes, it sounds silly, but it's difficult to suppress a smile and a giggle when just listening to a brief recording of a laughing club meeting.

Rod Martin, a humor researcher and director of the clinical psychology program at the University of Western Ontario in Canada, has taken a serious look at humor research. He concludes that rather than having *direct* health benefits, such as lowering blood pressure, humor has *indirect* benefits, such as helping people control their emotions or cope with difficulties. Martin believes that humor's greatest use is in psychology rather than in medicine.

In times of trouble and stress—such as the September 11 attacks, the War with Iraq, a weak economy, and terrorist alerts—people who feel overwhelmed have always needed an outlet, a way to relieve their tensions. Using humor is one way of helping people cope.[1] Sandra Ritz, a public health doctor, puts it this way: "The minute you can see the humor in a disaster or a trauma is the minute you know you're going to get better. That's how you know you have regained control."[2]

1. *USA Today*, 4 March 2003, p. 9D.
2. Ibid.

Sometimes a humorous quotation or story can lighten up a presentation. In announcing the possibility of salary and budget freezes to a group of faculty members, an academic dean said, "In the immortal words of 'Peanuts,' there's no problem too big we can't run away from." She then reworded a Woody Allen line—"If my films make one more person feel miserable, I'll feel I've done my job"—by saying, "To paraphrase Woody Allen, if my announcement makes all of you as miserable as I am, I'll feel I've done my job." Although both quotations emphasized the seriousness of a problem, both were greeted with laughter.

Notice how the previous examples related directly to the speaker and topic. Humor is not dumping a bunch of jokes into a presentation; it *is* finding a way to have fun while you are informing or persuading an audience. Appropriate humor makes your presentation more enjoyable both to give and to receive.

Hazards of Humor

Presenting humor is difficult. Most listeners will give you the benefit of the doubt if you don't hit their funny bone. And most audiences will forgive you if a joke or a humorous story doesn't come out as funny as was intended. There are, however, some approaches to humor that an audience will not and should not forgive. Offensive humor tops the list because it insults your audience and seriously damages your credibility. Irrelevant humor is a close second because it wastes the audience's time and makes you appear poorly organized. Stale, prepackaged humor comes in third. It's often irrelevant *and* offensive—a deadly combination. Chapter 21, "Special Presentations," explores these pitfalls in more detail.

Here we look at the link between humor and audience analysis. This is not about political correctness. It's about common courtesy and audience sensibilities. Sometimes the differences between appropriate and inappropriate humor are subtle. For example, look at the following pairs of jokes.[22] Which jokes have the potential to hurt someone's feelings?

Age:

> *Old? At Ruth's last birthday the candles cost more than the cake.*
>
> *There are three signs of old age. The first is lost memory.... The other two I forget.*

Banks:

> *A banker is just a pawnbroker in a three-piece suit.*
>
> *I think the reason banks have drive-up tellers is so the cars can see their real owners.*

Computers:

> *One of our clerks was let go because of a new software package that enabled a computer to do everything he used to do. The odd part was that his wife went out and bought one.*
>
> *We had a tough day at our office. The computers went down and everyone had to learn to think all over again.*

We hope you chose the second joke in each pair as the most appropriate. Just to make sure that you understand the characteristics of suitable humor, here are five general guidelines to follow when using humor:[23]

1. *Never use distasteful or insulting language.* Avoid curse words. Interestingly, and perhaps not surprisingly, male speakers can get away with saying *damn* and *hell* better than female speakers can. Use this simple test: Would you be likely to hear this word in a house of worship? If not, leave it out.

2. *Tiptoe around body functions.* The point is not what *you* think is acceptable but what your audience thinks is acceptable. Although body functions are a normal part of life, audience members may not appreciate comments about bodily fluids and private parts.

3. *Don't tease anyone in your audience.* Unless you are speaking at a *roast*—an event at which a series of speakers warmheartedly tease an honored guest—avoid singling out audience members for ridicule. Unless you're in a comedy club, your audience isn't there to be the brunt of your jokes.

4. *Never ever do ethnic or religious humor—unless you are making fun of yourself.* If, however, you decide to apply humor to your own ethnicity, race, or religion, make it very clear to your audience that you are laughing at *yourself.*

5. *Don't go overboard.* You are a presenter, not a comedian. Humor counts, but too much humor can be counterproductive. One study found that award-winning teachers use humor less often than average instructors.[24] Think about your best and most respected professors. What is more important—that you laugh at their jokes or that you appreciate and learn what they're teaching? Remember why you are speaking. Don't let the prospect of arousing audience laughter distract you from your purpose.

Humor for Beginners

Explaining how to be humorous is something like explaining how to ice skate. You can read about ice skating, and you can watch videotapes of Olympic skaters, but nothing will replace putting on a pair of skates and getting on the ice. Of course, your first few steps may leave you flat on your face or rear end. But with practice and some coaching, you can become quite comfortable and even graceful on ice. You may not become a gold medal winner, but you can learn to enjoy yourself. The same is true about using humor in a presentation. You can read about it and borrow funny lines from books and comedians. However, nothing replaces trying it in front of a real audience.

You don't have to begin with an entire humorous presentation to be funny. A few humorous lines in almost any kind of presentation can get you started. One of the easiest ways to become a humorous speaker is to begin with humor that pokes fun at yourself. You don't have to worry about offending anyone if you are the butt or target of your joke. You don't have to worry as much about forgetting details of a humorous story if it is based on something that happened to you. Real-life humorous stories are much easier to tell than stories you've made up or borrowed from a book.

Several comedians have their own signature jokes. David Letterman has his top-ten list. If you know your audience well, you can come up with a funny list of top-ten peeves or witticisms. When Johnny Carson hosted *The Tonight Show,* one of his signature routines was to impersonate a character called Karnak the Magnificent. After being told an answer, Carson would hold a sealed white envelope to his brow and guess the question it contained. Here's an example of a Karnak-style joke illustrating a publisher's nightmare: "The answers are 100,000, 100, and 100. What are the questions? How many copies of the publishing company's newest book were printed? How many were sold? How many were bought by the writer's mother?"

Both of us take great delight in telling our students about presentation aids that didn't work, about audiences that didn't behave the way we expected them to, and about embarrassing goofs we've made while speaking. We don't embarrass anyone but ourselves, and our students love it. Vice President Al Gore, a man regarded as straight-laced and formal, started telling jokes about himself as a way to humanize his image. How, he would ask, can you pick Al Gore out from the Secret Service agents around him? The answer: Al Gore is the stiff one.

With just a little exaggeration about the dog that wouldn't perform, the power saw that didn't work, the fish tank that broke, the exercise outfit that split, and the handmade poster that spelled an innocent word in a way that cannot be printed in a textbook, you too can turn an amusing story into a very funny one.

In most cases, you are your own best source of humor. Although you can buy books of jokes and handbooks on humor, their contents will rarely match the effectiveness of **self-effacing humor**—your ability to direct humor at yourself. Poking fun at yourself can lower the barrier between speaker and audience by showing the audience that you are an ordinary, fallible human being—just like them. At first, you may be at a loss. What can you poke fun at that's personal? Your job, your family, your experiences, and even your near-misses or failures can be a source of humor. But be careful that you don't poke too much fun at yourself. If you begin to look foolish or less than competent, you will damage your credibility, reduce your level of confidence, and weaken the power of your message.

One of the guidelines we use when looking for the "lighter side" of life is remembering situations where we've said, "I can't believe this is happening to me" or "Someday we'll laugh about this." Such situations can later be retold as humor. U.S. presidents are often remembered for their self-effacing humor. Ronald Reagan was well known for making fun of his age, an approach that also defused controversy about his being the oldest president in U.S. history. Here are two examples:[25]

> *I want to begin by saying how grateful I am that you've asked me here to participate in the celebration of the hundredth anniversary of the Knights of Columbus. Now, it isn't true that I was present at the first anniversary.*
>
> *There was a very prominent Democrat who reportedly told a large group, "Don't worry. I've seen Ronald Reagan, and he looks like a million." He was talking about my age.*

The Benefits of Audience Participation

One of the most powerful ways to keep an audience alert and interested is to ask audience members to participate actively in a presentation. Most audiences remember speakers who include them in the action. When audience members participate, they

Real World Real Speakers

Get Them Involved

Many respondents to our survey were eager to share their interest-generating techniques. Carol Herzog, an elementary school teacher in Warren, Indiana, often speaks to groups of educators and community members. She wrote, "I like to keep the audience actively involved during the presentation. My handouts are often an outline that needs filling in during the presentation. I have also done a personal growth speech where the audience writes themselves a postcard about a change they would like to make in their lives as a result of my talk. I mail the postcard six months later as a reminder of that change."

Dr. Rob Simpson, who works for the Salvation Army in Grand Rapids, Michigan, believes that he keeps audience attention by "beginning with humor, using professional visuals, including topics that require audience participation, linking theory to practical applications, using plain and simple language for all levels of audiences, and being thoroughly prepared." Note how these experienced speakers rely on varied techniques to keep their audiences interested and involved.

use more than their eyes and ears. They may speak, raise their hands, write, or reach out and touch someone or something. When a speaker interacts with audience members, they become more alert because they have to be prepared to participate.[26]

Audience participation is a common practice in religious services. Worshipers may engage in responsive reading, singing, kneeling, tithing, clapping, saying "amen," and going to the altar for special blessings or ceremonies. Great preachers know that audience involvement creates a sense of community and inspires loyalty to a congregation. The same kinds of involvement can be enlisted to serve a presenter. Audience participation involves audiences physically, verbally, and psychologically with your presentation. There are many ways to actively engage your audience.

FORMS OF AUDIENCE PARTICIPATION

- Ask questions
- Encourage interaction
- Involve their senses
- Do an exercise
- Ask for volunteers
- Invite feedback

Ask Questions

One of the easiest ways to involve audience members is to ask questions, pose riddles, or ask for reactions. Even if audience members do little more than nod their heads in response, they will have become part of a transaction with the speaker. Also, when audiences know that they will be quizzed or questioned during or after a presentation, they will be more alert and interested in what is said.

What's the Moral of this Story?

At a Virginia Press Association's Minority Job Fair in Richmond, Virginia, a speaker combined storytelling and audience participation into a highly effective presentation. Mr. Marvin Leon Lake, public editor of a Norfolk-based newspaper, the *Virginian-Pilot,* began his job fair presentation by announcing that he was going to tell a true story. And like all good stories, this one had a moral. But, he said, he wasn't going to tell his audience the moral. It was up to them to tell him what they thought the story meant.

He then told about a young journalism student who, at a previous job fair, had volunteered to be interviewed by a panel of strangers in front of an audience. The student went on to become a successful journalist. When he finished, Lake asked the audience: "What is the moral of this story?" One student raised her hand and said, "When given an opportunity—even in the face of public scrutiny—do it!" Another audience member said, "If you stand out in a crowd, you will be noticed." A third listener suggested that you should always be prepared, both physically and mentally, to accept a challenge. Lake said all of the answers were correct.

Lake engaged his audience by telling a relevant story and then involving them in a discussion about the story. The students attending the job fair had a lot to remember, but at the top of their list were Lake, his story, and its important lesson.

One special type of audience question, the poll, combines involving listeners and doing a quick form of audience analysis. Ask for a show of hands in response to simple questions such as "How many of you know someone who...?" "How many of you have visited...?" "Have any of you heard of...?" "Do we have anyone here who was born or raised in...?" The responses will tell you something about your audience and will also let the audience members know whether they share common experiences, opinions, and beliefs.

Encourage Interaction

As corny as it may seem, you can ask a general audience to shake hands or to introduce themselves to the people sitting on either side of them. Depending on the purpose of your presentation, you could add something beyond a handshake. For example, in a talk about childcare, you could request that audience members share the number, ages, and genders of their children with each other. If it's a business audience, ask members to exchange business cards. If you're addressing young college students, ask them to identify the high schools they attended or their career aspirations.

Involve Their Senses

Involve your audience by enlisting more of their senses. In addition to engaging their ears and eyes, let them use touch, smell, and/or taste. For example, asking your audience to write something down directly involves their sense of touch *and* reinforces your content. Encouraging your audience to touch, taste, or smell a product involves them directly with the subject of your presentation. Is your product softer, sturdier, and more effective than others? Does your chocolate chip cookie recipe produce a chewier, sweeter, and thicker cookie than another recipe? Does the old-fashioned rose smell better than the latest hybrid?

Do an Exercise

Both simple games and complex training exercises can involve audience members with your presentation and with each other. Most large bookstores have shelves filled with training manuals describing ways of involving audience members in games and exercises. They range from coming up with a name for a new product to suggesting solutions to hypothetical or real problems. Interrupting a presentation for a group exercise gives both the audience and the speaker a break during which they can interact in a different but effective way.

Ask for Volunteers

If you ask for volunteers from the audience, someone will usually offer to participate. Volunteers can help you demonstrate how to perform a skill or how to use a piece of equipment. They can engage in role-playing exercises. Some can even be persuaded to wear funny hats, sing songs, or leave the room. Most audiences love to watch a volunteer in action. If possible, find a way to reward volunteers—with a small prize or special thanks. Once audience members see that volunteering is a risk-free opportunity, they will be more willing to participate.

As long as everyone is involved, most audiences will go along with what they're asked to do. If you invite audience members to stand up and stretch, most of them will. If you ask them to write something down, most of them will pick up their pens. Both of us have learned that audiences will volunteer to do something as long as everyone is in it together. At the same time, don't force a volunteer or audience member to participate if you sense reluctance or apprehension. "Volunteers" who don't want to volunteer can become a hostile audience.

Invite Feedback

During or at the end of your presentation, you can invite questions and comments from the audience. Once interested audience members know that they can interrupt you with a question or comment, some will do just that. Of course, it takes a skillful presenter to allow this kind of interaction without losing track of a prepared presentation. Waiting until the end of a presentation for questions and comments is safer but doesn't involve the audience as much.

Encouraging audience participation requires skill and sensitivity. Respect any feedback from your audience. If audience members seem reluctant to participate, don't badger or embarrass them. If no one responds, go on and give your presentation without such involvement. In all likelihood, however, you will find most audiences ready, willing, and able to participate. The vast majority of audience members remember presentations in which they participated.

Summing Up Interest Factors

A study by John Daly and Anita Vangelisti sheds light on how presenters can convey interesting messages to others in clear and memorable ways.[27] After reviewing hundreds of research studies focused on this challenge, they drew two conclusions about what it takes to help listeners understand and recall messages.

FAQ How Do You Act in an Immediate Manner?

In Chapter 6, "Credibility and Ethics," we introduce the concept of **immediacy,** an audience's perceptions of physical and psychological closeness to the speaker. Whether you are telling a story, using humor, or explaining a highly complex phenomenon, use verbal and nonverbal immediacy strategies to engage your audience. In general, verbal immediacy is associated with a sense of humor, a willingness to engage the audience in conversation (even within a presentation), self-disclosure, using inclusive language (*we, us, our*), offering feedback, and seeking audience input.[1]

Nonverbally, immediacy is marked by closer physical distance (including coming out from behind a lectern), smiling, increased eye contact, natural body movement and gestures, touching audience members, a relaxed posture, and vocal expressiveness (variations in volume, pitch, and rate).[2]

1. John A. Daly and Anita L. Vangelisti, "Skillfully Instructing Learners: How Communicators Effectively Convey Messages," in *Handbook of Communication and Social Interaction Skills*, eds. John O. Greene and Brant R. Burleson (Mahwah, NJ: Lawrence Erlbaum Associates, 2003), p. 893.
2. Daly and Vangelisti, p. 893.

Daly and Vangelisti's first conclusion offers various communication strategies and skills to improve message comprehension, including the following:

- Create interesting messages (clear, vivid, suspenseful, humorous).
- Make sure that your messages are relevant to listeners.
- Beware of "seductive" details that, although interesting, distract listeners.
- Relate new content to prior knowledge.
- Encourage listeners to engage in self-questioning.
- Ask listeners to reformulate material in their own words.
- Use stories.
- Offer immediate and consistent feedback.
- Provide visual aids that enhance comprehension.
- Encourage effective note taking.
- Give listeners an opportunity to ask questions.
- Be clear by focusing on critical ideas, offering examples, and attending to any misunderstanding.
- Offer multiple, diverse examples of any important phenomenon, along with contrasting nonexamples.
- Use memorable analogies and metaphors.
- Provide organizing cues such as transitions, internal previews, internal summaries, and signposts.
- Use concrete language.

Daly and Vangelisti's second conclusion focuses on whether listeners *like* the speaker. Their findings suggest that when skillful presenters act in an *immediate* manner, audience members like them and, as a result, are more willing to listen to and remember what those speakers have to say. A speaker's immediacy, enthusiasm, and use of humor have a significant effect on audience interest, motivation, and recall.

Break the Rules

Many successful speakers break lots of the "rules" and "guidelines" in this textbook. Mainly, they're highly experienced speakers who know how far to push the limits. In some rare cases, they are inexperienced but inspired speakers who, despite lack of organization or a weak speaking voice, rise to an occasion and move an audience to tears or action.

Rules are *not* made to be broken. This book includes rules that represent our best advice as well as scholarly research about preparing and delivering effective presentations. We encourage following the rules until you gain enough experience to tailor them to your own needs and abilities. Keep the length of your presentations under twenty minutes until you know for certain that you can keep an audience interested for twice that long. Tell brief, one-character stories until you know that you can skillfully juggle multiple characters and plots. Break the rules when you know yourself and your audience well enough to also know when some rules don't apply.

Summary

▶ How do I interest audience members in my presentation?

Begin by addressing audience factors that inhibit interest: limited attention span and poor listening habits. Then focus on correcting speaker factors such as making excessively long presentations and poor delivery.

▶ Why are stories so interesting?

Well-delivered stories with simple story lines, limited characters, exaggeration, and audience links have the ability to captivate and educate because they create lasting images. Effective stories include background and character development, action or conflict, high point or climax, punch line, and a conclusion or resolution.

▶ How should I use humor into my presentation?

Humor should be used to make a point, not for its own sake. Effective humor is usually well prepared and well rehearsed. The best humor often pokes fun at the speaker. Make sure your humor is appropriate for your presentation's purpose, audience, and occasion.

▶ How can I directly involve my audience?

In addition to adapting to the results of audience analysis, ask questions, encourage interaction, involve their senses, do an exercise, ask for volunteers, and invite feedback.

Presentation Principles in Action

Take the Cartoon Caption Challenge

Directions: For several years, *The New Yorker* magazine has held a cartoon caption contest. The magazine publishes the illustrative part of a cartoon and invites readers to write a funny caption to complete it. Each year, the editors pick the best caption from the thousands of recorded entries. In 2001, the following drawing by Frank Cotham asked the question "Why would a man drive a car in circles in front of a garage?"

Here are a few entries that did *not* win the contest:

"Looks like operator error to me."

"Wait till you see the long program."

"Car Talk: The Movie"

"Bill Gates would call that a 'feature.' "

"I'm thinking mad-car disease."

What kind of caption would you submit for this cartoon? The editors look for a caption that is simple, elegant, and, of course, funny. Come up with a caption of your own. Then join a small group of students and share your results. Choose two or three of the best captions and be prepared to share them with the rest of the class. After sharing your "gems," discuss the following questions:

- Why was this task easy or difficult?
- What characteristics made the best captions funny?

Source: The New Yorker, 12 November 2001, p. 140. The annual cartoon caption contest usually appears in late November. Back issues of *The New Yorker* provide other examples to challenge your sense of humor and creativity. The winning caption for the 2001 contest and additional cartoons are provided in the *Instructor's Resource Manual.*

Assessing a Story

The following assessment instrument can help you evaluate how well you or someone else tells a story in a presentation. Use the following ratings to assess each of the criteria on the instrument:

E = Excellent G = Good A = Average F = Fair P = Poor

N/A = Not applicable to this presentation

Storytelling Assessment Instrument

CRITERIA	E	G	A	F	P	N/A
Purpose and Topic: Did the story have a clear and appropriate purpose?						
Audience Analysis: Was the story appropriate for the audience? Did the story adapt to audience characteristics, interests, attitudes, etc.?						
Credibility: Was the storyteller believable? Did the storyteller convey immediacy and enthusiasm?						
Logistics: Was the story appropriate for the occasion and place?						
Content: Did the story set the mood, place, and time? Were the characters and plot well developed? Did the storyteller create vivid images? Was the punch line clear?						
Organization: Did the story develop logically? Did the introduction establish a mood, motivate interest, and "set the stage"? Did the story end gracefully?						
Performance: Did the storyteller use appropriate form(s) of delivery: effective vocal and physical delivery, including eye contact? **Other:**						
COMMENTS:						

Source: The assessment instrument is based on storytelling criteria included in two sources: Rives Collins and Pamela J. Cooper, *The Power of Story: Teaching Through Storytelling,* 2nd ed. (Boston: Allyn and Bacon, 1997); and Joanna Slan, *Using Stories and Humor* (Boston: Allyn and Bacon, 1998).

Key Terms

attention span 294
expressiveness 296
forgetting curve 295
immediacy 312
narrative 303
punch line 302
self-effacing humor 308
story fidelity 304
story probability 304

Notes

1 Florence I. Wolff and Nadine C. Marsnik, *Perceptive Listening,* 2nd ed. (Fort Worth, TX: Harcourt Brace Jovanovich, 1992), p. 176.
2 Wolff and Marsnik, p. 176.
3 Douglas A. Bernstein et al., *Psychology,* 5th ed. (Boston: Houghton Mifflin, 2000), pp. 235–236.
4 Peggy Noonan, *Simply Speaking: How to Communicate Your Ideas with Style, Substance, and Clarity* (New York: HarperCollins, 1998), p. 9. Copyright © 1998 by Peggy Noonan. Reprinted by permission of HarperCollins Publishers, Inc.
5 Noonan, pp. 9–10. Copyright © 1998 by Peggy Noonan. Reprinted by permission of HarperCollins Publishers, Inc.
6 Alan M. Perlman, *Writing Great Speeches: Professional Techniques You Can Use* (Boston: Allyn & Bacon, 1998), p. 52.
7 Perlman, p. 53.
8 Thomas Leech, *How to Prepare, Stage, & Deliver Winning Presentations* (New York: AMACOM, 1993), p. 242.
9 Walter R. Fisher, *Human Communication as Narration: Toward a Philosophy of Reason, Value, and Action* (Columbia: University of South Carolina Press, 1987), pp. 64–65.
10 Rives Collins and Pamela J. Cooper, *The Power of Story: Teaching Through Storytelling,* 2nd ed. (Boston: Allyn and Bacon, 1997), p 2.
11 Joanna Slan, *Using Stories and Humor: Grab Your Audience* (Boston: Allyn & Bacon, 1998), pp. 5–6.
12 Eric Quinones, "Companies Learn the Value of Storytelling," *New York Times,* 1 August 1999, p. 4.
13 Malcolm Kushner, *Successful Presentations for Dummies* (Foster City, CA: IDG Books, 1997), p. 79.
14 Collins and Cooper, pp. 24–28.
15 Based on Slan, p. 116 and pp. 89–95.
16 Slan, p. 42.
17 Fisher, p. 24.
18 Fisher, p. 68.
19 Fisher, pp. 145–157.
20 Gene Perret, *Using Humor for Effective Business Speaking* (New York: Sterling, 1989), pp. 19–26.
21 Perret, p. 25.
22 Jokes are taken from Michael Iapoce's *A Funny Thing Happened to Me on the Way to the Boardroom: Using Humor in Business Speaking,* (New York: John Wiley & Sons, 1988), pp. 120, 125, 131.
23 We have added a fifth guideline to the four guidelines provided by Slan, pp. 170–172.
24 Valerie C. Downs, Manoochehr "Mitch" Javidi, and Jon F. Nussbaum, "An Analysis of Teachers' Verbal Communication within the College Classroom: Use of Humor, Self-Disclosure, and Narratives," *Communication Education* 37 (1988): 127–141.
25 Kushner, p. 350.
26 Ron Hoff, *I Can See You Naked* (Kansas City, MO: Andrews and McMeel, 1992), p. 106.
27 John A. Daly and Anita L. Vangelisti, "Skillfully Instructing Learners: How Communicators Effectively Convey Messages," in *Handbook of Communication and Social Interaction Skills,* eds. John O. Greene and Brant R. Burleson (Mahwah, NJ: Lawrence Erlbaum Associates, 2003), pp. 892–896.

part five

Performance

chapter fourteen

Performance and Practice

- What is a good performance?
- Should I use an outline or read my presentation word for word?
- How should I use notes when I speak?
- What's the best way to practice?

Perform is a verb that has several meanings, two of which apply especially well to presentations. *Perform* can mean to accomplish, carry out, or do something, as in "She performed her job efficiently and effectively." In this sense, performing a presentation carries out your purpose. Your performance is the final product. *Perform* also can mean to demonstrate an art in front of an audience. Actors, singers, and dancers perform. In this sense, performance is the way in which you use your voice and body to deliver your presentation. Just as you made decisions about the purpose and content of your presentation, you will have to make performance decisions that will affect how well you deliver your presentation and how well you achieve or carry out your purpose.

We use the term **performance** to refer to the effective vocal and physical delivery of your presentation. You've probably been impressed by speakers whose performances seemed natural, confident, and clear. And you've probably been distracted or annoyed by speakers whose performances were stilted, rushed, or filled with inappropriate gestures. It's all too easy to be a distracting presenter. Being a poised and powerful performer, though, takes effort and practice. You need to decide how you can best apply the performance techniques we discuss in this chapter and in the next three to your presentation purpose, your audience, the logistics, and yourself. We discuss specific techniques in Chapter 15, "Vocal Delivery," Chapter 16, "Physical Delivery," and Chapter 17, "Presentation Aids." In this chapter, we focus on the preparation and practice needed to deliver a strong presentation.

Choosing How to Deliver Your Presentation

You know what you want to say; now it's time to decide how to deliver your message. Whether you choose to rely on a few note cards or to read from a manuscript, your decisions about delivery will affect how you perform your presentation. You will need to decide which form of delivery to use: impromptu, extemporaneous, manuscript, memorized, or a combination of forms.

FORMS OF DELIVERY

Impromptu
Extemporaneous
Manuscript
Memorized

Impromptu Speaking

Impromptu speaking, also known as "off-the-cuff" speaking, occurs when you make a presentation without advance preparation or practice. You're called upon in class to answer a question or to share your opinion. Your boss asks you to summarize a report without giving you advanced warning. You're at a public meeting and decide to stand up and be heard on an important community issue. In impromptu situations like these, do you abandon all you've learned about preparing an interesting, well-organized presentation and blurt out whatever comes into your head? The answer is *no.* Even though you don't have enough time to stop and give a lot of thought to every detail of your presentation, you can very quickly think of a purpose and the ways in which you intend to organize and adapt your message to your audience. The more experience you have as a speaker, the more instinctive the "basics" become, even in impromptu speaking.

Although you can't prepare an impromptu presentation, you can *be prepared* by anticipating when you might have to give one. Most people do this kind of preparation when they are getting ready for an important job interview. Even if they don't know the interview questions, they prepare responses for the ones that might be asked. When an interviewer says, "Tell me about yourself," or "What would you do if you were confronted with...?" you are being asked to speak impromptu. Your impromptu speaking ability may be just as important for landing a good job as your credentials and references. Whether it's during an interview, an English class, or a staff meeting when you might have to speak, take a few minutes to consider what you may be asked to say or contribute. If you are going to a public meeting, give some thought to how you may want to respond if someone asks for questions or comments. As we explain in Chapter 21, "Developing Special Presentations," special techniques and

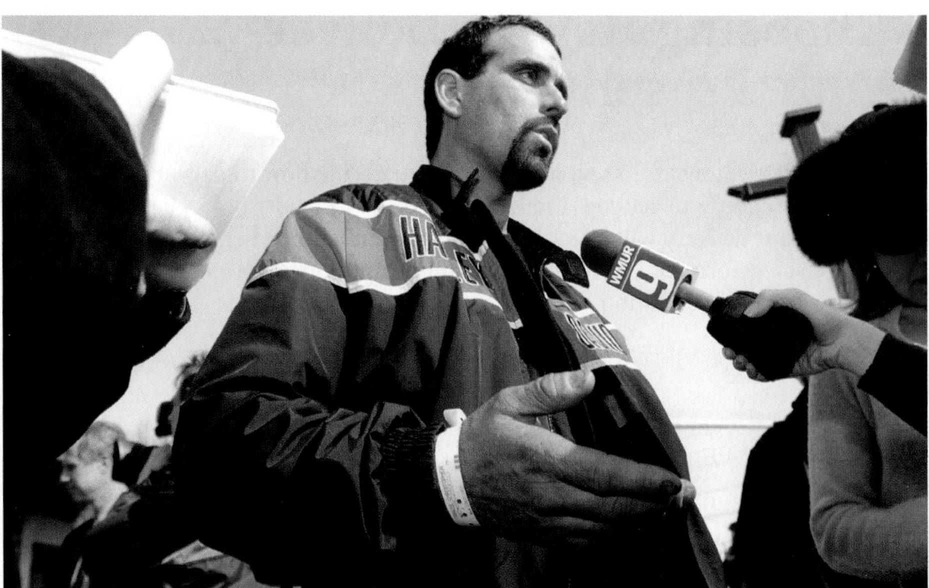

Reporters surround a survivor of the tragic nightclub fire in Rhode Island in which ninety-five people died. Answering questions in stressful situations requires clear thinking and effective speaking skills.

Figure 14.1

Impromptu Delivery

Advantages	Disadvantages
1. Natural and conversational speaking style.	1. Speaker may have nothing to say on such short notice.
2. Maximum eye contact.	2. Presentation anxiety may be very high.
3. Freedom of movement.	3. Limited or no time to prepare.
4. Easier to respond and adjust to audience feedback.	4. Limited or no time for audience analysis.
5. Demonstrates speaker's knowledge and skill.	5. Limited or no supporting material.
6. Performance can exceed audience expectations.	6. Only rudimentary organizational format.
	7. Delivery may be awkward and ineffectual.
	8. Difficult to gauge time.

standard organizational patterns can make an impromptu presentation a talk to be proud of.

Figure 14.1 lists the advantages and disadvantages of impromptu speaking as a form of delivery.

Extemporaneous Speaking

Extemporaneous speaking is the most common form of delivery. In **extemporaneous speaking,** you use an outline or a set of notes to guide yourself through your performance instead of reading aloud a written presentation word for word. Your notes can be a few key words on a single small card or a detailed outline on one or two sheets of paper. These notes will reflect the decisions you have made in the preparation process, but they will also give you the flexibility to quickly adapt your presentation to the audience and occasion.

In extemporaneous speaking you can combine the advantages of impromptu speaking (maximum eye contact, moving away from your notes, making mid-speech adjustments to the audience, setting, and occasion) with the advantages of a manuscript presentation (carefully planned organization, the opportunity to practice everything in advance, reduced nervousness). Classroom lectures, business briefings, and courtroom arguments are usually delivered extemporaneously. No other form of delivery gives you as much freedom and flexibility with preplanned material. An extemporaneous speaker can make last-minute adjustments much more easily than a speaker saddled with an inflexible manuscript can. Later in this chapter, we describe techniques for using notes effectively during an extemporaneous presentation.

Figure 14.2 lists the advantages and disadvantages of speaking extemporaneously, and as you can see, the advantages of extemporaneous speaking far outweigh the disadvantages. Extemporaneous speaking can give the audience the impression that you are speaking spontaneously. Because what you are saying is well planned and well rehearsed, you can change things around to adapt to the audience, the logistics, and the occasion. Because it's not restricted by a manuscript, a well-practiced extemporaneous presentation has an ease to it that makes both audience and speaker feel more comfortable.

Figure 14.2 Extemporaneous Delivery

Advantages	Disadvantages
1. It allows more preparation time.	1. Presentation anxiety may increase for sections not covered by notes.
2. Speaker can pay attention to purpose, audience, logistics, content, organization, credibility, and delivery.	2. Too many or too few notes can hamper fluency and physical delivery.
3. It seems spontaneous but is actually well prepared.	3. Language may not be well chosen or vivid throughout the presentation.
4. Speaker can monitor and respond to audience feedback.	4. It can be difficult to make extensive last-minute changes.
5. Speaker can respond to unforeseen events or logistical problems.	5. It can be difficult to estimate speaking time.
6. It allows more audience interaction and eye contact than manuscript delivery does.	
7. Practice can build confidence.	
8. Audiences respond positively to this delivery style.	
9. Speaker can choose concise language for key points and important ideas.	
10. With practice, it becomes the most powerful form of delivery.	

Manuscript Speaking

Manuscript speaking involves writing your presentation in advance and reading it word for word. Using a manuscript allows you to choose each word carefully. You can plan every detail. Manuscript use also gives you time to practice the same presentation over and over. It ensures that your presentation will fit within your allotted speaking time. For very nervous speakers, a manuscript can be a life-saving document that keeps them afloat throughout an entire presentation, even when they feel as though they're drowning. With all of these advantages, why do we discourage speakers from using manuscript delivery?

Manuscript presentations are hard for all but the most skilled and practiced speakers to deliver effectively. The most significant disadvantages of using a manuscript are inappropriate word choice, poor reading, and inflexibility. In manuscript delivery speakers often use the complex words, long sentences, formal style, and perfect grammar required for written reports and papers rather than the oral style that Chapter 12, "Engaging Language," recommends. *If you must use a manuscript, write it as though you are speaking.* You may even want to try speaking into a tape recorder and then transcribing what you have said, in order to make appropriate decisions about the words you select. Although most communication instructors and coaches don't encourage their students or clients to use manuscript delivery, many speakers continue to rely on it for important presentations.

Although we strongly recommend extemporaneous speaking in most situations, there are occasions when a word-for-word manuscript is either necessary or very helpful.[1] If the occasion is an important public event at which every word counts and time is strictly limited, you may have no choice but to use a manuscript. If you will be speaking "on the record" and do not want to be misunderstood or misinterpreted, you will want

Chrissy Gephardt, the openly lesbian daughter of Representative Dick Gephardt, relies on a limited set of note cards to talk about being gay, her partner, and what it's like to participate in a presidential campaign.

to make sure that you are quoted accurately. If the occasion is highly emotional, you may need the kind of support provided by a manuscript. Think of the ways in which a manuscript would be appropriate in the following situations:

- Legislative testimony
- Press statements
- Complex financial reports
- Synchronized multimedia scripts
- Presenting or accepting a prestigious award
- Eulogies

Figure 14.3 lists the advantages and disadvantages of using a manuscript to deliver a presentation. Learning how to read well from a manuscript lets you tap into the advantages and minimize the disadvantages of this form of delivery.

Even if you write your manuscript in an accessible oral style, it still may not sound that way when you read it. Lack of vocal expression and lack of eye contact with the audience can turn the reading of a manuscript into a dull and boring performance.

Figure 14.3

Manuscript Delivery

Advantages	Disadvantages
1. Speaker can pay attention to purpose, audience, logistics, content, organization, credibility, and delivery.	1. Delivery can be stilted and dull.
2. Speaker can choose concise and eloquent language.	2. Difficult to maintain sufficient eye contact.
3. Presentation anxiety may be eased by having a "script."	3. Limited gestures and movement.
4. Speaker can stay within the time limit.	4. Language can be too formal, lacking oral style.
5. Speaker can rehearse the same "script" every time.	5. Audience may conclude that the speaker has not adapted to them.
6. Speaker can ensure accurate reporting of speech content.	6. Difficult to modify or adapt to the audience or situation.

Effective manuscript delivery requires a lot of practice. The better you know the words that you've written and the more comfortable you feel with them, the easier it will be to concentrate on how you deliver them.

Despite its disadvantages, manuscript delivery is a fact of life. For a variety of reasons, speakers continue to rely on manuscripts for important presentations. Learning how to read from a manuscript is as important as learning how to speak impromptu or extemporaneously.

Memorized Speaking

A **memorized presentation** offers a speaker one major advantage over manuscript delivery and a major disadvantage when compared with the other three forms. The major advantage is physical freedom. You can look at your audience 100 percent of the time; you can gesture freely and even move around. There is no manuscript to keep you chained to a lectern or desk. The disadvantage, however, outweighs any and all advantages. What if you forget something? What if you go blank? If you can't remember your presentation and begin to rely on an impromptu style of delivery, the audience will know something is wrong. A bad situation will only feel worse. Unless you are a professional actor who can memorize a script and make it sound as if you just came up with the wording, forget about using the memorized style of delivering a presentation.[2]

Figure 14.4 lists the advantages and disadvantages of memorizing a presentation for delivery.

Figure 14.4

Memorized Delivery

Advantages	Disadvantages
1. Incorporates the preparation advantages of manuscript speaking and the delivery advantages of impromptu speaking.	1. Extensive time required to memorize the presentation.
2. Allows maximum eye contact.	2. Disaster awaits if memory fails.
3. Allows freedom of movement.	3. Can sound "canned," stilted, and insincere.
	4. Very difficult to modify or adapt to the audience or situation.
	5. Lacks sense of spontaneity unless expertly delivered.

Real World Real Speakers

What's the Worst that Can Happen?

A few years ago a well-known Shakespearean scholar was invited to speak at a local college. His hosts' mistake was failing to find out ahead of time whether he was a good speaker. The man had been scheduled to talk for thirty minutes; instead, he talked for an hour . . . in a monotone. Although he had been asked to speak to a general audience, he behaved as though he were addressing an audience of university professors. He had been asked to keep his talk informal; instead, he read a lecture, and read it badly. He had said he would not need a microphone, but he could barely be heard. His voice had no expression, and he never varied his delivery speed. Furthermore, he never looked at his audience, and the only movement he made was to sway back and forth as he read. The lecture was a total and terrible disaster.

We strongly discourage memorizing *entire* presentations. However, there's nothing wrong with trying to memorize your introduction or a few key sections, as long as you still have your notes to fall back on. An audience may be impressed by your skill at reciting a few lines of poetry or by your ability to put aside your notes, look them in the eye, and deliver a powerful ending. But don't count on remembering everything; the likelihood is that you will fumble or forget something important.

Using Notes Effectively

Regardless of what form of delivery you select, you should be prepared to use notes and to use them effectively. Even when you are speaking impromptu, you may find yourself using notes. A few quick words jotted down just before you stand to speak can help you through an unplanned talk. And if you are brave enough to try a memorized presentation, you should keep your manuscript nearby in case your memory or nerve fails you.

Not everyone can handle notes well. You've probably seen speakers lose the connection with their audience by awkwardly shuffling their pages or searching for a missing index card in the middle of a huge stack. You may have wished you could see a speaker whose face was buried in his notes! Fortunately, you can easily learn to use notes effortlessly and unobtrusively.

The look and scope of your notes will vary depending on what form of delivery you decide to use. In impromptu speaking, you may have little more than six words written on a scrap of paper. In extemporaneous speaking, you may use index cards or a presentation outline to guide you through your message. A manuscript or memorized presentation requires a carefully prepared, word-for-word manuscript that may include special symbols to remind you when to pause, when to increase or decrease your volume, when to cue up a slide, and when to emphasize a particular word or phrase.

Mix and Match

Learning how to deliver a presentation in extemporaneous, impromptu, manuscript, and memorized forms lets you select the method that works best for you and for your purpose and lets you vary your delivery within a presentation. You don't have to stay within the bounds of one form. An impromptu speaker can recite a memorized statistic or a rehearsed argument in much the same way that a politician responds to press questions. An extemporaneous speaker may read a lengthy quotation or a series of statistics and then deliver a memorized ending. A manuscript reader may stop and tell an impromptu story or may deliver memorized sections that would benefit from direct eye contact with the audience. A speaker can pause in a memorized presentation to repeat a key phrase or to re-explain an idea. Your decision about which delivery form or forms to use is important and, under most circumstances, it will be yours to make.

Karl Sprague of Corporate Finance Associates speaks about opportunities at his company to hundreds of business people at a seminar. Because his notes are placed on the lectern for easy reference, he can gesture naturally and establish direct eye contact with his audience.

Using Index Cards and Outlines. Extemporaneous speakers often use index cards to record key points and supporting material. Think of each index card as a visual aid. Provide yourself with just enough information to trigger an idea or to supply a vital piece of supporting material and its source. Figure 14.5 offers some tips for using index cards when making a presentation.

If you can't fit your notes on a few index cards, consider using a presentation outline. As we suggest on pp. 225–226 in Chapter 10, "Organizational Tools," a presentation outline can range from an 8 ½ × 11-inch version of your notes to a full-sentence outline in which your key points, supporting material, and sources are written out word for word.

Using a Manuscript. If you decide to write portions of or an entire presentation in manuscript form, you face a performance challenge. The disadvantages of

Figure 14.5

Using Note Cards

1. **Use key words.** Use only key words rather than complete sentences on each note card. Manuscripts do not fit or belong on note cards.
2. **Using fewer cards is better.** It's best when you can use one card for your introduction, one card for each key point, and one card for your conclusion.
3. **Using fewer words is better.** Don't overload the card with information or use small print.
4. **Use card stock.** Use sturdy card stock, not slips of paper.
5. **Use only one side of a note card.**
6. **Number the cards.** Doing this will keep the parts of your presentation in order or will allow you to rearrange key points at the last minute.
7. **Practice using your notes.** You may discover that you have too many cards or too much information on each card.

Figure 14.6 Using Manuscripts

1. **Make it readable.** Use large fonts (14–18 point) and double- or triple-space the manuscript.
2. **Number the pages.** Make sure that they stay in order.
3. **Use only the top two-thirds of the page.** That way, you don't have to bend your head to see the bottom of the page, a movement that will cause you to lose eye contact with your audience and will constrict your windpipe in such a way that your voice can sound muffled.[3]
4. **Use page breaks.** Make sure that your sentences do *not* run over to a new page. If paragraphs are short, give each one its own page.
5. **Use wide margins.** Wide margins give you a place to make last-minute changes or additions to your manuscript.
6. **Do not staple the pages together.** Instead, place your manuscript on one side of the lectern and slide the pages to the other side when it's time to go on to the next page. If you don't have a lectern, slide each page underneath the others as you finish.
7. **Practice using your manuscript.** Manuscript speaking requires a great deal of practice so that you can establish and maintain maximum eye contact with your audience without losing your place as you read.

manuscript speaking include difficulty maintaining sufficient eye contact as well as dull delivery. Figure 14.6 offers tips for manuscript delivery that can help you overcome some of these potential problems.

Marking up Your Notes. Many experienced speakers mark up their notes and manuscripts to help them with vocal and physical delivery, filling their pages with little marks as well as last-minute changes. Marking up your notes or manuscript provides additional "punctuation," telling you which words or phrases to emphasize as well as when to pause, gesture, or move.

Figure 14.7 lists some of the common graphics we've seen on presentation manuscripts, all of which are available on most word-processing programs.

In addition to using these or other symbols, you can underline or **bold** words that should be emphasized. Some speakers use a bright highlighting pen to make important words and phrases stand out. Or you can increase the font size to indicate a very important word or series of words.

Symbol	Meaning
/	short pause
//	medium pause
///	long pause
◄	speak louder
►	speak softer
▲	speak faster
▼	speak slower
★	key point or important sentence follows
✖	stop and look up for a reaction
☺	smile
☐❶	slide 1
☐❷	slide 2

Figure 14.7

Common Graphics Used to Mark up a Manuscript

Figure 14.8 Marking Up a Manuscript

Here's an example of how two sentences from President John F. Kennedy's Inaugural Address in 1961 may be marked up to enhance delivery:

▼And so / my fellow Americans // ask **not** / what your country can do for **you** // ask what **you** can do for your **country.** ✖

My fellow citizens of the **world** // ask **not** what **America** will do for **you** // but what **together** // **we** can do / for the **freedom** of **man.**

Bullet points also provide a convenient way of breaking up a list or series of words. Bullet points incorporated into a manuscript do more than highlight a list or series of ideas; they tell you when to take a breath and pause between those ideas.

Regardless of what form your notes take, put them on the lectern if you are provided with one. And don't let your notes hang over the front of a lectern. If you don't have a lectern, put the notes on a table or hold them in one hand. Also, hand-held note cards work much better than hand-held floppy paper. Regardless of whether you use full-size paper or index cards, slip each page or card behind the others when you're finished with it so that you don't end up revisiting the same information by mistake.

Practice

Athletes and musicians practice, and so do the best and most experienced speakers. Practice involves translating the decisions you make about performance into action. Practice is your best guarantee that you will perform well—in every sense of the word. Practice requires more than repeating your presentation over and over again. You must also pay attention to the fine points of your performance. Practice can tell you whether there are words that you have trouble pronouncing or sentences that are too long to say in one breath. In addition, it may help you discover that what you thought was a ten-minute talk takes thirty minutes to deliver. Practicing with presentation aids is critical, particularly if you've seen the embarrassing results that befall speakers who don't have their visuals in order. It's not a question of whether you should practice; rather, it's deciding what aspects of your performance need the most practice. Practicing is the only way to make sure that you sound and look good in a presentation. To put it another way, "give your speech *before* you give it."[4]

Some of the best speakers we know feel "naked" without their notes. Even though they are familiar with their material and have delivered the same message over and over, they still feel incomplete without a set of notes in hand. Great Britain's eloquent prime minister Winston Churchill was asked why he always had notes for his speeches, even though he rarely used them. He replied, "I carry fire insurance, but I don't expect my house to burn down."[1] Bringing notes with you is fine, particularly if you don't use them or only refer to them briefly. The problem occurs when well-prepared but insecure speakers bury their heads in their notes, even though the information is second nature to them.

1. Malcolm Kushner, *Successful Presentations for Dummies* (Foster City, CA: IDG Books, 1997), p. 204.

Practice can take many forms. It can be as simple as closing your door and rehearsing your presentation in private or as complex as a full, on-stage, videotaped rehearsal. The ways in which you can practice range from a quick look at your notes to a major dress rehearsal.

Depending on how much time you have, the length and importance of your presentation, and your familiarity with your material, there are several different ways to practice.

Rehearsing a presentation at home may feel awkward at first, but family and friends can offer useful suggestions and help you feel more confident about your upcoming talk.

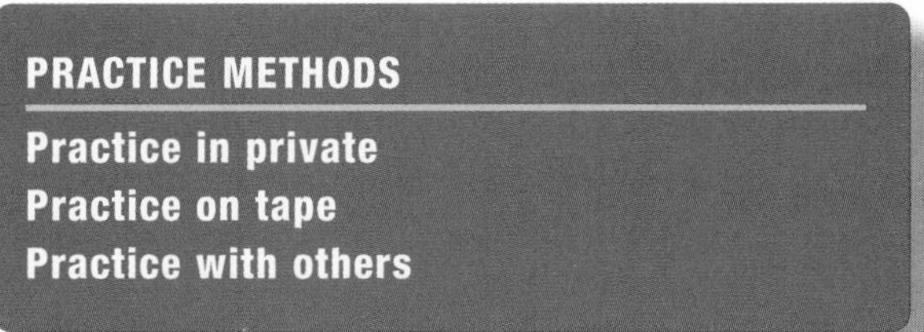

Practice in Private

Practice is usually a solo activity. You may go over your presentation as you drive your car, while you shower, behind a closed door in your home or office, or all by yourself in the room where you will be speaking. Regardless of where you practice, you should try to practice the way you want to sound and look in front of your audience. Speak at the volume and rate you intend to use, glance at your notes only occasionally, and use body movement that's appropriate for you and for your presentation. At first, you may feel a bit strange while talking to yourself. It may help to remember that musicians rehearse alone, athletes exercise alone, and actors recite their lines alone. Speakers must also learn to practice alone.

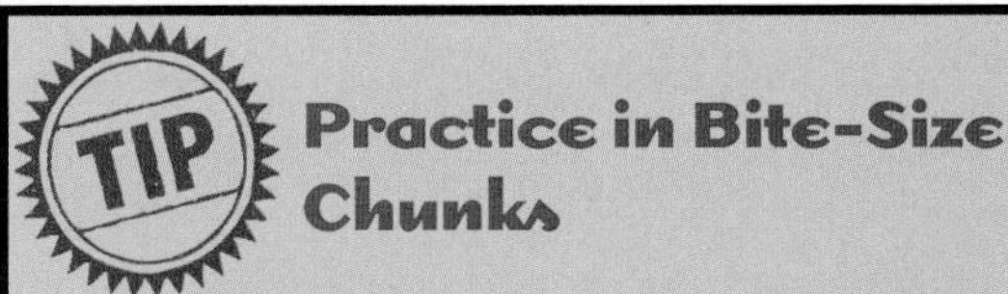

Practice in Bite-Size Chunks

Although it is important to do several complete run-throughs of your presentation, there is a lot to be said for breaking some of your practice sessions into smaller segments. Thomas Mira, author of *Speak Smart,* suggests using brief practice sessions during which you practice for only five or ten minutes at a time. He advises, "You can do anything for five or ten minutes. If you make practice a lengthy drudgery, you just won't do it. If you divide your practice time into manageable, bite-size chunks, you'll find yourself practicing more often and building confidence for each segment."[1]

1. Thomas K. Mira, *Speak Smart: The Art of Public Speaking* (New York: Random House, 1997), p. 91.

Should I Practice in Front of a Mirror?

Some speakers report that they like to practice in front of a full-length mirror, and many popular public speaking books recommend this practice technique. We do not share the general enthusiasm for this method. In fact, we discourage it. Try it, and you will see why. When you start talking to a mirror, you'll notice your face, your hair, your clothes, and your eyes. You will notice your mouth moving, your hands gesturing, and your posture. As a result, you'll think very little about your presentation.

In Chapter 3, "Building Presentation Confidence," we discuss how being too self-focused can heighten presentation anxiety. Mirrors are the ultimate in self-focus. Staring at your performance in a mirror takes you away from your purpose, your audience, and your setting. All it does is reflect how you look to yourself in the confines of a bathroom or bedroom.

Malcolm Kushner, who once taught speech communication classes at the University of Southern California, is the author of an amusing but substantive book, *Successful Presentations for Dummies*. He's also "anti-mirror." Kushner argues that practicing in front of a mirror is distracting and very unnatural. How many people, he asks, look at themselves while they're talking (other than the evil queen from *Snow White*)?[1]

At the same time, we recognize that there are pro-mirror people. So if you have rehearsed in front of a mirror and believe that doing so improves your performance, don't abandon this technique. Just make sure that it doesn't divert your focus from your purpose, your audience, and your message.

1. Malcolm Kushner, *Successful Presentations for Dummies* (Foster City, CA: IDG Books, 1997), p. 212.

Practice on Tape

If you practice in private, it's difficult to concentrate on delivering your presentation and to evaluate it at the same time. How do you know whether you are speaking clearly, maintaining enough eye contact, or fidgeting? An audiotape recording of your practice session can tell you a lot about what you are saying and how you sound. A video recording can tell you even more. Not everyone has access to a video camera, but most speakers can record themselves on audiocassette.

One of the first things you will notice in an audio recording is that your voice doesn't sound the way you thought it would. But remember, you hear your voice from the inside; your audience hears it projected across a room. The outside sound will be different. So instead of focusing on yourself, try to listen as an audience member would. Do you understand what is being said—the ideas and information as well as the individual words and phrases? You can time your presentation, check your pronunciation, and monitor your fluency.

If you can record yourself on videotape, you will also be able to assess how you look. Again, be aware that in all probability, you won't like what you see. At first, you may be distracted by the way your hair looks, the way you gesture, or the extra ten pounds you'd like to lose. If you're going to use a videotape, try watching it alone at first and then with a friend. A videotape can help you practice if you are able to look at it objectively.

Videotaping your practice session can tell you how to polish and improve your presentation before you speak. Videotaping your actual performance can tell you a lot about why you did or didn't achieve your purpose.

Practice with Others

With or without audiotaping or videotaping, you can practice your presentation in front of someone else. Your listener doesn't have to be a public speaking instructor to say, "I couldn't hear you," "You didn't look at me during the last section," or "I'm not sure what you were trying to prove with those statistics." Equally important, a friendly listener can reassure you and give you an extra dose of confidence. We often are our own harshest critics. Someone else's reaction can help you put the finishing touches on a well-prepared and well-practiced presentation.

Mid-Performance Decisions

You've reached that crucial moment that you've been preparing and planning for. After hours, days, even weeks of work, you're about to make your presentation. Even the most experienced speakers and speechwriters have described how it often takes one

Real World Real Speakers

View Yourself on Videotape

A few years ago, one of your authors taught a graduate course to a group of experienced and would-be college teachers who wanted to improve their classroom communication skills. Each student was videotaped giving a fifteen-minute lecture. No one else in the class viewed the tape. It was strictly for the private use of the speaker. In their final reports, even the most experienced professors made interesting and positive comments about the use of video as a practice tool.

Here's what one student wrote after viewing herself on video:

It took me three days to get up enough courage to watch my videotape. Then it took me three more days before I'd let my husband watch it. I guess I'll never be a TV personality. However, I really did learn a lot from the experience and from watching the tape. I never realized before how active my hands are while I'm lecturing. The gestures were appropriate, though, and I thought they helped me look at ease as I lectured. One problem I noticed after watching the video was that I focused more on the center of the room rather than on the sides. I will need to make a conscious effort to look around the entire classroom as I speak.

You, too, can learn more about yourself as a presenter by viewing yourself on tape.

hour of work to prepare for each minute of performance time. Is it worth it? You bet it is! You'll be so well-prepared that you will concentrate on communicating what you want to say, not on how you sound or look. You can concentrate your energy and will on achieving your purpose. You can put aside concerns about yourself and become an audience-focused speaker.

One of the most significant differences between good and great speakers is their ability to use audience feedback to make mid-performance adaptations. You don't have to wait until your presentation ends to get the audience's reactions. As you speak, you can see and hear how audience members react to your presentation and performance. Their facial expressions, their levels of concentration, and their responses to suggestions and humor are forms of feedback. What you decide to do with this information is critical. You can ignore the feedback and continue giving your performance exactly the way you did when you practiced it. Or you can modify your presentation.

These adaptations can be minor. You might slow down, increase your volume, or leave out a controversial story, a long quotation, or a complicated statistic. Sometimes, though, feedback can lead to major changes. You might modify or leave out a major argument, ask for or suggest a course of action that you hadn't intended to mention, make your general presentation style more or less formal, or spend more time demonstrating your competence.

How Much Should I Practice?

Generally, it's a good idea to practice your entire presentation several different times rather than to devote one long session to the process. Plus, brief five- to ten-minute sessions in which you practice smaller segments should ensure a good performance. Schedule and use at least three, but no more than five, complete run-through sessions. The reason for the upper limit is that too much practice can make you sound *canned,* a term used to describe speakers who have practiced their presentation so often or who have given the same presentation so many times that they no longer sound spontaneous and natural. Both of us have had to tell students and corporate speakers to stop practicing because they looked and sounded like robots.

Rather than prescribe the number of practice sessions, we offer this advice: Keep practicing until you feel satisfied. Then, practice with the goal of improving the fine points of your presentation. Then, stop!

Don't be afraid to make mid-course adjustments and corrections. Watch and listen to your audience as they watch, listen, and respond to you. If there's a noisy disruption in the room or nearby, increase your volume or stop and wait for the noise to end. If your audience laughs at a comment or applauds, stop and accept their response. If your talk runs longer than you've planned, and the audience is getting restless, do some quick thinking and shorten your presentation. Mid-course corrections in sailing are an accepted safety precaution. Mid-performance adjustments are just as important in order to deal with unexpected audience responses.

As the creator of your presentation, you have the right and power to change it at every decision-making point in the process. And if audience feedback tells you that an adaptation is needed, decide how to change, and do it.

Summary

What is a good performance?

A good performance helps you accomplish your purpose through the use of effective vocal and physical delivery and feedback-based adaptation.

Should I use an outline or read my presentation word for word?

Decide which form of delivery best suits your purpose, the audience, the logistics, the nature of the occasion, and your speaking style. Then choose from among impromptu, extemporaneous, manuscript, memorized, or a combination of these delivery forms.

How should I use notes when I speak?

If you are using index cards, an outline, or a manuscript, use them during every practice session. Make sure that your notes are easy to read, are in proper order, and suit the delivery form that you have chosen and the logistics of the setting.

What's the best way to practice?

Try practicing in three ways: in private, on tape, and in front of others. Each form can help you improve your performance.

Presentation Principles in Action

Punctuate the Presentation

Directions: Read the following excerpts from three famous speeches. Other than the capital letters at the beginning of sentences and final periods, punctuation marks have been removed. In addition to adding commas, dashes, or quotation and question marks, insert graphic symbols to help you read these excerpts out loud. When you have finished "punctuating" the presentation, practice delivering the manuscript excerpts in private. Be prepared to read them to others. When you listen to others read these excerpts, note how the ways in which they emphasize words and phrases affect the meaning of each excerpt. Also note how reading from a manuscript affects each speaker's delivery.

Excerpt from John F. Kennedy's Inaugural Address, January 20, 1961

Now the trumpet summons us again not as a call to bear arms though arms we need not as a call to battle though embattled we are but as a call to bear the burden of a long twilight struggle year in and year out rejoicing in hope patient in tribulation a struggle against the common enemies of man tyranny poverty disease and war itself. Can we forge against these enemies a grand and global alliance North and South East and West that you can assure a more fruitful life for all mankind.

Excerpt from General Douglas MacArthur's Address to Congress, April 19, 1951

Mr. President Mr. Speaker and distinguished Members of the Congress I stand on this rostrum with a sense of deep humility and great pride humility in the wake of those great American architects of our history who have stood here before me pride in the reflection that this forum of legislative debate represents human liberty in the purest form yet devised. Here are centered the hopes and aspirations and faith of the entire human race.

Excerpt from Jesse Jackson's Rainbow Coalition Speech at the Democratic National Convention, July 17, 1984

Our flag is red white and blue but our nation is rainbow red yellow brown black and white we're all precious in God's sight. America is not like a blanket one piece of unbroken cloth the same color the same texture the same size. America is more like a quilt many patches many pieces many colors many sizes all woven and held together by a common thread. The white the Hispanic the black the Arab the Jew the woman the Native American the small farmer the businessperson the environmentalist the peace activist, the young the old the lesbian the gay and the disabled make up the American quilt.

Source: Complete transcripts of each speech, with commentaries, can be found in James R. Andrews and David Zarefsky, *Contemporary American Voices: Significant Speeches in American History, 1945–Present* (New York: Longman, 1992)

Key Terms

extemporaneous speaking 321
impromptu speaking 320
manuscript speaking 322
memorized presentation 324
performance 319

Notes

1 Laurie E. Rozakis, *The Complete Idiot's Guide to Speaking in Public with Confidence* (New York: Alpha Books, 1995), p. 221. Also see Hall Persons with Lianne Mercer, *The How-To of Great Speaking* (Austin, TX: Black & Taylor, 1992), Chapter 11.

2 Marjorie Brody, *Speaking Your Way to the Top* (Boston: Allyn & Bacon, 1998), p. 113.

3 Rozakis, p. 222.

4 Peggy Noonan, *Simply Speaking: How to Communicate Your Ideas with Style, Substance, and Clarity* (New York: HarperCollins, 1998), p. 9. Copyright © 1998 by Peggy Noonan. Reprinted by permission of HarperCollins Publishers, Inc.

chapter fifteen

Vocal Delivery

- Can I improve my speaking voice?
- Can I speak loudly enough without feeling as though I'm shouting?
- Can I speak slowly enough to be understood without putting everyone to sleep?
- What's the best pitch for my voice?
- How can I avoid stumbling over words?
- How can I speak more clearly and accurately?
- How can I get rid of my accent?

Whether you like your speaking voice or not, it's *yours.* And like you, your voice is unique. Most of you can recognize your favorite singers or announcers on the radio because you know what their voices sound like. It's not unusual to telephone a friend and say, "Hi, it's me," and have that person recognize your voice.

Like fingerprints, each of our voices is one of a kind. As a result, there is little you can or should do to change it for a presentation. At the same time, you can *improve* your voice in order to make sure that your message is loud and clear. Although you must practice and want to improve, developing an effective speaking voice takes more than motivation and practice. You first must understand what it takes to make your voice an effective instrument for communication. In this chapter we start with the basics—the unique sound of your voice—and then move on to ways of improving its quality and effectiveness.

Developing an Effective Speaking Voice

Only a few lucky speakers are born with beautiful voices. Radio and television announcers often have natural voices that stand out in a crowd. Other speakers have learned Standard American English, the dialect used by the majority of outstanding educators, social and civic leaders, and prominent newscasters,[1] or grew up in an area of the country where it is spoken. Some people who do a lot of public speaking hire voice coaches for up to two hundred dollars an hour to help them improve the sound of their voices. In the musical *My Fair Lady,* professor Henry Higgins bets that he can change Eliza Doolittle's speech from that of a "gutter snipe" to that of a "lady" and thereby fool aristocratic society into thinking that she *is* a lady. Even with coaching, however, it can take years for a person to change the sound or quality of her or his voice.

Most of us don't have the money or time to hire a vocal coach, which is just as well. You probably don't need one anyway. What you *do* need is to know how to produce an effective voice and how you can monitor specific vocal qualities as you practice.

Think of your voice as the instrument that you use to produce sounds. Much like a musical instrument, the structure or anatomy of your vocal mechanism dictates the kind of sound you'll produce (see Figure 15.1). Men, for example, whose vocal cords are usually longer and thicker than women's, speak in a lower pitch. When your throat is swollen with a cold, your voice may be weaker or huskier. So before you try to sound like someone else, make sure that you comprehend the potential power and limits of your vocal instrument. Once you understand these factors, you can harness your vocal instrument for the task of producing clear and expressive speech.

Components of an Effective Voice

Being able to make a sound on a musical instrument (striking the keys on a piano, banging on a drum, or plucking a violin string) is not the same as making music. Knowing the notes on a keyboard is not the same as playing a tune and making that tune loud or soft, fast or slow, crisp or *legato* (smooth and connected). The same is true

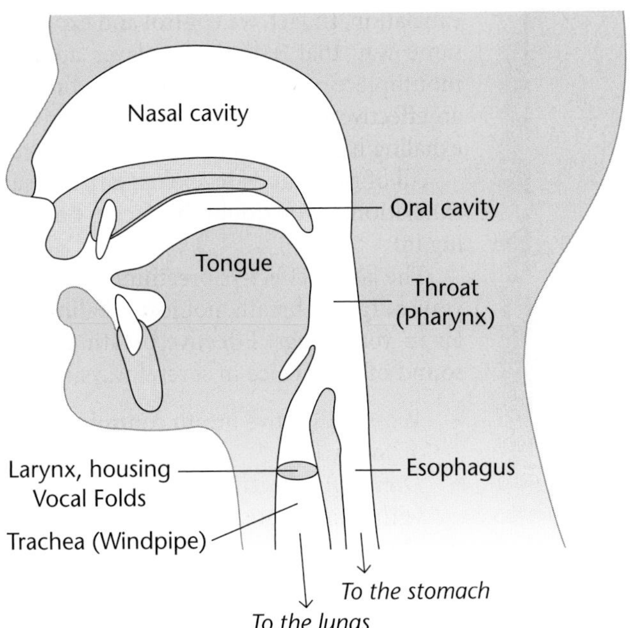

Figure 15.1

Voice Mechanism

The intermittent force of exhaled air from the lungs through the larynx produces vocal fold vibration. Much like the lips of a trumpet player forcing air against a mouthpiece, a controlled breath stream sets the vocal folds in motion to produce a vocal sound. The interaction of your lips, teeth, tongue, and oral cavity modifies that vocal sound to create the unique sounds of speech.

of the instrument called your *voice*. There are ways of "playing" your voice that improve its quality and vocal characteristics that you can control and practice.

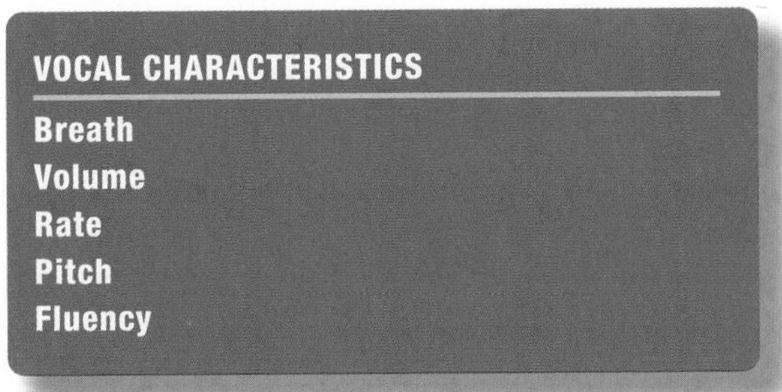

Developing a more effective speaking voice requires the same kind of time and effort that you would devote to improving any skill. You don't learn to be an accomplished carpenter, pianist, swimmer, writer, or speaker overnight. You need to learn the basics first.

Breath

Lyle Mayer, the well-respected author of a voice and articulation textbook, notes that "breathing to sustain life is primary and automatic—we're not always conscious of breathing."[2] Breathing for life, however, is not the same as breathing for speech. When we breathe to speak, we exercise conscious control of the processes of inhalation and exhalation. When we speak, we take in more air and control the release of air through

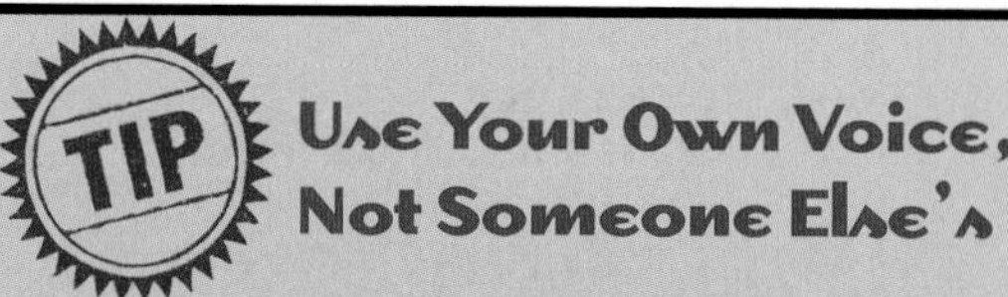

In the hope of impressing an audience, inexperienced speakers sometimes try to imitate another speaker's voice. Trying to sound like a speaker you admire or a famous person can have disastrous results. If nothing else, you will spend too much energy and concentration trying to mimic the other person instead of working to improve your natural voice. Rather than impressing your audience, you are likely to sound phony and insincere. Be true to your own voice; train it properly, and it will serve you well.

exhalation. In fact, we control and expend air in much the same way that a trumpet player applies breath to the mouthpiece of a trumpet. Thus, the first step in producing an effective vocal sound is inhaling enough air and then exhaling it in a controlled manner to produce speech.

All of the sounds in spoken language are made during exhalation. If you doubt this fact, try talking while breathing in!

The key to effective breathing for speech is controlling your outgoing breath, not just inhaling and holding more air in your lungs. Effective breath control improves the sound of your voice in several ways:[3]

- *Volume:* Effective breath control amplifies the loudness of your voice.
- *Duration:* Effective breath control lets you say more with a single breath.
- *Quality:* Effective breath control reduces the likelihood of vocal problems such as harshness or breathiness.

Voice coaches—whether they're teaching speakers or singers—always begin with breathing. Whether they call it "deep breathing," "abdominal breathing," or "diaphragmatic breathing," they insist that their students learn how to breathe more efficiently and effectively. Your breathing may be shallow and inefficient now, but you can learn how to change it.

The first step in learning to breathe for speech is to note the difference between the shallow, unconscious breathing you do all the time and the deeper breathing that produces a strong, sustained sound quality. Many speech coaches recommend the following exercise to learn abdominal breathing.

1. Lie flat on your back on a comfortable surface. Support the back of your knees with a pillow.
2. Place a moderately heavy hardbound book on your stomach. The book should sit right over your navel.
3. Begin breathing through your mouth. The book should move up when you breathe in and sink down when you breathe out.
4. Place one of your hands on the upper part of your chest in a "Pledge of Allegiance" position. As you inhale and exhale, this area should not move in and out.
5. Now, take the book away and replace it with your other hand. Is your abdomen moving up when you breathe in and sinking down when you breathe out?
6. Once you're comfortable with step 5, try doing the same kind of breathing while sitting up or standing.

Once you've learned how abdominal breathing feels, you can begin to add sound.[4] For example, try sighing the vowel *ahh* with each exhalation. Sustain the vowel for five seconds. Once you have mastered *ahh*, try counting from one to five, holding each number for a full second. Your progress may be slow, but your efforts will reward you with a stronger and more controllable voice.

Volume

If your audience can't hear you, you won't achieve your purpose. One of the best ways to make sure that everyone in your audience can hear you is to practice your presentation *out loud,* using the voice and volume you intend to use when making your presentation. **Volume** measures your voice's degree of loudness. The key to producing adequate volume is knowing the size of the audience that you will be addressing and the dimensions of the room in which you will be speaking. Experienced speakers know how to use these factors to adjust their volume automatically. You can do the same. If there are only five people in an audience, and they are sitting close to you, you can speak at a normal, everyday volume. If there are fifty people in your audience, you will need more energy and force behind your voice. Once your audience exceeds one hundred people, you may be more comfortable using a microphone. However, a strong speaking voice can project to an audience of a thousand people without any electronic amplification. Professional speakers, actors, and classical singers do it all the time, but they also have spent years developing the power of their voices.

If you are not a trained speaker, actor, or singer, how can you make sure that your voice is loud enough? One thing you should *not* do is practice in your head or in a whisper, nor should you do all of your practicing in a small room. You can practice most vocal characteristics in a quiet voice, but not volume.

Try to practice in a room that is about the same size as the one in which you will be speaking. Ask a friend to sit in a far corner and report back on your volume level. If you are not loud enough, keep increasing your volume until your friend is satisfied. Also note that a room full of people absorbs sound; you will have to turn up your volume another notch. Speakers who cannot be heard are a common problem. It's very rare, though, for a speaker to be too loud. Can we teach you to speak louder? The answer is, we don't have to; instead, let us convince you that it's okay to use your full voice. Have you ever yelled to someone in another room, called out to someone across campus, sung along full blast with a recording, or joined in a cheer at a game? Of course you have. Understand, however, that we are not suggesting that you yell at your

A speaker rallies employees protesting a bill that limits medical benefits. How would you adapt your delivery when speaking to a large crowd in an outdoor setting?

Using a Microphone

You may be thinking, "Well, if people can't hear me, why can't I just use a microphone to amplify my voice?" You can, but don't jump at every chance to use an amplification system. Most microphones don't reproduce a natural-sounding voice. Therefore, you may have to speak more slowly, articulate more clearly, and make sure that the system can accommodate changes in your volume. Microphones tend to be preset for one volume. If you speak too loudly, it may sound as though you are shouting at your audience. If you speak too softly, the "mike" may not pick up everything you say. An audience might forgive a few lost words under non-miked circumstances, but they will be less forgiving when you use a microphone since they will expect to hear you very well.

Sometimes, though, a microphone is essential. An audience or a room may be so large that you won't be heard without one. Or you may find yourself in a situation where microphones have already been set up for each speaker. Regardless of how you end up in front of a microphone, make the most of the technology.

The trick is to go against your instincts. If you want to project a soft tone, speak closer to the microphone and lower your volume. Your voice will sound more intimate and will be able to convey subtle emotions. If you want to be more forceful, speak further away from the microphone and project your voice. This technique minimizes distortions and will make your presentation sound more powerful.

Familiarize yourself with the specific microphone you'll be using.

- If you can, test the mike ahead of time. Ask someone to sit at the back of the room and monitor your amplified voice. Can you speak at a normal volume, or do you need to be louder?
- Determine whether the microphone is sophisticated enough to capture your voice from various angles and distances or whether you'll need to keep your mouth close to it.
- Microphones work best when placed about five to ten inches from the speaker's mouth. If you are using a hand-held microphone, hold it *below* your mouth at chin level.
- If you are using a clip-on lavaliere microphone (wired or wireless), test it carefully. Once it's clipped on, it can be difficult to readjust.
- Focus on your audience, not on the microphone. Stay near the mike, but don't tap it, lean over it, keep readjusting it, or make the *p-p-p-p-p-p* "motorboat sound" as a test. Experienced speakers make all the adjustments they need during the first few seconds that they hear their own voices projected through an amplification system.
- When your microphone is well adjusted, and you're feeling comfortable, speak in a natural, conversational tone.

Sometimes the *p* sound comes popping through a microphone, particularly if you speak straight into it instead of at an angle. Adjusting the position of the microphone usually eliminates the popping sound. If you hear the painful squeal of sound system feedback, try moving away from the speakers; you may be too close to them. Last, keep in mind that a microphone will not only amplify your voice; it will also amplify other sounds—coughing, throat-clearing, the shuffling of papers, or the tapping of a pen.

Learn to avoid these common microphone problems, and you'll sound like a pro! Microphones can be a valuable tool once you learn how to use them effectively.

audience. We're only pointing out that you already know how to speak loudly. The trick is finding and using the right volume level for your audience.

To reach all audience members, you need to learn to project. **Projection** is controlled vocal energy "that gives impact and intelligibility to sound. It involves a deliberate concentration and a strong desire to communicate with your listeners." When you project, your voice will reach the audience members sitting furthest away. A projected voice is beamed to listeners. It does not just reach them; it penetrates them.[5]

Like many other speakers, you may tend to speak to the people sitting right in front of you. You don't need a loud voice to be heard by someone five feet away. It's the person in the back row who will be straining to hear you. Simply looking at people in the back row and deliberately thinking about making them hear you can automatically increase your volume.

Here's an exercise that can help you learn to project. Ask someone to sit at the back of the room or auditorium in which you will be speaking. Then read a nonsense sentence in a voice that is loud and clear. The point, according to Lyle Mayer, is that by "practicing nonsense material, you'll quickly discover that loudness alone won't put it over."[6] You will need to tackle the consonants and vowels in the words with force and energy. Try to project your reading of the following sentences to someone sitting far away.

Samuel Hornsbee threw a turkey at the dragon's striped Chevrolet.

Karla Pavemore's heavy pen fell through the Earth's crust and reached New Zealand coated with magma.

Twenty-seven squirrels sang chants for the Christmas in April ball.

Using these nonsense sentences will ensure that your listener cannot anticipate the correct words. When asked to write down or repeat what you have said, your listener won't be able to guess a logical ending to your sentence. Thus, if you don't project with force and clarity, you won't be understood.

If your voice is too soft, you may need some direct coaching and confidence building before you speak. Don't wait until your presentation is over to find out that you couldn't be heard. Sometimes after a soft-spoken student has finished a presentation, we ask him or her to repeat the first ten seconds of the speech in a louder voice. After the student responds with some hesitancy and a slightly louder beginning, we ask for a louder one. And after that, we ask for an even louder one. In bewilderment, the student often says, "But I'm shouting." We then ask the class for a verdict and the answer is always the same: "You're not shouting; your volume is just right. That's how you should always speak." A quiet person is comfortable using a soft voice. What seems like a shout may be the perfect volume level for a presentation.

Practice your presentation at full volume. Give your speech at the same volume, observe your audience's reactions, and ask a friend to signal you if you need to increase your volume.

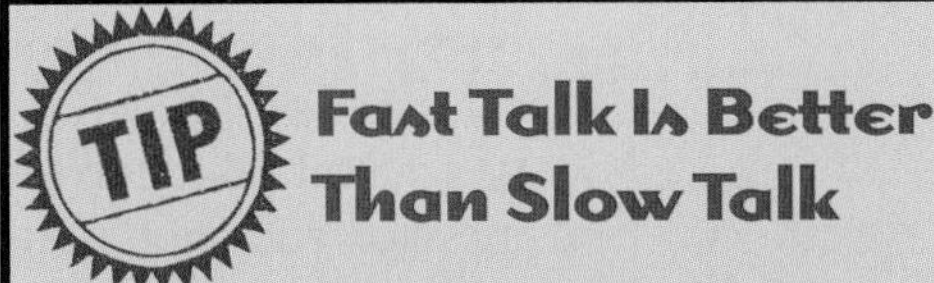

Fast Talk Is Better Than Slow Talk

In most cases, it's better to speak a little too fast than too slowly. Listeners perceive presenters who speak quickly and clearly as energized, competent, and interesting.[1] In every country that has been studied, according to linguist Deborah Tannen, people from the slower-speaking regions are stereotyped as stupid. She also notes that in the talk-focused culture of intellectual New Yorkers, intelligence is demonstrated by fast talk. Quick talk is taken as evidence of quick thinking, which is synonymous with smart thinking.[2]

Given the choice, it's better to speak too fast than run the risk of boring an audience. Too slow a rate can suggest that you are unsure of yourself or, even worse, that you are not very bright. There are, however, exceptions to this advice. It would be wise to speak at a slower rate when addressing older audiences—many of whom complain about the difficulty of following fast-paced talk—or international listeners who are not fluent in English. You should also vary your pace, particularly when making an important point. If you want to sound authoritative, slow down and articulate clearly. The change in pace and clarity will capture the audience's attention and add significance to your statement.

Since audiences can listen faster than you can talk, it's better to keep the pace up than to speak at a "crawl." Familiarize yourself with how it feels to speak at 145 to 180 words a minute so that you can monitor your rate during your presentation.

1. Michael Argyle, "Nonverbal Vocalizations," in *The Nonverbal Communication Reader: Classic and Contemporary Readings*, eds. Laura K. Guerrero, Joseph A. DeVito, and Michael L. Hecht, 2nd ed. (Prospect Heights, IL: Waveland, 1999), p. 141.
2. Deborah Tannen, "Hey, Did You Catch That? Why They're Talking as Fast as They Can," *Washington Post*, 5 January 2003, pp. B1 and B4.

Rate

We've all heard speakers who talked too fast or too slow. Your **rate** of speech equals the number of words you say per minute added to the number and length of pauses you use. There is no single "speed limit" for a presentation. But as in driving, for which there are different speed limits for different road and traffic conditions, there are various speech rates for various situations. Your natural speaking style, your presentation's mood, your vocabulary's complexity, and your audience's listening ability should affect your rate. Some general guidelines can help you determine whether you are speaking too slowly, too fast, or at just the right rate. First, you have to time yourself. This paragraph contains about 125 words. Read it out loud in the kind of voice you would use before an audience. How long did it take you to read it?

If it took you sixty seconds to read the previous paragraph, you're a slow speaker. If it took you thirty seconds, you are speaking at a rate of 250 words per minute (wpm), which is too fast for most audiences to follow easily.

Now read and time the previous two paragraphs. They contain about 170 words. Given that the material is fairly easy to read and unemotional, a total of sixty seconds (give or take a few) would be about right. Generally, anything below 125 wpm is too slow; 125 to 145 wpm is acceptable; 145 to 180 is better; 180 or higher exceeds the speed limit.[7] But don't carve these guidelines in stone. Your wpm depends on you, your message, and your audience.

Generally, presenters tend to speak too fast—they exceed the 180 wpm speed limit. Often speakers are so familiar with what they want to say that they forget that their audience is hearing it for the first time. Both of us have been accused of racing through presentations when we have had a lot to say. Even after years of making presentations, we still have to remind ourselves to slow down, slow down, slow down. Don't race; pace yourself.

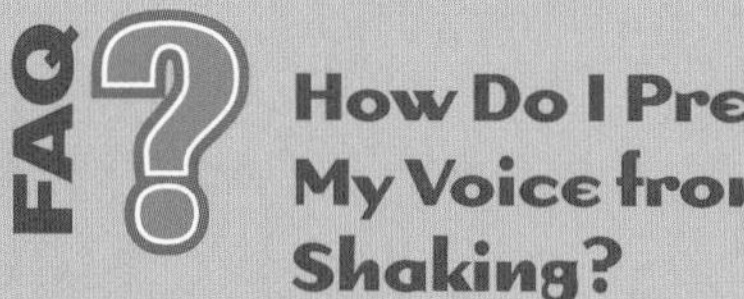

How Do I Prevent My Voice from Shaking?

One of our survey respondents, an assistant superintendent of schools in New York, wrote: "My problem—my voice quivers!" Many speakers believe that their voices quiver, but in fact, the audience hears nothing like a shake, rattle, or roll. When you speak loudly and forcefully, you perceive the sound of any vocal variation more intensely because your speaking voice is amplified in your head. Most of the time, the audience does not hear anything distracting in your voice. If that's the case, then don't worry about it. If, however, the shaking in your voice is obvious, you can take a few steps to reduce this phenomenon.

- Make sure that your volume is adequate, a situation which, in turn, ensures a strong and steady stream of air.
- Make sure that you are speaking at your optimum pitch.
- Review ways of reducing presentation anxiety, which may cause a trembling voice (see Chapter 3, "Building Presentation Confidence").

Pitch

Just like the notes on a musical scale, **pitch** refers to how high or low your voice sounds. Most men speak at a lower pitch than women do. Most adults speak at a lower pitch than children do. Anatomy determines pitch. Men have longer and thicker vocal cords (also known as vocal folds) than women do. Just as the longer, thicker strings on a piano produce lower notes, longer, thicker vocal cords produce a lower vocal pitch.

Americans seem to prefer low-pitched voices. They think that men and women with deeper voices sound more authoritative and effective. Men with a naturally high pitch may be labeled effeminate or weak, and women with very high speaking voices may be labeled childish or silly. To compensate for a high natural voice, some speakers push their voices down into a lower range of notes. However, this practice limits the voice's expressiveness, can make it sound harsh, and damages the voice by putting a strain on the vocal cords.

Like everyone else, you have a natural or **optimum pitch** at which you speak most easily and expressively. The hard part is finding it. Like many other speakers, you may have the habit of speaking at a too-low or too-high pitch. You need to rediscover your optimum pitch so that you can produce the strongest and clearest sound with the least amount of effort and strain.

Finding Your Optimum Pitch. Although there are several ways to find your optimum pitch, a method called "Sing *Sol-La*" works for many speakers. This exercise requires the ability to sing a musical scale or access to a musical instrument (and someone who can play a scale). Sing the lowest note you can sing. Then, sing up the scale—*Do-Re-Mi-Fa-Sol-La-Ti-Do*. Next, go back to your lowest note and sing up to *Sol*. Can you easily sing an octave above *Sol?* Try *La*. If you have to strain a little to reach the octave above *La*, go back to *Sol*. Your best pitch is probably the fifth (*Sol*) or sixth (*La*) note above your lowest note. Test your *Sol* or *La* note to see if you can increase its volume with minimal effort and strain. Then, sing an octave higher than that note. The sound should be clear and unstrained.[8]

Now, try to say a nursery rhyme or the Pledge of Allegiance very quickly at your optimum pitch. Can you produce the sound easily? Do you feel any strain? Is the sound higher or lower than the pitch at which you usually speak? If it is higher than your normal pitch, try raising your overall pitch when you speak. Finding this pitch doesn't mean that you should speak at only that one note. Instead, think of this pitch as "neutral," and use it as your base line for increasing the expressiveness of your voice. Then, establish your optimum pitch in your auditory memory and use it to project a clear and powerful speaking voice.

THE BENEFITS OF USING OPTIMUM PITCH

- **Your voice will be stronger and less likely to fade at the ends of sentences.**
- **Your voice will not tire easily.**
- **You will be less likely to sound harsh, hoarse, breathy, or squeaky.**
- **You will have "room to move" above and below that pitch, an absolute must for an expressive and energetic voice.**

Varying Pitch for Emphasis. **Inflection** is the changing pitch within a syllable, word, or group of words. Inflection makes speech expressive; lack of it is the culprit for what most people call a "monotone voice." A **monotone** voice occurs not because you use the wrong pitch or speak slowly but rather because you don't change the pitch of sounds within words or the pitch of words within phrases and sentences. Speaking in a monotone voice limits your expressiveness. In English, we tend to use a rising inflection when we ask questions, express uncertainty, or stress a word or syllable.[9] We tend to use downward inflections at the ends of phrases and sentences or when we're depressed or under stress. "I can't cope anymore" would not end with a rising inflection unless you were doing a "Valley Girl" imitation, in which almost every statement would end on the upswing.[10]

Inflection both helps you to avoid having a monotone voice and allows you to emphasize an important or meaningful word or phrase. When you're speaking from a manuscript, we recommend that you underline words that should receive extra stress or emphasis. More often than not, varying pitch sets a word apart from the rest of a sentence. A single change in inflection can change the entire meaning of a sentence, as is illustrated in the following examples.

I was born in New Jersey.	(You, on the other hand, were born in Maryland.)
I **was** born in New Jersey.	(No doubt about it!)
I was **born** in New Jersey.	(So I know my way around.)
I was born in **New Jersey.**	(Not in New York.)

Inflection may not seem very important since the resulting change in pitch can be a fraction of a note. Yet like the effects of any strong spice in a recipe, a small rise or drop in inflection can change the entire meaning of a sentence or the quality of your voice. Inflection is a key ingredient in making your voice more interesting, exciting, emotional, and emphatic.

FAQ

Should I Avoid Saying *Um* and *Uh*?

First, let's get one misconception out of the way about *ums* and *uhs*. There is nothing wrong with using an occasional *uh* or *um*. According to psychologist Nicholas Christenfeld, words like *uh* are universal speech fillers that are woven into the fabric of every language in the world. In Russian, it's *vot*. In Javanese, it's *nah,* and in German, it's *oder* or *nicht*. Such words are as much a part of the speech patterns of eloquent orators as of inarticulate mumblers. In fact, *um* seems to become part of our vocabulary before age three.[1]

Words such as *um, er,* or *uh* can help get the speech process going. You may use *ums* when you have several options for completing a thought while speaking. Using *ums, ers,* and *uhs* is also a way of filling silence so that someone doesn't interrupt you while you are talking. Thus, an *um* can mean that you're thinking about the way to phrase the next sentence or that you are searching for a word.

In a presentation, it is perfectly okay to have a few of these short filler phrases—not five or six per sentence, but an occasional interruption that makes your speech sound natural and conversational. You may think that *ums* are bad because you notice them when a speaker is bad. Eloquent speakers use them, too, but their *ums* go unnoticed because they are fluent, confident, and compelling.[2]

After putting your worries about using an occasional *uh* and *um* aside, you can start eliminating some of the more annoying filler phrases as well as reducing excessive use of *uh* and *um*.

1. National Geographic for AP Special Features, "The 'Um' Factor: What People Say Between Thoughts," *Baltimore Sun,* 28 September 1992, pp. 1D and 3D.
2. National Geographic for AP Special Features, p. 3D.

Fluency

Fluency is the ability to speak smoothly without tripping over words or pausing at awkward moments. Although an audience might not notice how fluent you are, they *will* notice when something interrupts the flow of your speech.

The more you practice your presentation, the more fluent you will become. Practice will alert you to words, phrases, and sentences that look good in your notes but sound awkward or choppy when spoken. You'll find out if you have included any words that you have trouble pronouncing. Practice lets you work on volume, rate, pitch, and articulation. With adequate practice, your voice will sound fluent.

Filler Phrases. Many people have the habit of using annoying filler phrases, a very common fluency problem. Annoying filler phrases, you know, like a, okay, break up, um, your fluency and, uh, drive your audience, right, like crazy. Everyone knows how annoying and distracting it can be to listen to a presentation loaded with filler phrases. Who hasn't sat in the back of a classroom or auditorium and counted the number of times a speaker said, "You know" or "okay"? Unfortunately, most speakers don't even know they're doing it.

In addition to filler words and phrases such as "you know," "okay," "like," and "right," some speakers have their own personal phrases—"Got it?" "There!" "Yup," and the unwarranted giggle that appears when it absolutely shouldn't. It doesn't matter what the phrase is. It only matters that you become aware of how often you use it and then try to stop.

Tape-record one of your practice sessions or an actual presentation and listen for filler phrases. Sometimes they appear only during your actual presentation, when you are most nervous and least aware of the extra phrases that can sneak into your speech. Then comes the hard part. In order to break the filler phrase habit, you must slow down and listen to yourself as you practice. At first, you will be less fluent, stopping at almost every phrase, correcting yourself. Monitor your practice sessions and performances as well as your everyday speech. Filler phrases cannot be turned off at the beginning of a presentation and allowed to reappear afterwards. As in breaking any habit, going "cold turkey" requires saying *no* to filler phrases in *all* speaking situations.

Run-on Sentences. The second cousins of filler phrases are run-on sentences. Sometimes, because a speaker is nervous and is trying hard to maintain fluency, she or he may have a tendency to connect all sentences with *and* or *uh* and keep going, even though there may have been several natural places to stop and begin another sentence during the speech. Notice how the last sentence could have ended after *uh* but instead used the word *and* to keep going. In a few cases, student speakers have managed to utter a seven-minute sentence rather than give a seven-minute presentation.

As with breaking the filler-phrase habit, you need to slow down and listen to yourself. Even better, tape-record your practice sessions and listen for run-on sentences. For practice purposes, write out a few sections of your presentation in manuscript form to make sure that your sentences are short. Practice those sections in order to get a feel for speaking in smaller units. Then apply that feeling to your entire presentation.

Clarity and Correctness

A strong, well-paced, optimally pitched voice that is also fluent and expressive may not be enough to ensure the successful delivery of a presentation. Clarity and correctness also matter. A million-dollar vocal instrument will have little value if you mumble and mispronounce words. Proper articulation and pronunciation are just as important as volume, rate, pitch, fluency, and inflection.

FACTORS AFFECTING CLARITY AND CORRECTNESS

Articulation
Pronunciation
Accents and dialects

Articulation

Articulation is a term that describes your diction or how clearly you make the sounds in the words of a language. Poor articulation is often described as "sloppy speech," "lazy tongue," or just plain mumbling. If friends ask, "What?" after you've said something, they are rarely asking you to speak louder; they are asking you to articulate.

You can improve and practice your articulation. Generally, it helps to speak a little more slowly and a bit more loudly and to open your mouth a little wider than you usually do. Speakers whose lips barely move and whose teeth barely part let their words get trapped and jumbled in their mouths. The result is mumbling.

Certain sounds account for most articulation problems. The culprits are combined words, "ing" endings, and final consonants. If someone said, "Firs, I'm gonna telya watsumata with sayin and readin thisenens," you might be able to translate it as "First, I am going to tell you what's the matter with saying and reading this sentence." Many of us combine words—"what's the matter" becomes "watsumata"; "going to" becomes "gonna." Some of us shorten the "ing" sound to an "in" sound: "sayin" instead of "saying." And others leave off final consonants such as the *t* in "first."

The final consonants that get left off most often are the ones that pop out of your mouth in a mini-explosion. Because these consonants—*p, b, t, d, k, g*—cannot be hummed like an "m" or hissed like an "s," it's easy to lose them at the end of a word. Although you can hear the difference between "Rome" and "rose," poor articulation can make it difficult to hear the difference between "rack" and "rag," "hit" and "hid," or "tap" and "tab," to give a few examples. Make a note of words that end with these consonants and practice articulating the final sounds.

Pronunciation

Pronunciation refers to whether you say a word correctly—whether you put all the correct sounds in the correct order with the correct stress. It can be embarrassing to mispronounce a common word. Once one of us heard a speaker give a presentation on the importance of pronunciation, but she undermined her effectiveness by referring to "pro*nounc*iation" throughout her speech! Finding a word's correct pronunciation is not difficult; look it up in a dictionary or listen to someone who knows how to pronounce the word. Speakers who don't take the time to check their pronunciation may find themselves embarrassed in front of an audience.

Pronunciation errors fall into five general categories. Speakers add sounds, subtract sounds, substitute sounds, reverse sounds, and misplace stress. Figure 15.2 shows examples of each kind of error.

Figure 15.2 Common Mispronunciations

Correct Spelling	Correct Pronunciation	Incorrect Pronunciation	Type of Error
across	uh-kraws	uhkrawst	Added sound
nuclear	nooklear	nookyoolear	Added sound
pronounce	pronauns	pronaunseate	Added sound
surprise	serprize	suprize	Subtracted sound
shouldn't	shoud'nt	shount	Subtracted sound
picture	pikcher	picher	Subtracted sound
deaf	def	deef	Substituted sound
chasm	kazm	chazm	Substituted sound
both	both	bof	Substituted sound
Detroit	det*roit*	*de*troit	Misplaced stress
theater	theater	the*a*ter	Misplaced stress
police	po*lees*	*po*less	Misplaced stress
larynx	larinks	larniks	Reversed sound
ask	ask	aks	Reversed sound
relevant	relevant	revelant	Reversed sound

Real World Real Speakers

Mispronunciations Can Be Costly

A professional colleague of ours told us this story about the importance of correct pronunciation:

I once attended a critical meeting with officers from a large corporate foundation and staff members from my college. We were seeking a substantial grant for our institution. Admittedly, the name of the corporation was long and difficult to pronounce. However, when introductions were being made around the conference table, a college official mispronounced the name of the foundation. It got worse and worse as each of the corporate officers was introduced with his or her corporate title. Within seconds, the rest of us at the table knew that we had jeopardized our chance for a donation. One mispronounced word cost us thousands of dollars.

Pronunciations can and do change. According to most pronunciation dictionaries, the word *often* should be pronounced "ofen," but many people now accept "of*t*en" as an acceptable pronunciation. The word *a* should be pronounced "uh," not rhyme with "hay," but many people now use both versions. When the word *the* appears before the sound of a consonant as in "the table" or "the dog," it should be pronounced "thuh." When *the* comes before the sound of a vowel, as in "the apple" or "the ambulance," it should be pronounced "thee." However, many people no longer make these distinctions. One way to look at pronunciation is to ask whether the way you pronounce a word will call attention to it. In front of a group of voice and diction teachers, "thuh apple" would be distracting and annoying. In front of a general audience, "thuh apple" might go unnoticed.

Accents and Dialects

When teaching or coaching speakers from other countries, we are often asked, "How can I get rid of my accent?" The honest answer to this question is that in most cases, you can't. The better answer is this: Why do you want to? An accent generally won't hinder your ability to communicate. Sometimes, in fact, an accent can add charm and interest to your presentation. In other cases, however, a heavy accent can distract an audience and can subsequently reduce your effectiveness. Before you try to change your accent, there are a few things you should learn about accents and dialects.

An **accent** is the sound of one language imposed on another.[11] Some Asian speakers have difficulty producing the "r" and "v" sounds in English. Spanish speakers often make the "i" sound in a word like *sister* sound like a long

FAQ

When Is It Acceptable to Use an Ethnic Dialect?

At first this may sound like a question that treads the dangerous territory of political correctness. After all, many southerners don't say, "Sho 'nuf," and most African Americans don't say, "My brother, he sick." Does that make southerners and African Americans who don't use these phrases better speakers than those who do?

For years a fierce debate has raged over whether there should be a standardized and official English language in the United States. It's not likely to be settled anytime soon. Those who want everyone to speak Standard American English argue that a common language will keep the country strong, literate, and unified. Those who argue against a common standard language recognize that such rules put immigrants and minority Americans at a significant disadvantage and take some of the richness out of our language. Didn't Lyndon Johnson, Martin Luther King Jr., and Jimmy Carter speak in southern dialects? Didn't John F. Kennedy speak with a Boston dialect?

In fact, it seems that some dialects are more acceptable than others. Is it okay to say, "Y'all come down now" but not acceptable to say, "He sick"? In the end, the answers depend on several factors. Ask yourself whether your decision to use an ethnic dialect in your presentation is suitable for the purpose, occasion, and audience. If you're not sure, monitor your presentation for "down-home" or "old-country" lingo that could offend or confuse your audience.

A tour guide without a microphone shows a group of visitors around the Roman and Byzantine ruins at Bet Shean, Israel. What kind of delivery challenges do such guides face?

"e" sound, as in *see.* Eastern Europeans may substitute a "v" for the "w" sound. Many non-English speakers have difficulty making the "th" sound. While listening to two colleagues—one from Thailand, the other from the former Yugoslavia—we heard the Thai speaker say that he was "wehwee worried" about a student and the Yugoslavian saying that she was also "very vorried." It's important to note that both of these speakers were rated as excellent teachers and communicators. Their accents did not inhibit the speakers from expressing themselves; nor did they prevent us from understanding what the speakers said.

Dialects differ from accents because they represent regional and cultural differences within the same language. What people call a southern accent is really a southern dialect. The phrase "pahking the cah in the Hahvahd yahd" demonstrates a Boston dialect, not an accent. Is it acceptable to say, "Y'all" and "Sho 'nuf" if you are a southerner? Is it acceptable for some African Americans and speakers of street lingo to say, "My brother, he sick"? If you answer these questions according to the rules of Standard American English,[12] the answer is *no.* Does that mean a speaker should never use "Y'all" and "He sick"? Again, the answer is *no.*

Although we can't answer all the arguments or resolve the debate about accents and dialects, we will take a position regarding presentation speaking. Whether standard or nonstandard, the language you use is a means to an end, a way of achieving the purpose of your presentation. Because words are the basic building blocks of a presentation, it is your choice which building blocks to use. If "y'all" or "he sick" is difficult for you to change or is the way you *want* to be heard, you run a risk. An audience that doesn't like or has trouble listening to that particular dialect may be distracted or even turned off by your presentation. In fact, a consistent finding across many research studies is that Standard American English speakers are judged as more intelligent, ambitious, and successful, even when the judges themselves speak

Real World Real Speakers

Learn the Local "Language"

I was born in Jersey City, New Jersey, and spoke in a very strong Jersey/New York dialect. When my family moved to a town where Standard American English was spoken, my speech was greeted with laughter. I decided that it was time for me to learn a second language—Standard American English. With the help of a tireless speech teacher, I learned the "proper" way to speak. But at the same time, I could speak pure Jersey whenever I was with my family and friends from New Jersey and New York.

I learned the same lesson when I spent a year teaching in Australia. I learned that a "subject" in Australian colleges is the same as a U.S. college course and a "course" is the same as a major or program. I learned to follow "timetables" instead of "schedules" and permitted my students to bring "rubbers" (erasers) to final exams. In order to be understood, I tried to speak Australian. Over time, even the sound of my American dialect changed. Although I will never sound like an Australian, at least I made the effort to sound less harsh to the Australian listener. So now I speak three "languages"—Standard American English, New Jersey, and a bit of Australian. Of course, all of these "languages" are different dialects of English. All of them are useful tools or building blocks that I can use in a presentation.

Isa Engleberg
Author

in a nonstandard American dialect.[13] On the other hand, an audience that expects to hear your natural dialect may think that you are talking down to them if you use Standard American English. As is so often the case, knowing your audience is the key to achieving your purpose.

If words are building blocks, the more blocks you have to choose from, the better. Just as you would dress differently for different speaking situations, you may sometimes want to change the way you use words. This can be a difficult but not impossible task, as both of us have learned during the course of living and working in many different places.

Having a strong accent or dialect does not stop anyone from being a strong speaker. Many years ago, one of us heard Dr. Elisabeth Kübler-Ross, who had a soft voice and a strong German accent, speak at a medical school graduation. Dr. Kübler-Ross's book *On Death and Dying* had brought her international attention and fame on the topic of caring for dying patients. During the first few minutes of her address, the audience strained to understand what she was saying. Yet her stories were so touching and her personality so compelling that the audience was soon captivated by her. Her accent made no difference at all.

At the same time, we don't want to minimize the importance of having an effective speaking voice. Esther-Ann Asch, a vice president with Federal Employment and Guidance Services in Manhattan, told us that she gives her voice credit for her success as a speaker: "My voice has always been the key to presenting. Because it is loud, forceful, and compelling, it gets and keeps the audience's attention."

You don't need a perfect voice to be a great speaker. You need a purposeful, well-organized message and a clear voice that helps you achieve the goal of your presentation. As long as your voice is loud enough and clear enough, you can concentrate your attention and energy on what you have to say.

Summary

Can I improve my speaking voice?

By further developing vocal characteristics that you already have—such as breath control, volume, rate, pitch, fluency, articulation, and pronunciation—you can improve the effectiveness of your speaking voice.

Can I speak loudly enough without feeling as though I'm shouting?

Yes, if you are willing to use your naturally loud voice and to project to the back of the room. Ask a friend or sympathetic listener to monitor your volume and to alert you to any problems.

Can I speak slowly enough to be understood without putting everyone to sleep?

Yes, if you time yourself and then try to adjust your speed to the message, room, and audience. Remember that most presenters speak too fast, not too slowly.

What's the best pitch for my voice?

Don't assume that a lower pitch is a better pitch. Instead, find your optimum pitch and try using it in all of your daily speaking situations. Make sure that syllables, words, and phrases receive the appropriate inflection and stress.

How can I avoid stumbling over words?

In addition to practicing your presentation, avoid using an excessive number of filler phrases and run-on sentences.

How can I speak more clearly and accurately?

Generally, you can improve your articulation by speaking a little more slowly and a bit more loudly and by opening your mouth a little wider than you usually do, while watching out for combined words, "ing" endings, and final consonants. Also, avoid mispronunciations by looking up questionable words in a dictionary before your presentation and by practicing words that are difficult to pronounce.

How can I get rid of my accent?

There is nothing wrong with having an accent or speaking in a dialect. If you speak clearly and accurately, your audience should understand you and your message.

Presentation Principles in Action

Customized Pronunciation Drills

Directions: The following chart lists some commonly mispronounced words. You may add other pronunciation errors unique to the area in which you live as well as those listed earlier in the chapter. Using the words on the list, create sentences that use as many of these frequently mispronounced words as possible. The sentences must be grammatically correct but can and probably will be unusual or nonsensical in content.

Example: Both Italian athletes were impotent once they were asked to take a picture of the wolf's larynx.

After reviewing the entire list of words and their correct pronunciations, read your sentences either to a small group or to the entire class. Listeners should identify any words that are mispronounced while also paying attention to the speaker's volume, rate, pitch, fluency, and articulation. It is important to note correct pronunciations of the word *the* before consonants ("thuh") and vowels ("thee") as well as the pronunciation of the word *a* as "uh" rather than "ay."

Practice these pronunciation drills outside of class as well. By repeating the correct pronunciations over and over, you can transform difficult-to-pronounce words into words that you routinely pronounce correctly.

Commonly Mispronounced Words

Substituting Sounds	Omitting Sounds	Adding Sounds	Misplacing Sounds	Reversing Sounds
anesthetist	Arctic	accompanist	applicable	entrepreneur
agile	asphyxiate	across	epitome	e pluribus unum
chasm	berserk	athlete	guitar	hundred
et cetera	Caribbean	corps	impotent	introduction
genuine	couldn't	escape	infamous	irrelevant
Italian	February	heir	mischievous	larynx
pitcher	library	nuclear	omnipotent	perspiration
pronunciation	picture	often	preferable	prescription
strength	recognize	schism	theater	professor

Source: Pronunciation word lists based on Lyle V. Mayer, *Fundamentals of Voice and Articulation,* 11th ed. (Madison, WI: Brown & Benchmark, 1996), pp. 154–263; and Lyle V. Mayer, *Fundamentals of Voice and Articulation,* 13th ed. (Boston: McGraw-Hill, 2004), pp. 256–260.

Key Terms

Notes

1 Lyle V. Mayer, *Fundamentals of Voice and Articulation,* 13th ed. (Boston: McGraw-Hill, 2004), p. 8.
2 Mayer, p. 18.
3 Ethel C. Glenn, Phillip J. Glenn, and Sandra Forman, *Your Voice and Articulation,* 4th ed. (Boston: Allyn & Bacon, 1998), pp. 30–31.
4 Jeffrey C. Hahner, Martin A. Sokoloff, and Sandra L. Salisch, *Speaking Clearly: Improving Voice and Diction,* 6th ed. (New York: McGraw-Hill, 2002), pp. 280–281.
5 Mayer (2004), p. 66.
6 Lyle V. Mayer, *Fundamentals of Voice and Articulation,* 11th ed. (Madison, WI: Brown & Benchmark, 1996), p. 62.
7 Authors of voice and articulation textbooks generally agree that a useful, all-purpose speaking rate is around 145 to 180 words per minute. See Lyle V. Mayer, *Fundamentals of Voice and Articulation,* 12th ed. (Boston: McGraw-Hill, 2004); Jeffrey C. Hahner, Martin A. Sokoloff, and Sandra L. Salisch, *Speaking Clearly: Improving Voice and Diction,* 6th ed. (New York: McGraw-Hill, 2002); Ethel C. Glenn, Phillip J. Glenn, and Sandra Forman, *Your Voice and Articulation,* 4th ed. (Boston: Allyn & Bacon, 1998).
8 Comprehensive descriptions of and guidelines for achieving optimum pitch can be found in a classic voice and diction textbook: Hilda B. Fisher, *Improving Voice and Articulation* (Boston: Houghton Mifflin, 1966), pp. 162–174.
9 Hahner, Sokoloff, and Salisch, p. 326.
10 A glossary of "Valley Girl Speak" can be found in Jim Crotty, *How to Talk American: A Guide to Our Native Tongues* (Boston: Houghton Mifflin, 1997), pp. 166–167.
11 Glenn, Glenn, and Forman (p. 8) define a dialect as a "variation pattern of speech features within a given language that is characteristic of certain native speakers. By contrast, an accent usually refers to patterns from a speaker's native language spilling over into the production of a second language; thus, a person from Paris might speak English with a French accent. Dialects can vary on a number of features including vocabulary, rhythm, and pronunciation. These variations may mark certain geographic areas (New Orleans, Boston, Brooklyn), ethnic and national groups (Black, Hispanic, Eastern European), and socioeconomic distinctions (upper class, working class)."
12 Glenn, Glenn, and Forman (pp. 8–9) point out that "in the United States, one particular dialect—Standard American English—has gained widespread acceptance.... Standard American English is a dialect, and in this country it is the dialect most commonly accepted and employed in the entertainment, education, business, and political worlds."
13 Glenn, Glenn, and Forman, p. 10.

chapter sixteen

Physical Delivery

- Why is eye contact so important?
- Can I control my facial expressions?
- Which gestures work best during a presentation?
- How should I stand and move during a presentation?
- How do I deliver a presentation on radio, on camera, or online?

A natural delivery style tells your audience a great deal about who you are and how much you care about reaching them. An audience-centered speaker is a natural speaker, and naturalness makes your personality an integral part of your performance. Audiences feel comfortable when *you* seem comfortable. When you appear competent and confident, they can relax and listen. Naturalness lets the real you come through. However, being natural doesn't mean "letting it all hang out." Rather, it means being so well prepared and well practiced that your presentation is an authentic reflection of you. During such a presentation, your eye contact, facial expressions, gestures, posture, and movement will not draw attention to themselves. Your movement will support and highlight your presentation's important words and ideas. In this chapter, we explain how to achieve this natural physical delivery style.

Making a Good Physical Impression

Audience members jump to conclusions about speakers on the basis of first impressions of their appearance. Even though such snap judgments may seem unfair, you've probably made them yourself. The ways in which you stand, move, gesture, and make eye contact will have a significant impact on your presentation.

Although you can change these aspects of your physical delivery, there's one thing you cannot change: your body. However, you *can* compensate for or adapt to the place where you will be speaking. If you are short, a small platform behind the lectern can make the difference between being hidden and being seen and will also let you see your audience. If you need glasses, wear them. Accommodate to the things you can't change, but control those you can. As in the case of your voice, special skills and strategies can help you practice and improve the way that you physically deliver a presentation.

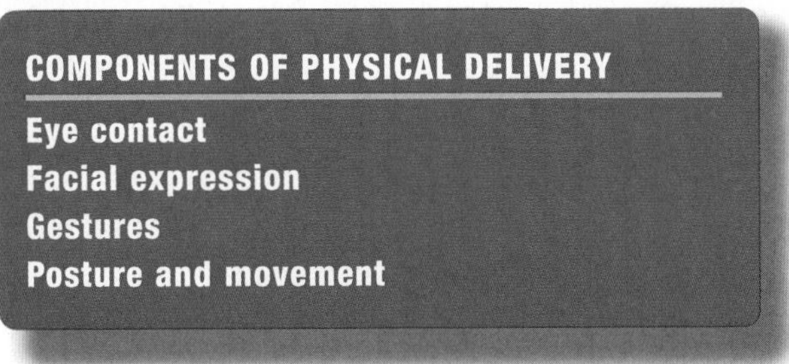

Eye Contact

Eye contact may be the single most important component of effective physical delivery. Quite simply, **eye contact** is establishing and maintaining visual links with individual members of your audience. Communication scholars, speech teachers, authors of popular public speaking books, and experienced presenters overwhelmingly agree that eye contact is critical because it initiates and controls communication, affects speaker credibility, and provides the speaker with a means of assessing listener feedback.

Control. When you want to speak with someone, you "catch her eye" to initiate communication. The same is true in a presentation. When you establish initial eye contact with your audience, you indicate that you are ready to begin speaking and that they should get ready to listen. Lack of eye contact communicates a message, too: It says that you don't care to connect with your audience. After all, if you don't look at your audience, why should they look at you?

Not only does eye contact initiate communication; it also has the power to make people listen. Every good teacher, preacher, police officer, and political candidate knows that "giving the eye" to inattentive listeners is one of the best ways to get and keep their attention. Direct eye contact says, "I'm talking to *you;* I want *you* to hear this." Direct eye contact transforms the speaker from an impersonal messenger into someone worth listening to.

Credibility. Eye contact can also have a direct and positive effect on your credibility.[1] It says:

- *I'm of good character.* I care enough to share this important message with you.
- *I'm competent.* I know this subject so well that I can leave my notes and look at you.
- *I'm charismatic.* I want to energize and connect with everyone in this room.

In everyday conversation, avoiding eye contact can indicate disinterest, insincerity, or deception. By looking directly at your audience, you demonstrate your dedication to open and honest communication. People who seek and maintain eye contact while speaking, whether face to face or before an audience of thousands, tend to be more believable.

Feedback. Making eye contact is the best way to gauge audience feedback during your presentation. At first, looking at your audience members eye to eye may distract you. Some people may smile, others may look bored or confused, and some may be looking around the room or passing notes to friends. With all of this going on in the audience, it's easy for you to become sidetracked wondering why you're getting so many different reactions.

Receiving all of those different responses can be unsettling until you realize that being aware of such responses is the very reason that you must establish and maintain eye contact. By looking at the individual members of your audience, you can tell whether they are interested, bored, delighted, or displeased. Speakers who don't look at their audiences rarely have a clue about why their presentations succeed or fail. Yes, audience reactions can be distracting, but they also give back more than they take. Eye contact gives you a wealth of information about the audience's reactions to you and your presentation. Moreover, when you see that your audience is attentive and interested, you may gain more confidence and enthusiasm.

Should I Imagine My Audience Naked?

Despite and perhaps because of its importance, eye contact has inspired numerous myths. We've had clients say that they've been told to look over and between the heads of the people in their audiences. Others have been told to find a spot on the back wall or one friendly face to look at throughout a presentation. Some have even been given the absurd suggestion that they should imagine their audience members without their clothes on—the best argument we've ever heard for *not* looking at your audience. Coming closer to receiving good advice—but not yet there—are the speakers who have been trained to move their gaze by looking at groups of people in every section of the room (a tactic which works well with audiences of one thousand but not with twenty listeners). Then there are those who have been told to move their gaze up and down or across every row. In all of these situations, the speakers were told not to look directly at individual listeners or to look at them as inanimate objects.

These myths and misconceptions about eye contact border on the ridiculous. They just don't work. Staring at a clock at the back of a room can make you look like a zombie or a sleepwalker. Imagining an audience naked not only insults the people you want to influence but also can be terribly distracting. Looking up and down every aisle is more suitable for mowing the lawn than for making a presentation. There's no "trick" to eye contact. Just look at individual people in your audience—eye to eye.

BENEFITS OF EYE CONTACT

Initiates and controls communication
Enhances speaker credibility
Provides feedback

Eye Contact Techniques. Talk to audience members in the same way that you would talk to a friend, coworker, client, or customer. This doesn't mean staring at them until they squirm in their seats; rather, it means catching their eye for a few seconds, saying something, and then moving on to someone else. Don't establish eye contact row by row as though you're taking roll. Move your gaze around the room, settle on someone, and establish direct eye contact. Then switch to someone else—someone sitting near the person whom you just looked at or someone all the way across the room.

Don't move your eyes in a rigid pattern but do try to establish eye contact with as many individual people as you can. It's very tempting to direct your eye contact at people sitting directly in front of you or at those who seem friendliest or most interested. Instead, try to look at the person seated farthest away from you just as often as you look at the person directly in front of you. Look at the people seated off to one side as often as you look at those in the center.

Amount of Eye Contact. Generally, the more eye contact you have with your audience, the more personal and responsive your presentation will be. So how much is enough? Ideally, you should maintain eye contact with your audience during most of your entire presentation. This is easiest to do in impromptu and extemporaneous presentations or in memorized speeches. Note that we said *most;* it would be unnatural to keep your eyes glued to your audience 100 percent of the time. An occasional look around the room, a glance at your hands, a peek at the clock, or a reference to a presentation aid adds naturalness and gives your eyes a brief rest.

Even when using a set of notes, you should maintain as much eye contact as you can—at least 75 percent of your speaking time. If you are using a manuscript, you should know your script so well that you can glance at the page, see a whole line of words, look up, and say them without having to read from the script word for word.

One useful method for maximizing eye contact when using detailed notes or a manuscript is called **eye scan.** Eye scan involves training your eyes to glance at a specific section of your notes or manuscript, to focus on a phrase or sentence, to glance back up at your audience, and to speak. Begin by placing your thumb and index finger on one side of the page to frame the section of your notes or the manuscript that you are using—to make sure that you don't lose your place on the page.[2] Then, as you approach the end of a phrase or sentence within that section, glance down again and visually grasp the next phrase to be spoken. Keep moving your thumb and index finger down the page as you move through each section. Eye scanning helps you maintain maximum eye contact without losing your place. Even when discussing a highly technical or complex topic, you should practice enough beforehand in order to be able to look at your audience most of the time.

With an audience of thirty or fewer people, it's usually possible to make eye contact with each person. In most cases, limit your eye contact to three to five seconds with any one person. Otherwise, the listener may become uncomfortable and feel singled out. If your audience is much larger than thirty or forty people, you may find it necessary to look instead at different sections of the audience. Focus on one or two individuals in the group of people closest to you; then look at a few people in the far corners of the room—to the right, center, and left. Even if the glare of stage lights prevents you from seeing anyone's face clearly, do your best to direct your eyes to different parts of the audience as if you could zero in on a single person. Many successful performers and public officials have mastered this technique. They appear to establish eye contact even when the spotlights are virtually blinding them. Making eye contact reassures listeners that you are trying to reach them with your message.

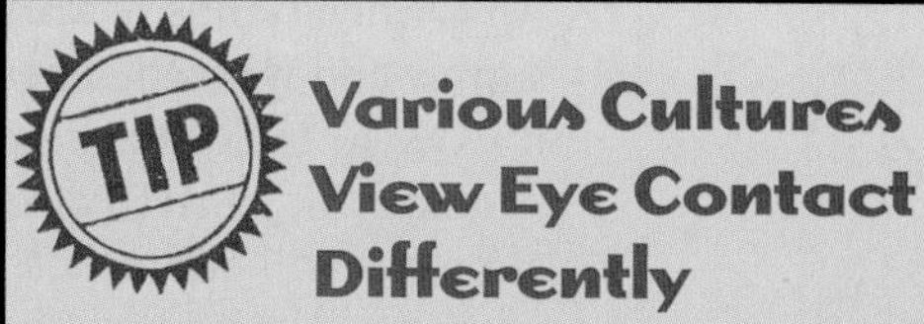

Various Cultures View Eye Contact Differently

Although many cultures place a high value on establishing and maintaining eye contact, not all do. For example, intercultural communication experts Guo-Ming Chen and William Starosta note that "direct eye contact is a taboo or an insult in many Asian cultures. Cambodians consider direct eye contact as an invasion of one's privacy. In ancient China, only a 'bad' girl or a prostitute would look straight into the eyes of males, whereas the English consider such gazing attentive listening." Likewise, they discuss how one source of racial tension in the United States may be differences in eye contact. They contend, "White Americans tend to look at their communication partner more when they are listening than talking, but African Americans use more eye contact when they are talking, than when they are listening."[1]

Direct eye contact with elders is perceived as disrespectful by some Native Americans and in some Asian cultures. Navajos avoid the direct, open-face gaze, even when shaking hands with someone whom they are very glad to see. To maintain direct eye contact is to display anger. [2]

Although various cultures view eye contact differently, most speakers in the United States try to maintain direct eye contact with most members of their audience. Why? Because, in general, U.S. audiences perceive such speakers as strong and effective presenters. At the same time, we urge you to be cautious when addressing a culturally diverse audience. If you sense discomfort when your establish eye contact with an audience member, look away. Experienced speakers have learned to sense when direct eye contact is appropriate while avoiding gazing directly at audience members who appear uncomfortable.

1. Guo-Ming Chen and William J. Starosta, *Foundations of Intercultural Communication* (Boston: Allyn & Bacon, 1998), p. 91.
2. Everett M. Rogers and Thomas M. Steinfatt, *Intercultural Communication* (Prospect Heights, IL: Waveland, 1999), pp. 174-175.

Facial Expression

Whether you are speaking to one person or to one hundred people, your audience will be watching your face, trying to read your facial expression. According to Mark Knapp and Judith Hall, experts in nonverbal communication, your face reflects your attitudes and emotional states, provides nonverbal feedback, and next to the words that you speak, is the primary source of information about you.[3]

Despite the enormous consequences of facial expression, it is difficult to control. Generally, we tend to display a particular style of facial expression. Some people show little expression—they have a serious, "poker" face most of the time. Others are "like an open book"—you have little doubt about how they feel. It's very difficult, therefore, to make a poker face into an open book—or vice versa. Adding to the difficulty are the effects of nervousness. A nervous speaker may be too distracted to smile, too frightened to stop smiling, or too giddy to register displeasure or anger when it's appropriate.

Unless your topic is very solemn or serious, we recommend that you try to smile. A smile shows your listeners that you are comfortable and eager to share your ideas and information. Smiles can even change behavior.[4] Audience members are more likely to smile if *you* smile. By smiling back, they reciprocate the positive bond that you, the speaker, have established.

Try this exercise. Read this short paragraph aloud while frowning. Then read it over again with a small smile on your face. Which version sounded better? In most cases, it's much easier to speak while smiling. So smile!

Although we sincerely recommend smiling, a smile can be inappropriate if it does not reflect what you feel or if it contradicts your message. A big goofy smile would clash with a presentation on the crisis of AIDS in prisons. At the same time, a small smile might relieve tension if you're talking about the discipline it takes to study for exams, lose weight, or stop smoking. But if you can't seem to smile naturally, don't.

An artificial smile is worse than no smile at all. In *Speak Smart,* Thomas Mira puts it simply and well when he writes: "If you're happy, it's important to smile. If you're sad, it's OK to look sad. If you're angry, it's fine to look angry. If you're frustrated, you should look frustrated. If you allow your face to communicate your feelings,... your audience will appreciate that you are being honest with them, even if they disagree with you."[5] In the end, the best advice we can offer is this: Let your face do what comes naturally. If you communicate your message honestly and sincerely, your facial expression will be appropriate and effective.

Gestures

A **gesture** is a body movement that conveys or reinforces a thought, an intention, or an emotion. Most gestures are made with the hands and arms, but the shrug of a shoulder, bending of a knee, and tapping of a foot are gestures, too. Gestures can clarify and support your words, help you relieve nervous tension, arouse audience attention, and function as a visual aid. Gestures make you more interesting to watch and therefore more interesting to listen to.

We can't really tell you how to gesture, in part because you already know how to do it. You gesture every day—when you speak to friends, family members, coworkers, and even perfect strangers. Sure, you may say, but that's not the same kind of gesture you need for a presentation. Remember, though, that a presentation is, first and last, speaking. Nevertheless, we've often seen naturally graceful and energetic people become stiff and straight as a stick when they speak in front of a group. Why? They become so worried about how they look and how to gesture that they stop doing what comes naturally. Sometimes we'll ask a stiff speaker a few easy questions at the end of a presentation, such as "Could you tell me more about this?" or "How did you first become interested in that?" In the blink of an eye, the speaker will start gesturing, moving naturally, and showing a lot of expression. This person will have stopped thinking about how he or she looks in order to answer our question.

What Should I Do with My Hands?

We hear this question all the time, and our answer is deceptively simple: Do what you normally do with your hands. If you gesture a lot, keep doing what comes naturally. If you rarely gesture, don't try to invent new and unnatural hand movements. Steve Allen, the comedian, songwriter, and author, put it this way:

> *Simply do with your hands what you would if you were talking to members of your family. Put one hand in your jacket pocket and gesture with the other.... Scratch your nose if it itches, make a gesture if it illustrates a story or point, or clasp both hands behind your back. It's not a big deal unless you make it one.*[1]

1. Steve Allen, *How to Make a Speech* (New York: McGraw-Hill, 1986), p. 67.

Effective Gestures. Despite our advice about "doing what comes naturally," there are some techniques that can liberate and animate your hands during a presentation. Begin by linking your gestures to a specific word, concept, or object. For example, introduce the number of main points in your presentation by holding up the correct number of fingers. Then, lift one finger for the first point, two fingers for the second, and so on. If you are describing an object, you can use your hands to trace its shape or size in the air. If you are telling a story in which someone scratches his head, points in a direction, or reaches into his pocket, you can do the same. If you're talking about alternatives, illustrate them on one hand and then on the other hand. But remember, if none of these gestures come naturally or improve with practice, avoid them.

Finally, try to adjust your gestures to the space in which you are speaking. If you are being videotaped close up or are talking to a small group, your gestures should be smaller and closer to your face. If you are speaking to a large audience in a large space, make your gestures bigger,

A police chief talks about the department's proactive style and open system of communication at a meeting with police administrators. How does his physical delivery reinforce his message?

broader, and more vigorous. An audience member a hundred feet away will have trouble seeing a small gesture. Conversely, an audience member sitting three feet away from you may have to duck if your gesture is too sweeping.

Peggy Noonan, former speechwriter for Ronald Reagan, describes a whole industry that exists to tell people how to move their hands while giving a presentation. It's one of the reasons, she maintains, why so many politicians and TV journalists look and gesture alike. "You don't have to be smooth; your audience is composed of Americans, and they've seen smooth. Instead, be you. They haven't seen that yet."[6]

Effective gestures are a natural outgrowth of what you feel and what you have to say. If you start thinking about your gestures, you are likely to appear awkward, unnatural, and forced. Rather than thinking about your hands, think about your message. In all likelihood, your gestures will join forces with your emotions in a natural and spontaneous mixture of verbal and nonverbal communication.

Ineffective Gestures. Unless you have a lot of speaking or acting experience, it's very difficult to plan your gestures. In fact, it's downright dangerous because most preplanned gestures look artificial and awkward. When speakers try to preplan their gestures in the same way that they would plan a dance step, the results can be ineffective and even comical. Figure 16.1 lists some common problem gestures.

Almost any gesture is acceptable if it occurs occasionally and appropriately. Clasping your hands in front of your body is okay if it isn't the only way you position your hands. Adjusting your glasses is fine if they need adjusting. The problem arises when you don't vary your gestures. If you use the same gestures over and over, your audience may begin counting them. As soon as your gestures fall into a pattern, your physical delivery becomes distracting.

As difficult as planned gestures are to execute well, becoming aware of unplanned, distracting ones can be even harder. A **fidget** is a small, repetitive movement, a physical filler phrase. Constantly pushing up on your eyeglasses, tapping a lectern with a pencil, jingling change or keys in your pocket, playing with a necklace or tie, swaying

Figure 16.1

Problem Gestures

	**The Fig Leaf**	Hands gripped together in front of the groin
	**The Handcuffs**	Hands gripped together behind the back
	**The Banker**	Rattling coins or keys in pocket
	**The Beautician**	Twirling a lock of hair, or continuously pushing hair away from face
	**The Gunfighter**	Both arms hanging stiffly away from both sides
	**The Death Grip**	White knuckled grip on the lecturn, pointer, or notes
	**The Optician**	Constantly adjusting eyeglasses
	**The Gadget Gripper**	Playing with pointers, pens, markers
	**The Church Builder**	Keeping hands in a steeple position in front of your face

back and forth, repeatedly hiking up your pants and tucking in your shirt, and pulling on a favorite ear lobe or hair curl are all fidgets. One of the easiest ways to stop fidgeting is to videotape and then watch your practice session. Once you see how often you jingle change or sway back and forth, you'll never want to inflict your fidgets on an audience again.

Gestures and Culture. People all over the world "talk" with their hands. The meanings of gestures, however, may be quite different in different cultures—both domestic and international. Everett Rogers and Thomas Steinfatt share a story about a U.S. professor teaching at Bangkok University in Thailand. The professor frequently put his hands in his pockets or held them behind his back while lecturing to his class. At the end of the semester, his polite Thai students gently informed him that individuals should hold their hands in front of them. They had been embarrassed and distracted by his nonverbal cultural error during the class.[7]

Most of our hand gestures are culturally determined. One of the best examples is a gesture that looks like this:

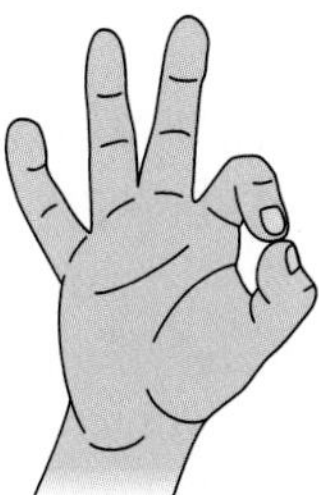

In the United States, this gesture usually means that everything is "A-okay." The same gesture can also be a sign for the sex act in some Latin American nations. To the French, the sign may indicate that someone is a "zero," and to people in Malta, it is an invitation to have homosexual sex.[8]

Even within the United States, similar gestures can have different meanings. For example, the vertical horn sign has different meanings to each of your coauthors.

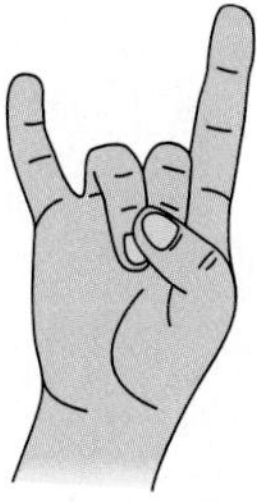

To one of us—a professor at the University of Texas at Austin—the sign represents the proud Texas Longhorn mascot of the university. To the other—born and raised on the East Coast—the gesture is a rude way of cursing someone or calling another person a cuckold, that is, a man married to an unfaithful wife.

In most speaking situations—both within and outside of the United States—certain gestures can trigger negative responses from an audience. Pointing or wagging the index finger at your audience, for example, may be seen as rude and offensive because it is associated with parental scolding. Several European leaders and commentators expressed irritation and even anger when President George W. Bush gestured this way while arguing for European support of military action against Iraq.

Instead of pointing your index finger at your audience, try gesturing with an open hand—fingers together, palm and inner wrist turned slightly toward the audience, forearm slightly bent and extended at about a 45-degree angle to the side (not aimed directly *at* the audience).[9]

If you have a favorite gesture, make sure that it serves its intended purpose. As with language, the meaning of gestures is not universal. Consider the characteristics and culture of your audience when you make decisions about how and when to gesture.

Posture and Movement

Posture and movement involve how you stand and move and whether your movements add to or detract from your presentation. Inexperienced speakers rarely worry about posture and movement because they believe that once they get behind a lectern, they are there to stay. They give little thought to whether they should move from behind the lectern. However, the authors of public speaking books written for the general public urge speakers to move away from the lectern. Author Ron Hoff says, "Podiums are poison. Lecterns are lethal."[10] We don't agree. Podiums and lecterns serve important functions but must be used appropriately and with skill.

Posture. Your posture communicates. If you stand comfortably and confidently, you will radiate alertness and control. If you are stooped and unsure on your feet, you will communicate apprehension or disinterest. Not only does good posture add to your credibility; it also aids proper breathing and gives you a strong stance from

John Ghidiu, a skating instructor and rep for Rollerblade, uses "body language" in his lesson to would-be rollerbladers in the parking lot at the State University of New York, Oswego.

which to gesture. We recommend that you stand straight but not rigidly. If you lock your knees, you may become lightheaded. Your feet should be about one foot apart. Lean forward just a little instead of rocking back on your heels. And then, like a good soldier—chest out, stomach in—you'll be ready to begin. And as long as we're using clichés, don't forget to keep your chin up. Doing so will open your airways and help make your voice both clear and loud.

Movement. Generally, a certain amount of movement is a good thing during a presentation. Although it's been said that "there's nothing more boring than something that never moves,"[11] we have listened to great speakers who plant their feet on the floor, practically glue their notes or manuscript to the lectern, and proceed to captivate and delight their listeners.

At the same time, you can move around the podium or occasionally around the room to attract attention, support and emphasize a point you are making, or channel nervous energy. Movement even gives you short pauses during which you can collect your thoughts or give the audience a moment to ponder what you have said. Both of us have used movement to direct attention to an important idea or piece of information.

Should I Sit or Stand?

When it's your turn to speak, you may or may not be able to choose whether you sit or stand. For panel discussions, participants often sit behind a table at the front of a room. Nervous students often ask whether they can sit during their presentations. There are good reasons why we say *no*. First and foremost is this: You are your own best visual aid. Why hide that advantage under a table? Standing up is a way of taking charge. It's also easier to breathe for speaking if you stand. It's easier to see your audience and maintain eye contact if you stand. And it's easier to gesture if you have your full body's length to use. In addition, it's easier to move from a standing position than to get up from a chair.

We even recommend that you find a way to stand when other speakers are sitting. Get up and use a flip chart or move to the head of a conference table. By standing when everyone else is sitting, you become the focus of attention. And that's exactly what you want to be during a presentation.

Delivering Mediated Presentations

Not that long ago, the average speaker would probably not have had to consider giving **mediated presentations** on the radio or on camera. Times have changed. Although it's still unlikely that the average speaker will "go prime time," the rise of local radio stations, public access cable, video presentations, teleconferencing, and distance learning means that you should know what to do if you end up in the studio or in front of the camera.

Before suggesting delivery techniques for each of these media, we do want to note their one common characteristic: Despite the fact that radio and television can reach huge audiences, they are still very personal and even intimate forms of communication. Most people listen to the radio or watch TV on their own turf—in their cars, living rooms, or bedrooms—so the voice from the speaker or the face on the screen seems to talk directly to them. In addition, the audience at the other end of the radio or television set is as close as a good friend or colleague. Consequently, mediated presentations can be more relaxed and conversational.

Radio

Speaking on the radio is, in a sense, easier than speaking in front of a television camera. Obviously, you don't have to worry about your appearance. You don't have to worry about the amount of eye contact you maintain with audience members.

Four people speak on The Group Room radio show for cancer patients at the Los Angeles Times Health Fair. What adaptations in delivery should these speakers make during their presentations?

And you don't have to worry about having adequate volume—that's adjusted for you electronically.

Christina Stuart, a speech consultant and author, rightfully notes that the most important factor on radio is your voice and its ability to communicate enthusiasm, sincerity, and vitality.[12] Just because an audience can't see you doesn't mean that your attitude or level of commitment changes. If you are being interviewed or are on a panel, speak to the interviewer or panelists in a conversational tone, the way you would if there weren't a microphone in front of each speaker. If you apply the Chapter 15, "Vocal Delivery," techniques for developing an effective speaking voice (well, most of them—you won't need to project your voice), your radio delivery will sound clear and natural.

Rely on the radio staff to show you how to use the microphone (the Mini-Module in Chapter 15 gives some tips, too). Some staffers will tell you to keep your elbows and forearms on the table as a way of keeping yourself from leaning into the mike. Other production engineers will tell you to ignore the microphone. Follow their advice. Radio technicians are there to make you and the radio show sound good.

Television

Being on TV adds the elements of physical delivery to those of vocal delivery. Because TV is primarily a visual medium, how you look matters a lot. Don't be surprised

FAQ ? Should I Look at the Camera?

If you have never been on TV, it can be confusing when the cameras start rolling. The key thing to remember is TV's intimate nature. If you are being interviewed, act as though you are having a conversation with that person and no one else. If you are on a panel, talk to the panel members, not to the camera. When other panelists are speaking, look at them. The camera may be shooting the entire panel at any time, so don't decide to adjust your clothes or look around the studio while you're not speaking.

The only time when you should look at the camera is when you are the only person on the set or when you are addressing the viewing audience directly, as candidates do in a political forum or debate. In these cases, talk directly to the camera as though it is a person rather than a machine connected to thousands of viewers. If you will be reading from a TelePrompTer, make sure that you have practiced reading your manuscript thoroughly and know which key words and phrases to emphasize. To keep your delivery natural and sincere, treat the TelePrompTer screen as you would your notes rather than following every word with your eyes.

Making Lecterns Work for You

If your presentation is formal or your audience large, you will probably have a lectern. For more informal talks and presentations to small groups, you may have nothing more than a place to stand. Given the choice, however, most presenters prefer and ask for a lectern. The key, of course, is learning how to take advantage of a lectern without falling prey to its perils. President Clinton has two distracting lectern habits. In his desire to connect with an audience, he often leans far forward over his lectern. Unfortunately, it looks as though he and the lectern are about to come crashing down into the audience. Even more distracting is his habit of pounding the lectern while he speaks. Since his microphone is often attached to the lectern, the pounding becomes a deafening and distracting noise.

Although a lectern can become a crutch or a protective barrier between the speaker and the audience, it offers many advantages if it's used well. We like lecterns because they give us a place to put our notes, a spot to focus audience attention, and even an electrical outlet for a light and microphone.

Coaches and consultants often advise their clients to speak without a lectern or to come out from behind the lectern and speak at its side. In this way, speakers remain close to their notes but also get closer to their audience.[1] We agree. Although you may begin your talk behind a lectern, there is nothing wrong with moving to one side of the lectern as you speak. At the same time, we recognize that audiences rarely remember whether a speaker stood behind, to the side, or in front of a lectern.

If you're going to move from behind a lectern, do it for a reason. After speaking from behind a lectern, we often move to its side or move out in front of it and toward the audience. Then we deliver an important part of our message: "And remember this..." or "Think about the impact of..." or "Let me say this again...." If you do this, your movement will put a huge exclamation point on your message.

Twenty years ago, a speaker could make camp and be quite comfortable behind a lectern. Today it is more difficult, given the extensive use of presentation aids and presentation software. Nowadays you may need to walk over and point to something on a screen or to get out of the way of a slide. Presentation aids in all of their forms have liberated speakers who at other times would have stayed behind a lectern. But as Chapter 17, "Presentation Aids," discusses, these tools must be used effectively so that they don't steal the show from the presenter.

If you're very nervous or feel more comfortable behind a lectern, then use one. The key is using it well. Don't be afraid to gesture when you're behind a lectern. Don't stay glued to your notes; make sure that you look up and establish eye contact. Don't grip the lectern as if it were the top railing of the sinking *Titanic*. Use it as it was intended to be used: as a center of focus where you and your notes can be stationed.

1. Thomas Leech, *How to Prepare, Stage, & Deliver Winning Presentations* (New York: AMACOM, 1993), p. 174.

if a studio's makeup artist pays you a backstage visit. Both men and women on television wear makeup. It helps reduce shine and can highlight facial features. As odd as you may think you look after a makeup session, you will be surprised by the positive results you will see on screen.

As we've indicated, radio and television are personal media. Of the two, television is the most intimate. Why? Because the camera can zoom in for a close-up. A full close-up of someone's face on television reveals every flicker of a smile, flinch, raised eyebrow, frown, or wince. Trying to hide those minute details will only result in an uninterested, deadpan look.

When you're on camera, your face is the main focus of attention—not your gestures, not your hands, not even your voice. If you gesture a great deal while you speak, remember that the television camera may be too close to pick up your hand movements. Consider gesturing closer to your face, being careful not to hide your face behind your hands. You may want to have a friend videotape you in close-up so that you can get a sense of how—or if—your gestures appear on-screen.

Whether you're part of a panel or appearing alone, make sure that you're dressed appropriately for television. Generally, this means wearing rather formal business attire, but if you're not sure, ask your contact at the station for advice. Because of the way that cameras work, some colors and patterns should be avoided.

- Black, dark gray, or midnight blue come out very dark on camera and can look too somber, even for a business program. Instead, choose a paler gray, gray-blue, or mid-blue.
- Bright white can be blinding. Choose cream, beige, or pale blue instead.
- Material with narrow stripes, small checks, or large patterns tends to vibrate or look jumpy. Plain colors look best on camera.
- Dangling earrings and fussy necklines tend to be distracting. Remember that most of the camera shots will be of your head and shoulders, so aim for a simple, plain, uncluttered look.[13]

If you know that you are going to be on television, you already have easy access to the best resource available on how to behave, how to move, where to look, and what to wear. Watch television. Watch news anchors. Watch Sunday morning news shows. Watch the weather channel. Watch shows in which real persons (talk-show guests and game-show contestants), not your favorite actors or sit-com characters, are talking.

U.S. Secretary of Defense, Donald Rumsfeld, and other officials meeting in a secure teleconferencing room at the Pentagon. How do teleconferences affect the ways in which speakers communicate with one another?

Real World Real Speakers

Super Prepare for Online Presentations

A colleague of ours provided us with her recollection of an online presentation, on behalf of a major computer company, that she had to prepare and deliver:

> *Once I had to deliver the keynote address to a conference of five hundred senior military and government officials attending a conference on learning, in Singapore. To make matters more interesting, I was in New York at the time delivering the address online. I had to select a mix of learning activities and supporting technologies to make this a high energy distance-learning experience. I wanted to have a different visual every three minutes and to vary the format of my presentation several times. I combined slides, live camera shots of myself, audience pools (we had a camera in the conference room in Singapore that fed to a monitor in New York), and still pictures. I also reserved about fifteen minutes after the speech for audience questions, which really made it feel as if we were in the same room. I built a website for the presentation with hundreds of links and resources so audience members could also follow up at their leisure.*
>
> *I was struck by how much energy it took to do the presentation online. I had to produce my own presentation as I was giving it by pointing and clicking the mouse on my laptop. Yet it paid off. I saved twenty-eight hours of travel for a forty-minute presentation. I saved our hosts a lot of money. Most important, though, the online format drove home the message about the power of technology-assisted learning.*

Videotape and Videoconferences

The use of videotape is no longer confined to broadcast and cable television. Many businesses—both large and small—now commonly videotape presentations for in-house use and videoconferences with colleagues at different locations. Regardless of whether you are being taped for an in-house video newsletter or are participating in an international videoconference, the "rules" are the same as those for appearing on television. One difference is that the equipment, the studio, and the technical support may not be broadcast quality. There is not a great deal you can do about technical quality. So if your presentation comes out looking a little grainy, and the camera never moves from a straight-on, medium shot, don't worry. As video presentations and videoconferencing become more common, knowing how to be comfortable while using and appearing on video will serve you well.

Webcasting and Online Presentations

The world of cyberspace has given us a new arena for speaking in front of audiences—online presentations. Many universities and corporations have turned to Webcasting online training as an efficient way to reach students and employees all over the world. What makes online presentations different from other types of mediated presentations is the level of preparation needed for coordinating and operating complex equipment while delivering a media-adapted presentation. Giving a successful online presentation takes more than just computer skill. The basic requirements of any good presentation still apply—you need a clear purpose, audience analysis, logistical planning, thorough preparation, good organization, and well-rehearsed delivery.

Putting It All Together

In order to understand how all of the elements of your physical delivery (eye contact, facial expression, gestures, posture, and movement) work together, let's follow you from the beginning to the end of a presentation.

First, you have to get to the place where you will speak or make your mediated presentation. You may be called on, introduced, take your turn, or just walk up and begin talking. When you stand up and walk to the lectern, desk, table, microphone, or open space, walk with confidence. Don't wince or make a face that says, "I'd rather not be doing this." Remember that your audience will "read" your posture and expression before they hear a word of your presentation. Let that first impression be positive!

Don't start speaking right away. Take a few seconds to get ready by rechecking your notes and scanning the room for potential problems such as a group of late arrivals. This pause also will give your audience a few seconds to settle down and prepare to listen to you. When you're ready, establish eye contact with several audience members. And then, start speaking without looking at your notes. The first few words of your presentation should be delivered to your audience, not to your note cards. To maintain maximum contact with your audience, refer to your notes as little as possible throughout the presentation. Let yourself become totally involved in your message.

Visualize Your Performance

In Chapter 3, "Building Presentation Confidence," we note how visualization can help reduce presentation anxiety. Visualization also can help improve your performance. Take a few minutes during the course of every practice session to imagine yourself giving your presentation from start to finish. If visualization works for Olympic and other topnotch athletes, it can work for speakers.

The key, writes Jean Williams, a sports psychologist at the University of Arizona, "is to engage all the senses in the imaging process."[1] As you visualize your presentation, imagine how you look, the way you gesture and move, the sound of your voice, the feel of your notes, even the smell of the room and the taste of the cold water you will sip between major sections of your presentation. Then go one step beyond your five senses and focus on positive emotions: how wonderful and exhilarating it feels to be a successful speaker. The more vivid you make your visualization, the more focused you can be on improving and controlling every detail of your performance.

1. Wendy DuBow, "Do Try This at Home," *Women's Sports and Fitness* 19 (May 1997):78.

As you deliver your presentation, visualize yourself reaching out to the audience with your message. Hear yourself emphasizing important words and ideas. Feel yourself gesturing and moving with confidence and ease. Notice how the audience looks at you when you look at them. See them nod in agreement, smile, and sit forward to concentrate. Feel the growing excitement that comes with knowing that you are making the most of your presentation.

Once you have finished your presentation, make a graceful and confident exit. Too often, nervous speakers are halfway to their seats before the last word has had time to reach the audience's ears. Just as you got ready before you began speaking, pause after you have finished, look at your audience, and then turn your gaze away from them and walk off with confidence.

After reading the previous few paragraphs, you may be thinking that we have described the perfect performance. In truth, we have also described a good practice session. You should practice every step of your presentation. A play director blocks a scene by telling the actors where, when, and even how to move. You can do the same thing. Practice walking to the podium. Practice the way in which you will handle your notes. Practice your presentation as though an audience were present. Only this kind of practice can give you the added confidence you can rely on when it's time for the real thing.

Summary

▶ Why is eye contact so important?

Eye contact may be the single most important element of physical delivery. Effective eye contact helps to initiate and control communication, enhances speaker credibility, and provides useful feedback. However, be cautious when addressing culturally diverse audience members who are uncomfortable with direct eye contact.

▶ Can I control my facial expressions?

Controlling your facial expressions is difficult because, in most cases, they naturally reflect what you are thinking and feeling. At the same time, something as simple as a smile can relax both you and your audience while also conveying your sincere interest in communicating your message.

▶ Which gestures work best during a presentation?

Gestures that reinforce a thought, an intention, or an emotion add to the effectiveness of a presentation. Usually, if you stop thinking about how to gesture and instead concentrate on your message, your gestures will be natural and communicative.

▶ How should I stand and move during a presentation?

An erect and confident posture and purposeful movements can enhance your credibility; give you a strong stance from which to gesture, support, and emphasize important ideas and information; and channel nervous energy.

▶ How do I deliver a presentation on radio, on camera, or online?

Remember that radio and television are very personal forms of communication. Speak as though you're talking to one other person rather than orating to thousands of listeners. Mediated presentations require practice and technical know-how as well as a thorough understanding of the basic principles of presentation speaking.

Presentation Principles in Action

The Two-Minute Performance Drill

Directions: As a way of understanding how all the elements of performance (practice, vocal delivery, and physical delivery) work together, prepare a short presentation using each of the four delivery modes as follows:

- *Memorized:* Recite thirty seconds of something you have memorized, such as a poem, the Pledge of Allegiance, song lyrics, a prayer, and so on.
- *Manuscript:* Read thirty seconds of any piece of prose, such as a passage from a book, newspaper, magazine, and so on.
- *Extemporaneous:* Spend sixty seconds talking about a personal experience, interest (such as a hobby) or opinion (such as your views on a political or campus issue).
- *Impromptu:* After you have completed the previous three presentations, someone in the audience will ask you a question. Answer the question in thirty seconds or less.

Members of the class should use the Performance Assessment worksheet to provide each speaker with an evaluation in the form of ratings and comments.

Performance Assessment

Speaker: ____________________

COMPETENCY	E	G	A	W	M	N/A	Comments
Preparation and Practice							
Extent of Preparation							
Evidence of Practice							
Effective Use of Notes							
Vocal Delivery							
Volume							
Rate							
Pitch							
Fluency							
Pronunciation							
Articulation							
Physical Delivery							
Eye Contact							
Facial Expression							
Gestures							
Posture and Movement							

COMPETENCY	E	G	A	W	M	N/A	Comments
Mode of Delivery							
Memorized							
Manuscript							
Extemporaneous							
Impromptu							
Summary							
Overall Performance							

E = Excellent G = Good A = Average W = Weak M = Missing NA = Not Applicable

Key Terms

eye contact 354
eye scan 356
fidget 359
gesture 358
mediated presentation 363

Notes

1 Steven A. Beebe, "Eye Contact: A Nonverbal Determinant of Speaker Credibility," *The Speech Teacher* 23 (1974): 21–25.
2 Marjorie Brody, *Speaking Your Way to the Top* (Boston: Allyn & Bacon, 1998), p. 113.
3 Mark L. Knapp and Judith A. Hall, *Nonverbal Communication in Human Interaction,* 4th ed. (Fort Worth, TX: Harcourt Brace, 1997), p. 332.
4 Knapp and Hall, p. 360.
5 Thomas K. Mira, *Speak Smart* (New York: Random House, 1997), pp. 25–26.
6 Peggy Noonan, *Simply Speaking: How to Communicate Your Ideas with Style, Substance, and Clarity* (New York: HarperCollins, 1998), p. 206. Copyright © 1998 by Peggy Noonan. Reprinted by permission of HarperCollins Publishers, Inc.
7 Everett M. Rogers and Thomas M. Steinfatt, *Intercultural Communication* (Prospect Heights, IL: Waveland, 1999), p. 174.
8 Rogers and Steinfatt, pp. 172; Guo-Ming Chen and William J. Starosta, *Foundations of Intercultural Communication* (Boston: Allyn and Bacon, 1998), pp. 81–92.
9 Lani Arredondo, *The McGraw-Hill 36-Hour Course: Business Presentations* (New York: McGraw-Hill, 1994), p. 238.
10 Ron Hoff, *I Can See You Naked* (Kansas City, MO: Andres & McMeel, 1992), p. 80.
11 Hoff, p. 83.
12 Christina Stuart, *How to Be an Effective Speaker* (Lincolnwood, IL: NTC, 1996), p. 213.
13 Stuart, p. 216.

chapter seventeen

Presentation Aids

- How can presentation aids help me as a speaker?
- What kinds of presentation aids should I use?
- What medium should I use?
- How do I design effective presentation aids?
- Are there tips for using my presentation aids?

Not that long ago, a speaker needed two things for a successful presentation: a good speech and a strong voice. Today you can use dozens of tools to enhance your presentation—ranging from scale models, flip charts, slide projectors, overheads, and computer-generated slides to multimedia presentations. In fact, in many business settings you are expected to use visual images throughout a briefing. From chalked notes on a blackboard to computer animation, a speaker's options seem endless. Deciding how to take advantage of such technologies, however, must be considered as part of your overall strategy for achieving the purpose of your presentation.

How Presentation Aids Can Help You

If a picture is "worth a thousand words," so is a chart, a map, a computer-generated slide, and a videotape. The reason that this old saying carries so much weight is that the brain processes most of the information that it receives visually. From early childhood on, humans rely on visual stimulation. Think of the books you "read" as a child. They were filled with pictures. Adult minds still prefer visual images. Most of us spend more time watching television than reading books. Waiting rooms are cluttered with photo-filled magazines, not journals.

Benefits of Presentation Aids

Although you can describe the car of your dreams in great detail, the color photos in a car dealer's brochure can do it better. Although you may be able to describe a good tennis serve, a live demonstration or a training videotape will be more useful to a player. You can try to persuade an audience that your key lime pie recipe is the greatest, but a sample taste can convince them in seconds.

Presentation aids are the many supplementary resources available to a speaker for presenting key ideas and supporting material. They give your audience an additional sensory contact with your presentation. Whether you intend to engage their sense of sight, hearing, touch, taste, or smell, presentation aids encompass a wide range of items and media—from homemade cookies to multimedia presentations.

Research studies conducted for the 3M Corporation found that when presenters used overhead transparencies, the audience remembered up to 10 percent more of the information presented. Subsequent research at the University of Minnesota showed that presenters who used computer-generated visual aids were 43 percent more persuasive.[1] In both of these studies, presenters who used some form of visual aid were perceived as better prepared, more professional, more credible, and more interesting than speakers who used no aids. Only a dozen or so years ago, a hand-drawn poster would have been an acceptable presentation aid in most situations. This is no longer the case. Learning to create and use sophisticated presentation aids is the responsibility of every effective speaker.

Functions of Presentation Aids

Presentation aids are more than a pretty picture or a "gee-whiz" graphic. They serve several functions, all of which support you and your message. Presentation aids can attract attention and can clarify, reinforce, supplement, compare, and illustrate information. They can help an audience understand, learn, and remember what you say. Thus, it's no surprise that some speakers claim as much as a 40 to 50 percent increase in communication effectiveness when they're using presentation aids. At the same time, the 40 to 50 percent gain can be reversed if those aids are poorly prepared or used.[2]

FUNCTIONS OF PRESENTATION AIDS

Gain attention
Clarify and reinforce ideas
Enhance comprehension
Improve efficiency

Gain Attention. Presentation aids attract attention. A clever cartoon, a bold headline, a soundtrack, an attractive or shocking picture, or any other compelling visual can gain and hold an audience's attention. Attention can wane, however, if the visuals are poorly prepared or irrelevant to the presentation. Margaret Rabb, an expert in designing presentation aids, writes that presentation aids "clarify the spoken word, help the audience identify the most important points, and rivet attention on the topic at hand. Subject matter is often more interesting and easier to understand when illustrated.... Colors, motion, and visual organization bring facts and figures to life."[3]

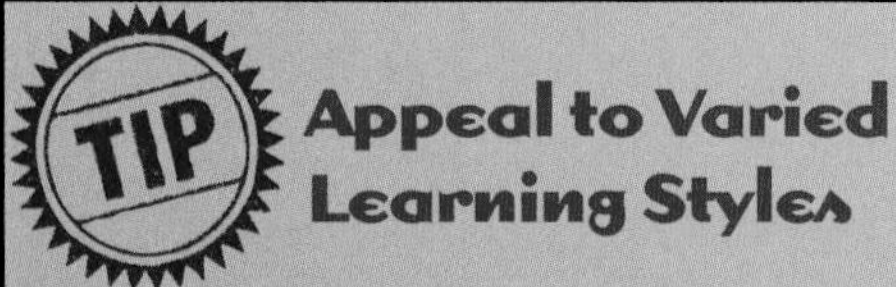

As the discussion of learning styles in Chapter 5, "Audience Analysis and Adaptation," points out, some audience members learn better by seeing and reading, some by listening, and some by doing. Using presentation aids adds a second channel of communication to your message and helps you adapt to your audience's different learning styles by engaging more of their senses. For audience members who learn better by seeing, you have many choices—ranging from charts to demonstrations. For physical learners, you may want to allow time for some hands-on experience. Let them sort through samples, help you demonstrate a product, or try out a technique or an exercise. Use a variety of presentation aids to ensure that you reach all kinds of learners.

Clarify and Reinforce Ideas. Depending on the subject, presentation aids can be more effective than words in conveying meaning. Complicated directions to a destination are often easier to give if you can point to a map. The intricacies of a business plan can be more simply explained if the plan can be charted. One of us once observed a benefits consultant helping a large group fill out a complicated preretirement form. His first presentation aid was a slide of the entire form. His second presentation aid zoomed in on the first two lines with an example of how to complete them. The third slide showed the next group of lines filled in—and so on through the last lines. Using a series of slides to move through the form in stages clarified and reinforced his verbal instructions.

In addition to clarifying and reinforcing a message for the audience, presentation aids can serve the same purpose for a speaker. If your visual aids follow an outline or the order of key points in your presentation, they can also function as speaking notes. Instead of using paper notes, you can speak from the visuals. You won't forget what you want to say, and your audience can follow along as you talk.[4]

Enhance Comprehension. Common sense and academic research arrive at the same conclusion: Visual information enhances learning. Imagine the impossibility of learning human anatomy without lifelike illustrations. Or the absurdity of studying music history without listening to recordings and following musical scores.

In some speaking situations, using presentation aids may be the best way to enhance learning and comprehension. Learning style theory tells us that audience retention improves when presentations include both sound and sight. Well-done and highly relevant visuals often increase audience involvement and, as a result, enhance comprehension.

Of course, not all visuals are created equal—some are more effective than others, and some sorts of presentations are enhanced more by visuals than others are.[5] For example, adding graphic organizers (outlines, matrixes, flow charts) improves recall—*unless* the information is simple and brief. Diagrams, if well designed, can make complex information easier to understand. They also allow audience members to process the information simultaneously—that is, they can see the whole picture. Researchers have also found that using speech alone or pictures alone is less effective than presenting speech and pictures together. The best illustrations are focused and clear. For example, it may be better to use line drawings than photographs to explain the human circulatory system.

In general, well-done presentation aids can enhance comprehension when

- You are presenting numbers and statistical data
- You are comparing and contrasting items or characteristics
- You are introducing or explaining a complicated process
- You are talking about something that is normally visual like a map, an architectural design, or a fine arts object such as a painting or sculpture
- You are giving complicated, step-by-step directions

Improve Efficiency. Presentation aids can save time, particularly when you use a graph, drawing, or chart to summarize a complex process or a set of statistics. As instructors and consultants, we often use overhead transparencies or computer-generated visuals to highlight important ideas. This way, we don't need to spend time writing on a board or flip chart, and we also save time by being able to point to the critical section of a pie chart or the key variable on a graph. If we give our listeners copies of our visuals, we will also save them the time it would have taken to write down what we said. By giving everyone the same material in written form, we have more confidence that the audience will "get" the message as we intend it.

The Basic Principle

As you consider the benefits and functions of presentation aids, keep in mind the most basic principle of all: *Presentation aids are aids.* They are not your presentation. Unfortunately, when some inexperienced speakers find out that they have to make a presentation, they immediately turn on their computers and start churning out PowerPoint slides. They have not yet determined their purpose, analyzed their audience, nor looked for or selected relevant supporting material. Just because they're using their favorite graphics template doesn't mean they're creating a cohesive, understandable presentation.

A D.A.R.E. instructor from the sheriff's department speaks to sixth grade students about the dangers of drugs. Are her "low-tech" visuals effective and appropriate for this audience?

A presentation aid is something that "aids" the speaker. You and your presentation come first; the aid helps you to achieve your purpose by supporting and supplementing your message. Don't let your aids and their technical razzle-dazzle steal the show. Today many business and professional presentations have become nothing more than narrated slide shows. The presenter simply reads what appears on a slide or transparency. By not taking the opportunity to connect with their audiences, such presenters have missed the point of making a live presentation in the first place.

Try this exercise the next time you have prepared a set of visuals for a presentation. Imagine that just as you are about to give your presentation, you misplace your visual aids, or the equipment breaks down. What would you do? Could you still communicate your message without the presentation aids? If the answer is *no,* or even "I'm not sure," then you're relying too much on your visuals. Your visuals are there to support you, not to take your place.

Messages and Media

Given the many different types of presentation aids and the enormous benefits of using them, it's important to understand how to select, shape, and use them effectively. When asked, "What kind of presentation aid should I use? Should I use slides? overhead transparencies? flip charts? scale models?" we answer, "Use whatever works best to communicate your message." As obvious as this response may be, it masks a complex decision-making process.

Not only do you need to decide what type of aid will work best, but you also need to decide which medium you want to create it in. For example, you could draw a graph on a blackboard or flip chart, display it on a transparency or computer screen, or distribute it as a handout. You could describe an accident with words or show a photograph or videotape of it. First, then, select the most appropriate and effective form to display your ideas and supporting material as presentation aids. Second, select the most appropriate medium for sharing those presentation aids with your audience.

Types of Presentation Aids

Presentation aids are a means of displaying supporting materials—facts, examples, statistics, and testimony—that clarify or reinforce your message. Presentation aids can take many forms: photographs, maps, diagrams, drawings, graphs, charts, tables, lists, models, and objects. Before deciding whether to power up your computer or buy a set of new markers, make sure that you have selected the most appropriate type of presentation aid.

Choosing the right form for a presentation aid is not as simple as choosing an item from a menu: "Should I use a single chart, a couple of graphs, or three drawings?" Your decision should be strategic. Which type of presentation aid will best achieve your purpose? Which type will be best for gaining and keeping audience attention, clarifying and reinforcing your message, and saving time? The first step in selecting an appropriate graphic is understanding that certain types of graphics work best for specific purposes. The following descriptions and guidelines can help you choose the most appropriate form for your presentation aid.[6]

TYPES OF PRESENTATION AIDS

- **Pie charts**
- **Graphs**
- **Text charts**
- **Tables**
- **Diagrams and Illustrations**
- **Maps**
- **Photographs**

Headline Your Visuals

A picture worth a thousand words can lose its impact if it doesn't have a title or headline. Gene Zelazny, a visual designer, writes, "Don't keep it a secret; let your message head the chart. In so doing, you reduce the risk that the reader will misunderstand, and you make sure he or she focuses on the aspect of the data you want to employ."[1] Zelazny uses the following pie chart to make his point.

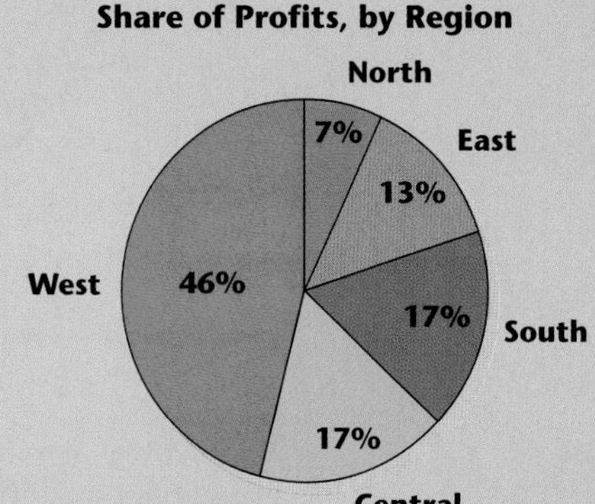

What is the significance of this pie chart? Most viewers would probably focus on the West, believing the message to be "West Accounts for Half of Profits." However, that may not be the point. Perhaps the reason the chart was developed was to show that the "North Generates Smallest Profits." Putting a more specific title on your visuals reinforces your message and ensures that your audience focuses on the aspect of the data you want to emphasize.[2]

Headlines should be conclusions, not topics. "Profits Are Up" is much more interesting than a slide title that reads, "Profit Figures."

1. Gene Zelazny, *Say It with Charts: The Executive's Guide to Successful Presentations* (Homewood, IL: Dow Jones–Irwin, 1985), p. 18.
2. Zelazny, pp. 18–19.

Pie Charts. **Pie charts** show *how much.* They show proportions in relation to a whole, or they depict relationships among related items. Each wedge of the pie usually represents a percentage, as in Figures 17.1 and 17.2. Most audiences comprehend pie charts quickly and easily.

When using a pie chart, try not to use more than six components. Why? Gene Zelazny, who advises executive-level presenters about the best ways to use presentation aids, notes that the pieces of the pie will be difficult to distinguish if you go beyond six.

Figure 17.1

Pie Chart

The pie chart shows that 5,311 students attending a local community college who also intend to transfer to a four-year college or university are enrolled in one of six program areas.

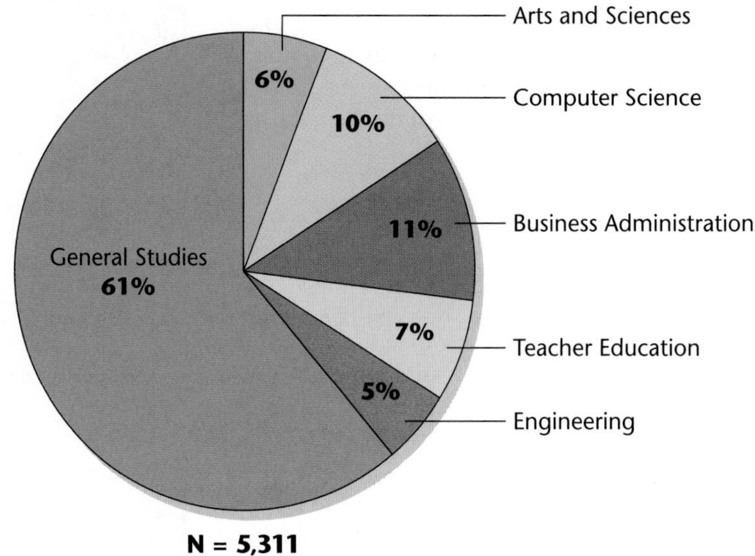

If you must have more than six pieces, select the most important components and group the remainders into an "others" category. Also, because the eye is accustomed to measuring in a clockwise motion, begin the most important segment of your pie chart against the 12 o'clock line. To add emphasis, use the most contrasting colors or the

Figure 17.2

Creative Pie Chart

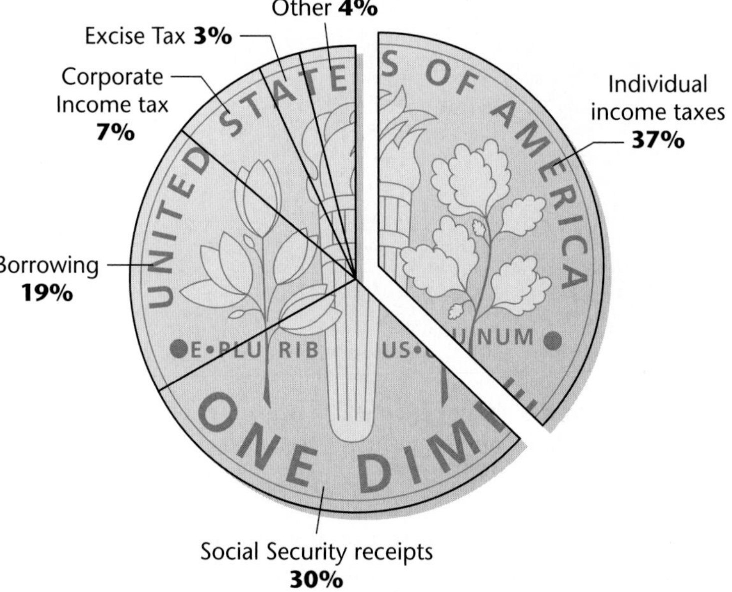

most intense shading pattern for consecutive slices of the pie chart to make sure that they are clearly separated.[7]

Graphs. **Graphs** also show *how much*, but they are primarily used to demonstrate comparisons. In addition, they can illustrate trends and can clearly show increases or decreases. Graphs, which can be displayed using bars or lines (see Figures 17.3a and

Figures 17.3a and 17.3b Bar Graph and Line Graph

Both bar graphs (a) and line graphs (b) chart trends over time. The bar graph tracks the number of high school graduates enrolled at a local community college. The line graph shows that the number of students enrolled in occupational programs exceeds the number of students intending to transfer to a four-year college or university.

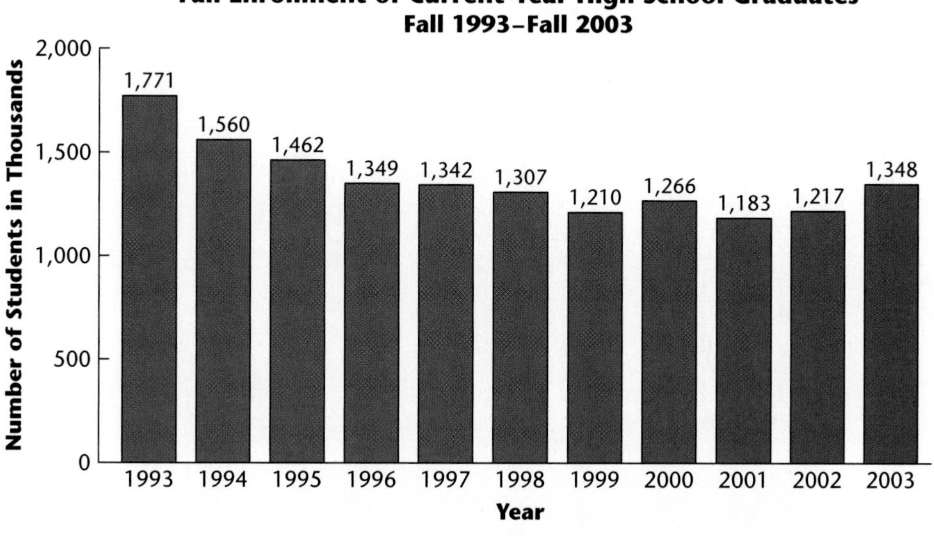

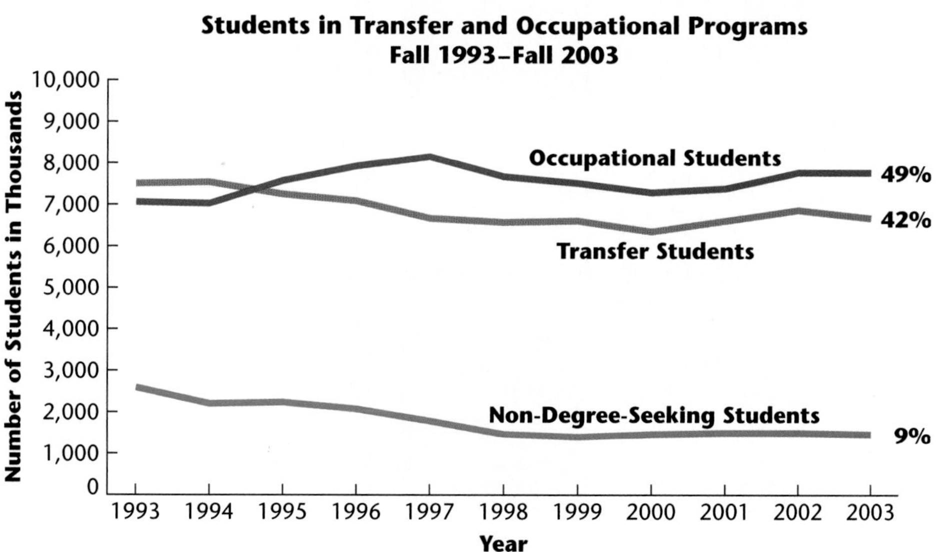

17.3b on page 379), usually represent countable things such as the number of different responses to a survey question or the number of products manufactured over a period of time. Stock market summaries on the nightly news are often presented in the form of graphs that extend over a week, a year, or even a decade.

Dennis McBride, author of *How to Make Visual Presentations,* notes that although "charts and graphs are the most widely used form of graphic visual display, ... anyone who wishes to make the most of these forms must first find the one that precisely fits the information to be presented. Otherwise, they can hurt a presentation more than help it."[8]

When using a bar graph, make the space separating the bars smaller than the width of the bars. Also, use the most contrasting color or shading to emphasize the most important item on the graph.[9] Figure 17.4 illustrates a creative way of displaying a lot of data without losing the basic characteristics of a bar graph.

Figure 17.4

Creative Bar Graph

"BULLETS" TAKE MANY FORMS

- • Circle
- ■ Box
- → Arrow
- ✔ Check mark
- ★ Star
- ☺ Happy face

Text Charts. **Text charts** list ideas or key phrases, often under a title or headline. Most of the "slides" in this book are text charts. They depict goals, functions, types of formats, recommendations, and guidelines. Items listed on a text chart may be numbered, "bulleted," or simply set apart on separate lines (see Figure 17.5).

Tables. **Tables** summarize and compare data (see Figure 17.6). In *The Presentation Design Book,* Margaret Rabb offers this advice: "When graphs aren't specific enough and verbal descriptions are too cumbersome, tables offer elegant solutions for showing exact numeric values."[10] Tables also can summarize and compare key features, as in the table on page 386 that summarizes the types of media most appropriate for small, medium, and large audiences.

Diagrams and Illustrations. **Diagrams** and illustrations show *how things work.* They can also be used to explain relationships or processes. They can be highly abstract, in the form of flow charts or organizational diagrams. In addition, they can chart a process—the steps involved in making a product, a cake, or even a presentation. Diagrams and illustrations (see Figures 17.7 and 17.8) also can chart timelines and can even "explode" a physical object so that you can see the inside of an engine, a heart, or a flower. The drawing in Chapter 1, "Presentation Speaking," of the Dynamic Model of Presentation Speaking (see Figure 1.1 on page 13) shows how the presentation speaking process works.

BASIC FACTS ABOUT THE SUN	
Mean distance from Earth	92,955,600 mi. (150 million km)
Period of rotation	27 days on average
Diameter relative to Earth	109 times
Temperature at core	27,000,000°F (15,000,000°C)
Temperature at surface	8,700°F (4,811°C)
Expected life of hydrogen fuel supply	6.4 billion years

Figure 17.5

Text Chart

Figure 17.6a

Tables

Simple Interest

Simple interest is computed on the amount of principal of a loan. That principal is multiplied by the rate of interest: the resulting figure is then multiplied by the time over which the loan will be repaid.

Simple Interest on a $100 Loan

	Annual Rate			
Time	*5%*	*10%*	*15%*	*20%*
1 month	$ 0.42	$ 0.83	$ 1.25	$ 1.67
6 months	$ 2.50	$ 5.00	$ 7.50	$10.00
12 months	$ 5.00	$10.00	$15.00	$20.00
24 months	$10.00	$20.00	$30.00	$40.00
36 months	$15.00	$30.00	$45.00	$60.00

Figure 17.6b

Compound Interest

Compound interest is computed by multiplying the sum of the principal and the accrued interest by the rate of interest. The calculation must be refigured each time the principal is compounded.

Compound Interest on a $100 Principal, Compounded Annually

	Annual Rate			
Time	*5%*	*7.5%*	*10%*	*12.5%*
6 months	$ 2.50	$ 3.73	$ 5.00	$ 6.25
1 year	$ 5.00	$ 7.50	$10.00	$12.50
2 years	$10.25	$15.56	$21.00	$26.56
3 years	$15.76	$24.23	$33.10	$42.38
4 years	$21.55	$33.55	$46.41	$60.18
5 years	$27.63	$43.57	$61.05	$80.20

Source: U.S. Department of Commerce.

Diagrams and illustrations can also depict physical objects and areas in the form of simple line drawings and scale drawings or as detailed schematics and blueprints. In Chapter 7, "Logistics and Occasion," we include a simple floor plan of a room to illustrate the proper placement of a screen for presentation aids (see Figure 7.2 on page 150). Even cartoons are a type of illustration that can be used to poke fun at or ridicule a real-life situation or issue highlighted in a presentation.

Maps. **Maps** show *where;* they "translate data into spatial patterns."[11] They also can be used to give directions or compare locations. Maps have more uses than

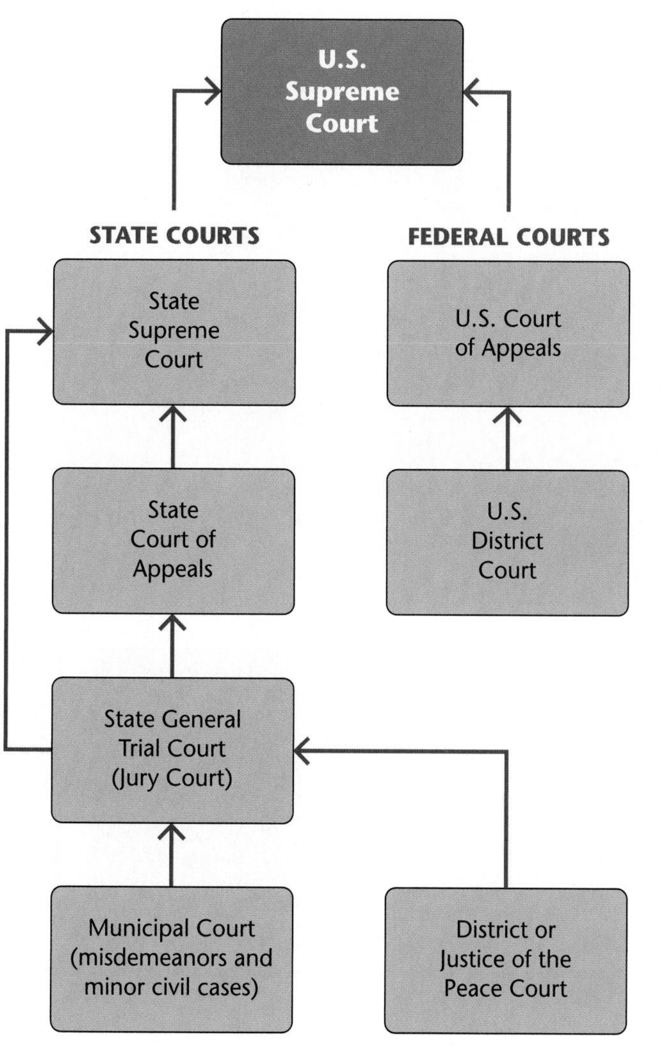

Figure 17.7

Diagram

those of your glove-compartment highway map or a geography textbook map. In presentations, maps can be used to locate and direct an audience's attention to a troubled traffic intersection, a complex battle scene, a proposed office complex, or a vacation destination. Maps can be divided into sections that link statistical data to population characteristics. For example, the map pinpointing states that rely on commercial nuclear plants for energy in Figure 17.9a could serve many purposes. Whereas one speaker could use the map to emphasize the vulnerability of such plants to terrorist attacks, another speaker could use the same map to defend or denounce the value and safety of nuclear energy. The simple map in Figure 17.9b could be used to guide audience members on a virtual or real tour of notable sites in Washington, D.C. In some cases, even the best-researched facts, statistics, descriptions, and examples will not equal the impact of showing a single map to an audience.

Figure 17.8 Illustration

Typical Orchestra Seating Plan

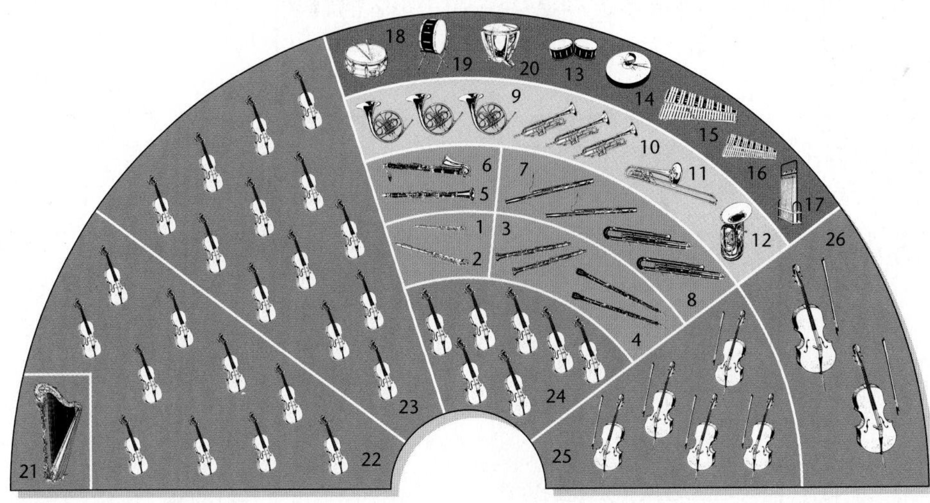

Woodwinds
1 Piccolo
2 Flutes
3 Oboes
4 Cor anglais
5 Clarinets
6 Bass clarinet
7 Bassoons
8 Contrabassoons

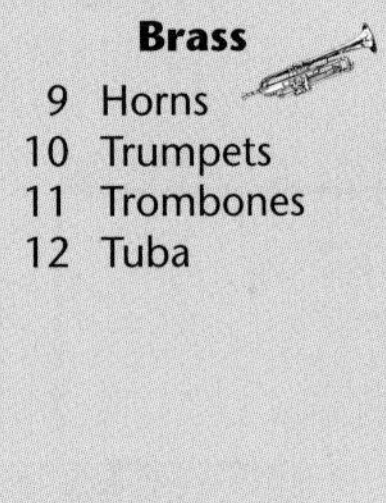

Percussion
13 Tam-tam
14 Cymbals
15 Xylophone
16 Glockenspiel
17 Tubular bells
18 Side drum
19 Bass drum
20 Timpani

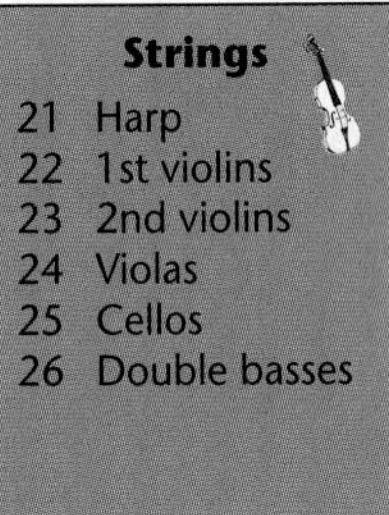

Photographs. Photographs portray reality. A real face or place is easily recognized through a photograph. Photographs also have the advantage of capturing emotions. Words such as *beautiful, dramatic, funny, heartbreaking,* and *awesome* can register in audience members' minds when a photograph is displayed.

Beyond Visual Aids. There are other forms of presentation aids—audio recordings, objects, handouts, and physical demonstrations. Regardless of the form or type, the key to selecting effective presentation aids is to make sure that they are relevant to your topic and purpose and that they have the potential to save time, gain attention, and clarify or reinforce your presentation's content.

Selecting the Media

Once you decide which type of presentation aid would best support your message, you can begin to consider which medium to use. Visual media fall into two basic types, projected and nonprojected. Projected, electronic media include overhead transparencies,

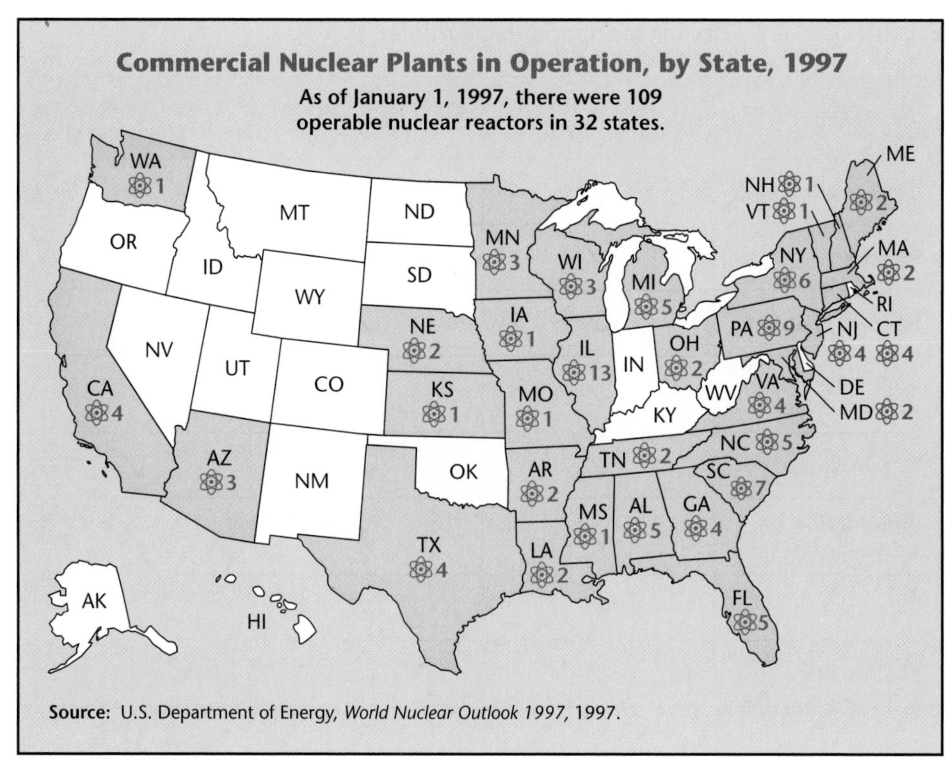

Figure 17.9

Maps

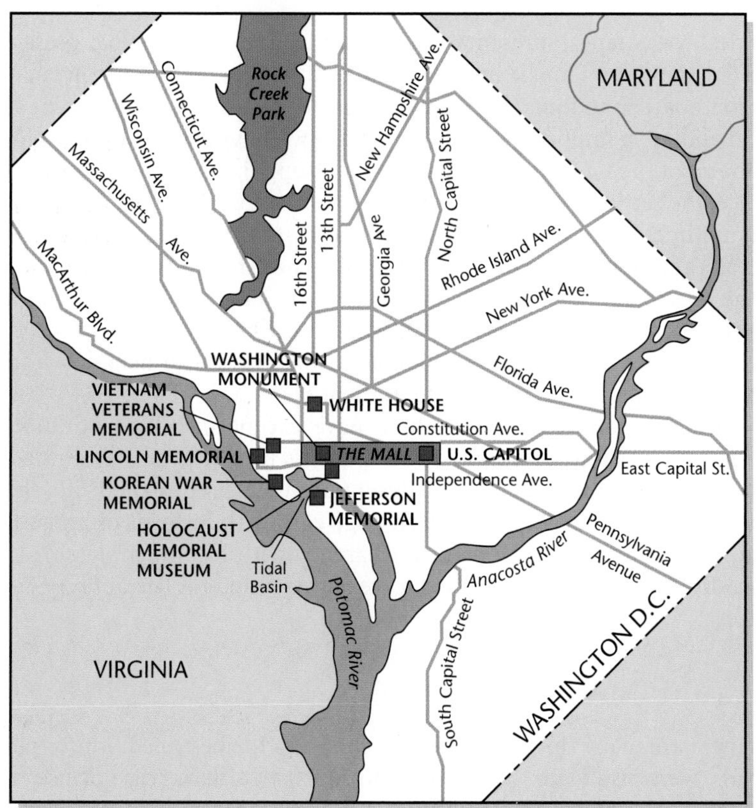

Figure 17.10 Selecting the Appropriate Medium

Media	Small Audience (50 or fewer)	Medium Audience (50–150)	Large Audience (150 or more)
Chalk/white board	✓		
Flip chart	✓		
Hand-held object	✓	✓	
Overhead transparencies	✓	✓	✓
35 mm slides	✓	✓	✓
Presentation software slides	✓	✓	✓
Videotapes	✓	✓	✓
Multimedia	✓	✓	✓

35mm slides, videotapes, presentation software, and multimedia presentations. Nonprojected, hard-copy media include more traditional types of displays such as flip charts, poster board, handouts, and chalk or marker boards.

The first and most important decision to make when preparing presentation aids is selecting the right media for the message you are supporting. Consider your purpose, the audience, the setting, and the logistics of the situation. As much as you may want to make a multimedia presentation, you may find that the room in which you're scheduled to speak cannot be darkened or that the facility cannot provide the hardware you need for the presentation. Writing detailed notes on a board or flip chart for an audience of hundreds will not make you any friends in the back row.

Figure 17.10 does not include all possible media, but it can help you understand how to select appropriate media for your audience.

Like all other recommendations, these have exceptions. A corporation's team presentation to a small group of prospective clients may require a multimedia presentation to compete with other team presentations. A predesigned flip chart with huge one- or two-word messages on each page can work in front of an audience of three hundred people. (An overhead transparency with too much data or tiny type would not.) But in general, certain media are better suited for certain types and sizes of audiences.

Criteria for Media Selection

Although there are many tips to offer about choosing the best medium for your presentation aids, we consolidate this advice into four key criteria: ease of use, audience expectations, availability, and adaptability.

Holding a remote control device, Steve Jobs enlists presentation software to display Apple Computer's year-end results.

Ease of Use. How familiar are you with the medium? If you love computers and understand software, then a computer-assisted medium such as PowerPoint or Astound may be a good choice. If, on the other hand, you are not comfortable or experienced with computer hardware, try overheads or flip charts. The day before a presentation is not the time to learn how to use new software or hardware.

Audience Expectations. Does your audience expect to see a computer-assisted multimedia presentation, or are they accustomed to flip charts? What have other speakers used when presenting to this audience? If your audience is expecting a presentation software slide show, make sure you can justify using something else.

Availability. Can you get the equipment you will need to the place where you will be speaking? Is the equipment available at the site? How much will it cost? Is the cost worth it? Recently one of our colleagues called to request a video playback unit from the hotel at which he was scheduled to make a professional presentation. He was told that it would cost one hundred dollars an hour to rent and set up the equipment.

Adaptability. If things go wrong, how quickly can you adapt? For example, if your computer shuts down, will you have time to get it going again? If the bulb on the projector blows, will there be a replacement handy? If your marker runs out of ink, will you have spare markers with you?

Overheads Can Cause Headaches

Slide and overhead projectors can be quite noisy. Often when we turn off an overhead projector in class, there's a brief and wonderful silent moment in which everyone enjoys the disappearance of the background hum. Try to approximate how loudly you'll need to speak over the noise of the projector. And if you're using a microphone, remember that the noise of the projector fan may be amplified just as much as your voice is. Also, make sure that you know where the vent on your overhead projector is located. Then be careful what you lay in front of it. Too often, speakers who are unaware of the powerful breeze caused by this fan can be unhappily surprised when their notes or transparencies sail off the table on which the projector rests.

Figure 17.11 Matching the Presentation Aid to Your Purpose

Purpose	Presentation Aids
Purpose: To explain the parts of an internal combustion engine	• Drawing of an engine • Pieces of an engine • Animated cartoon of engine operation
Purpose: To compare rap music and talking blues	• Audio excerpts of each musical form • Live performances • Chart listing music's characteristics
Purpose: To demonstrate how to separate egg whites from egg yolks	• Live demonstration • Still photos or slides • Audience participation
Purpose: To learn the causes and symptoms of sickle cell anemia	• Chart listing symptoms • Drawing of blood-cell action • Family tree tracing inheritance of the disease

Match the Medium to the Message

As we noted earlier in this chapter, some presentations are almost impossible to give without presentation aids. Try giving an informative talk on the sign language of the deaf without demonstrating a few signs. Try explaining the difference between major and minor musical keys without at least humming a tune. Figure 17.11 matches topics with some of the presentation aids a speaker could use to achieve her or his purpose.

Almost any kind of presentation can be supplemented by the use of a presentation aid. Deciding which kind of aid to use requires both creative and strategic thinking. For example, if you are fortunate enough to have all types of media available, how do you decide among them? Will a videotape demonstrate a product better than you can? Even though computer-generated slides may be attractive and easy to use, are they appropriate for your presentation?

When matching the medium to your message, make sure you consider the following:

- your purpose
- your audience
- your ability to use the medium with ease
- whether the medium is practical and appropriate for the occasion and place where you will be speaking

We next offer advice about using three common types of presentation aids: computer-generated slides, transparencies, and handwritten media such as flip charts and boards.

Computer-generated Slides. In general, computer-generated slides work best when the audience expects them, when color and pictures are key to achieving your purpose, and when you are unlikely to be interrupted during your presentation.

When computer-generated slides are well prepared, well organized, and well rehearsed, they can do wonders for a presentation. When poorly prepared, they can damage your reputation and undermine your message.

Transparencies. Sometimes a good set of overhead transparencies works just as well as slides and has the added advantage of flexibility. If you find yourself getting behind, you can skip some upcoming slides. If audience members have questions, you can return to a previous overhead with ease to provide an answer. Overhead transparencies also have the additional advantage of using simpler technology. As long as you have an extra bulb for the overhead projector, you're usually guaranteed a breakdown-free presentation.

Handwritten Media. Flip charts are wonderful aids, especially when a presentation encourages audience input and discussion. Flip charts and chalk/white boards are great tools if you plan to create graphics as you talk. Giving small groups of audience members a flip chart and marking pens guarantees audience input and involvement. Chalk/white boards, flip charts, or hand-held objects can outshine the latest high-tech equipment and presentation software when used effectively and appropriately.

Tips for Flips

Amidst all the high-tech options for presentation aids, flip charts—a large pad of paper on an easel—remain one of the most common media for displaying ideas and information. Not only do they work without electricity or software, but they also provide enormous flexibility. You can prepare your flip chart in advance or write on it as you speak. This flexibility allows you to involve the audience in generating ideas or filling in blanks. Flip charts also allow you to tear off pages and post them on walls as reminders or as templates for recording additional ideas. Both of us have participated in strategic planning sessions in which we were encouraged to add items to flip chart pages posted on the walls of a room. Marjorie Brody, a presentation speaking consultant and author, offers the following additional tips for using flip charts:[1]

- Flip charts work best during small-group presentations.
- Leave your flip chart covered until you are ready to use it.
- Black or dark blue markers are best—use a color like red only for emphasis.
- Write letters large enough so that those in the back of the room can read your words. Although your print size should vary with the room size, we recommend at least three-inch letters.
- Prewrite your flip chart pages lightly with pencil before you fill them in with markers.

You can even use flip charts as a form of speaker notes. Not only does the material on a flip chart serve as a master outline, but you can also write additional notes on a flip chart in light pencil in order to remind yourself to tell a story, share some statistics, or ask a particular question.

1. Marjorie Brody, *Speaking Your Way to the Top: Making Powerful Business Presentations* (Boston: Allyn & Bacon, 1998), p. 92.

Visual Design Principles

Regardless of the type of supporting material or the medium you choose to display, you can apply certain design principles to creating your presentation aids. In the following section, we use the general term *visual* to apply to any words or image that you put on a flip chart, slide, or computer-software template. In this way, we can generalize about design without referring to a specific medium.

VISUAL DESIGN PRINCIPLES

Preview and highlight
Exercise restraint
Choose readable typefaces and suitable colors
Use appropriate graphics
Build sequentially
Create an overall look

Preview and Highlight

Use your visuals to preview and highlight the most important and most memorable components of your message. The slides that accompany your presentation should not include every fact, statistic, and quotation that you include in your talk. What slides should do is preview what you want to say and highlight the most important facts and features of your presentation.

The RAND Corporation's guidelines for preparing briefings recommend using an outline slide near the beginning of a presentation and repeating it at transition points during the presentation. An outline slide gives a visual preview of your presentation. It is your presentation's table of contents. "When the slide first appears, it telegraphs the structure of the presentation, thereby increasing the audience's ability to understand and remember. When the outline slide reappears in the briefing, it reminds the audience of where they are in the structure. It can also underscore a substantive point by repetition."[12] Depending on how sophisticated your equipment is, you can incorporate a marker or change in color that moves down the outline as the presentation progresses.

Exercise Restraint

Presentation software has made it possible for speakers to use a dazzling array of graphics, fonts, colors, and other visual elements. At first, it's tempting to use them all. Resist that temptation. More often than not, a simple slide will be much more effective than a complex one. See Figure 17.12 for tips to help you create effective visuals.

We offer two general recommendations that apply to almost all types of presentation aids:

1. Make only one point on each chart or slide, and make sure the title of the slide states that point. Everything else on the visual should support the main point. It takes more time to explain one slide with a muddled message than to present two well-structured slides.[13]
2. Follow the **six-by-six rule.** Aim for no more than six lines of text with no more than six words per line. This rule of thumb allows your slide to contain the main heading and several bulleted lines below it without your having to fear information overload.[14]

These recommendations apply equally to the most sophisticated, computer-generated multimedia presentations and to hand-drawn posters and flip charts.

Please remember that an aid is only an aid; slides are not a presentation. They are not meant to be a script read word for word. In his book *TechEdge: Using Computers to Present and Persuade*, William Ringle recommends balancing "tersity" and diversity. By *tersity*, he means making visuals compact and concise while using them to add variety and interest. Finding this balance depends on understanding both the value of presentation aids and the pitfalls to avoid when adding technical "sizzle" to your presentation.[15]

Not only should you exercise restraint when creating each visual; you should also limit the number of presentation aids you use. Even the most alert and interested audience has its limits. Fifty slides do not necessarily hold more information than ten carefully selected and explained ones. Six pamphlets on energy conservation are not necessarily more persuasive than one. A musical excerpt may be enough; the entire song may be too much. Most audiences cannot absorb and retain a great deal of complex information, no matter how important it may be. In the end, do you want your audience to remember you and your message? Or do you want them to remember a blur of charts and outlines? The choice is yours.

Choose Readable Typefaces and Suitable Colors

After deciding what you want to put on a visual, you will need to select a typeface, or font. Again, exercise restraint. Using too many typefaces on a single slide will make your visual look amateurish. As a general rule, never use more than two different fonts on a single slide. As much as you may be tempted, avoid fancy but difficult-to-read fonts. You will be better off choosing common typefaces such as Helvetica, Arial, or Times Roman.

Type size is as important as font selection. Set up your visuals in the room where you will be speaking and walk to the back and sides of the room to determine whether your type is large enough and clear enough. When using computer-generated slides, try to avoid selecting type that is smaller than 24 points. If you find that you have more text than will fit on a slide, don't reduce the size of the type. Instead, reduce the amount of text on a slide. Remember the six by six rule. Reducing the size of the type to include more text not only results in a poor visual but also makes it less legible.

Choose colors with an eye to legibility, too. Contrast heightens legibility. If you are speaking in a bright, well-lit room, use a light background and dark text. If your visuals

Figure 17.12 Tips for Visuals

Beware of Seductive Details

A student of ours once asked to rehearse in class a business presentation that she was scheduled to give to an important group of clients. She had an absolutely stunning multimedia presentation filled with animation, bright colors, extraordinary sound effects, and delightful, even funny pictures. When it was over, the class had only one criticism: Most of her visuals had little to do with what she was talking about. She had fallen in love with her visuals and was committed to using them—even though they were not relevant.

During the 1980s, researchers found that emotionally interesting but irrelevant pictures actually *reduce* learning and comprehension among readers. The term **seductive details** has come to mean elements in a text that attract audience attention but do not support the writer's or speaker's key points. Instead of learning, audience members are "seduced" and distracted by interesting scenes, dramatic graphics, vivid colors, and engaging motion. Even when images *are* relevant to the presentation topic, they can make the information seem too easy and effortless to understand. Moreover, seductive details can confuse audience members about the meaning or purpose of the text.[1]

The best way to avoid negative seduction effects is to make sure that the images you use are directly relevant to the purpose and topic of your presentation. The time spent viewing relevant images can help audience members understand the concepts you are presenting.

There are several other ways to minimize the possibility of having your images act as seductive details.

1. Minimize the competition between pictures and written text. If you have a vivid picture or dramatic graphic, display the slide as accompanied by only the most important key words. Then follow the slide with a more detailed written explanation.
2. Avoid using background sound effects or music. They can distract an audience from you and your message.
3. Encourage visualization. When you want your audience to appreciate and learn a concept, give them just enough visual information so that they can construct or imagine their own version of the message. Just as radio shows and recorded books can serve as a medium of the imagination, effective presentation aids can encourage audience members to apply concepts and visualize consequences in their own lives, jobs, and world.

1. See Ruth Clark, "Six Principles of Effective e-Learning: What Works and Why," *The e-Learning Developers' Journal* (10 September, 2002), *www.e-LearningGuild.com*; Jennifer Wiley, "Cognitive Implications of Visually Rich Media: Images and Imagination," paper supported by grants from the Paul G. Allen Virtual Education Foundation and the Office of Naval Research, Cognitive and Neural Science and Technology Program, *www.vancouver.wsu.edu/fac/kendrick/loquent/eloquentjw.htm*; John Daly and Anita Vangelisti, "Skillfully Instructing Learners: How Communicators Effectively Convey Messages," in *Handbook of Communication and Social Interaction*, eds. John O. Greene and Brant R. Burleson (Mahwah, NJ: Lawrence Erlbaum Associates, 2003), p. 878.

are going to be projected on overhead transparencies or slides in a dark or poorly lit room, use a dark background with light text. If there is a lack of contrast in the background, the text tends to visually melt together, creating eyestrain for your audience.[16] No matter how sublime light blue letters on a lavender background may appear at your desktop, they will become nearly invisible when projected onto a screen.[17]

Also consider whether the color scheme will be appropriate for the situation and your purpose. If you are making a presentation on behalf of your college, using your school colors may be appropriate if they provide sufficient contrast. If you are making a presentation to a conservative business group, a very bright color scheme may not be appropriate unless you are trying to emphasize that your ideas are "not the same old thing." If you're in doubt about color, stick to proven color schemes. Most graphic software packages recommend colors that will sharply contrast with a background.

Use Appropriate Graphics

When choosing graphics, first ask yourself whether your audience really needs to see the picture you want to use. If you are making a presentation about a new medical device, showing the actual device or a drawing of the device would help your audience understand it. On the other hand, including a picture of a hospital would add little to your presentation.

In fact, artwork that doesn't have a specific purpose can get in the way of your presentation. Resist the temptation to use graphic elements just because you can. Not only does presentation software come with numerous clip-art images, but you also can buy clip-art books and software that specialize in certain types of images—such as job-related, sports, holidays, or around-the-world famous sites. However, more often than not, a clip-art graphic can get in the way of your message if the clip-art image doesn't reinforce the slide's meaning.

A man uses a large video screen in a training session on Adobe products at the DVD Expo in Los Angeles. What can the speaker do to focus audience attention in a crowded and noisy convention exhibit hall?

Build Sequentially

William Ringle, a presentation speaking consultant, refers to building sequentially as "progressive disclosure" and advises speakers to show relevant portions of material on a slide as seems appropriate.[18] For example, if you have a list of bulleted or numbered items and want to control how much the audience sees at one time, use progressive disclosure. If you want to build a chart or table by adding sections to it in a sequence, use progressive disclosure. By building your visual sequentially, you can build audience anticipation, focus on the point you are talking about, and save a "punch line" or conclusion until it is appropriate.

Create an Overall Look

Using presentation software to generate slides has become so common that many audience members can recognize common templates (backgrounds) by name. Your presentation software will let you select any of several dozen backgrounds or templates, too. Restraint is the key. A fireworks background can overpower your message. An under-the-sea template can drown your words. In most cases, it's better to choose a modest background that will spruce up your slides but not compete with your words, charts, or graphics. Use a consistent style and background from slide to slide.

Handling Your Presentation Aids

Using presentation aids well can make a dull topic interesting, a complex idea understandable, or a long presentation endurable. On the other hand, using presentation aids poorly can bore, confuse, and annoy your audience. Having spent the time and effort to plan and prepare presentation aids to enhance your message, you should make

Real World Real Speakers

Keep Your Slides in Sync

A friend of ours told a story about a young attorney who made a presentation to a group of prospective clients. He gave all his slides different backgrounds. He reasoned that since he wasn't that interesting a speaker, his slides would have to be really dazzling. Unfortunately, his listeners thought that the slides had been pulled from a number of prior presentations. Consequently, they were annoyed because they thought he hadn't taken the time or effort to prepare a presentation specifically for them.

When your slides have a consistent style, they convey a professional image and add credibility to your presentation. There's a saying in advertising: "It's a look." What this means is that it's better to have a consistent and identifiable "look" than to have an undistinguishable mishmash of images. The same is true of presentations. Keep the look of your visuals consistent.

sure you handle your aids smoothly and professionally. Certain delivery issues arise when speakers use presentation aids.

HANDLING YOUR PRESENTATION AIDS

Focus on your audience, not on your aids.
Timing is everything.
Begin with *you,* not your visual.
Be prepared to do without.

Focus on Your Audience, Not on Your Aids

Always focus on your audience, not on your presentation aids. Some speakers get so involved with their presentation aids that they forget they have an audience. Don't, for example, turn your back to the audience. Not only does this movement put you in a potentially unattractive pose and eliminates eye contact, but listeners also may not be able to hear you very well.

Remember that you control the presentation aid; it shouldn't control you. If you're explaining a chart or reviewing something on a screen (appropriately placed to the right of the audience), stand to its side, face your audience, and point with your left hand. Although this movement may feel awkward, it ensures that your audience can see both you and your aid. Also, don't stand in front of your screen or flip chart. Inexperienced presenters often forget that their audience cannot see through them.

If you're displaying an object or demonstrating a procedure, hold your head up as much as possible. Watch how the people who appear in commercials do it. They hold their products up near their faces. They wash floors, mow lawns, and eat candy with their eyes on the camera and its audience. They talk to you, not to their product. Please note, however, that we are not suggesting that you rigidly plant your feet and never move.

Real World Real Speakers

Watch Your Back

One of us once worked with an administrator who loved putting everything on transparencies. But as soon as she'd project something onto the screen, she'd turn around and point out the numbers she thought were important. She'd stand right between the screen and the overhead projector. As a result, most of the information was projected on her back. It was all we could do to keep from laughing at the way the numbers would move all over her back. It's an unflattering image that is difficult to forget.

In fact, turning toward your visuals can add emphasis. Generally, people will instinctively look wherever you are looking. Selecting one or two moments to "talk to your visual" can add emphasis, but it should not become the focus of your presentation.[19]

Timing Is Everything

There is a right time and place for each type of presentation aid. Appropriate background music before a presentation can set the right mood. Turning the music off right before you speak can signal to the audience that it's time for their attention. Setting up a photo display can provide an interesting introduction to your presentation, but you also should move the audience and their attention away from the display when your presentation begins.

It's equally important to know when to introduce your presentation aids, how long to leave them up, and when to remove them. Unfortunately, presenters often rush through their materials, forgetting that audience members would like to see them, study them, and understand them. Here's a rule of thumb: Any chart or slide needs to be displayed for at least the length of time it would take an average reader to read it twice. In other words, give your audience time to digest the message on your aid before you take it away. You should usually let the audience read the visual themselves—don't read your presentation from the screen or flip chart. The one exception to this rule is that when you want to underscore a specific aspect of your visual, it's appropriate to read those words out loud.

Try to avoid long pauses between slides. If you speak while showing a chart or graph and stop while changing the visual, you will send a signal that your presentation aids, not you, are driving the presentation. Keep talking as you move from one visual to another—it's a great time to make transitions or to give mini-summaries or previews.

Finally, when you've finished talking about a visual, get rid of it. Don't leave it on the screen or displayed on a flip chart as you move on to a new point. Likewise, don't reveal a new visual until you are ready to talk about it. When using electronic projection equipment, you may even want to insert or program a blank slide during the sections of your presentation that don't need visuals. And when you're nearly finished with your presentation, don't start to pack up your overheads, shut off your equipment, or take down your flip chart. Finish with a strong conclusion. You can clean up later.

Handling Handouts

Handouts are presentation aids. They can be a huge help when you're trying to explain difficult concepts and complex processes. Handouts also have the potential to enhance listener attention and understanding, keep the audience focused on the subject, present more information than can be covered in the presentation, and strengthen the speaker's credibility.[1] Generally, it's a good idea to use handouts if your presentation contains a lot of technical information or if you want your audience to take notes.[2] The problem with handouts is that many speakers don't know what to put in them or when to hand them out.

You can use handouts for many things: biographical information about yourself, copies of your presentation aids, checklists, drawings, references, article reprints, workshop exercises, an outline of your presentation, an evaluation form, and more. The nature and content of your handout should determine at what point you share it with audience members. Usually, distributing a handout during a presentation distracts the audience and takes their attention away from you.

In general, we recommend giving your audience handouts before you begin speaking or very near the beginning of your presentation—but not if your handout is a word-for-word copy of your presentation or if it outlines your ideas in minute detail. Both of us have left conference programs seconds before they began because presenters distributed and intended to read their research papers to the audience. What keeps us in a room are handouts that help us follow the presentation and/or provide additional information about the topic. Handouts that contain a skeleton outline of the presentation on which listeners can take notes can also be helpful. If you want audience members to have copies of your handout before you begin speaking, place them on each seat in the room, distribute them at the door as audience members enter, or place a stack on a table at the entrance to the room and tell them to pick one up before your presentation begins.

Distributing handouts at the end of a presentation can be awkward. Robert Pike, a nationally known communication consultant, describes a common and unfortunate scenario: "I've heard presenters say, 'Don't worry about taking notes. It's all in the handout you'll get at the end.' As the presentation continues and I see various visuals, I find myself wondering (meanwhile, not listening to the presentation), 'Will this be in the handout?' Not wanting to take a chance, I become more preoccupied with trying to copy all the visuals than I am in relating the visuals to the content being presented."[3]

There are only a few circumstances in which we'd recommend distributing a handout at the end of a presentation. As noted earlier, if your handout repeats your presentation, save it for the end. When the information or the handout is not an integral part of the presentation—such as publications or names and addresses to file for future reference—it can be passed out once you've finished speaking. Another appropriate circumstance is when the directions for an exercise, recipe, or procedure are written out in detail for future use. Notice that these are examples of information that will be useful in the future, not information that was needed to understand and appreciate a presentation. Handouts can make a difference if they are used wisely and well.

1. Robert W. Pike, *High-Impact Presentations* (Des Moines, IA: American Media, 1995), pp. 74–77.
2. Marjorie Brody, *Speaking Your Way to the Top: Making Powerful Business Presentations* (Boston: Allyn & Bacon, 1998), p. 104.
3. Pike, p. 78.

Begin with You, Not Your Visual

Always establish rapport with your audience before your start using presentation aids. The audience should know whom they are going to be listening to during the presentation. Your introduction should be you talking. After the audience has settled in and is comfortable with you, you can use your presentation aids.

Unfortunately, the increased use of computer-controlled presentations has made the "voice-from-the-darkness" delivery technique more common in professional settings.

Don't Speak in the Dark

A few years ago, one of your authors went to a very creepy presentation at a conference. The meeting room was nearly dark. At the front of the room was a large screen with the word *Welcome* in huge letters. After a few minutes, a shadow appeared in the front corner of the room. Through the sound system an amplified voice boomed, "I'm glad all of you could be here today. My name is Sandra James [the name has been changed], and what we will discuss today is..." At that point, a bright slide appeared with the words *Sandra James* on the first line and the title of the presentation on the second line. The presentation continued like this until the end, when the final slide popped up and said—you guessed it—"The End"! The room lights never came on, and the speaker never stepped forward to be seen, so the audience slowly left. To this day, audience members still wonder who the speaker *really* was.

We believe that too many presentations by disembodied speakers hiding in the dark corners of rooms make presentations dull and tiresome rather than interesting and energizing experiences. Unless your only purpose is to narrate, don't leave your audience in the dark. That doesn't mean turning the lights on and off for a few seconds between each visual—that would be worse. It means dividing your presentation into sections so that you can speak in the light and, when appropriate, narrate in a dimmed room.

The disembodied speaking voice can result in several problems:

- The presenter loses the principle advantage of a live presentation—the presence of a real speaker connecting with an audience.
- Speaker credibility can be eroded.
- Audience members may have more trouble comprehending the presentation because most of the speaker's nonverbal communication channels (eye contact, appearance, physical delivery) have been removed.
- A presenter can alienate an audience by seeming to be disconnected from his or her message.

Our advice: Always start and end your presentation by making direct and personal contact with your audience.

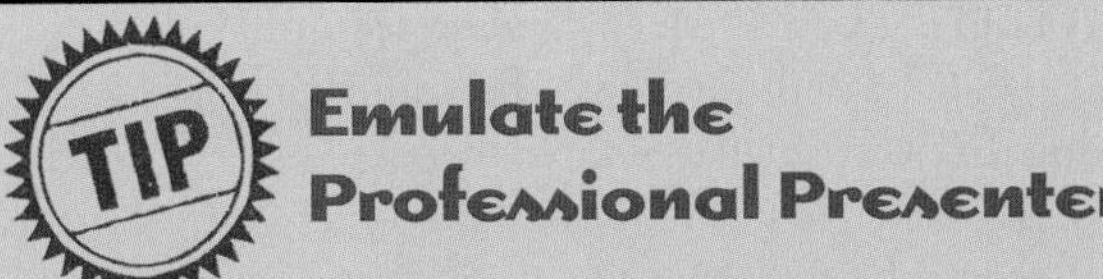

Emulate the Professional Presenters

In addition to the visual design principles and advice about handling your presentation, six techniques used by professional speakers can enhance the impact of your presentations aids:

1. **Paginate everything.** Page-numbered visuals ensure that your presentation aids are ready to go in the right order. Page numbers also help you identify specific visuals for modification and allow you to correctly reorder them for a subsequent presentation.
2. **Include source attributions.** Identifying your sources of information on a presentation aid can enhance your own and your message's credibility. It also gives you a permanent record of the place where you found the information for future use. Write your source attribution in the right- or left-hand corner of your slides as a way of consistently separating that information from the rest of the slide's content.
3. **Round off numbers.** Audience members cannot absorb and won't remember complex numbers. A visual displaying *$1 million* is much easier to remember than $982,896.25. The visual *50%* communicates more clearly than "51.678 percent."
4. **Avoid CAPS.** Use larger type size or bold print rather than all capital letters to communicate important words. In addition to being more difficult to read, capital letters may be interpreted as "shouting" or "anger" rather than as emphasis.

Professional speakers also exercise restraint. They make only one point on each chart or slide and follow the six-by-six rule whenever possible. They know that well-prepared presentation aids can be valuable assets while poorly designed aids can damage a speaker's credibility and sabotage her or his purpose.

Be Prepared to Do Without

The reason that we can tell sad tales about speakers using presentation aids is that no matter how

Using a Pointer

Pointers have become nifty high-tech toys. You can choose from among old-fashioned rubber-tipped wooden pointers; compact, retractable pointers; and illuminated laser-light pointers. Pointers can be very useful if you want to highlight or focus audience attention on a particular portion of your presentation aid. There are, however, some words of caution to consider when wielding a pointer.

- As a general rule, the "laser" pointers that flash a very small beam of light on a screen are not very effective. One of the respondents to our survey told us that he couldn't hold the pointer steady and ended up trying to circle the items with the light. The audience ended up feeling dizzy rather than enlightened.
- If you're using a rigid pointer, rest the pointer gently on the screen or flip chart at the place you want the audience to note. That way it won't move as you are talking. When using an overhead, use a sharpened pencil as your pointer. Point to the item right on the overhead, not on the screen. Lay the pencil down on the overhead, with the point aimed directly at the material you want your audience to note.
- When you have finished pointing, put the pointer down. Don't hold it in your hand as you continue to talk. Don't use it to point at the audience. Don't wave it about. Use it to point; then put it away. Almost nothing is more distracting than a speaker's gesturing into the air with a pointer or slapping it against his or her hand. Even worse, one of our classes was reduced to tears from laughing at a student who closed his retractable pointer against himself and got it caught in his belt buckle.

Marjorie Brody suggests a simple way to remember how to use a pointer. "Touch, turn, talk," she advises.[1] Use the pointer to touch the material on which you want your audience to focus its attention. Next, turn toward your audience. Then talk to your audience.

1. Marjorie Brody, *Speaking Your Way to the Top: Making Powerful Business Presentations* (Boston: Allyn & Bacon, 1998), p. 96.

well you plan and practice, something can always go wrong. Televisions can break, slide projectors can burn out, computers can lock up, and transparencies can be left at home. You can run out of pamphlets, samples, or chalk. Your faithful dog can refuse to perform its tricks. Your scale model can fall apart. Your assistant may forget to show up. Many speakers learn this lesson the hard way.

Consider the new architect who was giving her first presentation to her firm's partners. Her talk began confidently until she got to the first slide. It was upside down. She passed it off with a funny remark and went on to the next slide. Upside down again. This time she stopped and, with some embarrassment, took three minutes to turn all fifty slides right-side up. The third slide displayed a company's name. It came up backwards—totally unreadable, and unforgivable.

One way to avoid presentation aid disasters is to do a dry run, a special practice just to check your aids. A dry run would have averted the architect's problems with her upside-down and backwards slides. But practice cannot guarantee that a piece of equipment will work properly, nor will it create new transparencies. It will not change small visuals into large ones for a bigger-than-expected audience. So what should you do? You should have a "Plan B." Think about whether you could deliver your presentation without your presentation aids. In many cases you can. After all, if used properly, presentation aids are not the presentation. They are only there to help and assist you. You and your message should always come first.

Ethical Considerations

Technology not only makes it easier to create professional-looking presentation aids; it also makes it easier to appropriate the creative work of others for a presentation. When the creation of visual or audio images is a person's livelihood, the uncompensated use of such images raises ethical questions. Such unfair use may even be a violation of federal copyright laws.

An entire industry has developed to provide clip art, clip video, and clip audio for computer users. A user who purchases these packages has the right to make copies of the images and use them in presentations. Likewise, the visual and audio images that are included with presentation software can be used in your presentations. On the other hand, if you create a computer image by scanning the visual from another source, if you splice together video clips from a film or TV show, if you copy an audio excerpt from a CD, or if you obtain an image from the Internet, your conscience and your knowledge of copyright law must act as your guide. Remember our definition of *plagiarism*—using or presenting the ideas or writing of another person as your own. The same criteria apply to the unauthorized use of images and audio in presentation aids.

Summary

▶ How can presentation aids help me as a speaker?

Research has found that speakers who use appropriate presentation aids are perceived as more persuasive, better prepared, more professional, more credible, and more interesting. In addition, presentation aids can gain audience attention, clarify and reinforce ideas, enhance comprehension, and improve a speaker's efficiency.

▶ What kinds of presentation aids should I use?

Use the presentation aids that are most appropriate for you, your audience, your setting, and your message. Presentation aids include pie charts, graphs, text charts, tables, diagrams and illustrations, maps, and photographs as well as audiotape recordings, objects, handouts, and physical demonstrations.

▶ What medium should I use?

You may choose from a variety of media such as flip charts, slides, videotapes, or multimedia. Make sure that your choice matches the type of presentation aid that you are using and that it is appropriate for the setting and size of the audience.

▶ How do I design effective presentation aids?

When preparing presentation aids, you should keep several principles in mind: preview and highlight, exercise restraint, choose readable typefaces and suitable colors, use appropriate graphics, build sequentially, and create an overall look.

▶ Are there tips for using my presentation aids?

When delivering a presentation, remember to focus on the audience, not on your aids; to time your presentation aids for the appropriate moments; to begin with *you*, not with your visual; and to be prepared to do without the aids.

Presentation Principles in Action

Re-Envision the Visual

Directions: Use the design principles included in this chapter to redesign one or both of the following visuals as presentation aids. You can tackle this redesign challenge individually or work with a small group of other students. When you or your group has finished, be prepared to present your revision to the rest of the class. Explain your design decisions and why you think your design works better as a presentation aid than the example. Use both the Tips for Visuals listed below and the Visual Aid Assessment Instrument on page 402 to help you make sure that you have considered multiple redesign criteria.

Font Tips

- Use UPPERCASE sparingly
- Avoid using more than 2 fonts
- Use Helvetica, Arial, or Times Roman
- Use 24 point size or larger

Color Tips

- Choose legible colors
- Use bright colors to highlight
- Use light backgrounds with dark text
- Use dark backgrounds with light text
- Avoid red/green combinations

Design Tips

- Remember the 6 x 6 rule
- Use warm colors (oranges/reds) to excite
- Use cool colors (greens/blues) to calm
- Use ample spacing
- Use colors to organize slide elements

Consistency Tips

- Group related data or points
- Keep slide transitions consistent
- Keep background consistent
- Maintain a consistent color scheme
- Maintain consistent fonts

Visual Aid #1

Common Cents

Save half a buck a day in loose change	$ 15
Drink 12 fewer cans of soda per month	6
Order 20 regular coffees instead of cappucinos	40
Avoid ATM fees and credit card late charges	60
Eat out two fewer times a month	30
Borrow, rather than buy, a book or CD	15
TOTAL MONTHLY SAVINGS	$166

Source: America Saves

Visual Aid #2

Challenges We Face

We lost 3% of our market share last year

Our stock price is down by 7% from a year ago

Customer complaints are up by 14%

Retention of key people is down by 5%

The first chart was used in a *Newsweek* article to illustrate how saving $166 a month can help you build up your bank or retirement savings. The second visual was developed by one of your authors as a training activity. In addition to changing the design, you may change the wording (add, subtract, substitute other words) but not the basic meaning.

Visual Aid Assessment

The following visual aid assessment instrument can help you evaluate a single visual or a group of visual aids. This instrument does not evaluate a speaker's delivery or handling of presentation aids but instead focuses on the design and content of the aid itself. Use the following ratings to assess one or more visual aids:

E = Excellent G = Good A = Average F = Fair P = Poor

N/A = Not applicable to this visual aid

Visual Aid Assessment Instrument

CRITERIA	E	G	A	F	P	N/A	Comments
Preparation Factors							
Purpose. Specific and Appropriate							
Choice of Graphic. Graph, pie chart, table, drawing, etc.							
Choice of Media. Flip chart, object, slide, transparency, etc.							
Design Factors							
• Readable type							
• Appropriate fonts							
• Suitable colors							
• Suitable format/template							
• Contrasting background							
• Consistent design							
Page Factors							
• Effective headline							
• One point per page							
• Follows the 6 × 6 rule							
• Numbered pages							
• Provides sources							
• Avoids all capital letters							
• Rounds off numbers							
Summary Evaluation							
• Overall Evaluation of the Visual Aid							

Key Terms

diagrams 381
graphs 379
maps 382
pie charts 377
presentation aids 373
seductive details 392
six-by-six rule 390
tables 381
text charts 381

Notes

1 The 3M Meeting Management Team with Jeannine Drew, *Mastering Meetings: Discovering the Hidden Potential of Effective Business Meetings* (New York: McGraw-Hill, 1994), p. 140.
2 Thomas Leech, *How to Prepare, Stage, & Deliver a Winning Presentation* (New York: AMACOM, 1993), p. 128.
3 Margaret Y. Rabb, *The Presentation Design Book,* 2nd ed. (Chapel Hill, NC: Ventana, 1993), pp. 2–3.
4 Malcolm Kushner, *Successful Presentations for Dummies* (Foster City, CA: IDG Books, 1997), p. 159.
5 John A. Daly and Anita L. Vangelisti, "Skillfully Instructing Learners: How Communicators Effectively Convey Messages," in *Handbook of Communication and Social Interaction,* eds. John O. Greene and Brant R. Burleson (Mahwah, NJ: Lawrence Erlbaum Associates, 2003), pp. 882–885.
6 There are several useful guides for selecting effective types of visual aids. The following references were used to support this section of the chapter: Dennis McBride, *How to Make Visual Presentations* (New York: Art Direction Book Co., 1983); Margaret Y. Rabb, *The Presentation Design Book,* 2nd ed. (Chapel Hill, NC: Ventana, 1993); 3M Meeting Management Team with Jeannine Drew, *Mastering Meetings: Discovering the Hidden Potential of Effective Business Meetings* (New York: McGraw-Hill, 1994).
7 Gene Zelazny, *Say It with Charts: The Executive's Guide to Successful Presentations* (Homewood, IL: Dow Jones-Irwin, 1985), p. 28.
8 Dennis McBride, *How to Make Visual Presentations* (New York: Art Direction Book Co., 1985), p. 39.
9 Zelazny, p. 33.
10 Rabb, p. 154.
11 Rabb, p. 210.
12 RAND, *Guidelines for Preparing Briefings* (Santa Monica, CA: Rand, 1996), pp. 5 and 9. Also see *www.rand.org/publications/electronic/.*
13 RAND, p. 10.
14 William J. Ringle, *TechEdge: Using Computers to Present and Persuade* (Boston: Allyn & Bacon, 1998), p. 125.
15 Ringle, pp. 125–126.
16 Hinkin, p. 35.
17 Ringle, pp. 127–128.
18 Ringle, pp. 130–131.
19 Kushner, p. 273.

part six

Applications

chapter eighteen

Developing Informative **Presentations**

- How do informative and persuasive presentations differ?
- How can I respond to the unique challenge of informative speaking?
- What strategies can make my informative presentation more effective?
- How can I make my informative presentation stand out?

Of all the different types of presentations, informative speaking is the most common. Businesses use informative presentations to orient new employees, to present company reports, and to explain new policies. Colleges use informative presentations to advise new students, to teach classes, and to report to boards of trustees and funding agencies. Television presents news, documentaries, and "how-to" shows. Whether it's called an informative presentation, a corporate briefing, or an oral report, people speak to inform others in just about every context.

In addition to being the most common type of speaking, an informative presentation can be the most costly if not well planned and not well delivered. Poorly worded and inadequately explained informative messages have been linked to military disasters such as "friendly fire" incidents, transfusing patients with the wrong blood type, and deadly delays in responding to "911" emergency calls.[1] Informative speakers take on an enormous responsibility when faced with the task of sharing and explaining information to an audience.

What Is an Informative Presentation?

The primary purpose of an **informative presentation** is to instruct, explain, describe, enlighten, demonstrate, clarify, correct, or remind. An informative presentation can provide new information, explain complex concepts and processes, or clarify and correct misunderstood information. You will be asked to prepare and deliver informative presentations throughout your life and career, so learning how to do them well can give you a competitive edge.

Many of the speaking situations that our survey respondents described were informative. For example:

- Katie Smith Poole, a funeral director in Sandersville, Georgia, was invited by a church group to present a workshop on planning funerals.
- John Paguaga, a vice president and account executive at Fleet Bank in New York City, gave a presentation in England in which he explained the U.S. banking system to a large audience of executives from over one hundred British-owned banks.
- Captain Dr. Rob Simpson, a divisional finance secretary for the Salvation Army in Grand Rapids, Michigan, presented a paper titled "Enhancing Program Design Through Research" at a national social service conference.
- Ray Johnston, president of Top Hat Chimney Sweeps, Inc., in Altoona, Pennsylvania, talked about his background and professional experience in the chimney-sweep business to a group of insurance adjusters.
- Deanna Wolf, an assistant vice president of Platte Valley Bank in North Bend, Nebraska, gave a bank tour to a group of elementary school children.

- Joseph T. Mares, the director of Specialty Insecticide Development for Griffin L.L.C. in Valdosta, Georgia, gave a talk on fire ants at the local Rotary Club.
- Wendy Friedland, director of general accounting for Marriott International in Washington, D.C., made a presentation on new aspects of the accounting system to her colleagues.

As you can see, informative presentations can address a wide range of purposes and topics. Whether you're speaking to an audience of third-graders or an audience of CEOs, you can develop an informative presentation that helps them learn and understand.

Informative Versus Persuasive Speaking

The primary purpose of an informative presentation is to inform. As obvious as this may seem, it can be difficult to determine where an informative presentation ends and a persuasive presentation begins. Most informative presentations contain an element of persuasion. An informative presentation explaining the causes of acid rain may convince an audience that the problem is serious and should be addressed with stricter air pollution laws. Even an informative presentation demonstrating the proper way to change a tire can persuade an audience member not to call the local garage because changing a tire isn't as difficult as it looks. There is, however, a clear dividing line between informative and persuasive presentations: your purpose. As soon as you ask listeners to change their opinions or behavior, your presentation becomes persuasive.

The issue becomes even more complicated when your *private* purpose is considered. For example, if your presentation compares different brands of tires, it may slip over the boundary between informative and persuasive presentations if you manage a tire store that sells what you identify as the best brand. Advertisers often straddle this border. Statements such as "Laboratory tests show ...," "Three out of four doctors recommend ...," or "America's number one–selling brand ..." may be true, but their primary purpose is persuasive, not informative. Information can be persuasive. A persuasive presentation can and usually does inform. The factor that separates the two types of presentations is the speaker's purpose.

> **TIP**
>
> **Know If You're Asking or Telling**
>
> Your presentation's purpose directly relates to what you expect of your audience. If you're *telling* them something, it's informative. If you're *asking* them to change their opinions or behavior, it's persuasive. Michael Hattersley, a contributor to Harvard University's *Management Update*, suggests that the answer to "Are you telling them or asking them?" usually falls somewhere in between. His guideline for choosing the correct approach is to *tell*—in a polite way, of course—when you are in complete control of the necessary information and authority and to *ask* when you're in command of the information, but your audience retains the ultimate decision-making power.[1]
>
> 1. Michael Hattersley, "The Key to Making Better Presentations: Audience Analysis," *Management Update: A Newsletter from Harvard Business School Publishing*, Vol.1, no. 5 (Oct. 1999): 5.

The Unique Challenge of Informative Speaking

In many cases, persuasive presentations more easily capture and maintain interest than do informative ones. Controversy can arouse an audience. Listeners may be more alert when a speaker is trying to change their opinions or behavior. Informative speaking often requires a concerted effort to gain and then keep the audience's attention. In a communication class, students can choose exciting and interesting topics to involve their audiences. Most real-world informative speakers don't have this advantage. Imagine the awesome task confronting presenters with the following assignments:

Although an explanation of chiropractic treatment may seem unexciting, this speaker has engaged his audience's attention and earned smiles from most of his listeners.

- Explain a new piece of federal legislation to a group of city government workers.
- Instruct senior executives on the techniques for using a new phone system.
- Describe the procedures for preparing an audit report.
- Teach the names and functions of the cranial nerves.
- Compare the features of the health insurance policies offered by a company to new employees.

There's little that's inspiring here! In fact, it's probably easier to present such information in written form. You can address the challenge of informative speaking by including motivational elements in your presentation. Explaining to audience members why your topic should matter to *them* and how it can affect *their* success may be just as important as making sure that your presentation is well organized and well delivered.

James A. McComb, a senior consultant for the Centre for Strategic Management in Colorado, makes presentations for a living. Here's his advice about audience motivation: "I judge success the same way every time—did the majority of the audience leave having received value (as they perceive it) for the time and money they invested in me." Your audience will be ready, willing, and able to listen to information that's needed and highly relevant.

A **value step,** which uses the presentation's introduction to tell an audience why the information is valuable or important to them, is a powerful motivational tool. The value step gives your audience a reason to listen to the entire presentation. As described in Chapter 11, "Introductions and Conclusions," you can use your introduction to refer to the place or occasion—the reason that they are assembled. You can show them how a recent event has affected or will affect them directly. You can involve the audience by asking questions about their needs or telling a story about people just like them. If you decide to begin by describing a problem, make sure that your audience understands how that problem directly and significantly affects their lives.

FAQ: What Makes a Presentation Valuable?

Just because *you* love opera, bowling, or bidding on eBay doesn't mean audience members share your enthusiasm for and interest in such topics. In most informative presentations, you *know* more and *care* more about your presentation than your audience does. How, then, do you give them a reason to listen? What makes your presentation valuable?

Research on listening tells us that good listeners ask themselves a simple question when listening to a presentation: "What's in it for me?" In sales, the *What's In It For Them?* question is called WIIFT. If you cannot demonstrate that there's something of value for them in your presentation or product, why should your audience listen to you? Why should they care?

You can begin your search for a value step by making a mental or written list of the ways in which the information can benefit individual audience members. Ask yourself whether your presentation will provide:

- *Social benefits.* Will your presentation help listeners interact with others more effectively, become more popular, resolve social problems, or even throw a great party?
- *Physical benefits.* Will your presentation offer advice about improving their physical health, tips on treating common ailments, or expert recommendations on diet and exercise?
- *Psychological benefits.* Will your presentation explain common and interesting psychological topics, such as the causes and treatment of stress, depression, and anxiety, or descriptions of interesting—even seemingly bizarre—psychological disabilities? Will your presentation help audience members feel better about themselves?
- *Intellectual benefits.* Will your presentation help your audience learn difficult concepts or explain intriguing and novel discoveries in science? Will you demonstrate the value of intellectual curiosity and creativity?
- *Economic benefits.* Will your presentation help your audience make or save money? Will you explain or clarify monetary and economic concepts? Does your presentation offer advice about employment opportunities?
- *Professional benefits.* Will your presentation demonstrate ways in which audience members can succeed and prosper in a particular or general career field or profession? Will you provide expert instruction on mastering professional strategies and skills?

In addition to considering individual benefits to audience members, make a mental or written list of the interest factors you could include. Audiences often find intriguing stories compelling and memorable. They are impressed with new ideas and breakthrough discoveries. They enjoy humor and remember funny stories. The interest factors we discuss in Chapter 13, "Generating Interest," can help you turn a simple informative talk into a valuable and impressive presentation.

Note how this presenter uses a value step to motivate her audience to listen to a presentation about new evaluation plan forms, a topic that on first mention seems pretty dull:

> *Last year one of your colleagues was denied promotion. She was well qualified—better than most applicants. She received the highest recommendations. But she wasn't promoted. She didn't get her well-deserved raise. Why? Because she didn't use the new evaluation plan forms and missed the new deadlines. When it was time to give out promotions, her application wasn't in the pool of candidates. Don't let this happen to you.*

If there's a good reason for you to make a presentation, there should be a good reason for your audience to listen to it. Don't rely on the audience to figure it out, though. Tell them. Make it clear that the information has value. A value step may not be necessary in all informative presentations, but it can motivate a disinterested audience to listen to you.

Informative Strategies

Although each informative presentation you prepare may have a unique purpose, all will share the same goal: to help your audience better understand and become better informed about your topic. Informative goals are best achieved through a strategy that matches specific types of supporting material and organizational tools to audience characteristics.[2] That's why audience analysis is so critical to the success of an informative presentation.

Katherine Rowan, a professor of communication studies, suggests that there are two types of informative communication—*informatory* and *explanatory*. **Informatory communication** primarily aims at increasing audience awareness of some phenomenon. Much like news reporting, informatory communication creates awareness by presenting the latest information about some topic. **Explanatory communication,** on the other hand, aims at enhancing or deepening an audience's understanding of some phenomenon. Explanatory communication goes beyond "the facts" and helps audiences understand, interpret, and evaluate. Good explanatory presentations answer questions such as "Why?" or "What does that mean?"

Example of Informatory and Explanatory Communication

Informatory: Creates awareness	Explanatory: Deepens understanding
• Instruction booklets	• Textbooks
• Cake recipes	• Baking principles
• Simple directions	• Academic lectures
• Brief news stories	• In-depth news stories
• Sports trivia	• Game analysis
• Biographies	• Philosophies

Figure 18.1

Types of Informative Messages

Rowan goes on to provide the following examples of each type of informative communication. Instruction on how to shift bicycle gears would be an instance of informatory communication, whereas an account of how the gears are constructed or why bicycles stay upright when pedaled would be an instance of explanatory communication. An announcement about the day on which the Jewish holiday of Chanukah begins would be an instance of informatory communication; a brief lecture explaining why Chanukah is a minor holiday for Jews rather than a major one would be explanatory.[3] For other examples, see Figure 18.1.

Effective informative speakers understand when they need to report information and when they need to explain a more complicated concept or process. Not surprisingly, different types of informative messages require different communication strategies.

INFORMATIVE PRESENTATION STRATEGIES TO

Report new information
Explain difficult concepts
Explain complex processes
Overcome confusion and misunderstanding

Reporting New Information

Reporting new information can be the easiest informative presentation to prepare and present, particularly when an audience is eager to learn. As a type of informatory communication, sharing new information is much easier than struggling to explain a difficult, complex, or misunderstood concept. In informatory communication, listeners need only the facts. How you present those facts, however, will make a difference in how much the audience learns and remembers.

As Rowan notes in her explanation of informatory communication, reporting new information is what most news reporters do.[4] They report the *who, what, where, when, how,* and *why* of an event. They write about *who* is doing *what* to *whom*. They describe *how* or *why* something happened. You can find new information in daily newspapers and popular magazines, in textbooks and classroom lectures, and in encyclopedias and on specialized webpages.

When college students are asked to prepare and deliver an informative presentation in a communication class, they often choose topics that report new information. They try to find a topic that they, rather than the audience, know a lot about: the life of a great-grandmother, fly-fishing lures, shoeing a horse, fixing warped table tops.

You face two major challenges when reporting new information in a presentation. First, if your information is very new or unexpected, an audience may have trouble grasping your central idea. Second, you need to give the audience a reason to listen, learn, and remember such information. Why and what do they really need to know about your great-grandmother or about unwarping a table?

Four strategies can help you overcome the challenges of sharing new information with an audience. First, include a value step in your introduction. Second, use a clear and, if possible, creative organizational pattern to help your audience learn and remember what you say. Third, use a variety of types of supporting material to present the information in different forms. Use facts, statistics, testimony, definitions, analogies, descriptions, examples, and stories as described in Chapter 8, "Supporting Material." Fourth, relate the new information to audience interests and needs *throughout* the presentation. If they see no reason to learn or use the information, they are likely to stop listening.

STRATEGIES FOR REPORTING NEW INFORMATION

1. **Include a value step in the introduction.**
2. **Use a clear organizational pattern.**
3. **Use various types of supporting material.**
4. **Relate information to audience interests and needs.**

Informative presentations that report new information fall into several subtypes. Choosing one can help you clarify your purpose, select appropriate supporting material, and decide how to go about organizing your presentation. Informative presentations can report new information about objects, people, procedures, and events.

Informing Audiences About Objects. Students in public speaking classes often choose objects as the topic of their informative presentations. It's easy to see why: A tangible object can be described, touched, and even brought to the presentation, either in visual aid form or in the "flesh." Objects are often items very familiar to the speaker—a digital camera, a set of tools, or a favorite fishing pole. We've heard students report on their stamp collections, full-dress military uniforms, fishing lures, and exotic pets.

However, a topic alone is not a purpose statement or a central idea. Moreover, you won't have time to tell your audience everything there is to know about stamp collecting or fishing lures. So, as is the case in every presentation, you will need to focus your message on the characteristics that match your purpose, central idea, and organizational format. For example, this student used a spatial arrangement to develop an informatory presentation about fire-ant anatomy that also includes a value step:

An instructor in a factory talks to trainees near milling machines and lathes. What informative speaking strategies would make this kind of presentation interesting and memorable?

Topic Area:	Fire ants
Purpose:	To familiarize audience members with the external anatomy of a fire ant
Central Idea:	A tour of the fire ant's external anatomy will help you understand why these ants are so hard to get rid of.
Value Step:	Besides inflicting painful, sometimes deadly, stings, fire ants can eat up your garden, damage your home, and harm your pets and local wildlife.
Organization:	Spatial—a visual tour of the fire ant's external anatomy
Key Points:	A. Integument (exoskeleton)
	B. Head and its components
	C. Thorax
	D. Abdomen

Informing Audiences About People. Informatory presentations about people share common characteristics with presentations about objects. Like an object, people are tangible—in this case, flesh-and-blood personalities. A presentation about a person can focus on a historical or literary figure, a famous living individual, or someone whom you know. Regardless of whether you're developing an informatory presentation about a historical figure or about the person standing next to you, describe that person's life and accomplishments or select special stories about the person to tap audience interests and emotions. However, you need to be selective and focus your presentation on the personal characteristics or achievements that match your purpose and support your central idea. The following example presents a focused plan.

Topic Area: Early female blues singers
Purpose: To demonstrate the influence of four female blues singers of the 1920s on musicians in later eras
Central Idea: In the 1920s, Sippie Wallace, Edith Wilson, Victoria Spivey, and Alberta Hunter paved the way for other female blues singers.[5]
Value Step: If you call yourself an honest-to-goodness blues fan, you should know more about the major contributions made by the early *female* blues singers.
Organization: Stories and examples—brief biographies of four blues singers
Key Points:
A. Sippie Wallace
B. Edith Wilson
C. Victoria Spivey
D. Alberta Hunter

Informing Audiences About Procedures. Presentations about procedures can be among the easiest to plan and present—or they can be the hardest. It depends on the topic and whether your communication purpose is informatory or explanatory. If you are describing a fairly simple procedure, an informatory demonstration may be all that's necessary to achieve your purpose. If the procedure is complex and requires considerable expertise, you may have trouble deciding on the best way to approach and organize your explanation. Here are some sample topics that are well suited for an informatory presentation based on procedures:

How to complete an evaluation form

How to brew tea

How to prepare a meeting agenda

How to prune a tree

How to boil an egg

Note the use of the word *how*. Procedures focus on *how* to do something rather than on *what* to do or *why* to do it. Changing a tire, filling out a form, and sewing on a button are not necessarily easy procedures, but at least there are accepted and proper sets of steps for each of them. On the other hand, transplanting a heart and docking a space shuttle are highly complex procedures. There are no do-it-yourself manuals or "simple tips" to follow. These challenging topics require explanatory communication as well as information.

Make sure you know enough about your topic, particularly if it's a complex procedure, to properly explain it to your audience. If it's a simple procedure, make sure that you provide enough information to cover each step adequately. For example, anyone who has ever tried to cook a perfect hard-boiled egg knows that following the right procedure can make the difference between getting a hard egg and creating a mess of white albumen floating around in a pot of boiling water.

Topic: Cooking hard-boiled eggs
Purpose: To teach listeners how to make foolproof hard-boiled eggs
Central Idea: There are four steps to cooking perfect hard-boiled eggs.
Value Step: Rather than wasting or throwing away cracked eggs, you can use the proper procedure to make sure your hard-boiled egg is perfect.
Organization: Time Arrangement—step-by-step instructions

Key Points: A. Cold-water start
B. Stopping the boil
C. The fifteen-minute stand
D. The cold-water rinse

Informing Audiences About Events. You can base an informatory presentation on historical or recent events. History professors often center their lectures on an important event. Business executives may discuss a critical event to demonstrate how to handle a crisis. Politicians are often invited to commemorate an event. An event can be a single incident—such as the anniversary of the Columbine High School shootings, the winning of an Olympic gold medal by a particular athlete, or the dedication and opening of a new building. An event can also be a series of incidents or milestones that have become a historical phenomenon or institution—such as the Civil War, the race to the moon, or the founding of a company. Regardless of the date,

Tell, Show, Do

A physician friend of ours works in a large medical school and teaching hospital. He relates the way that he learned and now teaches most medical procedures. "Tell, Show, Do," he says. First, he *tells* students how to carry out a medical procedure by providing verbal and/or written instructions and advice. Then he *shows* them how to perform the procedure on a patient or volunteer medical student. Finally, he allows students to *do* the procedure under strict supervision.

The "Tell, Show, Do" technique can help you inform an audience about any basic procedure—from boiling an egg to installing software. This technique works well because it also adapts to the three basic learning styles we cover in Chapter 5, "Audience Analysis": tell (auditory learning), show (visual learning), and do (kinesthetic/tactile learning).

size, or significance of the event you select, the purpose of your informatory presentation will determine how you talk about that event.

The following example presents an approach to informatory speaking about an event.

Topic: Our company's fiftieth anniversary

Purpose: To preview the events scheduled for the company's upcoming fiftieth anniversary

Central Idea: The premiere events for our fiftieth anniversary will have something for everyone.

Value Step: Making our fiftieth anniversary celebration a success can bring more attention and—as a result—more business and profits to the company.

Organization: Topical—four major events

Key Points:
A. Dedication of the new office annex
B. Employee picnic and baseball game
C. Presentation by a nationally recognized speaker
D. Fiftieth anniversary gala

Explaining Difficult Concepts

Explaining a difficult concept presents special challenges for informative speakers. Unlike an object, person, procedure, or event, a concept is abstract—rarely can you touch it, demonstrate it, or easily define it in simple terms. You may be perplexed and bewildered for days trying to discover the essence of a concept and the most effective ways to explain it to an audience. Trying to explain quantum mechanics, the basic tenets of Islam, the relationship between nutrition and chronic disease, or the meaning of the word *rhetoric* would be a difficult task for any speaker.

Explaining a difficult concept requires more than reporting. It requires explanatory communication in which a speaker helps audience members understand and separate essential characteristics from nonessential features. What, for example, is the difference between concepts such as *validity* and *reliability, blues* and *jazz, ethos* and *ethics?* Why are corals classified as animals and not as plants?[6]

Shepherds looking at a flock of sheep will see things that we cannot see. They will be able to separate the old and young sheep, the males and the females, the healthy and the sick, the strong and the weak. With inexperienced eyes, we see only sheep. Your job as an informative presenter is to guide your audience to the distinctions that will help them better understand your topic.

If you are trying to explain a difficult concept to an audience, we recommend four strategies. First, define or list the concept's essential features. Whether you are using a presentation aid or are carefully defining the essence of a concept, make sure that you explain how it differs from

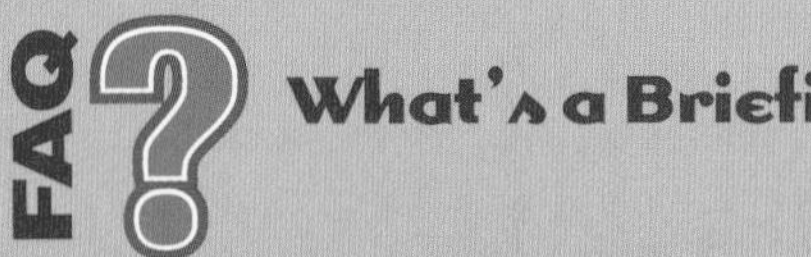

The word *briefing* should be familiar to those of you working in or seeking a career in business or government. A **briefing** is a type of informative presentation in which a speaker *briefly* reports about the status of an upcoming or past event or project in a business or organizational setting. In a business setting, you might be asked to present a short report to your colleagues or managers on what you learned at a recent conference or meeting. In a government setting, you might be asked to provide a brief update to staff members on the public response to an elected official's tax initiative or speech. The White House press secretary can often be seen on television providing a briefing to the press about the activities and reactions of the president.

Although briefings are—by their very definition—short, they may be the only way to inform an audience about a very important issue. Both of us have participated in briefings that were scheduled right before important events to make sure that all people involved were clear about their responsibilities and that any previously unforeseen problems were resolved before the event began.

other related concepts. Second, give a variety of typical examples of the concept. Third, discuss nonexamples or instances likely to be mistaken for examples. Can you show the audience that chaos theory is not the same as complete disorder or randomness? Can you explain that the opposite of communism is capitalism, not democracy? Finally, consider quizzing your audience's understanding. We aren't talking about a paper-and-pencil test (although you could, at the end of your presentation, give an anonymous quiz to see if you've made your point). Rather, pose questions about the concept and, after giving the audience time to think about answers, provide the answers yourself. You also may want to include a question-and-answer session at the end of your informative presentation to give the audience a chance to ask you questions.

Learning a difficult concept is just that—difficult. It's a challenge for both speaker and audience. By employing some of the strategies we've recommended, you are more likely to leave your audience with an accurate understanding of a concept that's difficult to grasp.

STRATEGIES FOR EXPLAINING DIFFICULT CONCEPTS

1. **Define essential features.**
2. **Use varied examples.**
3. **Discuss nonexamples.**
4. **Quiz the audience.**

In the following example, the concept of *heuristics* is explained in terms of its impact on persuasion.

Topic Area: Heuristics

Purpose: To explain how heuristics affect persuasion[7]

Central Idea: An understanding of the nature and uses of heuristics provides speakers with valuable persuasive tools.

Value Step: Understanding heuristics can help you persuade others and reject invalid arguments.

Organization: Topical plus questions to audience

A. Definition of heuristic messages
B. Examples of heuristic messages
   1. Use longer messages.
   2. Trust the speaker.
   3. Emulate respected sources.
C. Contrast heuristic messages with invalid arguments.
D. Quiz the audience about heuristic messages.

You may not be familiar with *heuristics*—the topic of this presentation—a term we define as shortcut decision-making rules, such as "Experts can be believed," that are correct often enough to be useful. (See the FAQ "What Are Heuristics?" in Chapter 19, "Understanding Persuasion.") Although this outline may not have explained heuristics to you, it does provide a good basis for developing an explanatory presentation that presents a difficult concept. When giving this talk, a speaker would provide examples of each type of heuristic message. For example, we know that celebrity endorsements and the behavior of others are often highly persuasive in some situations. We also know that audiences often buy more expensive items because they believe that the quality of products often correlates with their price. Explaining that heuristics are not the same as using poor evidence or unjustified emotional appeals could lead to audience questions about dubious arguments in political speeches and newspaper editorials.

Explaining Complex Processes

Explaining a complex process is not the same as explaining a difficult concept. In the case of difficult concepts, you are asking an audience to master the meaning and use of a certain term or principle. Processes tend to be multidimensional. With complex phenomena, you are asking audience members to unravel something that is complicated. Katherine Rowan explains the problem facing speakers who must explain the complex:

> *To the uninitiated, accounts of many phenomena often seem a mass of bewildering details. For instance, patients may wonder how antibiotics distinguish between "bad" versus "good" bacteria; people watching weather news may be confused about why El Niño events occur. Similarly, students encountering textbook material are daunted by dense, multipage accounts of how the human eye works, or the major types of Indo-European languages. In each case, these audiences are struggling to envision some complex structure or process.*[8]

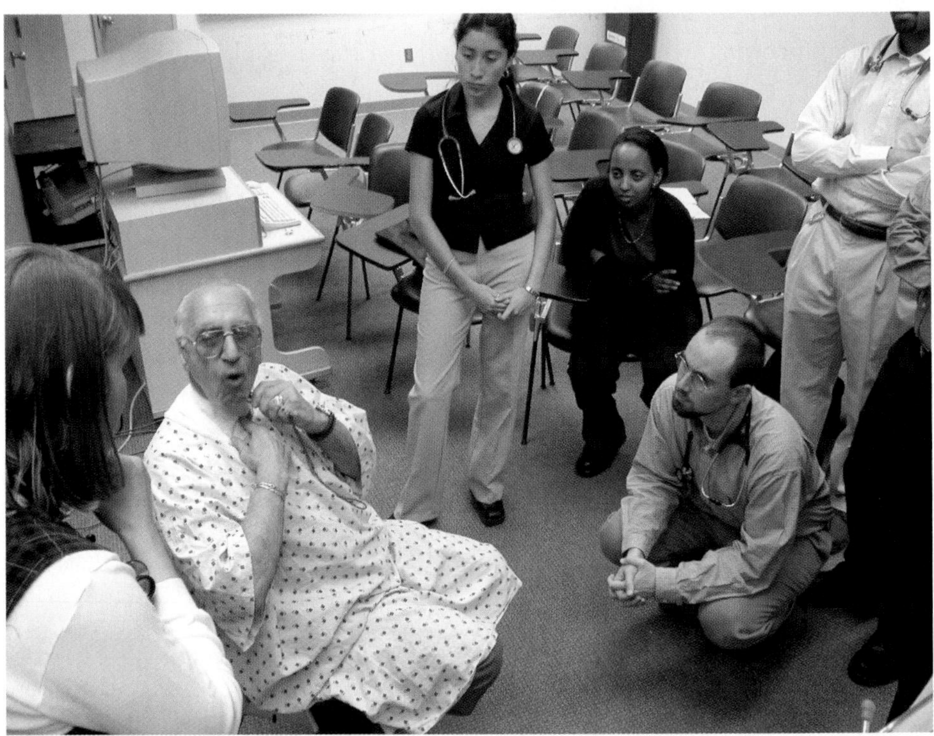

A laryngectomy patient speaks to a group of interested medical students about his symptoms and treatments. How does this kind of presentation make the topic more compelling?

Real World Real Speakers

Explain Complexity with Clarity

Mitchell Waldrop, author of *Complexity: The Emerging Science at the Edge of Order and Chaos*,[1] gave a guest lecture on complexity theory at one of our colleges. The lecture hall was packed with faculty and students eager to understand this much-talked-about but complex scientific process. Waldrop's talk was a great success. Why? Because he used several strategies to ensure that his explanation of "self-organizing systems" was clear and comprehensible.

He began by describing the essence of complexity theory by linking several well-known and intriguing events (the collapse of the Soviet Union, hurricanes, air traffic controller decision-making) to three key points about complexity theory. Then he used an analogy to compare and contrast his key points about order, complexity, and chaos to different states of water: ice, liquid, and steam. By displaying simple drawings of an ice cube, a country lake, and a steam bath, he reinforced the essential features of his key points. Finally, he used the example of national economies to illustrate order (economic stagnation), chaos (economic collapse), and a complex economy (strong and flexible).

Throughout his presentation, he linked his three key points to one another by using a variety of previews, transitions, and summaries and consequently led his audience to an understanding of a fascinating process.

1. M. Mitchell Waldrop, *Complexity: The Emerging Science at the Edge of Order and Chaos* (New York: W. W. Norton, 1989).

The first challenge when making an explanatory presentation is identifying the key components of the process. What's the "big picture"? We offer four recommendations that can help you find and describe the big picture to your audience. First, make sure that you are very well organized. Provide clear and well-supported key points. Second, use analogies to compare the unfamiliar concept you're presenting to something the audience already understands. Third, use presentation aids such as models and drawings to help your audience visualize or experience the process. Finally, use connectives frequently within your presentation. Transitions, internal previews, internal summaries, and signposts can reinforce and help your audience understand the interrelationship among key components (see Chapter 10, "Organizational Tools").

STRATEGIES FOR EXPLAINING COMPLEX PROCESSES

1. **Provide clear key points.**
2. **Use analogies, metaphors, and similes.**
3. **Use presentation aids.**
4. **Use connectives—transitions, previews, summaries, signposts.**

In the following example, the process of breathing for speech is outlined for a presentation designed to teach audience members how to improve the quality and strength of their voices.

Topic Area: Breathing for speech
Purpose: To explain how to breathe for speech in order to be a more effective and audible speaker
Central Idea: The ability to produce a strong and expressive voice requires an understanding and control of the inhalation/exhalation process.
Value Step: Learning to breathe for speech will make you a more effective and confident speaker.
Organization: Compare/Contrast—three components of the breathing process
Key Points: A. Active vs. passive exhalation
B. Deep diaphragmatic vs. shallow clavicular breathing
C. Quick vs. equal time for inhalation

By comparing something well known (breathing for life) to something less well known (breathing for speech), the speaker can help an audience understand this process. Throughout the presentation, the importance of breathing for speech can be explained by comparing it to playing a wind or brass instrument, by using presentation aids and demonstrations, and by making sure that transitions, previews, summaries, and signposts are used to connect the three key points.

Overcoming Confusion and Misunderstanding

In addition to instructing, explaining, and demonstrating, informative presentations can also help overcome confusion or misunderstanding. Why do people believe that going out into the cold without a hat will make them sick or that all dietary fat is harmful? People often cling to strong beliefs, even ones that are wrong. Informative speakers face the challenge of replacing old, erroneous beliefs with new, more accurate ones. The strategy is to first state the misconception; then acknowledge why it is believed; next, reject the misconception supported by evidence; and last, describe and explain the more acceptable belief. Let's keep it simple with an example about the fat content of our diets.

Topic: Fat in foods
Purpose: To explain that fat is an important element of everyone's diet
Central Idea: Our health-conscious society has all but declared an unwinnable and unwise war on food with high fat content.
Value Step: Eliminating fat from your diet can hurt you rather than help you lose weight.
Organization: Problem (misinformation)/Solution (accurate information)
Key Points: A. Many people believe that eliminating all fat from their diets will make them thinner and healthier.
B. This belief is understandable since fat is the very thing we're trying to reduce on our bodies.
C. Fat is an essential nutrient for your brain and body.
D. Fats are naturally occurring components in all foods that, in appropriate quantities, make food tastier and bodies stronger.

If you're thinking that an explanatory presentation designed to overcome confusion and misunderstanding is more persuasive than informative, you may be right. At the same time, it clearly fits within our definition of an informative presentation: one that seeks to instruct, explain, enlighten, demonstrate, clarify, correct, remind, or describe.

If it's successful, a presentation about fat in the diet will encourage an audience to rethink what they believe. The presentation does not advocate a change in diet, nor does it provide a chart spelling out recommended fat intake. Its primary purpose is to provide accurate information in the hope that an erroneous belief will be corrected. However, the borderline between informative and persuasive speaking can be elusive. As we note on page 408, what matters is your purpose. In this case, you're *telling* audience members about the beneficial role of dietary fat, not *asking* them to change their diets.

STRATEGIES FOR OVERCOMING CONFUSION AND MISINFORMATION

1. **State the belief or theory.**
2. **Acknowledge its believability.**
3. **Create dissatisfaction with the misconception.**
4. **State and explain the more acceptable belief or theory.**

Insider Secrets of Informative Presentations

By following the principles explained in this chapter, you can develop a successful informative presentation. However, you can apply some special techniques to take it to the next level. As teachers and presenters, we have listened to and evaluated thousands of informative presentations by students, colleagues, and corporate clients. We have vivid and long-lasting memories of some of them and absolutely no recollection of others. What made the memorable presentations exceptional? We're going to share some insider secrets of exceptional informative speaking.

INSIDER SECRETS OF INFORMATIVE SPEAKING

- **"KISS"**
- **Use one sensory image.**
- **Focus on your purpose.**

"KISS"

Keep it simple, speaker! Most audiences cannot absorb and retain complex information, no matter how important it may be. Can you identify the problem in the following exchange between a speaker and a listener?

Listener:	I heard your presentation on the new employee evaluation plan.
Speaker:	What do you remember about what I said?
Listener:	Well, you went through the plan page by page, explaining how the new provisions would apply.
Speaker:	What was one of the new provisions?
Listener:	Ah...well,...there was something about new forms, I think. I don't know—I'll look it up when I have to use it.

Exactly. The listener will look it up. The speaker's purpose—explaining the whole plan—was much too ambitious for a single, short presentation. Keep it simple, speaker! Audiences are intelligent, but they won't remember everything you say. In addition, most audience members are not highly skilled listeners. They can absorb only a few key ideas and facts during one sitting. Psychologists who study the capacity of short-term memory have concluded that most people can hold between five and nine chunks of information in their short-term memory.[9] Thus, an audience is unlikely to remember twelve recommendations or even ten good stories. Keep it simple if you want the audience to remember you and your message.

How could this speaker have presented the new evaluation plan more simply? First, she should have made sure that all employees already had a copy of the plan in their offices. Since many people don't read what they're given, the speaker would then have had to choose the essential elements to focus on during the presentation. She might have opted to explain the differences between the new and old plans or displayed the new forms that must be submitted at every deadline. Either option would have focused on one part of the plan only, but that would have been enough for a presentation. Keep it simple. Let the audience read the details.

How Do I Simplify a Complex Topic?

The "KISS" secret applies whether your presentation is informatory or explanatory as well as whether you're in a corporate setting or a communication class because most audience members don't have the listening skills or patience to accommodate every detail. Keep your topic tightly focused. Concentrate on one or two important details, not ten. The following examples illustrate how students narrowed their informative presentation topics into simpler messages by concentrating on just one aspect of a broader topic.

Broad Topic Area	Narrow Topic Area
Herbal Medicines	Chamomile
Mediation	Prehearing Preparation
The Vatican	The Vatican's Swiss Guard
Ice Hockey	The Goalkeeper's Protective Equipment
Islam	Sunnites and Shiites
Auto Maintenance	Changing the Oil
Insects	Fire Ants

Use One Sensory Image

What do you think of when you read the words *Ice Hockey* in the FAQ to the left? Fights, penalty boxes, screaming fans, chaos on ice, and body checks? Could one presentation incorporate all of these images? What do you start to imagine when you read *The Goalkeeper's Protective Equipment?* Perhaps you see a person bundled to near immobility or a menacing-looking face mask. A topic like "Herbal Medicines" can conjure up a witch's brew of images. "Chamomile" is easier to imagine—a strongly scented herb with tiny yellow blossoms.

You can make your informative presentation more interesting and memorable by focusing on one sensory image. Choose a topic that taps one of five senses.

When one of our students chose garlic as the subject of her informative presentation, she worried that there wouldn't be enough to say about her topic. After completing some initial research, she was overwhelmed with information, so she narrowed her topic to garlic's powerful odor. Although this topic can stimulate a visual image, the characteristic we all know and remember is garlic's strong and easily recognized odor. Her presentation focused on garlic's powerful smell and ways to get rid of that smell after eating a large dose. Even a talk on something as uninspiring as a new evaluation plan can benefit from the one-sensory-image tip. Visualizing a sample evaluation form with a deadline stamped across it is enough to provide the speaker with a clear central idea—and a memorable presentation aid. Choose one sensory impression—sight, sound, taste, smell, or touch—as the focus of your informative presentation.

Looking for one sensory image takes some creative thinking. If you wanted to give a presentation on baking chocolate chip cookies, you could begin by thinking of one sensory image for each of the five senses, then develop a central idea based on each.

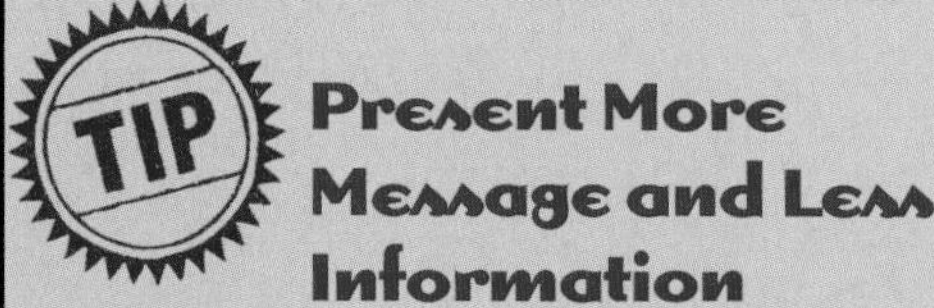

Present More Message and Less Information

Thomas Leech, a communication consultant and author, offers this tip for creating presentation aids: Present more message and less information. It applies equally well to developing informative presentations. Leech writes that "information overload is universally hated and, unfortunately, extremely common. The value of a presentation is to help listeners understand the essence of the subject."[1] Keeping your informative presentation simple and focused on the essentials helps you and your audience communicate successfully. You have a clear message you want to convey, and your audience receives that message.

1. Thomas Leech, *How to Prepare, Stage, & Deliver Winning Presentations* (New York: AMACOM, 1993), p. 139.

Sight: A thick brown cookie with visible chips
Sound: A cookie that doesn't snap when it's broken
Taste: A sweet cookie dough mixed with strong chocolate
Smell: A cookie that smells good while and even after baking
Touch: A soft and chewy cookie

An informative presentation could focus on how to make sure cookies are moist and chewy. Or you could emphasize the different tastes of different chocolates. Or you could identify the ingredients that make a cookie smell so good. How many of the five senses can you apply to the following topics: buying a new car, fire ants, explaining a company's mission statement, a school's discipline policy, the battle of Gettysburg, fighting oil well fires?

Focus on Your Purpose

In Chapter 4, "Purpose and Topic," we state that identifying your purpose is the critical first step in developing an effective presentation. First and foremost, you must know *why* you are speaking. Now we extend that advice to informative speaking. Not only must you identify your purpose, you must stick to it throughout your presentation!

As tempting as it may be to include a "neat" but irrelevant piece of information, or a "cool" but somewhat distracting visual, don't do it. Keep asking yourself whether your key points and supporting material directly support and advance the purpose and key points of your informative presentation. Don't go off topic. Focus on your purpose. Keep your eyes on the prize.

The final insider secret is that there isn't just one secret, any more than there's only one secret to the art of good painting, effective management, or skilled dancing. Insider secrets are nothing more than a series of good decisions that you make at key points in any process. First, you start with the basics. In dance, the basics involve a well-coordinated body, a sense of rhythm, and mastery of basic steps. In informative presentations, the basics involve all that we have discussed in the preceding chapters—clear purpose, audience analysis and adaptation, good research, effective organization, and skilled delivery. With these fundamentals well in hand, and with an understanding of informative speaking strategies and insider secrets, you can master the art of making interesting and effective informative presentations.

Summary

How do informative and persuasive presentations differ?

Although there can be a thin dividing line between informing and persuading, the speaker's purpose determines the difference. The primary purpose of an informative presentation is to instruct, explain, describe, enlighten, demonstrate, clarify, correct, or remind by sharing information with an audience. As soon as you ask listeners to change their opinions or behavior, your purpose becomes persuasive.

How can I respond to the unique challenge of informative speaking?

Include a value step in your introduction that gives your audience a reason to listen to the entire presentation.

What strategies can make my informative presentation more effective?

Decide whether the information you want to share requires informatory or explanatory communication. Then use appropriate supporting material and organizational tools, depending on whether you want to share new information, explain a difficult concept or complex process, or correct misinformation.

How can I make my informative presentation stand out?

After incorporating as many interest factors as you can, fine-tune your informative presentation by incorporating several insider secrets: (1) "KISS" ("Keep it simple, speaker!"), (2) highlight one sensory image, and (3) stay focused on your purpose.

Presentation Principles in Action

Values from A to Z

Directions: Develop a value step for one or more of the following topics. Try to find more than one reason why your audience should listen and remember a presentation on the selected topic(s). How will they benefit from listening? How will a presentation help them? Put yourself in their shoes and ask, "What's in it for me?"

Examples

Topic: Combating Fire Ants
Value Step: Helps you avoid painful, dangerous stings
Helps protect your garden
Helps protect your pets and local wildlife

Topic: Reading Music
Value Step: Helps you play musical instruments and sing
Helps you appreciate the complexity of good music
Helps you talk about music with other music lovers

Topics from A–Z

Auto Paint
Big Bang Theory
Chinese Language
Diatoms
Elevators
Fennel
Guiana
Hummingbirds
Ink
Jellyfish
Key Signature
Lent
Marxism
Nihilism
Opera
Parallax
Quarter Horses
Ramadan
Shingles
Tuskegee Airmen
Utilitarianism
Vishnu
Whiskey
Xenophobia
Yom Kippur
Zymurgy

Assessing Informative Presentations

The following informative presentation assessment instrument can help you evaluate the development of your own informative presentations as well as those made by other speakers. Use the following ratings to assess each of the criteria on the instrument:

E = Excellent G = Good A = Average F = Fair P = Poor
N/A = Not applicable to this presentation

Informative Presentation Assessment Instrument

CRITERIA	E	G	A	F	P	N/A
Purpose and Topic: Clear purpose, appropriate and narrowed topic						
Audience Analysis: Adapts to audience characteristics, interests, attitudes, etc.						
Credibility: Believable, trustworthy, competent, committed, etc.						
Logistics: Adapts to occasion and place of presentation, including use of equipment						
Content: Includes a variety of interesting and valid supporting material						
Organization: Clear organization and key points, effective introduction and conclusion, clear connectives						
Performance: Appropriate form(s) of delivery, effective vocal and physical delivery, including eye contact						
Presentation Aids: Effective choice, design, and handling of presentation aids						
Informative Strategies: Appropriate and effective strategies, a stated or implied value step						
Overall Evaluation:						

COMMENTS:

Key Terms

briefing 416
explanatory communication 410
informative presentation 407
informatory communication 410
value step 409

Notes

1 Katherine E. Rowan, "Informing and Explaining Skills: Theory and Research on Informative Communication," in *Handbook of Communication and Social Interaction Skills,* eds. John O. Greene and Brant R. Burleson (Mahwah, NJ: Lawrence Erlbaum Associates, 2003), p. 403.

2 Rowan, (2003), pp. 411–412. Also see Katherine E. Rowan, "A New Pedagogy for Explanatory Public Speaking: Why Arrangement Should Not Substitute for Invention," *Communication Education* 44 (1995): 236–250. We are indebted to Katherine E. Rowan, who has proposed a new pedagogy for informative speaking, one that focuses on understanding the differences between informatory and explanatory discourse and on adapting specific informative speaking strategies to the reasons for misunderstanding or confusion on the part of audience members.

3 Rowan (1995), p. 242; Rowan (2003), p. 411.

4 Rowan (2003), pp. 411–412.

5 See Daphne Duval Harrison, *Black Pearls: Blues Queens of the 1920s* (New Brunswick, NJ: Rutgers University Press, 1993).

6 Rowan, p. 241.

7 See James Price Dillard and Linda J. Marshall, "Persuasion as a Social Skill," in *Handbook of Communication and Social Interaction Skills,* eds. John O. Greene and Brant R. Burleson (Mahwah, NJ: Lawrence Erlbaum Associates, 2003), pp. 493–497.

8 Rowan (2003), pp. 422–423.

9 Douglas A. Bernstein et al., *Psychology,* 5th ed. (Boston: Houghton Mifflin, 2000), p. 223.

chapter nineteen

Understanding **Persuasion**

- What is persuasion?
- Will all audiences react to persuasive presentations in the same way?
- What's the best route to persuasion?
- How much persuasion can I achieve in a single presentation?
- How can marketing strategies be used to enhance persuasion?

Persuasive messages bombard us all from the time we wake up until the moment we end each day. Sometimes the persuasion is obvious—a commercial, a sales call, a political campaign speech. At other times it's less obvious—an inspirational sermon, an investment newsletter, a product sample in the mail. Businesses use persuasion to sell products. The armed forces use persuasion to justify their military budgets. Colleges use persuasion to recruit students and faculty. Even children use persuasive speaking to convince their parents to let them stay up late or to buy them the newest toy or breakfast cereal. In this chapter we explore how and why persuasion works. In the next chapter, "Developing Persuasive Presentations," we help you use this information to develop your own persuasive presentations.

What Is Persuasion?

Persuasion encourages audience members to change their opinions (what they think) or behavior (what they do). Figure 19.1 shows some opinions people may hold and the behaviors related to them. In informative presentations, a speaker *tells* something to an audience by giving directions, advice, explanations, or insights. In persuasive presentations, a speaker *asks* for something from the audience—their agreement or a change in their opinions or behavior. Just as information can be persuasive, a persuasive presentation can also inform. As we noted in Chapter 18, "Developing Informative Presentations," the speaker's purpose will determine which type of presentation he or she makes.

Figure 19.1 Opinions and Behavior

OPINION	BEHAVIOR
Nike makes the best athletic shoes.	Buy Nike shoes.
Vegetarian diets are good for your body—and good for the planet.	Cut red meat from your diet.
Your family is more important than your job.	Eat dinner with your family at least five times a week.
Stricter drunk driving laws and punishments are needed.	Write a letter to your state legislator supporting stricter drunk driving laws.

The Dynamics of Persuasion

Figuring out how to persuade audience members to change their opinions or behavior requires understanding why they may resist your efforts. Why don't you vote for the first candidate who asks for your support? Why don't you buy the cereal that a sports hero recommends? Why don't you change your job to one that offers more money? There are good answers to all of these questions, and that's the problem. All of the members of your audience can give you reasons explaining why they *won't* vote, buy, quit, or do any of the things you ask them to do. It's up to you to address these reasons.

Classify Audience Attitudes

Audience members vary greatly in their characteristics, learning styles, opinions, and behavior, as Chapter 5, "Audience Analysis and Adaptation," discusses. Therefore, no matter what your persuasive purpose is, you must understand and adapt to the people in your audience. For persuasive presentations, your audience analysis should pay special attention to people's attitudes. Whether their attitudes are positive, negative, or mixed, audience members will hold opinions about current issues such as abortion rights, affirmative action, and gun control as well as opinions about personal issues such as child rearing, religion, and patriotism. One way to clarify audience attitudes is to place the members of your audience along a spectrum of attitudes such as this one:

Strongly agree with me	Agree	Undecided	Disagree	Strongly disagree with me

Once you understand where audience members stand, you can develop persuasive strategies adapted to the people you're trying to persuade.

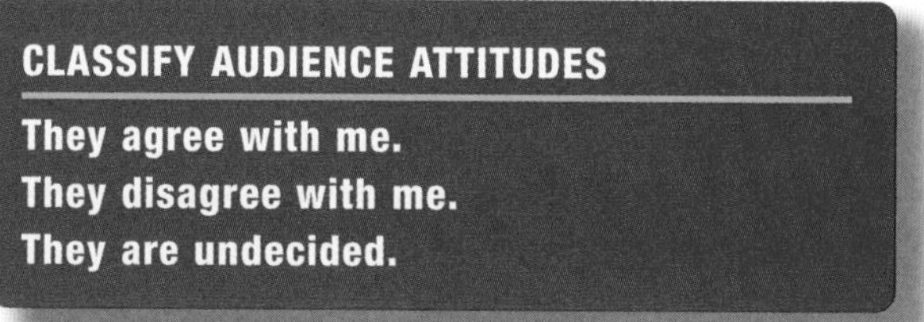

When Audience Members Agree with You

You may wonder if you even need to persuade an audience that already agrees with you. Although you don't have to sway them to your way of thinking, you can strengthen their existing agreement or use it to encourage behavioral change. Many audience members will agree that pollution is a problem, but most of them probably don't spend an hour a week cleaning up their neighborhoods or volunteering at a local recycling center. Persuasion can transform opinions into behavior. Several strategies can help you achieve your purpose with an audience that already agrees with you.

WHEN AUDIENCE AND SPEAKER AGREE, PERSUASION

- **Presents new information**
- **Strengthens audience resistance to counterpersuasion**
- **Excites the audience's emotions**
- **Provides a personal model**
- **Advocates a course of action**

An audience that already agrees with you will welcome *new* information that reminds them why they do and thus reinforces their agreement. In essence, the information persuades these audience members that they're "right" to feel the way they—and you—do.

Give them answers to the questions asked by those who disagree or those who can't decide. Show them the strengths of their position and the weaknesses of the positions of those who disagree. If, for example, your audience agrees that more regulations are needed to control air pollution, you can show them how to answer and even how to criticize industry denials.

At the Barton W. Stone Christian Home in Jacksonville, Florida, Representative Ray LaHood addresses senior citizen concerns. In order to achieve his persuasive purpose, Representative LaHood must adapt his message and delivery style to the attitudes, needs, and listening ability of his audience.

Preach to the Choir

People often use the expression "preach to the choir" to imply that speakers should avoid talking to friendly, supportive audiences. If they already agree, why preach to the choir? Yet members of the clergy preach to the choir all the time. In fact, choir members are often a congregation's truest believers. Every time a minister, priest, or rabbi delivers a sermon, he or she speaks to an audience that shares many of the same beliefs and agrees with most of what the sermon says. So why preach? It's because the strength and survival of a religious institution and its values lie with the faithful members—those who already believe. A preacher strengthens that bond by reassuring loyal members that their faith is well founded, encouraging them to stand by their religious beliefs and/or advocating good works. In much the same way, a persuasive presentation to an audience of "true believers" can build even stronger agreement with the speaker.

Excite audience members by being a cheerleader, a preacher, or a coach. Use examples and stories that demonstrate why they should feel pride, anger, happiness, or excitement about their shared opinions or behavior.

Also, be a model of the behavior you're advocating. Tell your audience what you've seen or done. Explain why and how they should pursue a similar course of action. Your example can persuade them to act—to sign a petition, write to a government official, report an incident to authorities, change their buying habits, or vote for a specific candidate.

When Audience Members Disagree with You

Audiences who completely agree with you are at one end of the spectrum; at the other end are audiences that don't agree with you at all. However, this disagreement doesn't mean that they will be hostile or rude. It *does* mean, though, that effecting a change in opinions or behavior becomes more challenging. In the face of disagreement, attempt to change only what *can* be changed.

WHEN AUDIENCE AND SPEAKER DISAGREE, PERSUASION

- **Sets reasonable goals**
- **Finds common ground**
- **Accepts differences of opinion**
- **Uses fair and respected evidence**
- **Builds personal credibility**

As much as you may want an audience that doesn't agree with you to come over to your way of thinking, a modest goal is more reasonable and realistic. You are unlikely to convince an audience full of avid meat-eaters to give up their steaks and become strict vegetarians. At best, you may be able to convince them that eating smaller meat portions is healthier. That alone would be a great accomplishment. Every small step taken in your direction can, in the long run, add up to a big change.

You also need to work on getting an audience that disagrees with you to listen. After all, you can't persuade an audience to change if they won't hear your recommendations. A good strategy here is to seek common ground with your audience. **Common ground** is a place where you and your audience can stand without disagreeing—it's a belief, value, attitude, or behavior that you and your audience share. Vegetarians and meat eaters usually agree that protein is important for a healthy diet. Smokers and nonsmokers may agree that smoking should be prohibited in and around schools. Literary and rhetorical scholar Kenneth Burke describes successful persuasion as the process of **identification,** in which the speaker and audience come to see that they share attitudes, ideas, feelings, values, and experiences.[1] Try to determine what you and your audience have in common. Identify with your audience by beginning on common ground before moving into potentially unfriendly territory.

You may also find common ground by accepting and adapting to differences of opinion. If your audience opposes censorship of any kind (and you're advocating curbs on hate speech), give them credit for defending the principle of freedom of speech. If your audience opposes a tax increase (and you're advocating one to build more elementary schools), acknowledge how difficult it can be to give up hard-earned money to the government.

An audience that disagrees with you will be highly critical, so it's vital that your supporting material be flawless. Choose your evidence from the most respected sources available and let your audience know where you found your information (see Chapter 8, "Supporting Material"). Also, make sure your sources aren't biased.

If you seek a reasonable goal, establish common ground, give the audience credit for their beliefs, and use fair and respected sources of information, your audience may come to like and respect you. Positive feelings about you may rub off on your arguments and help you to achieve your persuasive purpose. Your credibility can be a powerful tool to persuade an audience that disagrees with you.

FAQ

How Do I Find Common Ground?

Brainstorming can help you identify a belief or behavior that you share with your audience—a place where you both can stand without disagreement. Listed below are several controversial topics. Complete each sentence by stating an issue on which a speaker and audience would find common ground. For example, "Free speech advocates and antipornography groups would probably agree that... pornography should not be available to children."

1. Pro-capital-punishment and anti-capital-punishment groups would probably agree that ________________.
2. Opera lovers and rap music fans would probably agree that ________________.
3. Antitaxation groups and pro-education groups would probably agree that ________________.
4. National health insurance supporters and the American Medical Association would probably agree that ________________.
5. The National Rifle Association and gun control groups would probably agree that ________________.

The next time that you anticipate audience disagreement, write a similar fill-in-the-blank statement representing your position and your audience's viewpoint. Then generate as many endings for the sentence as you can. Did you find common ground?

When Audience Members Are Undecided

Some people may not have an opinion about a topic, or they may not be able to decide whether they agree or disagree. Audiences may be uncommitted for many reasons. Sometimes they're uninformed; at other times, they're unconcerned. Sometimes they're even adamantly neutral. Persuasion takes different courses, depending on the source of indecision.

Uninformed Audiences. An audience that doesn't know anything about a topic and hasn't formed an opinion about it is one of the easiest to persuade. All they need is information presented clearly and convincingly. Letting an uninformed audience know that Lyme disease and Rocky Mountain spotted fever are carried by ticks can persuade them to be more careful while walking in woods and fields. Telling uninformed employees that their credit union offers lower interest rates on loans than banks do can increase credit union membership. Sometimes information alone can persuade an uninformed audience.

WHEN AUDIENCE MEMBERS ARE UNDECIDED:

Persuade the uninformed by	• **providing information.**
Persuade the unconcerned by	• **gaining their attention and interest.** • **giving them a reason to care.** • **presenting relevant information.**
Persuade the adamantly neutral by	• **acknowledging both sides of the argument.** • **providing new information.** • **reinforcing old arguments.**

Unconcerned Audiences. When audience members see no reason to care or to have an opinion, the first step is getting their attention. Why should they listen to you if your topic doesn't affect them? If you can show them how the topic affects them personally, you are more likely to persuade them. Observe how this student speaker prepared her audience for a presentation on the importance of voting and taking political action:

> *How many of you applied for some form of financial aid for college? (More than half of the class raised their hands.) How many of you got the full amount you applied for or needed? (Fewer than one-fourth of the class members raised their hands.) I have some bad news for you. Financial aid may be even more difficult to get in the future. But the good news is that there's something you can do about it.*

This opening captured the audience's attention by asking them two questions about a situation that had affected many of them. Next, the speaker presented her arguments urging students to be more active in the political system. Once you have their attention and can arouse their motivation, you can use information to persuade an unconcerned audience.

When you get a flu shot or smallpox vaccination, you are being inoculated against a harmful illness. According to social psychologist William McGuire, protecting audience attitudes from counterpersuasion by the "other side" is like inoculating the body against disease.[1] By exposing the flaws in the arguments opposing your persuasive message, you can increase audience resistance to those arguments. By presenting the arguments of the opposition *and* then showing your audience how to refute them, you build up their resistance to counterpersuasion and create a more enduring change of attitude or behavior. **Inoculation** is most effective when audience members are highly involved critical thinkers because it first makes them aware that their attitudes are vulnerable to attack, then provides ammunition against or resistance to the attack.[2]

1. William J. McGuire, "Inducing Resistance to Persuasion: Some Contemporary Approaches," in *Advances in Experimental Psychology,* ed. L. Berkowitz (New York: Academic Press, 1964), pp. 192–229.
2. Robert H. Gass and John S. Seiter, *Persuasion, Social Influence, and Compliance Gaining* (Boston: Allyn & Bacon, 1999), pp. 195–196.

Adamantly Neutral Audiences. Adamantly undecided audiences can be difficult to persuade. Why? Because they've given the topic lots of thought. They understand both sides of the issue and either can't make up their minds or want to stay right where they are—in the middle. Some people can't or won't take a position for or against affirmative action, nuclear energy, capital punishment, or abortion. Because these are "hot" topics, this kind of audience knows the arguments on both sides. For example, audience members may be worried about the negative effects of television violence on children. At the same time, they oppose the censorship of program content by government agencies. They are caught between the pros and cons and, as a result, they cannot decide what should be done.

The first step with such an audience is to acknowledge how difficult it is to make a decision. Because this audience is already familiar with the issue, you should find *new* information that supports your position. Your task is to tip the balance. Maybe they don't know that the fears induced by scary television shows can spill over into a child's everyday life and interfere with otherwise normal activities.[2] No matter what side you're on, the key to persuading an undecided audience is to find something new. Then you can give new strength and force to your position by reminding them of all the other supporting arguments. Giving an adamantly undecided audience new information and then reinforcing old arguments leads to persuasion.

Why Does Persuasion Work?

More than in any other area of presentation speaking, researchers have devoted significant attention to developing theories that explain why persuasion works. One of the motives for this focus comes from the world of marketing and advertising. Theories of persuasion help advertisers develop effective marketing and sales campaigns. They also help speakers understand why enhancing their credibility can persuade some audiences while reinforcing logical arguments can persuade others. We know a lot about what does and doesn't work when messages are designed to persuade.

Here we offer four schools of thought about the nature of persuasion. Each one tries to explain why and how a particular persuasive strategy affects an audience.

Persuasive Proof

Skilled workers master the tools of their trades. A carpenter knows that nails and screws serve different functions. A good cook knows when to boil a sauce and when to turn off the heat. Just as there are tools of the trade for most tasks, the persuasive speaker has several basic tools that can be used to persuade an audience. Among the most critical is knowing why, when, and how to use persuasive proof to make an argument.

Like a lawyer arguing before a jury, the persuasive speaker must prove his or her case. The lawyer decides how to argue a case, but it's up to the jury to determine the argument's success. In the same way, when you try to persuade an audience, your success depends on whether or not the audience believes what you say. **Proof,** then, consists of the arguments you select and use to persuade an audience. Since audiences and persuasive situations

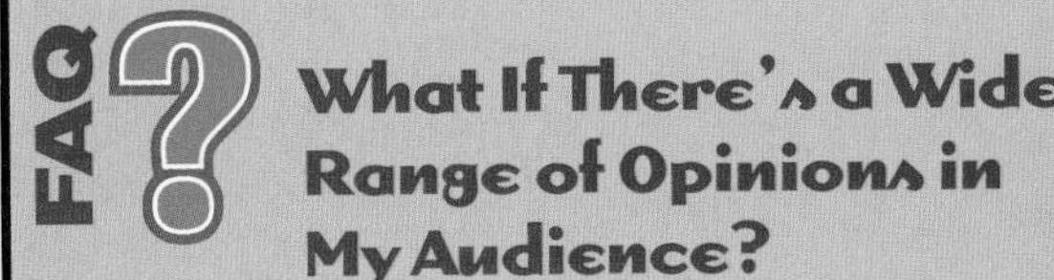

In the real world of presentation speaking, audience opinion will not be perfectly homogeneous. Rather, you're far more likely to face audiences consisting of some members who agree with you, others who don't, and still others who just aren't sure. Now what? You might want to focus your persuasive efforts on just one group—the largest, the most influential, or perhaps the easiest to persuade. Advertisers call this *targeting*. Or you might want to seek common ground among all three types of audience members. You could also try the persuasive strategy of providing *new* information from highly respected sources. Although especially suited to undecided audience members, this strategy can also encourage those who agree or disagree with you to change their opinions or behavior.

If you can get people who already agree with you to make it evident that they do (raise hands, clap, voice approval), others will join them.

Perhaps the best strategy of all is to acknowledge that you can't please everyone all of the time and to keep your persuasive message clear and consistent. Some members from each group will find your honesty, integrity, and resolve persuasive.

differ, so should your proof.[3] Thus, selecting the most appropriate forms of proof is just as important as developing valid arguments.

In the early fourth century B.C., Aristotle's *Rhetoric* proposed a theory that is still used as the basis for persuasion. By observing many persuaders at work in ancient Athens—in the law courts, the government, and the marketplace—Aristotle focused on what he called *artistic proofs* that a speaker could use to persuade.[4] Aristotle identified three major types of proof, which he labeled *ethos, pathos,* and *logos.* To that list we have added a fourth type of proof—*mythos.*

FOUR FORMS OF PROOF

Logos: Logical Proof
Pathos: Emotional Proof
Ethos: Personal Proof
Mythos: Narrative Proof

Logos: Logical Proof. **Logos** or **logical proof** asks if your arguments are reasonable and if your presentation makes sense. Logical arguments appeal to listeners' intellect, that is, their ability to think rationally and critically in order to arrive at a justified conclusion or decision. Note how the following speaker uses facts and statistics to prove logically that health care is too expensive for many Americans.

> *Many hard-working Americans cannot afford the most basic forms of health care and health insurance. Some 41 million Americans, 15.5 percent of the population, most of them lower-income workers or their families, live without health insurance—a necessity of modern American life. In New Mexico and Texas, 25 percent of the population is not covered by any form of health insurance. And contrary to popular belief, most of the uninsured are jobholders or their family members—the working poor.*[5]

The facts and statistics drive home the speaker's conclusion that the high cost of health insurance is seriously affecting the health and prosperity of many working Americans.

Logical proof, however, does not have to depend on supporting material. Often, appealing to your audience's common sense may be the best way to prove your point. Most audiences would accept the argument that everyone, whether rich or poor, needs good health care. Reasonable people will agree with reasonable arguments.

Logical proof can be divided into two major categories—deductive logic and inductive logic. Understanding each form can help you develop stronger arguments for your persuasive presentations.

- **Deductive logic.** When using deductive logic, you make your case by moving from accepted general premises to a specific conclusion. Consider this deductive argument for improving a company's customer service program:

Premise:	Successful companies emphasize customer service.
Premise:	We want to be a successful company.
Conclusion:	We should improve our customer service program.

  If the audience agrees with the general premises, it is likely they will also agree with the conclusion. Many smart persuaders use deductive logic by convincing an audience that there are certain criteria that ought to be applied to any proposed solution. For example, they may say, "Don't we all agree that any proposal ought to be cost-effective? Don't we also all agree that any proposal should build from our current strengths? And don't we all agree that any proposal should be easily implemented?" Because our savvy presenter just happens to have a proposal that meets all of these criteria, the audience is likely to be persuaded.

- **Inductive logic.** Whereas deductive proof moves from the general to the specific, inductive logic does just the opposite, moving from specific instances to a general conclusion.

Instance:	Our error rate is increasing monthly.
Instance:	Our competitors have new quality-control programs.
Instance:	Our customers are complaining that some of our products are shoddy.
Conclusion:	We need to develop a quality-control program.

Here you are building your argument piece by piece. If your audience agrees with each of your instances, they are likely to agree with your final conclusion.

Pathos: Emotional Proof. **Pathos** or **emotional proof** asks audience members to get in touch with their feelings. Audiences can experience various emotions—desire, anger, fear, pride, envy, joy, love, hate, regret, jealousy, or pity. Persuasion can be aimed at deep-seated feelings about qualities such as justice, generosity, courage, forgiveness, and wisdom.[6]

The following speaker uses a true story to touch the audience's emotions:

Kevin was twenty-seven years old and only two months into a new sales job when he began to lose weight and feel ill. After five weeks of testing and finally surgery, he was diagnosed with colon cancer. The bills were more than $100,000. But after his release from the hospital, he found out that his insurance benefits had run out.

As Kevin recalls, "Five weeks into the chemotherapy, I walked into my doctor's office, and he sat me down, put his hand on my knee, and told me there had been no payment. . . . Then he said that he could no longer bankroll my treatment. At one point in the middle of the whole thing, I hit bottom; between having cancer and being told that I had no insurance, I tried to commit suicide."

Instead of using logos to prove that many Americans suffer because they don't have dependable health insurance, the speaker tells a story of one person's suffering. Stories like this can persuade an audience that lack of health insurance can seriously affect the health and prosperity of many Americans in situations like Kevin's. Because audience members also know that the same thing *could* happen to them or someone they love, they are more likely to agree with the argument.

Many television commercials appeal to audience emotions. Telephone companies and fast-food restaurants use human interest stories and gentle humor. Insurance

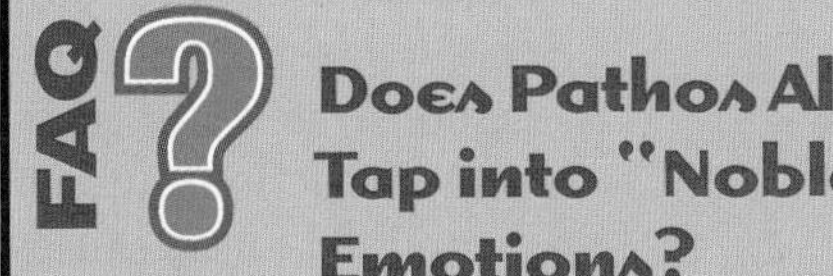

Does Pathos Always Tap into "Noble" Emotions?

Many advertisements, public service announcements, political ads, and magazine articles "go negative" as a persuasive technique. They try to persuade us by suggesting how bad things might be if we fail to take their advice. Do these fear appeals work? Yes. But they should be used both correctly and ethically. When a fear appeal is well justified, we are more open to being persuaded by it.

Fear appeals directed toward people we care about can also work well. Think of how many advertisements use this type of appeal. Life insurance ads suggest that you invest not for yourself but for those you love. Political ads tell you to vote for particular candidates because they will make the world better for your kids.

Fear appeals work best when they offer a way of avoiding the harms that are the centerpiece of the appeal. Consider public service announcements about AIDS. They don't say: "You will die of AIDS!" Instead, they say, "If you don't practice safe sex, you *may* die." An effective fear appeal tells listeners that they can do something to avoid what they fear.

companies may dramatize human tragedies to persuade you to buy more insurance protection. Perfect-looking people in beautifully filmed commercials may convince you to try a beauty product or a prepackaged diet. Whether we like it or not, commercials work because their creators understand the power of emotional proof.

Don't avoid emotional appeals because they seem to be illogical or irrational. Most of us have emotional responses to events and people, even though we cannot always provide a rational explanation for our reactions. The reasons that we are angry or sad or sympathetic or delighted can be quite understandable and justified.

Ethos: Personal Proof. As Chapter 6, "Speaker Credibility and Ethics," notes, audiences form an impression of each speaker they see and hear. This impression is based on many factors—the content of the speaker's message, the speaker's ability to effectively deliver that message, and the speaker's reputation and expertise on the topic. Remember, **ethos** has three major dimensions: competence, character, and charisma. Each of these dimensions can be enhanced as a form of **personal proof** in a persuasive presentation.

Audiences tend to be more easily persuaded by speakers with whom they can identify—people who are *similar* to them in attitude or background. You can build this perceived similarity in a number of ways. Try to dress in a way similar to your audience's style. If you are addressing a group of bankers, don't show up in jeans. Use examples and stories to demonstrate the similarity between your values and background and those of your audience. Highlight similarities, not differences.

In order to use personal proof, you can't just *tell* an audience to trust or to like you. Remember our pronouncement in Chapter 6: *Speaker credibility comes from your audience.* Only the audience can decide whether you are believable. Thus, you need to demonstrate that you are competent and of good character. Deliver your presentation with conviction. Audiences are more likely to be persuaded when the speaker seems committed to the cause.

Mythos: Narrative Proof. During the second half of the twentieth century, **mythos** or **narrative proof** has emerged as a fourth and significant form of persuasive proof. According to the communication scholars Michael and Suzanne Osborn, mythos addresses the values, faith, and feelings that make up our social character and is most often expressed through traditional stories, sayings, and symbols.[7] The Osborns maintain that the "unique function of mythos is to help listeners understand how the speaker's recommendations fit into the total belief and value patterns of their group."[8] In other words, narrative proof appeals to the ingrained beliefs and myths that audience members hold about themselves.

In America we are raised on mythic stories that teach us about patriotism, freedom, honesty, and national pride. President George Washington's admission—"I cannot tell a lie"—after cutting down the family's cherry tree may be a myth, but it has helped teach millions of young Americans about the value of honesty. The request "Give me your tired, your poor" from the Emma Lazarus poem inscribed on the base of the Statue of Liberty, the "Women and children first" directive for passengers on sinking ships, and the civil rights speech and song refrain "We shall overcome" are statements that have become part of American beliefs and values. Speakers who tap into the mythos of an audience form a powerful identification with their listeners.

One of the best ways to enlist mythos when trying to persuade is to tell stories. Religions teach many values through parables. Families bond through stories shared across generations. Effective leaders who inspire others are almost always excellent storytellers. Remember the two characteristics of a successful story that we described in

Fix It Before It Frays

One of your authors once heard an executive at a large manufacturing firm use a story to create a new company value. He told how he had recently been to Greece, where he visited an old monastery that stood at the top of a mountain. The mountain had sheer cliffs on every side. The monastery had been built there many centuries ago because it offered perfect protection for the monks. The executive discovered, however, that the only way to visit the monastery was to get into a large basket and have a monk slowly use pulleys to draw up the basket. He got in, he said, and as the monk pulled him up, he noticed that the rope was quite frayed. A little worried, he turned to the monk and asked, "When do you decide to change the rope?" The monk responded, "Whenever it breaks."

After the laughter died down, the executive became more serious and said, "In this company, we don't wait until the rope breaks. We don't even let it fray. We fix things before they become hazards." The story was used to create a new belief and value: Fix it before it frays. The hope was that every time an employee came across a potential hazard, she or he would recall the story of the monk and report or fix the problem. The story and the statement "Fix it before it frays" became a form of mythos at the company. And it made the executive's presentation more persuasive and memorable than any simple declarative sentence about safety could ever do.

Chapter 13, "Generating Interest"? A story that has both coherence (the story hangs together and has meaning) and fidelity (it's truthful or believable) can be applied to logical and emotional causes and will appeal to our imagination and feelings. And when told well, a story can be one of the most powerful persuasive tools we have.

The Elaboration Likelihood Model of Persuasion

Which forms of proof are the most effective—those based on emotion, those based on substantive evidence and logic, those centered on speaker credibility, or those built on stories? The answer is ... it depends. Two other factors, listeners' thinking abilities and motivations, became the focus of research by two social psychologists, Richard Petty and John Cacioppo. They developed the **Elaboration Likelihood Model of Persuasion,** which says that there are two "routes" to persuasion, depending on how able and willing an audience is to process a message.[9]

The term *elaboration* refers to whether an audience can engage in "elaborative" or critical thinking (see Chapter 2, "Listening and Critical Thinking"). Will they listen comprehensively and analytically to a message? Are they capable of analyzing the arguments in a message? Are they motivated to listen to a presentation about the issue? Do they see the issue as relevant to their lives? A presenter's answers to these questions can help him or her determine which route or persuasive strategy to follow.

Routes to Persuasion. Persuasion can take a central route or a peripheral route. When people are highly involved in an issue and when they are capable of thinking critically, the central route to persuasion is best. Highly involved critical thinkers do a lot of counterarguing when listening to a persuader. They may think, "I just read an article that proves the opposite" or "That may be fine in Arkansas, but it won't work in South Dakota." Thus, the best form of proof with these involved listeners is a logical one in which a speaker's claims are backed by strong and believable **evidence.** When audiences are highly involved, persuasion using the central route tends to be enduring, resistant to counterpersuasion, and predictive of future behavior.

When audiences are less involved or aren't interested in an issue, you're better off taking the peripheral route. Interestingly, these types of listeners are highly influenced by whether they like the speaker and whether they think the speaker is credible.[10] The peripheral route involves focusing on cues that aren't directly related to the substance of a message—catchy phrases, dramatic stories or statistics, the quantity (rather than quality) of arguments and evidence, and the credibility and attractiveness of the speaker. Figure 19.2 shows key aspects of both routes.

Figure 19.2 The Elaboration Likelihood Model of Persuasion

When your audience is motivated and able to think critically, the central route to persuasion works well. The peripheral route is better suited to less motivated, less critical audiences.

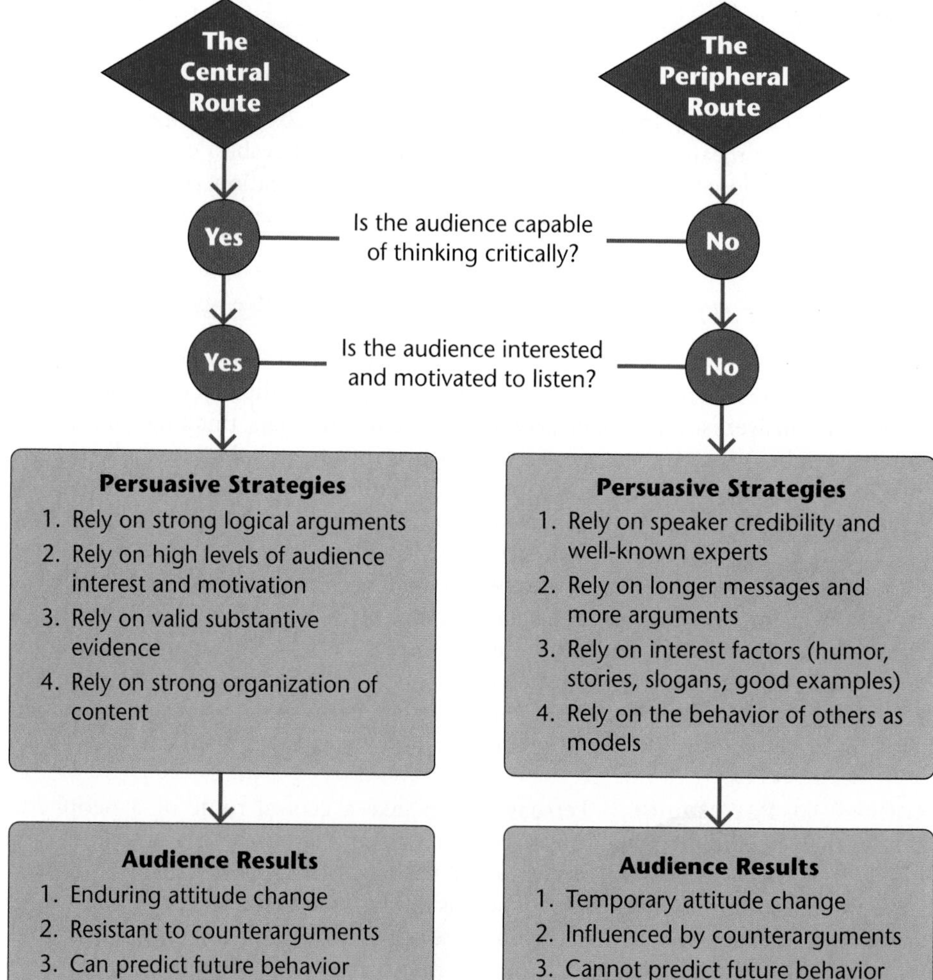

To better understand the two routes to persuasion, consider the Elaboration Likelihood Model from the listener's perspective. Let's suppose that you're very concerned about the traffic patterns in your neighborhood. You're tired of long waits at lights and slow-moving traffic. You attend a meeting where a county official is trying to convince the audience that traffic will not get worse in the future and that available funds would be better spent on parks and recreation. Since you're a good critical thinker and care about this issue, you're listening carefully and are probably generating a lot of counterarguments—traffic is awful, it's going to get worse, we need to spend money to alleviate traffic problems right now.

If the presenter wants to persuade you to adopt her point of view, she is going to have to come up with some good, logical arguments that take the central route to persuasion. Why? Because you're questioning almost everything she says. The only way that she can create a lasting change in your opinion is to present logically persuasive arguments that address your internal counterarguments directly.

Now, let's suppose that the person who's sitting next to you doesn't care that much about the traffic. He works at home and rarely drives during the busiest commuting hours. He's not very involved and is unlikely to do much critical thinking about this issue. How would the county official persuade him? The Elaboration Likelihood Model suggests that a peripheral route would be more effective. While logic and good evidence may be useful, the uninvolved listener might be more attuned to the speaker's emotional appeals as well as to her credibility and attractiveness ("she seems like a nice person," "she sounds as if she knows what she's talking about," "Lots of people here agree with her"). Interestingly, you often get only short-term attitude changes when using the peripheral route.

Applying the Elaboration Likelihood Model of Persuasion. Using the Elaboration Likelihood Model of Persuasion requires a deep understanding of your audience. As we've indicated, you begin by assessing their levels of personal involvement and their ability to think critically. If you think the majority of people in your audience are highly involved and will respond to the central route, develop a well-organized presentation with strong arguments buttressed by good evidence and sound reasoning. Imagine all the different objections and reservations that audience members may raise as they think critically about your message. Consequently, when you do address these reservations in your presentation, you are more likely to be persuasive than if you ignore them.

What Are Heuristics?

Heuristics is a word that does not appear in small dictionaries. It should, however, because understanding the nature of heuristics helps explain why and how persuasion works in everyday life and in persuasive presentations. **Heuristics** are shortcut decision-making rules that are correct often enough to be useful. For example, listeners often use simple decision-making rules such as "Experts can be trusted" or "Consensus implies correctness" to reach a conclusion without carefully scrutinizing the quality of persuasive arguments. Unfortunately, because some heuristics are widely believed, unethical persuaders use them to win agreement from their audiences even though their arguments are flawed.[1]

The peripheral route to persuasion in the Elaboration Likelihood Model often relies on hueristics such as the quantity (rather than the quality) of arguments or the credibility of the speaker. The following brief list includes common heuristics relevant to persuasive messages:

- Longer messages are strong messages.
- The quality of an item correlates with its price.
- We should trust those whom we like.
- The behavior of others is a good clue as to how we should behave ourselves.
- Confident speakers know what they are talking about.
- Something that is scarce is also valuable.

Think of how these heuristic cues are exploited in person-to-person sales. Successful salespeople appear confident, likable, and trustworthy and also provide multiple reasons for purchasing expensive, high-quality, limited-edition products that are very popular with discerning customers.

When you hear a message that is loaded with heuristic cues, be cautious. Analyze the arguments carefully before you succumb to their persuasive power.

1. See Alexander Todorov, Shelley Chaiken, and Marlone D. Henderson, "The Heuristic-Systematic Model of Social Information Processing," in *The Persuasion Handbook: Developments in Theory and Practice,* eds. James Price Dillard and Michael Pfau (Thousand Oaks, CA: Sage, 2002), pp. 195–211; James Price Dillard and Linda J. Marshall, "Persuasion as a Social Skill," in *Handbook of Communication and Social Interaction Skills,* eds. John. O. Green and Brant R. Burleson (Mahwah, NJ: Lawrence Erlbaum Associates, 2003), pp. 494–495.

Alternatively, if you think your audience members are far less involved and thus more responsive to the peripheral route to persuasion, concentrate your attention on your own credibility and attractiveness, emotional appeals, and the power of stories and traditions. Try to demonstrate how and why the issue affects each and every audience member. Something as simple as asking a rhetorical question—a technique that roughly one-third of all radio commercials use[11]—can motivate people to give more attention and thought to a message.

Many audiences, however, are composed of different people with different levels of interest in a topic or issue—and with different critical thinking and listening abilities. It may be necessary to use both routes to persuasion in a single presentation, even though the highly involved critical thinkers may become impatient with your peripheral strategies while less involved audience members may become lost or bored when you present detailed argumentation. If you must take both routes, be sure to balance the strategies.

Social Judgment Theory

Choosing the best proof or route to persuasion rests on understanding your audience, as we've seen. Yet a team of psychologists claims that you cannot really understand how people feel about an issue just by asking them about the strength of their attitudes. Even if two people say that they agree, you still can't conclude that they share identical attitudes. Why not? Because one person may hold that position more intensely than the other person. The first person strongly agrees and doesn't accept any alternative. The second person agrees but is not highly committed to the position. Although both hold the same position, one holds it more intensely.

According to the **Social Judgment Theory** proposed by psychologists Muzafer Sherif, Carolyn Sherif, and Robert Nebergall, people's reactions to persuasive statements are best reflected by ranges—what they call *latitudes of acceptance* (statements they agree with), *rejection* (statements they can't agree with), and *noncommitment* (statements that are neither acceptable nor nonacceptable).[12] Earlier in this chapter, we recommended ways to persuade audience members who agree, disagree, or are undecided. Social Judgment Theory highlights one very important and additional aspect of the persuasive process: the possibility that audience members who hold the *same* position on an issue might have very different views and tendencies for changing their opinions.

Consider two audience members, Charlene and Alonia. A local pollster asks their opinion about county funding and support for the public library system. Their response choices range from 1 (cut funding by 5 percent and close two library branches) to 7 (increase funding by 10 percent and build a new branch library). Both choose 4 (increase funding by 2 percent). They agree, right? Not necessarily. Figure 19.3 looks at their latitudes of acceptance, noncommitment, and rejection.[13]

Latitude of Acceptance. Charlene has a very narrow latitude of acceptance—she cannot agree with any response other than 4. Why? Although she frequently uses the library to borrow books and attend meet-the-author programs, she also feels overburdened by the county's property tax rate and doesn't want to see her taxes go up. Thus, even though she wants to support the library system, she cannot endorse anything more than a 2 percent increase in funding.

Alonia, on the other hand, has a large latitude of acceptance. If given good reasons, she could change her response to a 2 or 3—or even to a 5 or 6. She doesn't use the library very much, and because she rents her apartment, she doesn't feel the direct sting of

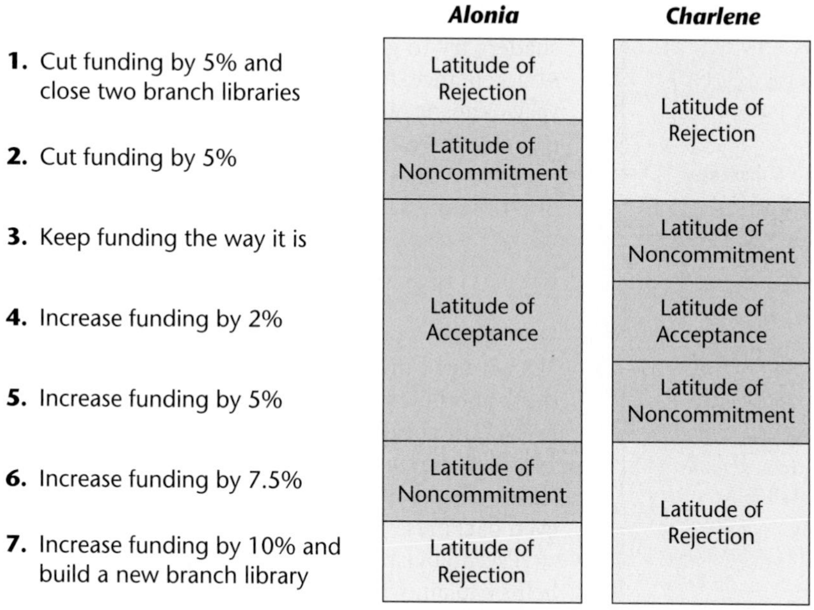

1. Cut funding by 5% and close two branch libraries
2. Cut funding by 5%
3. Keep funding the way it is
4. Increase funding by 2%
5. Increase funding by 5%
6. Increase funding by 7.5%
7. Increase funding by 10% and build a new branch library

Alonia

Latitude of Rejection

Latitude of Noncommitment

Latitude of Acceptance

Latitude of Noncommitment

Latitude of Rejection

Charlene

Latitude of Rejection

Latitude of Noncommitment

Latitude of Acceptance

Latitude of Noncommitment

Latitude of Rejection

Figure 19.3

Social Judgment Theory

Since listeners are easier to persuade within their latitudes of acceptance, almost impossible to persuade in their latitudes of rejection, and open to persuasion in their latitudes of noncommitment, what should a speaker do when trying to gain more support for the public library system?

property taxes. Because she wants to support what seems like a good cause, she joins Charlene at the 2 percent funding level but might accept other funding options as well.

Latitude of Noncommitment. Charlene, the tax-weary library patron, has a narrow latitude of noncommitment. A highly skilled persuader might get her to accept a 3 or 5, but doing so would be hard work. Alonia is different. Her latitude of noncommitment is large. She's okay with a 2 or even a 6. Give her a good reason to change her mind, and she will.

Latitude of Rejection. Their latitudes of rejection include all statements Charlene and Alonia cannot agree with. Charlene has a large one. She rejects almost everything but the choice she has made. She doesn't want to support a significant increase in funding but also doesn't want the library system to suffer or to cut services. On the other hand, Alonia's latitude of rejection is comparatively small. The only positions she can't imagine supporting would be 1 and 7. Charlene is far more emphatic about her position than Alonia.

Applying Social Judgment Theory. What does all this mean for you, the persuader? It means that in addition to having to address a range of opinions, you also may need to make sure that you don't give listeners grounds for rejecting your message. If you find yourself advocating a position that's in your listeners' latitude of rejection, try to establish some common ground, respect differences of opinion, and build your credibility by using fair and respected evidence. Both Charlene and Alonia would probably reject attending a public rally supporting the construction of a new library building, but they might be willing to join you in signing a petition urging elected officials to study the feasibility of expanding the library system. In general, try to advocate a position closer to your listeners' latitude of acceptance. Don't push too hard for a position that's too far from your listeners' current attitudes and feelings.

Launch a Persuasive Campaign

Think about how your attitudes and behaviors have changed over time. You probably find some things more acceptable today than you did ten years ago. Did your attitudes change overnight? No. Rather, you were probably exposed to a variety of persuasive messages over a period of time. Your latitude of acceptance slowly widened, and the range of what you found objectionable narrowed.

Can you identify the exact day on which you changed many of your attitudes, beliefs, and behaviors? With only a few dramatic exceptions such as the birth of a child or a startling revelation, you probably cannot pinpoint the moment. Consider this—people who move to South Florida gradually adapt to hot weather and then complain about freezing when they venture back to the North. Residents of the Southwest gradually learn to enjoy the hot, spicy foods of their region, whereas a Midwestern visitor may be overwhelmed by the burn of hot chili.

The same is true in persuasion. It usually takes time and many exposures to new ideas for us to change. A single broadcast of a television commercial rarely sells a new product. Persuasion often requires a **campaign**—a series of persuasive messages designed to achieve a specific social, political, or commercial goal.

In election campaigns you are bombarded with a wide range of sophisticated messages designed to influence your attitude and voting behavior. Often the candidate who can afford the most ads wins. Major military campaigns rely on a variety of messages from elected officials, supportive news media, and military spokespersons to sway public opinion about the necessity for intervention. Unrelenting warnings about weapons of mass destruction, terrorist links, perilous oil supplies, human rights atrocities, and the prospect of domestic terrorism gradually moved public opinion in the United States from skepticism to support of the U.S. invasion of Iraq.

Depending on your purpose and the disposition of your audience, you may need to launch a persuasive campaign if you hope to change audience opinions and behavior. You may have to speak to many different audiences on many occasions and prepare customized messages for those audiences in order to achieve your purpose.

Social Judgment Theory also tells us that effective persuaders try to gradually broaden their listeners' latitudes of acceptance. Although this takes time and effort, it is a very realistic approach. Social Judgment Theory thus gives one reason that persuasive campaigns—series of persuasive presentations—tend to be more effective than one-time messages.[14]

Psychological Reactance Theory

How would you feel if a speaker got up and declared, "Listen up! I'm here to tell you exactly what you should think and how you should behave." "Oh yeah?" you might reply, "Go ahead and try!" In addition to understanding why persuasion works, it's just as important to understand what happens when persuasion fails to work or even backfires on a speaker.

Psychologist Jack W. Brehm provides a theory that helps explain why telling an audience what *not* to do can produce the exact opposite reaction. **Psychological Reactance Theory** suggests that when you perceive a threat to your freedom to believe or behave as you wish, you may go out of your way to do the forbidden behavior or rebel against the prohibiting authority.[15]

If you tell an audience, "Do this" or "Don't believe that," you may run into strong resistance. After years of telling young people to "just say *no*," we have learned that preaching abstinence (from alcohol, drugs, premarital and unprotected sex, or junk food) doesn't work very well. Instead, we should recommend behaviors that reduce harm. For example, messages advocating the use of designated drivers and seat belts avoid saying, "Don't drink." Instead, they suggest moderation and responsible behavior to avoid the harms of drunk driving.

Even though the reactance response may be unreasonable or highly emotional, it does not make sense to ignore or fight it. Fighting reactance just throws more fuel on the fire. The effective persuasive message is one that does not give the impression of pressuring the audience or constraining their choices.[16]

If you believe that your audience may react negatively to your advice or directions, consider the following strategies as a means of reducing the likelihood of a reactance response:

- Avoid strong, direct commands such as "Don't," "Stop," and "You *must.*"
- Avoid extreme statements depicting terrible consequences such as "You will die," "You will fail," or "You will be punished."
- Avoid finger pointing—literally and figuratively. Don't single out specific audience members for condemnation or harsh criticism.

- Advocate a middle ground that preserves the audience's freedom and dignity while moving them toward attitude or behavior change.
- Use strategies appropriate for audience members who disagree, as described previously in this chapter.
- Respect your audience's perspectives, needs, and lifestyles.

Sonja Foss and Karen Foss build on this last strategy by suggesting that you can avoid rejection by creating a climate conducive to change. Rather than telling or selling, you should "invite your audience to see the world as you do and consider your perspective seriously."[17] When you take the audience's perspective, needs, and even fears into account, everyone gains a better understanding of the issue and of one another. Creating a climate conducive to change occurs when a "speaker sees audience members as having experiences and holding perspectives that are valuable and legitimate."[18] Under such circumstances, audience members feel *invited* to change rather than feeling as though the speaker is demanding compliance.

Applying Marketing Concepts to Persuasion

The idea of a persuasive campaign comes to us from the world of marketing. In fact, a great deal of our practical knowledge about persuasion comes from market researchers who study how to influence buyers in the marketplace. It's amazing how successful some marketing campaigns are in today's competitive business world. They succeed because their creators understand how persuasion works. Of the many strategies used by advertisers, five apply especially well to persuasive speaking.

MARKETING PRINCIPLES FOR PERSUASION

Create memorable slogans
Generate strong images
Focus on benefits
Address audience needs
Enlist celebrities

Create Memorable Slogans

We associate many products with their slogans: "Quality is job 1" (Ford), "A mind is a terrible thing to waste" (the United Negro College Fund), "Breakfast of champions" (Wheaties), and "Be all you can be" (U.S. Army). The word *slogan* comes from the Gaelic phrase *slugh gairm,* which means "battle cry." The best slogans are a product's battle cry in the marketplace. They are strong, are easily remembered, and conquer the competition. Slogans briefly summarize the message about a product's benefits in a short, easy-to-remember phrase.[19]

There is almost a magical quality to some advertising slogans. When we think of a product name or a slogan, all sorts of images and feelings come to mind. Marketers spend millions of dollars trying to create and get consumers to identify with the labels and slogans for their products. Good slogans "imbue the products with the positive qualities which, over time, become embedded in receivers' minds."[20] A slogan can even affect people's perceptions of a concept. For example, groups on both sides of the abortion debate call themselves "Pro-." After all, few people would want to be identified with an anti-choice or anti-life group.

Great persuaders understand the potential and power of words. They create and use memorable slogans with the hope that listeners will be persuaded when they are moved or inspired by a turn of phrase. When Dr. Martin Luther King Jr. proclaimed, "I have a dream," and when his supporters sang, "We shall overcome," both statements became battle cries for the civil rights movement.

A memorable phrase or statement can become a form of mythos—a way of proving an argument. Whether it's President Abraham Lincoln's "government of the people, by the people, for the people" or President John F. Kennedy's statement "Ask not what your country can do for you—ask what you can do for your country," the effect of the words can be powerful and persuasive.

Generate Strong Images

Ever notice how sleek the cars look in television ads? A car ad may show a new vehicle driving over dusty hills, through blizzards, and across streams. But at the end of the ad, the car is always perfectly clean. Does this look like your car? Probably not. Ads are designed to create an image. People buy images. So do audiences.

According to Karen Lawson, a communication consultant and instructor, "imagery is the use of words to create pictures in the minds of the audience. Good speakers draw the picture very carefully so that audience members can share the speaker's experience and remember the speaker's message."[21] Images do not have to be beautiful to be memorable and effective. When organizations are raising funds or recruiting volunteers for charitable causes, we often see or hear detailed descriptions of needy families, ill children, diseased or starving animals, drought-stricken states, hurricane-damaged communities, and war-torn countries. The more vivid the images you create—whether positive or negative—the more persuasive you can be.

Focus on Benefits

Think about the image of a car you'd like to own. Like any other car, it has four wheels, doors, a hood, and bumpers, among other parts. But is that why you want to buy this car? Few people buy a car because of its basic features. What, then, prompts them to want one car more than another? For one buyer, safety, affordability, and a minimal need for repairs might matter most. For another, gaining status among colleagues and friends could be more important than anything else. Having "made it" both socially and professionally, both buyers are now focusing on the benefits they associate with purchasing a particular car.

In marketing there are distinctions drawn between features, functions, and benefits. *Features* allow you to perform a *function* that generates certain *benefits.* When you are marketing an item, "you're not selling the product; you're selling the benefits of the product."[22] Effective persuasive speakers do the same. Audiences respond positively to presentations when they want the benefits you are describing. Skilled persuaders answer their listeners' most basic question: "What's in it for me?"

Address Audience Needs

Most of the purchases we make satisfy some need. We buy food for sustenance, homes for shelter, jewelry to give pleasure to ourselves or to the one we love, a car for

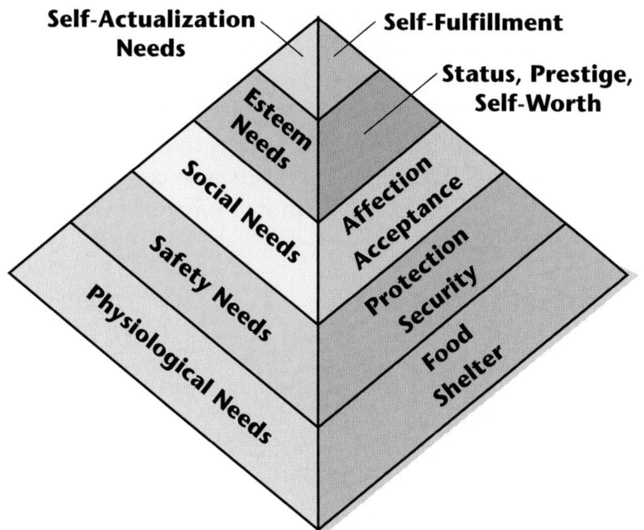

Figure 19.4

Maslow's Hierarchy of Needs

Persuasive speakers should appeal to deficiency needs when listeners are faced with threats to their physical survival, personal safety, and social development. When these needs have been met in an audience, speakers can then appeal to their listeners' fulfillment needs—their desires for esteem and self-actualization.

transportation (and perhaps also for status), and designer clothing to make an impression. Effective persuaders understand that if their proposals satisfy audience needs, they are more likely to succeed. Although there may be an infinite number of individual needs, we can classify most people's needs in terms of a few major types.

Psychologist Abraham Maslow has suggested one way of thinking about these needs: as a hierarchy (see Figure 19.4).[23]

At the lowest, most basic level of **Maslow's Hierarchy of Needs,** people have physiological needs. They need food and shelter. Beyond physiological needs are safety needs—a desire for protection and security. At the next level, there are social needs—a desire for affection and acceptance. These three levels are often called *deficiency needs* because if they are not met, we have difficulty surviving.

Beyond the three deficiency needs are two *fulfillment needs*—esteem needs (self-worth, prestige, status) and a need for self-actualization (for becoming self-fulfilled). When trying to persuade, you may think about these needs and use them as justification for the case you are making. For instance, a speaker making a presentation about exercise might note the value of exercise for health (physiological need), for the pleasant company of others (social needs), and for building confidence (esteem needs).

Another psychologist, William Schutz, has offered a second theory that focuses on psychological needs.[24] He proposes three basic needs in his **Fundamental Interpersonal Relationship Orientation (FIRO) Theory.**

- *Need for Inclusion:* To some extent, all of us have a need to be included. For instance, if we feel we've been excluded from a meeting, we may interpret any statement about the results of that meeting negatively. Effective persuaders make audience members feel included. They use plural pronouns such as *we, our,* and *us* rather than *I* and *my*. They ask audience members to *share, join,* and *participate.*
- *Need for Control:* Most of us think of ourselves as independent people. No one controls us; if anyone tries, we may rebel. The expression "I've gotta be me" is really everyone's theme song. Persuaders know this. If they push too hard, they will create resistance in their audiences. As Psychology Reactance Theory notes, telling an audience that you're going to change their minds about something can make them more resistant to persuasion. You are threatening their sense of

control. Using statements such as "It's your decision," "You can make a difference," and "It's up to you" can speak to listeners' control needs.

- *Need for Openness:*[25] Most of us want to be liked and appreciated. Usually, when someone doesn't like you, it bothers you. And you're not likely to listen or be persuaded by this person. Effective persuaders try to make sure that audience members feel well liked and respected. Speakers who communicate openly with genuine affection for their audiences are more likely to be successful persuaders.

Enlist Celebrities

Celebrity endorsements work in advertising. In one study, ads with testimonials from celebrities scored 11 percent higher than the average in terms of whether potential buyers noticed the ad and its product.[26] On the other hand, testimonials from noncelebrities actually earned below-average scores in terms of whether they were noticed. Thus, Jane and John Doe's endorsement of milk will not have the same impact as the entire cast of a popular television show posing with milk "mustaches" on their upper lips.

What do such research findings mean for you as a speaker? First, they should encourage you to use testimony from famous people who, at the very least, can attract listener attention. As we noted when explaining the Elaboration Likelihood Model of Persuasion, endorsements by celebrities work best when you're using the peripheral route to persuasion, but the results may not be long-lasting. Finding a respected celebrity who agrees with your position will enhance your persuasiveness. Thus, when President Clinton was trying to move the proposal to join NAFTA (the North Atlantic Free Trade Alliance) through Congress, he called on every living president—both Republicans and Democrats—to publicly support the proposed trade agreement. Bipartisan "endorsements" from such esteemed figures left Congress little choice but to give in and join the alliance.

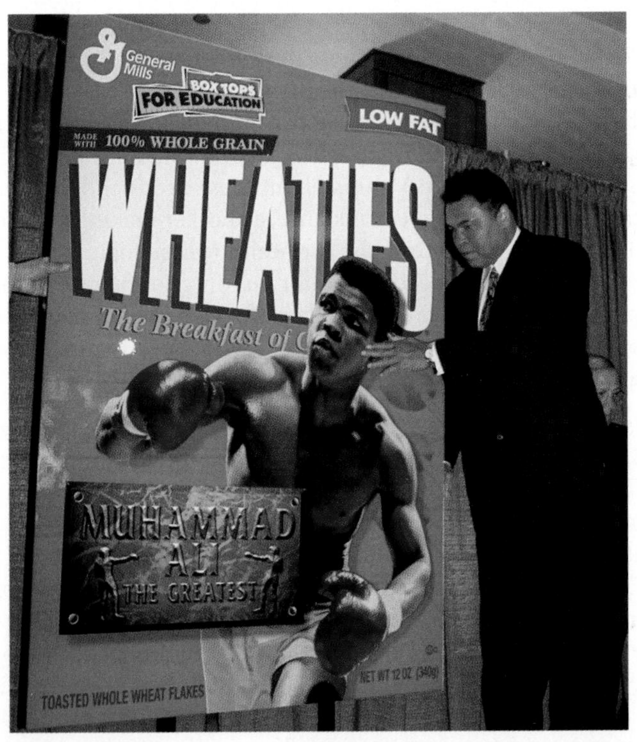

Muhammad Ali with a display of the special edition Muhammad Ali Wheaties box that marks the cereal's 75th anniversary. The slogan "The Breakfast of Champions" and celebrity endorsements have sold millions of boxes of cereal for General Mills.

Aristotle's forms of proof, the Elaboration Likelihood Model of Persuasion, Social Judgment Theory, Psychological Reactance Theory, hierarchical and psychological needs theories, and marketing research all try to explain why and how persuasion works. Although such theories and research do not tell you *what* to say in a specific persuasive presentation, they can help you identify the most effective persuasive strategies. In Chapter 20, "Developing Persuasive Presentations," these models and theories will serve as the foundation for choosing specific strategies and speaking techniques that will help you become a more effective persuasive speaker.

Summary

What is persuasion?

Persuasion attempts to change opinions (what people think) and/or behavior (what people do) by using effective logical, emotional, personal, and/or narrative appeals.

Will all audiences react to persuasive presentations in the same way?

Audience reactions to persuasive presentations can vary significantly, depending on the differences and strengths of their attitudes, their abilities and willingness to listen critically, their basic and psychological needs, and whether their opinions are narrowly focused or open to change. Effective persuaders use their understanding of audience attitudes to select the most appropriate persuasive strategies.

What's the best route to persuasion?

According to the Elaboration Likelihood Model of Persuasion, there are two routes to persuasion. For audience members who are able and motivated to listen critically, a carefully constructed, logical presentation will produce long-lasting results. For audiences unable or unmotivated to listen critically, a presentation that relies on speaker credibility and attractiveness, celebrity endorsements, and numerous arguments will persuade an audience in the short run but may not sustain long-lasting results. In either case, avoid threatening or demanding statements that could produce a negative reactance response.

How much persuasion can I achieve in a single presentation?

According to Social Judgment Theory, listeners' reactions to persuasive messages are reflected in varying degrees of acceptance, rejection, and noncommitment. A series of persuasive presentations designed to broaden listeners' latitudes of acceptance may be more effective than a single presentation.

How can marketing strategies be used to enhance persuasion?

Marketing strategies such as creating slogans, presenting vivid images, focusing on benefits rather than on features, addressing audience needs, and enlisting celebrity testimony can enhance persuasion.

Presentation Principles in Action

When *Don't* Means *Do*

Directions: Psychological Reactance Theory suggests that effective persuasive messages do not give the impression of pressuring the audience or constraining their freedom of choice. The following message urges college students to limit their alcohol consumption. The message is designed to create a negative reaction by being forceful, directive, and paternalistic.

Use your textbook's strategies for reducing negative reactance to rewrite this message. Try to create a climate conducive for change by granting the listeners more options and freedom to make their own decisions.

Responsible Drinking: You Have to Do It

The conclusion is crystal clear: There is unequivocal evidence that overconsumption of alcohol is implicated in reducing school performance, sexual violence, secondary effects on others, and physical harm to the drinker. In fact, any reasonable person has to agree that overconsumption of alcohol is a serious campus problem that demands immediate attention. No other conclusion makes any sense. Stop the denial. There is a problem, and you have to be part of the solution. So if you drink, drink responsibly. Three drinks is a safe, reasonable, and responsible limit, and it's the limit that you need to stick to. Do it.

Revision

Title: ______________________________

____

____

____

____

____

____

____

____

____

____

____

Source: The sample paragraph is taken from a 2002 unpublished master's thesis by L. Shen at the University of Wisconsin–Madison that is referenced in James Dillard and Linda J. Marshall, "Persuasion as a Social Skill," in *Handbook of Communication and Social Interaction Skills,* eds. John O. Green and Brant R. Burleson (Mahwah, NJ: Lawrence Erlbaum Associates, 2003), p. 501. The *Instructor's Resource Manual* for this textbook provides a rewritten paragraph that uses less forceful, directive, and paternalistic language and, as a result, may avoid eliciting a variety of negative responses.

Key Terms

campaign 444
common ground 432
deductive logic 436
Elaboration Likelihood Model of Persuasion 439
emotional proof 437
ethos 438
evidence 440
Fundamental Interpersonal Relationship Orientation (FIRO) Theory 447
heuristics 441
identification 433
inductive logic 437
inoculation 434
logical proof 436
logos 436
Maslow's Hierarchy of Needs 447
mythos 438
narrative proof 438
pathos 437
personal proof 438
persuasion 429
proof 435
Psychological Reactance Theory 444
Social Judgment Theory 442

Notes

1 Kenneth Burke, *A Rhetoric of Motives* (New York: Prentice-Hall, 1950).
2 Joanne Cantor, *Mommy, I'm Scared: How TV and Movies Frighten Children and What We Can Do to Protect Them* (San Diego: Harcourt Brace, 1998), p. 20.
3 Charles U. Larson, *Persuasion: Reception and Responsibility,* 8th ed. (Belmont, CA: Wadsworth, 1998), p. 180.
4 Larson, p. 58.
5 U.S. Bureau of the Census, *Statistical Abstract of the United States: 1997,* 117th ed. (Washington, D.C.: U.S. Bureau of the Census, 1997).
6 Larson, p. 60.
7 Michael Osborn and Suzanne Osborn, *Public Speaking,* 4th ed. (Boston: Houghton Mifflin, 1997), pp. 458–460.
8 Osborn and Osborn, p. 460.
9 Richard Petty and John Cacioppo, *Communication and Persuasion: Central and Peripheral Routes to Attitude Change* (New York: Springer-Verlag, 1986). For a detailed explanation of the Elaboration Likelihood Model of Persuasion, see Daniel J. O'Keefe, *Persuasion: Theory and Research* (Newbury Park, CA: Sage, 1990), Chapter 6. Also see the Heuristic-Systematic Model, which contrasts heuristic processing (superficial and simplistic) with systematic processing (analytical and contemplative) as presented in Shelly Chaiken et al., "Heuristic and Systematic Processing Within and Beyond the Persuasive Context," in *Unintended Thought,* eds. J. S. Uleman and J. A. Bargh (New York: Guilford, 1989), pp. 212–252.
10 Daniel J. O'Keefe, *Persuasion: Theory and Research* (Newbury Park, CA: Sage, 1990), p. 97.
11 Sharon S. Brehm, Saul M. Kassin, and Steven Fein, *Social Psychology,* 4th ed. (Boston: Houghton Mifflin, 1999), p. 183.
12 See Muzafer Sherif and Carolyn Sherif, *Attitude, Ego Involvement and Change* (New York: Wiley, 1967); Muzafer Sherif, Carolyn Sherif, and Roger Nebergall, *Attitude and Attitude Change: The Social Judgment–Involvement Approach* (Philadelphia: W. B. Saunders, 1965). A detailed explanation of Social Judgment Theory can be found in Daniel J. O'Keefe, *Persuasion: Theory and Research* (Newbury Park, CA: Sage, 1990), Chapter 2.
13 Robert H. Gass and John S. Seiter, *Persuasion, Social Influence, and Compliance Gaining* (Boston: Allyn & Bacon, 1999), p. 106.
14 Gass and Seiter, p. 107.
15 Jack W. Brehm, *A Theory of Psychological Reactance* (New York: Academic Press, 1966). Also see Michael Burgoon et al., "Revisiting the Theory of Psychological Reactance," in *The Persuasion Handbook: Developments in Theory and Practice,* eds. James Price Dillard and Michael Pfau (Thousand Oaks CA: Sage, 2002), pp. 213–232; James Price Dillard and Linda J. Marshall, "Persuasion as a Social Skill," in *Handbook of Communication and Social Interaction Skills,* eds. John O. Greene and Brant R. Burleson (Mahwah, NJ: Lawrence Erlbaum Associates, 2003), pp. 500–501.
16 James Price Dillard and Linda J. Marshall, "Persuasion as a Social Skill," in *Handbook of Communication and Social Interaction Skills,* eds. John O. Greene and Brant R. Burleson (Mahwah, NJ: Lawrence Erlbaum Associates, 2003), p. 501.
17 Sonja K. Foss and Karen A. Foss, *Inviting Transformation: Presentational Speaking for a*

Changing World, 2nd ed. (Prospect Heights, IL: Waveland Press, 2003), pp. 6–7.

18 Foss and Foss, p. 11.

19 J. Thomas Russell and W. Ronald Lane, *Kleppner's Advertising Procedure,* 14th ed. (Upper Saddle River, NJ: Prentice-Hall, 1999), p. 462.

20 Gass and Seiter, p. 59.

21 Karen Lawson, *Involving Your Audience: Making It Active* (Boston: Allyn & Bacon, 1999), p. 95.

22 Russell and Lane, p. 465.

23 Abraham H. Maslow, *Motivation and Personality* (New York: Harper & Row, 1954).

24 William C. Schutz, *FIRO: A Three-Dimensional Theory of Interpersonal Behavior* (New York: Holt, Rinehart, & Winston, 1958).

25 Since publishing his three-dimensional theory of interpersonal behavior (FIRO-B) in 1958, Schutz has renamed the third dimension. Instead of *affection,* he uses the term *openness.* Thus, like inclusion and control, openness is a behavior (rather than an emotion) which, when enacted, can convey feelings of likability and affection. See Will Schutz, *The Human Element* (San Francisco, CA: Jossey-Bass, 1994), pp. 49–70.

26 Russell and Lane, p. 466.

chapter twenty

Developing Persuasive **Presentations**

- What constitutes a good persuasive presentation?
- What are the characteristics of a persuasive argument?
- What's the best type of evidence to use in a persuasive presentation?
- What's the best way to organize a persuasive presentation?
- What are the common fallacies of argument?

As we note in Chapter 19, "Understanding Persuasion," persuading people to change their attitudes or behavior is among the more complex challenges of presentation speaking—and is certainly among the most widely studied. Communication scholars, psychologists, and master marketers all offer theories and research to explain why people react to persuasive messages in so many ways. In this chapter, we help you put these theories into practice in your own persuasive presentations.

Purposeful Persuasion

In order to prepare and deliver an effective persuasive presentation, you must know *why* you are speaking. Four critical steps can help ensure that your persuasive presentation achieves a specific purpose. You need to determine *what* you want your audience to believe after hearing your presentation, *why* your audience should believe it, and *what evidence* supports the claims you're advocating.

PURPOSEFUL PERSUASION

- **Match your purpose to your passion.**
- **Build strong arguments.**
- **Clarify your claims.**
- **Use persuasive evidence.**

Match Your Purpose to Your Passion

What are you trying to achieve when you make a persuasive presentation? This question involves more than asking which attitudes or behaviors you are trying to change. It asks *why* you are trying to change them.

Are you making a persuasive presentation because you believe the audience needs changing or because you have been asked to give a persuasive speech? If you believe that people who take a CPR course will be able to save more lives, you can justify the time needed to prepare a talk on this topic. If you decide to make a presentation on the need for CPR training because you think it will be an easy topic to research, your presentation may not be very convincing to your audience. A health insurance manager told us she speaks two or three times a month to a variety of audiences. Here's how she describes the link between purpose and passion: "I believe the success of any speaking engagement is to *love* and *believe* what you are talking about. In my case, it's my company's Healthy Lifestyles Program."

Choose a topic you care about. It will be hard to convince your audience that they should change their opinions or behavior if you don't believe in the change yourself. Even though there may be plenty of information available on topics such as capital punishment, abortion, gun control, cigarette smoking, and the need for regular exercise, don't select one of them unless you have strong feelings about it and are willing to do a lot of thorough research. The most effective presentations are often the most personal:

"Contribute to the local charity that helped my family after Hurricane Isabel." "Stay out of the harmful sun so you don't get melanoma like I did." "Help clean up the neighborhood we all call home." A passion for your topic will give you a compelling reason for addressing an audience. Most audiences can tell if you honestly care about your topic; your passion can help convince them. At the same time, Social Judgment Theory cautions that no matter how passionately *you* feel about a topic, you may not be able to persuade your audience if your purpose lies deep in their latitudes of rejection.

Note how the following student speaker directly addresses the question about the purpose of his presentation.

> *I am tired of being called a monster and murderer because I'm a deer hunter. Most people think I'm out there killing cute little Bambi when, in fact, I'm helping to protect the deer herds from disease and starvation. Sure, I enjoy hunting, but I do it safely and legally. If people knew more about deer hunting, they might not be so critical of it.*

A speaker who cares about a topic will work harder to prepare an effective presentation. A speaker with strong feelings about a topic will spend hours practicing because the outcome matters to her or him.

Build Strong Arguments

Passion for your purpose is only a prelude to developing an effective persuasive presentation. Persuasion also requires the development of strong, valid arguments.

Arguments are not disagreements between people; they are claims supported by evidence and reasons for accepting them. Stephen Toulmin, a philosopher and the author of *The Uses of Argument,* developed a way of looking at arguments that has become a mainstay in communication studies.[1]

This model helps both speakers and listeners to understand the basic structure of an argument. **The Toulmin Model of an Argument** maintains that a claim is only one part of a complete argument. To be complete, an argument also requires evidence, a warrant, backing, reservations, and qualifiers.[2]

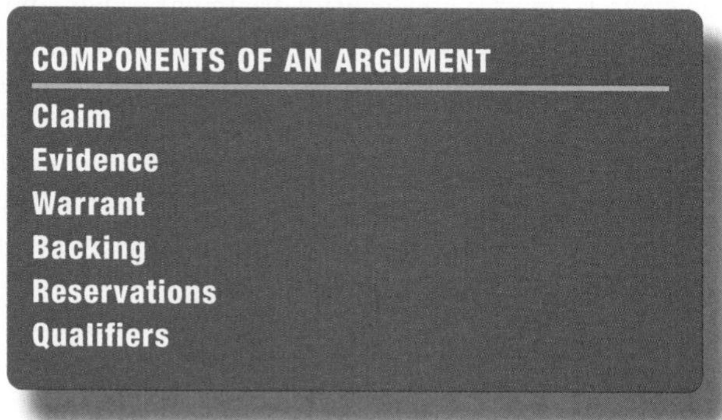

Claim. In Chapter 2, "Listening and Critical Thinking," we define a *claim* as a statement that identifies your position on a particular issue or topic. In persuasive speaking, a **claim** is the conclusion or position a speaker advocates. It is the idea a speaker wants the audience to believe or accept. For example, a speaker could claim that "keeping a food-intake diary is the best way to monitor a diet," that "communication skills are the most important characteristics to look for when recruiting new employees," or that "capital punishment deters criminals."

Evidence. Speakers support and prove the claims they advocate by providing information, data, and opinions as evidence. **Evidence** answers the questions "How do you know that?" and "What do you have to go on?" A sound argument relies on strong evidence, which can range from statistics and multiple examples to the advice of experts and generally accepted audience beliefs. For example, if you claim that keeping a food-intake diary is the best way to monitor a diet, you might share the results of a study conducted at a major medical school which concluded that food-intake diaries produce the best results. Or you might tell stories about how your many attempts to lose weight failed until you spent two months keeping a food-intake diary. You might even distribute examples of food-intake diaries to the audience to show them how easy it is to surpass a 30-gram fat allowance during a "day of dieting." Without good evidence, your audience may be reluctant to accept your claims.

Although supporting a claim and proving an argument require some form of evidence, not all evidence is logical or substantive. For instance, a speaker may use evidence based on audience knowledge and beliefs. Remember the first question that evidence tries to answer in an argument: "How do you know that?" Sometimes, when an audience "knows that," you can use their beliefs as evidence. For example, doesn't "everyone know that" a 150-pound person who rarely exercises will gain weight if he or she consumes 4,000 calories a day? Doesn't "everyone know that" running five miles a day is a more vigorous form of exercise than walking a half mile? By using such audience beliefs as evidence, you can claim that restricting calories combined with vigorous exercising will help you lose weight.

A speaker may also use her or his expertise about the topic or the expertise of an information source as evidence. For example, if we recommend an exercise for improving the quality of your speaking voice, we hope that you will take our advice because we are professors and authors who have spent most of our professional lives studying communication. Sometimes, to strengthen a claim, we will also provide a quotation from a study or a book written by other communication experts.

In many cases, your audience's beliefs, knowledge, and sympathies can be powerful forms of ready-made evidence. For example, if you have learned that most members of your audience believe that controlling guns will reduce violent crime, you can use that belief as evidence to support a gun-control argument. When appealing to audience members familiar with the findings of a government task force or a renowned psychologist on the impact of gun violence, you can use their knowledge to support your argument. You could also quote a well-known and sympathetic victim of gun violence such as James Brady, who in 1981, was shot and paralyzed in an assassination attempt on President Reagan and then became an advocate of gun control. In Toulmin's model, evidence can take many forms: audience motives, values, and beliefs; speaker credibility or source expertise; and traditional forms of supporting material such as statistics and examples.

Warrant. Strong claims supported by good evidence, however, may not be enough to make an argument believable. The third component in Toulmin's argumentation model is the warrant. The **warrant** explains why the evidence is relevant and why it supports the claim. For example, the warrant might say that the author of the article on food-intake diaries has been recognized as one of the country's leading nutrition experts. Rather than asking, "What do you have to go on?" the warrant wants to know "How did you get there?" and "What gives you the right to draw that coclusion?" Figure 20.1 illustrates how the Toulmin model represents the evidence, warrant, and claim of an argument.

The previous argument, then, would sound like this: "Want to lose those extra pounds for good? Keep a food-intake diary. Dr. Nathan Carter, the lead researcher in a

Figure 20.1 Basic "T" of the Toulmin Model

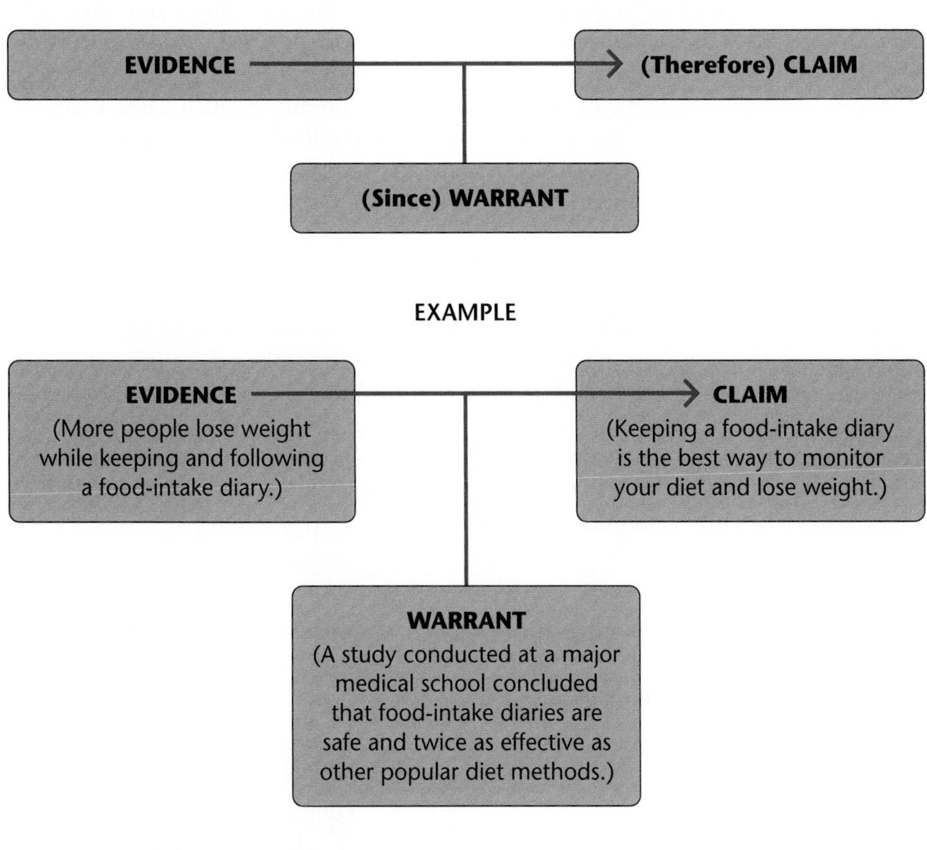

medical school study, has reported that patients who kept food-intake diaries were twice as likely to lose weight as were patients who used any other method." Warrants can demonstrate the logical relationship between the evidence and the claim. They can also prompt audiences to move from the evidence to the claim on the basis of the speaker's expertise or on the basis of their shared beliefs. Evidence and claims will remain separate unless warrants build a mental bridge between them.

Backing. **Backing** provides support for the argument's warrant. Backing is not needed in all arguments, but it can be crucial if an audience questions why the warrant should be accepted as the link between the evidence and the claim. While the warrant answers the question "How did you get there?" the backing answers the question "Why is this the right way to get there?" Backing can be in the form of more information about the credibility of a source: "Dr. Nathan Carter and his colleagues received two national awards for their contributions to weight-loss research." Backing can also describe the methodology used in the weight-loss study that determined the effectiveness of food-intake diaries.

Reservations. Not all claims are true all of the time. The **reservation** component of the Toulmin model recognizes exceptions to an argument or indications that a claim may not be true under certain circumstances. For example, a food-intake diary is only as good as the limits placed on daily food intake. Setting a limit of 4,000 calories and 100 fat grams a day for a 150-pound person won't do it. Moreover, there are some people whose weight problems have hormonal or genetic causes. The reservations could be stated this way: "Food-intake diaries must be well calibrated and may not work if there are genetic or hormonal causes of obesity. In such cases, keeping a standard food-intake diary may not be sufficient." Not only does a reservation make an argument more reasonable; it can also serve as an exception to an argument because it acknowledges that under certain circumstances, a claim may not be warranted.

Qualifiers. When the argument contains reservations, the speaker may have to qualify it. The **qualifier** states the degree to which a claim appears to be true. Qualifiers usually include the words *likely, possibly,* or *probably.* This could be a claim with a qualifier: "Unless there are medical reasons for seeking other therapies, using and following a food-intake diary calibrated to your own dietary goals is *probably* the best way to lose weight." Speakers need qualifiers when the evidence or warrant is less than certain and when audience members are likely to have doubts. Qualifiers soften a claim and therefore can make an argument more acceptable to a skeptical audience. Figure 20.2 maps out a complete argument.

Figure 20.2 The Toulmin Model of an Argument

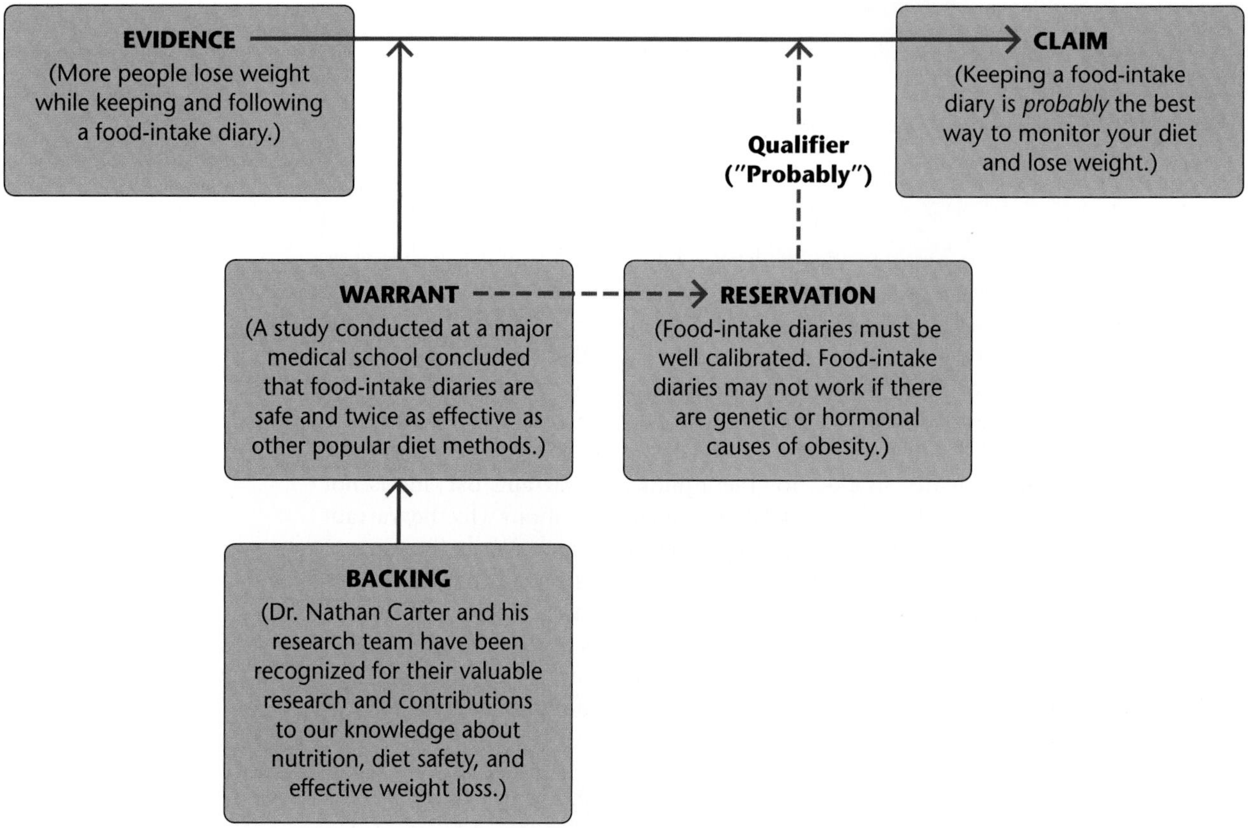

Use the Toulmin model to think critically about the basic components of any argument. When you develop a presentation, this model can help you test your own claims and arguments to determine whether they need to be strengthened or qualified. By recognizing that situations may alter the certainty of a claim, you can advocate more reasonable positions and thereby help audience members decide what to do or believe about your message.

The Toulmin model also supplies audience members with questions to ask about a speaker's claims. It can help listeners recognize when a speaker makes an unsupported claim that they may reject for lack of evidence. If the speaker provides evidence, the model helps listeners question the evidence's relevance and whether it warrants the claim.

Clarify Your Claims

Having decided why you are speaking as well as how to build strong arguments, you can now concentrate on clarifying your claims in light of their persuasive potential. As you begin planning a persuasive presentation, list all the possible arguments you could use—all the reasons that the audience should agree with you. The speaker who was planning a presentation on hunting as a means of controlling the growing deer population listed several reasons:

The enormous deer population
is starving and dying of disease.
is eating up crops, gardens, and forest seedlings.
is carrying deer ticks that cause Lyme disease in people.
is causing an increase in the number of highway accidents.

Although there may be several arguments for advocating hunting to reduce the deer population, the speaker should use only the arguments that, based on an analysis of his audience, would most likely persuade that audience.

In Chapter 2, "Listening and Critical Thinking," we identify four types of claims. Here we explain how clarifying each of these claims can enhance persuasion. Whatever arguments you choose, ask whether your claims answer questions of fact, value, conjecture, or policy. The answers will help you determine how best to make your case.

CLARIFY YOUR CLAIMS

Do they address questions of fact?
Do they address questions of value?
Do they address questions of conjecture?
Do they address questions of policy?

Questions of Fact.

An argument based on a **question of fact** addresses claims about whether something is true or false, whether an event did or didn't happen, or whether a circumstance was caused by one thing or another. Even though questions of fact are not concerned with whether something is good or bad, or likely or unlikely, they are not easy to answer, particularly when audience members are neutral or disagree with your position. Most friendly audiences will accept what you say as fact.

TIP: Use All Four Types of Questions

Basing arguments on all four types of questions within a single presentation can be especially effective! For example, whether you are supporting or condemning capital punishment, you might start with questions of fact: How many people are executed in the United States each year? What crimes are punishable by death? Which state leads the nation in executions? Then you could move to questions of value: Is it right for a state to take the life of a prisoner regardless of how serious the crime? Is capital punishment cruel? Is "a life for a life" a moral position? Questions of conjecture, the third type, require predictions about the future: Will the number of executions increase in the future? Will criminals be deterred from committing crimes if all states have mandatory capital punishment laws for similar crimes? Finally, you could ask a question of policy: Should capital punishment be expanded (or curtailed or abolished)?

Most persuasive presentations deal with more than one type of claim. If you don't adequately address the questions about the facts of a situation, the values held by your audience, future implications, and possible audience reactions to a proposed course of action, you may get a disappointing reaction to your persuasive presentation.

On the other hand, skeptical audience members will want you to demonstrate that your facts are accurate and true.

The factual question "How has enrollment changed at your college during the past ten years?" can require answers to a series of subquestions about the enrollment of women and ethnic groups or the status of part-time and full-time students. When you are trying to develop an argument that answers questions of fact, you must look for the best evidence you can find and then closely scrutinize that information. If you are trying to persuade an audience that something is true or that evidence points to a particular conclusion, be sure that your facts are accurate, credible, and relevant. Use the tests of evidence that we offer in Chapter 8, "Supporting Material."

Questions of Value. An argument based on a **question of value** makes judgments about whether something is worthwhile—is it good or bad; right or wrong; moral or immoral; best, average, or worst? It's hard to address questions of value because your success hinges on your ability to modify well-established attitudes and beliefs of audience members. In many cases, the answer to a question of value may be "It depends." Is a public college a better place to begin higher education than a prestigious private university? It depends on a student's financial situation, professional goals, academic achievement record, work and family situation, and beliefs about the quality of education offered at each type of institution. Convincing an audience of parents who hold advanced degrees from Ivy League schools that their children would be better off beginning their higher education at the local community college requires more than presenting facts about the quality of schooling available at a particular two-year college. It requires changing their attitudes about the value and benefits of attending a less prestigious school. Changing listeners' perceptions about

A speaker addresses an American Indian rally supporting Native-American rights. How would his message differ if he were addressing a non-Native-American audience?

strongly held values requires an understanding of and respect for your audience and—depending on the critical thinking ability and motivation of your audience—requires either a central or a peripheral route to persuasion.

Questions of Conjecture. An argument based on a **question of conjecture** asks whether something will or will not happen. Unlike a question of fact or value, only the future holds the answer to this type of question. Instead of focusing on *what is,* you are asking the audience to consider possibilities: *what could be* or *what will be.* Will John Doe be the next president? Will the stock market go up? Will our hometown get an expansion football team? Even though it's impossible to know what the future will bring, you can address questions of conjecture by basing your predictions as much as possible on statistical trends, past history, and expert opinion.[3] Answers to questions of conjecture should also consider the values held by audience members. A stockbroker trying to convince an audience to invest in mutual funds or in a particular company is dealing with facts about the past and present as well as audience hopes and fears about the future. The key to convincing an audience about arguments based on questions of conjecture is to discover how to use facts and scenarios that touch their interests, needs, and values.

Questions of Policy. An argument based on a **question of policy** asks whether or not to take a particular course of action. A persuasive presentation that looks at a policy question focuses on the issues that arise when people are asked to change how things are or should be done. We often ask ourselves questions of policy when trying to make difficult decisions. We weigh the pros and cons of choosing a particular college, accepting a new job, or making a major purchase.[4] When used for a persuasive presentation, arguments based on policy questions ask an audience to do something or to support a course of action. Should you vote for Jane Doe? Should you speak out against the college's proposed tuition increase? Should you spend more time with your family and work less overtime at your job? Should you support more funding for the public library system?

When asking an audience to take action, try to determine whether your listeners are able and willing to think critically about your arguments. If they are, using a central route to persuasion is more likely to produce long-lasting behavioral change. For less critical and less motivated audience members, taking a peripheral route to persuasion may be the only way to induce even a temporary change in their behavior.

Use Persuasive Evidence

In explaining Toulmin's Model of Argument, we defined *evidence* as the information, data, or audience beliefs used to support and prove the claim of an argument. In Chapter 8, we illustrate how to use valid supporting material to help explain and/or advance a central idea and key points. When supporting material is used to strengthen the persuasive claim of an argument, it becomes evidence.

In persuasive speaking, evidence verifies and strengthens the proof you use to secure belief in an argument. It is the backup material that justifies why an audience should accept or reject a claim. If you claim that millions of Americans cannot afford health insurance, a statistic from a reputable source can help to justify your claim. If you argue that responsible environmentalists support deer hunting, you'd better have a reputable quotation or survey to prove your point. If you are trying to demonstrate the benefits of early diagnosis of diabetes, you may want to tell two contrasting stories—one about a person who was diagnosed early and one who wasn't diagnosed until the disease had ravaged her body. Be strategic. Select your evidence according to the type of argument you are trying to prove, the attitudes and needs of your audience, and whether you're seeking a central or a peripheral route to persuasion. Moreover, evidence is most persuasive when it is novel, believable, or dramatic.[5]

PERSUASIVE EVIDENCE IS

- **Novel**
- **Believable**
- **Dramatic**

Novel Evidence. Very often the best persuasive evidence is information that is new to your audience. If they have heard a piece of evidence before, they've already considered its implications when forming an attitude. The best persuaders constantly look for new evidence to support their arguments. How many times have you seen someone at a swimming pool stand next to a sign that reads, "No diving" and then dive right into the pool? Overly familiar evidence just doesn't work that well. By the way, this is one of the reasons that advertisements on television keep changing: Once an ad is very familiar, viewers don't pay as much attention to it.

The theories of persuasion that we discussed in Chapter 19 reinforce the value of novel evidence. When you're speaking to a primarily friendly audience, new evidence can strengthen their resolve and provide answers to any questions asked by audience members who disagree. When audience members are uninformed or undecided, new evidence can tip the balance in favor of your position. And if you are seeking a central route to persuasion, audiences will expect to hear new, well-researched evidence to support your arguments.

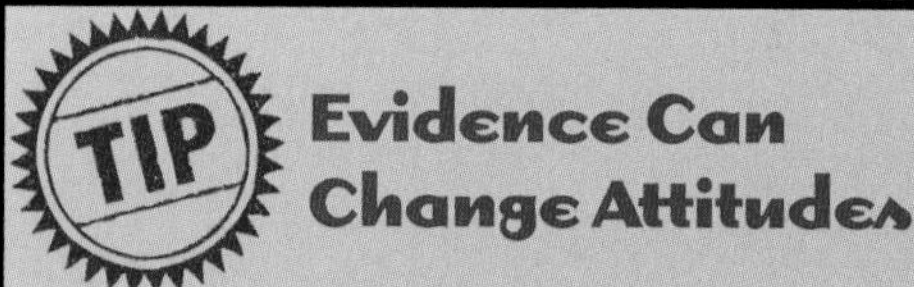

According to Martin Fishbein, an expert in how people form attitudes, evidence can affect attitude change in three ways.[1] First, information can alter the believability, or weight, of a particular belief: "Given this evidence, I will now believe it or reject it more strongly than ever." Second, information can change the direction of a belief: "The evidence supports just the opposite belief. I've been wrong about this." Third, information can add new beliefs: "I had no idea that was the case! But I believe it now."[2]

1. Martin Fishbein, *Readings in Attitude Theory and Measurement* (New York: Wiley, 1967). Also see Martin Fishbein and Icek Ajzen, *Belief, Attitude, Intention, and Behavior* (Reading, MA: Addison-Wesley, 1975).
2. Steven W. Littlejohn, *Theories of Human Communication*, 5th ed. (Belmont, CA: Wadsworth, 1996), p. 140.

Believable Evidence. Even if the evidence is completely accurate, well understood, and novel, it still will not be persuasive if people don't believe it. If your audience doubts the believability of your evidence, take the time to explain why it's true or provide other sources of evidence that support the same conclusion. If you think the source of your evidence has high credibility, you should mention that source *before* presenting your evidence. On the other hand, if you think that naming the source will not add to the evidence's believability, mention it *after* you've presented the evidence.

As we note in Chapter 19, if an audience disagrees with your position, it is vital that your evidence be fair and respected. Establish the credibility of your evidence in order to strengthen your own credibility. If you demonstrate that the sources of your evidence are highly respected, you will have found a way to take both the central and the peripheral routes to persuasion.

Dramatic Evidence. When using evidence, especially statistics, for a persuasive presentation, find ways to

Adapting Persuasion to Cultural Differences

In Chapter 5, "Audience Analysis and Adaptation," we include a Mini-Module titled "Adapting to International Audiences" that discusses guidelines for adapting your speaking style to listeners from other countries. In this Mini-Module, however, we look at some of the ways in which different cultures respond to persuasive appeals. As was the case with presentation speaking style, we lack significant research in this area of study. At the same time, you should make every effort to understand, respect, and adapt to the ways in which culturally diverse audience members may respond to persuasive messages.

As we have noted, even within the United States, there are members of microcultures (Native-American Indians, African Americans, Hispanic/Latino Americans, Asian Americans, and various religious groups) that coexist within mainstream society. The members of these groups may be as collectivist and high context as audience members from other countries. In a highly individualistic culture such as that of the United States, listeners value individual achievement and personal freedom. In collectivist cultures (those of Asian and Latin American countries), audience members are more likely to value group identity, selflessness, and collective action. Audiences in collectivist cultures place less importance on the opinions and preferences of the individual than do audiences in individualistic cultures.[1] In the United States, appeals that benefit individuals—personal wealth, personal success, personal health and fitness—may be highly persuasive while appeals that benefit society and families are often overlooked. Think about the commercials that you see on television. They often focus on how *you* can become more successful, more attractive, and healthier; they rarely address collective benefits. When addressing a collectivist audience, however, you should think about collective benefits. How does your position help your collectivist audience's families, businesses, and communities?

Now let's explore how different persuasive strategies may be applied to audiences from high-context cultures in contrast with strategies used with low-context audiences in the United States. In low-context cultures such as those of the United States, England, and Germany, audiences expect messages to be explicit, factual, and objective. Words are valued and believed. For example, in the United States, persuasive appeals are often direct—do this; buy that; drink this; avoid that; just do it! In advertising, this would be termed a *hard-sell* approach to persuasion.

In contrast, high-context cultures such as those of Japan, China, and Mexico expect messages that are implied and situation specific. Nonverbal behavior is valued and believed more than words. A soft-sell approach would be a better persuasive strategy. When addressing a high-context audience, encourage listeners to draw their own conclusions. Demonstrate benefits and advantages rather than advocating action.

Differences between cultures are very real. At the same time, be cautious about how you interpret and use this information. You cannot assume that all members of a culture conform to one or more cultural dimensions. Are all Japanese collectivist and high context? Many young Japanese business professionals are learning and embracing American ways that include a more direct and self-centered approach to communication. Are all Australians individualistic? Although Australians are very independent and value personal freedom, they also live in a culture in which power distance is minimal. Public displays of achievement or wealth are frowned upon.[2] One of your authors lived in Australia for a year and was introduced to the *tall poppy syndrome.* If, in a field of poppies, one red blossom grows higher than the others, you chop it off. When people show off or try to rise above others, you cut them down to size, too. "He thinks he's a tall poppy" is used to describe someone who—in American terms—is "too big for his britches."

Unfortunately, the lack of significant research on attitude and behavior change in other cultures makes it difficult to provide universal guidelines or strategies for persuasion. There is no question, however, that differences do exist. Effective speakers spend extra time and energy investigating the attitudes, beliefs, and values of a culture before speaking in order to ensure that they understand, respect, and do their best to adapt to their listeners.

1. Sharon Shavitt and Michelle R. Nelson, "The Role of Attitude Functions in Persuasion and Social Judgment," in *The Persuasion Handbook: Developments in Theory and Practice,* eds. James Price Dillard and Michael Pfau (Thousand Oaks, CA: Sage, 2002), p. 150.
2. Shavitt and Nelson, p. 150.

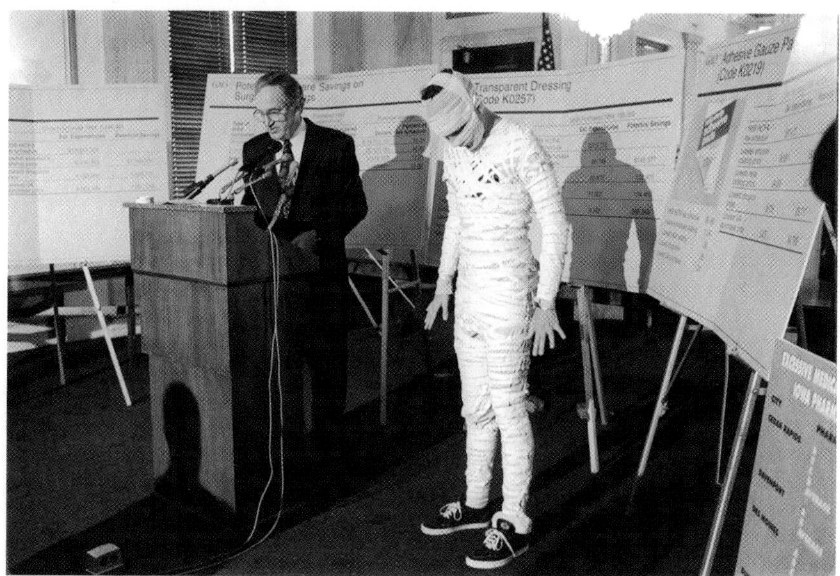

Senator Tom Harkin of Iowa (on the left) went ballistic in 1995 when he learned from the Government Accounting Office that Medicare paid $2.32 for surgical gauze that could be bought wholesale for 19 cents. To dramatize his criticism of Medicare payment practices, the senator had an aide dress himself in surgical gauze.

make it memorable. Instead of saying that your proposal will save the organization $250,000 dollars during the next year, you could say that it will save a quarter of a million dollars next year, the equivalent of the entire travel budgets of the three largest divisions of the company.

Statistics are often more dramatic when they are used in attention-getting comparisons. For instance, a study by an advocacy group for better road maintenance reported that motorists spend twice as much to repair cars damaged by potholes and pavement cracks as governments spend to fix the same holes and cracks. Why not save motorists a lot of money, they proposed, by investing in better road repair?[6] Or consider this comparison made by Robert Reich, former secretary of labor in the Clinton administration. Writing about the increasing income disparity between the rich and the poor in the United States, Reich noted that Bill Gates's net worth roughly equaled the combined net worth of the least wealthy 40 percent of American households.[7] That comparison brings home the point far better than relying solely on statistical evidence would. Presenting such statistical comparisons visually can heighten their impact. Imagine the chart or graph Reich could have used to dramatize his evidence!

Organizing Your Persuasive Presentation

You have a topic you care about; a list of potential arguments; an understanding of how your arguments answer questions of fact, value, conjecture, and policy; and evidence to support your arguments. You've reached a key decision-making point. It's time to put these elements together to form an effective persuasive message.

In addition to the organizational patterns discussed in Chapter 9, "Organization," there are some additional formats particularly suited to persuasive presentations.

PERSUASIVE ORGANIZATIONAL PATTERNS

Problem/Cause/Solution
Better Plan
Overcoming Objections
Monroe's Motivated Sequence
Persuasive Stories

Problem/Cause/Solution

A **Problem/Cause/Solution organizational pattern** is exactly what its name implies. First, you describe a serious problem, explain why the problem continues (the cause), and offer a solution. The basic outline for a Problem/Cause/Solution presentation looks like this:

I. There is a problem.
  A. The problem is serious and/or
  B. The problem is widespread.
II. The problem is caused by…
III. There is a solution to the problem.
  A. This solution can and will work.
  B. This solution will not create new problems.

In the following outline, the speaker uses a Problem/Cause/Solution organizational pattern to propose a national health care system for all U.S. citizens.

I. Americans are not getting needed medical care.
  A. Serious diseases (cancer, heart disease, diabetes, sexually transmitted diseases) are going undetected and untreated.
  B. Millions of Americans do not see a doctor for regular checkups.
II. The high costs of health care and health insurance prevent a solution.
III. A national health care system can guarantee medical care for all citizens by providing free health care for those in need without eliminating private care for those who can and want to pay extra.
  A. This plan works well in other modern countries.
  B. This plan will not cause problems such as low-quality care or long waiting lines.

The Problem/Cause/Solution pattern of organization works best when you are proposing a specific course of action to solve a serious problem. The previous outline's primary arguments addressed a question of policy: What should be done to guarantee medical care for all citizens? Depending on the results of audience analysis, the speaker would use logical arguments and substantive evidence if the audience was able and motivated to think and to listen critically. However, with an unmotivated audience that would be unwilling to listen, personal stories and the opinions of well-known, respected experts would be more likely to persuade. Regardless of the type of evidence, however, the basic outline for the Problem/Cause/Solution pattern works well for many kinds of audiences.

Better Plan

If a problem is complex and difficult to solve, a **Better Plan organizational pattern** may be a better way to structure your persuasive presentation. In this pattern, you present a plan that will improve a situation or help to solve a problem while acknowledging that a total solution may not be possible. The basic outline for a Better Plan follows.

I. There is a plan.
   A. What is it?
   B. How will it work?
II. This plan will be better than current plans.
   A. It will be better because...
   B. It will be better because...
   C. It will be better because...

In the following outline, the speaker contends that more hunting is a Better Plan for alleviating the serious problems caused by the growing deer population. The speaker is arguing that hunting is a better way to control deer populations than letting them die of starvation and disease. Although animal rights and anti-hunting advocates may disagree, the speaker is trying to show that increasing deer hunting is a better plan than doing nothing.

I. There is a plan that will help to reduce the deer population.
   A. The deer hunting season should be extended.
   B. States should allow hunters to kill more female than male deer.
II. This plan will reduce the problems associated with a large deer population.
   A. It will reduce the number of deer deaths from starvation and disease.
   B. It will save millions of dollars now being spent to repair crop, garden, and forest seedling damage.
   C. It will reduce the number of deer ticks carrying Lyme disease, which endangers humans.

The strategic advantage of using a Better Plan organizational pattern is that it can anticipate audience resistance and inoculate them against counterarguments. Unlike the Problem/Cause/Solution pattern—which says, "Here's the solution to the problem"—the Better Plan pattern offers a course of action acknowledging that it may be difficult, if not impossible, to "solve" the problem. Audience members who engage in critical thinking may respond positively to a speaker who admits that he or she doesn't have all of the answers. Audience members who are neutral or who disagree may find the Better Plan easier to accept as an option and easier to adopt as a reasonable solution.

Overcoming Objections

Sometimes an audience agrees that there is a problem and even knows what should be done to solve it. Yet they do not act because the solution is frightening, expensive, or difficult to implement. At other times, an audience disagrees with a speaker and comes prepared to reject the message before hearing it. With both types of audiences, you must deal with and try to overcome their objections. The basic outline for an **Overcoming Objections organizational pattern** has three sections.

I. People should do X.
 A. Most people know that doing X is a good idea.
 B. Many people don't do X.
II. There are several reasons why people don't do X.
 A. Reason #1
 B. Reason #2
 C. Reason #3
III. These reasons can and should be overcome.
 A. Overcoming Reason #1
 B. Overcoming Reason #2
 C. Overcoming Reason #3

In the following example, the speaker uses the Overcoming Objections organizational pattern to encourage listeners to donate blood. The audience already knows about the need for well-stocked blood supplies. They also know that people's donating more blood is the best way to solve the blood shortage problem. However, the speaker needs to overcome the audience's barriers to giving blood, deal with their counterarguments, and persuade them to act.

I. People should give blood but often don't.
 A. Most people think that giving blood is a good idea, but...
 B. Most people don't give blood.
II. There are several reasons that people don't give blood.
 A. They're afraid of pain and needles.
 B. They're afraid that they could get a disease from giving blood.
 C. They claim that they don't have time or know where to go to give blood.
III. These reasons can and should be overcome.
 A. There is little or no pain involved in giving blood.
 B. You can't *get* a blood disease by *giving* blood. You can get one only by *receiving* blood carrying a disease.
 C. The Red Cross makes it easy and convenient to give the gift of life.

Remember the Elaboration Likelihood Model of Persuasion from Chapter 19? Logical proof backed by strong evidence is effective when well-informed audience members are likely to do a lot of counterarguing. If you ignore their objections and concerns, you are not likely to persuade them. Take the central route to persuasion by addressing their reservations head-on and inoculating them against counterpersuasion. Overcoming Objections is also a useful pattern for strengthening the resolve of audience members who agree but still need motivation before they will take action.

Monroe's Motivated Sequence

In 1935, a communication scholar and teacher named Alan Monroe took the basic functions of a sales presentation (attention, interest, desire, and action) and transformed them into a step-by-step method of organization that could be used for all kinds of speeches.[8] The five basic steps in **Monroe's Motivated Sequence** have been used quite successfully by many persuasive speakers.

I. *The Attention Step:* Get the audience's attention.
II. *The Need Step:* Show the audience that there is a problem related to their individual interests and needs that should be solved.
III. *The Satisfaction Step:* Propose a plan of action that will solve the problem and satisfy audience needs.
IV. *The Visualization Step:* Describe what the audience's life and/or the lives of others will be like once the plan of action is implemented.
V. *The Action Step:* Ask the audience to act in a way that demonstrates their personal commitment to the solution.

In the following example, a student used Monroe's Motivated Sequence to focus on the problem of geographic illiteracy and to urge listeners to support the teaching of geography in public schools.

I. The Attention Step: Half of all Americans don't know where Columbus landed.
II. The Need Step
    A. Americans need to know more about geography for environmental, economic, and political reasons.
    B. Citizens of other countries are much more literate about geography than Americans are.
III. The Satisfaction Step
    A. Integrate geography into the curriculum.
    B. Offer geography workshops for teachers.
    C. Reinstate geography as a separate subject.
IV. The Visualization Step
    A. Heather Hill Elementary School's successful geography classes.
    B. U.S. students would know as much about geography as foreign students now do.
V. The Action Step
    A. Increase parent-student involvement.
    B. Put pressure on local and national education agencies.

The unique visualization step in Monroe's Motivated Sequence makes this organizational pattern particularly suitable for neutral audience members who are uninformed, unconcerned, and unmotivated to listen or for listeners who are skeptical of or opposed to the proposed course of action. By encouraging listeners to project themselves into the future to "see" the results of taking or failing to take a particular course of action, you can strengthen the impact of your message. The more you involve your listeners' senses in the visualization and the more realistic you make that future scenario, the more likely you will be able to persuade them.[9] The visualization step intensifies the audience's willingness and motivation to believe, feel, or act in a certain way.

An added advantage of Monroe's Motivated Sequence is its focus on audience needs. We noted in Chapter 19's discussion of Maslow's Hierarchy of Needs and Schutz's FIRO Theory that appealing to the deficiency, fulfillment, or psychological needs of audience members can enhance the persuasiveness of a message. Monroe's organizational pattern is perfectly suited to that purpose.

Persuasive Stories

Stories are a powerful type of supporting material (see Chapter 8) that can capture and hold audience interest (see Chapter 13, "Generating Interest") and serve as a persuasive form of proof (see Chapter 19). So why not use stories that represent the central idea of your persuasive presentation as an organizational format? When using a **Persuasive Stories organizational pattern,** you rely on narrative proof (mythos) to organize your presentation along with emotional proof (pathos) to show how people, events, and objects are or can be affected by the change you are seeking. The Persuasive Stories outline is fairly simple:

I. The following stories show why people should change their opinions and/or behavior about X.
   A. Story A
   B. Story B
   C. Story C
II. Unless people change their opinions and/or behavior about X, there will be more (or fewer) stories like A, B, and C.

Note how the following speaker uses a series of persuasive stories to convince an audience to support programs designed to help political refugees. By telling real stories about refugee families, the speaker relies on emotional proof, going beyond logical appeals based on newspaper summaries and government statistics about the refugee problem.

I. The stories of three refugee families demonstrate the need for and the value of migration ministries.
   A. Story of Letai Teku and her family (Cambodia)
   B. Story of Peter Musooli and his family (Ethiopia)
   C. Story of Nasir Rugova and his family (Kosovo)
II. More support for migration ministries can save even more families who are fleeing foreign tyranny and persecution.

The Persuasive Stories organizational pattern may not be very effective for convincing those audience members who are well informed about this topic, opposed to extending more aid to refugees, or critical thinkers. Their counterarguments may range from "The speaker has used only three examples—maybe it's not such a big problem" to "The speaker is trying to manipulate me by using emotional appeals."

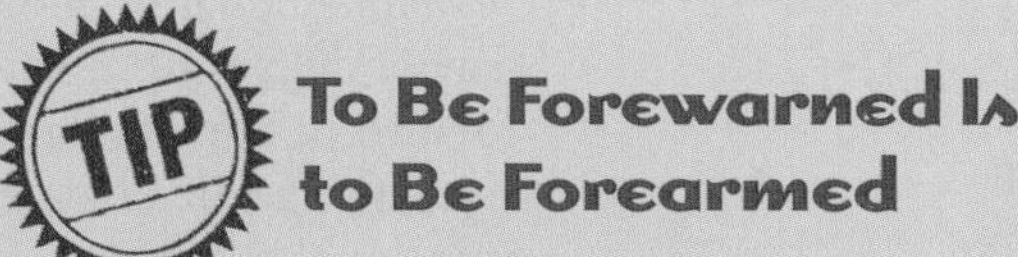

To Be Forewarned Is to Be Forearmed

Throughout this textbook, we advocate the use of message previews as part of the introduction to your presentation as well as a statement of your central idea. In some persuasive situations, however, this advice may be counterproductive. William L. Benoit warns that audience members may resist persuasion if you announce that you want to persuade them.[1] Think of it this way: If someone tells you that you need to think or act differently, she or he may be implying that your thinking is faulty or that your behavior is improper. As we note in Chapter 19, Psychological Reactance Theory predicts that under such circumstances you may defy the speaker's advice because you feel threatened.

So should you forewarn an audience that you are going to try to persuade them and run the risk that they will be forearmed to resist? The research indicates that forewarning an audience can result in rejection. How, then, do you approach an audience with a persuasive purpose?

Benoit suggests that you do the following:

- Avoid creating the perception that you want to change your audience's attitudes and behavior.
- Focus on informing your audience about your topic.
- Show the audience how the information is relevant and important to their lives.
- Let your arguments unfold rather than showcasing them up front.
- Create a climate conducive to change by inviting audience members to draw their own conclusions about the information you share with them.
- Acknowledge that there are two sides to the argument and then refute the other side.

When you encourage audience members to draw their own conclusions, they are more likely to be persuaded.

1. William L. Benoit, "Forewarning and Persuasion," in *Persuasion: Advances Through Meta-Analysis,* eds. M. Allen and R. W. Preiss (Cresskill, NJ: Hampton, 1998), pp. 139–154.

The Persuasive Stories organizational pattern, however, can be a very effective way of delivering a persuasive message to neutral audience members who are uninformed or are unable or unwilling to listen critically. By adding your personal reactions to and involvement in these stories, you can use the Persuasive Stories organizational pattern as an effective peripheral route to persuasion.

Fallacies of Argument

Critical thinking is essential for both persuasive speakers and effective listeners. If you are preparing a presentation, you must understand and be on guard against obstacles to clear thinking and purposeful persuasion. If you are listening to a presentation, you must be alert for unsound or unfair arguments. Although poor organization, uninspired language, and weak delivery can reduce the power of a persuasive presentation, the fallacies of argument can totally derail a speaker from achieving her or his purpose.

At the National Rifle Association's annual convention, a speaker directs his remarks to a friendly audience. What persuasive strategies work best with an audience that already agrees with you?

Rosie O'Donnell offers encouragement at the Million Mom March, during which participants demand that the U.S. Congress pass commonsense gun control. How would Rosie's message differ from that of an NRA member offering encouragement at an NRA convention?

According to the *American Heritage Dictionary of the English Language,* a fallacy is "a statement or an argument based on a false or an invalid inference." It also is "incorrectness of reasoning or belief" and "the quality of being deceptive."[10] The word *fallacy* comes from the Latin verb *fallere,* which means "to deceive." **Fallacies,** then, are invalid arguments or misleading statements that can deceive an audience. Fallacies can be intentional or unintentional. However, whether an unethical speaker misuses evidence or reasoning for the purpose of deceiving an audience or whether a well-meaning speaker misinterprets evidence or draws erroneous conclusions, the result is still the same: A deceived audience is led to believe something that is not true or justified.

One way to keep fallacies from creeping into your presentations (with or without your knowledge) is to become familiar with them. Once you are, you'll start noticing fallacies everywhere—in product advertisements, in political campaign commercials, and in everyday conversations!

COMMON FALLACIES

Faulty cause
Attacking the person
Hasty generalization
Selected instances
Bandwagon
Begging the question
Victory by definition

Faulty Cause

The **faulty cause** fallacy has a Latin name: *Post hoc, ergo propter hoc* or, in shortened form, the *post hoc* fallacy. It means "After this; therefore, because of this." Think of it as the superstition fallacy. If you walk under a ladder, you will have bad luck. In politics, the *post hoc* fallacy is often used to blame elected officials for problems that they didn't cause: When Juan Diaz became our mayor (after this), juvenile delinquency increased (because of this). College students are not immune to this fallacy: Just because you spent four hours in the library (after this) does not mean that you are ready for the test (because of this).

Unfortunately, the *post hoc* fallacy is often difficult to detect, in part because it is so common. When you are constructing an argument for your presentation or listening to a speaker making claims about causality, make sure that the *post hoc* fallacy isn't clouding the issue. Here are some questions to ask about faulty causality:

- Have you or the speaker identified the real cause?
- What else could explain why this has happened?
- Are there multiple causes instead of just one?

Attacking the Person

The fallacy of **attacking the person** also has a Latin name: *ad hominem,* which means "against the man." Thus, the *ad hominem* fallacy involves attacking a person rather than the substance of that person's argument. Attacking a person diverts audience attention from the person's argument and damages the person's credibility. Calling someone a cheat or a racist doesn't make the charge true, but it does plant seeds of doubt. Negative campaign ads take advantage of this phenomenon. Making *ad hominem* attacks on a rival candidate rather than addressing the issues has helped many politicians get elected. Name calling, labeling, and attacking a person rather than the substance of his or her argument are unethical practices as well as fallacies of argument. Here are some questions to ask about the *ad hominem* fallacy:

- Does the person deserve this negative criticism?
- Is the person's character linked in any way to the substance of the issue?
- Is the argument valid and justified regardless of who supports it?

Hasty Generalization

All of us occasionally make hasty generalizations. We go to a restaurant with a friend and have a good meal, so we recommend the restaurant to a colleague. A few days later she comes to work with a tale of terrible service and tasteless food. It's possible we might have made a hasty generalization. Because we had liked the dishes we ate at our first and only meal at the restaurant, we assumed that all of the dishes were excellent. All it takes to commit a **hasty generalization** fallacy is to jump to a conclusion based on too little evidence. For example, you could be making a mistake if you avoid taking a class from a certain professor just because you've heard a disgruntled student complain about that professor. When developing a persuasive presentation, make sure that you have surveyed the research and opinions on your topic. If the first study or opinion you find supports your position, do more research to make sure that other studies and experts also agree. Here are some questions to ask to ensure against making hasty generalizations:

- Is the conclusion based on enough or typical examples?
- Are there more comprehensive studies or surveys that arrive at the same conclusion?
- Are there a significant number of exceptions to this conclusion?

Selected Instances

The fallacy of **selected instances** is the opposite of a hasty generalization and more sinister because the speaker usually knows exactly what she or he is doing. This fallacy occurs when a speaker purposely picks atypical examples to prove an argument. Let's say that you are trying to convince a pro-environmental group that they should help elect a candidate to Congress. You know that the candidate whom you support has had an anti-environmental voting record in the state legislature, yet you choose to tell the audience only about the one time he voted *yes* on a pro-environmental bill. You are using the fallacy of selected instances.

When issues are highly controversial, some speakers will go out of their way to prove a point by using only selected instances. A speaker who's against gun control may tell carefully selected stories about gun owners who thwarted robbers rather than sharing the many more documented stories about accidental shootings and crimes of passion committed with guns in the home. Here are some questions to ask about the use of selected instances:

- Are these rare or infrequent examples?
- How many times has the opposite occurred?
- Why did the speaker choose these particular stories or examples?

Bandwagon

The **bandwagon** fallacy is an appeal to popularity. Its Latin term is the *ad populum* fallacy, which claims that something is good, right, or desirable because it is popular. "Join the smart crowd" and "Everyone's doing it" are typical bandwagon appeals. Whether you were buying the latest

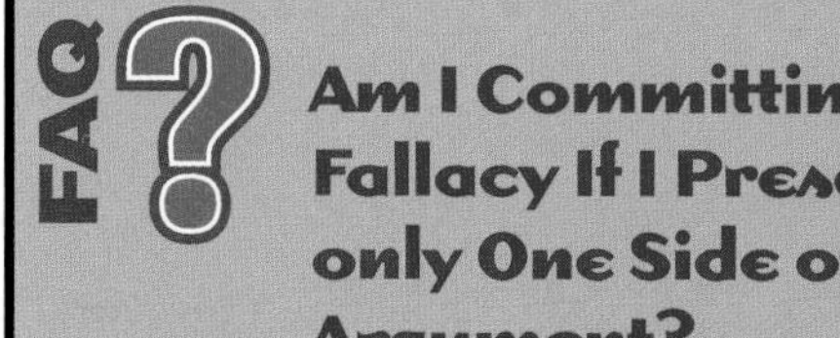

Am I Committing a Fallacy If I Present only One Side of an Argument?

This question often comes up when speakers realize that presenting only one side of an argument may appear manipulative. It seems as though the speaker is concealing the reasons why there is disagreement on an issue. For example, advertisers rarely present both sides of an argument—TV ads won't tell you that the active ingredient in Bayer aspirin is exactly the same as the one in less expensive generic aspirin.

At first glance, you may be tempted to tell an audience only your side of the story. Don't give in, though. Deceiving an audience by presenting only one side of an argument is unethical. There may be good reasons that several members of your audience cannot or should not change their opinions or behavior. The wisest move is to acknowledge both sides of an issue.[1] Both the Better Plan and the Overcoming Objections organizational patterns acknowledge that there are other viewpoints and other approaches to an issue.

When you present the other side, though, also refute it. Inoculate your listeners with a refutational message: "Here is my position. My opponent will tell you this, but let me tell you why I think my opponent's position is incorrect or misleading." (Of course, your "opponent" would likewise explain why your position is just as incorrect or misleading.) Because you have acknowledged that legitimate differences of opinion exist, your audience will see you as more credible for mentioning other points of view. Also, remember that when audience members are well informed but undecided about an issue or are likely to engage in counterarguing, it's a good idea to acknowledge both sides of the issue. When your arguments are strong, a two-sided approach will enhance your persuasiveness.

1. Robert H. Gass and John S. Seiter, *Persuasion, Social Influence, and Compliance Gaining* (Boston: Allyn & Bacon, 1999), pp. 191–193.

fashion or wishing for the newest hot car, at some point you probably have succumbed to the bandwagon fallacy. In a persuasive presentation, a speaker may state or imply that audience members are "out of it," "behind the times," or "not in step" if they fail to join the majority and support a particular issue. Sadly, the bandwagon appeal has been used to justify and recruit people for hate groups, unscrupulous financial schemes, and illegal "thrills." Here are some questions to ask about a bandwagon appeal:

- Is this proposal right or best just because it's popular?
- Is popularity a relevant criterion for making a decision?
- What are the disadvantages of following the crowd in this case?

Begging the Question

The **begging the question** fallacy assumes that an unproven fact in an argument is true. Here are some examples: Have you stopped cheating on your spouse? When did you first smoke marijuana? How did you manage to deceive the IRS? These questions assume you did cheat on your spouse, smoke marijuana, and deceive the IRS. In *Begging the Question*, Douglas Walton writes that this fallacy uses "deceptive tactics to try to get a respondent to accept something as a legitimate premise that is really not, and to slur over the omission, to disguise the failure of any genuine proof."[11] Here are some questions to ask about begging the question:

- Does the question assume that something unproven is true?
- Does any direct answer to the question get the subject into trouble?
- Does the speaker presume to know what you think or what you have done?

Victory by Definition

Victory by definition is a fallacy that makes the definition of a word self-serving. For instance, during the 1998 impeachment proceedings against him, President Clinton's definition of the term *sexual relations* provided him with a way of "telling the truth" about his inappropriate encounters with Monica Lewinsky. The more abstract or emotional a term, the easier it is to make its definition suit a persuasive purpose. For example, when asked whether a marketing campaign had been successful, a manager reported that the competition had seen only a 2 percent rise in sales compared with his company's 4 percent. Therefore, the campaign worked. Unfortunately, though, the marketing department had predicted an 8 percent increase! By defining *success* as an

Figure 20.3 Testing Arguments

- ——— Am I feeling manipulated or confused by the speaker? If I am, why?
- ——— Does this statement make sense? Is it reasonable?
- ——— Does the speaker use valid and relevant evidence to support claims?
- ——— Is this statement consistent with what I already know and believe? If it's not, how credible are the speaker's sources?
- ——— Will the speaker directly benefit if I am persuaded?
- ——— Does the speaker appeal to emotions (pity, amusement, disgust) that have little to do with the substance of the argument?
- ——— Is the speaker telling only one side of the story?

increase "twice as high as that of any competitor," the manager was able to avoid mentioning that the marketing department had missed its projected mark by half. Here are some questions about victory by definition:

- Is this the accepted definition of the word?
- Is this the definition that the speaker used at other points in this argument?
- Would using other definitions change the speaker's conclusion?

Knowing that so many fallacies exist should forewarn you that speakers with the best of intentions can still fall prey to a lurking fallacy. Whether you're a speaker or an audience member, do your best to test what you say or hear before delivering or believing a message. The tests of evidence that we discuss in Chapter 8, "Supporting Material," can be applied to arguments, too. Use the checklist in Figure 20.3 to test an argument's overall validity.

When a fallacy unintentionally enters a persuasive presentation, we can usually forgive the speaker and hope that she or he will recognize the error and avoid making it in the future. What we should not forgive is the intentional use of fallacies. Being able to identify the fallacies of arguments is the first step in making sure that we avoid using them and condemn them when we hear them being used by unethical speakers.

Summary

What constitutes a good persuasive presentation?

Begin with a topic and purpose that are important to both you and your audience. Then develop your arguments while considering whether your claims are asking the audience to believe questions of fact, value, conjecture, and/or policy.

What are the characteristics of a persuasive argument?

According to Toulmin's Model of Argument, a persuasive argument should include a clear claim, valid and relevant evidence, reasoning that warrants the conclusion, and—in some cases—backing for the warrant, acknowledgment of reservations, and qualified claims.

What's the best type of evidence to use in a persuasive presentation?

Assuming that you have already collected valid supporting material for your presentation, select evidence that is novel, believable, and dramatic.

What's the best way to organize a persuasive presentation?

Adapt your persuasive organizational pattern to the beliefs and needs of your audience. In addition to standard formats, consider the following organizational patterns: Problem/Cause/Solution, Better Plan, Overcoming Objections, Monroe's Motivated Sequence, and Persuasive Stories.

What are the common fallacies of argument?

Some of the most common fallacies of arguments include faulty cause, attacking the person, hasty generalization, selected instances, bandwagon, begging the question, and victory by definition. Regardless of their names, fallacies are invalid arguments or misleading statements, made during a persuasive presentation, that intentionally or unintentionally deceive an audience.

Presentation Principles in Action

Clarify Your Claims

Directions: Identify the following statements as claims of *fact, value, conjecture,* or *policy.*

Type of Claim	Claim
1. ________	The United States will adopt a universal health care program for all citizens.
2. ________	Intelligent life exists on other planets.
3. ________	Homosexual relationships are immoral.
4. ________	The assassination of President John F. Kennedy was the result of a conspiracy involving the CIA.
5. ________	Lance Armstrong won his fifth straight Tour de France in 2003.
6. ________	All public school teachers should be required to pass a competency examination before being certified to teach.
7. ________	The number of people enrolled in college education will increase by 10 percent in the next five years.
8. ________	President Clinton was impeached for his conduct with Monica Lewinsky.
9. ________	Private schools provide students with a better education than public schools do.
10. ________	A catastrophic earthquake will destroy significant portions of California's coastal cities.
11. ________	Students should be required to wear school uniforms in elementary school.
12. ________	Drivers over the age of seventy-five should be required to complete a driver's examination every two years.
13. ________	Volunteering provides personal satisfaction and important service to your community.
14. ________	O. J. Simpson murdered his ex-wife.
15. ________	Premarital sex violates religious principles.

Assessing Persuasive Presentations

The following persuasive presentation assessment instrument can help you evaluate the development of your own presentation as well as those made by other speakers. Use the following ratings to assess each of the criteria on the instrument:

E = Excellent G = Good A = Average F = Fair P = Poor
N/A = Not applicable to this presentation

Persuasive Presentation Assessment Instrument

Criteria	E	G	A	F	P	N/A
Purpose and Topic: Clear purpose, reasonable goals, appropriate and narrowed topic						
Audience Analysis: Adapts to audience characteristics, interests, attitudes; adapts to different types of listeners						
Credibility: Believable, trustworthy, competent, committed, charismatic						
Logistics: Adapts to occasion and place of presentation, including use of equipment						
Content: Includes valid arguments supported by strong evidence and reasoning						
Organization: Clear and strategic organization, effective introduction and conclusion, clear connectives						
Performance: Appropriate form(s) of delivery, effective vocal and physical delivery, including eye contact						
Presentation Aids: Effective choice, design, and handling of presentation aids						
Persuasive Strategies: Appropriate and strategic choices of persuasive strategies						
Overall Evaluation:						

COMMENTS:

Key Terms

argument 455
attacking the person fallacy 472
backing 457
bandwagon fallacy 473
begging the question fallacy 474
Better Plan organizational pattern 466
claim 455
evidence 456
fallacy 471
faulty cause fallacy 472
hasty generalization fallacy 473
Monroe's Motivated Sequence 467
Overcoming Objections organizational pattern 467
Persuasive Stories organizational pattern 469
Problem/Cause/Solution organizational pattern 465
qualifier 458
question of conjecture 461
question of fact 459
question of policy 461
question of value 460
reservation 457
selected instances fallacy 473
Toulmin's Model of Argument 455
victory by definition fallacy 474
warrant 456

Notes

1 Stephen Toulmin, *The Uses of Argument* (London: Cambridge University Press, 1958).
2 We have taken liberty and departed from some of Toulmin's terminology for the layout of an argument. We also have used elements of the Toulmin model as modified by Donald Ehninger and Wayne Brockriede to explain the different types of proof that can be used to support an argument. See Douglas Ehninger and Wayne Brockriede, *Decision by Debate* (New York: Dodd, Mead, 1963), Chapters 8–11. Also see Douglas Ehninger and Wayne Brockriede, *Decision by Debate,* 2nd ed. (New York: Harper and Row, 1978), Chapters 4–6; Sonja K. Foss, Karen A. Ross, and Robert Trapp, *Contemporary Perspectives on Rhetoric* (Prospect Heights, IL: Waveland Press, 1985), Chapter 4.
3 Dennis S. Gouran, "Effective Versus Ineffective Group Decision Making," in *Managing Group Life: Communicating in Decision-Making Groups,* eds. Lawrence R. Frey and J. Kevin Barge (Boston: Houghton Mifflin, 1997), p. 139.
4 David L. Vancil, *Rhetoric and Argumentation* (Boston: Allyn & Bacon, 1993), p. 26.
5 See Donald D. Morley, "Subjective Message Constructs: A Theory of Persuasion," *Communication Monographs* 54 (1987): 183–202. In addition to Morley's concept of *novel evidence,* we use the term *believable* for Morley's concept of *plausibility.* Morley's *importance* construct is discussed throughout this textbook in terms of the validity and relevance of good evidence. Also see Donald Dean Morley and Kim B. Walker, "The Role of Importance, Novelty, and Plausibility in Producing Belief Change," *Communication Monographs* 54 (1987): 436–442.
6 *Washington Post,* 6 November 1998, p. F3.
7 *New Yorker,* 30 November 1998, p. 32.
8 Alan H. Monroe, *Principles and Types of Speech* (Chicago: Scott, Foresman, 1935), pp. vii–viii, x. Various applications of Monroe's Motivated Sequence can be found in Bruce E. Gronbeck et al., *Principles and Types of Speech Communication,* 13th ed. (New York: Longman, 1997).
9 Gronbeck et al., pp. 186–187.
10 *The American Heritage Dictionary of the English Language,* 4th ed. (Boston: Houghton Mifflin, 1992), p. 658. Copyright © 2000 by Houghton Mifflin Company. Reproduced by permission from *The American Heritage Dictionary of the English Language, Third Edition.*
11 Douglas N. Walton, *Begging the Question: Circular Reasoning as a Tactic of Argumentation* (New York: Greenwood, 1991), p. 285.

chapter twenty one

Developing Special **Presentations**

- What kinds of special presentations should I know how to make?
- How do I introduce a presenter?
- How should I welcome an audience or a group of guests?
- What's the best way to make a toast?
- How do I prepare and deliver a meaningful eulogy?
- How can I apply the principles of presentation speaking to sales?
- What should I do if I'm asked to make a humorous presentation?
- How do I handle question-and-answer sessions?
- Can I *prepare* for impromptu presentations?

Although most presentations inform, persuade, and/or entertain, a special group of presentations resists such strict classification. Sometimes called special occasion speeches or ceremonial speaking because of the unique occasions that prompt their use, special presentations have specific names that tell you a great deal about their unique purpose, audience, setting, and preparation requirements. For example, a toast celebrates someone at a special event, humorous comments can lighten the atmosphere at a retirement dinner, and welcoming remarks at a ribbon-cutting ceremony can kick off the dedication of a building or monument. This chapter focuses on how to prepare and deliver several kinds of special presentations that you are likely to encounter as a speaker and listener.

Special Presentations

The purpose of most **special presentations** is to bring people together, to create social unity, to build goodwill, to answer questions, or to celebrate.[1] There are many types of special presentations.

SPECIAL PRESENTATIONS COME IN MANY FORMS

- Welcomes
- Acceptance speeches
- Award presentations
- Eulogies
- After-dinner speeches
- Impromptu remarks
- Sales presentations
- Nominations
- Toasts
- Dedications
- Commencement addresses
- Question-and-answer sessions
- Retirement roasts
- Introducing a speaker

At this point you may be wondering why the chapters on informative and persuasive speaking won't provide you with enough strategies to master these forms of presentation speaking. Actually, they will—if you are a quick-thinking, highly adaptable speaker who has tremendous confidence. If you're at a wedding or a retirement dinner, and someone asks you to offer a toast, you will have to think quickly and adapt your toast to what you know about the bride and groom or about the retiree. It also helps to have a great deal of confidence if you're confronted with such a speaking opportunity. Most guests can't pull a toast out of their hats with ease.

Special presentations often come with their own sets of rules—rules that a speaker is expected to follow. If you're asked to make a toast, nominate a candidate, or present an award, many of your decisions will have already been made for you. If you're presenting an award, for example, you can't choose the person or organization that will receive the award—that will already have been done. The audience and the place where you will be speaking will also have been predetermined. And you will have a very specific purpose that will require specific types of preparation and planning. Generally, you will be expected to praise the award recipient, cite reasons that the recipient deserves the award, and deliver your presentation in a positive, uplifting style.

Most of you will never nominate a presidential candidate at a national convention, but you might nominate a classmate or coworker for an office in your student government or a professional association. Most of you will never have to dedicate a public memorial or building, but you may be asked to say a few words at the opening of a new branch office. We don't have enough space in this text to give you specific advice for every type of special presentation. However, if you apply the basic principles of presentation speaking, you can adapt to any type of situation, no matter how monumental or modest the occasion may be.

Introducing a Presenter

When you're invited to **introduce a presenter,** you are being asked to make brief remarks about the speaker and the presentation in order to motivate the audience to listen. You are the warm-up act for the speaker who follows you. Introducing a speaker, a very common type of special presentation, is, unfortunately, often dismissed as an easy chore by those who do it. After all, it's the presentation that's given *after* the introduction that everyone has come to hear. Instead of thinking about introducing a speaker as a necessary but unimportant trifle, you should look upon your comments as a golden opportunity to prepare an audience for the main event and as a way of enhancing your own credibility.

When you introduce a presenter, your purpose is to make listeners *want* to hear the person being introduced. You can share information that makes listeners interested in and curious about the person or give details that can create admiration and respect for him or her. Your introductory comments will also set the stage for the upcoming presentation. Remember the goals of a presentation's introduction from Chapter 11, "Introductions and Conclusions"? They can be exactly the same for introducing a presenter except that you are achieving these goals for someone else rather than for yourself. Introducing a presenter can (1) gain audience attention and interest, (2) connect the presenter to the audience, (3) enhance the presenter's credibility, (4) introduce the presenter's purpose or topic area, and (5) set the appropriate mood for the upcoming presentation.

The introduction of a presenter should "warm up" an audience and make the speaker seem interesting and human. Sometimes, however, an introducer can go overboard and heap so much praise on a speaker that he or she would have a lot of trouble living up to the introduction.

Creating effective remarks to introduce a presenter takes preparation. Let's consider some of the basic decisions you'll need to make and a few guidelines specific to this type of special presentation.

Basic Decisions About Introducing a Presenter

Although on the one hand, you can view an introduction of a presenter as a presentation's introduction, on the other hand, it helps to consider it as a complete mini-presentation. You can apply the seven basic principles of presentation speaking to your introductory comments, making a few adjustments for this type of special presentation.

Purpose: Your purpose is clear-cut: to introduce a particular presenter to a specific audience. In addition, ask yourself, "How can I make the listeners respect and want to hear the person being introduced?"

Audience: As with any other presentation, you'll need to research the characteristics and needs of your audience. In particular, ask yourself, "What do the listeners already know or need to know about the presenter?"

Credibility: Because your introduction should focus the audience's attention on the presenter, not on you, your comments should likewise bolster the presenter's credibility—although one of the best ways to do this is to transfer some of your own credibility to the speaker. Ask yourself, "What can I say that will impress the audience about the presenter's competence and character?"

Logistics: A presentation that calls for a formal introduction by someone else—you!—will already have had many of its logistic decisions made. It's up to you to find out what they are. Ask yourself, "How formal is the occasion, and how formal should the introduction be?" "Where and when will I speak?"

Content: The content of your introduction needs to include details about the person you're introducing. Ask yourself, "What background information do I need to have about the presenter (accomplishments, experiences, education, titles, personal information, and so on)?"

Organization: Even though the introduction of a presenter should be brief, it needs to be well organized instead of being a random collection of unrelated comments. Ask yourself, "How can I review, regroup, reduce, and refine the key points I want to make in a well-organized introduction?"

Performance: Once you have prepared your introduction, you'll need to decide what's the best way to deliver it. Ask yourself, "What form of delivery—other than impromptu—is best for this occasion and presenter?" Then, practice! At this point, one of your most critical questions will be "Can I pronounce the presenter's name correctly and easily?"

Guidelines for Introducing a Presenter

Your answers to the previous questions will help you introduce a presenter. We also offer the following guidelines, developed over years of hearing wonderful and not-so-wonderful introductions.

1. An introduction should be carefully prepared; don't try to make one impromptu.
2. Begin your introduction by acknowledging and thanking the speaker.

3. An introduction should *appear* to be spontaneous and natural. If you're using a manuscript, practice your delivery in order to maximize eye contact instead of reading it word for word.
4. During the body of the introduction, look at the audience. Don't talk to the person being introduced.
5. The introduction should be short. You aren't the main attraction; the speaker is. In most cases a one- or two-minute introduction will be enough. If the audience knows the presenter very well, it can be even shorter.
6. Don't speak at length on the presenter's subject; that's the speaker's job.
7. Play a supportive role. Don't steal the show or embarrass the presenter with extravagant compliments.
8. Avoid using clichés such as "Tonight's speaker needs no introduction" or "So without further ado..."
9. Make sure that your introduction is appropriate for the presenter. If the speaker is not your close friend, don't describe him or her as one.
10. At the end of your introduction, begin applauding until the presenter reaches the lectern or podium. Then, when the speaker begins the presentation, listen closely. You might have to respond to a thank-you for a great introduction!
11. Ask the presenter what she or he wants you to say. Doing this can save you a lot of preparation time and can answer most of your questions.

Because including good information is the key to making a good introduction, it's better to collect too much information about the person whom you will be introducing rather than not enough. Often the best source of this information will be the speaker, and the best way to get that information is to conduct an interview (see the mini-module in Chapter 8, "Supporting Material"). You can ask the presenter one or more of the following questions:[1]

- What do you hope to accomplish with your presentation?
- How did you become interested in your topic?
- What are the two or three most important things that the audience should know about you or your topic?
- Whom should I contact to hear some good stories about you?
- Is there anything that you specifically want me to mention or not to mention?
- Is there anything else that you thought I was going to ask?

1. Malcolm Kushner, *Successful Presentations for Dummies* (Foster City, CA: IDG, 1997), p. 310.

Welcoming an Audience

Welcoming remarks are one of the most common and most underappreciated forms of special presentations. Although making them may look easy, they require significant preparation and thought. You may be asked to welcome a speaker or a special guest, which is not the same as introducing a presenter. Rather, you will be welcoming that person on behalf of the audience. Welcoming remarks also kick off special events. For instance, when a group visits a college, company, or organization, someone usually has been asked to welcome the audience.

What makes giving this type of special presentation difficult is that there isn't much to say if you haven't done your homework. You stand up, look at the audience, and say, "We are delighted to welcome you to (insert the name of the event)." Now what? "On behalf of the entire organization, we are pleased you chose (insert the name of your organization) to host your meeting." Now what? "Thank you, and have a great day." Those three sentences may constitute a welcome, but they won't do much for you or your organization—or for your credibility as a speaker.

When you welcome an audience, you create a critical first impression of yourself and your organization. If your welcome is dull, the audience may regard *you* as dull.

If your welcome says nothing about the audience or their organization, your listeners may decide that you are a poor speaker who has no interest in whether or not they are there. Although welcoming remarks can be brief, they can provide a lot of benefits for speakers and their organizations.

Basic Decisions About Welcoming Remarks

Effective decisions about welcoming an audience are based on the material you know or have collected about a group or the reason that audience members have been assembled. Paying attention to a series of basic questions can help you make your remarks memorable.

Purpose: How can I link my welcoming remarks to the goals of the organization that *I* represent?

Audience: What are the audience's expectations and interests? What is the organization's goal or history? What kind and size of audience will attend?

Credibility: What can I say to demonstrate that I share the audience's interests, beliefs, or values?

Logistics: How formal is the occasion, and how formal and long should my welcome be?

Content: What specific content should I include that relates to the assembled group, its purpose, and the occasion?

Organization: How can I use a simple organizational pattern to accomplish my purpose?

Performance: What form of delivery is best for this occasion? Regardless of what form I choose, can I deliver my remarks naturally, with maximum eye contact?

Guidelines for Effective Welcoming Remarks

Your answers to the previous basic questions will help you prepare and present successful welcoming remarks. The following guidelines can help you make them even better.

1. Don't throw your welcoming remarks together at the last minute. If you do, you run the risk of making a "one-size-fits-all-groups" welcome that basically says, "I don't know anything and didn't have time to learn anything about you, but in any event, I'm glad you're here."
2. Link your own or your organization's goals to those of the group. If you can, show that you share their interests and values. Also, use the opportunity to share information about your own organization.
3. Acknowledge the group's leader or leaders by name somewhere in your welcoming remarks.
4. Make sure that you correctly pronounce the name of the group that you are welcoming.
5. Stick around after you finish your welcoming remarks. Don't rush out the door. Someone may have a question or need your help. Even if you do nothing more than stand at the back of the room for a few minutes, you will be further extending the goodwill created by your welcome.

Making a Toast

If you've ever been at a wedding, retirement party, or special banquet, you've probably been asked to lift your glass and toast the newlyweds, guest of honor, retiree, employee, or family member. A **toast** consists of remarks that accompany an act of drinking to honor a person, a couple, or a group. Most of you, at some point, will be asked or inspired to make a toast. Whether you're drinking champagne or orange juice, a toast is a way to publicly honor, recognize, or thank someone or something. Yes, you can make a toast to a thing: Here's a toast to our tenth anniversary in business!

Basic Decisions About Toasts

Even though many toasts are impromptu in form, you can still prepare and practice them. Here, too, there are basic decisions to make. Some of them involve the basic principles of presentation speaking. However, the answers to some additional questions can help you to prepare and present a successful toast.

A maid of honor offers a toast at a wedding reception. Although she speaks without notes, her short toast should be well prepared and well rehearsed.

Find a "Hook" for Your Toast

The *Wall Street Journal* has spotlighted British Ambassador Christopher Meyer, known on Washington's Embassy Row for his witty and literate toasts.[1] Where does he get his inspiration? He credits websites that specialize in trivia and "useless" knowledge. That's where he finds a "hook" for his remarks—a birthday, battle, or other historical event that occurred on the toast day.

Ambassador Meyer has given thousands of toasts in his more than thirty-year career. He has developed several rules for his routine: He always makes toasts at the end of the meal, after his audience has been warmed up by wine and dinner conversation. He always talks for five to seven minutes. During the first half of his toast, he tries to make people laugh. "It engages their emotions so [that] when you do come to the serious bit, you have their attention," he says. And if you get off to a bad start (one sign: the guests start chattering with their neighbors), keep the volume up. This is the best way to regain their attention. "Project your voice across the room," he advises. "You can recover."

1. *Wall Street Journal,* 19 February 2003, p. D1. *Note:* Several websites offer trivia and historical events by date. As we write this text, the following site provides a good example of the kind of information used by Ambassador Meyer: *www.coolquiz.com/trivia/.*

Purpose: How can I help the audience join in and celebrate the reason that we are here?

Audience: What do the listeners already know and feel about the person or object being honored?

Credibility: What can I say that will show the audience how wonderful this person or cause is?

Logistics: How formal is the occasion, and how formal should my toast be?

Content: What can I discover or share in my toast that will celebrate the person, group, or occasion (special stories, accomplishments, personal experiences)?

Organization: How can I use a series of stories or experiences to support the key points in my toast?

Performance: What style of delivery would best suit this occasion?

Why Is It Called a Toast?

Apparently the term *toast* comes from an old English tradition of putting a spiced piece of toast in an alcoholic drink to add more flavor. In speaking situations, the toast brings attention to something special at an event—it "spices up" and adds a joyous flavor to a celebration. Thus, a toast is a way of focusing on a special guest or event. From the word *toast,* we have *toastmaster,* a term that has come to mean the person who introduces a speaker or who serves as a master or mistress of ceremonies at a special event.

Guidelines for Great Toasts

A toast can be as solemn as a prayer or as risqué as a wedding-night joke. A toast can remind an audience why they are celebrating or remind a person why he or she is being honored. Because toasts are supposed to make everyone feel good, they can be more emotional, inspiring, and joyful than other types of presentations. Toasts can be memorable and great fun if you take the time to make appropriate decisions and follow a few simple guidelines.

1. Carefully prepare your toast. Don't try to make it impromptu if you know in advance that you will be expected to make a toast.

2. A toast should have a purpose and make a point.
3. A toast should sound and look spontaneous and natural; never *read* a toast unless you are reading a special poem or quotation.
4. When making a toast, look at the audience *and* at the person or group whom you are toasting. This isn't an introduction—it's a celebration.
5. Keep it short and simple; your audience will get tired of holding their glasses up.
6. Be direct and sincere; your job is to say what everyone else is feeling.
7. Make sure your comments are appropriate for the person, group, or occasion you are honoring.

Delivering a Eulogy

Eulogies are tributes that praise the dead. Most people think of a eulogy as a speech delivered shortly after a person's death. Some eulogies, however, may be delivered years later to commemorate the anniversary of a death or to celebrate an important person's historical achievements.

A eulogy can honor a person's life, offer comfort to those who mourn, awaken personal remembrances, celebrate a person's accomplishments, and/or urge others to embrace the deceased person's values and goals. Given the emotional circumstances of a eulogy, speakers face the difficult task of dealing with their own emotions as well as those of their audience. (The Appendix includes a eulogy delivered by Senator John McCain in which he honors Mark Bingham, one of the brave United Airlines Flight 93 passengers who lost his life on September 11, 2001.)

A speaker raises his hands during a eulogy at a gravesite. The speaking notes in his left hand ensure that he is able to express his thoughts in a distressing situation.

Basic Decisions About Delivering a Eulogy

Use the following principles to prepare and present an appropriate and meaningful eulogy.

Purpose: Make sure your purpose is specific, appropriate, and achievable. Do you want to comfort those who grieve and/or focus your presentation on paying tribute to the deceased person? Do you need to familiarize audience members with the person's background and accomplishments, or do you want to celebrate the values the person held? Eulogies are most effective when they set out to accomplish a limited number of goals.

Audience: Understand the relationship of the audience to the person being eulogized. Is the audience composed of family members, close friends, colleagues, or acquaintances? What do the listeners already know and feel about the deceased person? In some cases, you may need to give the audience biographical information about the person. In other cases, you can assume that everyone knew the person well.

Credibility: When presenting a eulogy, you may face the daunting task of maintaining your composure throughout the presentation. No one in the audience will think less of you if you cannot finish a eulogy, or if you falter in its delivery because you are overcome with emotion. They will think a great deal more of you if you handle this difficult speaking task with serenity and skill.

Logistics: Eulogies often take place in formal settings—at memorials, funerals, and religious services. The speaker and audience are usually dressed conservatively. Eulogies rarely require special logistical arrangements other than a microphone for large audiences. In some cases, a set of photographs, honors, or personal effects may be displayed and can be used to reference personal attributes or achievements.

Content: Most eulogies are personal and reflect the speaker's most cherished memories and experiences with the deceased person. They are usually delivered by someone who knows a great deal about the deceased person. However, there are occasions—such as a memorial at a work site—when the speaker has limited information about the person beyond the work environment. In such cases, a little bit of research can help you speak with authority.

Organization: Most eulogies employ a simple organizational pattern. Use a series of stories to highlight the deceased individual's achievements, values, or personal qualities. Select some meaningful quotations to describe someone when your own words seem inadequate. Relate experiences in chronological order to document the length and depth of your relationship.

Performance: Given the emotional nature of a eulogy, many speakers decide to read their remarks from a well-prepared manuscript. In other cases, a short list reminding you of a few personal stories may be all that you need to deliver a meaningful eulogy. Concentrate on keeping your voice steady and loud enough to be heard by your audience.

Guidelines for Meaningful Eulogies

Much like a toast, a eulogy can be as solemn as a prayer or as amusing as a funny anecdote. Grieving audiences often appreciate a speaker who can bring a little humor into a solemn occasion. Depending on your purpose, your eulogy can be highly emotional, inspiring, or even joyful. The following guidelines can help you develop and deliver a meaningful eulogy.

1. Carefully prepare your eulogy. Maintaining your composure can be difficult during the presentation.
2. Focus on one or two key points. Keep the eulogy short and simple, particularly if there are multiple speakers.
3. Pay careful attention to the words you choose. Family members often ask speakers for copies of their eulogies, so make sure that your words are the ones you want preserved for posterity.
4. If appropriate, acknowledge and offer sympathy to the family and close friends of the deceased person during the eulogy.
5. Personalize the eulogy. Anyone can read a list of a person's accomplishments—only *you* can talk about your relationship with the deceased person.
6. Practice a eulogy many times so that you feel confident about being able to deliver it under highly emotional conditions.
7. Make sure that your clothing and delivery style are appropriate for the occasion.

Sales Presentations

The **sales presentation** is a unique form of speaking that combines the strategies and skills of informative and persuasive presentations. Even if you never work in retail sales, you can benefit from learning how effective salespeople achieve their goals in the marketplace. Whether you are selling Girl Scout cookies to your neighbor, promoting the services of a major law firm to a corporate client, or even selling yourself at an important job interview, the art of selling can be very profitable for you and others.

Basic Decisions About Sales Presentations

Successful sales professionals excel as strategic speakers and motivated listeners. They know how and when to apply presentation speaking principles to achieve their business goals. Use the following seven principles to prepare and present an effective sales presentation.

Purpose: Expert sales professionals look for a match between their product and the needs and interests of the buyer. A purpose statement for a sales transaction must be specific. "I want to sell cars" is not specific. "I want to demonstrate why our dealership is best equipped to understand and meet this customer's personal and financial needs" is much more specific and can lead to a wide variety of sales strategies. When establishing your purpose for a sales presentation, remember one of the key points for persuading an audience that disagrees with you: Set reasonable and appropriate goals.

Customers Come in Many Varieties

One of the most important questions to ask about your audience is this: "What connections do I have with this person or group?" Sales connections come in many different varieties.

- *Prospects.* People who can afford and can benefit from buying the product.
- *Leads.* People who have the potential to become prospects.
- *Past customers.* People who have benefited from the product and may be inclined or persuaded to buy it again.
- *Existing customers.* People who buy the product on a regular or contractual basis.
- *Competitors' customers.* People who have the potential to be wooed away from another product.
- *Referrals.* People who have been recommended by business associates, marketing research groups, existing customers, or past customers.

Each type of customer is different and requires different adaptations in a sales presentation. Promising and providing responsive and high-quality service may be the key to keeping an existing customer, whereas improving a product or offering a better financial package may interest a past customer. Investigating customer complaints about a competitor's product may give you the arguments you need to attract that customer to your product. Telephoning leads and referrals with a well-prepared sales pitch can hook a few new customers from the large sea of potential buyers.

Audience: Regardless of the size of an audience (a single customer, a family, a business, or millions of TV viewers), successful sales professionals are audience focused. They focus on customer needs and try to figure out WIIFT—What's In It For Them?

Credibility: Many people have seen or experienced sleazy, dishonest, high-pressure salespeople. You can avoid producing this perception of yourself and your sales presentation in several ways. Make sure that you are a product expert. Demonstrate your competence in customer service: Return your phone calls promptly, take time to get to know your customers, and handle complaints without becoming defensive. Buyers also want salespeople of good character—professionals who are honest, friendly, and fair. Are you willing to tell customers that a product won't work for them, that they don't need an expensive repair, or that an outfit doesn't flatter them? If you are willing to lose a sale, you may have gained a loyal customer. Finally, consider ways to demonstrate your enthusiasm about the product. If you don't like what you're selling, why should the buyer?

Logistics: How will the sales transaction occur—face-to-face, before a group, on the phone, or via e-mail? Each medium requires different tactics. In a face-to-face meeting, you can zero in on the particular needs of a buyer. In a presentation to a large group, you have to consider differences and similarities in audience interests, needs, and financial resources. In mediated transactions, your writing and graphic displays must effectively compete against the information from competitors.

Content: All salespeople must be content experts. They must know their product inside and out, be able to describe the product using different forms of supporting material (facts; statistics; and examples of, testimony from, and stories about satisfied customers). If your listeners sense that you don't know your product and can't answer their questions, you won't make the sale.

Organization: Organizing a sales presentation is very similar to organizing a persuasive presentation. Persuasive organizational patterns are particularly well suited to sales. For example, the Problem/Cause/Solution pattern works well with prospective customers who are looking for a product to solve a problem. The Better Plan pattern can be used to demonstrate why your product is better than the competition's. The Overcoming Objections pattern can dispel concerns and fears about making a major purchase. The Persuasive Stories pattern can influence potential buyers who have the time and are interested in hearing well-told tales about satisfied customers. The most applicable persuasive pattern, though, may be Monroe's Motivated Sequence because it is based on sales techniques.

1. **The Attention Step.** Capture attention, establish your credibility, clarify your purpose, and draw attention to the customer's needs.
2. **The Need Step.** Ask questions about or discuss individual or group needs. Relate your product to the needs and interests of your customers.
3. **The Satisfaction Step.** Provide a compelling description of your product or service. Describe its benefits. WIIFT—What's In It For Them?
4. **The Visualization Step.** Vividly describe what their lives will be like if they make the purchase. Show how the benefits will be realized. Try to intensify their willingness to buy. Help them visualize a better or less problematic future.
5. **The Action Step.** Close the sale. Summarize the benefits. Arouse their determination. Ask if they have any questions.

Performance: Generally, it's a good idea to speak extemporaneously during a sale. That means being well prepared but able to adapt to customer feedback. If you use presentation aids, don't overuse them, and make sure that they are as accurate and professional looking as possible. Don't talk your customers to death. Know when to stop and listen.

Guidelines for Listening to Customers

The most successful sales professionals are motivated listeners. The more a customer talks, the more you can learn about the person's needs, concerns, tastes, and financial resources. Listening also gives you time to think about what you want to say and how you want to say it. Several listening techniques can enhance your ability to serve customers.

1. In addition to listening to what they say, "listen" to their nonverbal behavior. Even when they say they're not interested, their nonverbal behavior may tell you the opposite.
2. Listen *comprehensively* when a customer seems confused or reticent. If a potential buyer believes that you are trying to learn about her or his needs and concerns, the buyer is more likely to trust you.
3. Listen *analytically* when a customer is skeptical or critical. Then try to answer the person's objections without belittling her or his concerns.
4. Listen *empathically* when a customer is describing a problem or concern. Genuine concern for your customer translates into trust.
5. Listen *appreciatively* when a customer seems enthused and interested in your product.

Humorous Presentations

What's the most difficult kind of presentation to prepare and present? As you might guess from the location of this question, our vote goes to the **humorous presentation,** sometimes called an after-dinner speech, a "roast" of a friend, or a speech to entertain.

Following the basic principles of presentation speaking requires a lot of work; trying to be funny at the same time requires even more work—with a dash of talent added to the mix.

Life without humor would be pretty dull. Some researchers even claim that humor can prevent or cure illness. The saying "laughter is the best medicine" may have some basis in fact. We do know that humor can reduce stress. In fact, it's so effective at relieving muscle tension that people often fall down laughing.

As we note in Chapter 13, "Generating Interest," a little humor in an otherwise "straight" presentation can relax the speaker as well as ease audience tensions. It can also capture and hold an audience's attention. It can even defuse anger and stimulate action. Audience members tend to remember humorous speakers positively, even when they aren't enthusiastic about the speaker's message. In this chapter, we look at making humor the centerpiece of a presentation.

With so much to be said about the advantages of using humor as a component of a presentation or as the centerpiece of a talk, why don't more speakers give humorous presentations? For one thing, many presenters don't think they can deliver a humorous presentation well. For another, many people have no idea how to go about being funny. However, it's easy to learn what pitfalls to avoid and what guidelines to follow for using humor well.

The Pitfalls of Humorous Speaking

What are some of the mistakes that speakers make when they're trying to be funny? A few common pitfalls stand out.

THE PITFALLS OF HUMOROUS SPEAKING

- **Offensiveness**
- **Irrelevance**
- **Poor delivery**
- **Using prepackaged humor**

Offensive Humor. We shouldn't have to say this, but we will: Don't use humor that has the potential to offend your audience. Avoid telling stories or jokes that could be interpreted as racist or sexist. We are astounded at how many speakers think it's okay to tell stories or jokes about a "priest, minister, and rabbi," "a ditzy blond," or a trio of "deaf, blind, and crippled" people. This point is not about political correctness. It's about common courtesy and audience sensibilities. There are plenty of ways to be funny without being insulting or offensive. Don't even think about using humor if there's any chance that it would offend your audience.

Deciding whether a one-liner, story, or joke is offensive or inappropriate isn't always easy. Most of us can recognize a joke that is blatantly racist or in poor taste. But it's harder to make a call on the borderline ones. If you have any doubts, heed them! Malcolm Kushner, a speaker, author, and former communication instructor, provides this simple test for making sure that your humor is appropriate for an audience: "Picture a front-page headline in your hometown newspaper describing your use of the joke in a presentation. Would you be embarrassed? If the answer is 'yes,' then don't use the joke."[2]

One of the reasons that ethnic and sexist jokes are popular is that they're based on very funny ideas. One way to take advantage of such humor—and to make it less offensive—is to tailor the object of the joke to the audience or occasion. For example, try filling in the blanks for jokes such as "How many_____s does it take to_____?" or "What do you call a_____?" With apologies to our academic colleagues, we offer a couple of examples: "How many professors does it take to change a curriculum?" (We don't know. They're still in committee.) "What do you call a professor who yells at the dean?" (Tenured.) If you don't get these feeble jokes, don't worry. They're aimed at an academic audience. They're also a good example of the self-effacing humor we discuss in Chapter 13. By making fun of yourself, you can use humor to make a serious point. Depending on where you work or live, you can substitute any group you work with or belong to. At the same time, make sure you don't make *too* much fun of the group and its members. They may not be amused.

Irrelevant Humor. Why do speakers often begin or end a presentation with a joke? We guess that there are two major reasons. One is that they don't know how to create an effective introduction or conclusion. The other is that they think they're expected to begin and end with a joke—even if it has nothing to do with the presentation. We dislike pointless humor. When a humorous story or joke is irrelevant to your message, it can distract an audience and waste their time. And what happens if the audience doesn't find your opening or closing statement funny? Just when you should be making a good first and last impression, you've bombed! Humor—regardless of its form—should support your presentation by tying in to a specific point. Just because you've heard a good joke, don't assume that's any reason to share it with the world—particularly in a presentation that has nothing to do with the characters or topic of the joke.

Poorly Delivered Humor. Don't use humor unless you feel comfortable telling jokes and humorous stories. Do you have trouble remembering a joke or the punch line of a funny story? Are you confident enough to tell a long joke without jumping over some parts of the story ("So, anyway, this happens four or five more times and then . . .")? Do you ramble through a joke ("And then this guy says, . . . and then she says, . . . and then the guy says, . . . and then . . .")? Do you laugh at your own humor before you get to the funny part? Do you apologize for lacking the skill to tell a good joke? Do you spoil the joke by telling everyone when the funny parts are coming up? If you aren't skilled at delivering humorous material, think twice before taking on the challenge of creating and delivering a humorous presentation.

Prepackaged Humor. Some speakers use other people's humor. You can buy books on humor and look up jokes in alphabetized categories such as *Advertising, Age, Television, Unions,* or *Women.* Many of the jokes, stories, and one-liners in these books are funny, but they may not be appropriate for your audience. They can't possibly reflect the specifics of the audience you're addressing. Or you may not feel comfortable telling them. Many of these jokes are dated and stale. Despite these cautions, speakers persist in using prepackaged jokes without realizing how obvious it is that they're telling jokes that they found in a book.

Guidelines for Humorous Presentations

Before you turn in your jokes at the door and avoid using humor at all, be reassured that humor can be delivered easily if you use it in a way that's appropriate for you and for your presentation. Very few people can tell a lengthy joke well, but most people can deliver meaningful one-liners, tell humorous stories, or make fun of themselves. For those of you who want to use humor but are nervous about giving it a try, we offer some guidelines to help you decide when and how to prepare and deliver a humorous presentation.

GUIDELINES FOR HUMOROUS PRESENTATIONS

Focus on one humorous idea.
Let the humor suit you.
Practice until you drop.

Focus on One Humorous Idea. Whether you are inserting humor into a presentation or preparing an entire speech to entertain, you can develop quite a few funny lines by focusing on and researching one humorous idea. One student decided to meet the challenge of creating an entire presentation about what would happen if doctors decided to advertise. The following excerpt was part of it.

> *Since no healthy, red-blooded American can resist a bargain—a rash of sales will develop. Surgeons could have grand opening sales. Of course, the same is true of obstetricians and Labor Day sales—20 percent off on all deliveries. And, of course, if you're going to run sales, that means advertising in the print media. Organ donor banks might have their own section in the classified ads, right behind "Used Parts—Auto."*

The previous examples illustrate an idea allowed to run wild. The result, by the way, was a presentation that won first place at a national speech tournament.

Let the Humor Suit You. Some speakers are good storytellers; others are known for their ability to tell jokes. Some presenters are masters at making puns; others do great imitations of friends and famous people. When you use humor, make sure it suits you and your speaking style. If you're not good at delivering one-liners, don't use them. If you can take a common situation and exaggerate it into a hilarious episode, you have found your niche.

Gene Perret, author of *Using Humor for Effective Business Speaking,* strongly believes that humor should begin with the speaker, not the joke. "Rarely will you find a chunk of comedy that you can retell as is. A joke or a story is a naked thing. It has no relation to you, to your audience, or to your message. You have to work to make it personal."[3] In other words, don't contort yourself to fit your material; adapt the material to fit your personality and your style.

Practice Until You Drop. Of all the forms, types, kinds, and styles of presentation speaking, humorous speaking needs to be practiced the most in order to ensure a good performance. It involves more than just knowing the content of your presentation. It requires comic timing—knowing when and how forcefully to say a line, when to pause, and when to look at the audience for their reactions. To pull off a humorous presentation, you have to practice, practice, and then practice some more. The result will be a very funny speech that looks as if it's easy and enjoyable to perform.

Answering Audience Questions

At first, answering audience questions may not seem like a type of special presentation, but it qualifies in every way. The **question-and-answer session** (often called "Q-and-A") is a special type of impromptu talk that is limited and directed by questions. Other types of presentations may have planned or spur-of-the-moment Q-and-A sessions that follow them. Very often, audiences report that they liked the Q-and-A sessions better than the presentations. Why? As Chapter 14, "Performance and Practice," notes, speakers often talk and move more naturally while answering audience questions because they have stopped thinking about how they sound and look. Instead, they are thinking about how to answer the questions. Some speakers report that they don't think of a question-and-answer session as a presentation or speech, so they have less to be nervous about.

Audience members often measure a speaker's character and competence—the ultimate test of credibility—by the way in which she or he answers questions. Whereas most presentations are prepared in advance and rehearsed, a question-and-answer session may seem more personal and authentic—the *real* speaker is revealed.

Audiences like Q-and-A sessions because they can get their specific questions answered and can interact directly with the speaker instead of remaining quiet and passive. If some speakers like this form of speaking, why don't other speakers? The reason is that some speakers are afraid of answering or don't know how to answer questions. The key to making a question-and-answer session a positive experience is to be prepared.

PREPARING FOR A QUESTION-AND-ANSWER SESSION

Predict and practice.
Have ready-made remarks.
Have a ready-made closing.

Be Prepared

Did you know that U.S. presidents take days to prepare for press conferences? Certainly, they have other important things to do, yet no one argues about the need to prepare and practice for a press conference. All speakers should heed the advice of press conference veterans. Advance preparation is the best way to ensure that you can and will answer questions effectively. Here's how you do it:

Predict and Practice. Predict which issues you think will be most important to your audience. Ask your friends or coworkers what questions they would ask or what kinds of questions have been asked in similar situations. Ask the chairperson of the meeting or the person who invited you to speak what questions the audience might have. Once you have identified these questions, practice answering them.

Also, you may want to announce the fact that there will be a question-and-answer session at the end of your presentation (and how long it will be). This announcement can affect the way in which an audience listens to you. If audience

Connecticut State Treasurer Denise Napier leads students in an open discussion on the importance of saving money. Her eager audience has many questions that she will try to answer in a short period of time.

members don't understand something you say or feel you've left out something that concerns them, they know they can ask you questions about it later.

Have Ready-Made Remarks. Be prepared with a few interesting statistics, stories, examples, and quotations that you can use in an answer. You may not use any of them, but at least you will know that you'll have something in reserve to support the ideas you express.

Have a Ready-Made Closing. When audience questions begin winding down or when it's time to stop the Q-and-A session, make a concluding remark that you've prepared in advance. Saying "thank you" is polite, but it doesn't take advantage of the opportunity to end with a memorable statement. Marjorie Brody, author of *Speaking*

Handling Hostile Questions

Depending on your topic and the people in your audience, you may be faced with one or more hostile questions. Although this is a rare occurrence, it does happen. Before you panic, think about this: Even when an audience doesn't agree with you, they will usually be sympathetic and supportive if one of their members badgers you or asks hostile questions. They wouldn't want to be in your shoes and therefore may become your best allies if someone goes after you. Fortunately, there are strategies to help you deal with a hostile question from an antagonistic audience member.

- Take your time before answering. Listen carefully. And don't strike back. Don't get drawn into a raging argument with one person. Taking a few seconds to think first can help you stay under control and avoid an embarrassing response. Hostile questioners are trying to provoke you. Don't let them. Be diplomatic and keep your cool.
- Paraphrase the question. Rephrasing the question, even when it's a friendly one, is not a bad idea. Making sure you understand the question also gives you time to think of an appropriate answer. When rephrasing a hostile question, don't repeat it word for word. Instead, try to put the question in more neutral or even positive terms.
- If you aren't sure how to answer a hostile question, admit it. Audience members are more likely to respect speakers who admit that they can't answer a question rather than those who try to derail a hostile question by faking their way through an answer.
- If possible, try to empathize with a hostile questioner. Very often hostile questions come from frustrated audience members. If a questioner has been treated poorly, has a personal stake in the outcome of your presentation, or is offended by something you have said, you shouldn't dismiss that person's feelings.
- Perhaps the best suggestion for dealing with a hostile questioner is to seek common ground with the questioner (see "When Audiences Disagree" in Chapter 19, "Understanding Persuasion"). Find an area in which you and the questioner agree and build your answer from there: "Then we both agree that customers are waiting much too long in line with their purchases. We just differ on how to speed up the checkout process." In addition, use fair and respected evidence when you support the answer to a question. Accept differences of opinion. Work to build personal credibility by treating your audience with respect and by answering their questions as specifically as you can.
- Finally, there may come a point at which you have to be more assertive with a hostile questioner. As we indicated, an audience will become just as tired of listening to a harangue as you will. When a questioner is being abusive, offensive, or threatening, it's often effective to suggest that the person talk to you after the presentation and then to quickly move on to the next person who has a question. And don't let a hostile questioner ask a follow-up question. Again, move on to other audience members who have questions.

Your Way to the Top, suggests that you return to the central idea, make references to the conclusion of your presentation, or talk about next steps.[4] Even if your concluding statement is short, it can neatly and professionally wrap things up.

Answer the Question

Once you feel well prepared for a question-and-answer session, the most important piece of advice we can offer is this: Answer the questions. Unless a question is technical and demands a lengthy response, each answer should be no longer than three sentences, and we don't mean run-on sentences. Be direct. Don't ramble or change the subject. Be honest. Audiences can tell if you're dodging an issue or fudging an answer; they won't like you any better if you evade their questions. Be specific but be brief. That doesn't mean giving superficial answers. It means answering a question directly without using up so much time that no other listener has a chance to ask you anything else.

The following set of guidelines can help ensure that you are answering the right question with the right answer.

1. Listen carefully to the question. Enlist all four types of listening—comprehensive, analytical, empathic, and appreciative—to make sure that you fully understand the nature of the question.
2. Pause before answering. Unless you believe that an instant response is appropriate, reflect on the question. Audience members respect speakers who give visible, thoughtful consideration to their questions.
3. Repeat or rephrase the question before answering. If some audience members can't hear the question, repeat it for them. Even better, rephrase it. Not only can you make the question easier to answer if you put it in *your* own words; you may also be able to substitute positive or neutral phrases for negative ones. Instead of repeating, "Why does our PR Office do such a lousy job of publicizing our achievements?" you could reword the question as "What can our PR Office do to better publicize our achievements?"
4. If appropriate, thank the questioners. But be careful to avoid insincere flattery. Don't use a statement such as "That's an excellent question" after every question. The audience will know that your compliments are not sincere. Instead, when you hear a very good question or one that supports your purpose, you can thank the questioner for asking an important question and then demonstrate its value.
5. Seek confirmation. When you rephrase a difficult or important question, ask, "Did I get it right?" The last thing you want to do is answer the wrong question.
6. Link your answer to your key points. Use the question as a bridge to your purpose. Employ audience questions to reinforce your arguments or to share additional information relevant to your topic. If you let an audience sidetrack you, they may lose touch with your central idea and the key points that you want them to remember.

Respect Your Questioners

Most questioners are good people seeking answers to their questions. Even if they don't word their questions well, you will sense what they want or need to know. A few questioners, however, fall into a different category. They can be highly opinionated or incomprehensible. Nevertheless, you should treat all of your questioners with respect. The following suggestions can help you give questioners the respect they deserve.

1. Don't make the questioner feel embarrassed or stupid. Even if you think the question is absurd, foolish, or just plain dumb, treat the questioner with respect.
2. Assist a nervous questioner. Like speakers, audience members may experience speech anxiety when they get up to ask a question. Help them through their nerve-wracking moment in the spotlight. Encourage, praise, and thank them.
3. One very common problem is the overexcited questioner who tries to give a speech rather than ask a question. After a minute or two of the questioner's speech, interrupt

(if you can) and politely ask what the question is. If the speaker keeps going, you may find audience members joining you and asking the questioner: "What's your question?"

4. Recognize questioners by name. If you know a questioner's name or can see it on a name tag, use it. Saying their names when you answer their questions personalizes the exchanges.
5. Control your body language. Looking bored, annoyed, impatient, or condescending while a questioner is speaking sends a negative nonverbal message. If the questioner or audience senses your negative response, your credibility will be damaged. To avoid this, make full eye contact, smile, and lean toward the questioner.

Because Q-and-A sessions are so common, being well prepared for them is just as important as being well prepared to make a full-scale presentation.

What If No One Asks a Question?

What should you do at the beginning of a question-and-answer session if no one asks a question? Say, "Great!" and sprint off the stage? Effective speakers use a variety of techniques that encourage audience members to ask questions.

Never open a Q-and-A session with "Are there any questions?" This is a *yes*-or-*no* question. If audience members do *not* have a question in mind, they may just sit there. Instead begin by asking questions that assume there *are* questions, such as "What are your questions?" or "Who has the first question?"

If no one answers at this point, pause and wait. Inexperienced speakers often feel uncomfortable waiting the several seconds it takes for audience members to come up with questions. Even a five-second pause can seem like five minutes. Think about this challenge from the audience's perspective. Just as *you* may need a few seconds to organize your thoughts for an answer, audience members may need even more time to frame their questions. If you still don't get any questions after a significant pause, be prepared with some of your own. You could say, "One of the questions I often hear after my presentation is..." or "If I were in the audience, I'd want to know..."

Once an audience member asks the first question, you may find yourself facing the opposite situation. You may get an overwhelming number of questions and not have enough time to answer them all. As you near the end of your allotted time, or when you determine that the question-and-answer session has gone on long enough, bring the questioning to an end by saying, "I have time for two more questions." Then do just that. Answer two more questions and thank the audience for their participation. If necessary or convenient, you may want to ask audience members to continue the conversation in another location. In this way, other audience members can ask their questions after you've cleared the stage or room for other speakers and activities.

Impromptu Speaking

In much the same way that you can prepare for a Q-and-A session without knowing precisely what questions you may have to answer, you can prepare to speak impromptu whenever the opportunity arises. As we noted in Chapter 14, "Performance and Practice," **impromptu speaking** calls on you to present without advance practice and with little or no preparation time.

Of all the forms of speaking, impromptu speaking has the potential to be the most nerve-wracking. Also known as "off-the-cuff" speaking, this type of special presentation shouldn't be feared. In fact, Laurie Rozakis, a professor and communication consultant, contends that "being a good impromptu speaker is very beneficial because of its everyday usefulness. Mastering this skill will help you feel more comfortable thinking—and speaking—on your feet."[5]

In many ways, preparing to speak impromptu is similar to preparing for a question-and-answer session. You may be called on to share your opinion in class, be asked by your boss to summarize a report with no advance warning, be moved to speak at a public forum, or be asked during a job interview to describe your accomplishments to a panel of interviewers. In each case, the response you make will be a mini-impromptu speech. You can apply many of the same techniques to a variety of off-the-cuff speaking situations. Try to predict the topic you may be called upon to discuss. Then practice speaking on that topic. Know as much as you can about the topic and have a few ready-made remarks handy.

Political candidate Antonio Villaraigosa talks to supporters during a backyard campaign fundraiser. The content of his impromptu remarks is based on weeks of speaking to similar audiences.

In addition to taking these preparation steps, you will have to make some important decisions right before or during an impromptu presentation. Speakers who sound as fluent during an impromptu presentation as they do during a memorized presentation have mastered two techniques. They have come equipped with ready-to-use organizational patterns, and they know how to make the best use of their time.

Ready-to-Use Organizational Patterns

Successful impromptu speakers always have a handful of standard organizational patterns to fall back on. In an impromptu situation, you won't have a lot of time to think about which pattern is best suited to your topic. So try fitting your response into a simpler pattern, one that clearly separates the key points. In impromptu speaking, *sounding* organized is critical to appearing organized.

Suppose someone asked you to talk about the value of a college education. How would you structure your ideas and opinions with one of these ready-to-use organizational patterns?

ORGANIZATIONAL PATTERNS FOR IMPROMPTU SPEAKING

Past, Present, Future
Me, My Friend, and You
Opinion, Reason, Example, Belief

Past, Present, Future. This pattern is a variation of the time arrangement discussed in Chapter 9, "Organization." In such a pattern, you could begin by explaining that at the turn of the twentieth century, a college education was not necessary for most jobs and was something that only the rich and gifted could afford to pursue. By the end of the last millennium, jobs that once required only a high school diploma required at least an A.A. or a B.A. degree. In this century, our best hope for prosperity in a more competitive world will be a better educated work force. As you can see, time arrangement can be as focused as yesterday, today, and tomorrow or as long-reaching as from the Stone Age to the "dot-com" era.

Me, My Friend, and You. In this pattern, you begin by explaining how the topic affects or has affected you, tell how it affects or has affected another person, and conclude with how it can affect everyone in your audience. When advocating a college education, you can start with your own story—why you went to college, what you have gained from your experience, and why you like or liked it. Then you can tell a story about someone else who did or didn't go to college. Finally, you can draw general conclusions about the importance of a college education for everyone in your audience. The key in this pattern is moving from your personal experiences to establishing common ground with your audience.

Opinion, Reason, Example, Belief. In this pattern, you follow four steps: (1) Here's my opinion, (2) here are the reasons that I have this opinion, (3) here are some examples to explain and support these reasons, and (4) that's why I believe this way. For instance, you may state that, in your opinion, a college education is valuable. Then you offer reasons supported by examples. A college education can prepare you for a career (examples of various careers), can inspire you to become a lifelong learner (examples of respected and learned people), and can help you meet interesting people who will be your good friends for the rest of your life (examples of your best friends). Then you sum up your presentation by explaining that these are the reasons that you strongly believe in the value of a college education.

Time Management

Time is precious to the impromptu speaker. If you're lucky, you may have a minute to collect your thoughts and jot down a few ideas before speaking. In most cases, though, you will only have a few seconds to prepare. Manage the brief amount of time you have to your advantage.

Use Your Thought Speed. This technique is borrowed from the listening research we discuss in Chapter 2, "Listening and Critical Thinking." Remember that most people can think much faster than they can speak. If you speak at 150 words per minute, your brain can race ahead of what you are saying because you can think as fast as 500 or 600 words per minute. The very fact that you can listen to a speaker while writing a note or thinking about something else demonstrates your ability to think faster than a person can speak.

The best impromptu speakers think ahead. As they get up to speak, they're deciding on their two or three key points and which organizational pattern they will use. When they reach the podium or lectern, they're formulating an attention-getting beginning. As they start talking, they're thinking ahead to their first key point. They trust that the words will come out right, even though their thinking is divided between what they are saying now and what they want to say in the next few seconds. No wonder impromptu speakers feel exhausted after a successful presentation!

The best way to master using your thought speed to full advantage is to get plenty of impromptu speaking practice. While you are alone, with no pressures from an audience, practice your impromptu speaking with one part of your thinking focused on what you are saying and another part focused on what you will say next. Make sure to practice out loud—you won't become comfortable using this technique any other way.

Buy Time. In the few seconds between the time you're asked to make impromptu remarks and the moment when you start speaking, you have to plan and organize your entire presentation. You can stretch those seconds by following a few suggestions.[6]

1. *Pause thoughtfully.* Give yourself a few seconds to think before you speak. This technique can enhance your credibility. As Malcolm Kushner, a communication consultant and author, notes, "The audience assumes that your words will now be carefully considered rather than the first thoughts that flew into your head."[7] Of course, your audience may now expect something better than random thoughts.

2. *Rephrase the question.* As we suggested in our discussion of Q-and-A sessions, paraphrasing serves many functions. In addition to ensuring that you heard and understood the question or topic for comment, it also gives you more time. As the questioner answers you, you can be thinking ahead to your next response.

3. *Use all-purpose quotations.* Most of us know a few quotations by heart—from the Bible, from Shakespeare or a favorite poet, from song lyrics, or the tag lines from famous commercials. Try memorizing a few all-purpose quotations that can apply to almost any speaking situation. Not only does quoting someone make you sound intelligent; it also gives you a little extra time to think about what you want to say. Both of us have our own stockpile of quotations to call up when we have to speak off-the-cuff.

Throughout your life you will make many different kinds of presentations. You will give informative and persuasive presentations, and you will be asked to introduce speakers, welcome guests, deliver eulogies, offer toasts, sell products, answer questions, and speak impromptu. The strategies and skills that you use for such presentations can also be applied to other situations in which you are asked to give and accept awards, speak at special events, deliver tributes, or nominate a colleague for a professional office. The key to success in any speaking situation is understanding how to apply the basic strategies and skills you have learned from this textbook to the unique characteristics of each presentation you will make. As these strategies and skills become second nature, you will improve your speaking ability and will become a more polished and successful presenter.

Summary

What kinds of special presentations should I know how to make?

Some of the most common special presentations include introducing a presenter, welcoming an audience, delivering a eulogy, making a toast, selling a product, entertaining an audience, answering audience questions, and speaking impromptu.

How do I introduce a presenter?

Think of the introduction of a presenter as being similar to the introduction to a presentation. Try to gain audience attention and interest, connect with the audience, indicate the topic of the presentation, enhance the presenter's credibility, and set the appropriate tone for the presentation. Remember that your purpose is to motivate the audience to respect and listen to the person whom you are introducing.

How should I welcome an audience or a group of guests?

Apply the basic principles of presentation speaking in such a way that you link yourself and your organization's goals to the characteristics, interests, needs, and expectations of the group that you are welcoming.

What's the best way to make a toast?

Because toasts are more emotional, inspiring, and joyous than other types of presentations, you should be more personal in both the content and the delivery style used for this special presentation.

How do I prepare and deliver a meaningful eulogy?

Make sure that you understand the relationship of the audience to the person being eulogized. Given the emotional nature of a eulogy, you may want to read from a well-prepared and frequently rehearsed manuscript.

How can I apply the principles of presentation speaking to sales?

Successful sales presentations focus on *W*hat's *I*n *I*t *F*or *T*hem, the customers. Demonstrate your character and competence to gain customer trust by being an ethical communicator and a product expert. Listen carefully to customers in order to learn about and adapt to their needs, concerns, tastes, and financial resources.

What should I do if I'm asked to make a humorous presentation?

Unless you're comfortable making this type of presentation, avoid them. If you want to ensure your success, use humor that is relevant, appropriate, and well delivered.

How do I handle question-and-answer sessions?

Preparation is the key. Predict and practice answering possible questions. Plan ready-made responses and have a ready-made closing. Make sure that you answer the questions and show respect for your questioners.

Can I *prepare* for impromptu presentations?

Effective impromptu speakers employ ready-to-use organizational patterns and use what little time they have to plan and organize their remarks.

Presentation Principles in Action

Impromptu Toast

Directions: Choose a subject for an impromptu toast in class. Take ten minutes in which you prepare to toast a classmate, the instructor, a person who has inspired you, a member of your family, a famous person, or an important event such as an anniversary, wedding, graduation, and so on. As you prepare your toast, consider the following guidelines.

- Use a conversational style. Do not read your remarks unless you are including a brief quotation or poem that you may not be able to remember.
- Keep your toast short and simple. Make a point. Don't ramble.
- Focus on the positive qualities of your subject.
- Consider telling a brief but memorable story or recount an experience that represents the subject's qualities.

Assessing an Impromptu Toast

The following assessment instrument can help you evaluate an impromptu toast. Use the following ratings to assess each of the criteria on the instrument.

E = Excellent G = Good A = Average F = Fair P = Poor
N/A = Not applicable to this presentation

Impromptu Toast Assessment Instrument

CRITERIA	E	G	A	F	P	N/A
Purpose: Did the toast help the audience appreciate and/or honor the subject?						
Audience Analysis: Was the toast adapted to what the audience knows or feels about the subject?						
Credibility: Did the toast enhance the speaker's and subject's credibility?						
Logistics: Was the toast adapted to the logistics and occasion?						
Content: Did the toast include appropriate supporting material and/or stories?						
Organization: Was the toast clearly and effectively organized?						
Performance: Was the style of delivery suitable for a toast?						
Overall Evaluation:						

COMMENTS:

Key Terms

eulogy 487
humorous presentation 491
impromptu speaking 499
introducing a presenter 481
question-and-answer session 495
sales presentation 489
special presentations 480
toast 485
welcoming remarks 483

Notes

1 Laurie E. Rozakis, *The Complete Idiot's Guide to Speaking in Public with Confidence* (New York: Alpha, 1995), p. 181.
2 Malcolm Kushner, *Successful Presentations for Dummies* (Foster City, CA: IDG, 1997), p. 327.
3 Gene Perret, *Using Humor for Effective Business Speaking* (New York: Sterling, 1989), p. 88.
4 Brody, *Speaking Your Way to the Top: Making Powerful Business Presentations* (Boston: Allyn & Bacon, 1998), p. 158.
5 Rozakis, p. 193.
6 Kushner, pp. 315–316.
7 Kushner, p. 315.

chapter twenty two

Developing Group **Presentations**

- What kind of speaking will I have to do in groups?
- How do I prepare for a group presentation?
- What's the best way to organize group decision making?
- How can I become a more effective group member?
- How do groups communicate electronically?

Up to now, we've been exploring the strategies and skills you need for preparing and making *presentations,* which we define in Chapter 1, "Presentation Speaking," as any time speakers use verbal and nonverbal messages to generate meanings and establish relationships with audience members. We have focused on your role as a single speaker trying to achieve a specific purpose in front of a particular audience. We now turn our attention to the speaking skills needed to be successful in small group settings. Understanding how the basic principles of presentation speaking apply to this setting is critical in the world of work as well as to social and civil harmony.[1]

What Are Groups?

No matter what you do or where you go, you feel the influence of people who join groups to make decisions, solve problems, share information, and build friendships. Think of how many groups you belong to. Depending on your current situation in your college or professional career, you may list family, friends, study groups, car pools, roommates, class project groups, sports teams, coworkers, campus clubs, religious groups, neighborhood groups, service clubs, management teams, governing boards, political committees, or professional association memberships.

We use the term **small group communication** in this chapter to refer to the interaction of three or more interdependent people working toward a common goal.[2] The expression "Two's company; three's a crowd" recognizes that a conversation between two people is quite different from a three-person discussion. In fact, each person who is added to a group significantly affects the interaction. We believe that the ideal size for a group is five to seven members.

Group members come together for a reason. It is this collective reason or goal that defines and unifies a group. The label doesn't matter—*goal, objective, purpose, mission,* or *assignment.* Without a common goal, groups wonder: Why are we meeting? Why should we care or work hard? The importance of a group's goal can't be underestimated. If there is one single factor that separates successful from unsuccessful groups, it's having a clear goal.[3] Small groups achieve their goals by talking and working together.

Types of Groups

Most groups work in private—in face-to-face meetings, in teleconferences, or via the Internet. In private groups, the interpersonal interactions that occur among members are vital to achieving the group's goal. So, too, are presentation speaking skills. Group members use speaking skills to give reports at staff meetings, to present recommendations to organizational groups, and to offer remarks at social gatherings. We inform, persuade, and even entertain our supervisors, colleagues, associates, friends, and families in group settings in which the "audience" can be as small as two or three people.

Although most groups and their products may be visible to the public at some point, members usually meet, discuss, and make decisions behind closed doors. There are, however, two other types of group situations in which members must develop and make presentations to audience members outside the group. In order to understand how the purpose and logistics of small group communication require presentation speaking strategies, we consider three types of group presentations: public group presentations, team presentations, and working group presentations.

- **Public Group Presentations:** One or more group members make a presentation with or on behalf of a group for the purpose of informing or persuading a public audience.
- **Team Presentations:** Group members make a coordinated presentation as a cohesive team for the purpose of influencing an audience of key decision-makers.
- **Working Group Presentations:** Group members make informative or persuasive presentations to others within the confines of a private group meeting.

All three types of presentations require attention to the seven basic principles of presentation speaking. The factors that make each type of group presentation different include the presentation's purpose, the type of audience, the logistics of the occasion, and type of performance required by the situation. Understanding and adapting to these differences can help you become an effective and respected group member.

Public Groups

Public groups engage in discussion in front of and for the benefit of the public. Their meetings usually occur in open settings in which group participants may be judged by an audience of listeners. Regardless of the type of public group presentation, speakers must make critical decisions about purpose, audience, credibility, logistics, content, organization, and performance. As you will see, public groups vary in terms of their purpose, which affects subsequent decisions about applying the principles of presentation speaking.

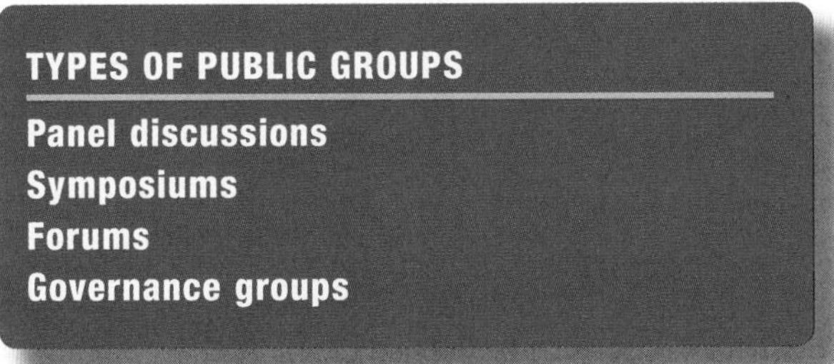

Panel Discussions.

A **panel discussion** involves several people who interact with one another about a common topic for the benefit of an audience. Panel discussions are very common on television and range from tabloid-style talk shows to heated discussions of current events. The participants in such discussions talk with one another in the hope that they will educate, influence, or entertain an audience. A moderator usually tries to control the flow of communication.

Symposiums.

In a **symposium,** group members present short, uninterrupted presentations on different aspects of a topic for the benefit of an audience. For example, a college may sponsor an AIDS symposium in which a doctor, medical researcher, AIDS activist, and health department official each give uninterrupted talks about the status of AIDS research and treatment. Symposium members apply the strategies and skills of presentation speaking to prepare their contributions.

Forums. A **forum,** which provides an opportunity for audience members to comment or ask questions, frequently follows a panel or symposium. Some forums invite open discussions, letting audience members share their concerns about a specific issue. Other forums give the public an opportunity to ask questions of and express concerns to elected officials and experts. A strong moderator may be needed to ensure that all audience members have an equal opportunity to speak. In Chapter 21, "Developing Special Presentations," we discuss a variety of techniques for responding to audience questions. You can apply these strategies and skills to participating in forums, too.

Governance Groups. Public policy decisions are made in public by **governance groups.** State legislatures, city and county councils, and the governing boards of public agencies and educational institutions must conduct their meetings in public. The U.S. Congress cannot deny the public access to congressional debate. Unfortunately, most government watchers know that the "real" decisions are often made in private and that public debate is just for show. At the same time, though, an elected or appointed official's vote is not a secret. Governance group members know that if their votes differ from their public positions, they could be accused of pandering to voters and dishonesty.

When participating in any public group—whether it's a panel discussion, symposium, forum, or governance group—remember that you are "on stage" all the time, even when you aren't speaking. If you look bored while another member is presenting, the audience may question your commitment to the group's goals. If one member of a panel or symposium rolls his eyes every time another group member speaks, it sends the audience a mixed message about the credibility and civility of the speakers. Try to look at and support the other members of your group when they speak—and hope that they will do the same for you.

Participating in panel discussions, symposiums, forums, or governance groups gives you an opportunity to advance yourself and your group. Making an effective presentation as a member of a public group is something you can learn to do with skill and confidence by employing the presentation speaking strategies and skills described in this textbook.

Team Presentations

When a person prepares a presentation, he or she must make dozens of decisions. When an entire group has to prepare a presentation together, the task becomes much more complex. Unlike panel discussions, symposiums, forums, or governance group discussions—which are designed to inform general audiences—team presentations tend to have different goals. A **team presentation** is a well-coordinated, persuasive presentation made by a cohesive group of speakers who aim to influence an audience of key decision-makers. Organizations as diverse as nonprofit agencies and international corporations rely on team presentations to offer marketing proposals, to compete for major contracts, and to request funding.

Team presentations can demonstrate whether a group or company is competent enough to perform a task or take on a major responsibility. When organizations seek support and endorsements, they must present a united front. Team presentations often have high stakes.[4] Here are some examples:

- A professional football team seeks backing for a new stadium by bringing a well-rehearsed group of executives and star players to a public meeting at which they explain how the stadium will enhance the economic development and prestige of the community without adversely affecting the surrounding neighborhoods.

Bendita Malakia explains one of seven Kwanzaa principles while other group members wait to talk about the other six principles. A well-prepared team presentation can make its message memorable and moving.

- Companies making the "short list" of businesses considered for a lucrative government contract make team presentations to the officials who will award the final contract.
- In a presentation to the state legislature's appropriations committee, a state university's board of trustees chairperson, the university president, an academic vice president, and a student representative are given a total of twenty minutes to justify their request for more state funding.

A team presentation is not a collection of individual speeches; it is a team product. Although a symposium is a coordinated presentation, symposium speakers do not necessarily present a united front or have a strategic, team goal as their purpose. In many ways a team presentation is the ultimate group challenge because it requires efficient and effective decision making as well as coordinated performances. Groups that work well in the conference room may fall apart in the spotlight of a team presentation.

Fortunately, the presentation speaking strategies and skills in this textbook can direct a group through the critical decision-making steps needed to develop an effective team presentation. Much as a single speaker does, a team should apply the basic principles of presentation speaking:

- *Purpose:* Determine the team presentation's overall purpose or theme.
- *Audience:* Adapt the presentation to a specific group of decision makers.
- *Credibility:* Enhance the team's credibility by demonstrating the team's expertise and trustworthiness.
- *Logistics:* Adjust to the time limits and the place where the team presentation will be delivered.

- *Content:* Prepare and share appropriate supporting materials.
- *Organization:* Plan the introduction, body, and conclusion for each team member's presentation as well as those for the entire team's presentation.
- *Performance:* Practice until the team's performance approaches perfection.

Team presentations require a great deal of time, effort, and money to prepare and make. Marjorie Brody, author of *Speaking Your Way to the Top,* writes:

> *To be effective, team presentations must be meticulously planned and executed. They must be like a ballet, in which each dancer knows exactly where to stand, when to move, and when to exit from the stage.... If a team works like a smooth, well-oiled machine, if one member's presentation flows into the next presentation, and if all members present themselves professionally and intelligently, the impression left is one of confidence and competence.*[5]

High-stakes team presentations can have equally high payoffs. For instance, Thomas Leech, a management communication consultant, reports that following team presentations by several companies, the Department of Energy awarded a $2.2 billion contract for environmental cleanup to a team headed by Fluor Corporation. Then-Assistant Energy Secretary Leo P. Duff said Fluor made the best impression. "All the firms had capabilities, but how the team works as a team in the oral presentations is a key determining factor."[6] The awarding of a $2.2 billion contract should convince anyone who doubts the value of effective team presentations.

Working Groups

Despite the importance of presentation speaking within a group, most communication in small groups is more interactive. Although you *may* be asked to be part of a public group or team presentation, you *will* be a member of many working groups in which you must present your ideas and opinions to others.

A group of teachers discusses ways to improve student proficiency in writing.

Figure 22.1 Types of Working Groups

The common goal of each type of working group determines its membership and function.

Type of Working Group	Membership	Function
Primary Group (family, friends)	People who are close, intimate friends or relatives	Provides members with affection, support, and a sense of belonging
Social Group (athletic teams, hobby groups, sororities, fraternities)	People who enjoy interacting with others while pursuing social or recreational goals	Allows members to share common interests in a friendly setting or participate in social activities
Self-Help Group (therapy groups, Weight Watchers, Alcoholics Anonymous)	People who hope to overcome problems by sharing their personal concerns with people who have similar concerns	Offers advice and encouragement to members who want or need support with personal problems
Learning Group (study groups, book groups, fitness classes)	People who share an interest in understanding concepts or mastering particular skills	Helps members acquire information and develop skills
Service Group (labor unions, Kiwanis, civic associations)	People who see value in using a group to help themselves or others	Dedicated to worthy causes that help people both within and outside the group
Work Group (committees, work teams, task forces)	People who work in groups in order to make decisions, solve problems, and carry out assigned tasks	Responsible for performing specific tasks and routine duties on behalf of a business or organization

The members of **working groups** exert collective efforts to achieve a shared goal. They work in private settings in order to benefit the group rather than to benefit a public audience or external decision-makers. Working groups can range from the most personal and informal types of groups to more formal types. And like their individual members, each type of group has different characteristics and concerns. As Figure 22.1 shows, each type of group can be recognized by its membership (who is in the group) and by its function (what the group does).

Communicating in Small Groups

Regardless of whether you are speaking within a working group or to an audience of public listeners or decision makers, most of the time that you spend in groups will be taken up in discussions focused on achieving a common goal. That goal may focus on resolving routine staff meeting issues or planning a high-stakes team presentation. Asking group-focused questions about the basic principles of presentation speaking can help ensure that your group and its meetings are productive and provide a positive experience for all members.

Real World Real Speakers

Perfect Your Team Presentation

Rosa Vargas, Human Resources Manager for The Topps Company in New York City, was introduced to team presentations in graduate school. She wrote:

During my MBA studies, I was part of a team, and our purpose was to launch a new product to market. I feel that preparation and rehearsal are key to a successful team presentation. I was nervous in the beginning of our presentation (we presented to a panel of professors and students), but as the presentation progressed, I relaxed a bit. Our group had practiced, and I know this helped us give a more focused presentation.

Another respondent was less fortunate. She wrote that her work-based team presentation was unsuccessful because "people hadn't gotten together beforehand, and hence there was unnecessary repetition in the group presentation." Successful team presentations must be meticulously planned and practiced.

GROUP COMMUNICATION PRINCIPLES

- ***Purpose:*** **What is the group's goal?**
- ***Audience:*** **Who will benefit from the discussion?**
- ***Credibility:*** **How can members enhance their believability?**
- ***Logistics:*** **Where and when does the group do its work?**
- ***Content:*** **What does the group need to know?**
- ***Organization:*** **How should the group organize its task and its meetings?**
- ***Performance:*** **What delivery skills will enhance the group's performance?**

Purpose

As we indicate earlier in this chapter, successful groups clearly understand their goals. A group's goal is similar to a speaker's purpose and asks this question: What does the group want to achieve?

The first and most important task all groups face is to make sure that everyone agrees with and understands the group's purpose. One way to develop a group's purpose is to word it as a question. In Chapter 20, "Developing Persuasive Presentations," we suggested framing the claims of arguments as questions of fact, value, conjecture, or policy. The same advice holds true in groups. Not only do such questions identify

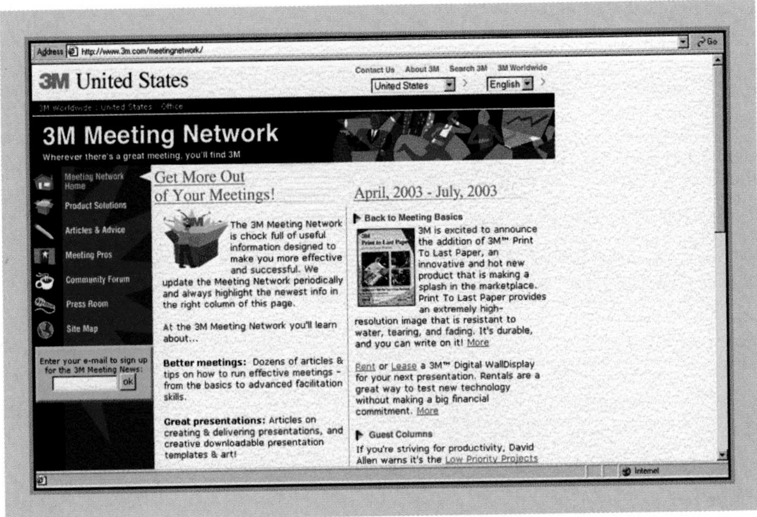

The 3M Meeting Network, www.3m.com/meetingnetwork, provides a wealth of material on small group communication. The subjects range from improving basic communication skills, to interviews with small group communication experts, to advice about overcoming common obstacles to meetings' efficiency and effectiveness.

the discussion topic, but the answers to the questions also become clear statements of the group's goal.

Note how the following questions give you a clear idea of the topic that the group will be discussing as well as an understanding of the group's ultimate goal.

Questions of Fact:	What foods have the highest fat content?
Questions of Value:	Is a community college a better place to begin higher education than a prestigious university?
Questions of Conjecture:	Will inflation increase by 5 percent next year?
Questions of Policy:	How should we improve our customer service?

Whether you're leading a strategic planning team for a major corporation or trying to choose a topic for your classroom discussion, make sure that everyone in your group understands the group's goal.

Audience

Like all audiences, group members have demographic characteristics, motives, interests, knowledge, attitudes, and learning styles. You are part of that "audience" when the other group members speak. They become the "audience" when you speak. However, your relationship with listeners in a working group differs from that of a speaker addressing a one-time audience. In most working groups, you can count on the same people attending every meeting. Your ability to get along with these members matters as much as your ability to adapt to them as listeners.

In addition to having all the characteristics of any group of listeners, group members assume group roles. Very often, by understanding the roles they play within your group, you can predict how members will react to what you say. Figure 22.2 shows two categories of roles found in most groups.[7] Group **task roles** affect a group's ability to achieve its goals by focusing on behaviors that help get the job done. Group **maintenance roles** affect how group members get along with one another while pursuing a shared goal.

Brainstorming in Groups

When students have trouble coming up with a topic for an in-class group discussion, we suggest that they brainstorm for ideas. When working groups need to generate ideas for a project—determining the goal of a fundraising campaign, choosing possible themes for an advertising campaign, nominating members for a special committee assignment, selecting reasonably priced holiday gifts for support staff—they often begin by brainstorming for ideas. **Brainstorming** is a tool for generating as many ideas as possible in a short period of time.[1] When a group is asked to generate a list of suggestions, explanations, or solutions, brainstorming can be used to increase the number and creativity of suggestions. The following guidelines can help.

- *The more, the better:* Suggest as many ideas as you can. Quantity is more important than quality.
- *Be creative:* Free your imagination. Wild and crazy ideas are welcome and often generate breakthroughs.
- *Never criticize:* During the brainstorming session, don't analyze, oppose, praise, or laugh at another member's ideas. Also, don't discuss, defend, clarify, or comment upon your own suggestions. Evaluation occurs only *after* the brainstorming session is over.
- *Hitchhike:* Build on or modify ideas presented by others. Someone else's wild ideas can trigger a creative suggestion.
- *Combine and extend:* Combine two or more ideas into a new idea.

Although groups often use brainstorming, its success depends on the nature of the group and the characteristics of its members. If a group is self-conscious and sensitive to implied criticism, brainstorming can flop. If a group is comfortable with such a freewheeling process, brainstorming can enhance creativity and produce valuable ideas and suggestions.

1. Alex F. Osborn, *Applied Imagination*, rev. ed. (New York: Scribner's, 1957).

Depending on your group's goal, the nature of its task, and the characteristics of its members, you could function in several different roles. When each of the roles is assumed by at least one group member, the group is more likely to achieve its goal.

Credibility

When group members communicate with one another, their comments and behavior determine how credible they are in the eyes of other members. Chapter 6, "Speaker Credibility and Ethics," notes that audiences believe and trust credible speakers more often. The same holds true for groups. Highly credible groups exhibit the three components of ethos we described in Chapter 6: competence, character, and charisma.

Competence. *Competence* means being prepared, in advance, for a group discussion or presentation. You wouldn't make a presentation without preparing for it. Why, then, do some group members show up for meetings with little or no preparation? Participants in group discussions must be well prepared to deal with a host of predictable as well as unpredictable issues and people. Depending on the topic of a group discussion or meeting, preparation may involve reviewing documents, drafting a proposal, or doing library or online research. All of the research strategies and skills described in Chapter 8, "Supporting Material," can help you prepare for a group discussion or meeting.

Figure 22.2 Group Task Roles and Group Maintenance Roles

Group Task Roles	
Initiator:	Proposes ideas and suggestions, provides direction
Information Seeker:	Asks for needed facts, requests explanations
Information Giver:	Researches, provides, and presents needed information
Opinion Seeker:	Asks for others' opinions, tests validity of group opinions
Opinion Giver:	States personal beliefs, shares feelings, offers analysis
Clarifier:	Explains ideas to others, reduces confusion, summarizes
Evaluator:	Assesses ideas, arguments, and suggestions; diagnoses problems
Energizer:	Motivates group members, helps create enthusiasm

Group Maintenance Roles	
Encourager:	Praises and supports group members, listens empathically
Harmonizer:	Helps resolve conflicts, emphasizes teamwork
Compromiser:	Offers suggestions that minimize differences, helps the group reach decisions
Tension Releaser:	Alleviates tension with friendly humor, relaxes the group
Gatekeeper:	Monitors participation, encourages equal participation
Observer:	Explains and interprets what others are trying to say, paraphrases
Follower:	Supports the group and its members, accepts assignments

Character. Having *character* means making a commitment to act and accept responsibility before, during, and after a group discussion or group presentation. Whereas competence requires planning, critical thinking, and time, character depends on your attitude toward and commitment to the group's goal and its members. Assuming appropriate task and maintenance roles is one way to demonstrate your support for and dedication to your group and its goal.

Charisma. *Charisma* refers to your ability to communicate both your message (a product of your competence) and your commitment to the group (a product of your character). Being prepared and committed to your group may have little effect if you do not communicate effectively. Group members must be able to speak and listen during a discussion. At a more personal level, they need to be able to relate to the feelings and needs of others. And, of course, group members must be able to make effective presentations in, for, and with their group.

Logistics

Although the logistics of working groups differ from those individual speakers face, they require just as much attention if a group expects to achieve its purpose. Answering two basic questions can help a group begin the process of planning an effective meeting: When should we meet? Where should we meet? In many cases, a group will meet

Doctors discuss a variety of issues at a family medical center. A common agenda and well-prepared reports can help groups deal with a wide variety of issues in a short period of time.

at the same time in the same room, one that already contains the furniture and equipment the group needs. In other cases, a group will first have to find out when members are available, then reserve a room that matches the purpose and size of the meeting. The room should be large enough, clean, comfortable, and far from distractions such as ringing phones or noisy conversations.

Once the group has secured a comfortable and quiet place to work, someone should be responsible for distributing necessary reading material and an agenda far enough in advance so that everyone has time to prepare. Also plan on having extra copies available at the meeting. In addition, make sure that supplies and equipment such as flip charts or projectors are available and in working order.

Content

Researchers investigating the reasons that some groups achieve their goals while others fail emphasize that the quantity and quality of information available to a group is a critical factor in predicting its success. Randy Hirokawa, a group communication researcher, concludes that "the ability of a group to gather and retain a wide range of information is the single most important determinant of high-quality decision-making."[8] Sometimes, when group members have preconceived notions about which decision is best, they may reject information that does not support their conclusions. As a result, the group will fail to fully understand an issue or to consider other options. Overlooking useful information or accepting inaccurate information will produce poor decisions and frustrated group members.[9]

If you want your group to succeed—regardless of its purpose, audience, or setting—make sure that you have collected appropriate ideas and information from credible sources. Chapter 8, "Supporting Material," covers how to research and use supporting material. All of these strategies and skills apply equally to small group communication as well as to individual presentations.

Organization

Some groups have tasks that are fairly easy to accomplish—deciding when to meet again, what to include in a monthly report, or to whom to assign a routine job. Other group tasks are much more complex and difficult—determining the group's common goal, whom to hire or fire, where to hold a major convention, or how to plan a team presentation. As difficult as it can be to make a personal decision or solve a personal problem, these challenges are much more complex for groups. On the other hand, achieving a group's goal through a well-organized decision-making process can be highly satisfying and worthwhile. Although there are many different ways to organize a group discussion, we have narrowed our focus to two: the standard problem-solving agenda and the working agenda.

The Standard Problem-Solving Agenda. The founding father of problem-solving procedures was a U.S. philosopher and educator named John Dewey. In 1910, Dewey wrote a book titled *How We Think,* in which he described a set of practical steps that a rational person should follow when trying to solve a problem. These guidelines have come to be known as *Dewey's reflective thinking process.*[10]

Dewey's ideas have been adapted to the process of solving problems in groups. The reflective thinking process begins with a focus on the problem itself and then moves on to a systematic consideration of possible solutions. Figure 22.3 shows an expanded, modified approach to this process—the **Standard Problem-Solving Agenda**—developed by three communication scholars, Julia Wood, Gerald Phillips, and Douglas Pedersen.[11]

Before a group can solve a problem, members must understand the group's assignment. The task clarification step answers questions such as these: What are we being

Figure 22.3 The Standard Problem-Solving Agenda

PROBLEM-SOLVING STEPS	GOALS
1. Task Clarification	*Goal:* To make sure that everyone understands the group's task or assignment
2. Problem Identification	*Goal:* To make sure that everyone understands the nature of the problem and why it must be solved
3. Fact Finding and Problem Analysis	*Goal:* To collect and analyze facts, claims about causes and effects, and value judgments about the seriousness of the problem
4. Solution Criteria and Limitations	*Goal:* To develop realistic criteria for a solution, including an understanding of solution limitations, be they financial, institutional, practical, political, and/or legal in scope
5. Solution Suggestions	*Goal:* To generate a list of possible solutions
6. Solution Evalution and Selection	*Goal:* To discuss the pros and cons of each suggestion in light of the agreed-upon criteria for a solution and to select the solution that rises to the top of the list
7. Solution Implementation	*Goal:* To plan the implementation of the decision, including an assignment of responsibilities

asked to do? Why is it important to do this? What are we trying to achieve? During the second step—problem identification—the group should make sure that everyone understands the nature of the problem, possibly by wording the issue as a question of fact, value, conjecture, or policy. During the fact-finding and problem-analysis step, group members should investigate facts, opinions, and value judgments about the seriousness and causes of the problem. At this point, group members may be tempted to skip the fourth step—solution criteria and limitations. But if the group has a limited budget or short time period for implementation, some proposed solutions may not be reasonable or even possible.

Once a group has analyzed a problem in light of realistic criteria, members can become fully involved in step five—suggesting as many solutions as possible. Then comes the hard part. The sixth step of the standard problem-solving agenda requires group members to discuss the pros and cons of each suggestion in light of their agreed-upon criteria for a solution. Some solutions will be rejected quickly, but others may be argued until one or more rise to the top of the list. Agreeing on a solution, however, is not the end of the process. At this point, the group has one more challenge: How should they implement the solution? Despite all the time a group spends trying to solve a problem, it may take even more time to organize the task of implementing the solution. Fortunately, groups that follow the seven steps in the standard problem-solving agenda will have a much better solution to implement.[12]

Working Agendas. In *Effective Meetings: The Complete Guide,* Clyde Burleson maintains that two of the most powerful tools in meeting management are agendas and minutes.[13] A **working agenda** is the outline of items to be discussed and the tasks to be accomplished during a discussion or meeting. A well-prepared working agenda can serve many purposes. First and foremost, it's a road map for the discussion and helps group members focus on their task. When used properly, a working agenda helps participants get ready for a meeting by telling them what to expect and even how to prepare. Most important of all, an agenda provides a detailed outline for a discussion, indicating what issues will be discussed and in what order. By following a well-constructed agenda, a group is much more likely to reach its goal. In fact, the 3M Management Team states that a "written agenda, distributed in advance, is the single best predictor of a successful meeting."[14] There are two basic types of working agendas, a business meeting agenda and a task-specific agenda. Each type has a specific purpose and a specific format.

Business meeting agendas follow a standardized format that lists, in a specified order, several items for discussion and/or decision. The meeting's chairperson or convener usually prepares and distributes the agenda to all members in advance. The following example shows a formal business meeting agenda. The notes in parentheses explain the functions of particular agenda items.

Business Meeting Agenda

I. Call to order (The chairperson officially opens the meeting.)
II. Approval of meeting agenda (Members may vote to add, subtract, or modify agenda items.)
III. Approval of previous meeting's minutes
IV. Officers' reports
V. Committee reports
VI. Unfinished business (issues and business from previous meetings)
VII. New business (new issues and business to consider)
VIII. Announcements
IX. Adjournment

Whereas business meeting agendas offer a general framework on which to build any formal meeting, a task-specific agenda helps a working group share complex information, discuss a problem, or make a decision about one particular issue. Working groups use such agendas for project planning, decision making, and team meetings. Students in communication classes use this type of agenda to organize their in-class discussions. The following agenda could be used by a management team to discuss a company's website problem.

Task-Specific Agenda

I. The current situation
  A. Current responsibility for website
  B. Existing Web policy and procedures
II. The problem
  A. Poor quality of the website
  B. Out-of-date and erroneous information
III. The possible causes
  A. Lack of authority and assigned responsibility
  B. Inadequate maintenance staff
  C. Poor design
IV. Solution criteria
  A. Cost
  B. Speed of response
  C. Quality control of content
V. Solutions
  A. Option A: Hire full-time webmaster and assign support staff
  B. Option B: Contract Web design and maintenance to outside sources
  C. Other options
VI. Decision
VII. Implementation

Notice how this agenda includes every component of the standard problem-solving agenda. Ensuring that a group understands the nature of a problem as well as the criteria or limitations affecting its solution makes the successful implementation of an agreed-upon solution much more likely.

Taking Minutes. The **minutes** of a meeting are the written record of a group's discussion and decisions. Instead of describing a group's discussion in detail, minutes include brief, clear statements that summarize the main ideas and actions. In many cases, an hour's worth of discussion may be recorded as only a few statements in the minutes! Despite their brevity, minutes must record decisions and task deadlines in the exact wording that the group uses, in order to avoid future disagreements and misunderstandings. In formal meetings, minutes are legal documents as well as part of the historical record of an organization.[15] If there is any question about what to include in the minutes or how to word an item, the person taking the minutes should ask the group for clarification.

Most important of all, the minutes of a meeting must be objective. They should neutrally report the facts and accurately represent all sides of a discussion. They should never include the minutes-taker's personal opinions.[16] Minutes should reflect the experience of the entire group, not just that of the person chosen to document it.

Performance

When we talked about performance in Chapter 14, "Performance and Practice," we noted that *perform* is a verb that has several meanings. Although it can refer to the way

Figure 22.4

Negative Group Roles

The Aggressor. Puts down other members, is sarcastic and critical, takes credit for other people's work or ideas

The Blocker. Stands in the way of progress, presents uncompromising positions, uses delay tactics to derail ideas or proposals

The Dominator. Prevents others from participating, interrupts others, tries to manipulate others

The Recognition Seeker. Boasts about personal accomplishments, tries to be the center of attention, pouts if he or she doesn't get enough attention

The Clown. Interjects inappropriate humor, seems more interested in goofing off than working, distracts the group from its task

The Deserter. Withdraws from the group, appears to be "above it all" by acting annoyed or bored with the discussion, stops contributing

---

in which a speaker delivers a presentation, it also can mean to accomplish, carry out, or do something. The same applies to the way in which you perform during a group discussion. Certainly the vocal and physical delivery skills you would use in a presentation also have value in groups. Although you may not speak with as much volume, you still should speak clearly and with appropriate vocal emphasis. Although you may not gesture broadly and walk around a stage, your eye contact and gestures will still communicate a significant portion of your meaning.

Performing well in a group also means knowing how to deal with the inevitable obstacles that prevent a group from achieving its goal. Rarely do the biggest obstacles arise from technical problems—short deadlines, technical errors, or limited resources. Rather, the biggest problems in groups relate to their members' behavior. Next, we offer some suggestions for overcoming two common obstacles: difficult members and hidden agendas.

Difficult Members. Although most groups can handle an occasional encounter with a difficult member, constant problems caused by such people can be disruptive. The negative group roles listed in Figure 22.4 depict a few of the most common "people" problems encountered in groups.[17]

Several strategies can help a group deal with difficult people. A group can accept, confront, or even exclude a troublesome member. If the behavior won't detract from the group's ultimate success or if the member's positive contributions far outweigh the inconvenience or annoyance of putting up with the negative behavior, a group may tolerate the behavior and allow it to continue. For example, a "clown" may be disruptive on occasion but may also be the group's best report writer. A person who is often late for meetings may put in far more than her fair share of work during or after the meeting.

When it becomes impossible to accept or ignore behavior that threatens the effectiveness of the group and its members, the group must take action. At first, it may try to reason with the wayward member. Group members may even talk about him or her during the discussion: "If we disregard Barry's objections, I think the rest of us are ready to decide." In a moment of extreme frustration, one member may say what everyone else is thinking: "Darn it, Lisa. Why can't you let me finish a sentence?" Although such a confrontation may make everyone uncomfortable, it can put a stop to disruptive behavior.

Finally, when all else fails, a group may exclude a difficult member. A group can ignore what a disruptive member says or does. The member may be assigned a solo task to keep her or him away from everyone else. Finally, a group may expel a member to be rid of the troublemaker. Being asked to leave a group or being barred from participating is a humiliating experience that all but the most stubborn members would prefer to avoid.

Hidden Agendas. Most groups have a shared goal or clear agenda. They know what they want and how they intend to go about achieving their goal. When, however, a member's private goals conflict with the group's goals, that member has a **hidden agenda.** Hidden agendas represent what people *really* want instead of what they *say* they want. When people's hidden agendas become more important than a group's agenda or goal, the situation can lead to frustration and failure.

For example, someone serving on a selection committee may dislike a job applicant for very personal reasons that he may not want to share with the group. Instead, he will look for ways to criticize the candidate for things that have nothing to do with his reason for disliking the person. Another member of the selection committee may be a good friend of the candidate but may not want anyone to know it. Instead, she will look for ways to heap praise on the candidate and will refute any suggested weaknesses. Both of these committee members' agendas bury the real issues and concerns and let pseudo-issues dominate the discussion.

Recognizing the existence of hidden agendas can make groups more effective. When group members refuse to compromise, or if group progress is unusually slow, look for hidden agendas. Groups can resolve some of the problems caused by hidden agendas through early agreement on the group's goal and careful planning of the discussion process. Rodney Napier and Matti Gershenfeld, experts in group behavior, suggest that up-front answers to three questions can help counteract the blocking power of hidden agendas:

1. What are the open and shared goals of the discussion?
2. Do any members have any up-front personal concerns or possible hidden goals?
3. What does each participant want from the discussion?[18]

Discussing these questions openly can be productive if a group recognizes the inevitability and purpose of hidden agendas. Hidden agendas don't always cause problems or prevent a group from achieving its goal. However, recognizing and understanding them can help explain why some members are not ready, willing, or able to participate in a group discussion.

Presenting in Virtual Groups

A new type of group is taking over the workplace. This new group is called a **virtual group,** one whose members use technology to communicate, often across time, distance, and organizational boundaries. Our definition recognizes that some members of virtual groups may be separated by thousands of miles and several hours of time while others may work in the same room but use computer technology and software to enhance their interaction and problem solving. In fact, after the September 11 attacks and then the 2003 outbreak of Severe Acute Respiratory Syndrome (SARS) in Asia, U.S. companies increased their use of teleconferences, videoconferences, and webcasts to present and discuss business proposals with international colleagues and customers.[19]

At first, presentation speaking may seem inappropriate for a virtual environment. However, just the opposite is true—group participants are often asked to present their ideas and opinions electronically as though they are making face-to-face presentations. Two of the fastest-growing forms of virtual presentations involve videoconferencing and the use of collaborative presentation technology.

Videoconferences

Videoconferences are much like phone conferences except that a visual component is added. Thus, videoconferences permit both oral and visual communication.

Setting up a videoconference requires a considerable amount of preplanning and technical support. The most sophisticated videoconferences take place in specially designed studios equipped with professional lighting, cameras, and a crew of technicians. It is also possible to conduct videoconferences using less expensive digital cameras connected to personal computers.

In addition to advice on delivering mediated presentations in Chapter 16, "Physical Delivery," there are several additional strategies and skills you can use when preparing for a presentation in a videoconference setting:

- All participants and speakers should be briefed about the operation of the videoconferencing system.
- All participants and speakers should have an agenda and any necessary documents well in advance.
- If you want to interact with audience members at other sites, look directly at the camera, not at their images on a television monitor.
- Use the microphone discretely. In a videoconference, the microphone is always listening. Avoid the temptation to lean over and whisper something to the person sitting next to you. Although the people across the room may not be able to hear you, everyone at the other end of the videoconference can.
- Dress appropriately. See page 366 in Chapter 16, "Physical Delivery," for television wardrobe guidelines.

The primary advantage of videoconferencing is that it allows group members to see and hear each other much as they would during a face-to-face discussion or presentation. As more businesses and institutions embrace the efficiency of videoconferencing, speakers will be required to master new presentation skills for speaking in this virtual environment.

Collaborative Presentation Technology

When you see the term *presentation technology,* PowerPoint slides may come to mind. Adding the word *collaborative* to this phrase moves it beyond individual slide presentations and into the realm of technology-enhanced, interactive group presentations.[20] **Collaborative presentation technology** enables group members to project an idea or graphic onto a screen, wall, or whiteboard so that both face-to-face and/or virtual participants can interact with the presentation.[21] Collaborative presentation tools make it possible to display information without being physically present with other group members. The use of these technologies also allows members to review, revise, edit, and finalize documents.

Sophisticated meeting rooms now come fully equipped with the tools necessary for collaborative presentations: projection screens, computer slide projectors, whiteboards, video cameras and monitors, laptop computers, and even old-fashioned flip charts and overhead projectors. One of the most useful collaborative presentation technologies is the **electronic whiteboard.** Computer-based electronic whiteboards allow members to work on the same document or drawing simultaneously. Anything written on the whiteboard is instantly digitized. This means that it can be stored, printed, and displayed in face-to-face and remote locations. Thus, group members can pose ideas, suggest modifications, draw links among ideas, edit text, draw a design, or format documents.

When electronic whiteboards are used in virtual or face-to-face settings and are combined with audio and video capabilities, the potential for effective collaboration increases significantly. State-of-the-art electronic whiteboards offer a great deal of flexibility and choice in sharing ideas, building presentations, and creating documents. Whether presenting full-fledged multimedia productions or simple text and graphics to be discussed at a staff meeting, electronic whiteboards make presentations, interactions, and collaboration more efficient and effective.

Summary

▶ What kind of speaking will I have to do in groups?

In addition to interacting as a member of small working groups, you may have to make presentations to group members during meetings, make presentations on behalf of a group to public audiences, or be part of a team presentation directed to a group of important decision-makers.

▶ How do I prepare for a group presentation?

You use the presentation speaking principles described in this textbook while also making sure that you help your group achieve its shared goal. In the case of a team presentation, you should pay meticulous attention to individual presenters and to the team's presentation as a whole.

▶ What's the best way to organize group decision making?

Using the standard problem-solving agenda and using a working agenda are two ways to ensure that your group will make a better-informed and better-reasoned decision. Group members must understand the nature of an issue or problem that they are discussing before they make a decision or select a solution to a problem.

▶ How can I become a more effective group member?

Develop your credibility by being well prepared (competence), willing to make a commitment to the group and its task (character), and skilled at communicating your message and commitment (charisma).

▶ How do groups communicate electronically?

In addition to face-to-face meetings and presentations, groups are using e-mail, teleconferences, videoconferences, and collaborative presentation technology to communicate across time, distance, and organizational boundaries.

Presentation Principles in Action

Creative Brainstorming

Directions: Review the guidelines for brainstorming presented in the Mini-Module "Brainstorming in Groups" presented in this chapter. After the class forms groups of five to seven students, each group should select a recorder to write down all of the group's ideas. Each group is given a paper clip and then has five minutes to generate all the potential uses for it. After the brainstorming session, the recorder should recount the number of ideas generated by the group and be prepared to share the list with the rest of the class.

After hearing the list generated by each group, the class should discuss the following questions.

- What were some of the unique ideas suggested during the brainstorming?
- Do you think individual group members would have generated as many ideas if they had been working alone?
- Was it difficult to follow some of the guidelines for brainstorming? If so, which ones were difficult?
- In what types of group situations would brainstorming be most useful?

Group Participation Assessment Instrument

The following assessment instrument can help you evaluate a group and its members. Regardless of the *type* of group you are in (public group, team presentation group, working group) or your group's goal (informing a public audience, persuading key decision-makers, conducting private meetings), several criteria can help you assess the value of your own participation as well as the participation of other group members. Use the following ratings to assess each of the criteria on the instrument:

E = Excellent G = Good A = Average F = Fair P = Poor
N/A = Not applicable to this presentation

Group Assessment Instrument

CRITERIA	E	G	A	F	P	N/A
Purpose: Is the group's goal clear and supported by all members?						
Audience: Do members adapt to one another or to the audience with appropriate task and maintenance roles?						

CRITERIA	E	G	A	F	P	N/A
Credibility: Does each group member exemplify character and competence?						
Logistics: Is the meeting place well prepared and appropriate for the group and the occasion?						
Content: Are all members well prepared for the discussion or presentation?						
Organization: Does the group follow a clear agenda or plan for its presentation?						
Performance: Do members communicate effectively and adapt to any difficulties that may arise?						
Overall Evaluation:						
COMMENTS:						

Key Terms

brainstorming 515
collaborative presentation technology 523
electronic whiteboard 524
forum 509
governance group 509
hidden agenda 522
maintenance roles 514
minutes 520
panel discussion 508
public group 508
small group communication 507
Standard Problem-Solving Agenda 518
symposium 508
task roles 514
team presentation 509
videoconferences 523
virtual group 522
working agenda 519
working groups 512

Notes

1 A significant portion of the material in this chapter is based on or selected from Isa N. Engleberg and Dianna R. Wynn, *Working in Groups: Communication Principles and Strategies,* 3rd ed. (Boston: Houghton Mifflin, 2003), by permission of the authors and publisher.
2 Engleberg and Wynn, pp. 4–6.
3 Carl E. Larson and Frank M. J. LaFasto, *TeamWork: What Must Go Right/What Can Go Wrong* (Newbury, CA: Sage, 1989), p. 27.
4 Thomas Leech, *How to Prepare, Stage, & Deliver Winning Presentations* (New York: AMACOM, 1993), p. 278.
5 Marjorie Brody, *Speaking Your Way to the Top: Making Powerful Business Presentations* (Boston: Allyn & Bacon, 1998), p. 81.
6 Leech, p. 288.
7 In 1948, K.D. Benne and P. Sheats published in the *Journal of Social Issues* an essay, "Functional Roles of Group Members," which labeled and described the functional roles they had observed in groups. The list in this textbook is based on a modification of the Benne and Sheats list. See Isa N. Engleberg and Dianna R. Wynn, *Working in Groups: Communication Principles and Strategies,* 3rd ed. (Boston: Houghton Mifflin, 2003), pp. 50–53.
8 Randy Y. Hirokawa, "Communication and Group Decision-Making Efficacy," in *Small Group Communication: Theory and Practice,* 7th ed., ed. R. S. Cathcart, L. A. Samovar, and L. D. Henman (Madison, WI: Brown & Benchmark, 1996), p. 108.
9 Randy Y. Hirokawa and Dirk R. Scheerhorn, "Communication in Faulty Group Decision-Making," in *Communication and Group Decision Making,* eds. R. Y. Hirokawa and M. S. Poole (Beverly Hills, CA: Sage, 1986), pp. 73–74.
10 John Dewey, *How We Think,* revised and expanded ed. (Boston: Houghton Mifflin, 1998).
11 Julia Wood, Gerald Phillips, and Douglas Pedersen, *Group Discussion: A Practical Guide to Participation and Leadership,* 2nd ed. (New York: Harper & Row, 1986).
12 Engleberg and Wynn, pp. 210–213.
13 Clyde W. Burleson, *Effective Meetings: The Complete Guide* (New York: Wiley, 1990), p. 25.
14 3M Management Team with Jeannine Drew, *Mastering Meetings: Discovering the Hidden Potential of Effective Business Meetings* (New York: McGraw-Hill, 1994), p. 26.
15 Engleberg and Wynn, pp. 362–365.
16 Burleson, p. 88.
17 Engleberg and Wynn, pp. 52–53. Engleberg and Wynn have modified a list of negative, self-centered roles that first appeared in K. D. Benne and P. Sheats, "Functional Roles of Group Members," *Journal of Social Issues* 4 (1948): 41–49.
18 Rodney W. Napier and Matti K. Gershenfeld, *Groups: Theory and Experience,* 6th ed. (Boston: Houghton Mifflin, 1999), p. 182. Napier and Gershenfeld's questions have been modified to suit the specific nature of a group discussion.
19 *USA Today,* 8 April 2003, p. B1.
20 Engleberg and Wynn, pp. 340–341.
21 David Coleman (Ed.) Groupware: Collaborative Strategies for Corporate LANs and Intranets (Upper Saddle River, NJ: Prentice Hall, 1997), p. 266.

CREDITS

Text Credits

Chapter 1: p. 6, definition of "public" copyright © 2000 by Houghton Mifflin Company. Reproduced by permission from *The American Heritage Dictionary of the English Language, Fourth Edition;* p. 23, The National Communication Association Credo for Ethical Communication. Used by permission of the National Communication Association; p. 25, GENE Scale, developed by Janes Neulip and James C. McCroskey from Neulip, *Intercultural Communication: A Contextual Approach,* 2nd ed. (Boston: Houghton Mifflin, 2003). Copyright © 2003 by Houghton Mifflin Company. Reprinted with permission; p. 27 *Simply Speaking: How to Communicate Your Ideas with Style, Substance, and Clarity* by Peggy Noonan. Copyright © 1998 by Peggy Noonan. Reprinted by permission of HarperCollins Publishers, Inc. **Chapter 2:** p. 38, screenshot copyright © 1999 by Houghton Mifflin Company. Used with permission; p. 41, definition of "criticize" copyright © 2000 by Houghton Mifflin Company. Reproduced by permission from *The American Heritage Dictionary of the English Language, Fourth Edition;* p. 41, Figure 2.3, Isa Engleberg and Dianna Wynn, *Working in Groups,* Second Edition. Copyright © 2000 by Houghton Mifflin Company. Reprinted with permission; p. 45, William V. Haney, *Communication and Interpersonal Relationships: Text and Cases* (Homewood, IL: Irwin, 1992). Reprinted by permission of the author. **Chapter 3:** pp. 58, 59, 61, from Virginia P. Richmond and James C. McCroskey, *Communication Apprehension, Avoidance, and Effectiveness,* 5th ed. (Scottsdale, AZ: Gorsuch Scarisbrik, 1995). Reprinted by permission of the publisher. **Chapter 5:** p. 115, Reprinted by permission of Gallup Organization. **Chapter 6:** p. 129, definition of "credibility" copyright © 2000 by Houghton Mifflin Company. Reproduced by permission from *The American Heritage Dictionary of the English Language, Fourth Edition;* p. 137, definition of "ethics" copyright © 2000 by Houghton Mifflin Company. Reproduced by permission from *The American Heritage Dictionary of the English Language, Fourth Edition.* **Chapter 7:** p. 153, definitions of "lecturn" and "podium" copyright © 2000 by Houghton Mifflin Company. Reproduced by permission from *The American Heritage Dictionary of the English Language, Fourth Edition.* **Chapter 8:** p. 171, the definition of "blues" © 2003 by Encyclopaedia Britannica. Reproduced by permission from *The New Encyclopaedia Britannica, Fifteenth Edition;* p. 185, definition of "plagiarize" copyright © 2000 by Houghton Mifflin Company. Reproduced by permission from *The American Heritage Dictionary of the English Language, Fourth Edition;* pp. 188–189, exercise based on John Chafee with Christine McMahon and Barbara Stout, *Critical Thinking, Thoughtful Writing,* 2nd ed. (Boston: Houghton Mifflin, 2002), pp. 534–536, 614. Copyright © 2002 by Houghton Mifflin Company. Reprinted with permission. **Chapter 10:** p. 226, screenshot printed with permission; p. 235, adapted from Lee Towe, *Why Didn't I Think of That? Creativity in the Workplace* (West Des Moines, IA: American Media, 1996), pp. 8–12. Reprinted by permission of the author. **Chapter 11:** p. 243, screenshot courtesy of Quotable Quotes. **Chapter 12:** p. 265, definition of "language" copyright © 2000 by Houghton Mifflin Company. Reproduced by permission from *The American Heritage Dictionary of the English Language, Fourth Edition.* **Chapter 13:** p. 295–296, *Simply Speaking: How to Communicate Your Ideas with Style, Substance, and Clarity* by Peggy Noonan. Copyright © 1998 by Peggy Noonan. Reprinted by permission of HarperCollins Publishers, Inc. **Chapter 17:** p. 378 figure 17.2, p. 380 figure 17.4, p. 381 figure 17.5, p. 385 figures 17.9a and 17.9b, p. 382 figure 17.6, p. 383 figure 17.7, p. 384 figure 17.8, and page 385 figure 17.9 from *Scholastic Kids' Almanac for the 21st Century,* a Blackbird Graphics Book. Copyright © 1999 by Blackbird Graphics, Inc. Reprinted by permission of Scholastic, Inc.; p. 401, figure 1, Newsweek, March 24, 2003, p. 60. © 2003 Newsweek, Inc. All rights reserved. Reprinted by permission. **Chapter 20:** p. 471, definition of "fallacy" copyright © 2000 by Houghton Mifflin Company. Reproduced by permission from *The American Heritage Dictionary of the English Language, Fourth Edition.* **Chapter 22:** p. 514, reprinted by permission of the 3M Meeting Network. **Appendix:** pp. A12–A14, address by Candace Corlett, President, 50+ Marketing Division. Candace Corlett is a Principal at WSL Strategic Retail in New York, NY; pp. A15–A18, "Looking Through Our Window: The Value of Indian Culture" is reprinted with the permission of Chief Executive Marge Anderson and the Mille Lacs Band of Ojibwe Indians; pp. A18–A21, reprinted by permission of Dr. Herb Simpson, President and CEO, Traffic Injury Research Foundation; pp. A21–A22, reprinted by permission of Vivian Hobbs.

Photo and Cartoon Credits

Netscape browser frame, software, and website © 2002 Netscape Communications Corporation. Screenshots used with permission.

Chapter 1: p. 2, © David Young-Wolff/PhotoEdit; p. 5, AP/Wide World Photos; p. 16, © Ellen Senisi/The Image Works; p. 17, © Syracuse Newspapers/C.W. McKeen/The Image Works; p. 20, © Syracuse Newspapers/Dick Blume/The Image Works. **Chapter 2:** p. 28, © Bill Varie/Corbis; p. 35, AP/Wide World Photos; p. 42, © Tony Freeman/PhotoEdit; p. 51, © John Neubauer/PhotoEdit. **Chapter 3:** p. 57, AP/Wide World Photos; p. 60, © Mark Richards/PhotoEdit; pp. 63, 70, © Bob Daemmrich/The Image Works; p. 72, A. Manis/NYT Pictures. **Chapter 4:** p. 82, © Tony Robert/Corbis; p. 89, © Lara Jo Regan/Getty Images; p. 90, © Jeff Greenberg/PhotoEdit; p. 95, © Syracuse Newspapers/The Image Works. **Chapter 5:** p. 100, © Judy Gelles/Stock Boston; p. 108, Kevin Anderson/Kansas City Star; p. 111, © Susan Van Etten/PhotoEdit; p. 113, © Geri Engberg/The Image Works. **Chapter 6:** p. 128, © E. Fornaciari/Gamma Press; p. 131, © Bob Daemmrich/Stock Boston; p. 135, AP/Wide World Photos; p. 137, © AFP/Corbis. **Chapter 7:** p. 146, © Jeff Greenberg/PhotoEdit; p. 148, © A. Ramey/PhotoEdit; p. 155, AP/Wide World Photos; p. 156, AP/Wide World; p. 160, © A. Ramey/ PhotoEdit. **Chapter 8:** p. 168, © Mario Tama/Getty Images; p. 174, © Reuters NewMedia Inc./Corbis; p. 186, AP/Wide World Photos. **Chapter 9:** p. 192, © Jose Luis Pelaez, Inc./Corbis; p. 196, © David Young-Wolff/PhotoEdit; p. 201, © Jonathan E. Pite. **Chapter 10:** pp. 211, 216, 231, AP/Wide World Photos. **Chapter 11:** p. 237, © Cleve Bryant/PhotoEdit; p. 240, © Michelle Bridwell/PhotoEdit; p. 245, © David Young-Wolff/PhotoEdit. **Chapter 12:** p. 263, © Peter Hvizdak/The Image Works; p. 275, © Reuters NewMedia Inc./Corbis; p. 282, Hulton Archive/Getty Images. **Chapter 13:** p. 292, © Dick Blume/The Image Works; p. 297, © Eastcott-Momatiuk/The Image Works; p. 305, © Robert Nickelsberg/The Image Works; p. 314, © The New Yorker Collection 2001 Frank Cotham from cartoonbank.com. All Rights Reserved. **Chapter 14:** p. 318, © Bob Daemmrich/The Image Works; p. 320, © Chet Gordon/The Image Works; p. 323, AP /Wide World Photos; p. 326, AP/Wide World Photos; p. 329, © Mark Burnett/Stock Boston. **Chapter 15:** p. 335, © Joe Traver/Getty Images; p. 339, © Bob Daemmrich/The Image Works; p. 438, © Dave G. Houser/Corbis. **Chapter 16:** p. 353, © Dick Blume/The Image Works; p. 359, © Syracuse Newspapers/Dick Blume/The Image Works; p. 362, © Randi Anglin/The Image Works; p. 364, © David Young-Wolff/PhotoEdit; p. 366, © David Hume Kennerly/Getty Images. **Chapter 17:** p. 372, © Stan Godlewski/Getty Images; p. 376, © Syracuse Newspapers/The Image Works; p.387, © Sam Sargent; p. 393, © David Young-Wolff/PhotoEdit. **Chapter 18:** p. 406, © Arnold Gold/New Haven Register/The Image Works; p. 409, © Bill Bachmann/PhotoEdit; p. 413, © Michael Rosenfeld/Stone/Getty Images; p. 418, © Susan Van Etten/PhotoEdit. **Chapter 19:** p. 427, © Davis Barber/PhotoEdit; p. 431, © Journal-Courier/Steve Warmoski/The Image Works; p. 448, AFP/Corbis. **Chapter 20:** p. 453, AFP/Corbis; 460, © Bob Daemmrich/Stock Boston; p. 464, Paul Hosefros/NYT Pictures; p. 470, © Reuters NewMedia Inc./Corbis; p. 471, © Reuters NewMedia Inc./Corbis. **Chapter 21:** p. 479, AP/Wide World Photos; p. 485, © Susan Van Etten/PhotoEdit; p. 487, © Tony Freeman/PhotoEdit; p. 496, © Peter Hvizdak/The Image Works; p. 500, © Michael Newman/PhotoEdit. **Chapter 22:** p. 506, © Jose Luis Pelaez, Inc./Corbis; p. 510, © Syracuse Newspapers/Suzanne Dunn/The Image Works; p. 511, © Elizabeth Crews; p. 517, © Mark Richards/PhotoEdit.

Sample Presentations

STUDENT PRESENTATIONS

Informative Presentation

The Sound of Muzak

Julie Borchard, Student

Julie Borchard, who now works as a public education specialist for the U.S. Treasury Department, developed the following informative presentation when she was still in college. She was looking for a topic that would provide new and interesting information about a subject familiar to everyone. She found such a topic in Muzak. In addition to conducting research, Julie visited a large Muzak franchise, where she interviewed the company's president and collected a wide variety of supporting materials from its library and marketing department. Her use of language is powerful because it is clear and simple, as well as direct and vivid, through her use of personal pronouns and alliteration. In Chapter 10, "Organizational Tools," we present the mind map Julie used to organize her presentation, as well as her complete outline.

Julie Borchard is a graduate of Prince George's Community College and the Universtiy of Iowa (Editorial Note: *Some of the information in* The Sound of Muzak *has been updated.)*

Julie began her presentation by turning on a demonstration tape that played excerpts of music from Muzak. After a few opening bars, she began speaking carefully chosen words that described people's positive and negative reactions to Muzak. This paragraph also introduced her first use of alliteration ("vacant volumes of vapid violins"), many more of which would follow.

It's been referred to by its creators as "sonorous design" and "sound energy, attractively arranged." On the other hand, to much of the American public, this product conjures up images of "spineless melodies" with "vacant volumes of vapid violins." In short, it's Muzak. And what you're now hearing is an actual demonstration tape of Muzak. But Muzak isn't just any old song. According to its creators, it can reduce your stress, boredom, and fatigue, and increase your productivity.

Julie offered a short definition of Muzak, and for audience members unfamiliar with the concept of a trademarked brand name, she used *Kleenex* to provide an analogy.

Muzak is actually a trademarked brand name for background music, much like Kleenex is for facial tissue. Although the background music industry is composed of several independent companies, according to Allen Smith, president of Muzak's Washington, D.C., franchise, "Muzak dominates the field by over 70 percent."

In one sentence, Julie linked her three key points to the Central Idea of the presentation. She used the personal pronouns *your* twice and *you* once to begin the process of involving her audience.

By understanding how pervasive Muzak is, how it originated, and how it supposedly lifts your spirits and productivity, you can become a little more enlightened [the] next time it's playing your song.

Julie supported her first key point by providing a lot of statistics. Amidst all the numbers, she included the word *you* four times. She also ended the paragraph with a well-written sentence ("In short, you may be able to avoid the IRS . . .") that served to spice up her internal summary. This paragraph also featured Julie's use of words that had musical connotations ("lend Muzak a thoughtful *ear,*" "interest you to *note,*" "sweet *strains* of Muzak").

Now, even if you don't care to lend Muzak a thoughtful ear, it may interest you to note that this $200 million a year business can be heard in over 250,000 locations in the United States and in 15 foreign countries. Each day, more than 80 million people listen to Muzak in one form or another. And amazingly, according to independent surveys reported in *USA Today,* at least 90 percent of these people actively like what they hear. A recent list of the 150 largest industrial corporations, retail companies, and commercial banks in this country showed that only seven were not plugged into Muzak somewhere within their organization. In short, you may be able to avoid the IRS, outwit the FBI, and even fool Mother Nature, but you can't escape the sweet strains of Muzak.

This section begins with a well-written transitional phrase that anticipates the third key point as it introduces the second one. In this section, Julie presented her historical information in chronological order. She used stories as well as research statistics as supporting material. The paragraph also continues her clever use of words and phrases to make her presentation more interesting..

Before explaining how Muzak claims to put a smile on your face, energy in your work effort, and a song in your heart, let's step back in time to 1922 to see how this dynasty developed. Muzak was the creation of Major George O. Squier, Chief Signal Officer of the U.S. army during World War I. Before the success of commercial radio, he patented a plan to use electric power lines for transmitting news, music, and advertising directly into homes—the same idea being used today for cable television. In the 1930s Muzak began piping in music—via telephone lines—to hotels and restaurants. But the big break came in 1937 when two British industrial psychologists, S. Wyatt and J. Langdon, released a study called "Fatigue and Boredom in Repetitive Work." Their studies contained evidence that music cheers up workers sapped by the monotony of the assembly line. Muzak had found its niche. According to Professor Russell Nye of the University of Southern Florida, by 1945, 75 percent of the war industry had Muzak in its plants. The U.S. Army claimed Muzak helped spur defense workers onto new heights of wartime productivity. And as postwar industry boomed, so did Muzak.

This section brought the research on Muzak into the present and focused on an extended example of how Muzak was used by two companies. Into this somewhat technical information, she inserted her reaction to statistics ("A little mind-boggling, wouldn't you say?") that also asked the audience for their reaction.

In slightly more recent history, a 1972 controlled experiment was conducted at a Manhattan Blue Cross and Blue Shield Company, where workers were processing an average of 90,000 Medicare claims by computer each week. A little mind-boggling, wouldn't you say? But nothing that Muzak couldn't handle. After Muzak was installed, Blue Cross reported a 100 percent jump in worker productivity. In a major cosmetics firm, Muzak is credited with decreasing errors by 16.4 percent and lowering absenteeism by 29.9 percent.

Thus, to many office and factory subscribers, Muzak is as beneficial to their work environment as good lighting and air conditioning. Now, if all this is true—and dozens of studies have verified these results—why don't companies just install their own stereo systems and play a local radio station or an old Lawrence Welk album? The reason they don't is that Muzak does something unique to its music, and thus does something unique to you. In order to appreciate how Muzak works, it's necessary to understand what happens to a worker on the job.

This paragraph represents a transition from one section to another. It was used to introduce the characteristics that explain Muzak's unique form and function.

Researchers have concluded that most of us arrive at work in the morning at a certain energy level, which drops in mid-morning and picks up with thoughts of lunch. This pattern is repeated in the afternoon. To counteract these sluggish periods, Muzak designed what they call "stimulus progression." Stimulus progression involves alternating 15 minutes of music with 15 minutes of silence to offset periods of fatigue in listeners. According to *USA Today,* Muzak's stimulus progression nudges workers during the 11 A.M. droop and perks them up in the later afternoon. These 15-minute segments are selected from a computerized music library housing more than 200,000 recorded melodies, each with an assigned "stimulus quotient" of between 0 and 7. These values are determined by such factors as the music's tempo and intensity. A typical music segment might start with a soothing song that would rate a 1 or 2, and end with a toe-tapping rendition of a popular tune rating of 6 or 7. Thus we can see how Muzak carries and maintains a worker's energy level throughout the course of the day.

The next two paragraphs covered the more technical sections of the presentation in which Julie explained the "stimulus progression" and "dulled" features of Muzak. By now, she had warmed up her audience, involved them, and could let her performance style and personal credibility (character, competence, and charisma) serve her and her purpose.

In addition to subjecting you to these mood-enhancing progressions, Muzak's music takes a distinct musical form. It is more than just adding violins. The arrangements are "dulled" by electronically chopping off the high and low tones in a recording. The sharp contrasts and other techniques used by composers and musicians to catch your attention are smoothed over so the music slips by with little notice. Janis Jarvis, a Muzak executive, explains: "If listeners say they like a song it means the presentation has been too distracting and it is taken out of circulation right away." All that matters to Muzak is that you experience increased energy, higher productivity, and improved morale. No wonder Muzak has so many fans—fans like AT&T, IBM, and Xerox, who use it in their paper processing divisions. It's also big in the federal bureaucracy where it not only soothes stressed file clerks but aids in drowning out CIA spy talk.

Beginning with the phrase "In addition to . . .," Julie made a smooth transition to her next key point. By using a quotation and brief examples, she explained how and why Muzak "dulls" its sound.

Muzak isn't restricted to the office, however. Restaurants employ it to drown out the buzzing of competing dinner table conversations, and supermarkets use Muzak to encourage shoppers to linger and buy on impulse. Even hospitals have introduced Muzak to their sterile corridors. Dr. Frank B. Flood, Chief of Cardiology at St. Joseph's Hospital in Yonkers, New York, reported that "recovery rates among coronary patients improved when the intensive-care unit was bathed in homogenized Beatles and Bacharach."

Julie provided additional examples in this section to extend the range and influence of Muzak.

However, not only clients are soothed by Muzak. John Mose, Professor of Industrial and Organizational Psychology at George Washington University, separates people into two categories—those who crave external stimulation, "like the people you see jogging around the streets with headphones," and those capable of entertaining themselves with private reverie. For the second group, Muzak can be an annoyance. And although the *New York Times*

Opening with a transition ("However, not only clients are soothed . . .,"), Julie explained why some people like listening to Muzak whereas others are annoyed. She used quotations to verify her claims.

subscribes to Muzak, many of the editors turned it off in their area. One savings and loan officer told me, "Most managers don't like Muzak." Nor, studies conclude, do most people with relatively interesting jobs.

With a name like "Bing" Muscio, Julie felt that she had to include a quotation from Muzak's former president. She searched through her research to find the statistics and quotation that best fit this final portion of her presentation. The quotation also gave her the lead in she needed for a conclusion. Using alliteration (Vic Damone-Valium, Paul Simon-Penicillin), she offered a final summary and ended with a little play on words that referred to *The Sound of Muzak*.

But the president of Muzak, "Bing" Muscio, has little difficulty defending the sound of his music. Muzak is used by more than 100,000 organizations. There are some 250 franchises around the world and a Muzak franchise can sell for as much as $2 million. But Mr. Muscio's plans extend even further:

> *We know it can affect the heartbeat and the pulse rate. We know it can be effective in dealing with people under stress. Just think what it might mean if we could begin to substitute music for the incredible number of invasive drugs we put into our systems.*

Imagine Vic Damone instead of Valium. Paul Simon instead of penicillin. Impossible? Well, given what you've just heard about Muzak's pervasiveness, development, and techniques, nothing should surprise you. Yes, the sound of Muzak is here to stay.

Informative Presentation

CliffsNotes

John Sullivan, Student

"For all the trust I put in CliffsNotes, *I don't know one thing about them" was the sentence that inspired this informative presentation on* CliffsNotes. *John Sullivan, who now works for the American Association of Retired Persons as director of Information Technology, External Partner Solutions, translated his very personable speaking style into a delightful and interesting presentation. When he discovered that very little had been written about* CliffsNotes, *he phoned the company's headquarters in Lincoln, Nebraska, and interviewed the managing editor, Gary Carey. John Sullivan graduated from Prince George's Community College and the University of Maryland.* (Editorial Note: *Some of the information in* CliffsNotes *has been updated.)*

Eight o'clock Wednesday night. I have an English exam bright and early tomorrow morning. It's on Homer's *Iliad.* And I haven't read page one. I forego tonight's beer drinking and try to read. Eight forty-five. I'm only on page 12. Only 482 more to go. Nine thirty, it hits me. Like a rock. I'm not going to make it.

The way I see it I have three options. I can drop the class, cheat, or go ask Cliff. Because I'm not a quitter, and because I don't think cheating is the right thing to do, I borrow a copy of the *CliffsNotes* from a friend.

Yet for all the trust I put in *CliffsNotes,* I couldn't have told you one thing about them. Even though, according to no less a prestigious source as *People Magazine,* over fifty million of these yellow and black pamphlets have been sold, you probably don't know too much about them either. After exhausting *People Magazine,* the *Nebraska Sunday World Herald Magazine,* and *Forbes Magazine,* I had to turn to Cliff himself. Yes, there is a Cliff behind *CliffsNotes* and no, his last name is not Notes. After two interviews with Gary Carey, the managing editor of *CliffsNotes,* it became clear to me that *CliffsNotes* was truly an American success story.

At one time, the notes were nothing more than simple plot summaries. But today, they offer the reader much more in terms of character analysis and literary criticism. To better appreciate this unique publishing phenomenon, it is necessary to trace the history of *CliffsNotes,* note some of the changes they have undergone, and finally, understand why Cliff and his notes get put down by teachers and praised by students.

Mr. Cliff Hillegass, owner and founder of *CliffsNotes,* literally started the business in the basement of his home as a mail-order company. As an employee of the Nebraska Book Company, he happened upon a Canadian publisher who had a full line of study guides. Upon returning home from a trip to Canada, he brought with him the notes to sixteen Shakespearian plays. He immediately made three thousand copies of each and sent them throughout the U.S. Book store managers were very receptive to the idea and put the Notes on sale.

When *CliffsNotes* first splashed onto the scene in 1958, 18,000 copies were sold. By 1960 sales had increased to 54,000. By the mid-60s, the magic number was two million and soon everyone wanted a piece of the action. By 1968, no less than thirteen other companies were in the market. Mr. Hillegass was confident through it all that none could overtake him. He told his sales staff not to worry. He said, "I believe most of our competition are large publishers for whom the study guides would never be more than one item in their line."

He couldn't have been more correct. By 1968, just two years later, only three competitors were left. And as competition went down, sales went up. By the mid-1980s, *CliffsNotes* was grossing over $4 million a year with over 200 titles in print. In 1988, *CliffsNotes* sold 5 million copies and brought in revenues of $11 million. By 1992, sales exceeded $13 million.

Even with 200-plus titles, it is the original 50 titles that constitute 70 percent of sales. Obviously certain titles have remained relatively constant through the years. In fact, Cliff keeps a top ten for every year. The following list represents the Top Ten in 1992. As I list them in descending order, try and think what might be number one. And, as a hint, keep in mind that most *CliffsNotes* are sold to high school juniors and seniors.

10. *To Kill a Mockingbird*
9. *The Scarlet Letter*
8. *Great Expectations*
7. *A Tale of Two Cities*
6. *Romeo and Juliet*
5. *The Great Gatsby*
4. *Julius Caesar*
3. *Macbeth*
2. *Huckleberry Finn*
1. *Hamlet*

According to Mr. Carey, *CliffsNotes* first went intercontinental in 1983. In Europe they were first sold in France and Italy—in the land down under, in Australia and New Zealand. They entered the Chinese market in Beijing and Hangzhou. *CliffsNotes* are now sold in thirty-eight foreign countries.

What next, you may wonder. Well, in another interview with Mr. Carey, he told me that the next development will be the expansion of *CliffsNotes* into several new languages. In addition to Spanish, Portuguese, and Greek, *CliffsNotes* will soon be read right to left, in Hebrew. In 1998, IDG Books Worldwide, Inc., the people who publish the . . . *for Dummies* books, acquired the little company that Cliff built. *CliffsNotes* now takes on other challenges, such as how to prepare for the GMAT test, how to master computer technology, and how to manage your finances.

Yet despite international inroads and domestic success, *CliffsNotes* has its critics. Questions have been raised concerning the quality of the literary criticism within *CliffsNotes,* the claims of copyright infringements, and the academic ethics of using *CliffsNotes* in place of the real thing.

Mr. Hillegass, no writer himself, commissions the writing of the notes to scholars and teachers. At the college level, he uses Ph.D.'s or grad students who have experience with the work. For example, the notes on *The Iliad* were penned in 1986 by Dr. Elaine Strong Skill of the University of Oregon. The consulting editor was Dr. James L. Roberts from the University of Nebraska.

Cliff did find, however, that Ph.D.'s and grad students sometimes write above the level of high school students. As a result, many of the high school notes are written by secondary school teachers who use the work in question, year in and year out.

Cliff also has had his share of problems with publishers. In 1966 Random House filed suit against *CliffsNotes* for quoting too extensively from some of its copyrighted Faulkner titles. Both sides had lawyers poised and ready to do combat. It could have become a landmark case. Instead Cliff and some of the people from Random House solved their problems out of court.

Cliff believes that this was a turning point for both himself and his company. It forced them to take a fresh look at the notes. As a result, the classics were revamped to the point that they are now approximately 50 percent text summary and 50 percent critical analysis.

For example, the notes on *Macbeth,* Act I, scene 1, discuss the witches' famous lines "When shall we three meet again" and "In thunder, lightening, or in rain?" These lines take up only two lines in the play. The *CliffsNotes* analysis is many times that length, with commentary on such things as the dramatic creation of mood, the use of time as a key theme, and the language of paradox and prophecy.

Cliff no longer has problems with publishers, but his academic critics are still there. Certainly you have heard (or can easily imagine) teacher complaints that *CliffsNotes* allow students to avoid reading the original text.

In an article about *CliffsNotes* published in the *Nebraska Sunday World Herald Magazine,* one educator said, "Reading *CliffsNotes* is like letting someone else eat your dinner. They deprive students of the pleasure of discovering literature for themselves."

Mr. Carey countered such criticism in the same article by stating: "Teachers' apprehensions concerning *CliffsNotes* may have been well founded twenty years ago when they were simple plot summaries. But, today, they are mainly composites of mainstream literary criticism that are of little value to students who have not read the book."

An informal survey at Creighton University and the University of Nebraska has indicated that Mr. Carey may be correct. Where students' older brothers and sisters may have used *CliffsNotes* in place of the real thing, more than 80 percent of those students interviewed said they never used *CliffsNotes* by themselves. They only used them to accompany the reading of the required text. If anything, the *CliffsNotes* helped them discover the pleasure of reading the literature.

But then again . . . I did pass my exam, and I have yet to read *The Iliad.* And I'm sure there are plenty of students out there who have missed the delights of *Huckleberry Finn* or the pathos of *The Grapes of Wrath.* "To be or not to be," "Friends, Romans, Countrymen," and "Out out damn spot" very well could be the only lines of Shakespeare that some students know.

So the controversy continues. But at least you know that, unlike Ronald McDonald, Cliff is a real person and he has not dodged the issues. He will go on explaining the finer points of his 200-plus titles. Because as long as teachers assign the classics of literature, the racks of yellow and black will continue to grow and prosper.

Persuasive Presentation

Asleep at the Wheel

Camille Dunlap, Student

Camille Dunlap, an honors student at Prince George's Community College, took a direct route to persuasion in this highly successful presentation. The beginning of her persuasive speech embodied all of the elements of an effective introduction. She gained attention and interest with a tragic and personal story. She asked students questions that connected her topic to their busy, tired lives, and she established a serious emotional tone for her presentation.

The presentation included three main points. First, she explained why everyone needs a good night's sleep every night. Then she addressed the harmful effects of insufficient sleep. Finally, she offered "a few simple ways" to get adequate sleep.

Two sections of the presentation impressed her audience more than the others did. In her introduction, she compared driving while drowsy with driving while intoxicated. This comparison hit home for students with busy and tiring life schedules. Her audience also became personally involved when she posed questions to determine if they were suffering from sleep deprivation.

Ms. Dunlap's well-researched and skillfully organized presentation used clear and engaging language. She incorporated effective stories and a sense of humor into her presentation. Most important of all, her message spoke to each and every listener in the classroom.

On June 23 at 7:43 P.M., a smoldering car was found twisted around a tree. Two dead bodies. One adult. One baby.

Why did this happen? Was it drunk driving? No. Adverse road conditions? No. A defect in the car? No.

Something else took the life of my best friend and her baby brother. Something quite simple, quite common, and deadly: She fell asleep at the wheel.

"Fall asleep crashes" account for 100,000 car accidents and 1,500 deaths every year. Everyone knows about the dangers of drunk driving, but very few of us know about the dangers of sleep deprivation.

How many of you would drive home with a 0.1 blood-alcohol concentration? That's the legal limit in most states. Now answer this: How many of you have pulled an all-nighter studying for an exam or writing a paper, and then driven to school in the morning? According to experts from the National Sleep Foundation, if you drive without sleep for twenty-four hours, you are in the same condition as someone driving at the 0.1 blood-alcohol level. But you don't have to pull an all-nighter to be impaired. If, like me, you wake up at 5:00 A.M., go to work, and then attend class until 9:30 P.M., you're putting in a very long day. The National Sleep Foundation reports that when I drive home tonight, I will be driving at the equivalent of a 0.05 blood-alcohol level. I wouldn't think of having a drink before heading home, but I may be driving as if I did.

A good night's sleep is essential for your health, well-being, and safety. Sleep restores your body's physical and mental reserves. When you fail to get enough sleep, you do more than put yourself at risk. You also risk the lives of others.

There was a time when sleep was as natural as the setting and rising of the sun. No more. We live in a fast-paced, high-tech world that operates twenty-four hours a day. Grocery stores, banks, restaurants, and many other services are accessible to us around the clock. Television, radio, and movie channels broadcast day and night. The Internet is oblivious to time. As a result, we often trade needed sleep for catching up on work from the office and school or engaging in leisure activities such as surfing the Net, playing video games, and late-night partying. Is it any wonder we're short on sleep?

Everyone needs a certain number of sleep hours each day in order to function effectively. According to Berkman and Breslow in *Health and Ways of Living,* our natural sleep patterns are controlled by an internal clock called a "circadian clock." This genetically-controlled "clock" also regulates body temperature, hormone levels, heart rate, and other vital body functions. Lack of sleep impairs these functions and your overall health. Lack of sleep is hazardous—for you and for others.

Even your emotions need sleep. Without adequate sleep, you can become upset more easily as well as more frustrated and irritable. I, for one, can vouch for that. I stand before you today deprived of sleep after working on this presentation—and I'm feeling stressed out and grumpy.

If occasional grumpiness were the only problem, I wouldn't have much more to say. But sleep deprivation has other serious consequences. It also affects your productivity and concentration. When you're tired, it's more difficult to concentrate and perform tasks that require memory. When you're sleepy, it takes you longer to get things done. Some mornings, it takes me forty-five minutes to make breakfast—normally, it takes five to ten minutes.

Lack of sleep also affects your physical health. You become more susceptible to disease and infection, stress, tension headaches and fatigue. Insufficient sleep can also be fatal—as was the case with my best friend. Even the Chernobyl nuclear reactor meltdown and the Exxon Valdez oil spill have been linked to severe sleep deprivation.

So why is sleep so important? According to the National Sleep Foundation, deep sleep allows your body to repair tissues, reenergize organs and muscles, and replace old cells with new ones. Sleep provides relief from physical activity by slowing your body's metabolism, heartbeat, and respiration. Most of these important functions occur between the seventh and eighth hour of sleep. So if you're sleeping fewer than seven hours every night, you're missing out on the most important opportunity to repair and prepare your body for the coming day. In fact, Donald Hall, a sleep researcher, notes that people who sleep fewer than seven hours do not live as long as those who sleep seven or more hours a day. So here's a maxim to remember: Sleep longer, live longer.

But, you may be saying, I'm one of the exceptions. *I* really don't need seven hours of sleep. I'm not grouchy or ill or nonproductive. So here are a few questions you can ask yourself to determine if you're suffering from sleep deprivation:

1. Do you crave naps or doze off during the day?
2. Do you find yourself zoning out during meetings, study sessions, or (heaven forbid) your professor's lectures?
3. Do you hit the snooze button several times in the morning?
4. Do you have difficulty solving problems, being creative, or thinking critically?
5. Do you feel lethargic or groggy, especially when you're less active?

If you answered *yes* to any of these questions, take a good look at your sleep schedule. What is robbing you of needed sleep?

As students, we may be among the most sleep deprived. In addition to our classes, many of us work—full-time and part-time. I know that some of you are married. A few of you are single moms raising families. Those of you with children or young brothers and sisters know how cranky kids can get when they're tired. The same may be true of you.

So what can you do to ease your tired body and soul? The answer is simple but not easy. Getting more sleep is difficult when you have so much else to do. I urge you to try—even for a couple of weeks—to see what a difference a good night's sleep can mean for you and others. Here are a few simple ways to start:

1. Decide how many hours of sleep are right for you by keeping a sleep log. Jot down the number of hours you slept and how you felt during the next day.
2. Create a comfortable sleep environment. Is your mattress firm? Is there good air circulation? Is your room dark and quiet?
3. Do not try to fall asleep on a full or empty stomach. Cut back on fluids before you go to sleep.
4. Exercise. It promotes good sleep. But make sure you exercise at least three hours before going to bed. Otherwise, your body will not have had sufficient time to wind down.
5. Do not drink alcohol or caffeinated beverages before bedtime. Avoid cigarettes as well.
6. Establish a relaxing bedtime ritual that will allow you to unwind. Avoid bright lights. Take a hot bath. Try going to bed around the same time each night.
7. Last and most difficult of all, do not take your troubles to bed with you. If you can't fall asleep after thirty minutes, don't toss and turn. Get up! The National Sleep Foundation suggests listening to soothing music or reading a book until you feel sleepy. May I suggest reading my economics textbook—it works every time!

Recognizing that you may be sleep deprived is the first step. The hardest thing to do is to alter your habits. Retraining yourself to follow a more normal sleep pattern isn't going to happen overnight. But once you discover that a few extra hours of sleep will help you feel more rested, relaxed, and revitalized, giving up that extra hour on the Internet will have been worth it. There's so much in life to enjoy. And remember: Sleep longer, live longer.

Persuasive Presentation

What's Fair Is Fair

Regina Smith, Student

Regina Smith is a "nontraditional" college student. She is a working adult who holds a full-time job with the Federal government and attends college in the evenings. While exploring topics for her persuasive presentation, she realized that a speech defending affirmative action in college admissions might not convince an unfriendly or bored audience. She understood that, on the surface, affirmative action may seem unfair when less qualified minority students are admitted to institutions of higher education. Rather than confronting the affirmative action controversy head on, she chose a subtler, peripheral route to persuasion that examined the "other" preferences in college admissions—preferences that most students don't know about or are only marginally aware of.

Ms. Smith is African American. She believed that she would be more persuasive if she approached her topic in an indirect way. In addition to presenting very well-researched information, she relied on her well-established personal credibility as a good student and speaker to strengthen her arguments. Her frequent use of the word fairness *and the statement "That seems unfair" evoked a value shared by most students.*

Her conclusion is purposely disingenuous. Although she strongly believes that eliminating affirmative action preferences would hurt students and our colleges as well as the society at large, she hoped that her audience would see that absolute fairness can be a poor and hypocritical standard for achieving genuine equality and social justice. Regina Smith delivered this persuasive presentation in an honors communication course at Prince George's Community College.

Americans love fairness. It's a wonderful ideal. Our country was built by people who were given the equal opportunity to work hard and succeed. So I understand why affirmative action upsets the American idea of fairness. I understand why some of you may feel that way.

You may believe that affirmative action gives some black students an unfair opportunity for a college education, an opportunity that others deserve because they have worked hard and succeeded in high school. You may be right—affirmative action gives some black students a preference. But despite what you may think, I'm not going to try to justify affirmative action. Nor am I going to deny its apparent unfairness. Instead, I'm going to focus on the *other* preferences. Yes, there are other preferences that give other kinds of students the same unfair opportunity for a college education. It's really quite curious that *these* preferences are given so little attention. So I'm going to give them attention here in the name of that important ideal of American fairness.

Let's start with the oldest type of preference. They're called *legacy admissions.* Legacy admissions give students special consideration in admittance to a college or university if one of their parents graduated from the same institution. Legacies were started in the 1920s by elite Eastern schools to give the children of old wealthy white families a preference over the children of Jewish people and immigrants, who were outscoring them on entrance exams. Today, your grade point average could be 2.0, and your family legacy could get you admitted to the University of Pennsylvania instead of the student with a 3.5 grade point average. You could live outside of the state of Virginia, yet your family legacy could get you admitted to the University of Virginia before an in-state student with higher grades. Your SAT score could be lower than three fourths of your classmates, but your family legacy could still get you admitted to Harvard University. Legacies give an edge to applicants who are clearly less qualified.

In 2002, the University of Pennsylvania had a special alumni admissions office that lobbied for alumni children. The result: Forty-one percent of the students accepted at the University of Pennsylvania are legacies. At the University of Virginia, 52 percent of freshmen are legacies, and a whopping 57 percent of students accepted to Notre Dame University—home of the "Fighting Irish"—are legacies. In addition, legacies can give some degree of preference to graduates' grandchildren and siblings as well as nieces and nephews. Even our esteemed President Bush was a legacy admission to high school, college, and even—the White House. Legacy admissions seem unfair.

Let's move on to another preference. Most of us believe that no one should be admitted to higher education unless they have high SAT scores and a good grade point average. That seems fair. Yet, historically, most college athletes have been held to a lower standard than other students. Even under the new academic requirements set by the National Collegiate Athletic Association (NCAA), the standards are not much better. In 1986–1987, under Proposition 48, the NCAA required high school graduates to present a 2.0 grade point average (G.P.A.) in eleven core courses and a minimum SAT score of 700. In 1996–1997, the NCAA tightened the eligibility under Proposition 16 by requiring two more core courses. In addition, athletes need an SAT score of 1010 if their G.P.A. was 2.0 or an SAT score of 850 if their G.P.A. was 2.5. Is it fair when you have to earn a much higher G.P.A. and SAT score than an athlete?

Many athletic programs would collapse without the talented athletes who are given preference in admissions. And if that's not enough, athletes often get more academic assistance than the average student—special advisors and paid tutors, careful course placement and schedules, even pressure that's placed on tough teachers to "go easy" on the superstars. With all that support, shouldn't they earn higher grades and have a higher graduation rate? Not so. The average graduation rate of college athletes is dismal. In 2001, Division I football players graduated at a 51 percent rate and Division I basketball players graduated at only 40 percent. In a system of approximately 3,700 athletes, roughly half get a college degree. Hasn't higher education failed when so many athletes fail to graduate? Yet athletes are given preference in college admissions over students with higher G.P.A.s and SATs. That seems unfair.

Fortunately, there are exceptions to athlete preferences. Duke University admits student athletes who are academically prepared and provides them with academic support. Consequently, Duke has a 90 percent graduation rate for scholarship athletes. The average combined SAT score of its football players is 1140. In addition, Duke's athletes have access to tutoring, coaching in study skills, and time management. Duke's formula demonstrates that students can win championships and have academic success—without preferences.

So why do we have athletic preferences? The answer: It's the money. The NCAA signed an eleven-year, $6 billion television contract with $187 million distributed to 320 Division I schools. Because of the focus on money, academically qualified students are passed over for physically gifted athletes. Both sets of students are cheated out of an education. That seems unfair.

Finally, special preferences are given to students with a socioeconomic disadvantage. The University of California system factors in economic status and challenging life circumstances such as family illness, immigration hardships, and living in high-crime neighborhoods. But what about blue-collar and middle-income students whose parents are just one paycheck from the streets yet struggle to provide a quality education for their children? Too often, their "just making it" paycheck cannot squeeze out enough to pay for tuition, room, and board. Why shouldn't their children be given a preference for their hard work in school and their parents' hard work on the job that pays just enough to get by but not enough to pay that tuition? That seems unfair.

There are other advantages extended to special groups, but my goal is not to point out all of the preferences available to college students. My goal is to question why affirmative action is singled out. I'm not arguing about whether affirmative action is fair or unfair. But I do challenge the justification for getting rid of affirmative action without also doing away with all of the other preferences. Now that would be fair.

Ron Wilson, an African American representative in the state of Texas, understood this irony when he persuaded the Texas legislature to pass a law requiring any school in the Texas system that has a minimum G.P.A. for athletes to use the same low minimum G.P.A. for all applicants. Wilson argued that it's a great hypocrisy when courts allow selective universities to relax their academic standards for athletes and children of alumni but not for African Americans.

In the name of fairness, let us stop giving preferences to the children of alumni. Let us stop offering preferences to athletes. Let us offer encouragement to economically disadvantaged students, but no preferences. If your culture is not represented in higher education, we'll give you your very own month to celebrate, but no preferences for a college education. Let's be fair. Let's not give preferences in higher education to anyone. Yes, many deserving students will not have access to higher education. Yes, college athletic programs will suffer or be abolished. Yes, diverse-looking and diverse thinking student bodies will become a thing of the past. But at least our society, our precious American way of life, will be viewed by the world as being fair.

REAL WORLD, REAL SPEAKERS

Informative Presentation

Marketing to Women 50+ on the Internet: Promote the Upside of Aging

Address by Candace Corlett, Principal, 50+ Marketing Directions, A Service of WSL Strategic Retail, NY, NY
Delivered to the World Research Group Conference, Orlando, Florida
May 27, 1999

Most *informative presentations are prepared for extemporaneous delivery. The language is usually informal with a focus on clarity rather than on eloquence. This is seen in an address on marketing to women over age 50 on the Internet by Candace Corlett that is presented next in outline form.*

The content of Ms. Corlett's presentation reinforces the importance of audience research, analysis, and adaptation as keys to developing strategic messages. Because Ms. Corlett was addressing an audience of marketing professionals interested in her topic, she did not have to spend time addressing audience needs. Nor did she need a value step or a section devoted to establishing her credibility. She did, however, have to prepare a very well-organized presentation in order to cover the wealth of information she wanted to share with her audience. Given her credibility as principal of the 50+ Marketing Directions, a service of WSL Strategic Retail, she did not identify the sources of her information.

The presentation is very *well organized. Her introduction uses a song lyric as an attention getter, helps her listeners visualize a foot-stamping group of demanding consumers, and identifies why it's important for the audience to understand the consumer over age fifty. Two major key points are well supported. Ms. Corlett uses facts, statistics, testimony, definitions, analogies, descriptions, examples, and stories to support her conclusions and recommendations.*

The subpoints under each key point are also well organized. Clear statistics and an audience involvement quiz are used in the first key point to help the audience understand the demographic characteristics of the 50-plus consumer market. The second key point is divided into three subsections. The first describes three separate target markets in the 50-plus population. The second subpoint describes seven market indicators for "getting to know" the 50-plus market. The final subpoint offers three guidelines for speaking to the 50-plus consumers.

Although the presentation is well organized, the supporting material and subpoints do not always address the speech's purpose and central idea. Very often, Ms. Corlett's supporting material applies to all *consumers over fifty (not just women) and their buying habits in general (not just on the Internet). Yet to the extent that women belong to these groups, the speaker implies that the research and advice can be applied to the needs and interests of women over age fifty who use the Internet.*

The informal style and clever use of terms lend the speech vigor and a sense of humor. Key words or phrases in parentheses provide reminders of how to explain or describe each point.

Notice how the presentation incorporates many informative speaking strategies: using a clear organizational pattern and key points, presenting various types of supporting material, defining essential features, using typical and contrasting examples, quizzing the audience, using appropriate transitional phrases, and providing information that overcomes misinformation.

The conclusion is short but invites listeners to take on the challenge of advertising to an older generation of consumers.

Marketing to Women 50+ on the Internet: Promote the Upside of Aging

I. Introduction
Baby boomers are not a generation to be ignored. What's that song lyric, "I know what I want and I want it now"? You can almost see them stamping their feet and demanding new products and services: skin creams to erase lines, medications to manage menopause, biotechnology to replace damaged body parts. That is why we are all here today, because the 50-plus population, even before the onslaught of the baby boomers, is a significant target audience that is getting attention. Why?

II. Central Idea and Preview
- A. Several strategies that can help you approach women over 50 with products and services on the Internet
- B. Key Points
  Understand 50+ consumer demographics
  Three steps to successful internet marketing to women over 50:
  - Define your target audience
  - Get to know them
  - Speak to them in a voice they will hear

III. Demographics are too compelling to ignore any longer.
- A. Characteristics of 50+ Consumers
  - Represent 38% of the total U.S. adult population
  - 70 million people strong
  - Control 55% of the discretionary spending in our economy
  - 77% of U.S. assets in their name
  - 80% of U.S. savings dollars in their name
  - Because women live longer than men, the over-50 population is skewed: 52% women versus 48% men.
  - The over-50 consumers have money to spend, but they demand service, information, and value.
  - 68% of online buyers are over 40, and they spend 38 hours a month online, more than any other demographic group does.
- B. "Test Your Assumptions" Quiz About Consumers over 50
  - What percent of baby boomers expect to work at least part-time during retirement? (Answer: 80%)
  - What percentage of people age 50-plus use a computer at home? (Answer: 40%)
  - What percentage of 50-plus computer owners access the Internet? (Answer: 25%)
  - What percentage of people over age 50 feel that these years are the best years of their lives? (Answer: 54%)

IV. Three Steps to Successful Internet Marketing to Women over 50
- A. Define your target audience
  1. G.I. Generation of Women
     - 74+ years old
     - Housekeepers, dependent on husband-providers, traditional roles and values
     - Most do not use computers

2. The Anything-but-Silent Generation
   - 54–73 years old (22 million women)
   - Caught between homemakers and those affected by the liberation of women
   - Many use computers and the Internet
3. The Boomers—a demanding, demanding, demanding generation
   - 40–53 years old (26 million women)
   - Businesses are adjusting to this large market
   - Majority use computers and the Internet

B. Get to know them (Women consumers between 40–73 years old)

1. Characterized by
   - The liberation of women
   - Identities apart from family and children
   - Freedom to choose
2. Seven indicators of the mature market consumer
   - Lifestyle changes (after children leave and retirement)
   - The self regains importance ("Now it's time for me")
   - Spirits are renewed (Take time for yourself—live a richer life)
   - New time needs to be filled (need ideas on how to fill time)
   - Money has new dimensions (no mortgage, no tuition = more spending)
   - Bodies send new messages (want products to help compensate for an aging body)
   - Purchases are viewed with new perspective (released from peer pressure, have more time to comparative-shop)

C. Speak to them in a voice they will hear

1. Talk about what is of interest to them.
   - You can talk about hush-hush topics on the Internet (Example: Menopause)
   - Offer information about how to make the most of aging.
2. Promote the upside of aging
   (Transition: People are all too familiar with the downside of aging. You don't need to remind them. Sell to them with the promise of the second stage of their life!)
   - Vitality (How to live a long, fulfilling life—Example: Club Med)
   - Glow (Everything good will glow: glow of good health, glow of skin)
   - Growth (Personal, financial muscle, and hair growth—not weight)
   - Advertising copy (*First* will replace *new* because people want to experience firsts; use call-to-action words—*begin, start, fast, instantly*)
   - Graphics (Small, tightly spaced type is illegible—**LARGE BOLD TYPE IS OFFENSIVE.**)
   - Models (Use "ageless," 45-year-old models)
   - Use active symbols (Replace golf carts with sail boats, bicycles, hiking boots, walking sticks, carpentry tools, exercise)
3. Avoid ageism in advertising—Insensitivity to aging will replace racism and sexism as fatal offenses.

V. Conclusion

Will it be very much fun to get old? Of course not; but if advertising can make it appear fun to be a teenager or starting out young and single in your twenties, then why not the fifties, sixties, or seventies?

Persuasive Presentation

Looking Through Our Window: The Value of Indian Culture

Marge Anderson, Chief Executive, Mille Lacs Band of Ojibwe

Ms. Anderson's March 5, 1999, presentation on the value of Indian culture reflects many of the strategies for generating interest discussed in Chapter 13, "Generating Interest." It was delivered to the First Friday Club of the Twin Cities and sponsored by the St. Thomas Alumni Association, St. Paul, Minnesota. As you read Ms. Anderson's words, analyze how she

- *Accommodates the audience's attention span by limiting the length of her presentation*
- *Adapts to the audience's level of motivation and listening habits*
- *Enlists the power of language. Look, for example, at her second paragraph and note the simple words, short sentences, active voice, numerous personal pronouns, and repetition of the word* about
- *Tells two stories—one real, one mythic*

Ms. Anderson uses informative speaking strategies to persuade. By explaining "what it means to be Indian," "how my People experience the world," and "the ways in which our culture differs from yours," she takes a peripheral route to persuasion (see the Elaboration Likelihood Model of Persuasion in Chapter 19, "Understanding Persuasion"). Thus, she informs her audience about her culture and helps them understand why they "should care about all this." For example, note how she

- *Relies on her competence, character, and charisma to enhance her credibility*
- *Uses St. Thomas Aquinas and the story of Jacob wrestling with the angel as a theme and a form of mythos*
- *Avoids statistics and a "laundry list"of Indian problems and complaints*
- *Lists ways the Indians have "given back"*
- *Uses mythos as persuasive proof*
- *Acknowledges and respects differences between Indians and non-Indians*

Aaniin. Thank you for inviting me here today. When I was asked to speak to you, I was told you are interested in hearing about the improvements we are making on the Mille Lacs Reservation, and about our investment of casino dollars back into our community through schools, health care facilities, and other services. And I do want to talk to you about these things, because they are tremendously important, and I am very proud of them.

But before I do, I want to take a few minutes to talk to you about something else, something I'm not asked about very often. I want to talk to you about what it means to be Indian. About how my People experience the world. About the fundamental way in which our culture differs from yours. And about why you should care about all this.

The differences between Indians and non-Indians have created a lot of controversy lately. Casinos, treaty rights, tribal sovereignty—these issues have stirred such anger and bitterness.

I believe the accusations against us are made out of ignorance. The vast majority of non-Indians do not understand how my People view the world, what we value, what motivates us.

They do not know these things for one simple reason: they've never heard us talk about them. For many years, the only stories that non-Indians heard about my People came from other non-Indians. As a result, the picture you got of us was fanciful, or distorted, or so shadowy, it hardly existed at all.

It's time for *Indian* voices to tell *Indian* stories.

Now, I'm sure at least a few of you are wondering, "Why do I need to hear these stories? Why should I care about what Indian People think, and feel, and believe?"

I think the most eloquent answer I can give you comes from the namesake of this university, St. Thomas Aquinas. St. Thomas wrote that dialogue is the struggle to learn from each other. This struggle, he said, is like Jacob wrestling the angel—it leaves one wounded and blessed at the same time.

Indian People know this struggle very well. The wounds we've suffered in our dialogue with non-Indians are well-documented; I don't need to give you a laundry list of complaints.

We also know some of the blessings of this struggle. As *American* Indians, we live in two worlds—ours, and yours. In the 500 years since you first came to our lands, we have struggled to learn how to take the best of what your culture has to offer in arts, science, technology and more, and then weave them into the fabric of our traditional ways.

But for non-Indians, the struggle is new. Now that our People have begun to achieve success, now that we are in business and in the headlines, you are starting to wrestle with understanding us.

Your wounds from this struggle are fresh, and the pain might make it hard for you to see beyond them. But if you try, you'll begin to see the blessings as well—the blessings of what a deepened knowledge of Indian culture can bring to you. I'd like to share a few of those blessings with you today.

Earlier I mentioned that there is a fundamental difference between the way Indians and non-Indians experience the world. This difference goes all the way back to the Bible, and Genesis.

In Genesis, the first book of the Old Testament, God creates man in his own image. Then God says, "Be fruitful, multiply, fill the earth and conquer it. Be masters of the fish and the sea, the birds of the heaven, and all living animals on the earth."

Masters. Conquer. Nothing, *nothing* could be further from the way Indian People view the world and our place in it. Here are the words of the great nineteenth century Chief Seattle:

"You are a part of the earth, and the earth is a part of you. You did not weave the web of life, you are merely a strand in it. *Whatever you do to the web, you do to yourself.*"

In our tradition, there is no mastery. There is no conquering. Instead, there is kinship among all creation—humans, animals, birds, plants, even rocks. We are all part of the sacred hoop of the world, and we must all live in harmony with each other if that hoop is to remain unbroken.

When you begin to see the world this way—through Indian eyes—you will begin to understand our view of land, and treaties, very differently. You will begin to understand that when we speak of Father Sun and Mother Earth, these are not new-age catchwords—they are very real terms of respect for very real beings.

And when you understand this, then you will understand that our fight for treaty rights is not just about hunting deer or catching fish. It is about teaching our children to honor Mother Earth and Father Sun. It is about teaching them to respectfully receive the gifts these loving parents offer us in return for the care we give them. And it is about teaching this generation and the generations yet to come about their place in the web of life. Our culture and the fish, our values and the deer, the lessons we learn and the rice we harvest—everything is tied together. You can no more separate one from the other than you can divide a person's spirit from his body.

When you understand how we view the world and our place in it, it's easy to appreciate why our casinos are so important to us. The reason we defend our businesses so fiercely isn't because we want to have something that others don't. The reason is because these businesses allow us to *give back* to others—to our People, our communities, and the Creator.

I'd like to take a minute and mention just a few of the ways we've already given back:

- We've opened new schools, new health care facilities, and new community centers where our children get a better education, where our Elders get better medical care, and where our families can gather to socialize and keep our traditions alive.
- We've built new ceremonial buildings, and new powwow and celebration grounds.
- We've renovated an elderly center, and plan to build three culturally sensitive assisted living facilities for our Elders.
- We've created programs to teach and preserve our language and cultural traditions.
- We've created a small Business Development Program to help Band members start their own businesses.
- We've created more than twenty-eight hundred jobs for Band members, people from other tribes, and non-Indians.
- We've spurred the development of more than one thousand jobs in other local businesses.
- We've generated more than fifty million dollars in federal taxes, and more than fifteen million dollars in state taxes through wages paid to employees.
- And we've given back more than two million dollars in charitable donations.

The list goes on and on. But rather than flood you with more numbers, I'll tell you a story that sums up how my People view business through the lens of our traditional values.

Last year, the Woodlands National Bank, which is owned and operated by the Mille Lacs Band, was approached by the city of Onamia and asked to forgive a mortgage on a building in the downtown area. The building had been abandoned and was an eyesore on Main Street. The city planned to renovate and sell the building, and return it to the tax rolls.

Although the Band would lose money by forgiving the mortgage, our business leaders could see the wisdom in improving the community. The opportunity to help our neighbors was an opportunity to strengthen the web of life. So we forgave the mortgage.

Now, I know this is not a decision everyone would agree with. Some people feel that in business, you have to look out for number one. But my People feel that in business—and in life—you have to look out for *every* one.

And this, I believe, is one of the blessings that Indian culture has to offer you and other non-Indians. We have a different perspective on so many things, from caring for the environment, to healing the body, mind and soul.

But if our culture disappears, if the Indian ways are swallowed up by the dominant American culture, no one will be able to learn from them. Not Indian children. Not your children. No one. All that knowledge, all that wisdom, will be lost forever.

The struggle of dialogue will be over. Yes, there will be no more wounds. But there will also be no more blessings.

There is still so much we have to learn from each other, and we have already wasted so much time. Our world grows smaller every day. And every day, more of our unsettling, surprising, wonderful differences vanish. And when that happens, part of each of us vanishes, too.

I'd like to end with one of my favorite stories. It's a funny little story about Indians and non-Indians, but its message is serious: you can see something differently if you are willing to learn from those around you.

This is the story: Years ago, white settlers came to this area and built the first European-style homes. When Indian People walked by these homes and saw see-through things in the walls, they looked through them to see what the strangers inside were doing. The settlers were shocked, but it makes sense when you think about it: windows are made to be looked through from both sides.

Since then, my People have spent many years looking at the world through your window. I hope today I've given you a reason to look at it through ours.

Mii gwetch.

Source: Reprinted with the permissions of Chief Executive Marge Anderson and the Mille Lacs Band of Ojibwe Indians.

Persuasive Presentation

Drunk, Dangerous, and Deadly

Herb Simpson, Ph.D., President and CEO, Traffic Injury Research Foundation

Dr. Simpson's persuasive presentation, delivered to the American Legislative Exchange Council's annual meeting on August 12, 1999, resembles some of the better student presentations we have heard about drunk driving. It is well organized in a Problem-Cause-Solution organizational format. Part of what makes Dr. Simpson's talk different, however, is that he does not document every piece of supporting material he uses. As president and CEO of the Traffic Injury Research Foundation, he relies on his authority and expertise to make claims about the problem, its causes, and potential solutions. The presentation is heavy with statistics, but that is what a research foundation provides to the public and policy makers. Yet by including four brief stories, he puts a human face on the numbers. His language is direct, and his presentation of statistics is clear. Dr. Simpson openly acknowledges that some of his foundation's research has been supported by grants from the Anheuser-Busch Corporation. His introduction begins with a blunt statement of the problem rather than leading up to his Central Idea with an attention-getting device. His conclusion is just as blunt.

Despite the impressive gains that have been made in the fight against drunk driving, a dangerous minority, called the Hard Core, keeps bucking the trend. This group repeatedly takes to the road after consuming large amounts of alcohol, placing themselves and others at very great risk. They often have blood alcohol concentrations (BACS) that are double or triple the legal limit, causing a majority of drinking and driving deaths.

As a result, they continue to make headlines in the most regrettable ways: A Florida man was convicted of driving under the influence (DUI) manslaughter in the deaths of five people. He had a BAC of .25—a level that is two and a half times the legal limit in most states. His license had been suspended and even revoked in three states for prior drinking and driving offenses.

Or consider the case of a North Carolina man who was recently convicted of second-degree murder in the death of a young woman who was a sophomore in college and also the mother of a two-year-old. He had a BAC of .26 and had two previous drunk driving convictions.

In another tragic case, a thirty-one-year old Tennessee woman and her unborn child were killed when a drunk driver ran his truck up on a curb, pinning the woman against a light pole. The man driving the car had a BAC of .28. His license had already been revoked because of two previous drunk driving convictions.

Unfortunately, these are not rare, isolated events but are all too familiar. However, it is only in recent years that hard core drinking drivers have received serious attention by policy makers. Contemporary focus on the problem began in the U.S. at the beginning of this decade with the publication of what has become an internationally acclaimed study entitled *The Hard Core Drinking Driver.* Conducted by the Traffic Injury Research Foundation (TIRF), under a grant from Anheuser-Busch, this research documented the extent of the problems caused by this group and identified it as a target for special attention by policy leaders.

Several years later, TIRF, again with support from Anheuser-Busch, provided a comprehensive review of effective and promising programs and policies for dealing with hard core drinking drivers. This study urged lawmakers to better enforce laws already on the books and use proven methods to deal with these troublemakers.

Since then, many organizations, both public and private, have joined the fight in dealing with these extremely dangerous drivers. Recognition is growing, not only of the severe threat they pose to public safety but also of the challenge they present. This is underscored by the fact that they have numerous convictions. This is a double-edged sword from a public policy standpoint. The system is obviously having some success because hard core drinking drivers keep getting caught; at the same time, the system is failing because the same offenders are frequently caught again and again. Obviously, they are not receptive to traditional appeals and are even resistant to changing their behavior in the face of usual sanctions. New approaches are needed.

In part, the challenge presented by this group lies in identifying them. Studies have shown that the hard core represents less than one percent of all night-time drivers. Being such a small group, it can be very challenging to target them through traditional enforcement.

However, this small group is a significant threat, causing as many as 65 percent of the serious collisions. The major reason for this is that they drive with very high BACS, which has a profound effect on their risk of being in a serious traffic accident. A driver with a BAC of .20 or higher is 460 times more likely to be involved in a fatal crash than a driver with no alcohol, or very low amounts of alcohol, in his or her system.

But as indicated earlier, the hard core does fall into the arms of the criminal justice system with great regularity, so it is imperative that the most be made of these opportunities to address them with effective policies. And, research shows that there are very real limits to the ability of stiffer monetary fines and longer jail sentences to induce changes in their drinking and driving behavior. Fortunately, there is an emerging consensus that the strategic application of a diversity of proven measures can have a significant positive impact. And, there are proven measures at our disposal. Let me briefly describe a few of them.

At the top of the list is rehabilitation. Because so many of the hard core are alcohol abusers or dependent—up to 75 percent of second time offenders—there is a need to get offenders into treatment. To ensure that officials prescribe the most appropriate treatment for offenders, a reliable screening and assessment technique should be used to identify the nature and severity of their problems.

And, treatment works. It has a significant impact on re-offense rates and alcohol-related crashes. But a note of caution is warranted. Because it is a long-term process and by no means perfectly effective, treatment should be provided in combination with other sanctions and not used as a substitute for, or a means to circumvent them.

One of those other sanctions is license suspension. It has been one of the most popular and effective sanctions for drunk driving. However, many offenders are not deterred by the loss of their license; up to 75 percent drive anyway. And, some continue to drive and drink. This behavior can be remarkably persistent. For example, a motorist in New York City was recently stopped making an illegal U-turn. During this, the police discovered the driver was the "phantom motorist" whose license had been suspended 633 times since 1990. This motorist had eluded capture for four years, and it took the computer nearly two hours to generate a written report of the motorist's driving record.

For such hard core offenders, the next logical step is to deny them access to their vehicle, or to ensure that if they do drive, they have not been drinking. Actions against the vehicle have been gaining popularity in the past few years.

In general, these vehicle-based measures are designed to limit the mobility of the offender. At one end of the spectrum is the alcohol-ignition interlock, a device that still allows offenders and their family to use the vehicle but only if they are sober. At the other end of the spectrum is vehicle immobilization, which denies the offender and family access to the vehicle.

The ignition interlock is a small breath test device installed in the vehicle to measure the driver's BAC. The driver is required to provide a zero or low-BAC breath sample to operate the vehicle. Technological improvements in these devices over the past several decades prevent virtually all of the known ways to "fool" the system.

Ignition interlocks work. Evaluation studies have consistently demonstrated that interlocks are effective—the re-arrest rate among offenders with an interlock device has been found to be as much as 75 percent lower than among those without the device.

Obviously, with an interlock on the vehicle, family members and the offender can drive. But some vehicle sanctions allow only the family to use it, not the offender. These typically involve special license plates, such as blaze-orange or zebra-striped, primarily to alert police to the fact that this is the vehicle of a convicted drunk driver. Ideally, the legislation that permits the use of these plates empowers the police to stop such a vehicle and verify that the driver is not the offender.

The most severe form of vehicle-based sanctions includes immobilization or impoundment, and forfeiture. Depending on the jurisdiction, the vehicle can be seized by the police if the driver is under suspension for any reason, or for an alcohol-related offense, or is driving under the influence of alcohol. The vehicle is then either placed in a secure compound for a period of usually one or two months or is immobilized with a device such as a "club" on the steering wheel, often in the offender's driveway.

There is solid evidence that these programs have a significant impact on the prevalence of driving while under suspension as well as on alcohol-related collisions. In Canada, a federally funded study by TIRF showed there was a 12 percent decrease in drunk driving fatalities when vehicles were impounded, along with a 50 percent decrease in DUI offenses. Most importantly, there was a 27 percent decrease in repeat driving while suspended offenses, a category that many hard core drinking drivers all fall into. Evaluations of programs in California, Ohio and Minnesota have also produced positive results.

The toughest vehicle sanction program was recently introduced in New York City. The ordinance began making headlines because the vehicle of anyone stopped for drunk driving, most of whom do not fit the hard core drunk driving descriptions, was seized and forfeited. This very aggressive approach has not yet been evaluated, but the attention the law has gathered, from both fans and critics, underscores an important lesson we should not forget in dealing with this problem. Too frequently countermeasures are embraced as the silver bullet, magic elixir or panacea for the problem. If we have learned one lesson in the long struggle to deal with this problem, it is that there is no single solution. It requires a diversity of complementary measures. License suspension became for many "the solution" of the 80s; hopefully, vehicle forfeiture will not become "the solution" of the 90s. Both work but they are only part of the puzzle.

Drinking and driving declined dramatically during the 1980s and has continued to show some, albeit more modest, progress in the 90s. Many have argued that we've already achieved the easy gains because responsible, social drinkers have gotten the message. Hard core drinking drivers have not. Many do not care about the threat they pose to others, or even about being punished. They are the single largest challenge in the continuing battle against impaired driving and must be a priority if further meaningful progress is to be made. A key to that progress is the widespread use of effective measures for dealing with hard core drinking drivers.

Source: Reprinted by permission of Dr. Herb Simpson, President and CEO, Traffic Injury Research Foundation

Special Presentation

Commencement Address

Vivian Hobbs, Attorney

Vivian Hobbs, an alumnus of Prince George's Community College, was invited to be the 1991 Commencement Speaker. In 1972, at the age of seventeen, Ms. Hobbs was involved in an automobile accident that left her paralyzed from the neck down. Her doctors told her that she would never be able to move, talk, or breathe without a respirator. Since this pronouncement, Vivian Hobbs became a prominent Washington attorney and partner in the law firm of Arnold and Porter and raised three children. She passed away in 1997 from complications related to her disability.

Ms. Hobbs's commencement address was a moving testament to her college. Not only was she a celebrated alumnus, but her presentation also earned her enormous credibility with the audience. Her competence was unquestioned, her character was unassailable, and her quiet, heartfelt delivery bestowed on her an inspiring form of charisma.

Good evening. My name is Vivian Hobbs. I can't begin to tell you how honored I am to have been asked to speak at this commencement ceremony.

Prince George's Community College has played a very special part in my life and holds a very special place in my heart.

I was in an automobile accident just after high school, which left me in a wheelchair. I was trying to deal with that, a new marriage, and other personal and financial problems, not the least of which was an uncertainty about what I could do, about the extent of my own potential.

Even then, in 1975, Prince George's Community College took a real leadership position in serving the community and meeting the special needs of each student. In my case, this did not stop with meeting the basic obligation of making the campus accessible to a wheelchair. Professors helped me study and gave me oral exams because I cannot use my hands to write. New rules and procedures were developed to help me get through lab courses. Many other adjustments were made to help me succeed.

But, most of all, I received support and encouragement from every staff member, every member of the administration, and every one of my professors. They made me feel that my problems were their problems—that their mission was to help me and all of this college's students to realize our full potential, whatever the obstacles.

For example, my biology professor spent a great deal of time and patience helping me to get slides just right under a microscope so that I could see various organisms and processes. My chemistry professor showed equal patience in helping me through chemistry lab experiments. My history professor allowed me to tape, rather than to write, my exams. This required him to spend much longer grading my examinations, because it takes longer to listen to a tape than to read a written exam. Other professors let me take exams orally, instead of having to write them. And some professors even allowed me to take my exams home on an honor system.

Ultimately, I left Prince George's Community College with a renewed confidence in myself, with a stronger sense of purpose, and with a greater awareness of my own potential. This has helped hold me together as I have gone on in life through less supportive institutions and tougher problems, both personal and in my career.

I finished my Bachelor of Science degree at the University of Maryland. I went to Georgetown Law Center, and I'm now a partner at the biggest and, I think, the best law firm in Washington, D.C.

Prince George's Community College was the first and most important step in my career and in my adult life. I succeeded largely because of the support and help I got here. This college provides all kinds of special help and support for all kinds of special problems. So much so, that it's not even special. Here it's just routine. Child care for students who are parents, financial aid to those who need it, evening and weekend classes for those who work, developmental classes for those who may not have been given the academic background they need, counseling and career planning as well as tutorial programs for those who need extra guidance and assistance.

I feel that I have a lot in common with many of you. Many of you have had to struggle with other problems and obligations while earning your degree. Many of you have families—spouses or children—who take up a lot of your time. You may have had to work while going to college to support yourself or your family. Many of you have had to go to school at night after working long, hard days, or have had to come on weekends or give up time with your family. You may have found it difficult to afford the time, money, and energy that has been required of you.

Some of you have started your college careers with doubts about the extent of your own potential. Like me, many of you have come from families where no one else has had a college degree.

But you hung in there. You kept working and learning and growing, because you knew you deserved the better life that this degree can give. Some of you will leave here for careers in nursing, computer technology, accounting, business, education, engineering, law enforcement or other professions or careers. Others will transfer to four-year colleges or universities. Still others will leave the job market to raise families. But, wherever you choose to go from here, you will take a new, stronger sense of your own value and potential.

Through your work and success at Prince George's Community College, you have set yourselves apart from the vast majority of people who just didn't have the right stuff to get this far. Many of you have done this despite tremendous obstacles and at great personal cost. You have proved that you do have the right stuff. From here, you can, and will go on to do anything, to make and live your lives according to your own dreams.

I hope that you will remember Prince George's Community College. You will go on to other endeavors and higher achievements. Many of you will go on to earn degrees at more prestigious colleges and universities. But Prince George's Community College is the place where we all got our start—the place where we changed our lives and goals forever.

I am very honored and humbled to have been asked to share this celebration with each of you, in this new beginning. And I do honor each and every one of you. Thank you.

Special Presentation

Eulogy in Honor of Mark Bingham

Senator John McCain
San Francisco, CA, September 22, 2001

On September 22, 2001, Senator John McCain delivered a eulogy honoring Mark Bingham, one of the brave passengers on United Flight 93 who "grasped the gravity of the moment, understood the threat, and decided to fight back at the cost of their lives."

The eulogy begins with a reference to Bingham's personal support for McCain during the recent presidential campaign. Although this reference may seem self-serving, it allows McCain to establish his personal connection to Bingham. He also admits that his fixation with winning or losing distracted him from giving more attention to those who put their trust in his candidacy.

McCain organizes the eulogy by moving from his personal connection to Mark Bingham to praising the courageous passengers on United Flight 93 who gave their lives to prevent further injury to others—including McCain, who was working in the plane's designated target—the U.S. Capitol. Again, McCain links himself directly to the hero he eulogizes.

In keeping with his plain-spoken style, John McCain's language is clear, simple, and appropriate. Most sentences are direct and short. He frequently repeats short phrases to emphasize an idea or communicate an emotion (e.g., "I wish I had," "We will prevail"). The pronoun we *helps McCain communicate shared emotions while* I *emphasizes his connections—particularly as a Vietnam War hero—to the brave passengers on Flight 93 and to the sacrifice of New York's emergency personnel. Words such as* honor, God, *and* love *are frequently used to pay tribute to a fallen hero and to invoke God's love as a source of strength and comfort to the family and friends of Mark Bingham.*

I didn't know Mark Bingham. We met once briefly during my presidential campaign, yet I cannot say that I knew him well. But I wish I had. I wish I had. You meet a lot of people when you run for president. I was fortunate to have had the support of many Americans who were, until then, strangers to me. And I regret to say, that like most candidates, I was preoccupied with winning or losing. I had not thought as much as I should have about what an honor, what an extraordinary honor it was to have so many citizens of the greatest nation on earth place their trust in me, and use our campaign as an expression of their own patriotism. They were the best thing about our campaign, not me. Had I been successful, my greatest challenge would have been to prove myself worthy of the faith of so many good people.

I love my country, and I take pride in serving her. But I cannot say that I love her more or as well as Mark Bingham did, or the other heroes on United Flight 93 who gave their lives to prevent our enemies from inflicting an even greater injury on our country. It has been my fate to witness great courage and sacrifice for America's sake, but none greater than the selfless sacrifice of Mark Bingham and those good men who grasped the gravity of the moment, understood the threat, and decided to fight back at the cost of their lives.

In the Gospel of John it is written that "Greater love hath no man than this, that a man lay down his life for his friends." Such was the love that Mark and his comrades possessed, as they laid down their lives for others. A love so sublime that only God's love surpasses it.

It is now believed that the terrorists on Flight 93 intended to crash the airplane into the United States Capitol where I work, the great house of democracy where I was that day. It is very possible that I would have been in the building, with a great many other people, when that fateful, terrible moment occurred, and a beautiful symbol of our freedom was destroyed along with hundreds if not thousands of lives. I may very well owe my life to Mark and the others who summoned the enormous courage and love necessary to deny those depraved, hateful men their terrible triumph. Such a debt you incur for life.

I will try very hard, very hard, to discharge my public duties in a manner that honors their memory. All public servants are now solemnly obliged to do all we can to help this great nation remain worthy of the sacrifice of New York City firefighters, police officers, emergency medical people, and worthy of the sacrifice of the brave passengers on Flight 93.

No American living today will ever forget what happened on September 11, 2001. That day was the moment when the hinge of history swung toward a new era not only in the affairs of this nation, but also in the affairs of all humanity. The opening chapter of this new history is tinged with great sadness and uncertainty. But as we begin, please take strength from the example of the American we honor today, and those who perished to save others in New York, Washington, and Pennsylvania. The days ahead will be difficult, and we will know more loss and sorrow. But we will prevail. We will prevail.

Pay no heed to the voices of the poor, misguided souls, in this country and overseas, who claim that America brought these atrocities on herself. They are deluded, and their hearts are cramped by hatred and fear. Our respect for man's God-given rights to life, liberty, and the pursuit of happiness assures us of victory even as it made us a target for the enemies of freedom who mistake hate and depravity for power. The losses we have suffered are grave, and must not be forgotten. But we should all take pride and unyielding resolve from the knowledge that we were attacked because we were good, and good we will remain as we vanquish the evil that preys upon us.

I never knew Mark Bingham. But I wish I had. I know he was a good son and friend, a good rugby player, a good American, and an extraordinary human being. He supported me, and his support now ranks among the greatest honors of my life. I wish I had known before September 11 just how great an honor his trust in me was. I wish I could have thanked him for it more profusely than time and circumstances allowed. But I know it now. And I thank him with the only means I possess, by being as good an American as he was.

America will overcome these atrocities. We will prevail over our enemies. We will right this terrible injustice. And when we do, let us claim it as a tribute to our liberty, and to Mark Bingham and all those who died to defend it.

To all of you who loved Mark, and were loved by him, he will never be so far from you that you cannot feel his love. As our faith informs us, you will see him again, when our loving God reunites us all with the loved ones who preceded us. Take care of each other until then, as he would want you to. May God bless Mark. And may God bless us all.

Special Presentation

Speech at "Ground Zero"

President George W. Bush
September 14, 2001

On September 14, 2001, President Bush took a short helicopter tour of the devastation at "Ground Zero" and then walked the site. He talked with volunteers, firefighters, and police officers. Hearing chants of "U.S.A.! U.S.A.!" he grabbed a bullhorn, climbed to the top of a pile of rubble, and put his arm around a firefighter and delivered a short but highly successful ten-sentence speech. As we note in the Real World, Real Speakers feature in Chapter 7, "Logistics and Occasion," logistics played a critical role in Bush's presentation, particularly when a place such as 'Ground Zero' speaks more loudly than words.

CROWD: U.S.A.! U.S.A.!

BUSH: Thank you all. I want you all to know—

QUESTION FROM CROWD: Can't hear you.

BUSH: I can't talk any louder. (Laughter) I want you all to know that America today—that America today is on bended knee in prayer for the people whose lives were lost here, for the workers who work here, for the families who mourn. This nation stands with the good people of New York City, and New Jersey, and Connecticut as we mourn the loss of thousands of our citizens.

QUESTION FROM CROWD: I can't hear you.

BUSH: I can hear you. (Applause) I can hear you. The rest of the world hears you. (Applause) And the people who knocked these buildings down will hear all of us soon. (Applause)

CROWD: U.S.A.! U.S.A.!

BUSH: The nation sends its love and compassion to everybody who is here. Thank you for your hard work. Thank you for making the nation proud. And may God bless America. (Applause)

CROWD: U.S.A.! U.S.A.! (Bush waives a small American flag to audience cheering and applause.)

GLOSSARY

Abstract word A word referring to an idea or concept that *cannot* be observed or touched. (268)

Accent The sound of one language imposed on another. (347)

Acoustics The science of sound; the sound characteristics of the room in which you will be speaking. (150)

Active voice The subject of a sentence performs the action, as in "Bill read the book." (279)

Alliteration A figure of speech in which a series of words all begin with the same sound. (281)

Analogy A comparison that identifies similarities in things that are alike or similar in function. (172)

Analytical listening A type of listening that focuses on evaluating whether a message is reasonable and/or whether an argument is valid. (31)

Antithesis A statement that juxtaposes two contrasting ideas to create a kind of balance between parallel words or phrases. (284)

Appreciative listening A type of listening that focuses on how well a person expresses an idea or opinion. (31)

Argument A claim supported by evidence and reasons for accepting it. (455)

Articulation How clearly you make the sounds in the words of a language; your diction. (345)

Attacking the person fallacy A fallacy that involves criticizing or attacking a person instead of the substance of the argument. (472)

Attention span The amount of time audience members can be attentive to sensory stimulation. (294)

Audience analysis The ability to understand, respect, and adapt to audience members before and during a presentation. (101)

Audience attitudes A measure of whether audience members agree or disagree with a speaker's purpose statement as well as how strongly they agree or disagree. (107)

Backing The component of the Toulmin model of an argument that provides support for an argument's warrant. (457)

Bandwagon fallacy The fallacy of making an appeal to popularity. (473)

Basic terms Words that immediately come to mind when you see an object, such as *car* or *van*, instead of more abstract words such as *vehicle*. (268)

Begging the question fallacy The fallacy of making an unproven assertion in an argument that is assumed to be true. (474)

Better Plan organizational pattern An organizational pattern that presents a plan to improve a situation or help to solve a problem, while acknowledging that a total solution may not be possible. (466)

Biased Having an opinion so slanted or self-serving that it may not be objective or fair. (174)

Boolean search A research technique that helps you focus and narrow a computerized search by using terms such as AND, OR, and NOT as well as other search-limiting techniques. (181)

Brainstorming A technique that encourages group members to generate as many ideas as possible in a nonevaluative atmosphere. (515)

Briefing A type of informative presentation in which a speaker briefly reports about the status of an upcoming or past event or project in a business or organizational setting. (416)

Campaign A series of persuasive messages designed to achieve a specific social, political, or commercial goal. (444)

Captivating language Language that attracts and holds an audience attention and interest by virtue of its beauty or brilliance. (281)

Causes and effects arrangement An organizational format that identifies a situation, object, or behavior and then describes the results of that situation, object, or behavior. (202)

Central idea A sentence or thesis statement that summarizes the key points you want your *audience* to understand. (198)

Channel The medium in which a message exists; using the senses of sight, hearing, touch, taste, and/or smell as a medium for transferring messages. (15)

Character A component of speaker credibility that relates to a speaker's honesty and goodwill. (130)

Charisma A speaker's level of energy, enthusiasm, vigor, and/or commitment; a speaker's dynamic qualities. (132)

Chunking The process of sorting your ideas and supporting material for a presentation into unique categories or "chunks." (215)

Claim The conclusion or position a speaker is advocating. (43, 455)

Claims of conjecture Claims that predict whether something will or will not happen in the future. (43)

Claims of fact Claims that something is true, that an event occurred, that a cause can be identified, or that a theory accurately explains a phenomenon. (43)

Claims of policy Claims recommending a particular course of action. (44)

Claims of value Claims asserting that something is worthwhile; good or bad; right or wrong; or best, average, or worst. (43)

Cliché A trite and overused expression that has lost its freshness. (280)

Closed-ended question A question that forces respondents to choose an answer from a limited list. (118)

Cognitive restructuring A presentation-anxiety therapy that attempts to change the way a speaker thinks about speaking, so that positive thinking replaces worrisome, irrational, nonproductive thoughts. (68)

Collaborative presentation technology Technology that enables group members to project an idea or graphic onto a common surface so that both face-to-face and virtual participants can interact with one another about a presentation or written document. (523)

Common ground A belief, attitude, or experience shared by the speaker and the audience; a "place" where both the speaker and the audience can stand without disagreeing. (249, 432)

Communication model An illustration that shows the interactions of essential components of the communication process in order to clarify relevant relationships and to help predict outcomes. (11)

Communication transaction Communication in which speakers and listeners exchange messages in order to share meaning. (12)

Comparison-contrast arrangement An organizational format that uses similarities and differences between two things or concepts as a method of arranging ideas. (204)

Competence A component of speaker credibility that relates to the speaker's expertise and abilities. (130)

Comprehension questions Questions asked by a speaker during a presentation as a way of involving the audience, assessing their understanding, and maintaining control of the situation. (124)

Comprehensive listening A type of listening that focuses on accurately understanding spoken and nonverbal messages. (30)

Concrete word A word referring to specific things that can be perceived by our senses. (268)

Connectives Devices that link key points, remind the audience of the speaker's direction, and preview or summarize major sections of a presentation. (226)

Connotation The emotional responses and personal thoughts connected to the meaning of a word. (268)

Context The surrounding environment—both physical and psychological—that can affect every aspect of a presentation. (12)

Creativity The process of searching for, separating, and connecting thoughts as a way of combining previously unrelated elements. (231)

Critical thinking The particular kind of thinking we use to analyze what we read, see, or hear in order to arrive at a justified conclusion or decision. (41)

Culture The common characteristics and collective perceptions that distinguish one group of people from another. (19)

Decoding The process of comprehending a message as influenced by audience characteristics, motives, interests, knowledge, attitudes, and learning styles. (12)

Deductive logic Proving a persuasive argument by moving from accepted general premises to a specific conclusion. (436)

Definition A statement that explains or clarifies the meaning of a word, phrase, or concept. (171)

Demographic information Information about audience characteristics such as age, gender, marital status, race, religion, place of residence, ethnicity, occupation, education, and income. (103)

Denotation The objective, dictionary-based meaning of a word. (267)

Description A statement that creates a mental image of a scene, concept, event, object, or person. (172)

Diagrams Presentation aids that show how things work or explain relationships or processes. (381)

Dialect Regional and cultural differences within the same language. (348)

Documentation The practice of citing the sources of supporting material used in a presentation. (183)

Elaboration Likelihood Model of Persuasion A model stating that persuasive proof should be selected based on considering "two routes to persuasion." The central route requires strong, logical arguments; the peripheral route depends on simpler cues based on emotional, personal, and narrative proofs. (439)

Electronic whiteboard Computer-based projection that allows group members to work on the same document or drawing simultaneously. (524)

Emotional proof Proof that appeals to the audience's emotions and feelings. (437)

Empathic listening A type of listening that focuses on understanding and identifying with a person's situation, feelings, or motives. (31)

Encoding The process of making decisions about how to create and send a message. (12)

Entertainment speaking A presentation designed to amuse, interest, divert, or "warm up" an audience. (91)

Ethics A speaker's moral values and personal principles of correct conduct. (137)

Ethnocentrism A belief that your culture is superior to others. (21)

Ethos Aristotle's term for personal proof—proof that relies on the competence, character, and charisma of a speaker. See personal proof. (137, 438)

Eulogy A tribute that praises the dead. (487)

Evidence The information, data, or audience beliefs used by a speaker to support or to prove the claim of an argument. (440, 456)

Example A reference to a specific case or instance; examples are often items, facts, or instances that represent an entire group. (172)

Exclusionary language Language that uses biased terms that reinforce stereotypes or belittle other people. (276)

Explanatory communication Communication that enhances understanding of a topic the audience may be aware of but does not fully comprehend. (410)

Expressiveness The vitality, variety, and sincerity that a speaker puts into the delivery of a presentation. (296)

Extemporaneous speaking A well-prepared presentation delivered from an outline or set of notes. (321)

Eye contact The establishment and maintenance of visual contact with individual members of your audience. (354)

Eye scan A method for establishing maximum eye contact while using detailed notes or a manuscript form of delivery. (356)

Fact A verifiable observation, experience, or event. (170)
Fallacy An invalid argument or misleading statement that deceives an audience. (471)
Faulty cause fallacy The fallacy of making an erroneous claim that something was caused by an event or action that preceded it. (472)
Feedback The verbal and nonverbal responses made by audience members as they listen to and interpret the meaning of a presentation. (15)
Fidget Small, repetitive body movements that function as physical filler phrases. (359)
Figurative analogy A way to compare two things that are not in the same class but that have basic attributes in common. (205)
Fluency The ability to speak smoothly without tripping over words or pausing at awkward moments. (344)
Formal outline A comprehensive written framework for a presentation that follows established conventions of content and style. (221)
Forgetting curve The tendency for audience members to forget a large portion of what they have seen or heard in a presentation (295).
Forum A public meeting in which audience members express their concerns and address questions to public officials and/or experts. (509)
Framing An organizational process in presentation speaking that is similar to the way a picture selects and organizes critical content. (195)
Fundamental Interpersonal Relationship Orientation (FIRO) Theory A theory containing three interpersonal needs (inclusion, control, and openness) that can be addressed in a persuasive presentation. (447)

Gesture A body movement, usually made by the hands and arms, that conveys or reinforces a thought, an intention, or an emotion. (358)
Gobbledygook Language that is unclear or uses jargon. (278)
Golden listening rule The principle that you should listen to others as you would have them listen to you. (34)
Governance group A group that makes policy decisions in public meetings. (509)
Graphs Presentation aids that show comparisons and trends. (379)

Hasty generalization fallacy The fallacy of drawing a conclusion based on relevant but insufficient evidence or examples. (473)
Heuristics Shortcut decision-making rules without carefully scrutinizing the quality of an argument. (441)
Hidden agenda An individual group member's private motives and goals that may conflict with and affect the achievement of a group's common goal. (522)
Humorous presentation A presentation in which the speaker's primary purpose is to entertain the audience or to use humor as a means of making a serious point. (491)

Identification A persuasive strategy in which the speaker encourages audience members to see how they all share common attitudes, ideas, feelings, values, and experiences. (433)
Immediacy Perceptions of physical and psychological closeness to a speaker including both verbal and nonverbal behaviors that, taken together, enhance learning and motivation. (132, 312)
Impromptu speaking A presentation for which the speaker has little or no time to prepare or practice. (320, 499)
Inductive logic The process of making a persuasive argument by moving from specific instances to a general conclusion. (437)
Inference The process of drawing a conclusion based on claims of fact. (44)
Inflection A change of pitch, within a word or group of words, that adds emphasis or meaning. (343)
Informative presentation A presentation designed to instruct, enlighten, explain, share, demonstrate, clarify, remind, or interpret. (91, 407)
Informatory communication Communication that creates awareness of the latest information about a topic; for example, news reports. (410)
Inoculation A persuasive strategy in which a speaker presents the opposition's argument and then refutes it in order to build audience resistance to counterpersuasion. (434)
Internal preview A connective phrase or sentence that introduces the key points of a presentation or tells an audience what will be covered in what order. (228)
Internal summary A connective phrase or sentence that concludes a section of a presentation, summarizes major ideas, or reinforces important ideas and information. (228)
Introducing a presenter A presentation in which a speaker provides information about a presenter who is about to speak, as a means of motivating the audience to listen. (481)

Judgment A statement that expresses your opinion or makes an evaluation. (170)
Jargon The specialized or technical language of a profession or homogenous group. (278)

Key points The most important issues or the main ideas that you want your audience to understand and remember during and after your presentation. (196)

Language A system of arbitrary signs and symbols used to communicate thoughts and feelings. (265)
Language intensity The degree to which your language deviates from bland, neutral terms. (280)
Learning styles The characteristic strengths and preferences exemplified in the way you take in and process information. (110)
Lectern A stand that serves as a support for the notes of a speaker. (153)
Listening The ability to understand, analyze, respect, and respond to the meaning of another person's spoken and nonverbal messages. (29)
Logical proof Proof that appeals to the intellect; proof appealing to the rational side of an audience. (436)
Logistics The strategic planning, arranging, and use of people, facilities, time, and materials relevant to a presentation. (147)

Logos Aristotle's term for logical proof. See logical proof. (436)

Maintenance roles Group roles that affect how members get along with each other while pursuing a shared goal. (514)

Manuscript speaking A presentation written out in advance and delivered word for word. (322)

Maps Presentation aids that show *where* or translate data into spatial patterns. (382)

Maslow's Hierarchy of Needs A specific sequence of needs (physiological, safety, social, esteem, and self-actualization) that can be addressed in a persuasive presentation. (447)

Mediated presentation A presentation that relies on electronic media to support or convey the speaker's message. (363)

Memorized presentation A presentation for which the speaker memorizes a manuscript and then delivers it without notes. (324)

Memory aids arrangement An organizational format that uses easily remembered letters of the alphabet, words, or common phrases to arrange the key points of a presentation. (205)

Message The content of a presentation; the way a speaker's purpose is transformed into words and action. (12)

Meta search engine A search engine that builds listings by tapping several basic search engines all at once. (181)

Metaphor A figure of speech that makes a comparison between two things or ideas without directly connecting the resemblances with words such as "like" or "as." (282)

Microculture Members of a culture that coexist within mainstream society. (19)

Mind mapping An organizational technique for discovering the key points and connections among the ideas in a presentation without forcing a predetermined organizational scheme on them. (217)

Minutes The written record of a group's discussions and decisions that occur during a meeting. (520)

Monotone A voice with very little variety in pitch. (343)

Monroe's Motivated Sequence Alan Monroe's five-step sequence (attention, need, satisfaction, visualization, and action) for motivating an audience to change its opinions or behavior. (467)

Mythos A term used to denote various forms of narrative proof. See narrative proof. (438)

Narrative The process, art, and techniques of storytelling. (303)

Narrative proof Proof that appeals to the values, faith, and feelings that make up our social character and is most often expressed through traditional stories, sayings, and symbols. (438)

Noise In the communication process, anything that inhibits a message from reaching and being understood by its listeners as it was originally intended. (16)

Nonverbal communication Messages we send using means other than words. (36)

Occasion The reason why an audience assembles at a particular place and time. (154)

Open-ended question A question that allows respondents to provide specific or detailed answers. (118)

Optimum pitch The natural pitch at which you speak most easily and expressively. (342)

Organization A strategy or method that determines what to include in a presentation as well as how to arrange the ideas and information in an effective way. (194)

Organization tree An organizational technique that puts ideas and information in a hierarchical order, shows whether there is adequate supporting material for each key point, and ensures that key points are directly related to the central idea. (220)

Overcoming Objections organizational pattern An organizational pattern in which each key point attempts to overcome an objection or to refute an argument that prevents the audience from accepting the speaker's position. (467)

Panel discussion A group discussion in which participants interact with one another on a common topic for the benefit of an audience. (508)

Paraphrasing Rephrasing what a person has said as a way of indicating that the listener has understood what the speaker means and feels. (37)

Passive voice The subject of a sentence receives the action, as in "The book was read by Bill." (279)

Pathos Aristotle's term for emotional proof. See emotional proof. (437)

Performance The effective vocal and physical delivery of a presentation. (319)

Personal proof Proof that relies on the credibility and attractiveness of the speaker. (438)

Personification The process of providing a human example of an abstract concept or complex idea. (285)

Persuasion Communication that seeks to change audience attitudes or behavior by using logical, emotional, personal, and/or narrative appeals. (429)

Persuasive presentation A presentation designed to change or to influence an audience's opinion and/or behavior. (91)

Persuasive Stories organizational pattern An organizational pattern using stories to illustrate each key point of the central idea of a persuasive presentation. (469)

Pie charts Presentation aids that show *how much* or show proportions in relation to a whole or to comparable items. (377)

Pitch How high or low your voice sounds. (342)

Plagiarism Using or passing off the ideas or writing of another person as your own. (185)

Podium An elevated platform on which a speaker stands. (153)

Powerful speech Speech consisting of simple and direct words that express your confidence, as opposed to powerless speech that conveys uncertainty. (274)

Prejudices Negative attitudes toward a cultural group as a whole, based on little or no direct experience with that group. (21)

Preliminary outline An initial planning outline that puts the major pieces of a message in a clear and logical order. (213)

Presentation aids Mediated ways of sharing key ideas and supporting material during a presentation. (373)

Presentation anxiety A speaker's individual level of fear or anxiety associated with either real or anticipated communication to a group of people or an audience. (59)

Presentation software Software designed to help presenters prepare visual aids for projection or distribution. (224)

Presentation speaking When speakers use verbal and nonverbal messages to generate meanings and to establish relationships with audience members, who are usually present at the delivery of a presentation. (8)

Primacy effect The fact that an audience is more likely to recall what speakers say in an introduction than what they say in the body of a presentation. (238)

Primary source The document, testimony, or publication in which information first appeared. (180)

Private purpose The personal goal of your presentation. (86)

Problem/Cause/Solution organizational pattern An organizational pattern that describes a problem and its possible causes, then offers a solution. (465)

Problem-solution arrangement An organizational format that describes a situation that is harmful (the problem) and then offers a plan to solve the problem (the solution). (201)

Projection Controlled vocal energy that gives impact and intelligibility to sound. (340)

Pronunciation Putting all the correct sounds in the correct order with the correct stress in a word. (346)

Proof The strategies, evidence, and/or arguments you select in order to persuade an audience. (435)

Protocol The expected format of a ceremony or the etiquette observed at a particular type of ceremony or event. (157)

Psychological Reactance Theory A theory stating that when you perceive a threat to your freedom to believe or behave as you wish, you may go out of your way to do the forbidden behavior or rebel against the prohibiting authority. (444)

Public group A group that engages in discussion in front of or for the benefit of the public. (508)

Public purpose The publicly stated goal of your presentation. (86)

Public speaking A type of presentation speaking that occurs when speakers address public audiences in community, government, and/or organizational settings. (8)

Punch line A sentence or phrase that communicates the climax of a story or joke. (302)

Purpose The outcome that you are seeking as a result of making your presentation. Purpose answers the question "What do I want my audience to know, think, feel, or do as a result of my presentation?" (84)

Purpose statement A sentence that clearly states the specific, achievable, and relevant goal of your presentation. (87)

Qualifier The component of the Toulmin model of an argument that states the degree to which a claim appears to be true. (458)

Question of conjecture A question that asks whether something will or will not happen. (461)

Question of fact A question that asks whether something is true or false, whether an event did or did not happen, or whether a circumstance was caused by one thing or by another. (459)

Question of policy A question that asks whether a particular course of action should be taken. (461)

Question of value A question that asks whether something is worthwhile (good or bad; right or wrong; moral or immoral; best, average, or worst). (460)

Question-and-answer session A situation in which a speaker responds to audience questions. (495)

Rate Your speaking speed; the number of words you say per minute added to the number and length of pauses that you use. (341)

Receiver The communicator who interprets a message and responds to its perceived meaning. (12)

Recency effect The fact that an audience is more likely to recall what speakers say in a conclusion than what they say in the body of a presentation. (250)

Research A search or investigation designed to find useful and appropriate ideas, opinions, and information. (176)

Reservation The component of the Toulmin model of an argument that recognizes exceptions to an argument or indications that a claim may not be true under certain circumstances. (457)

Rhetoric According to Aristotle, rhetoric is the ability to discover "in the particular case what are the available means of persuasion," such as logical arguments, emotional arguments, and/or speaker credibility. (7)

Rhetorical devices Language-based communication strategies that help speakers achieve their purpose. (284)

Rhetorical questions Questions to which no answer is expected. (285)

Rhyme Words that correspond to other words in terminal sounds and may give a phrase a singsong quality. (285)

Rigid rules Strongly held misconceptions about what makes a presentation good or bad. (62)

Sales presentation A unique form of speaking that combines the strategies and skills of informative and persuasive presentations. (489)

Scientific method arrangement An organizational pattern that follows the well-established steps that are the mainstay of scientific reporting. (203)

Search engine A Web service that matches key words to websites that include those terms. (181)

Secondary source A source that reports, repeats, or summarizes information from one or more other sources. (180)

Seductive details Elements in a presentation aid that attract audience attention but do not support the speaker's key points. (392)

Selected instances fallacy A fallacy that occurs when a speaker chooses atypical examples to prove an argument. (473)

Self-effacing humor The ability to direct humor at yourself or to poke fun at yourself. (308)

Sign Something that stands for or represents something specific and may look like or depict a symptom of the thing it represents. (265)

Signposts Short phrases that tell or remind an audience of the speaker's current place in the organizational scheme of a presentation. (229)

Simile A figure of speech that makes a direct comparison between two things or ideas, usually by using words such as "like" or "as." (282)

Situation-specific introductory methods Ways of beginning a presentation that adapt to the interests and concerns of a specific audience in a particular setting or situation. (242)

Six-by-six rule The rule that you should aim for no more than six lines of text with no more than six words per line on any slide or presentation aid. (390)

Skills The most basic abilities needed to prepare and to perform a presentation. (19)

Small group communication The interaction of three or more interdependent people working toward a common goal. (507)

Social Judgment Theory A theory stating that audience reactions to persuasive statements are best reflected by ranges: latitudes of acceptance (statements they agree with), latitudes of rejection (statements they cannot agree with), and latitudes of noncommitment (statements that are neither acceptable nor unacceptable). (442)

Source The communicator who creates a message and sends it to one or more receivers. (12)

Space arrangement An organizational format that arranges ideas, objects, events, people, and/or places in a physical pattern, location, or space. (200)

Speaker credibility Ethos; the characteristics of a speaker that determine whether the audience believes the speaker and the message. (129)

Special presentations Unique types of presentations that are used to bring people together, to create social unity, to build goodwill, to answer questions, or to celebrate. (480)

Standard Problem-Solving Agenda A procedure that guides a group through problem solving by using the following steps: clarifying the task, understanding and analyzing the problem, assessing possible solutions, and implementing a decision or plan. (518)

Statistics A system of organizing, summarizing, and analyzing numerical data that have been collected and measured. (170)

Stereotypes Oversimplified conceptions, opinions, or images of a person or a group of people that are often based on demographic characteristics. (21, 104)

Stories Accounts or reports about some things that have happened. (172)

Story fidelity The quality referring to whether a story seems truthful and believable. (304)

Story probability The quality referring to whether a story "hangs together," whether it is coherent and makes sense. (304)

Strategy A plan of action selected to help achieve the purpose of a presentation. (19)

Style The manner in which a presenter uses language to express a message, including vocabulary, sentence structure and length, grammar and syntax, and delivery techniques used. (269)

Subordinate terms The most concrete words that provide specific descriptions. (269)

Superordinate terms Abstract words that group objects and ideas together very generally. (268)

Supporting material Ideas, opinions, and information that help explain and/or advance a presentation's key points and purpose. (169)

Survey A series of written questions designed to gather information about audience characteristics and opinions. (114)

Symbol An arbitrary collection of sounds and letters that stand for a concept but do not have a direct relationship with the things they represent. (265)

Symposium A group presentation in which participants give short, uninterrupted presentations on different aspects of a topic for the benefit of an audience. (508)

Systematic desensitization A presentation anxiety therapy that teaches speakers how to relax before and during a stressful speaking situation. (67)

Tables Presentation aids that summarize and compare data; they may show exact numeric values. (381)

Task roles Group member roles that affect a group's ability to achieve its goals by focusing on behaviors that help get the job done. (514)

Team presentation A presentation by a cohesive group of speakers trying to influence an audience of decision makers. (509)

Testimony Statements or opinions that someone has said or written. (171)

Text charts Presentation aids that list ideas or key phrases, often under a title or headline. (381)

Theory A principle that tries to explain and to predict events and behavior. (19)

Thought speed The speed (words per minute) at which most people can think, as contrasted with the slower speed at which most people speak. (33)

Time arrangement An organizational format that orders ideas and information according to time or calendar dates. (200)

Toast Spoken remarks that accompany an act of drinking to honor a person, a couple, or a group. (485)

Tone The feeling or impression that an audience derives from a presentation based on the speaker's language, performance, and attitude. (286)

Topic The subject matter of a presentation. (89)

Topical arrangement An organizational format that divides a large topic into small subtopics. (199)

Topic-specific introductory methods Ways of beginning a presentation that rely on topic-related supporting material. (241)

Toulmin's Model of Argument A model stating that a complete argument is composed of evidence, a claim, and a warrant and may include backing, reservations, and qualifiers. (455)

Transitions A connective in the form of a word, phrase, number, or sentence that helps a speaker move from one key point or section to another. (228)

Tree outline An organizational technique that compares the central idea, key points, and supporting materials to the trunk, limbs, and branches of a tree. (218)

Triangle of terror A representation of the three interacting components of presentation anxiety and how they affect your head, heart, and habits. (74)

Valid Well founded, justified, or true (used to describing ideas, information, or opinions). (173)

Value step A section in the introduction of a presentation that explains why the information is valuable or important to the audience. (409)

Values Beliefs that guide how you think about what is right or wrong, good or bad, just or unjust, and correct or incorrect. (92)

Victory by definition fallacy A fallacy that occurs when a self-serving definition of a word is used to benefit the speaker and the speaker's argument. (474)

Videoconferences A meeting in which members use audio and visual technology to communicate. (522)

Virtual group A group in which members use technology to communicate, often across time, distance, and organizational boundaries. (522)

Visualization A procedure that encourages people to think positively about presentation speaking by imagining what it would be like to go through an entire successful speechmaking process. (69)

Vividness effect The ways in which colorful language elicits strong images in the minds of listeners. (270)

Volume Your voice's degree of loudness. (339)

Warrant The part of an argument that explains why the evidence supports a claim. (456)

Welcoming remarks A presentation in which a speaker representing one organization welcomes the public or a group from another organization to an event or place. (483)

Working agenda An outline of the items to be discussed and the tasks to be accomplished during a meeting or discussion. (519)

Working groups Private groups in which members exert collective effort to achieve a shared goal. (512)

Writing apprehension The fear or anxiety associated with writing situations and topic-specific writing assignments. (264)

INDEX